THE JOURNAL OF INDUSTRIAL ECONOMICS

VOLUME XXXII
1983–84

ISSN 0022-1821

BASIL BLACKWELL
OXFORD

THE JOURNAL OF INDUSTRIAL ECONOMICS

Volume XXXII SEPTEMBER 1983 No. 1

BO CARLSSON
Industrial Subsidies in Sweden: Macro-Economic Effects and an International Comparison 1

R. DIXON
Industry Structure and the Speed of Price Adjustment 25

RAPHAEL KAPLINSKY
Firm Size and Technical Change in a Dynamic Context 39

HIROYUKI ODAGIRI
R & D Expenditures, Royalty Payments, and Sales Growth in Japanese Manufacturing Corporations 61

NEIL DORWARD, MIKE POKORNY and RAY BAYLDON
The UK Truck Market: An Investigation into Truck Purchasing Behaviour and Changing Market Shares 73

MARCEL BOYER and MICHEL MOREAUX
Consistent Versus Non-Consistent Conjectures in Duopoly Theory: Some Examples 97

SSN 0022-1821
BASIL BLACKWELL OXFORD ENGLAND

THE JOURNAL OF INDUSTRIAL ECONOMICS
Volume XXXII September 1983 No. 1

INDUSTRIAL SUBSIDIES IN SWEDEN: MACRO-ECONOMIC EFFECTS AND AN INTERNATIONAL COMPARISON*

Bo Carlsson

I. PURPOSE

Like many other countries, Sweden was hit by severe economic problems in the mid-1970s. In the deep cyclical downturn in the world economy after the oil crisis 1973–74, the shipping, shipbuilding, steel and mining industries were particularly hard hit. In Sweden, certain parts of the forest-based industries also suffered from acute difficulties. Together, these crisis-stricken industries accounted for some 35% of total Swedish exports. Many firms and even whole industries were facing bankruptcy or drastic cutbacks. This situation created strong political demands for action on the part of the government. Thus, "in order to prevent or delay unacceptable reductions of employment in an industry or an enterprise or to facilitate re-structuring which can yield long-term profitability"[1] the government took direct action to save the threatened firms.

What has been the magnitude and orientation of this industrial subsidy program in the 1970s? How does this program compare with similar measures in other countries? What are the macroeconomic effects of the subsidies to ailing firms? What alternative measures could have been taken? These are the main questions in the present paper which is based on a recently published study. (Carlsson, Bergholm, and Lindberg, [2].)[2]

The paper is organized in the following way. Section II presents a brief discussion of industrial subsidies as an element of industrial policy in general and distinguishes between general and specific subsidies. Section III gives an overview of the magnitude and orientation of the Swedish industry subsidy program in the 1970s. In section IV an attempt is made to make an international comparison of industrial subsidy programs. The comparison is limited

* An earlier version of this paper was presented to the European Association for Research in Industrial Economics (EARIE) conference in Basel, Switzerland, September 16–18, 1981. I would like to thank my colleagues Fredrik Bergholm and Thomas Lindberg for their work in connection with this study and especially the book that preceded it. I am indebted also to Robert M. Grant and Alfredo del Monte for furnishing me with data for the United Kingdom and Italy, respectively. I would also like to thank William S. Comanor, Richard R. Nelson, Burton H. Klein, and Wilhelm Paues for valuable comments on earlier versions of this paper. All remaining errors and shortcomings are, of course, my own.

[1] According to the Directives given to the Government Committee on Industrial Subsidies.

[2] The study was commissioned and financed by the Government Committee on Industrial Subsidies (Industristödsutredningen). Financial support in the form of computer time provided by Industriøkonomisk Institutt, Bergen, Norway, is also gratefully acknowledged.

to a numerical description of the size and character of subsidy programs in various countries; no attempt is made to evaluate the performance or degree of success. Section V turns to a description of the selective subsidies given to certain industrial firms in Sweden during the 1970s, and section VI investigates the macro-economic effects of these firm-specific subsidies. Section VII presents a summary and some concluding remarks.

II. INDUSTRIAL SUBSIDIES—AN ELEMENT OF INDUSTRIAL POLICY

Government policy regarding industrial subsidies is but one element of what may loosely be referred to as industrial policy. Without going into the thorny question of how "industrial policy" is or should be defined, it is clear that the objectives of such policies vary greatly among countries and therefore also the means used to achieve those ends. It is also clear that, in addition to industrial subsidies, among the elements constituting industrial policy in various countries, the following are usually to be found, in varying degrees: (1) tariff policy and other forms of protection; (2) direct government ownership of means of production; (3) economic planning at the national level; (4) manpower policy broadly defined; (5) regional policy; (6) government procurement policy; and (7) policies regarding research, development and technical training. Thus, it is obvious that any attempt to evaluate the policies and performance of a given country as regards industrial subsidies is bound to give only a partial picture of the country's overall performance in industrial policy in general. The role of industrial subsidies in overall industrial policy also varies.[3]

Restricting ourselves henceforth to considering industrial subsidies, it is useful to distinguish between *general subsidy schemes* and *specific schemes*. General subsidies are those schemes under which the subsidy is given under certain standard rules of procedure to determine the eligibility of applicants and within those rules is available to all comers. On the other hand, specific or tailor-made subsidies are given to particular persons or firms for a particular purpose. (Whiting, [17, p. 1].) Examples of general subsidies would be tax deductions for investments of a particular type or in a particular region, grants or tax deductions for research and development expenditures, or loans offered below market rates to small and medium size firms.

Specific subsidies typically involve support for a specific project or product or for the restructuring or re-equipment of a firm. The philosophy behind general subsidies is that their availability and value are readily calculable by firms, who can therefore take them into account in planning their activities. They are also relatively straightforward, quick and cheap to operate [17, p. 2].

[3] In addition to these industrial policies, most countries pursue with varying vigor policies to maintain competition and efficiency and to fight collusion and monopoly.

Specific subsidies, on the other hand, involve more discretion and more top-level decision making on the part of the government, and the results are much less predictable and calculable.

For these reasons, industrial subsidies have tended to be of the general rather than the specific kind in the countries investigated here. However, in the face of the severe structural adjustment problems that arose during the 1970s the emphasis seems to have shifted significantly towards more specific policies.

III. MAGNITUDE AND ORIENTATION OF THE SWEDISH INDUSTRY SUBSIDY PROGRAM

Sweden provides a good example of this shift in emphasis from general to specific schemes during the 1970s. Structural adjustment policy has played an important role in the Swedish economy since the 1950s. The principal means has been labor market policy which has been designed to alleviate the continuous adjustment generated by the pressures of international competition. Thus, Sweden's labor market policy can be seen as a complement to the country's extensive social welfare programs. But in addition, the "solidaric wage policy" favored by the Confederation of Trade Unions (LO) has actually reinforced the adjustment need by putting increased pressure on low-wage, low productivity firms. This philosophy of the complementary role of adjustment policy and the role of labor union wage policy originated in the so-called Rehn model of economic policy in Sweden which was developed in the early 1950s by LO economists and which placed considerable emphasis on the need for active intervention by government in the labor market (OECD, [12, p. 189]).[4]

However, in the face of the extremely large structural adjustments necessitated by the developments, both international and domestic, in the wake of the first oil crisis, it was widely felt that labor market policy alone was inadequate to deal with the situation, and the political pressure to intervene more directly mounted. The means chosen was dramatically increased selective subsidies to ailing firms and industries.

The changing structure and magnitude of the Swedish industrial subsidy program in the course of the 1970s is reflected in Figure 1. There it can be seen that the industrial subsidies rose from a modest 1.3% of GDP (or 4.9% of value added in mining and manufacturing) in 1970 to an extraordinary 3.6% of GDP (16% of V. A. in mining and manufacturing) in 1978 (production valued at market prices), declining somewhat in 1979. Virtually the whole increase can be attributed to an increase in firm specific subsidies of a very selective kind; these grew from practically zero to a peak of 2.0% of GDP in 1978.

[4] For a survey of Swedish industrial policies in the postwar period, see Ohlin [14] and Eliasson and Ysander [6].

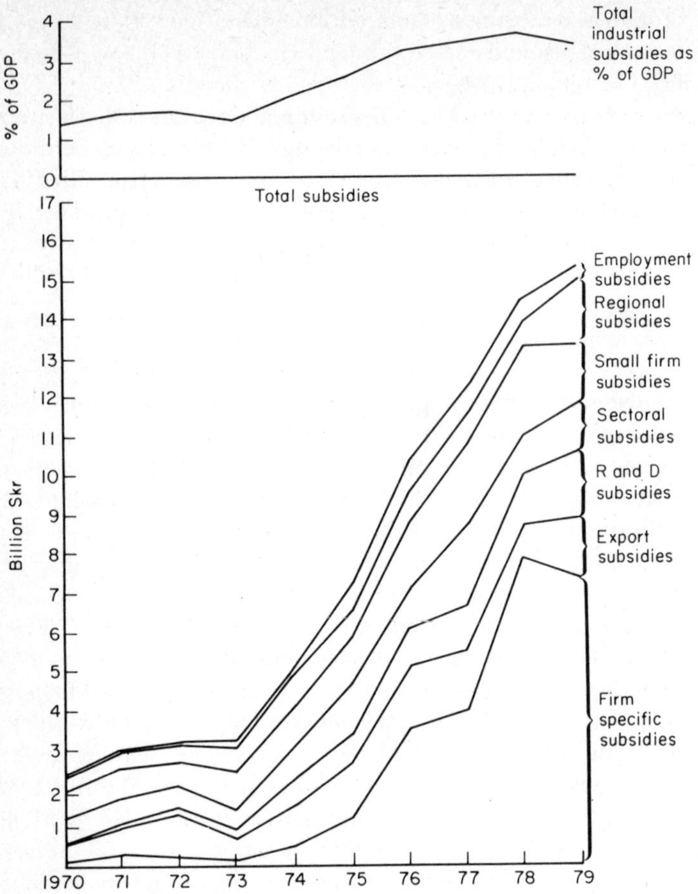

FIGURE 1

Swedish Industrial Subsidies 1970–79
(Paid-out amounts in current prices)

The Swedish subsidy figures presented in this paper (including those in Figure 1) refer to amounts actually paid out and include both grants and loans. The reason why no distinction is made here between grants and loans is primarily that it is often difficult to draw the line between them, as e.g. in the case of so-called conditional loans. It is common also in other cases that soft loans are converted into grants. As indicated in Table A in the Appendix, about 58% of the Swedish industrial subsidies during the 1970s were given in the form of loans. The loan figures, too, represent paid-out amounts; no attempt has been made to calculate the subsidy element by comparing the conditions of the loans to commercial loan conditions.[5]

[5] On the other hand, all forms of guarantees are excluded from the presentation here, except insofar as incurred losses have had to be covered. Still outstanding guarantees are not included.

According to this definition, the total amount of industrial subsidies rose from 2.3 billion Skr (equivalent to .44 billion US dollars) in 1970 to 15.4 billion Skr (3.71 billion US dollars) in 1979. As shown in Figure 1, up until 1973 the level of expenditures was rather stable, and the amount of firm specific subsidies was negligible. However, since then expenditures have risen very fast: more than a doubling (in current prices) between 1973 and 1975, then a doubling again between 1975 and 1978. Over the entire decade of the 1970s a total amount of 75 billion Skr was paid out in industrial subsidies. Measured in 1979 prices this is equivalent to about 100 billion Skr or about 10 billion Skr per year (equal to 2.4 billion US dollars), on the average.

For comparison it may be mentioned that the cost of labor market measures during the period 1970–79 amounted to about 50 billion Skr (in current prices). At the same time, non-industrial policy measures (including e.g. subsidies and other measures directed at the agricultural sector, policies to promote forestry, commerce, and the social infrastructure—e.g. the state railroad system, the postal service, road services, and the energy supply system) came to a total of about 110 billion Skr. Thus, the total cost to the government of economic policy measures directed at the business sector was about 235 billion Skr for the whole decade.

Within the industrial subsidy program, as shown in Figure 1, the type of measure that has increased the most is *firm specific subsidies*, i.e. direct measures to save ailing firms. The amount spent for this purpose rose from a modest 127 million Skr in 1970 to almost 8 billion Skr in 1978. Altogether during the decade about 26 billion Skr (out of which 37% in the form of loans) was spent for this purpose, i.e. about one-third of the total industrial subsidy program. It is this type of expenditure with which we are primarily concerned in this study. A more detailed description of the composition and distribution of these firm specific subsidies is presented below.

There are several forms of general subsidies. *Regional subsidies* include both grants and loans. *Small firm subsidies* consist mainly of loans issued by financial institutions such as Industrikredit and Företagskredit and, after 1978, the so-called regional development funds. *R&D subsidies* consist mainly of grants made to the State Board for Technical Development (STU), tax exemptions from corporate income tax obtained by firms for R&D expenditures, and grants for energy research and energy conservation in the business sector. *Export subsidies* consist predominantly of export credits issued by AB Svensk Exportkredit. *Sectoral subsidies* consist mainly of loans issued by the Swedish Investment Bank.

In addition to the above measures, all of which have been financed via the budget of the Department of Industry, certain programs administered by the Labor Market Board (AMS) have been directed at firms—although the bulk of the Board's activities are directed at individuals in the labor force rather than at firms and therefore are not considered here. The total of the *firm-oriented actions of the Labor Market Board* amounted to 3.4 billion Skr during the period

1970–79 and included *i.a.* support of certain training programs and inventory build-up during 1972 and 1975–76.

It is apparent from the material presented so far that the bulk of the industrial subsidies in Sweden have been designed to promote industrial development in general and small and medium-sized firms in distressed regions in particular. But large and expanding firms have also received support, especially via tax exemptions for R&D expenditures and via export credits. The impact of these general and permanent subsidy programs is difficult to evaluate, since the conditions for receiving support have varied strongly, and since it is difficult or impossible to characterize the recipients. Therefore, it is virtually impossible to specify an alternative policy with which the actual program could be compared. Perhaps the most relevant comparison one could make would be to view these general subsidies as a form of tariff.[6] In any case, the empirical investigation of Swedish industrial subsidies in the 1970s summarized below is confined to rescue operations to certain crisis-stricken firms only.

IV. INDUSTRIAL SUBSIDY PROGRAMS—AN INTERNATIONAL COMPARISON

But before we analyze the Swedish data further, how does the Swedish industrial subsidy program compare to those in other countries? In order to answer this question, we undertook a data collection, the results of which will be presented below.

First of all, it must be stated at the outset that collecting data on government subsidies is a difficult, if not impossible, task. The virtual absence of international comparative studies on this topic testifies to this. Data on government subsidies is one type of information which most governments are not eager to divulge or whose diffusion they sometimes actively prevent. The transparency, and thus the quality, of the data we have been able to obtain, therefore, varies a great deal from one country to another. Accordingly, the figures presented here represent only a first attempt to pull together information which has been made available to us and must be interpreted with extreme care. For example, there are some glaring omissions in the data we have obtained; the institutional arrangements vary greatly, particularly with regard to the tax system, and it is therefore difficult to classify certain measures under any given heading. Also, in some countries, such as e.g. France and Germany, tax exemptions play an important role as a supplement to direct subsidies. However, the impact and magnitude of tax exemptions obviously depend on the characteristics of the tax system, the study of which would take us too far afield. Therefore, except in the German case, we have tried to exclude tax exemptions

[6] For a discussion of the equivalence of tariffs and subsidies, as well as an empirical investigation of their relative importance in Germany and Britain, see Corden and Fels [3].

and included only paid-out or appropriated amounts.[7] The reasons why tax exemptions in Germany are treated differently from those in other countries are (1) that they seem to be much more specific than those, e.g., in the Scandinavian countries and therefore play a role very similar to that of direct subsidies in these countries; (2) that the German government itself obviously views these tax exemptions as being very similar to direct subsidies; and (3) that estimates of the (gross) cost to the government's budget of tax exemptions are available for Germany but not for other countries.

Secondly, it should be pointed out again that the degree to which government industrial policy relies on subsidies varies among countries. As indicated in section II, industrial subsidies constitute but one aspect of industrial policy. This means, more specifically, e.g., that the role of indirect subsidies in the form of government procurement arrangements and rules as well as that of trade barriers protecting domestic firms may vary substantially among countries. Such effects are not considered here.

Thirdly, and perhaps most importantly, the aim in presenting this comparison is neither to evaluate individual governments' subsidy programs, nor to assess the role of subsidies in overall adjustment policies. The goal is rather more modest, namely to get a rough idea of the magnitude and orientation of such subsidy programs in various countries, and to find out to what extent they differ.

Being aware of all these limitations, let us turn now to the information at hand, summarized in Table I. According to the table, the subsidy programs of various countries vary substantially in magnitude, with Britain and West Germany at the low end of the spectrum (1.0 and 1.6% of GDP, respectively), and Sweden at the high end with 3.5%, Norway and Italy being in between. It is perhaps surprising that the British subsidy program is found to be the smallest in the comparison. However, this is due partly to the fact that there was a substantial reduction in the British subsidy program from a peak in 1978–79.

Roughly one-half of the industrial subsidies in Italy, Norway and Sweden are of the general type, while general subsidies account for significantly higher shares in the United Kingdom (64%) and West Germany (82%). Regional and small firm support programs seem to be the most important types of general subsidies and R&D subsidies the second most important type, with Germany leading in both categories. Export subsidies turn out to be the kind of general subsidy that varies the most in relative magnitude. However, since most export subsidies are given in the form of loans for which the actual subsidy element and the institutional arrangements vary a great deal, the large differences here probably mostly reflect the poor quality or at least poor comparability of the data. General investment and employment subsidies seem to

[7] It has not been possible, except in the case of Italy (see note to Table I below), to obtain estimates of "the subsidy element" of loans given at less than market rates of interest. Therefore, the "gross" amounts are included in Table I.

TABLE I

INDUSTRY SUBSIDIES IN GREAT BRITAIN (1979–80), ITALY (1978), NORWAY (1979), SWEDEN (1979) AND WEST GERMANY (1980)

	Great Britain 1979–80 million £	%	*Italy 1978 billion lire*	%	*Norway 1979 million Nkr*	%	*Sweden 1979 million Skr*	%	*West Germany 1980 million DM*	%
"*General subsidies*"										
Export subsidies	376	19.4	1,688	31.3	152[a]	3.2	1,507	9.8	1,750	8.0
R&D subsidies	267	13.8	75	1.4	614	12.8	1,643	10.7	4,450	20.3
General investment subsidies	2	.1	240	4.4	395	8.2	—	—	650	3.0
Employment subsidies to firms	209	10.8	—	—	125	2.6	396	2.6	—	—
Regional and small firm support	388	20.0	725	13.4	1,205	25.2	3,134	20.3	12,000	54.8
Subtotal	1,242	64.1	2,728	50.5	2,491	52.0	6,680	43.4	18,850	86.1
"*Rescue operations*"										
Sectoral subsidies	77	4.0	—	—	1,109	23.1	1,255	8.1	2,650	12.1
Specific firm subsidies	620	31.9	2,671	49.5	1,192	24.9	7,464	48.5	400	1.8
Subtotal	697	36.0	2,671	49.5	2,301	48.0	8,719	56.6	3,050	13.9
Total subsidies	1,939	100.0	5,399	100.0	4,792	100.0	15,399	100.0	21,900	100.0
Total as % of GDP		1.0		2.6		2.0		3.5		1.6
Total as % of value added in mining and manufacturing		3.6		7.1		7.6		16.0		4.0[b]
"General subsidies" as % of value added in mining and manufacturing		2.3		3.6		4.0		6.9		3.4[b]
"Rescue operations" as % of value added in mining and manufacturing		1.3		3.5		3.6		9.1		.6[b]

[a] The figure given represents only a minor fraction of total export subsidies.
[b] Estimated figure.

Sources for Table I

Great Britain: Public Expenditure White Paper, [15, Table 2.4]. I would like to thank professor Robert M. Grant, The City University Business School, London, for furnishing me with these data and for helpful suggestions for classification of the data.

Italy: Bank of Italy [1]; Istituto Centrale di Statistica [10]. I am indebted to Professor Alfredo Del Monte, University of Naples, for collecting and furnishing me with these data.

According to calculations made by Prof. Del Monte, the financial cost to the government budget of the industry subsidy program (calculated as the difference between the market rate at which the government borrows and the favorable rate on the loans offered under the available schemes times the amount of loans outstanding, plus capital grants given during the year) amounted to 1,375 billion lire in 1978.

Norway: Industrifondet, [8] and [9].

Sweden: Data from Industristödsutredningen (Government Committee on Industrial Subsidies) as reported in Carlsson, Bergholm, and Lindberg [2].

West Germany: Deutscher Bundestag [4] (*7th Subsidy Report*); Sjöström and Olofsson [16].

The German figures were obtained in the following way. The basic source for the allocation of various support programs to the types of programs in Table I is the *7th Subsidy Report.*

From the total figure for Federal financial support of the industrial sector given in that *Report* (4,006 million DM 1980), support programs for energy and raw material acquisition were excluded. To the remaining Federal financial support of 3,618 million DM were added an estimated 2,000 million DM in state and local aid, and 2,039 million DM in ERP (= European Recovery Program) measures, all of which were classified as regional and small firm support". The total tax exemption figure for the industrial sector given in the *7th Subsidy Report* is 9,802 million DM (4,616 Federal aid and 5,186 million DM state and local). However, after excluding certain measures applying to the financial sector and certain programs relating to the housing sector, the remaining tax exemption total is 9,184 million DM.

In addition, based on Sjöström and Olofsson [16], 1,700 million DM in export credit by the Kreditanstalt für Wiederaufbau were added, and also an estimated 3,000 million DM in R&D support in programs financed via the Bundesministerium für Forschung und Technologie, Bundesministerium für Wirtschaft, defense agencies, etc., which are not included in the *7th Subsidy Report.*

The figures for West Germany in the Table were also checked against those reported by Jüttemeier and Lammers [11].

GDP, *Value Added in Mining and Manufacturing:* OECD [13].

be relatively unimportant. Under the heading "employment subsidies to firms" we have tried to include only anticyclical measures aimed at firms, as well as labor market subsidies available not just to firms in acute difficulties.[8]

It should be pointed out, of course, that the classification of certain types of subsidy schemes is wrought with many problems. This is particularly true of sectoral subsidies. It might be argued, for example, that government support of the aerospace industry is a sector-oriented type of program and should be thus classified. Yet we have chosen to classify such support under "R&D subsidies", while support of the steel and shipbuilding industries, perceived to be of a rather different, "rescue type" character, are regarded as sectoral subsidies. In some countries, support of the steel industry has been industry-wide, while in others it has been firm specific. Therefore, it has been judged more useful to distinguish between "rescue operations" and other types of industrial subsidies than to try to differentiate between industry-wide and firm specific subsidies to, say, the steel industry. Hence the division into "rescue operations" (rather than "specific subsidies") and "general subsidies" in Table I.

What is left, then, under "rescue operations" is principally support of ailing firms and industries. But because of lack of sufficiently detailed data, it is possible that there are some other elements also included here. The sector composition varies greatly: two-thirds of the rescue operations in Germany are directed toward the coal mining industry, which is also a large receiver in Britain, along with autos, shipbuilding and steel. In Norway, about one-half of the rescue operations involve the shipbuilding industry. In Sweden, as we will see in more detail below, three-fourths of this type of selective measures are directed toward shipbuilding and steel. It has not been possible to determine the distribution by sector in Italy.

It appears from the table that the Swedish subsidy program in 1979 was substantially larger than that of any other country in the comparison. This is true for both general subsidy schemes and rescue operations, but particularly for the latter. Could it be that the Swedish figures are simply more complete than the others—or are the differences genuine? Could it be that Sweden, traditionally a proponent of free trade, faced greater difficulties during the 1970s than the other countries and, having disarmed itself of other protective measures, had to resort to subsidies as a remedy? The answer is that we just do not know. Before any firm conclusions can be drawn from an international comparison such as this, it is clear that substantially more work is required to ensure the quality and comparability of the data. The effort made in this paper is only a beginning.

[8] In addition to the figures reported here, an estimate has been made by J. P. Foresti for France (1979), based on information obtained from the French Ministry of Budget. The total figure for industrial subsidies is approximately 26 billion francs, corresponding to 1.1% of GDP and 3.9% of value added in mining and manufacturing. Over 70% of these subsidies were classified as "rescue operations". Thus, the French subsidies appear to be of the same general magnitude as those in Britain and Germany, but they also appear to be much more selective in nature.

V. DISTRIBUTION BY SECTOR OF THE SWEDISH SPECIFIC FIRM SUBSIDIES

Let us turn now from the international comparison to a closer examination of the Swedish subsidy program in the 1970s. More specifically, we are concerned henceforth only with rescue type operations, leaving aside all general subsidy schemes.

As already noted, the firm specific industrial subsidies in Sweden amounted to about 26 billion Skr during the 1970s, all but a minor fraction being paid out during the latter half of the decade. According to Table II, over 20 billion Skr was paid out during 1977–79. As already noted, three-fourths of this amount went to the shipyards and the steel industry and the remainder to the forest-based industry, the mining industry, and the textile and apparel industry. The shipyards alone received nearly half of these firm specific subsidies.[9] During the three-year period 1977–79 the shipbuilding subsidies corresponded to 120% of the total wage bill, or approximately 280,000 Skr per employee. During 1978 and 1979, the subsidies actually exceeded the value added in the shipbuilding industry—i.e., inputs in the production process were worth more when they arrived at the shipyards than they were when they left in the form of newly built ships (Hamilton, [7, pp. 8–9])! In the steel industry and the mining industry, the subsidies corresponded to 30–40% of the wage bill or about 100,000 Skr per employee for the three-year period as a whole. Since nearly all of the steel subsidies have gone to the commercial steel sector, which represents one-third of total employment in the industry (specialty steel making up the remaining two-thirds), it turns out that the subsidies to the commercial steel industry were nearly as large as those to the shipyards, measured per employee.

TABLE II
FIRM SPECIFIC SUBSIDIES BY RECEIVING SECTOR IN SWEDEN 1977–79
(Sum of grants and loans. Paid-out amounts. Credit guarantees not included.)

		In relation to		
	Million Skr	*Value added* %	*Total wage-bill* %	*No. of employees, thousands of Skr*
Shipyards	9,094	72.3	120.2	282
Steel	4,880	35.6	33.4	92
Forest-based	2,012	11.2	12.4	32
Mines	1,666	32.9	41.2	100
Textile and apparel	1,125	9.5	11.6	21
All manufacturing	20,238	6.9	8.5	21

[9] The shipyards also received some "general subsidies", but their share of total subsidies was considerably smaller than their share of firm specific subsidies. For a more detailed analysis of the subsidies to the shipbuilding industry, see Hamilton [7].

The subsidies to the forest-based industry have gone mainly to three firms, where they represented about 40% of the total wage bill 1977–79. Given its prominent place in the political debate, it may seem surprising that the textile and apparel industry ranks lowest among the subsidized industries. Nevertheless, that is the case; the number of recipient firms in the industry is also fairly large.

The following comparisons may be helpful in getting an idea of the magnitude of the subsidies given to crisis-stricken firms:

– Government revenue in the form of corporate income tax 1970–79 amounted to 13.8 billion Skr—i.e., about one-half of firm-specific subsidies during the same period.
– During the period 1977–79, the total industrial subsidies (both general and specific) were somewhat larger than the total appropriations for national defense. At the same time, the firm specific subsidies corresponded to one-half of the payroll tax paid by all industrial firms.
– During the same period (1977–79), the firm specific subsidies corresponded to 2,500 Skr (about US$500) per individual in Sweden or about 5,000 Skr (US$1,000) per person employed in the whole economy. Nearly half of this went to the shipyards.

VI. MACRO-ECONOMIC EFFECTS OF FIRM-SPECIFIC SUBSIDIES

What, then, has been the macro-economic impact of the firm-specific subsidies? In order to answer that question one needs to specify some alternatives to which the implemented policy can be compared. This can be done with the aid of a model. A model can also be used as an analytical tool in trying to understand the basic mechanisms at work in various policy alternatives.

The model used in the present study is a micro-(firm-)based simulation model of the Swedish economy.[10] For a brief description, see Appendix 2. One of the central features of the model, which distinguishes it from other models, is that it is based on data for individual firms. It is possible to characterize firms within the model and study how they behave under various conditions. Thus, what happens in the markets is determined endogenously in the model rather than directly via assumptions.

There are normally about 140 real firms in the model, covering about 70–75% of Swedish manufacturing output. In the present simulations we

[10] The model, which is named MOSES, has been described in several publications, especially in Eliasson [5]. A brief presentation of the model with special application to the present subsidy simulations is found in Carlsson-Bergholm-Lindberg, [2, esp. Ch. 4]. A more detailed description is given in the appendices to the same volume: "The Investment Finance Decisions" (by Thomas Lindberg), "The Development of Sales" (by Fredrik Bergholm), and "An Example of Firm Behavior" (by Thomas Lindberg). The programming of the model is done in APL, but if it were FORTRAN, the program would require some 5–10,000 lines. About 50 variables are determined each quarter for each firm in the model. A 15-year simulation requires about 30 CPU minutes on a DEC 20 computer.

THE JOURNAL OF INDUSTRIAL ECONOMICS

VOLUME XXXI
1982 – 83

ISSN 0022-1821

BASIL BLACKWELL
OXFORD

CONTENTS

VOLUME XXXI

Numbers 1/2, *September/December* 1982 PAGE

Spatial Competition and the Theory of Differentiated Markets: An Introduction, by LOUIS PHLIPS AND JACQUES-FRANÇOIS THISSE 1

I. UNIFORM F.O.B. PRICING: THE HOTELLING-LÖSCH APPROACH

List of Abstracts 11

Spatial Competition à la *Hotelling: A Selective Survey*, by DOMINIQUE GRAITSON 13

Product Differentiation and the Consistency of Monopolistic Competition: A Spatial Perspective, by DENNIS R. CAPOZZA AND ROBERT VAN ORDER 27

Innovative Entry: Profit Hidden Beneath the Zero, by KELVIN LANCASTER 41

Competitive Behaviour in Chain-Linked Markets, by R. ROTHSCHILD 57

Product Proliferation in Characteristics Space: The UK Fertiliser Industry, by R. W. SHAW 69

Existence and Computation of Mixed Strategy Nash Equilibrium for 3-Firms Location Problem, by A. SHAKED 93

Differentiated Products, Consumer Search, and Locational Oligopoly, by KONRAD STAHL 97

Product Differentiation with Income Disparities: An Illustrative Model, by J. JASKOLD GABSZEWICZ AND J.-F. THISSE 115

II. DISCRIMINATORY PRICING: THE GREENHUT - OHTA APPROACH

List of Abstracts 131

Recent Developments in the Analysis of Spatial Competition and Their Implications for Industrial Economics, by NEIL DORWARD 133

Dynamic Market Strategy under Threat of Competitive Entry: An Analysis of the Pricing and Production Policies Open to the Multinational Company, by GEORGE NORMAN AND NANCY K. NICHOLS 153

Spatial Price Duopoly Under Uniform Delivered Pricing, by RICHARD E. SCHULER AND BENJAMIN F. HOBBS 175

Pricing Policies Under Conditions of Spatial Competition, by MENAHEM SPIEGEL 189

Number 3, March 1983

Industrial Concentration: A Survey, by B. CURRY AND K.D. GEORGE 203

The Performance of Merging Firms in Japanese Manufacturing Industry: 1964 – 75, by KATSUHIKO IKEDA AND NORIYUKI DOI 257

The Causes and Consequences of Abandoned Mergers, by J.F. PICKERING 267

A Note on Conglomerate Merger and Behavioural Response to Risk, by NORMAN J. IRELAND 283

Anatomy of a Price Leadership Challenge: An Evaluation of Pricing Strategies in the Australian Newspaper Industry, by WILLIAM J. MERRILEES 291

Innovation in a Labor-Managed Firm: A Membership Perspective, by JOHN P. BONIN 313

Number 4, June 1983

An Empirical Analysis of Stockholder Injury Under §2 of the Sherman Act, by MALCOLM R. BURNS 333

Regulation of 'Administered' Prices: An Empirical Analysis of the Microeconomics of Price Movement in Finland 1972 – 77, by BJÖRN WAHLROOS 363

Joint Costs and Intra-Tariff Cross-Subsidies: The Case of Liner Shipping, by J.A. ZERBY AND R.M. CONLON 383

An International Comparison of the Fiscal Treatment of Shipping, by BERNARD GARDNER AND PETER MARLOW 397

An Analysis of Cost and Supply Conditions in the Liner Shipping Industry, by J.E. DAVIES 417

Co-operative Agreements and the Organization of Industry, by P. MARITI AND R.H. SMILEY 437

The Impact of Joint Ventures on the Market for OCS Oil and Gas Leases, by ALAN ROCKWOOD 453

Economic Effects of Non-Binding Constraints, by REX L. COTTLE AND MYLES S. WALLACE 469 have added eight subsidized firms: two based on data for two forest-based firms (Södra Skogsägarnas Cellulosa AB and NCB), one based on data for the merged commercial steel company (Svenskt Stål AB), one based on data for the Swedish shipyards (Svenska Varv), and four textile and apparel "firms", each representing a subsector within that industry.

The purpose of the simulations has been to illustrate a few fundamental relationships which illuminate the macro-economic effects of subsidies, not to simulate the actual development or the impact on individual subsidy recipients. The experiments on the model represent an attempt to estimate the order of magnitude and the distribution over time of the macro-economic effects after allowing for the adjustments made as a result of the subsidy program, i.e., taking into account both direct and indirect effects. All such calculations are necessarily hypothetical in nature. However, we are not aware of any other way to illustrate and quantify the macro-economic impact than through a model based on the behavior of micro units.

The point of departure for the simulations has been to compare the result of the policy actually conducted with that of other alternatives. All exogenous variables have been exactly the same in all the simulations except the specification of the subsidy program. In all cases, the simulations have covered 18 years beginning in the base year 1976, i.e., they have covered the period up through 1994.

The subsidy program actually carried out has been characterized in the following way. The eight subsidized firms in the model have been given temporary wage subsidies of a magnitude corresponding to the total level of actual support during the period 1977–79. The subsidies have been given in the form of that percentage of the total wage bill, which corresponds to the actual level for each recipient firm. This level of support has been assumed to continue for another three years and then be reduced to two-thirds in 1983 and one-third in 1984 and eliminated completely thereafter.

The subsidies paid out through this program during the entire subsidy period 1977–84 amount to 70 billion Skr. The program is financed in the model through a percentage increase in the level of the income tax applicable throughout the entire 18-year period 1977–94. Thus, the economy is stimulated at the beginning of the period through the subsidy program but at the same time held back through the income tax rise. However, most of the income tax revenue comes towards the end of the simulation, i.e., after the subsidies have been phased out.

The object of the simulations has been to compare this policy package to other alternatives, keeping the magnitude and time profile of the subsidy program constant (about 70 billion Skr during the period 1977–84), changing only the type of policy measures used.

As an alternative to the extremely selective actual subsidy program (support given to specific firms in specific circumstances) we have specified a more general alternative, namely where subsidies are given to all firms as a percentage reduction of their total wage bill in proportion to the rate at which they increased their exports in the preceding quarter. This is referred to as the *export subsidy case*. It should be noted that support is not necessarily given to the largest exporters or to the firms with the largest export share but rather to those which *increase* their exports at the highest rate.

An even more general alternative is to give wage subsidies to all manufacturing firms in proportion to their wage bill during the same period as the selective subsidy. This can be regarded as either a (temporary) *general wage subsidy* or a (temporary) *reduced payroll tax*. It turns out that in order to reach the same magnitude as the actual subsidies, the general wage subsidy would have to be about 10%. Alternatively, the payroll tax would have to be reduced from about 40% to about 20% of the total wage bill.

In summary, the subsidy experiments can be described in the following way. We have studied the macro-economic impact of a temporary stimulus in the form of wage subsidies to either a) a group of non-competitive firms, b) a group of rapidly growing export oriented firms, or c) all manufacturing firms, all other things being equal.

As a contrast to subsidy policies with varying degrees of selectivity we have also constructed a *laissez-faire* case in which no measure is taken, i.e., no subsidies are given at all. In this case, there is of course no need to finance a subsidy program; therefore there is no need for an income tax increase either.[11]

Through the selective subsidies, the recipient firms survive in the simulation at least until the subsidies begin to be phased out in 1983. In 1983–84 in this simulation, one of the forest based firms as well as the commercial steel firm and the shipyards are closed down. The other recipient firm in the forest based industry is closed down in 1988 and one of the textile firms in 1990. The other textile and apparel "firms" survive throughout the whole simulation.

But what happens if these firms are *not* subsidized? In the laissez-faire case, the largest among them (the shipyards, the commercial steel and the two forest based firms) are eliminated during the first few years of the simulation, while the textile and apparel firms are phased out more gradually. But even in the cases when the selective subsidies are replaced by more general subsidies, the shipyards, steel and forest firms are forced to close down rather quickly. In the export subsidy case, the textile firms also gradually fail, but in the general subsidy (reduced payroll) case, three of the four textile "firms" survive throughout the simulation.

The conclusion to be drawn from this is that it would have been difficult to maintain employment in the crisis-stricken firms, or even to prevent these firms from failing, without direct subsidies. But what are the more general effects of

[11] Yet another case of selective subsidies to ailing firms but on conditions that differ from those in the selective subsidy case mentioned above has also been examined but is not reported on here for reasons of brevity and clarity of exposition.

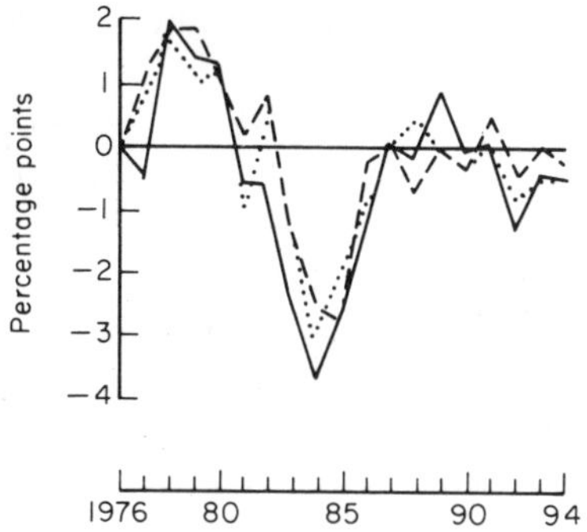

FIGURE 2a
Unemployment, difference between the simulations
(Percentage points, selective policy = 0)

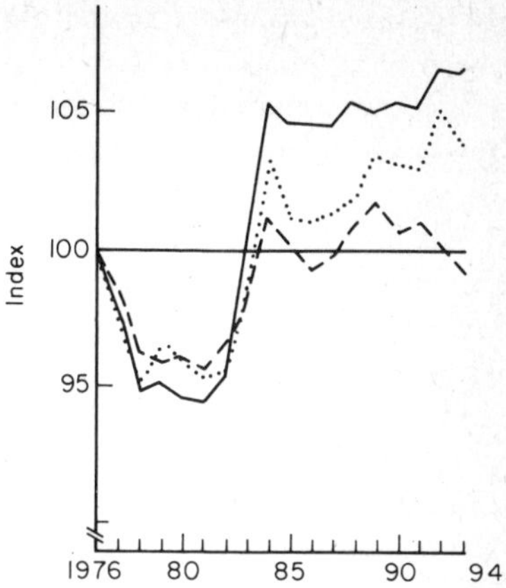

FIGURE 2b
Manufacturing output
(Index, selective policy = 100)

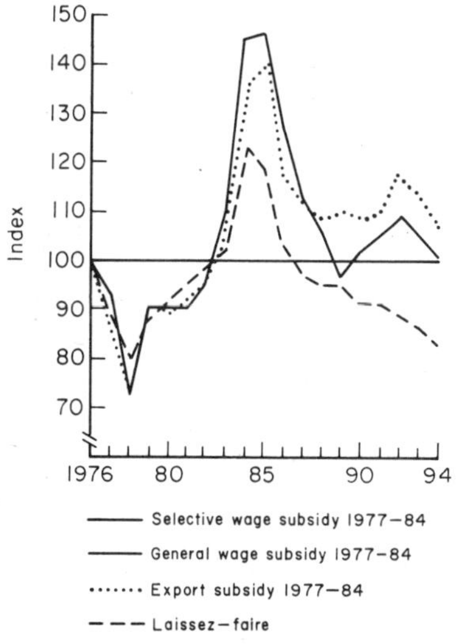

FIGURE 2c
Net Trade Balance in Percent of GNP
(Index, selective policy = 100)

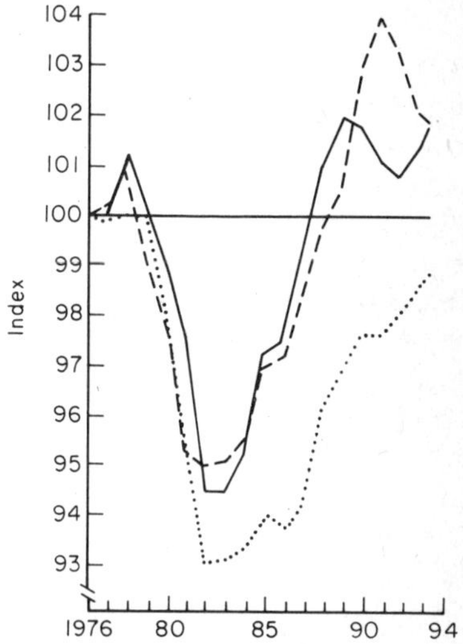

FIGURE 2d
Private consumption
(Index, selective policy = 100)

these selective policies? What, e.g., would have happened to unemployment in the longer run?

As shown in Figure 2a, closing down several of the ailing firms at the beginning of the period would have led to considerable unemployment for a few years at the end of the 1970s. However, the additional unemployment would have been smaller than the number of people employed initially in the closed-down firms, because approximately one-third as many jobs would have been created elsewhere in the manufacturing sector during the first couple of years.[12]

One of the main reasons for this result is that when the wages in non-competitive firms are subsidized, these firms maintain their employment. Non-subsidized firms therefore have to raise their wage offers in order to be able to recruit people from either the subsidized firms or the unemployment pool (which is reduced because of the subsidies). This causes generally higher wages, lower profits in non-subsidized firms, and therefore fewer incentives for expansion. The result is that the adjustment to changing external circumstances which necessitated the subsidies in the first place is delayed.

The basic reason why the unemployment rate becomes substantially higher during the first half of the '80s in the selective subsidy case than in the other cases is that when the subsidies are phased out, most of the recipient firms fail. In order to rescue them permanently, the subsidies would either have had to be larger or be continued for a longer period than we assumed. Thus, in our simulations the effect of the subsidies as far as unemployment is concerned is largely to delay unemployment and hold back expansion outside the subsidized firms.

Of course, in the absence of direct subsidies to crisis-stricken firms, industrial production would have been lower for a few years but would then have been higher for the rest of the simulated period after the subsidies are phased out, for reasons similar to those given above. See Figure 2b. This conclusion does not hold for the laissez-faire case, however. In that case, the production lost during the subsidy period is not made up later.

It is worth noting that even if subsidies had been given of the same order of magnitude but of a less selective type, it would have taken some time before industrial production started to rise. Most of the large recipient firms would have been forced to close down, as already noted. This would have meant a further loss of demand in addition to that created already by the extremely low trough in the international business cycle. This would have resulted in large overcapacity which would have delayed the expansion and increase in investment for which the subsidies *per se* would have provided stimulus. Even though profits would have increased, firms would have waited to increase their investment until an acceptable level of capacity utilization had been reached. Only towards 1980–81 would a rise in investment have occurred, resulting in a strong expansion in production in 1981–82, according to Figure 2b. In conjunction with the phase-out of the subsidy program in 1983 and 1984, further expansion is held back. Nevertheless, the level of industrial production

[12] Public sector employment is assumed to be the same in all of the simulations.

after 1983 is substantially higher and grows faster in the general wage subsidy (reduced payroll) case than in the selective subsidy case.[13]

If direct subsidies had not been given to the ailing firms, the balance of trade would also have suffered a relative decline during the first few years. See Figure 2c. This is due to the fact that several of the firms receiving subsidies, e.g., the shipyards, are large exporters. Therefore, when the subsidies are phased out and several of the subsidized firms close down, the trade balance suffers. After the elimination of the subsidies, the more general subsidy policies turn out to yield a more positive trade balance than the selective policy. Again, the laissez-faire policy turns out to perform less well. Looking over the entire simulated period, both export subsidies and a general wage subsidy (reduced payroll tax) are clearly more favorable as regards the trade balance than the selective policy.

However, as far as private consumption is concerned (see Figure 2d), the selective wage subsidy policy may be said to yield the most favorable development over the simulated period as a whole and especially during the period of the subsidy program. This indicates that direct subsidies to crisis-stricken firms is a more effective means of maintaining capacity utilization and therefore also private consumption than the other policy alternatives. On the other hand, as just pointed out, these other alternatives are more successful in improving the trade balance.

An alternative policy might have been to impose tariffs or import quotas in the stricken industries. However, such a policy has not been investigated because import restrictions would not be of much use in these heavily export oriented industries and have never been contemplated in the Swedish debate. Roughly 3/4 of the output of Swedish shipyards and 2/3 of the output of forest products is exported. Even prohibitive tariffs on imports would not guarantee a large enough domestic market for the sick firms in these industries to survive. Also, such tariffs would violate GATT rules and would run counter to the whole postwar development. It is likely that the distortions resulting from such a policy would have been even worse than those resulting from subsidies because import restrictions would have led to both lower domestic consumption (through higher prices) and higher costs to using sectors, as well as a home-market bias (see Corden and Fels [3, pp. 215–22]) detrimental in the long run to the international competitiveness of Swedish industry. In other words, the negative impact on firms' incentives seems likely to be greater when tariffs are imposed than when subsidies are used—but this is clearly a question for future research.

[13] The fact that the decline in industrial production is smaller in the laissez-faire case relative to the selective policy alternative than that in the other policy cases is explained by 1) the fact that there is no income tax raise suppressing total demand, and 2) the fact that general subsidies are relatively powerless in the poor cyclical conditions during the first few years of the simulation.

VII. SUMMARY AND CONCLUSIONS

Summing up, if we first confine the discussion to the stated objectives of the subsidy program, it is quite clear that in terms of the first objective, that of preventing or delaying unacceptable reductions of employment, the selective wage subsidies have favorable short-run effects relative to all other alternatives investigated here. But in the longer run, this policy performs worse than the other alternatives (except the laissez-faire case) even in pure employment terms. And in terms of the second objective, that of facilitating re-structuring, this policy is worse than both export subsidies and general wage subsidies.

If we broaden the evaluation to include more than just employment effects, the conclusions are rather similar. The selective wage subsidy yields higher industrial production and exports during the first few years than the alternative policies investigated, because the subsidized firms, most of which are heavily export oriented, do not fail as in the other policy alternatives. However, both export subsidies and general wage subsidies lead to more favorable long-term effects on industrial production as well as trade performance (and unemployment). In comparison with these alternatives, therefore, the selective subsidy program yields negative long-run effects.

Compared to the laissez-faire case, the effects of the selective policies are very favorable in the short run and yet not particularly costly in the long run. The virtual absence of long-term (allocative) effects in the selective relative to the laissez-faire case is explained by several circumstances: (1) that the subsidies are actually phased out after eight years and that the firms which fail then are allowed to close down; and (2) that the subsidies are limited and non-negotiable. The recipient firms receive "only" a certain percentage of their total wage bill—even though this percentage is very high in some cases. They are not allowed to negotiate for more subsidies. Therefore, their incentives are not destroyed. It is not likely that such constraints apply in the real world. In other words, it is likely that the negative long run effects of the selective subsidy policy relative to the laissez-faire policy are underestimated. However, a laissez-faire policy seems neither politically attractive nor economically or socially desirable, based on the results of our investigation.

It should perhaps also be pointed out that the whole issue of how subsidies affect the incentives of firms has not been dealt with adequately in this study. While using a micro-based model for the analysis offers considerable advantages compared to conventional macro models, the question of incentives *within* firms has been handled here only by assumption. Thus, here remains an important topic for further research.

A comparison of the development of industrial production in the various policy alternatives shows that the selective policy gives an immediate stimulus while more general measures take longer before they yield results; on the other hand, the long-term results are much more favorable. Expressed differently, a dosage of temporary wage subsidies to all manufacturing firms yields more favorable long-term effects than a similarly large dosage of temporary subsidies to non-competitive firms. However, as far as the short-run effects are concerned, the reverse is true, since the non-competitive firms would have failed without subsidies and their production, exports, and employment would have been lost.

Thus, our study sheds light on some of the issues involved in industrial policy making. The results show that it is difficult, if not impossible, to both prevent unemployment in the short run and facilitate re-structuring with one single policy. They bring out the differences in the consequences of selective and general policies. And they illuminate the conflict between short run and long run policies. There is little doubt that the political choices made in Sweden in the latter part of the 1970s concerning adjustment policy have involved highly selective, short run policies. These policies have undoubtedly allowed Sweden to escape in the short run from certain adjustment problems at the cost of delayed adjustment and slower future growth. The question is how long it will take to reverse these policies, and how much permanent damage will have been done in the process. The problem for the future is exacerbated by the fact that Sweden's subsidy program appears to have been both considerably larger in terms of industrial output and more heavily oriented towards rescue operations than those in other European countries, creating greater destruction of incentives and contributing to greater uncertainty for firms' decision making in Sweden than elsewhere.

BO CARLSSON,
The Industrial Institute for Economic and Social Research,
Grevgatan 34,
114 53 Stockholm, Sweden

ACCEPTED JUNE 1982

APPENDIX 1

TABLE A
SWEDISH INDUSTRIAL SUBSIDIES 1970–79
Billion Skr, current prices

	Grants	*Loans*	*Total*
Firm-oriented employment subsidies	3.4	—	3.4
Regional subsidies	3.1	3.6	6.7
Small firm subsidies	.4	13.0	13.4
Sectoral subsidies	1.1	8.5	9.6
R&D subsidies	7.1	—	7.1
Export subsidies	.7	10.0	10.7
Firm specific subsidies	16.1	9.6	25.7
Total, billion Skr (%)	31.9 (42)	44.7 (58)	76.6 (100)

APPENDIX 2

BRIEF DESCRIPTION OF THE MODEL

The model used in the analysis of Swedish industrial subsidies is a micro-(firm)-based simulation model of the Swedish economy, named MOSES. What follows is a short description of some of the most central features of the model designed to facilitate the interpretation of the results reported in the main text. For a more complete description of the model, the reader should turn to the references given in footnote 10.

The model is oriented mainly toward analyzing industrial growth. Therefore, the manufacturing sector is the most detailed in the model. Manufacturing is divided into four industries (raw material processing, semi-manufactures, durable goods manufacturing, and manufacture of consumer nondurables). Each industry consists of a number of firms, some of which are real (with data supplied mainly through an annual survey) and some of which are synthetic. Together, the synthetic firms in each industry make up the differences between the real firms and the industry totals in the national accounts. The 147 real firms (including the eight "crisis-stricken firms"—see next paragraph) in the model cover 70–75% of industrial employment and production in the base year, 1976. The model is based on quarterly data.

In addition to the real firms which are normally included in the data base, certain "crisis-stricken firms" have been added in the present runs: two forest-based firms (Södra Skogsägarnas Cellulosa AB and NCB), the consolidated company formed by merging the three large Swedish commercial steel firms in 1977 (Svenskt Stål AB), the consolidated Swedish shipyards (Svenska Varv), and four textile and apparel "firms", each representing a subsector within that industry. Together, these firms received the great bulk of industrial subsidies during the 1970s, with the exception of the iron ore mines. The mining sector is outside manufacturing in MOSES and therefore is not analyzed here.

Firms in the model constitute short and long run planning systems for production and investment. Each quarter they decide on their desired production, employment and investment. Armed with these plans they go into the labor market where their employment plans confront those of other firms as well as labor supply. The labor force is treated as homogeneous in the model, i.e., labor is recruited from a common "pool". However, labor can also be recruited from other firms. This process determines the wage level, which is thus endogenous in the model. Even though the labor market is homogeneous, wages vary among both firms and industries without any tendency to converge. Since the labor market is not subdivided into industries or regions, mobility in the labor market is probably overestimated. This is important in interpreting the results.

Domestic product prices and the production volume in the four product markets are determined through a similar process. The export volume is determined endogenously in the following way.

Each quarter the firms determine their production volume in two steps. First, they determine their desired production volume, taking into account desired changes in their inventories of finished goods, based on their expected total sales (including exports) which are in turn based on the firms' historical experience. This first production plan is revised by the firms with regard to profit targets, capacity utilization, and the expected labor market situation. After this revision, the production plan is executed. The production volume is distributed to the export and domestic markets according to an export share which is dependent on that for the previous quarter but which also depends on the difference during the previous quarter between the export price and the domestic price. If this export price (which is exogenous) was higher than the domestic price, the firms try to increase their export share during the present quarter. However, the adjustment takes place over several quarters, not instantly. If the export price is lower than the domestic price, the firms do not try to lower their export share but rather maintain it at a constant level. In spite of this assymetry concerning the effect of positive or negative price differences between exports and the domestic market, it turns out that the export shares in the various markets can both increase and decrease. This depends on whether firms with high export shares fare better or worse than other firms in the market.

The import share in the four markets is also determined by the difference between the export and domestic prices with a certain time delay. High domestic prices relative to foreign prices lead to increasing import shares.

Since the adjustment of both export and import shares takes place over several quarters, price differences between the domestic and export markets can arise and last for several years. This is a source of cycles in the model: if the export price exceeds the domestic price, firms try to increase their exports. Since they are always able to sell their export supply at the going (exogenous) export price, this provides stimulus to the firms. However, the stimulus is limited by the fact that the price difference between the domestic and export market has been constrained to $\pm 2\%$. This causes the export and import shares to be relatively stable. As far as exports are concerned, this is not too surprising, since the export prices have been assumed to change smoothly. But there is considerable turbulence on the import side in these runs which arises when certain large firms are not able to reach their profit target and use up their equity capital so that they are forced to close down. This causes a loss of supply which leads to a price rise in the domestic market. Since the price differential has been constrained to be less than 2%, and since the change in the import share is not instantaneous, only *some* of the supply loss is replaced with increased domestic production in other firms and with increased imports. In order to satisfy domestic demand in spite of this, temporary "extra imports" are allowed which do not affect the "regular" import share and which remain until domestic demand can be satisfied through domestic production and "regular" imports.

There is also a capital market in the model where firms compete for investment resources and where the rate of interest is determined. However, in the present runs the rate of interest has been determined exogenously. At this given interest rate firms invest as much as they find it profitable to invest, given their profit targets. The absence of competition among firms for capital causes the effect of subsidies on investment to be more favorable than would otherwise be the case.

The public sector is treated in the following way. Public sector employment is determined exogenously, and the rate of wage increase in the public sector has been set equal to the average wage change in manufacturing. Therefore, the public sector can be said to be neutralized in these runs. The reason for neutralizing this block in the model is that it simplifies the analysis of the industrial development. Thus, public sector employment is the same regardless of the size and direction of subsidies.

The exogenous variables which drive the model are the rate of technical change (which is specific to each sector and raises the labor productivity associated with new, best practice investment) and the rate of change of prices in the export markets. The rates of change of these variables are identical in all runs reported here.

In contrast to most econometric macro models, domestic prices and wages are determined endogenously in MOSES. These in turn influence the firms' profits and therefore their production plans, the allocation of sales to the domestic and export markets, their investments, and therefore their productivity. This is the main mechanism through which resource allocation is determined in the model. These features make the model especially suited for analyzing the effects of policy measures which can be expected to influence the expectations and plans of firms and which influence the development of prices and wages. The advantage of a micro-based simulation model is that one can introduce various policy measures affecting individual firms rather than industries and analyze the effects. In more traditional macro models one is usually forced to make assumptions regarding the resource allocation effects, i.e., one has to *assume* a large portion of the results.

REFERENCES

[1] Bank of Italy, *Annual Report*, 1978.
[2] Carlsson, B., Bergholm, F., and Lindberg, T., *Industristödspolitiken och dess inverkan på samhällsekonomin* (The Industrial Subsidy Program and Its Macro-Economic Impact). (Industriens Utredningsinstitut, Stockholm, 1981).
[3] Corden, W. M. and Fels, G., *Public Assistance to Industry. Protection and Subsidies in Britain and Germany*. (Macmillan, London, 1976).
[4] Deutscher Bundestag, *Bericht der Bundesregierung über die Entwicklung der Finanzhilfen und Steuervergünstigungen für die Jahre 1977 bis 1980 gemäss § 12 des Gesetzes zur Förderung der Stabilität (Siebter Subventionsbericht)* (Report of the Federal Government on the Development of Financial Aid and Tax Subsidies for the Years 1977 through 1980 According to the Law Concerning Promotion of Stability (Seventh Subsidy Report), Drucksache 8/3097, Bonn, 1979.
[5] Eliasson, G. (ed.), *A Micro-to-Macro Model of the Swedish Economy*. Papers on the Swedish Model from the Symposium on Micro Simulation Methods in Stockholm, Sept. 19–22, 1977, IUI Conference Reports 1978:1. (Industriens Utrednings-institut, Stockholm, 1978).
[6] Eliasson, G. and Ysander, B.-C., *"Picking Winners or Bailing Out Losers? A Study of the Swedish State Holding Company and Its Role in the New Swedish Industrial Policy"*. IUI Working Paper No. 37. (Industriens Utredningsinstitut, Stockholm, 1981).
[7] Hamilton, C., "Public Subsidies to Industry. The Case of Sweden and Its Ship-building Industry". Seminar Paper No. 174, Institute for International Economic Studies, Stockholm, 1981.
[8] Industrifondet, "Offentlige/halvoffentlige selektive finansielle virkemidler for industrien" (Public/Semi-public Selective Financial Resources to Industry). Mimeo, Oslo, December 1980.
[9] ———, "Offentlige midler tilført industrien og endringer i garantier 1975–1979" (Public Disbursements to Industry and Changes in Guarantees 1975–1979). Mimeo, Oslo, 01.10.80.
[10] Istituto Centrale di Statistica, *Rendiconto Finanziario dello Stato 1978* (State Financial Accounts 1978).
[11] Juttemeier, K. H. and Lammers, K., *Subventionen in der Bundesrepublik Deutschland* (Subsidies in the Federal Republic of Germany). Kiel Discussion Papers 63/64 Institut für Weltwirtschaft, Kiel, 1979.
[12] OECD, Technical Sub-Group on Transparency of the Special Group of the Economic Policy Committee on Positive Adjustment Policies, "Appraisal and Reporting Methodologies on Certain Types of Direct Government Intervention Used in Selected OECD Member Countries", Draft Report by the Secretariat, CPE/PAP/TR(80) 1, Paris, 1980.
[13] ———, *National Accounts of OECD Countries 1962–1979*. OECD, Paris, 1981.
[14] Ohlin, G., "Sweden", in Vernon, R. (ed.), *Big Business and the State. Changing Relations in Western Europe*. Harvard University Press, Cambridge, MA., 1974.
[15] Public Expenditure White Paper, *U.K. Parliamentary Papers*, Cmnd. 8175. HMSO, London, March 1981.

[16] Sjöström, L. H. and Olofsson, B., "Statligt industristöd i Västtyskland" (Government Industrial Subsidies in West Germany), Swedish Embassy in Bonn PM 1981.03.05. Mimeo, Bonn, 1981.

[17] Whiting, A. (ed.), *The Economics of Industrial Subsidies.* Papers and Proceedings of the Conference on the Economics of the Industrial Subsidies held at the Civil Service College, Sunningdale, February 1975. (Department of Industry. HMSO, London, 1976).

THE JOURNAL OF INDUSTRIAL ECONOMICS
Volume XXXII September 1983 No. 1

INDUSTRY STRUCTURE AND THE SPEED OF PRICE ADJUSTMENT*

R. Dixon

I. INTRODUCTION

Recent work has suggested that there is an association between the degree of concentration in an industry and the speed at which prices adjust to changes in prime costs (Cagan [8], Domberger [12, 13], Scherer [21], p. 356 and the references cited therein). Apart from its intrinsic interest to students of industrial economics, there would seem to be three reasons for investigating this association. First, to see what light, if any, it throws upon the influence of industrial structure on the price level together with the rate (and process) of inflation. Secondly, to test the assumption made in some influential studies (e.g. Godley and Nordhaus [15]; Coutts, Godley and Nordhaus [10] and Haig and Wood [18]) that the size of the lag between cost and price changes is solely dependent upon the length of the fabrication, production and delivery period in the various industries. The third reason is a 'belief', held by the author, that distributed lag coefficients in econometric studies should be subject to analysis and not left 'hanging in the air'.

As part of the development of a large scale econometric model of the Australian economy (the IMP model) a team of researchers (under the direction of Dr Brain) at Melbourne University have estimated price–prime cost equations for 43 manufacturing sectors, using annual data referring to the period 1948/49–1973/74.[1]

The estimating equation is of the form:

$$\ln P_{i,t} = \lambda_i(\ln \beta_{i,t} + \ln PC_{i,t}) + (1 - \lambda_i)\ln P_{i,t-1}$$

where: P_i = price index for industry i output allocated to domestic markets.
β_i = a (flexible) markup percentage, which may assume different values in different periods.
PC_i = actual industry prime costs (defined to equal labour plus materials costs) per unit of output in any period.
λ_i = lag parameter.

* I am grateful to Neville Norman, Ian McDonald, Tony Thirlwall and an anonymous referee for helpful comments on an earlier draft. The methodology adopted in this study is analogous to that of Griliches [16] as modified by Dixon [11].

[1] The structure of the model is described in Brain [5]. The procedure used to estimate the price–prime cost equations which are the basis for the present paper are discussed in Brain [6] and [7].

TABLE I
ESTIMATED LAG COEFFICIENTS (λ)

	ASIC[a]	*Lag parameters*[b]	*t-value*
Milk products	212	0.985	17.138
Fruit and vegetable products	213	0.740	5.730
Margarine, oils and fats	214	0.880	12.456
Flour mill and cereal food products	215	0.632	7.312
Bread, cakes and biscuits, sugar and other food products	216–8	0.867	7.482
Beverages and malt	219	0.656	4.761
Tobacco products	221	0.482	4.390
Prepared fibres	2311–3	0.466	2.332
Man-made yarns and fibres	2314–9, 2322	0.983	21.751
Textile finishing	2321	1.061	14.762
Textile floor coverings and other textile products	233	0.868	8.675
Knitting mills	241	0.940	13.680
Joinery and wood products	2514, 2516	0.995	15.238
Furniture	252	1.108	16.550
Printed matter	262	0.974	13.851
Industrial chemicals	271	0.767	10.181
Paints	2722	0.949	12.288
Soap	2725	0.342	5.361
Other chemicals	272—(2722 + 2725)	0.667	4.710
Petroleum and coal products	273–4	1.023	15.154
Glass and glass products	281	0.766	9.907
Clay products	282	0.526	5.096
Cement and concrete products	283	0.683	10.901
Other non-metallic mineral products	284	0.852	9.770
Basic iron and steel	291	0.840	16.425
Non-ferrous metal basic products	292–3	0.904	6.596
Fabricated structural metal products	311	0.923	14.771
Metal containers, sheet metal products	312	0.958	11.745
Motor vehicles and parts	321	0.883	6.852
Other transport equipment	322	1.013	18.256
Appliances and electronic equipment	331 + (3321–3)	0.681	8.197
Leather products	341	0.968	7.307
Rubber products	342	0.905	13.058

[a] Australian Standard Industrial Classification code number.
[b] The mean value of the lag parameter is ($\lambda =$) 0.827 which implies a mean lag of $2\frac{1}{2}$ months.
Source: Brain [7, Table 1].

In estimating the (home) price equation, the markup (β_i) is not assumed to be constant[2] but is specified to be a log-linear function of an index of the price of capital, the capital–output ratio, the ratio of an international trade (in commodity i) price index to domestic costs per unit of output, the percentage deviation of output from capacity and a time trend.

[2] In this respect the price–prime cost relationship which forms the basis for the present study is superior to that of most other studies (e.g. Domberger [12] and [13]) in that they assume that the markup is constant. Whilst the price equations reported in our study do not exclude this possibility (i.e. we allow for the possibility of zero coefficients on the variables which are hypothesised to account for variations in the markup) they are more general than fixed markup equations.

Although 43 industries were studied, the lag coefficient was constrained to equal unity in the price equation for ten of these industries, and so we are left with 33 estimated lag coefficients to be explained. Table I reports on the estimated lag coefficients together with their standard errors. It is important to note that the higher is the magnitude of the lag coefficient (λ) the shorter is the length of the lag, that is, the greater is the size of the lag parameter, the faster is the speed of adjustment of price to changes in prime costs.[3]

II. THEORIES OF THE LAG

Two theories have been advanced, or may be culled from the literature, by way of attempts to account for the speed of adjustment of prices in an industry to changes in prime costs. One approach (stressed by Godley and Nordhaus [15]) focuses upon the length of the production period. A second approach, stressed by industrial organisation literature, focuses upon the degree of concentration within an industry.

(a) *The length of the production period*

Where inputs and stocks are valued according to historical cost (FIFO), and especially where this is accompanied by a lengthy production or gestation period, we would expect there to be a relatively long lag between changes in costs and changes in prices (Godley and Nordhaus [15, p. 862] and Coutts, Godley and Nordhaus [10, p. 36f]).

If the production process were such that all inputs entered progressively we might depict it as a triangle, the base of which represents the length of the production period (θ) and the height of which represents the cumulative value of inputs (plus notional profits). The height of the R.H.S. of the triangle at the end of the production period measures the value of sales.

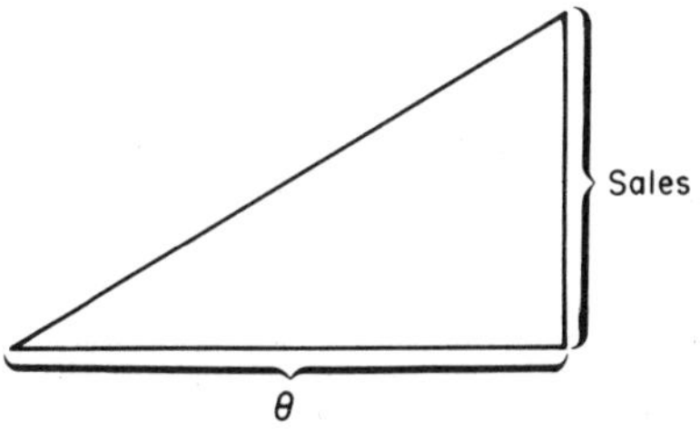

The area of the triangle will also equal the total value of stocks of work in progress (SWIP) at any point in time, assuming that the production process is continuous. That is:

$$\text{SWIP} = \tfrac{1}{2}(\theta \cdot \text{Sales})$$

[3] The presence of a lagged dependent variable may be rationalised on one or other grounds. First, as an outcome of an adaptive expectations hypothesis (i.e. firms forecast prime-costs) or, secondly, as an outcome of partial adjustment of actual price to desired price. It is the second rationalisation which shall be explored in this paper.

It follows that in the event that all inputs were added progressively and the production process were continuous, we could measure the length of the production period as:[4]

$$\theta = \frac{2(\text{SWIP})}{\text{Sales}}$$

As Godley and Nordhaus [15, p. 864f] point out, it may not be the case that all inputs are added progressively, indeed it is common for some raw materials to enter at the beginning of the production run. In this event the measure of the length of the production period has to be adjusted to take into account the initial entry of some (if not all) materials. Godley and Nordhaus show that the appropriate measure would be:

$$\theta = \frac{2(\text{SWIP})}{\text{Sales}(1 + \alpha\beta)}$$

where: α = share of materials costs in sales revenue.
β = proportion of the materials costs which are incurred at the beginning of the period.[5]

In this paper the length of the 'production period' is arrived at by adjusting the above measure to account for the stockpiling of raw materials (prior to the commencement of the production process) and the holding of output as stocks of finished goods. We will assume that stocks of raw materials are added to, and depleted, continuously, such that at any point in time the measure of the value of stocks of raw materials will be approximately equal to the product of their turnover period times the monthly rate of usage. We will assume that finished goods are produced 'to order' (in the Carlson [9] sense) in that they are accumulated until an order arrives and are then shipped in a batch.[6] Thus we shall measure the 'production lag' as:[7]

$$\text{PLAG} = \left[\frac{\text{SM}}{\text{U}}\right] + \left[\frac{2(\text{SWIP})}{\text{Sales}(1 + \alpha\beta)}\right] + \left[\frac{2(\text{SFG})}{\text{Sales}}\right]$$

[4] See Carlson [9] and Coutts *et al.* [10].

[5] Coutts, Godley and Nordhaus [10] use the length of the production period, as estimated by this technique, to determine the lag profile prior to and as a constraint upon the specification and estimation of the price equations for U.K. manufacturing. They assume that $\beta = 0.66$.

[6] In the event that stocks entered and left at the same (continuous) rate we would model stocks of finished goods in the same (rectangular) way as we have treated stocks of raw materials. In treating them 'triangularly' we are following Carlson [9] and Coutts *et al.* [10]. We did experiment with the alternative specifications and it may be reported that our results are not at all sensitive to the treatment of stocks.

[7] There is a possible problem here, which arises from the fact that the price equations are estimated with a single lag imposed whereas our measure is of the longest lag (i.e. the period from purchase of the materials to sale of the product). This will not coincide with the 'lag' in passing on changes in wage costs alone which (assuming FIFO accounting) will be determined by the length of the last two terms in our expression.

where: SM = stocks of materials
SFG = stocks of finished goods
U = Usage rate of materials
$\beta = 0.66$ (by assumption)

Figures for the 'production' lag for each industry are given in Table II.

TABLE II
MEASURES OF THE PRODUCTION LAG

ASIC	PLAG[a]	ASIC	PLAG[a]
212	0.10	2725	0.40
213	0.71	272—(2722 + 2725)	0.46
214	0.28	273–4	0.17
215	0.25	281	0.87
216–8	0.14	282	0.49
219	0.29	283	0.25
221	1.06	284	0.32
2311–3	0.34	291	0.33
2314–9, 2322	0.44	292–3	0.35
2321	0.21	311	0.34
233	0.39	312	0.37
241	0.28	321	0.32
2514, 2516	0.26	322	0.53
252	0.25	331 + (3321–3)	0.47
262	0.36	341	0.61
271	0.45	242	0.27
2722	0.39		

[a] Expressed as a proportion of a calendar year.
Source: Australian Bureau of Statistics [3].

(b) *The degree of concentration*

Stigler [23] has argued that the fewer the number of firms in an industry, the easier it is for secret price cutting to be detected. This is because the fewer the number of rivals (*ceteris paribus*) the more discernible will be the effect of price cutting upon the sales of any one firm. Instead of limiting the theory to the consideration of cuts in absolute prices we may regard it as (potentially) applicable to the case where firms might be tempted to 'lag' behind when prices are adjusting to previous increases in costs.[8] Thus the theory might be taken to predict that adjustments will be faster (and more orderly) in industries which have fewer firms as against those in which the number of firms is larger. The relevant variable to account for the length of the lag would

[8] This may be construed to be a hypothesis relating to the 'orderliness' of price changes (i.e. λ_i/σ_i) as much as the speed of adjustment (i.e. the size of λ). Common sense would suggest that oligopolies would take advantage of changes in prime costs (especially if these were known (i.e. signalled) be to be industry wide) to put up prices in an orderly fashion, and also to take advantage of such an event in order to 'catch-up' for previous increases in demand, advert. expenses or 'firm-specific' events. (Labini [19, p. 156f].)

TABLE III
INDICES OF MARKET STRUCTURE

ASIC	n^a	CR^b	m^c
212	252	0.22	0.9
213	130	0.34	5.8
214	31	0.72	21.2
215	118	0.51	0.7
216–8	2058	0.32*	6.0
219	577	0.38	8.5
221	6	1.00	16.6
2311–3	51	0.92*	17.1
2314–9, 2322	234	0.63*	33.1
2321	108	0.55	0.0
233	374	0.37	25.5
241	407	0.23	8.5
2514, 2516	2043	0.14*	3.9
252	1696	0.16	1.6
262	2655	0.23	11.4
271	144	0.47	29.5
2722	163	0.60	2.0
2725	156	0.61	4.6
272—(2722 + 2725)	461	0.30*	14.2
273–4	40	0.68*	32.7
281	47	0.95	23.2
282	269	0.32	14.4
283	547	0.34	0.2
284	364	0.47	10.3
291	255	0.83	8.5
292–3	240	0.45	6.2
311	1429	0.16	6.1
312	913	0.33	2.4
321	806	0.68	22.0
322	529	0.26	56.5
331 + (3321–3)	754	0.36*	28.1
341	442	0.29	20.0
342	112	0.74	17.0

[a] Number of firms in the industry.
[b] Four-firm concentration ratio.
Source: Australian Bureau of Statistics [4].
* Estimated by author.
[c] Imports as a percentage of domestic sales.
Source: Australia. Committee . . . [2].

therefore appear to be the number of firms in the industry (n_1),[9] or some transformation of n_i, such as $[n(n-1)]$ since that is a measure of the number of inter-connections between n firms in an industry. Stigler indicates that, once the number of firms are weighted by size, the appropriate explanatory variable would be the Herfindahl index. We will use the 'top-four-firm share of sales' concentration ratio as an approximation to the Herfindahl index whilst attempting to adjust the 'sales-based' four-firm concentration ratio to take

[9] Phillips [20] also stresses that the number of firms may act as an index of the effectiveness of price-fixing behaviour.

account of the importance of imports as a source of supply.[10] Figures for the concentration ratio, the proportion of sales accounted for by imports together with the number of firms within each industry (all as at 1968–69)[11] are presented in Table II.

It is important at this point to note that what empirical evidence we have on the role of concentration in influencing the rate of adjustment of prices to changes in prime costs is conflicting. Domberger, in his study of U.K. manufacturing industries, asserts that in "highly concentrated oligopolistic sectors, characterised by low costs of search and communication between sellers, price changes can be effectively co-ordinated and the adjustment of equilibrium speeded up" [12, p. 96]. He found [12 and 13] finds a significant and positive relationship between the size of the lag parameter and indices of the degree of concentration indicating that the more concentrated the industry, the faster the speed of adjustment of prices to changes in costs.[12] On the other hand Yordon [24, p. 292] found for U.S. industry that ". . . there is almost no support for the view that the degree of concentration . . . affects [the] rate of price response to cost changes." Scherer cites a number of other authors as demonstrating that ". . . there is a tendency for concentrated industries to pass on, in the year they occurred, a smaller fraction of cost increases . . . than atomistically structured industries". (Scherer [21, p. 356].)

III. THE EMPIRICAL ANALYSIS

Theory suggests that the speed of adjustment of price changes to cost changes should be related to the period of production (assuming FIFO accounting) and to the degree of interdependencies between firms in the industries. Our econometric work shall deal with the investigation of the relationship between the lag parameters (λ), and various explanatory variables mentioned above: i.e., with equations of the form:

$$\lambda_i = f(\text{PLAG}_i;\ \text{CR}_i;\ \ldots).$$

[10] Our measures of interdependence and concentration are 'national' indices and need to be adjusted on two counts: First, they neglect the role of overseas supplies in domestic markets, and the exportation of domestic production. Secondly, they need to be adjusted in those industries (such as printing, cement, etc.) whereas geographic fragmentation is important. Various indices of the importance of exports and of fragmentation were experimented with but all proved to be insignificant and unsatisfactory. The only adjustment which proved to be worthwhile was to include import rates as an additional explanatory variable. Implicitly we are assuming that either we are dealing with undifferentiated oligopolies or that the degree of differentiation is constant across industries and sample period.

[11] Data on concentration are available only for the years 1968–69 and 1972–73. Since data for 1968–69 lie nearer to the mid-point of our study period statistics for that date have been taken as those most appropriate for our purposes. Other 'point' measures were then measured at this date. It would appear as though there has been little change in the relative rankings of industries with respect to each of our industries throughout the study period.

[12] Domberger used a dummy variable which took the value of unity for engineering industries and zero for all other industries, supposedly reflecting the longer period of production in engineering. The coefficient of the lag parameter on the dummy is significant and negative.

TABLE IV
(WEIGHTED) REGRESSIONS OF THE LAG PARAMETER ON VARIOUS EXPLANATORY VARIABLES

Explanatory variable	*Coefficients and t-values*[a]		
Weight[b]	0.993	1.034	0.942
	(14.15)*	(13.85)*	(13.97)*
$PLAG_i$[c]	−0.342	−0.442	−0.498
	(1.94)***	(2.32)**	(2.83)*
CR_i[d]		−0.165	
		(1.33)	
$n(n-1)_i$[e]			3×10^{-7}
			(1.90)***
m_i[f]		0.005	0.005
		(2.31)**	(2.65)**
SER[g]	2.269	2.106	2.046

[a] * Significant at 0.01 level.
** Significant at 0.05 level.
*** Significant at 0.10 level.

[b] All equations are estimated with a constant in the original (unweighted) form. This constant becomes, after weighting, a vector of $(1/\sigma_i)$ across industries.

[c] A measure of the length of the production lag (from Table II).

[d] The four-firm sales-based concentration ratio (from Table III).

[e] A measure of the number of interdependencies between firms, where n = number of firms in each industry (from Table III).

[f] The proportion of domestic sales accounted for by imports (from Table III).

[g] Standard Error of the Regression.

However, we must note that because our dependent variable (λ_i) is itself a coefficient estimated from its own 'fitted' equation, we would expect the different observations of λ_i to each have their own, and not identical, standard errors. In other words in our 'explanatory' regressions the use of λ_i alone would introduce heteroscedasticity into the estimating equation.[13] For this reason our estimating equations will be based upon weighted least squares, of the form:

$$\frac{\lambda_i}{\sigma_i} = f\left(\frac{\text{PLAG}}{\sigma_i}, \frac{\text{CR}}{\sigma_i}; \ldots\right)$$

where σ_i = standard error of the estimate of λ_i.

Results of weighted least squares regressions are reported in Table IV, for three cases: first, where the length of the production lag[14] alone is used as an

[13] See Dixon [11], and the references cited therein.

[14] Alternative measures of the production lag were experimented with, e.g. allowing for production 'to stock' rather than 'to order'. The results were essentially the same as those reported here.

explanatory variable; secondly, where the production lag together with the four-firm concentration ratio[15, 16] (adjusted for imports) are used as explanatory variables; and, thirdly, where the production lag together with the potential number of interdependencies between firms[17] (adjusted for imports) are used as explanatory variables. The last two are meant to include alternative measures of 'fewness'. In all of the regressions reported in Table IV the production lag (together with the other explanatory variables) is assumed to be linearly related to the size of the lag parameter. It is likely, however, that the relationship is non-linear, especially in so far as the production lag is concerned. The mean value of the lag parameter in months is (negatively) exponentially related to the size of the lag parameter[18] which suggests that if the production lag is measured in months, there will be a linear relationship between the size of the lag parameter and the logarithm of the length of the production lag.

Table V reports the results of weighted regressions of the lag parameter on the explanatory variables, with all variables entering in a linear fashion except the production lag (in months) which enters non-linearly.

We find that the coefficient of the lag parameter on the length of the production period is negative in all cases.[19] indicating that the longer the period of production the slower the speed of adjustment of prices to variations in prime costs. This is as we would expect.

F tests indicate that the explanatory power of the regressions are enhanced by the use of variables representing industrial structure in addition to the production lag. There is no warrant therefore for accepting the view, implicit in the work of Coutts, Godley and Nordhaus [10] and Haig and Wood [18] for example, that the length of the lag between changes in prime costs and changes in prices solely reflects the effect of stock turnover periods and the length of the period of production.

Turning to the role of the variables representing industrial structure, we find that the coefficient on the concentration ratio is negative, albeit insignificant, whilst the coefficient on the potential number of interdependencies

[15] Only the four-firm concentration ratio is reported. The degree of association between the 4-firm and the 8-firm ratio is so high that conclusions drawn with respect to one apply equally well to the other.

[16] Domberger [12] and [13] includes, as variables to explain interindustry differences in the lag parameter, measures of the change in the Concentration Ratio (and the H-index) over the sample period. However, to do this contradicts the assumption that the lag parameter is not time dependent. This assumption lies behind the estimation procedure which is used to estimate the lag parameter, as it is regarded to be a constant in the original price equation. One cannot estimate it as a constant (over-time) parameter, and then 'explain' it as if it were not a constant over time.

[17] Alternative measures of interdependence were tried, including the number of firms (n) and the inverse of the number of firms (n^{-1}). In no case were the results better than those reported here.

[18] The formula for computing the mean lag in years, given the value of the adjustment coefficient for any industry is: mean lag = $[(1 - \lambda)/\lambda]$, which is a non-linear function of λ.

[19] With one observation (Soap) excluded (that being the only major outlier in the regressions) the coefficient on the production lag when it is the lone explanatory variable does become significantly different from zero at the 5% level.

TABLE V
(WEIGHTED) REGRESSIONS OF THE LAG PARAMETER ON VARIOUS EXPLANATORY VARIABLES

Explanatory variable	*Coefficients and t-values*[a]		
Weight[b]	0.703	0.684	0.533
	(9.29)*	(5.55)*	(5.56)*
Log of $PLAG_i$[c]	−0.124	−0.171	−0.197
	(1.91)***	(2.47)**	(3.06)*
CR_i[d]		−0.176	
		(1.46)	
$n(n-1)_i$[d]			4×10^{-7}
			(2.13)**
m_i[d]		0.005	0.006
		(2.44)**	(2.85)*
SER[d]	2.273	2.084	2.009

[a] * Significant at 0.01 level.
** Significant at 0.05 level.
*** Significant at 0.10 level.

[b] All equations are estimated with a constant in the original (unweighted) form. This constant becomes, after weighting, a vector of $(1/\sigma_i)$ across industries.

[c] Logarithm of the production lag measured in months (so as to allow for non-linearity) (from Table II).

[d] See notes to Table IV.

between firms [$n(n-1)$] is positive and significantly different from zero at the 10% level. Although one could hope for more precision in the estimates, the results do indicate that (contrary to Stigler's hypothesis, and Domberger's findings for U.K. manufacturing [12, 13]) the rate of adjustment of prices to prime costs is slower the more concentrated the industry [i.e. the higher the concentration ratio the lower the value for the lag parameter (λ)] and that the smaller the number of firms in the industry the slower is the rate of adjustment (i.e. the lower n, the lower the value for λ).

The positive coefficient on the import share variable (m) may be rationalised by seeing this variable as adjusting the concentration and interdependence measures to take account of competition from foreign suppliers. Thus the concentration ratio tends to overstate the true degree of concentration and this requires an offsetting on the import variable. Likewise the number of firms variable [$n(n-1)$] taken alone, will understate the potential rivals where foreign suppliers are operating in the market, and this requires a 'boost' from the coefficient on the imports variable.

IV. IMPLICATIONS AND CONCLUSIONS

First, it must be noted that our results[20] tend to give support to the hypothesis that the length of the production lag affects the length of the lag between

[20] These findings must be regarded as tentative. We must recognise that our results are time and place specific. Also that our results may be an artifact of the particular technique used to estimate the lag parameter in the original price–cost equations. The sensitivity of the results to the

changes in unit costs and changes in prices, but it does not appear to be the sole determinant of the length of the lag.

Secondly, Stigler's hypothesis that the extent of price cutting is inversely related to the number of firms in an industry (insofar as it may be extended beyond (absolute) price 'cutting' to (relative) price 'lagging') is not supported by our evidence, indeed it appears to be contradicted by it.[21]

Thirdly, our findings would also suggest that in order to understand the rate of (and the processes involved in) inflation, attention *must* be given to characteristics of the production process and to the structure of industry. This is in marked contrast to much recent work on inflation (e.g. that surveyed by Hagger [17]) which makes little or no mention of microeconomic or industrial organisation matters.

Fourthly, our findings seem to indicate that there may be a tendency for 'fewness' to be associated with 'slowness' of adjustment. Even tentative acceptance of this hypothesis would seem to have disturbing implications for the likely success of macroeconomic stabilisation policies and for the 'side-effects' which might accompany such (especially, monetarist) policies.

In an interesting paper published some time ago J. K. Galbraith argued that, because of the economic power of oligopolistic firms, and their slower rate of adaptation of prices to changes in demand conditions, ". . . that both monetary and fiscal policy must have a markedly differing impact on different parts of the economy, and this will be different at different times depending on the state of adaptation. This is especially true of monetary policy." [14, p. 130.] He goes on to say that; "By monetary policy we seek to control inflation by denying to the small business cum competition sector the credit on which growth depends. . . . By both monetary and fiscal policy we reduce prices and profits in the competitive sector by methods which leave them unaffected in the oligopolistic sector. As a centralizing influence in the economy it is possible to imagine that an active and continuing monetary policy is not less effective than, say, the repeal of the antitrust laws." [14, p. 133.] In addition to Galbraith, Ackley [1], Sellekaerts and Lesage [22] and Coutts *et al.* [10] (amongst others) have discussed the consequences (in terms of higher unemployment than would otherwise be the case) of the exercise of monetarist anti-inflationary policy in a world where prices are insensitive to variations in

---

specification of the original price–prime cost estimating equation, and its associated lag structure should be considered. (Indeed, there may be advantages to treating the rate of adjustment as an endogenous variable in the original price–prime cost estimating equation.) In addition it will be recalled that the lag parameter was derived from estimating equations fitted to annual data, the results may be sensitive to the use of annual rather than quarterly or monthly data. Furthermore, it may be that our maintained hypothesis "that the lag parameter is a 'partial adjustment coefficient'" is incorrect, and that it ought properly be regarded as an 'expectations coefficient'. Also some allowance has to be made for the presence of differentiated oligopoly.

[21] It may be argued (see n.8, above) that Stigler's hypothesis is really an explanation of the 'orderliness' of price changes, i.e. that firms in an oligopolistic industry will tend to change their prices together. In this guise the hypothesis is to do with the variance of the response in addition to, or instead of, the length of the response (on average). This hypothesis is also rejected by the evidence as neither the standard error of the lag parameter (σ_i), nor a measure of the variance around the 'average' response in each industry, (σ_i/λ_i) are significantly related to the industry concentration variables [CR, $n(n-1)$ and m].

the pressure of demand. Our results may give some support to these arguments.

A final implication of our results concerns the Keynesian predilection for wages *and* prices policies as an appropriate panacea for stagflation. Our findings would indicate that there may be considerable resistance to these policies from (oligopolistic) firms. We have seen that prices tend to lag behind costs[22] and thus, where wage and price inflation has been going on it is likely that firms in oligopolistic industries will very strongly resist the application of price controls, the more so if price controls are intended to be applied simultaneously with wage controls. The firms will argue that, at any point in time, they need to catch-up on past increases in costs, i.e. that there is a cost (wage)-price 'overhang'. Organised labour on the other hand will press strongly for the absence of wage controls or, as a second best strategy, they will press for the *simultaneous* application of wage and price controls (partly by way of an attempt to freeze the wage-share at a 'relatively' high level). The situation is clearly one of inherent conflict between parties capable of wielding considerable ecomomic and political power.[23] Further, it is important to recognise that the introduction of an incomes policy into this environment will not be, and will not be seen to be, an action which will resolve or prevent conflict, rather the reverse.[24] It may well be the case that because of the degree of resistance from firms and unions in concentrated industries (for the reasons mentioned above) that an incomes policy will be ineffective in all but the more 'competitive', relatively un-unionised, industries.

R. Dixon
Economics Department,
University of Melbourne,
Parkville,
Victoria 3052, Australia

ACCEPTED MAY 1982

REFERENCES

[1] Ackley, G., 'Administered Prices and the Inflation Process', *American Economic Review* (May 1959), pp. 419–30.

[2] Australia. Committee to Advise on Policies for Manufacturing Industry, *Policies for the Development of Manufacturing Industry, Volume Two* (Australian Government Publishing Service, Canberra, 1975).

[22] And also that there is a tendency for this lag to be even more pronounced, the fewer the number of firms in the industry.

[23] All the more so because of the tendency for high seller concentration to be matched by a high degree of unionisation in an industry. (See Scherer [21, p. 358–62] and the references cited therein.)

[24] The introduction of an incomes policy may well result in the worsening of the position of poorly organised labour in 'competitive' industries. This may occur as: (i) their money wage relative to other workers is likely to decline because they are less well organised and have less economic power, and (ii) since prices adjust more rapidly to costs in those industries they will not have the possibility (and it is no more than that) that a wage-price freeze (initiated once inflation has been under way) will allow the maintenance of a relatively high wage-share.

[3] AUSTRALIAN BUREAU OF STATISTICS, *Manufacturing Establishments: Details of Operations by Industry Class 1968–69* (Canberra, 1973).

[4] AUSTRALIAN BUREAU OF STATISTICS, *Industry Concentration Statistics 1968–69* (Canberra, 1974).

[5] BRAIN, P., 'The Institute Multi-Purpose Model: An Outline', *Australian Economic Review* (no. 39, 1977), pp. 47–64.

[6] BRAIN, P., 'Why Do Model Results Differ?', paper presented to the *Eighth Conference of Economists*, La Trobe University, 1979.

[7] BRAIN, P., 'Price and Income Determination in Australian Manufacturing in *Structure of the Australian Economy* (forthcoming).

[8] CAGAN, P., 'Inflation and Market Structure 1967–1973', *Explorations in Economic Research* (Spring 1975), pp. 203–16.

[9] CARLSON, J. A., 'The Production Lag', *American Economic Review* (March 1973), pp. 73–86.

[10] COUTTS, K., GODLEY, W. A. H., and NORDHAUS, W. D., *Industrial Pricing in the United Kingdom* (Cambridge University Press, London, 1978).

[11] DIXON, R. J., 'Hybrid Corn Revisited', *Econometrica* (September 1980), pp. 1451–61.

[12] DOMBERGER, S., 'Price Adjustment and Market Structure', *Economic Journal* (March 1979), pp. 96–108.

[13] DOMBERGER, S., 'Mergers, Market Structure and the Rate of Price Adjustment in K. Cowling (*et al.*), *Mergers and Economic Performance* (Cambridge University Press, Cambridge, 1980), pp. 343–68.

[14] GALBRAITH, J. K., 'Market Structure and Stabilisation Policy', *Review of Economics and Statistics* (May 1957), pp. 124–33.

[15] GODLEY, W. A. and NORDHAUS, W. D., 'Pricing in the Trade Cycle', *Economic Journal* (September 1972), pp. 583–82.

[16] GRILICHES, Z., 'Hybrid Corn: An Exploration in the Economics of Technological Change', *Econometrica* (October 1957), pp. 501–22.

[17] HAGGER, A. J., *Inflation: Theory and Policy* (Macmillan, London, 1977).

[18] HAIG, B. D. and WOOD, M. P., 'Tracing Price Changes Through Stages of Production: Australia, 1968 to 1977', *Review of Income and Wealth* (March 1979), pp. 1–30.

[19] LABINI, P. SYLOS, 'Industrial Pricing in the U.K.', *Cambridge Journal of Economics* (June 1979), pp. 153–63.

[20] PHILLIPS, A., *Market Structure, Organisation and Performance* (Harvard University Press, Cambridge, Mass., 1962).

[21] SCHERER, F. M., *Industrial Market Structure and Economic Performance* (Rand McNally, Chicago, Second Edition 1980).

[22] SELLEKAERTS, W. and LESAGE, R., 'A Reformulation and Empirical Verification of the Administered Prices Inflation Hypothesis: the Canadian Case', *Southern Economic Journal* (January 1973), pp. 345–60.

[23] STIGLER, G. J., 'A Theory of Oligopoly', *Journal of Political Economy* (February 1964), pp. 44–61.

[24] YORDON, W., 'Industrial Concentration and Price Flexibility in Inflation', *Review of Economics and Statistics* (August 1961), pp. 287–94.

THE JOURNAL OF INDUSTRIAL ECONOMICS
Volume XXXII September 1983 No. 1

FIRM SIZE AND TECHNICAL CHANGE IN A DYNAMIC CONTEXT

RAPHAEL KAPLINSKY

I. THE PROBLEM

THE relationship between firm size and technical change has long been a pre-occupation in the literature, preceding the flurry of macroeconomic studies which followed the discovery of the 'residual factor' by Solow, Dennison and others. Although this concern goes back at least to the writings of Marx, it was Schumpeter who first emphasized the relationship between firm size and technical change. Schumpeter [19], writing in 1942, pointed out that market imperfections—namely the ever-increasing trend towards oligopolistic market structures—did not necessarily result in sub-optimal levels of invention and innovation.

> "Thus it is not sufficient to argue that because perfect competition is impossible under modern industrial conditions—or because it always has been impossible—the large-scale establishment or unit of control must be accepted as a necessary evil inseparable from the economic progress which it is prevented from sabotaging by the forces inherent in its productive apparatus. What we have got to accept is that it has come to be the most powerful engine of that progress of the long-run expansion of total output not only in spite of, but to a considerable extent through, this strategy which looks so restrictive when viewed in the individual case and from the individual point of time. In this respect, perfect competition is not only impossible but inferior, and has no title to being set up as a model of ideal efficiency" (Schumpeter [19, p. 101]).

For some years this assertion of Schumpeter's was widely accepted. But then a number of detailed empirical studies were undertaken resting on 1950s data (Scherer [17] and [18] and 1960s data (Shrieves [20]). These began to suggest that beyond a certain size (roughly 5,000 employees, according to Scherer) inventive activity rose less than proportionately with bigness. Soete [22], in an important study, has questioned these conclusions, resting his argument on more recent 1970s data, with a different sample (i.e. excluding oil companies) and a different indicator of inventive activity (i.e. R and D as % of sales rather than numbers of R and D workers or patents registered). Soete's conclusions are unequivocal and, *at a macroeconomic level and within a restricted time period (1974–6)*, wholly believable—there is clearly a positive relationship between size and the effort expended in changing technology.

By contrast, and more recently, Rothwell and Zegveld [16] assembled a variety of country studies, some of which suggest that small and medium sized firms (that is those employing less than 500 people) are relatively invention- and innovation-intensive in some sectors and in some countries.

We are faced therefore with contrasting sets of views on the relationship between firm size and technical change.[1] Although to some extent these conflicting views arise as a consequence of using different indicators of technical change—i.e. input measures (number of employees or % of sales in R and D) versus output measures (patents)—there remains a residual set of views which directly conflict with each other. The purpose of this paper is to argue, by illustration with a single sector, *computer-aided design* (CAD), that the above-mentioned studies reach their varying conclusions in a largely static framework. Thus, whilst there is always a tendency towards concentration in capitalism, the relationship between firm size and technical change is a dynamic one, ensuring that static generalisations at any single point of time are not very helpful.

In the following section we describe the market structure in the CAD sector and analyse how this has changed over the past decade.[2] In section IV we analyse the nature of the barriers to entry in this sector and illustrate how these are typical of other emerging software-intensive microelectronic-based sectors. Finally in section V we return to the earlier discussion on the relationship between firm size and inventive activity.

II. COMPUTER AIDED DESIGN TECHNOLOGY

CAD is a particularly good example of a software intensive industry. Building on a fairly standard set of microelectronic hardware (predominantly minicomputers) and peripheral components (television screens, computer memory, drawing devices and digitising boards[3]) systems are available to undertake a wide range of tasks to assist designers and draughtspersons in their work. This assistance is of two major sorts. The first involves *basic graphic software* which speeds up the process of drawing;[4] the second involves a wide variety of *applications programs* to meet particular design needs in all sectors of engineering (electrical, civil, mechanical, chemical), cartography, business analysis and animation.

The price of these systems starts from around $30,000 for a single termina system which is suitable only for drawing, to around $1.5 m for a 30 termina system which provides both a wide variety of analytical applications programs

[1] See also Kamien and Schwartz [12] for a survey of additional literature in this subject.
[2] Much of the detailed case-study material is drawn from Kaplinsky [14].
[3] These are flat surfaces which are used to convert drawing specifications to the digital format utilised by electronic systems.
[4] Or the reproduction of design information in other forms which may be relevant e.g. paper tape for CNC machine tools.

and a capability to undertake numerous, unrelated batch processing tasks such as payrolls and customer billing. Of these prices, around 30 percent is hardware; the rest comprises overheads and a considerable input of software.

The origins of this industry lay in the aerospace and defence sectors in the late 1950s and 1960s. By the early 1970s CAD began to be used in the electronic sector, diffusing to mechanical engineering and cartography over the past five years. The industry expects the civil engineering and architectural sectors to be the major growth point in the second half of the 1980s. The growth of this sector has been quite remarkable. Having reached around \$80 m in 1976, the sector 'took off' with the value of output reaching around \$1 b in 1980. Projections of sales value for 1984 are between \$5 b and \$8 b. By comparison, the projection for global sales of robots is only \$2 b by 1990, and only \$4 b for Colour TVs in the USA in 1984. As another indicator of the phenomenal growth of the CAD sector, if the industry had grown at the same rate as IBM between 1976 and 1980, its sales would have only been around \$120 m in 1980, and if it had followed the same growth path as DEC (the most successful of the mini-computer firms, the 'success story' of the 1970s), its size in 1980 would only have been around \$250 m.

III. MARKET STRUCTURE

Potentially the market for CAD systems is segmented into three major divisions, namely:

(i) mainframe based systems which are partly used for graphics and partly for information processing and analytical tasks;
(ii) minicomputer based systems dedicated to graphics use, which can undertake a variety of different applications programs but with limited ability to perform complex analytical programs;
(iii) microcomputer based systems with a basic draughting software and dedicated to a few applications programs with a very limited analytical capability.

Each of these systems could be made available by turnkey suppliers, selling complete systems of hardware and software, or by specialised vendors which provide software alone. However the running so far over the past decade has been made almost entirely by the minicomputer-based turnkey systems, with the exception of IBM (whose presence[5] has hitherto largely been limited to very large companies each using a relatively large number of graphics terminals with the processing mainframe also being used on a batch-basis for additional heavy-analytic and data-processing activities) and the emerging

[5] However IBM markets only its mechanical software. Its electronic software is not marketed outside of affiliates since IBM are concerned that this would divulge proprietary information regarding component, integrated circuit and computer architecture.

TABLE I
MARKET SHARES (%) AND CONTROLLING SHAREHOLDINGS OF MAJOR US TURNKEY CAD SUPPLIERS

	Market Shares (%)				
	1976	*1977*	*1978*	*1979*	*1980*
Applicon	14.5	15.1	10.9	9	8.8
Auto-trol	10	11.4	13	10.6	8.9
Calma	14.3	15.5	16	13.6	13.8
Computervision	28.1	25.6	25.8	32.6	33.2
Gerber	3.6	1.3	2.6	3.2	4.1[a]
IBM	21.4	18.2	13.6	12.7	12.2
Intergraph	8.2	8.3	12	9.3	9.8
Unigraphics			3.3	2.4	2.3
Other					6.9

[a] Excluding estimated sales of PC800 dedicated electronic systems sold by a different division, Gerber's share falls to 2.3% in 1980.

	Shareholdings	
	Control	*Other significant*
Applicon	Original founders	General Electric owns 28%; will divest due to purchase of Calma
Auto-trol	Hillman Foundation (c75%)	25% public + employees
Calma	General Electric (100%)	
Computervision	Founding president and vice president (22%)	Institutions
Gerber	Gerber Scientific (80%)	Public (20%)
IBM	Public 100%	
Intergraph	Eight directors and employee fund[b] (40.6%)	Public (13.2%) Employees (46.2%)
Unigraphics	McDonnel Douglas (100%)	

[b] Voting rights of employees fund held by founder and his wife.

sales of software systems such as those of Cambridge Interactive Systems[6] and Compeda,[7] both of the UK.

Currently seven US firms dominate this turnkey market[8]—the shares of these individual firms are shown in Table I for the period 1976–80. The most significant factor which emerges from this tabulation is the growing dominance of the market by Computervision whose share grew from 28.1% in 1976 to 33.2% in 1980, at the expense of all of the other turnkey vendors except Inter-

[6] CIS markets, with increasing success, a 3D modelling capability and a basic draughting system. Annual sales are less than $10 m.

[7] Compeda, a UK government sponsored firm, markets a very successful 3D system (PDMS) to check interference between pipes in process plant design. Its annual turnover is less than $5 m.

[8] We refer, here, to the market for CAD systems in the engineering (electronic, mechanical, civil and structural) architecture, retailing and publishing sectors. Excluded are the fields of business graphics (which according to one source—the Harvard Newsletter on Computer Graphics [9]—was worth $200 m. in 1981) and animation.

graph. It is significant that the extraordinarily high growth rate of the industry means that despite a 78.4% annual growth in sales between 1979 and 1980 a firm like Auto-trol was faced with a declining market share, or that Gerber, with a 31.4% p.a. growth rate over the same period[9] must be seen as struggling for survival!

Given the paucity of data on the various firms operating in this sector it is not easy to be precise in describing the evolving market structure. Nevertheless it is possible to distinguish between four distinct periods in the industry's development.

(a) *Pre 1969: Industry Origins*

In this initial period of industry development the running was made almost entirely by existing large firms in the defence, aerospace and aeronautical industries with the collaboration of mainframe computer manufacturers such as IBM. The first technical breakthrough (the light pen and screen, allowing for interactive use) occurred in the 1950s during the development of the SAGE early-warning radar system. By the 1960s the aerospace industry became the major user, pushed by the US Air Force which actively attempted to widen applications to other manufacturing industries in the late 1960s. During this latter period General Motors began the development of its DAC ('Design Augmented by Computers') programme.

In summary, therefore, during this early period there was hardly any 'market' for CAD, with most developments occurring to assist own-use by large, technologically advanced mechanical-engineering corporations in the US and (to a lesser extent) in the UK.[10]

(b) *1969–74: Dynamic new firms*

In this short second period, the industry began to change its nature significantly by rapidly diffusing its product to the electronics sector. The primary impetus for this were new small firms begun by software writers spinning off from other industries. These comprised two groups. The first were those with specific experience in CAD software in the aerospace and automobile sectors—a particularly influential group moved west to Southern California and formed a company called Systems Science Software which over the years provided the basic software for many of the current turnkey vendors; another Huntsville Alabama firm was established by ex IBM employees feeding off displaced software manpower as the neighbouring Apollo moon-programme was wound down. The second source of software writers were those emerging

[9] Excluding estimated sales of $10 m for the dedicated electronics system produced by an affiliate.

[10] According to Radar and Wingert [15], the UK CAD industry was more advanced than the German industry in the 1960s due to the relative strength of the UK aircraft industry.

from the electronics sector itself (especially IBM) who were attracted by the low barriers to entry and the obvious future potential of the CAD sector.

The consequence was a variety of new firms, initially making digitising equipment and subsequently moving to the supply of complete turnkey systems. This group includes all of the current major US turnkey vendors except IBM and Gerber (whose origins lie in computerised plotters and cutters for the garments industry). By contrast in Europe (and especially the UK) the emergent CAD capability in this time period arose directly within established electronics firms (such as Racal, Plessey and ICL) who produced equipment for their own needs.

In summary, therefore, this second period of industry development saw the emergence of new, independent firms and the rapid diffusion of the technology out of the defence, aerospace and automobile sectors to the electronics industries.

(c) *1974–80 The trend to concentration*

By around 1974 most of the major suppliers were established, protected (as we shall see in section IV) by a large investment of software in a suite of specialised applications programs. At this point CAD equipment began to penetrate manufacturing industry. The rate of diffusion proved to be so rapid in this sector that the aggregate industry growth rate increased from around 55% p.a. to around 80% p.a. All the vendors, despite different specialisations (e.g. Intergraph and Auto-trol in cartography, Calma in electronics; Computervision and Applicon in both electronics and mechanical engineering) adopted a similar strategy of expanding their range of applications programs to provide comprehensive cover to all industries. But this diversification, together with the cost of financing such heady rates of expansion, necessitated the raising of financial resources. In the case of Auto-trol and Applicon, this meant recourse to venture capital.[11] But all firms—including those owned by venture capital—were forced both to sell shares in the stock market and into long and short-term debt.

At the same time as these established CAD suppliers were raising funds, predators were emerging amongst established Corporations. First McDonnel Douglas took over United Computing in 1974 changing its name to Unigraphics. Then around 1975, Gerber, a major name in the garments sector, expanded its range of operations, buying in software from Systems Science Software. But most significant was the action of US-based General Electric (GE), one of the largest mechanical engineering corporations in the world. Initially GE had taken a 28% share of Applicon as a speculative investment. Then in the late 1970s GE changed its chairman—the new incumbent was

[11] Such was the growth rate of the industry, that the $50,000 (plus commercial loans of $3.6 m) invested by the Hillman Foundation (a family trust seeking 'explosive growth sectors') in Auto-trol in 1973 was worth over $100 m by 1981.

struck by the outdatedness of GE's technology and its vulnerability to Japanese and European competition. Already a joint venture of Fujitsu Fanuc and Siemens had made very heavy inroads into the US machine tool numerical control sector eroding GE's former dominance and achieving a 15% market share within five years. Consequently GE has begun radically to alter its structure moving up the technological stream towards the 'factory of the future'.[12] This involved the acquisition of a semiconductor firm (Intersil) for $235 m, the beefing up of its machine-tool NC capability (costing $31 m) and buying Calma.[13] GE paid around $170 m for Calma in 1981—its previous owners, United Telecom, had boughtout Calma for a mere $17 m two years earlier.

There are reasons to believe that GE will be setting a trend. Whilst the remaining independent vendors all profess to want to maintain their independence, this may not be possible. For example, because of fund raising issues in the stock market, the founding two shareholders of Computervision, the market leader, now control only 22% of its shares—the remainder being held by the public, predominantly institutions. Computervision is therefore now extremely vulnerable to a takeover bid. The remaining independent firms—Applicon and Intergraph are still controlled by their founders. It must be an open question whether they, too can withstand acquisition offers.[14]

Therefore one pressure towards concentration has already been described, namely vertical and horizontal integration by enterprises in other sectors. A second tendency towards concentration is the organic tendency within the CAD sector itself, namely the growing market presence of Computervision (and Intergraph) at the expense of industry minors. Computervision has not only increased its market share (from 28% to 33% between 1976 and 1980) but is in the process of becoming a TNC itself with the decision to set up a manufacturing subsidiary in Europe.

To summarise, therefore, this third phase of industry development was associated with the growing size of CAD firms, the growing organic trends towards concentration within the sector, and a tendency for formerly independent CAD firms to be swallowed by existing TNCs.

(d) *Post 1980. Maturity*

In the most recent development which is only just emerging we can once again see the emergence of new, small firms spun-off from larger, older and established firms. To understand their significance we need to go a little deeper into the nature of CAD technology. CAD systems, as we have seen, are built around two sets of software, basic graphics and applications oriented. The

[12] See Business Week [3] and [5].
[13] Having done so GE is forced to divest itself of the holding in Applicon.
[14] Indeed Applicon was itself taken over by a French Transnational, Schlumberger, in early 1982.

advantage of *mainframe* based systems is that they are not only able to cope with the heaviest requirements of particular applications programs, but they are also able to undertake complementary batch processing tasks such as payroll and inventory controls. Their disadvantages are that they are costly (an entry cost of over $500,000 with unit-terminal costs of around $60,000), that they are vulnerable to breakdown of the centralised host computer and memory, and that the mainframe suppliers have hitherto developed only a limited range of applications programs. By contrast the *mini-computer based turnkey vendors* have developed the most comprehensive range of applications software, most of which can be used independently from mainframe computers. They have lower entry costs (around $200,000) with lower unit terminal costs. The major disadvantage is their weaker processing capability which limits their use for heavy-analytical applications programs and hinders their response rate to users.

But recently, as the CAD vendors have penetrated a wider user base, a 'space' has begun to emerge for dedicated systems. That is amongst users (e.g. engineering firms using printed circuit boards and draughting firms) who have no need for a comprehensive suite of applications programs and whose engineering data processing requirements are not extensive. Their needs can be met by microprocessor driven systems which provide basic graphics software with a single (or small number of) applications programs. Such systems, based upon already 'mature' applications programs developed by the turnkey vendors are rapidly beginning to emerge, selling for around $30,000 each. The vendors are new firms begun by ex-employees of existing CAD vendors. For example, Avera Inc., was set up by two ex-Applicon employees (one had worked there for seven years) and one ex Intel employee. Set up with $150,000 of capital the single-terminal systems are sold for $39,250. One of the ex-Applicon founders described its origins in the following way:

> "While at Applicon, request-upon-request would come in for design automation equipment priced at $50,000 or less".
> (Harvard Newsletter on Computer Graphics, [10]).

To summarise, therefore, this most recent stage of industry development has seen two divergent trends—a continued tendency to concentration and an opposing tendency for the entry of new small firms selling limited capability dedicated systems.

IV. BARRIERS TO ENTRY

The key to the discussion of firm size and technical change lies in the barriers to new entrants. For, in the context of constrained market growth, the expansionary momentum of existing enterprises provides a constant tendency towards concentration of ownership and production. This momentum can be undermined only if space exists for new entrants into the industry. We therefore consider the problem of entry barriers in the CAD industry at some length, partly because we believe the discussion throws some light on the emerging software-intensive industries and partly because it illuminates the discussion of our central concern, namely the relationship between firm size and innovative activity.

Investment in the CAD sector is a relatively profitable activity, both in relation to potential income streams[15] and in appreciation of capital stock. Consequently the incentive to new entrants is substantial. Yet given the small number of firms which dominate the industry, it is evident that there must be barriers to entry.

The primary barrier to entry in the CAD industry is technology.[16] It is now widely accepted that technology is a "free" or "public" good, that is it is not used-up in consumption and is available for multiple and indefinite use. (Arrow [1]). Therefore unless some mechanisms can be found to protect proprietary rights over technology, there will be no incentive, under a market system, for the generation of new technology. In the case of embodied technology—for example, machinery—this function is partly performed by the patent system which gives exclusive power for exploitation to the owner of the patent or its licensees. But, as has recently emerged in a series of well publicised court-cases, software cannot be patented;[17] it can only be copyrighted which is easily circumventable. Yet for the CAD industry to have maintained such dramatic changes in technology, there must by necessity have been a process of *effective* appropriation, whatever the *legal* rights may have been.

The primary factor protecting existing producers from new entrants has been the scale of software inputs necessary to offer a competitive package of applications programs. In Table II we detail the extent of R and D inputs of those firms for which information exists; in Table III we detail (without mentioning the names of firms to avoid disclosing proprietary information) the current numbers of software writers they employ and, where available, the accumulated input of software person years in their system. It can be seen from Table II that compared to US industry in general, the CAD industry invests a very large proportion of sales in R and D. This proportion is high even relative to information processing in general where the 1979 average was only 6.1% of sales (Business Week [4]) and the 1980 average was 2%. From Table III it can be seen that most CAD suppliers currently employ over 100 software writers per year, expanding these numbers at well over 30% p.a. Some of the vendors

[15] Computervision and Intergraph, for example, have had significantly higher return on equity than either DEC or the Fortune 500 average (Kaplinsky, [14]).

[16] There are only insignificant economies of scale in production at the level of output of most of the relevant firms. Only IBM and Computervision make their own computers and even they buy-in the peripherals from external suppliers.

[17] However, a very recent ruling (May, 1981) of the US Supreme Court has determined that 'firmware' (a form of software written into particular pieces of hardware—see later), can be patented. This is almost certainly likely to have a profound impact upon the direction of technological change in the whole of the electronics sector.

TABLE II
R AND D AS % OF SALES

	R and D as % of sales											
	1969	*1970*	*1971*	*1972*	*1973*	*1974*	*1975*	*1976*	*1977*	*1978*	*1979*	*1980*
Applicon								11	8.4	12.8	8.9	11.2
Auto-trol[a]						22.8	13	14.6	12.6	15.7	14	12
Computervision	671	28	4.4	6.4	9.7	11.8	12.3	8.9	9.6	8.3	8.8	
Intergraph								6.5	5.7	7.6	10.1	11
Gerber												15.9
All US industry	2.2	2.2	2.1	2	2	1.9	1.9	1.9	1.9	1.9	1.9	2

Source: Interviews, annual reports, Soete [21], Soete [22] and Business Week, June editions.

[a] In 1980, Auto-trols ratio of R and D expenditure to sales (which at 12% of sales, was the lowest ratio for the firm since 1974) was the fourth highest ratio of the 744 US Corporations surveyed by Business Week; its R and D expenditure per employee was the third highest of the sample.

TABLE III

1980 SOFTWARE STAFF AND ACCUMULATED PERSON YEARS OF SOFTWARE[a]

Firm code	*Numbers employed*	*Accumulated years of software in system*
a	40	130 person years post bought-in package in 1974
b	150–200	1000 person years
c	103	NI
d	345	NI
e	125	NI
f	120	NI
g	110	600 person years in 2D draughting package plus 400 person years in bought-in mechanical outline
h	88	500 person years of software; 7 million lines of software.

Source: Interviews.

[a] Excludes personnel on hardware development, but includes those working on operating systems of minicomputers.

Note: firm code is not in the same order as in previous tables.

were able to detail their stock of software—over 1,000 person years in some cases and over 7 m lines of code in others.

These absolute sunken R and D expenditures are in themselves not a sufficient deterrent to entry. After all in 1980 prices, even Computervision had accumulated less than $80 m of R and D, and some of that was in the development of their own minicomputer; compare this with the $1.5 b profits earned by General Electric in 1980 alone. The critical protective factors are that this software development occurs in a relatively specialised sector in the context of a general shortage of software writers. But more importantly, much of the necessary software development is sequential—as one of the founders of Computervision describes it, "One can't make a baby in one month with nine women".[18]

Although these accumulated R and D expenditures are a significant form of appropriation and consequently an effective barrier to the entry of new firms, some CAD firms nevertheless take additional steps to avoid the disclosure of proprietary software information to competitors;[19] this involves control over the software itself and over the movement of personnel.

(a) *Control over software*

Software programs can basically be divided into two segments—object code (usually referred to as machine code), which is made up of a string of 0's and 1's (i.e. binary code) and sourcecode which is a higher level of

[18] A similar example can be drawn from the automobile industry. When Agnelli, the head of Fiat, was asked whether selling the Fiat 124 design to the Russians would not provide fatal competition to his firm, he answered "If we are still producing the Fiat 124 in 5 years time, we will go bankrupt anyhow"!

[19] These observations are based on visits made to 13 vendors and 24 users in the UK and the US in early 1981. For a full description see Kaplinsky [14].

programming language, which assembles the object code into less cumbersome bundles of instructions. None of the CAD firms objected to the release of object code to users (since it is an essential requirement for the functioning of their hardware) except for IBM which does not market its electronic CAD software. But significant differences were displayed in the attitude of firms towards the release of sourcecodes. Four of the CAD supplying firms had no objection to its release, although one observed that the sourcecode itself would be inoperable without a particular item of hardware over which it maintained tight and exclusive control; a second of these firms had merged with a parent which had developed its own software, and observed that even though it had unfettered access to this software with the full cooperation of its affiliate, it took years to unravel; a third firm only released sourcecode if the user entered a "Proprietary Software Agreement".

The remaining firms retained tight physical control over the sourcecode, despite their general observations that they would not feel unduly threatened if their competitors obtained access to it. In one of these companies, which employs over 100 software programmers, only 4 people have access to the full store of sourcecode; in another case a user reported that the CAD suppliers applications engineers came and physically removed the sourcecode which they had "inadvertently obtained".

(b) *Control over personnel*

The flow of manpower, holding firm-specific rather than individual-specific knowledge is an important concern for all CAD firms, although of diminishing importance as the stock of software grows and individual specific knowledge becomes increasingly differentiated from firm specific knowledge.[20] There are a number of notable examples of the gains and losses flowing from such mobility. In the mid-1970s, a team of West Coast software writers prepared the basic mechanical applications package for Computervision having earlier performed a similar task for Gerber. When the 1975 recession forced economies on Computervision, the head-office in the Boston-area tried to regain control over these programmers and wanted them to return to the East Coast. With few exceptions they refused and the recalcitrants formed their own company, Systems Science Software, later taken over by Calma. Computervision responded with a law-suit alleging (i) unfair competition, (ii) breach of contract not to compete (iii) Contractual interference and (iv) "conspiracy". Calma counter-sued for $127.5 m punitive damages (under the Sherman anti-trust act), but both claims were eventually dismissed without damages.

[20] A major method through which CAD suppliers appropriate the individual knowledge of programmers is by insisting on the use of structured programming techniques. These involve the use of standard procedures for software writing which are easily intelligible and assimilable by other software writers.

However the upshot was a damaging delay (until 1978) in the development of Calma's own mechanical applications package since Calma had to ensure that it would not lay itself open to further litigation. A second example is that of the recent move by the ex-head of Computervisions European marketing division to Intergraph.[21] And a third example is that of Gerber, anxious to establish a strong package of mechanical applications software, which has recently 'poached' 12–15 software writers from Unigraphics which has developed over the years a strong suite of relatively bug-free mechanical applications programmes.

Reflecting the importance, albeit declining, of this transfer of personnel is a repeated tendency to increase the costs to individuals of leaving the company. Intergraph requires its newly appointed European marketing manager to resell his stock to the company if he leaves their employment; the same company specifically sees its employee stock option and bonus plans as a way of reducing employee turnover. In another case of a CAD bureau control was kept over one key software writer by the granting of a concessionary mortgage for the purchase of a house. But these safeguards are not always wholly effective: one user pointed out that whole sections of the software manuals of two different suppliers were almost identical, reflecting the mobility of manpower between these firms.

(c) *Firmware*

It is an increasingly common occurrence in the electronics industry for software-intensive firms to wire-in particular sets of software into hardware. In part this reduces the input of programming, which both saves costs and speeds-up processing time. But more importantly it 'hides' software from potential competitors, and following a recent US Supreme Court ruling, unlike software, firmware is patentable. For example Intergraph has a major competitive advantage over its competitors in being able to insert and withdraw information rapidly from its storage discs; the substance of this advantage is wired-in to a separate set of hardware called a "scanner-processor" which Intergraph makes itself under carefully protected conditions. The move to increasing firmware is a major area of effort by all of the CAD vendors.

In conclusion therefore it is clear that whilst legal proprietary rights over CAD technology are of little effect, CAD suppliers are nevertheless increasingly able to maintain proprietary control over their software. Applicon, which has two US patents for hardware, recognises the limited utility of these and of patents in general.

[21] As an incentive to change firms this individual was given the opportunity to purchase 45,000 shares at $4.17 each prior to public flotation. Two weeks after the public issues these shares were worth $30, giving him a stock appreciation of $1.16 m. (See Dean Witter Reynolds Inc [7, p. 22]).

> "The company does not consider that its success will depend upon its ability to obtain and defend patents, but rather on its ability to offer its customers high-performance products at competitive prices" (Blyth Eastman Paine Webber [2, p. 19]).

Auto-trol comes to an identical conclusion:

> "The company does not hold any patents or licenses covering its graphics systems. It may be possible for competitors of the company to copy aspects of its systems even though the company regards such aspects as proprietary. However the Company believes that, because of the rapid pace of technological change in the electronics industry, patent protection is of lesser significance than factors such as the knowledge and experience of the Company's management and personnel and their ability to develop and market its products".
> (Hambrecht and Quist [9, p. 20]).

In the face of this effective appropriation of technology, of the sequential imperative in software development and the minimum scale in input required to develop a wide-ranging set of applications programs, the barriers to entry are high (but not insurmountable). A number of examples illustrate this:

(a) *General Electric*

General Electric is one of the largest industrial corporations in the world with a 1980 turnover of $25 b, and is considered to be the largest user of CAD systems in the world. Its various divisions currently use over 100 systems,[22] and plan to purchase an additional 25 systems per annum. In the face of increasing technology-based competition in all of its markets, the company has made a major decision to upgrade its own technology and in particular, through association between its new semiconductor division, its machine-tool division and the CAD affiliate (now all grouped in its Industrial Controls Group), to develop the "factory of the future". An essential ingredient of this was a CAD/CAM capability—instead of starting afresh GE tried to increase its 28% speculative holding in Applicon, which had a particularly strong capability in mechanical engineering CAD software. When this failed it switched its attention to Calma which was a less attractive proposition since its historic strength lay in electronics applications.

(b) *IBM*

In the mid-1970s IBM made a decision to expand its mechanical applications CAD capabilities for two major reasons. The first was the need to extend sales growth in the face of declining hardware prices; the second

[22] In the order of Computervision and Applicon, with Calma a poor third, being used predominantly for electronic systems.

was its own need for CAD/CAM applications as it struggled to keep abreast of competition within its own sector. Despite having around 150 person years of software in their system, they preferred to buy-in Lockheeds software package since it had a track-record of successful main-frame based users. Lockheed are currently reputed to have around 120 people upgrading and maintaining this package.

(c) *Gerber*

As we have seen, Gerber was an early entrant to the CAD/CAM market, having bought in the basic mechanical software from Systems Science Software in 1973, and investing over 70 person years of software to upgrade it by 1979. However their effort languished for some years and it was only when a new president was recruited from United Technologies in 1978 that their CAD activities began to expand significantly. This was followed by the separation of Gerber Systems Technology (now the CAD division) from Gerber Scientific in 1979, and the sale of 20% of its equity to the public in March 1981. Since 1979 Gerber has been struggling to increase its market share through, by its own admission, extensive price-discounting and the widening of software applications programs. But the costs of this have been substantial:[23] just prior to the sale of 20% of its stock to the public in March 1981, GST had

- accumulated losses (by 31/12/80) of $1.453 m and expected these to increase until at least May 1981.
- GS had written-off $4 m of debt by GST in exchange for 320,000 shares.
- $2.081 m of the expected stock issue of $7.1 m would go to repay additional debt to GS.
- Additional long term debt of $4.5 m.
- these losses were incurred despite the sale of a technology licence to a Japanese firm which netted $1 m in advance, plus an annual minimum royalty on sales, plus a share of its licensee's pre-tax profits.

These barriers to entry are most substantial in relation to the comprehensive application program systems offered by the existing turnkey suppliers using mini and mainframe computers. There is, however, an emerging space for microprocessor driven systems which has been made possible by two factors. The first, and obvious, precondition, is the development of increasingly powerful microprocessors. The second is the maturity of specific applications programs which significantly lower the barriers to entry in these limited areas.

[23] See Hambrecht and Quist [9].

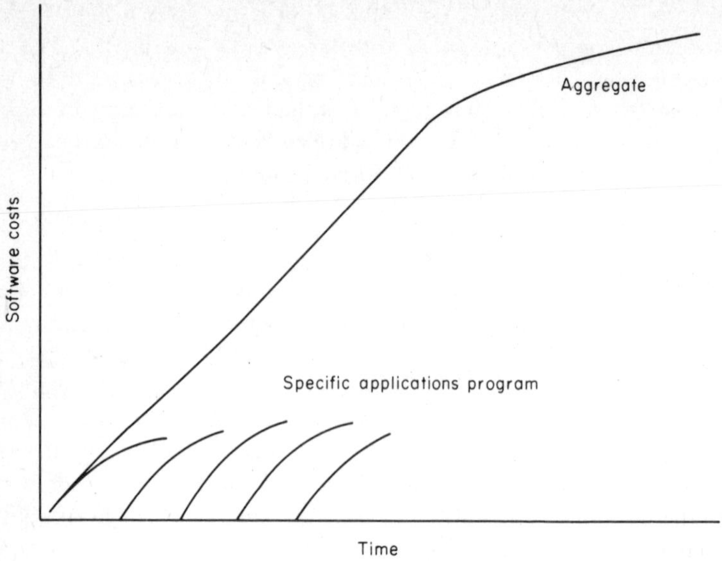

FIGURE 1
Software development—Aggregate and applications curves

In order to grasp the significance of this latter point it is necessary to understand that in the CAD industry there is a distinction between the *average* and *marginal* cost of systems. This distinction partly arises from the imperative to all CAD suppliers to employ a large overhead of software writers. These software writers are in general divided into three groups. The first is committed to the development of operating systems, the second into a small number who upgrade and maintain existing applications programs and the larger number who are involved in developing the new applications programs which are necessary to keep an all-round presence in the industry. From each supplier's point of view, therefore, the software development process takes the form as represented by Figure 1: a constant overhead investment in software, made up of a family of matured packages and an increasing family of new packages. Evidence of the existence of this type of mature packages is provided in Figure 2 for three specific applications, sculptured surfaces and view independent construction developed by one particular supplier, and orthographic piping developed by another.

Microprocessor driven CAD systems are aimed at this market of matured applications programs, of which basic graphics capabilities (that is, the ability to draw lines, arcs and so on which are necessary for computer-aided draughting) is the most obvious. From the vendor's point of view the software needs little attention and the system can be sold at a price which is close to its marginal cost, that is the cost of the hardware input.

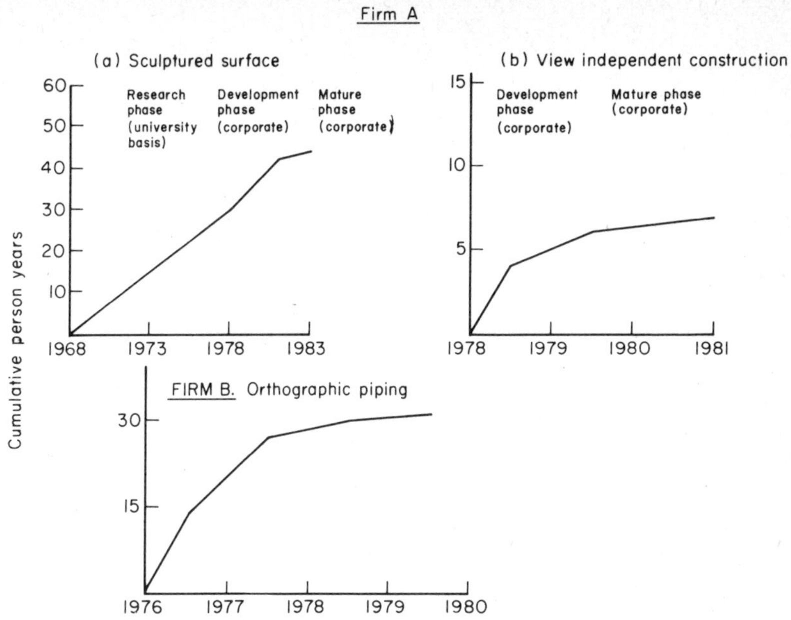

FIGURE 2

Examples of matured applications programmes

Source: Interviews with CAD Supplying Firms

There are a great number of such small firms springing up in North America[24] and Europe. Many of them offer basic graphics capabilities with perhaps one applications program, often an auto-routing electronics program. Many of these firms are started by former employees of established turnkey suppliers who recognised that these turnkey firms were overstretched and unable to satisfy the limited needs of small-scale users.

V. FIRM SIZE AND TECHNICAL CHANGE IN RELATION TO INDUSTRY GROWTH CURVES

We have gone into some detail in describing the genesis and growing maturity of the CAD industry. This has been done because we believe that it throws light on the relationship between firm size and technical change. In Figure 3 we attempt to chart the nature of this industry growth curve,[25] which we believe to be representative of other software intensive microelectronic sectors. In general the radical nature of the technology has meant that the origin of these industries is to be found in larger user-firms who innovate to meet their own

[24] Where according to one estimate there are at least 60 different suppliers.

[25] This pattern is particularly evident for the US electronics sector, only in recent years has it begun to emerge in Europe and Japan.

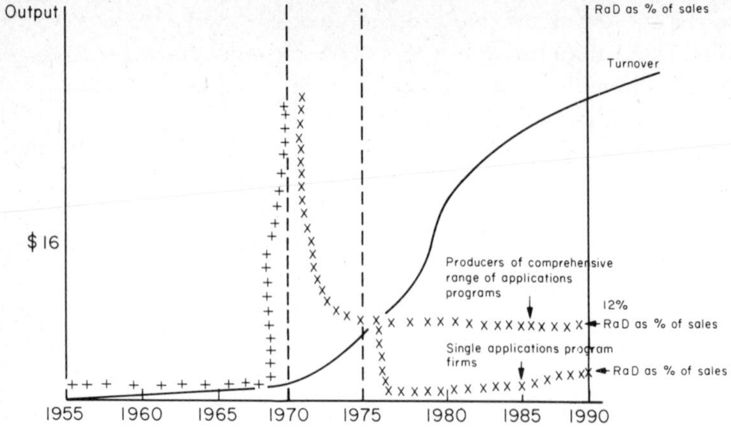

	Industry origins	Dynamic new firms	Trend to concentration	Maturity
Diffusion of product	Defence, aerospace	Electronics	Mechanical engineering	Mechanical engineering Civil engineering Business graphics
Source of innovation	For own use	External sales Own use	External sales Own use	External sales Own use
Innovative firms	Very large firms	New small firms	Medium firms	Large and very large firms New small firms

FIGURE 3

Industry Growth Curve for Software Intensive Industries Based on Actual and Projected Growth of CAD Industry

product needs. Thereafter, in the second phase, key individuals spin-off from the pioneers to establish new small firms dedicated to the development of the product. During the third phase these firms grow and become less vulnerable to new entrants as accumulated software protects them from new entrants. At the same time their strong growth potential and their key strategic value attracts large predators from other sectors. In the final phase new small entrants begun by people spinning off from existing CAD suppliers, find a role within particular mature applications programs.

It is believed that this growth pattern is largely representative of other software-intensive industries. For example in the word-processing sector the industry appears to be rapidly moving into the third phase (trend to concentration), with new entrants from outside the subsector (e.g. Exxon) and organic growth from within (e.g. Wang). By contrast the automatic testing equipment has already passed through the stage of concentration and the industry is now seeing the emergence of small firms producing dedicated sets of equipment. A third example is that of microcomputers where the entrance of IBM, Zerox and the Japanese firms appears to signal the transition between the second and third phases.[26]

In many ways this notional growth curve of software intensive industries proximates that of the pre-microelectronic era. There is one crucial difference, however. In the earlier pre-microelectronic period, the mature phase was not characterised to the same extent by the emergence of new small firms. This was because concentration was underpinned by economies of scale in production (e.g. automobiles). The industries under discussion are distinctive because their relatively high input of software, with its associated variation between average and marginal costs of production, allows for economies of scale only in relation to new products. The manufacture of existing products (e.g. mature applications programs) is therefore open to new entrants if they can gain access to the technology itself. And in many cases, as we have seen in the CAD and automatic testing equipment industries, there are bits of the technology (e.g. particular applications programs) which are often individual, rather than firm, specific, thereby providing the opportunity for new entrants.

V. TECHNICAL CHANGE AND FIRM SIZE RECONSIDERED

In the above discussion we have deliberately characterised the problem loosely as being one of 'technical change' or more loosely innovation, rather than R and D or patents. With respect to patents, we have observed that there is little scope for patenting in these types of industries. In relation to R and D, this measure is not a very useful indicator of innovation. Historically R and D levels in the CAD industry (as we can see from Figure 3) have varied and show no constant relation to industry growth or the introduction of new products—they more clearly reflect the changes in the phase on the industry growth cycle.

This observation enables us to return to the debate on firm size and technical change. Our argument is that the existing studies in this area are largely static—they observe a particular relationship at one point of time (perhaps a period of 2–3 years) and then project this as characterising a trend. The 'truth' is rather more complicated—it is not possible to determine whether large or small firms are inherently more innovative since it depends so largely on which period of industry life-cycle one is measuring. For example in the CAD sector in the 1950s large firms were relatively innovative; in the late 1960s and early 1980s new small firms played an important role, whereas in the mid-1970s medium-sized firms were most prominent.

It might well be argued that however valid these observations are at a sectoral level, when observations are aggregated across a large number of sectors we might nevertheless expect a trend to emerge. In answering this we

[26] G de Jonquieres [11].

are drawn to the debate on long-wave cycles where Freeman [8] and Clark *et al.* [6] argue (convincingly, in our view) that we can distinguish long-wave cycles associated with major heartland technologies which provide big-wave effects to overwhelm the average of a large number of observations (Kaplinsky [13]). Each of these has an expansionary upswing of new product development and a rationalising downswing of cost-reduction, product improvement and reduction of lead-time. Thus in the same way that we can expect the relationship between firm size and technical change to vary between the different phases of an industry growth cycle, so we can expect it to vary between different phases of the long-wave cycle. For example the upswing is likely to be dominated by new firms expanding organically, and later to be taken over by existing firms or to grow themselves into very large firms (e.g. IBM) as the cycle moves into the downswing.

RAPHAEL KAPLINSKY,
The Institute of Development Studies,
University of Sussex,
Brighton, Sussex BN1 9RE

ACCEPTED APRIL 1982

REFERENCES

[1] ARROW, K. J., Economic Welfare and the Allocation of Resources for Invention, in the *Rate and Diffusion of Inventive Activity: Economic and Social Factors*, National Bureau of Economic Research, Princeton University Press, 1962.
[2] BLYTH, EASTMAN PAINE WEBBER INC., and ALEX BROWN AND SONS, 20 July 1980, Prospectus for Issue of 1,000,000 Shares of Common Stock of Applicon.
[3] *Business Week*, 'GE's New Input for "Factories of the Future"' 22nd December, 1980.
[4] *Business Week*, Survey of R and D, June 30th, 1980.
[5] *Business Week*, 'Attacking GE's Grip on Controls', 16th March, 1981.
[6] CLARK, J., FREEMAN, C. and SOETE, L., 'Long Waves and Technological Developments in the 20th Century', mimeo, Brighton, 1980.
[7] DEAN WITTER REYNOLDS INC, and THE ROBINSON-HUMPHREY COMPANY INC., Preliminary Prospectus for Issue of 1,500,000 Shares of Common Stock of Intergraph Corporation, 25th February, 1981.
[8] FREEMAN, C., 'The Kondratiev Long Wave, Technical Change and Unemployment', *Proceedings of OECD Meeting of Experts on Structural Determinants of Employment and Unemployment*, (OECD, Paris, 1977).
[9] HAMBRECHT and QUIST, Prospectus for Issue of 500,000 Shares of Common Stock of Auto-trol Technology Corporation, San Francisco, 24th January, 1979.
[10] *Harvard Newletter on Computer Graphics*, Vol 3 No 4, 1981, and Vol 3 No 9, 1981.
[11] G. DE JONQUIERES, 'Personal Computers Come of Age', *Financial Times*, 21st Auguest, 1981.
[12] KAMIEN, MORTON I. and SCHWARTZ, NANCY L., 'Market Structure and Innovation: A Survey', *Journal of Economic Literature*, 3, No 1 (March 1975), pp. 1–37.
[13] KAPLINSKY, R., 'Radical Technical Change and Export-Orientated Industrialisation: The Impact of Micro-electronics, *Vierteljahresberichte*, Probleme der Entwicklungslander, No 83, (March 1981), pp. 81–99.

[14] KAPLINSKY, R., *Computer Aided Design—Electronics, Comparative Advantage and Development*, (Frances Pinter, London, 1982).
[15] RADER, M., and WINGERT, B., *Computer Aided Design in Great Britain and the Federal Republic of Germany—Current Trends and Impacts*, (Karlsruhe, Kernforschungszentrum, 1981).
[16] ROTHWELL, R. and ZEGVELD, W., *Industrial Innovation and Public Policy: Preparing for the 1980s and the 1990s*, (Frances Pinter, London, 1982).
[17] SCHERER, F. M., 'Size of Firm, Oligopoly and Research: A Comment', *Canadian Journal of Economics and Political Science*, Vol 31 No 2 (May, 1965) pp. 256–66.
[18] SCHERER, F. M., 'Firm Size, Market Structure, Opportunity and the Output of Patented Inventions', *American Economic Review*, Vol 55 No 5, (December 1965), pp. 1097–25.
[19] SCHUMPETER, J. A., *Capitalism, Socialism and Democracy*, (Harper and Bros, New York, 1942).
[20] SHRIEVES, R. E., 1978, 'Market Structure and Innovation: A New Perspective' *Journal of Industrial Economics*, Vol 26, No 4, (June 1978), pp. 329–47.
[21] SOETE, L. L. G., 'Size of Firm, Oligopoly and Research: A Reappraisal', *Extrait de Reseaux*, Nos 35–36, 1977.
[22] SOETE, L. L. G., 'Firm Size and Inventive Activity', *European Economic Review*, Vol 12, (August, 1979), pp. 319–40.

THE JOURNAL OF INDUSTRIAL ECONOMICS
Volume XXXII September 1983 No. 1

R & D EXPENDITURES, ROYALTY PAYMENTS, AND SALES GROWTH IN JAPANESE MANUFACTURING CORPORATIONS

HIROYUKI ODAGIRI*

I. INTRODUCTION

THIS paper empirically analyzes the relationship among R & D expenditures, patent royalty payments, and the rate of sales growth in large Japanese manufacturing corporations. Such an analysis will enable us to answer several interesting questions. For example, does R & D really contribute to sales growth? Which is more effective to growth—making research inside of the company or acquiring licenses for patents from outside? Are R & D expenditures and royalty payments substitutes or complements? That is, does introducing outside patents reduce the necessity of making research internally or increase it by requiring internal research to utilize the patents? Is there any reverse causality such as sales growth affecting R & D expenditures or royalty payments? If so, is the effect positive or negative? Are there industrial differences on these effects? For instance, in which industries is R & D most effective to sales growth?

A rich stock of studies is available concerning the relationship between R & D and market structure (see Kamien and Schwartz, [4]). However, there are only a few on the effects of R & D on growth. Earlier supports to the contribution of research on sales growth were given by Scherer [8] who found a positive association between the number of patents issued during a year as a ratio to sales and the rate of sales growth after the year in his cross-section study of 365 firms, and by Mansfield [6] who found a positive effect of successful innovations on corporate growth in the steel and petroleum industries. However, not all research yields patents or successful innovation and whether expending on research always contributes to growth has not been answered by these writers.

A more extensive study on this subject is Leonard's [5] cross-industry study, which found the correlation coefficient between the ratio of company R & D spending to net sales and the rate of sales growth not only positive and significant but also increasing in the length of growth period, for instance, 0.619 for the correlation between the R & D intensity in 1957 and the sales growth during 1958–61 and 0.818 for that during 1958–67. This latter fact, he argued, suggests a causality from research to growth and not the reverse of it, because the higher correlation with longer-run growth presumably resulted

* Research assistance by S. Hatakeyama and T. Shimizu is acknowledged.

from the growing proportion of sales represented by new and improved products created through R & D. Branch [2], using a distributed lag model and pooled data of cross section (across firms) and time series in each of seven industries, used the ratio of the number of patents received in a given year to sales as the measure of research intensity and found its effect on the rate of sales increase positive and significant in every industry, similarly to Scherer's results. In another study [1], using the data of 166 firms in eight industries, Branch also found a positive and significant (at 5% level) correlation between the ratio of the number of patents given in a year to assets averaged over 1954–68 and the rate of sales growth during 1950–64. Presuming four-year lag between reducing an innovation to practice and receiving a patent on it, these two variables are for the same period and thus the direction of causality is unclear.

Though principally aimed at inquiring into the effect of market structure on research, Rosenberg [7] and Doi [3] both considered the relation between research and growth by including the rate of sales growth besides market share, etc., as a variable to explain the level of R & D. Rosenberg, on the one hand, in a cross-section study over 100 U.S. companies, found the effect of sales growth during 1958–63 on the percentage of total employment allocated to professional R & D personnel in 1964 positive and significant at 1% level whereas the correlation between sales growth during 1964–69 and the same R & D variable was significant at 2% level, suggesting past growth stimulating R & D which in turn stimulates future sales growth with the first effect a little stronger. Doi, on the other hand, made a cross-section study over 350 Japanese manufacturing companies and found a negative effect of sales growth during 1967–72 on R & D expenditures in 1972 or its ratio to sales. This negative correlation was sustained when the number of patents received during 1973–75 was alternatively used as a research variable. Doi did not investigate the correlation between R & D expenditures and the rate of growth following the research.

Thus, there seem to exist positive effects of R & D on growth and of growth on R & D in the United States but a negative effect of growth on R & D in Japan. However, the researches are too few, particularly in Japan, to claim this result final and more fact findings are desired. No study has been made on the correlation between research and post-research growth in Japan. Neither has been made a study of the relation between patent royalty payments and growth in any country as far as the author knows. Because firms can make a choice between making research themselves and acquiring licenses for outside patents, royalty payments should be considered as an alternative means of paying for research; hence, it is more logical to include royalty payments as an alternative R & D variable. This study aims to fill these needs—an addition of new finding and a new approach to the analysis of relation between R & D and corporate growth.

II. DATA AND VARIABLES

Our sample consists of 370 Japanese manufacturing firms that satisfy two conditions; first, listed on the first market of Tokyo Stock Exchange through 1966 to 1980,[1] and second, without any merger that substantially changed the size of the firm (e.g., by more than a quarter) during the same period. All the data were taken from company financial reports.

Three kinds of variables were used; *GSLS* is the rate of sales growth, *RS* is the ratio (in percentage) of R & D expenditures to sales, and *PS* is the ratio (in percentage) of patent royalty payments to sales. *GSLS* was calculated for the 12 year period that starts in 1969 and ends in 1981. *RS* and *PS* were calculated for the first four years during this 12 year period (named *RSPRE* and *PSPRE*, respectively) and for the last four years (named *RSPOST* and *PSPOST*, respectively). Thus, although there is a four-year overlap, we may say that *RSPRE* indicates the R & D intensity before the period for which *GSLS* was measured and *RSPOST*, after the period, and similarly for *PSPRE* and *PSPOST*. These variables were calculated as an average over the four years to eliminate the effect of yearly fluctuation. Because of this time setting, we expect that *RSPRE* and *PSPRE* may affect *GSLS* but *RSPOST* or *PSPOST* may not, and that *GSLS* may affect *RSPOST* and/or *PSPOST* but may not affect *RSPRE* or *PSPRE*. This fact will be used to estimate the causality between research and growth from statistical results.

GSLS was obtained as the slope coefficient (minus one) of the equation with time as the independent variable and the logarithm of sales as the dependent variable. This measure has an advantage over another popular measure, the ratio of sales in the ending year to that in the starting year, in that all the sales figures during the period are utilized and that the figures in the ending and starting years do not unduly influence the growth rate. Still, we report here that as a precaution all the following analyses have been also made using this alternative measure of growth rate with essentially the same results.

Several other remarks are quickly made. First, many firms had zero values for *RS*, *PS*, or both. We did not give any separate treatment to them. Since zero is the corner solution, there is a possibility of some bias here. Second, we did not include the R & D expenditures financed by the government. Because the transfer of R & D funds from the government to businesses is almost zero in Japan,[2] this exclusion is harmless. Third, industrial classification follows that of Tokyo Stock Exchange. Admittedly there are instances in which this classification does not truly reflect the activity of a firm. Fourth and finally,

[1] Since 1961, Tokyo Stock Exchange has been separated into two markets. The first market is more prestigious with stricter listing requirements and lists all the big, well-known Japanese corporations.

[2] Among the R & D performed by businesses only 2 percent is financed by the national and local governments. See Japan, Office of the Prime Minister, *Report on the Survey of Research and Development*.

TABLE I
DATA

Industry	*Mean Values of* *GSLS*	*RSPRE*	*RSPOST*	*PSPRE*	*PSPOST*	*Number of Observations*
Food	5.493	0.231	0.382	0.0426	0.0308	30
Textiles	3.477	0.395	0.424	0.0258	0.0396	35
Paper	5.493	0.185	0.268	0.0253	0.0131	14
Chemical	6.072	0.886	1.126	0.192	0.103	54
Drugs	5.867	3.976	6.573	0.580	0.529	15
Petroleum Refinery	10.371	0.0339	0.0343	0.00114	0.000293	7
Rubber, Glass and Cement	5.648	0.209	0.302	0.127	0.0872	29
Iron and Steel	5.533	0.0850	0.115	0.0630	0.0242	27
Nonferrous Metal and Metal Products	4.693	0.325	0.531	0.0488	0.0197	29
Machinery	4.553	0.371	0.551	0.401	0.260	43
Electrical Equipment	5.440	0.575	0.870	0.538	0.384	42
Transportation Equipment	6.124	0.157	0.328	0.0719	0.156	33
Precision Equipment	6.692	1.160	1.885	0.420	0.524	12
All Manufacturing	5.427	0.562	0.839	0.204	0.158	370
Innovators	5.892	1.183	1.777	0.380	0.292	123
Noninnovators	5.195	0.253	0.373	0.117	0.0914	247

because we used R & D expenditures and royalty payments as reported by companies in their financial statements, the definition on these categories may differ across firms and the figures may not accurately indicate the extent of research activity of firms. Due to the lack of any other source of data, however, we have to rely on these.

Table I summarizes the data. It gives the means of five variables, *GSLS*, *RSPRE*, *RSPOST*, *PSPRE*, and *PSPOST*, for 13 industries and for all the manufacturing. Perhaps most prominent is the exceptionally high rate of growth in the petroleum refinery industry. This reflects the steep rise in oil prices after the oil crisis of 1972–3, because the growth rate is in terms of nominal, but not real, sales volume. Also noticed is that the same industry has the lowest research intensity in terms of both R & D/sales and royalty/sales. These facts combined suggest a negative influence on the correlation coefficient between *GSLS* and any research variable when industries are aggregated, possibly biasing the whole result. In order to examine the extent of this bias, we redid the statistical analysis to be presented in the following section excluding from sample the seven refining companies. The result suggested little bias; that is, the results are hardly affected by the exclusion of the refining companies except that in many cases *t*-values were slightly decreased.

As is observed in many countries, the drug industry is most and exceptionally research intensive. It spent 4 percent of its sales revenue to R & D in 1969–72 and 6.7 percent, in 1977–80, which are more than three times the percentage in the precision equipment industry, the second most research intensive industry. The *PS*s in the drug industry were much smaller than *RS*s; merely one seventh in 1969–72. Still, it was the largest among the 13 industries. Thus, relatively to the volume of sales, the drug industry not only spent most in making research inside the companies but also in obtaining licenses for outside patents, which are mostly from foreign companies. In terms of *RS*, it is followed by the precision equipment, chemical, and electrical equipment industries. These four industries are the only ones with *RSPRE* and *RSPOST* greater than the averages over all manufacturing industries, implying a skewed distribution of research intensity across industries. We will hereafter aggregate these four industries under the name of the *innovators* and the other nine industries, the *noninnovators*. This classification is similar to that of Scherer [9] in which 14 industries were classified to electrical, chemical, moderates, and unprogressive. Roughly speaking, the first two are here innovators and the latter two, noninnovators. We will show that there are important behavioral differences between innovators and noninnovators.

On average, the innovators spent 1 to 2 percent of sales revenues in R & D and the noninnovators, 0.2 to 0.4 percent. Both spent less on royalty. In all the manufacturing, for a dollar in R & D, the companies spent only 36 cents on royalty in 1969–72. In 1977–80, this figure dropped to 19 cents suggesting that Japanese firms are relying less and less on patent licenses and more and more on internal research efforts, due perhaps to the technological catch-up of Japanese manufacturing companies and the fewer opportunities to introduce patents from foreign companies.

III. RESULTS

Table II gives the estimated coefficients of correlation between *GSLS* and the four alternative research variables. In all the manufacturing, we find the correlations with *RSPRE* and *RSPOST* positive and significant at 5 percent level, and the correlations with *PSPRE* and *PSPOST* negative but insignificant even at 10 percent level. The four innovative industries all have positive coefficients with *RSPRE* and *RSPOST* and only these plus the nonferrous metal and metal products industry have the coefficients with *RSPRE* greater than 0.2. This fact is consistent with the positive and significant correlation between *GSLS* and *RSPRE* for the innovators as a whole. Another finding about the innovators is that the correlation with *RSPRE* is stronger than that with *RSPOST*, which may suggest a stronger effect of research on growth than that of growth on research, although, individually taken, *RSPOST* is slightly more correlated with *GSLS* in the chemical and precision equipment industries. Interestingly, the correlation with *PSPRE* and that with *PSPOST* are

TABLE II
CORRELATION COEFFICIENTS BETWEEN *GSLS* AND FOUR ALTERNATIVE RESEARCH VARIABLES

	Variables			
Industry	*RSPRE*	*RSPOST*	*PSPRE*	*PSPOST*
Food	0.055	−0.077	0.109	0.118
Textiles	−0.029	−0.055	0.023	0.364**
Paper	0.152	0.150	0.125	0.110
Chemical	0.362*	0.380*	0.235**	0.100
Drugs	0.233	0.187	−0.053	0.634*
Petroleum Refinery	0.141	0.271	0.363	0.446
Rubber, Glass and Cement	0.000	0.020	0.150	0.050
Iron and Steel	0.080	−0.001	−0.013	−0.172
Nonferrous Metal and Metal Products	0.327**	0.256	0.321**	0.338**
Machinery	−0.182	−0.202	−0.177	−0.147
Electrical Equipment	0.202	0.117	−0.148	−0.379*
Transportation Equipment	−0.007	−0.377*	0.062	−0.292**
Precision Equipment	0.403	0.426	−0.083	0.144
All Manufacturing	0.125*	0.102*	−0.019	−0.065
Innovators	0.222*	p.173**	−0.069	−0.177**
Noninnovators	−0.110**	−0.153*	−0.074	−0.075

Notes: * (**) indicates significance at 5 (10) percent level.

both negative among the innovators, the former being insignificant and the latter being significant only at 10 percent level, weakly suggesting a negative effect of growth on royalty payments. We may thus speculate that in these industries a firm with slower sales growth tends to pay more to obtain patent licenses so as to recover their deteriorating position in the market. It needs be noted, however, that in the drug industry *GSLS* is strongly positively correlated with *PSPOST*, suggesting that a growing drug company tends to pay more for patent royalty, whereas strong negative correlation between *GSLS* and *PSPOST* is found in the electrical equipment industry.

Among the noninnovators, by contrast, the correlations with *RSPRE* and *RSPOST* are both negative and *RSPOST* is more strongly correlated with *GSLS* than *RSPRE*. Thus the causality reverse to that for innovators, slower growth in sales stimulating research, is suggested. The correlations with *PS*s are negative but insignificant, with a slightly larger absolute value for that with *PSPOST*. A conjecture is therefore made that a noninnovator with a lower growth rate seeks to foster growth by making more innovative efforts, with expending for research internally preferred to obtaining patent licenses from outside as the means to achieve innovation. This differs from the estimated behavior of innovators that depend on outside patents when sales growth is slow.

Looking at individual noninnovative industries, only a few coefficients are significant. In the nonferrous metal and metal products industry, *GSLS* is positively and significantly (though only at the 10 percent level) correlated with three of the four research variables, unlike in the noninnovators as a whole. In the transportation equipment industry, *GSLS* is negatively and significantly correlated with *RSPOST* and *PSPOST* but not with *RSPRE* and *PSPRE*. The correlation coefficients, particularly between *GSLS* and *PS*s, are positive and rather large in the petroleum refinery industry, though not significant due at least partly to the fewness of samples.

We have observed a very important behavioral difference between the innovators and the noninnovators. To analyze further, we present in Table III the estimation result in which *GSLS* is regressed to *RSPRE* and *PSPRE* or to *RSPOST* and *PSPOST*. (Only the results for the innovators and the noninnovators are presented here to save space.) This confirms our findings above.

TABLE III
MULTIPLE REGRESSION RESULTS
(WITH *GSLS* AS THE DEPENDENT VARIABLE)

	Coefficients for				
Industry	*RSPRE*	*RSPOST*	*PSPRE*	*PSPOST*	Adjusted R^2
Innovators	0.256† (2.653)		−0.263 (1.172)		0.044
Innovators		0.153* (2.358)		−0.548* (2.395)	0.059
Noninnovators	−0.475 (1.611)		−0.392 (0.978)		0.008
Noninnovators		−0.521* (2.184)		−0.345 (0.574)	0.017

Notes: In parentheses are *t*-values.
† (*) indicates significance at 1 (5) percent level.

Particularly, because among the innovators the coefficient for *RSPRE* is not only positive and significant but also with a larger *t*-value than that for *RSPOST*, we can estimate that the innovators' research contributes to their sales growth. For the noninnovators, on the contrary, the effect of *RSPRE* on *GSLS* is insignificant and negative. We also observe that the partial correlation between *GSLS* and *PSPOST* for the innovators and the partial correlation between *GSLS* and *RSPOST* for the noninnovators are both negative and significant, suggesting again that under slower growth in sales the innovators tend to rely on patent licenses whereas the noninnovators tend to expend on research within the company. To confirm this hypothesis, however, requires the estimation of regression equations with *RSPOST* or *PSPOST* as the dependent variable.

Table IV presents the estimation result of regressions with *RSPOST* as the dependent variable. They include *RSPRE* as an explanatory variable since some continuity in research activity is expected. In fact, the coefficient for *RSPRE* turned out to be highly significant in every equation explaining more than sixty percent of the variation in *RSPOST*. The coefficient for *GSLS* is

TABLE IV
THE DETERMINANTS OF *RSPOST*

Industry	Coefficients for *RSPRE*	Coefficients for *GSLS*	Adjusted R^2
Innovators	1.272† (18.382)		0.734
Innovators	1.278† (17.944)	−0.0248 (0.374)	0.732
Noninnovators	1.009† (20.608)		0.633
Noninnocators	0.999† (20.375)	−0.0181** (1.701)	0.635

Notes: In parentheses are *t*-values.
† (**) indicates significance at 1 (10) percent level.

significantly negative at the 10 percent level among the noninnovators but not significantly different from zero among the innovators. Thus, sales growth negatively affects the intensity of R & D within the firm in the case of the noninnovators but may not do in the case of innovators.

Table V similarly presents the regression result with *PSPOST* as the dependent variable. Again, its earlier rate, *PRPRE*, is highly significant. The coefficient for *GSLS* is significantly negative among the innovators but insignificant among the noninnovators, giving a sharp contrast to the result

TABLE V
THE DETERMINANTS OF *PSPOST*

Industry	Coefficients for *PSPRE*	Coefficients for *GSLS*	Coefficients for *RSPOST*	Adjusted R^2
Innovators	0.642† (9.608)			0.428
Innovators	0.633† (9.560)	−0.0515** (1.949)		0.441
Innovators	0.631† (9.317)		0.0195 (0.991)	0.428
Innovators	0.617† (9.197)	−0.0585* (2.184)	0.0275 (1.397)	0.445
Noninnovators	0.449† (13.660)			0.430
Noninnovators	0.448† (13.562)	−0.00284 (0.539)		0.428
Noninnovators	0.431† (13.020)		0.0536† (2.788)	0.445
Noninnovators	0.431† (12.973)	−0.00081 (0.154)	0.0532† (2.733)	0.443

Notes: In parentheses are *t*-values.
† indicates significance at 1 percent level;
* at 5 percent level; and ** at 10 percent level.

concerning *RSPOST*. That is, sales growth negatively affects the intensity of royalty payments in the case of the innovators but may not do in the case of the noninnovators.

Table V also presents the result when *RSPOST* is added as an explanatory variable. It is found that, with or without *GSLS* as another explanatory variable, the effect of *RSPOST* on *PSPOST* is positive in both of the two industrial categories but significant only among the noninnovators. It is therefore estimated that internal research and patent introduction are complements rather than substitutes; that is, a firm with a larger expenditure on internal R & D tends to pay more for royalty payments. This may be because a research intensive firm tends to utilize both of the two means to achieve innovation or because introducing a patent from outside requires internal research efforts to comprehend the new technology implied in the patent and apply it to meet the company's own needs, experiences, and equipment. In the case of the noninnovators, we may conjecture that a decrease in the rate of sales growth increases internal research effort which in turn increases or accompanies royalty payments. This indirect negative effect of *GSLS* on *PSPOST* is consistent with the negative (though insignificant) correlation coefficient between the two variables.

IV. SUMMARY AND CONCLUDING REMARKS

This paper analyzed the correlation among R & D expenditures (per sales revenue) *RS*, patent royalty payments (per sales revenue) *PS*, and the rate of sales growth *GSLS*, using the sample of 370 Japanese manufacturing corporations. Two variables were defined for *RS* (*PS*) depending on the period—*RSPRE* (*PSPRE*) which measures research intensity around the beginning of the period in which the rate of growth is measured and *RSPOST* (*PSPOST*) which measures it around the end of the period. It was found convenient to separate the entire sample into two categories, innovators and noninnovators, depending on whether the research intensity is above or below average, respectively. We found important differences between the two in our results.

The major findings are as follows: (i) Both *RSPRE* and *RSPOST* are positively correlated with *GSLS* with a stronger correlation between *RSPRE* and *GSLS* [for the innovators only]. (ii) *PSPOST* is negatively correlated (rather weakly) with *GSLS* [innovators]. (iii) *RSPOST* is negatively correlated with *GSLS* [noninnovators]. (iv) The correlation between *PSPRE* and *GSLS* is negative but insignificant [both innovators and noninnovators]. (v) *RSPOST* positively affects *PSPOST* [significantly for noninnovators; insignificantly for innovators].

Combined with the *a priori* reasoning that timewise while *RSPRE* or *PSPRE* (or both) can affect *GSLS*, *RSPOST* or *PSPOST* cannot, we conclude that the positive effect of research on growth was confirmed only among the innovators, namely, those firms in the chemical, drug, electrical equipment, and precision equipment industries, and that the effect on growth of paying for patent licenses is dubious. It is also estimated that, faced with slow growth, the innovators tend to rely on patent licenses whereas the noninnovators tend to expend on internal research which may be reinforced by the introduction of outside patents.

This result raises an interesting question on the rationality of corporations. If R & D expenditures are effective to growth but royalty payments are not, why do innovators tend to rely on the latter rather than the former when sales growth is slow? Also, if the noninnovators' R & D expenditures do not contribute to their sales growth, why do they tend to spend more on R & D when sales growth is slow? There may be a cumulative effect here: A badly performing (in terms of sales growth) innovator (noninnovator) tends to rely on patent licenses (internal research) which actually are hardly effective to sales growth and thus may well hurt its performance further through the increased cost. Or it may be that the relative effectiveness of the two means of innovation changed between 1970 and 1980 and the corporate managers accurately foresaw it. This study cannot answer which.

Another interesting question is whether the result is mainly due to differences across industries or to differences across firms. One way to answer this is to analyze the cross-industry data. We calculated the correlation coefficient between *RSPRE* and *GSLS* using the mean values for the 13 industries in Table I, and found it −0.0209 and insignificant even at the 10 percent level. Also in a multiple regression using these industrial data with *GSLS* as the dependent variable, we found the coefficients for *RSPRE* positive and for *PSPRE* negative with the *t*-values 0.194 and 0.351, respectively, which needless to say are insignificant. Therefore, we infer that the results presented in this paper are mostly due to the differences across firms, suggesting the importance of utilizing company data in the analysis of research activity.

Hiroyuki Odagiri
International Institute of Management,
Platz der Luftbrücke 1–3,
D-1000 Berlin 42,
West Germany

ACCEPTED DECEMBER 1981

REFERENCES

[1] BRANCH, BEN, "Research and Development and Its Relation to Sales Growth," *Journal of Economics and Business*, **25** (2) (Winter 1973), pp. 107–11.

[2] BRANCH, BEN, "Research and Development Activity and Profitability: A Distributed Lag Analysis," *Journal of Political Economy*, **82**(5), (September/October 1974), pp. 999–1011.

[3] DOI, NORIYUKI, "Firm Size, Market Power, and Research and Development," *The Journal of Economics of Kwansei Gakuin University*, **31**(3), (October 1977), pp. 99–123, in Japanese.

[4] KAMIEN, MORTON I. and SCHWARTZ, NANCY L., "Market Structure and Innovation: A Survey," *Journal of Economic Literature*, **13**(1), (March 1975), pp. 1–37.

[5] LEONARD, WILLIAM N., "Research and Development in Industrial Growth," *Journal of Political Economy*, **79**(2), (March/April 1971), pp. 232–56.

[6] MANSFIELD, EDWIN, *Industrial Research and Technological Innovation*. (W. W. Norton, New York, 1968).

[7] ROSENBERG, JOEL, B., "Research and Market Share: A Reappraisal of the Schumpeter Hypothesis," *Journal of Industrial Economics*, **25**(2), (December 1976), pp. 101–11.

[8] SCHERER, FREDERIC M., "Corporate Inventive Output, Profits, and Growth," *Journal of Political Economy*, **73**(3), (December 1965), pp. 190–7.

[9] SCHERER, FREDERIC M., "Firm Size, Market Structure, Opportunity, and the Output of Patented Inventions," *American Economic Review*, **55**(5), (December, 1965), pp. 1097–125.

THE JOURNAL OF INDUSTRIAL ECONOMICS
Volume XXXII September 1983 No. 1

THE UK TRUCK MARKET: AN INVESTIGATION INTO TRUCK PURCHASING BEHAVIOUR AND CHANGING MARKET SHARES

Neil Dorward, Mike Pokorny and Ray Bayldon

The empirical analysis of market performance within industrial economics is still predominantly focused on market structure—performance relations. When applied to cross-section industrial studies, this approach implicitly assumes that industries are insignificantly dispersed from their respective short-run equilibrium positions and that each industry (or market) is homogeneous in terms of the behaviour of buyers and sellers. However, these assumptions will not be appropriate in the case of markets experiencing market share instability to the extent that the relative positions of competitors are changing. Structural adjustments towards new equilibrium positions resulting from competitors having different degrees of market success suggests that corporate market behaviour has an effect on market performance independent of any market structure variable.

Recently, there has been a small, but growing, recognition of the importance of the behavioural mechanism in determining corporate market performance which is reflected in the work of Hatten and Schendel [6], Dorward [3], [4] and Caves and Porter [1]. These studies suggest that corporate behaviour has an independent effect on short-run market performance. Such an effect is particularly likely in the case of product differentiated industries where the market performance of competing manufacturers is affected by their relative success in matching planned product characteristics to buyer preferences. The importance of heterogeneous buyer preferences in explaining the variation of such variables as market share and profitability between firms means that detailed buyer requirements must be analysed in addition to the different competitive strategies of manufacturers. Thus, rather than assuming the complete structural dependence of the behavioural mechanism, empirical research needs to investigate the role of buyer and seller behaviour in affecting market performance.

This paper focuses on the relationship between the purchasing behaviour of truck operators and the changing market performances of UK medium and heavy truck manufacturers between 1976–79. While this is a relatively short period for the analysis of structural change, there have been substantial changes in fortune for some of the leading manufacturers. In the 7.5–20 tonne gross vehicle weight (gvw) sector, Bedford, the market leader, had a decline in market share from 39.7 to 29.7 percent and in the over 20 tonne sector Leyland, the market leader, saw its share fall from 27 to

19.4 percent. However, the extent of the heterogeneity of truck operators in terms of fleet size, type of operational requirement, and the multiplicity of transport applications, makes it inappropriate to generalise about the reasons for the varying levels of manufacturer performance without an analysis of data collected at the level of the individual truck purchaser. Aggregated market share data are too superficial for the analysis of structural change in product differentiated industries, as the concept of the 'average purchaser', which the use of such data implies, is largely meaningless.

This paper attempts a quantification of the extent of the product and operational heterogeneity of truck purchasers by the use of data drawn from a sample of 51 truck fleet operators between January and March 1979. Section I presents details of the survey questionnaire and the sample. Section II outlines the sample market performance of UK truck manufacturers between 1976 and 1979, including the effect of replacement cycles on sales penetration. This is followed in Section III by an attempt to explain the differential manufacturer market performances in terms of purchasing behaviour, with specific reference to buyer loyalty, the diverse pattern of truck usage applications, and buyers preferences in terms of product characteristics.

I. THE SURVEY

The population was defined as those fleet operators listed in the Freight Industry Yearbook (5) (1978) which is estimated to cover some 80 percent of all operators in the UK. In view of our intention to interview a large proportion of the respondents for the purpose of deriving attitudinal information affecting the truck purchasing decision, we initially selected the sample frame from the London region. A total of 200 truck operators were approached by telephone, of which 43 agreed to co-operate and returned questionnaires. Extended personal interviews were carried out with 20 of these respondents. At these interviews a further 12 subsidiaries were identified, all located outside London. As these subsidiaries were autonomous with respect to the truck marque purchased, they were added to the sample and 8 responded, making a total return of 51 questionnaires (24 percent).

The questionnaires requested information on each truck in the fleet in excess of 7.5 tonnes (those trucks for which heavy goods vehicle licences are required) detailing; the manufacturer brand (marque), gvw, make and type of engine, number of axles, year of first registration, year of delivery, whether leased, and the major type of freight application. The same information was requested for trucks currently on order and in addition, where the trucks were replacements, which existing trucks they were to replace. Respondents were also required to identify the factors considered important when selecting a particular truck marque, and the extent to which these factors varied by the weight of truck.[1]

In total, data were obtained for 13,018 trucks, of which 1,042 were on order at the time of the survey. The fleet sizes ranged from 5 to 2,531 trucks with an average of 235 trucks per fleet. Eighty percent of the respondents had fleets of 20 or more vehicles and 92 percent of all trucks in the sample were in fleets of greater than 100. It is impossible to derive corresponding population data as the Department of Transport Survey (4) defines a "commercial vehicle operator" as a holder of an operator's licence and a separate licence is required for each of the 11 Traffic Areas in which a firm has an operating centre. Thus, a firm operating in all Traffic Areas would be counted as 11 different operators. The Department of Transport Survey for 1978 indicates that vehicles in excess of 7.5 tonnes gvw were operated by approximately 100,000 holders of operators' licences. Unfortunately, it is impossible to quantify the extent to which this figure overestimates the actual number of fleet operators. The census also indicates that there were approximately 380,000 trucks of over 7.5 tonnes gvw registered in the UK in 1978. Again it is impossible to break this figure down into operator fleet sizes.

Although the survey generated a large amount of data, it constitutes only 3 percent of the total population of trucks. Further, the impossibility of deriving a comparable size distribution by fleet operator from the total population together with its diverseness in terms of operator size and transport application means that our sample provides a weak basis for drawing any precise inferences about that population. Rather than use it to draw inferences about the population (although some plausible patterns and implications do emerge) this paper has the less ambitious task of identifying inter-relationships between buyer behaviour and market performance within the sample. In effect, the sample is being treated as "the population". However, the results will be suggestive of relationships likely to be present in the true population and so indicate directions for further research.

II. SAMPLE PERFORMANCE OF MANUFACTURERS IN THE UK MEDIUM AND HEAVY TRUCK MARKET, 1976–79

A typical starting point for an investigation of manufacturer market performance is to calculate market shares. The sample was segmented into two sub-markets, the medium sector ranging from 7.5 tonnes to 20 tonnes gvw and the heavy sector covering trucks in excess of 20 tonnes gvw. Although essentially arbitrary, this division roughly corresponds to the

[1] When piloting the questionnaire discounting was found to be a widespread phenomenon. However, it proved impossible to ascertain a generally agreed rate of discount and so price was not included as a systematic question. Instead, we decided to examine the role of price informally when questioning respondents about the factors determining the choice of supplier.

TABLE I
SAMPLE MARKET SHARES OF MAJOR MANUFACTURERS OF MEDIUM TRUCKS: 1976–79 (%)

Manufacturer	*1976*	*1977*	*1978*	*1979*
Leyland	20.1	44.8	34.5	51.4
Ford	23.7	15.0	11.1	12.1
Chrysler	5.2	2.7	3.3	4.7
Bedford	49.9	30.7	43.1	21.4
Seddon-Atkinson	0.9	4.9	7.5	4.6
Foreign	0.2	1.9	0.5	5.8
Total Number of Vehicles	541	674	858	828

division between rigids and tractor units and between four and six-wheeled vehicles.[2] As such it permits some examination of the extent and effect of market segmentation. This segmentation gave 6,111 medium trucks and 6,907 heavy trucks. Tables I and II give the sample market shares of the main marques in the medium and heavy sectors, respectively, from 1976 to 1979.[3]

The major features of the medium sector are the variable but generally declining market share trends of Bedford and Ford, together with the fluctuating but generally rising market shares of Leyland and the Foreign marques. In the heavy sector, the main features are the consistent and steep decline in the market shares of Leyland and the strong performances of ERF and Seddon-Atkinson. The foreign manufacturers in the heavy market increased their total share from 12.2 percent in 1976 to 21.4 percent in 1978, although this share fell back somewhat to 14.1 percent in 1979.[4]

[2] We experimented with a number of alternative segmentations but finally decided upon this two-way segmentation as it provides sufficient observations in each weight category for the analyses that follow.

[3] None of the vehicles that were being replaced in our sample had a year of first registration more recent than 1976. We therefore assumed that none of the respondents had disposed of any post-1976 registered vehicles; that is, the vehicles registered in each of the years 1976 to 1978 were the total of the vehicles purchased. The 1979 figures were derived from the vehicles either already received at the time of the survey or the vehicles that were expected to be received during 1979. Thus, as our sample includes only a proportion of the vehicles actually purchased prior to 1976 (total purchases minus disposals), the sample totals pre- and post-1976 are not comparable. And more seriously, not even the market shares are comparable as this would require assuming that the replacement cycles across truck marque were identical—that is, not only that each truck marque is replaced, on average, after the same number of years but that the variation in these replacement cycles is constant across truck manufacturers. Even *a priori* we considered this an unreasonable assumption and the evidence in our sample confirms that this is the case. See Table III and Footnote 5 below.

[4] We include the population market shares in the Appendix. A comparison of some of the sample and population market share levels confirms our earlier reservations about the size of our sample. Clearly the sample is biased towards purchasers of UK manufactured trucks and, in particular, purchasers of Leyland trucks. However the trends in the sample and population are less divergent. Certainly some of the trends are exaggerated by the sample, and some are missed, but the dominant trends are replicated—notably Bedford's decline in the medium sector and Leyland's decline in the heavy sector.

TABLE II
SAMPLE MARKET SHARES OF MAJOR MANUFACTURERS OF HEAVY TRUCKS: 1976–79 (%)

Manufacturer	*1976*	*1977*	*1978*	*1979*
Leyland	64.5	48.8	33.9	27.1
Ford	0.9	4.8	1.1	3.5
Chrysler	0.5	1.2	0.1	—
Bedford	1.2	—	0.2	—
Foden	5.6	1.7	1.0	1.0
Seddon-Atkinson	4.1	15.3	21.0	31.8
ERF	11.0	12.0	21.1	22.4
Volvo	5.4	7.2	5.5	6.3
DAF	3.0	6.5	10.3	5.2
Other Foreign	3.8	2.5	5.6	2.6
Total Number of Vehicles	802	1031	979	764

However, aggregate market share data alone are of limited value in describing manufacturer performance in a capital goods market. Because truck purchases are a mixture of replacements and additions to truck fleets a manufacturer's market share at a point in time will partly reflect performance in previous time periods. As there are fixed costs in switching marques (see section III below for a fuller discussion) truck purchasers will to some extent be induced to maintain the marque composition of their fleets when purchasing new vehicles. Thus, for example, a manufacturer's market share may increase from one year to the next simply because a large number of its trucks are due for replacement (reflecting high market shares in previous periods) and a substantial proportion of these are replaced by vehicles of the same marque. However as the manufacturer attains only a proportion of its potential replacement sales it is losing penetration in the replacement market—poor current performance is being disguised by high sales levels in previous periods.

These considerations are particularly relevant when using market share trends to compare the performance of well-established manufacturers, such as Leyland, with the performance of the newer foreign entrants. As a recent entrant will have few, if any, replacement sales its market share movements will closely mirror its current competitiveness. For well-established manufacturers this direct link between market share movements and current market performance cannot be assumed.

As the survey provided data on replacement purchases, it was possible to examine replacement cycle differences across manufacturers and to gauge their effect on changing market shares. In total, 525 trucks were being replaced in the medium sector and 446 in the heavy sector. Table III gives the mean and the standard deviation of the age of trucks being replaced.

TABLE III
AVERAGE AGE AND STANDARD DEVIATION OF TRUCKS BEING REPLACED BY MANUFACTURER AND SIZE

	Medium Trucks		*Heavy Trucks*	
Manufacturer	*Average Year of Purchase*	*Standard Deviation (Years)*	*Average Year of Purchase*	*Standard Deviation (Years)*
Leyland	1970.5	1.64	1971.3	1.70
Ford	1973.4	2.60	**	**
Chrysler	1972.6	2.12	**	**
Bedford	1972.3	3.04	1968.2	0.94
Seddon-Atkinson	*	*	1969.2	0.85
Other	—	—	1973.9	1.58
Total	1971.6	2.68	1971.3	1.95

* Only one observation.
** Included in 'other' category because of small number of observations

From Table III it can be seen that the average age of medium and heavy vehicles is about the same, with trucks being replaced every 7 to 8 years. However, the replacement cycles of medium trucks appear to be more variable than those of heavy trucks with considerable differences existing between manufacturers, in terms of both the length and variation of the cycle.[5]

Comparing the market shares of the trucks being replaced with the shares of those on order provides some indication of the extent to which each manufacturer is maintaining its market position. For example, if a manufacturer accounts for a larger share of the vehicles on order than of the vehicles being replaced, then this would indicate an improvement in its competitive position. The simplest way of presenting these data is to express each manufacturer's share of new replacement purchases as a ratio of that manufacturer's share of trucks being replaced. We will refer to this ratio as an index of replacement penetration. Table IV presents these indices for the larger manufacturers in both the medium and heavy sectors. A value in excess of 1.00, then, indicates an improved penetration of the replacement market and a stronger market position, and conversely for a value of less than 1.00.

The indices in Table IV are a summary measure of a single purchase decision. Ideally a time series of these indices would provide a detailed description of manufacturer performance. However, few respondents kept sufficiently detailed records to allow the extraction of such data. None the

[5] Presumably the explanation of these differences is more complex than arguing that they just reflect price and quality differences. Vehicle replacement policies may vary across purchasers and there is no reason for this variation to average out across all marques. A further possibility is that certain marques are more suited to certain applications and it is the variation of applications across marques that in part explains the variation in replacement cycles.

TABLE IV
AN INDEX OF REPLACEMENT
PENETRATION: 1979

Manufacturer	*Medium Trucks*	*Heavy Trucks*
Leyland	1.49	0.12
Ford	1.03	3.22
Chrysler	1.58	0.92
Bedford	0.09	0.00
Seddon-Atkinson	3.00	11.20
ERF	—	48.00
Foden	—	0.00
Volvo	—	9.57
DAF	—	10.25
Other Foreign	—	5.00

less Table IV does permit a fuller interpretation of the market share movements given in Tables I and II. And further, as a series of past purchase decisions are linked to current market shares by the replacement cycle mechanism, the replacement penetration indices also provide an indication of future market share movements.

In the medium sector, the increased market shares between 1978 and 1979 of Leyland, Ford, Chrysler and the foreign marques are all amplified by their respective replacement penetration indices. This implies future market share improvements for these manufacturers.[6] These improvements would appear to be at the expense of Bedford, whose decreasing market share between 1978 and 1979 is emphasised by its replacement penetration index of only 0.09.

In the heavy sector, Leyland has a very low index suggesting a continuing decline in its market share, which clearly contrasts with its performance in the medium sector. Excluding Chrysler and Bedford which have only small shares of the heavy sector, providing very few observations, the remainder of the manufacturers all have high replacement penetration indices. However, these indices vary considerably and it is useful to interpret them in the context of the market share trends in Table II. Seddon-Atkinson, Volvo and DAF all have indices of about the same magnitude but display quite different market share trends—Seddon-Atkinson increases its share by about 50 percent between 1978 and 1979, DAF experiences a decrease in its share by about the same proportion and Volvo increases its share by just under 20 percent. Part of the explanation for this divergent market share behaviour is the differing replacement cycles between these three manufacturers—relatively more Seddon-Atkinsons are being replaced than DAFs and Volvos,

[6] Seddon-Atkinson's market performance index results from just 3 vehicles on order and 1 vehicle being replaced. The bulk of the Seddon-Atkinson's trucks making up the 1979 market share had in fact already been received at the time of the survey.

thus inflating Seddon-Atkinson's market share. The implication of the similar indices for these three manufacturers is that their future market share trends will remain broadly the same. In the case of ERF, there is a very modest market share increase between 1978 and 1979 but it has easily the highest replacement penetration index. Again, the implication is that this current high level of replacement penetration will lead to more substantial long-run improvements in market share. Essentially the replacement penetration indices are likely to provide a closer correspondence with the competitive strengths and weaknesses of the different marques than aggregate market shares. This is particularly so in the case of a change in market leadership where the competitive weakness of the former leader has been partially disguised by market shares dominated by high levels of replacement sales.

III. SOME EXPLANATIONS FOR THE SAMPLE DIFFERENCES IN MANUFACTURER MARKET PERFORMANCE

Purchasing Behaviour and Buyer Loyalty

In his account of competition within the UK heavy commercial vehicle industry Rhys [9] placed considerable emphasis on the role of buyer loyalty in influencing the range of vehicles offered by manufacturers, the price premium that could be charged, and the height of the entry barrier. Dorward [3] in his study of the West Germany medium-sized truck market found a significant positive relationship between a manufacturer's market share and its level of buyer loyalty, with the latter explaining up to 40 percent of the inter-firm market share differences. The measure of buyer loyalty was derived from repeat purchase probabilities estimated by applying a first-order Markov model to a time series of market shares over a 13 year period. However, Dorward's quantitative analysis is based on the assumption that repeat purchasing behaviour is a satisfactory proxy for buyer loyalty.

There has been a long debate in the marketing literature over the conceptual definition of buyer loyalty and its distinction from repeat purchase behaviour.[7] Despite a large number of operational definitions there is no generally agreed conceptual definition of buyer loyalty. However, most usages of the term imply an attitudinal as well as a behavioural dimension in that loyal buyers have a positive preference towards the product and as such the decision to repeat purchase is based on rational choice and not on automatic (reflex) behaviour. This rationalised positive preference distinguishes buyer loyalty from those reflex aspects of repeat purchasing based on inertia and conservatism as well as from market imperfections caused by high fixed costs of switching brands.

[7] For example, see Jacoby and Kyner [8], Jacoby [7] and Tarpey [10].

It is most unlikely that factors such as inertia, reflex buying or mere conservatism are important in explaining repeat purchasing behaviour in the truck market. Trucks are capital goods and are likely to be subject to normal investment criteria so that repeat purchasing would imply a positive preference related to the opportunity cost of capital. However, while a positive preference is a necessary condition for establishing the equivalence of repeat purchasing and buyer loyalty it is not a sufficient condition. Repeat purchasing is simply a two period sequence of purchasing a given brand while buyer loyalty implies repeat purchasing over several periods. For example, if a truck manufacturer induced operators to repeat purchase by reducing prices either to run down stocks of an old model or to dispose of a cancelled order, this would equate with buyer loyalty only if the low price became an integral product characteristic lasting over several years. Any return to 'normal' pricing in the year following the price reduction would cause these operators to seek out other 'reduced price' marques. So repeat purchasing lasting for only two years could imply a response to factors other than buyer loyalty, whereas repeat purchasing over, say, three or four years would suggest the presence of buyer loyalty.

There remains the final problem of distinguishing buyer loyalty from high fixed costs of switching truck marques. As many operators undertake their own truck maintenance and repair work, the advantages resulting from fleet standardisation are important factors in the truck purchasing decision. Fleet standardisation on one marque gives economies in the stocking of spare parts, permits taking advantage of quantity discounts when purchasing spare parts, and minimises the costs of staff training for truck maintenance. There will, of course, still be an incentive, especially for the larger operator, to make one-off purchases of other marques in order to investigate their relative reliability and efficiency. But the costs of such experimentation will be high. Thus, the fixed costs of switching truck marques together with buyer loyalty provide the two main explanations of long-term repeat purchasing. Therefore, evidence of sustained repeat purchasing behaviour can only be indicative of, and not equivalent to, buyer loyalty. However, the cost advantages of fleet standardisation are factors contributing to a positive preference for a manufacturer's truck range and hence can be considered as contributing to the formation of buyer loyalty. But this loyalty derives from the joint-cost economies in operating several trucks of the same marque rather than deriving from any integral characteristic of a given marque. Nevertheless this interdependence of buyer loyalty and fleet standardisation suggests that long-run repeat purchasing can be considered to be dominated by buyer loyalty considerations.

Although our sample data allowed for an examination of each operator's purchasing behaviour over the four year period 1976–79 the data were not suitable for calculating unambiguous indices of repeat purchasing or buyer loyalty. Essentially, the problem of deriving acceptable repeat purchasing indices, and hence useful buyer loyalty measures, derives from the following reasons: truck purchasers generally do not purchase the same number of vehicles on each purchase occasion; purchases are generally a mixture of replacements and additions to fleets (or subtractions from fleets in the case of purchases being less than disposals); operators tend to switch marques progressively rather than abruptly, giving rise to the difficulty of interpreting trends; and the number of marques purchased can vary between purchase occasions.

Despite these difficulties the data do allow some insight into the strength of buyer loyalty and brand switching. Given the complexity of identifying repeat purchase and loyal behaviour we do not attempt to capture these phenomena via single indices or simple numerical measures. Rather we present and analyse the data in a variety of ways and thereby attempt to capture the multidimensional nature of buyer loyalty.

Inter-Marque Differences in Repeat Purchasing

The pattern of truck purchasing by respondents for the 1976 to 1979 period is presented in Table V for the medium and heavy sectors. Only those respondents purchasing in both 1976 and 1979 are included, providing 21 purchasers of medium trucks, 13 of whom purchased more than one marque, and 26 purchasers of heavy trucks, 23 of whom purchased more than one marque. Marques which had less than 5 purchasers are not shown separately in Table V, although their effect is included in the column totals.

TABLE V
REPEAT PURCHASE PATTERNS AMONG TRUCK OPERATORS: 1976 TO 1979

Market Sector and Marque	*Number of Operators Purchasing Marque in 1976 (1979)*	*Proportion of Operators Purchasing Same Marque in 1976 as in 1975*	*Proportion of Operators Purchasing Same Marque in 1979 as in 1978*	*Proportion of Operators Continuously Purchasing Marque Over Whole Period 1976 to 1979*
Medium Trucks				
Bedford	14 (14)	0.78	0.71	0.71
Leyland	8 (9)	0.88	0.89	0.75
Ford	8 (7)	0.75	0.86	0.63
Total (All marques)	36 (36)	0.75	0.81	0.61
Heavy Trucks				
Leyland	19 (9)	0.79	0.89	0.42
Seddon-Atkinson	6 (9)	0.67	0.89	0.83
ERF	8 (10)	0.38	0.60	0.50
Volvo	5 (6)	0.40	0.83	0.40
Other Foreign	8 (8)	0.38	0.50	0.13
Total (All marques)	60 (50)	0.58	0.70	0.38

The behaviour of purchasers of medium trucks shows remarkable stability in contrast to the pattern of market shares (Table I). Each marque was repeat purchased by an average of 75 percent of the respondents between 1975 and 1976, and by an average of 81 percent of the respondents between 1978 and 1979. With at least 63 percent of these respondents continuously purchasing one of the three leading marques between 1976 and 1979, a high level of buyer loyalty is indicated. So the decline in sample market share experienced by Bedford and Ford over the period would appear to be more a result of repeat buyers making fewer purchases rather than a reduction in the number of buyers—buyers appear to have remained loyal, but with a reduced commitment. Leyland would seem to be in the strongest position of all the manufacturers with nearly 90 percent of its purchasers repeating; this was associated with a rising market share.

In the heavy truck sector there appears to have been a substantial increase in repeat purchasing behaviour between 1976 and 1979 which was shared by all the leading marques. Even Leyland, which lost half its buyers over the sample period, had a repeat purchasing rate of 89 percent in 1979. In fact, the four leading marques in 1979 had an average rate of repeat purchasing in excess of 80 percent, which is comparable with the high rates achieved by the leading marques in the medium sector. Therefore, the relatively low rates in column five of Table V indicate a high rate of inter-marque switching earlier in the period; only half the respondent operators purchasing marques in 1976 were still purchasing the same marque in 1979. We seem to be observing a major shift in buyer preferences which by 1979 was showing signs of stabilising, at least in terms of the rates of repeat purchasing. However the average rate of repeat purchasing for all marques remains distinctly lower for the heavy sector leading to an expectation of a relatively lower buyer loyalty than the medium sector.

The greater specialist nature of the heavy sector with its emphasis on custom building is reflected in the greater tendency for multi-marque purchasing. Aggregating for 1976 and 1979, there was an average of 2.1 marques per respondent as against 1.7 marques for the medium sector.

The substantial drop in Leyland's market share is reflected in the decline in its purchasers from 19 in 1976 to 9 in 1979. Leyland is both losing buyers in the heavy sector as well as selling fewer vehicles to those who purchase. The substantial market share gains of Seddon-Atkinson and ERF seen in Table I are associated with an increasing number of purchasers and a substantial rise in their rates of repeat purchasing.

Inter-Marque Differences in Buyer Loyalty: A Subjective Approach

In an attempt to evaluate the extent of buyer loyalty within the sample, as distinct from the level of repeat purchase behaviour, we subjectively allocated the respondents into five behavioural groups. This subjective approach, in which a set of criteria are considered rather than a single quantitative measure, should encompass most of the multi-dimensionality of buyer loyalty.

Specifically, only those respondents with at least three years purchasing data were analysed (most of the respondents had data available for all four years). For each respondent, we observed the number of occasions on which each marque was repurchased, the shares of each marque on each purchase occasion, the trend in these shares over the purchase period, and the changes in the relative shares over the period. The five loyalty groups that emerged are defined as follows:

> *GROUP A: Absolute loyalty on one or two marques.* One or two marques accounted for 100 percent of all purchases and were purchased each year over the three or four years considered.
>
> *GROUP B: Loyalty to one marque and occasional purchases of other marques:* One marque was purchased every year, accounting for 100 percent of purchases for at least two years. Other marques were purchased for one year only. There must be no discernible trend away from the loyal marque.
>
> *GROUP C: Reduced loyalty on one or more marques.* Respondents repeat purchased the marque(s) every year, but at a reduced rate over time. The purchase of other marques must be more than occasional with evidence of some repeat purchasing.
>
> *GROUP D: Switching with evidence of buyer loyalty towards the end of the period.* There must be evidence of switching out of a marque which the respondent initially repeat purchased, together with a building up of loyalty on one or more other marques.
>
> *GROUP E: Switching with little or no evident buyer loyalty.* The repeat purchasing that occurred was between two years only, and there was no evidence of loyalty being built up on any marque.

As might be expected not all respondents fell unambiguously into just one of these groups. Where doubt arose, reference was made to the 1975 purchase data in order to determine a final classification. However, in all cases, the use of 1975 data confirmed the initial classification. Indeed, the classification of respondents into these five loyalty groups proved robust to modifications in the stringency of application of the criteria.

A frequency representation of respondents in the loyalty group is presented in histogram form in Figure 1, for both the medium and heavy markets. The classification is based on the data for 27 purchasers[8] in both the medium and heavy sectors.

[8] The larger number of firms used in this analysis compared to the analysis of Table V results from all firms with at least three years of data between 1976 and 1979 being considered, thus including those firms that may not have had observations for 1976 or 1979.

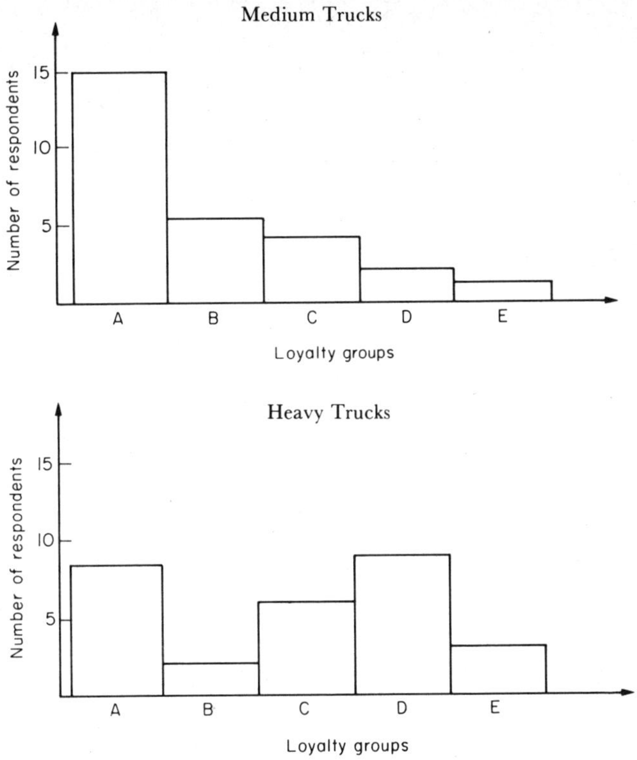

FIGURE 1

Classification of respondents into loyalty groups: medium and heavy trucks

With a progressive movement from Group A to Group E indicating a lowering of commitment to any given marque, the dominant feature of Figure 1 is the greater tendency to loyal behaviour exhibited by medium truck purchasers as compared to heavy truck purchasers. Of the medium truck purchasers 55 percent were absolutely loyal to one or two marques (Group A) as against 26 percent of heavy truck purchasers, while 33 percent of heavy purchasers switched loyalties (Group D) compared to 7 percent of medium truck purchasers. These results are consistent with the data given in Table V where the rate of continuous repeat purchase behaviour between 1976 and 1979 was higher among medium truck purchasers.

The classification of respondents into the five loyalty groups can be used to investigate whether truck manufacturers experienced varying levels of buyer loyalty and the implications that this may have for manufacturer performance.

TABLE VI
BUYER LOYALTY BY MANUFACTURER: MEDIUM AND HEAVY TRUCKS

Vehicle Category and Marque	Number of Vehicle Purchasers				Number of Purchasers
	Exhibiting Strong Loyalty (Groups A, B)	Exhibiting Reduced Loyalty (Group C)	Switching Out from Marque (Groups D, E)	Switching Into Marque (Groups C, D)	
Medium Trucks					
Bedford	9	2	1	—	12
Leyland	7	3	2	1	13
Ford	3	2	1	1	7
Heavy Trucks					
Leyland	4	3	7	2	16
Seddon-Atkinson	1	1	—	7	9
ERF	2	—	1	7	10

The distribution of respondents by loyalty group for each manufacturer[9] in both the medium and heavy sectors is given in Table VI.[10] In the medium sector, Bedford appears to be in the strongest position with 75 percent of its purchasers being in the strong loyalty Groups A and B. This is consistent with the results in Table V indicating that Bedford's loss of market share primarily derives from its loyal buyers purchasing less rather than from a loss of buyers. While Leyland appears to be in a relatively weaker position with only 54 percent of its purchasers falling into Groups A and B only two purchasers were switching out of the marque. As in the case of Table V, the overall picture is one of relative behavioural stability.

Again, greater behavioural instability is shown in the heavy sector with no one manufacturer benefiting from a dominance of strong loyalty in respondents' purchasing behaviour. Leyland appears to be in the weakest position with 44 percent of former repeat purchasers having switched out of the marque. Indeed, 63 percent of its total purchasers either reduced their loyalty to the marque or switched out completely. As ERF and Seddon-Atkinson have only two loyal purchasers each, the increase in their market shares resulted primarily from buyers switching into these marques. These results confirm those of Table V with the high rate of inter-marque switching suggesting that a major shift in loyalties took place between 1976 and 1979. It would appear that the new truck ranges introduced by ERF and Seddon-Atkinson during the second half of the 1970s achieved a better match with operators' haulage requirements than their former technologically outdated products. As such they could be in the process of converting high rates of repeat purchasing into strong buyer loyalty.[11]

The effect of repeat purchasing and buyer loyalty on manufacturer performance would appear to be different in the medium and heavy sectors. In the heavy sector, Leyland's declining sample market share and its major loss of replacement penetration was associated with a halving in its number of purchasers and a low level of buyer loyalty. Thus the reduced loyalty of continuing purchasers and the considerable switching out from the marque were important explanatory factors in terms of sales performance. Although the marques with rising market shares and high replacement penetration indices such as Seddon-Atkinson, ERF, and Volvo did not have high levels of

[9] Only those marques with more than 5 purchasers are presented in Table VI.

[10] Only those purchasers indicating a strong preference for or against a marque were included in the table. While the identification of purchasers behaving in accordance with the criteria of Groups A, B and C is straightforward, purchasers in Groups D and E were included only if they switched out of a marque after repeat purchasing it at least once at the beginning of the period and switched into a marque to the extent of repeat purchasing it at least once at the end of the period.

[11] An anonymous referee suggested that the improved position of ERF and Seddon-Atkinson evident in Tables V and VI was consistent with a 'strong latent goodwill' as customers return to their previous suppliers consequent on an improvement in their products. However, this could be tested only by detailed purchasing data covering the whole of the 1970s. Certainly the results of Table V do not lend much support to this hypothesis as one would expect 'latent goodwill' to be evident in terms of high rates of repeat purchasing in 1975–76.

buyer loyalty, their rapidly rising rates of repeat purchasing and the dominant switching by operators into these marques offer important explanations of market performance. Further, the changing repeat purchasing position is suggestive of the building up of high buyer loyalty on those marques. Thus high and increasing rates of repeat purchasing, together with high buyer loyalty, serve to strengthen market performance in the heavy sector.

Such a relationship was not evident in the medium truck sector. Bedford and Ford maintained high rates of repeat purchasing; nearly as high as that of Leyland, even though their market shares were falling (Leyland's share was rising). Bedford was also rapidly losing replacement penetration. By retaining both its buyers and their loyalty, Bedford, and to a lesser extent Ford, would be expected to have exhibited satisfactory market performances and not the loss of sales penetration observed. This lack of an obvious positive relation between buyer loyalty behaviour and market performance[12] requires an investigation of other possible explanations.

Haulage Applications and Manufacturer Specialisation

Given the extensive range of haulage applications in the road transport industry it is necessary to evaluate the extent to which each truck manufacturer specialises in particular applications and therefore whether changes in the relative growth rates of the different haulage applications can explain, in part, the variation in manufacturer performance. For this purpose respondents were requested to indicate the applications for which each of their vehicles were used. A total of 72 specific applications were identified which we subsequently collapsed into eight general application categories.[13] The sample data did in fact reveal a number of changes in user demand over the period 1976 to 1979 and the main trends are shown in Table VII.

In order to determine whether these changes have influenced manufacturer performance Table VIII and Table IX provide market share breakdowns within these application categories for the medium and heavy sectors respectively.

From Table VIII it can be seen that Bedford is the dominant supplier to the Bulk Goods Transportation market in the medium sector where it has performed consistently well over the four year period. On average, 52 percent of Bedford's medium trucks were supplied for Bulk Goods Transportation and hence it is the manufacturer to suffer most from the contraction in this application area. Further, Bedford has performed inconsistently in the

[12] This is not to deny that such a relationship existed in the medium sector. In fact, Table V showed a direct association between the proportion of operators continuously purchasing each marque between 1976 and 1979 and the market shares in 1979. Also Leyland had the highest rate of repeat purchasing.

[13] General Haulage, Bulk Liquid Transportation, Refrigerated Transportation, Bulk Goods Transportation, General Food and Containerised Drink Delivery, Container Transportation, General Non-Food Delivery, Petrol Transportation.

TABLE VII
TRUCK PURCHASES BY APPLICATION CATEGORY
MEDIUM AND HEAVY TRUCKS
1976 TO 1979 (Percent)

Application and Weight Category	*1976*	*1977*	*1978*	*1979*
Medium Trucks				
General Haulage	45.9	42.8	58.6	60.5
Bulk Goods Transportation	28.0	21.8	15.3	16.4
Other	26.1	35.4	26.1	23.1
Heavy Trucks				
General Haulage	33.7	27.9	24.6	23.7
Petrol Transportation	42.8	40.8	49.0	56.2
Other	23.5	31.3	26.4	20.1

expanding General Haulage market. Thus while Bedford has maintained a high percentage of loyal buyers they are concentrated in the declining segments of the market. Leyland has performed strongly in the expanding General Haulage market, which has taken an average of 67 percent of its medium trucks since 1976. Ford performed poorly in General Haulage thereby contributing to its overall declining share in the medium sector.

Table IX highlights some of the difficulties experienced by Leyland in the heavy sector. Its share of both application groups has declined rapidly over the period, the more serious being its decline in the expanding Petrol Transportation market. By contrast, both ERF and Seddon-Atkinson have expanded rapidly into Petrol Transportation—69 and 65 percent, respectively, of their heavy trucks were supplied to this market in 1979 compared with only 11 and 9 percent in 1976.

TABLE VIII
SHARES OF MEDIUM TRUCKS BY APPLICATION AND MANUFACTURER
1976 TO 1979 (Percent)

Marque	*Application*	*1976*	*1977*	*1978*	*1979*
Leyland	General Haulage	27.8	43.9	39.9	80.0
	Bulk Goods Transportation	0.7	8.2	1.5	0.7
Ford	General Haulage	30.6	32.1	15.4	8.8
	Bulk Goods Transportation	5.3	1.4	0.8	7.4
Chrysler	General Haulage	1.2	2.1	3.0	4.0
	Bulk Goods Transportation	11.9	4.8	2.3	—
Bedford	General Haulage	38.3	19.9	41.3	7.0
	Bulk Goods Transportation	82.1	84.9	93.8	91.9

TABLE IX
SHARES OF HEAVY TRUCKS BY APPLICATION AND MANUFACTURER
1976 TO 1979 (Percent)

Marque	*Application*	*1976*	*1977*	*1978*	*1979*
Leyland	General Haulage	28.9	27.2	12.1	6.7
	Petrol Transportation	96.2	59.8	39.9	25.0
Seddon-Atkinson	General Haulage	2.2	16.7	47.5	44.1
	Petrol Transportation	0.9	23.8	17.7	36.3
ERF	General Haulage	23.0	4.9	4.2	22.3
	Petrol Transportation	2.9	13.6	33.2	27.6
Foden	General Haulage	15.2	—	0.8	—
	Petrol Transportation	—	1.7	—	0.9
Volvo	General Haulage	10.4	23.7	17.9	22.9
	Petrol Transportation	—	1.2	0.4	0.9
DAF	General Haulage	8.9	20.6	12.1	—
	Petrol Transportation	—	—	8.8	9.2

This brief analysis of haulage applications has provided an explanation for the variation in market performance in the medium sector. Although most manufacturers experienced high levels of buyer loyalty, there appears to have been considerable variation in the ability of manufacturers to adequately adjust their product-market strategies consistent with the shifts in the patterns of user demand that occurred. In the heavy sector a number of manufacturers appear to have compensated for their low loyalty by being able to identify and respond to the changes in user requirements, which presumably will result in increased loyalty levels in the future.

Product Characteristics and the Requirements of Fleet Operators

In an attempt to investigate the nature of the loyalty factor in the truck purchasing decision, respondents were requested to list in rank order those factors they considered important when purchasing medium and heavy trucks. The question was asked in an open-ended form, rather than presenting respondents with a pre-determined set of factors. Factors such as "loyalty" and "standardisation", for example, may have different meanings for different respondents. A total of 42 respondents completed this section of the questionnaire resulting in 19 different factors being identified as important in the medium sector and 18 in the heavy sector. These were collapsed into 11 sets of factor groups in both vehicle sectors. Although most respondents identified factors in order of importance the information is presented here in terms of the number of times each factor grouping was mentioned. Weighting these factor groupings according to order of importance had little

TABLE X
IMPORTANCE OF FACTORS IN THE TRUCK PURCHASE DECISION

Medium Trucks		*Heavy Trucks*	
Factor	*Number of Times Mentioned*	*Factor*	*Number of Times Mentioned*
Reliability	10	Standardisation	17
Price	10	Back-up Service	16
Standardisation	10	Reliability	15
Back-up Service	9	Price	11
Availability	9	Availability	9
Operational Suitability	7	Operational Suitability	8
Running Costs	7	Running Costs	8
Weight	7	Weight	8
Driver Preference	3	Quality	6
Past Experience	3	Buy British	6
Appearance	2	Driver Preference	4

effect on the ordering of the factors given in Table X.

In the medium sector, reliability, price, standardisation (including the cost of spare parts), manufacturer back-up, and the availability of the vehicle (delivery time) are the dominant factors. Of these, reliability, standardisation and back-up can be considered as largely contributing to buyer loyalty. Yet as they do not totally dominate; with factors such as price, availability, operational suitability and running costs being important, one would expect there to be less loyalty and a greater propensity for switching than in the heavy sector where all three positive buyer loyalty factors dominate. The implication is that the *potential* for loyal behaviour does indeed exist in the heavy sector and apparently to a great extent than in the medium sector. The observation that the *actual* level of repeat purchase and loyal behaviour was lower in the heavy sector suggests that the heavy sector was undergoing fundamental changes in the relative competitiveness of the truck marques.

The heavy truck sector is a diverse and complex market with many specialist sub-sectors which has given opportunities for the smaller specialist producers to survive. This range of specialist sub-sectors and the considerable product differentiation existing within them has led to large price differentials across marques. In evaluating the competing marques within each specialist sub-sector, the truck operator has to adjust manufacturer prices for the perceived differences in truck characteristics between marques. When the operator's estimated characteristic (or quality)-adjusted price for a given marque is lower than that of competing marques he will buy that marque to the extent that he is profit maximising (or cost minimising). If the characteristic adjusted price remains the lowest he will repeat purchase and eventually become a loyal purchaser. However, if the marque, relative to competing marques, becomes technologically dated, declines in reliability, back-up service deteriorates or the level of quality drops then the operator's estimated characteristic-adjusted price will rise. Unless the truck specifications are improved he will switch into a competing marque. Effectively, the higher characteristic-adjusted price will have eroded his positive preference for the marque and loyalty to the marque will be lost.[14] It would appear that during the late 1970s the heavy truck market was experiencing fundamental changes in the inter-marque structure of characteristics-adjusted prices. Manufacturers were having different degrees of success in matching product characteristics to changing buyer preferences.

Leyland appears to have been the main cause of the destabilisation of the heavy truck sector leading to high marque-switching and lowered buyer loyalty. Its serious loss of market share associated with its relatively low buyer loyalty in a sector where buyers put a premium on factors contributing to high loyalty suggest that its trucks were increasingly failing to meet the requirements of fleet operators. During interviews with respondents, there were frequent complaints concerning Leyland's poor after-sales service, its slow response in the supply of spare parts, and the unreliability of certain truck components. It is Leyland's poor product-market strategy which seems to have destabilised the heavy sector, causing a higher propensity for switching between marques.[15] The result has been an increase in price and non-price competition as Seddon-Atkinson, ERF and the foreign marques achieved a better match between their truck ranges and the product preferences of a wider group of fleet operators. However, Leyland's eventual response in March 1980, with the launching of the new Roadtrain range of heavy trucks, should go some way towards halting its decline in market share and replacement penetration. If this new range is successful, it will lead to operators switching back to Leyland and out of the other British and foreign marques. Thus, it could take some time before actual buyer loyalty approaches its potential level.

IV. CONCLUSIONS

The sample data have indicated marked differences in the market share trends for the leading UK truck manufacturers between 1976 and 1979. However, this paper has demonstrated that aggregate market share data do not necessarily closely correspond to the changing competitive strengths of manufacturers when important replacement cycle effects are present. The use of replacement penetration indices has shown that Bedford and Leyland in the medium and heavy sector, respectively, were in a far worse plight than that suggested by their declining sample market shares. The lack of correspondence between market shares and replacement indices was particularly noticeable

[14] We wish to acknowledge the contribution of an anonymous referee to the presentation of this argument.

[15] An anonymous referee raised the possibility of Leyland losing buyers loyal to AEC and Scammell when these marques were phased out. Many of these buyers switched to non-Leyland rather than Leyland marques.

for those marques experiencing major changes in competitiveness, notably, Bedford in the medium sector and Leyland, Seddon-Atkinson, and ERF in the heavy sector. The main value of the replacement penetration indices is to provide a 'lead' indicator of future trends in market share under *ceteris paribus* conditions and so more accurately reflect current competitiveness.

The examination of buyer behaviour at the level of the individual truck purchaser has revealed a complex market exhibiting substantial behavioural heterogeneity across operators in terms of repeat purchasing and buyer loyalty, ranging from absolute loyalty at one extreme to high switching between marques at the other. These results are consistent with those of Dorward [4] who found significant local and regional differences in truck purchasing behaviour for West Germany.

The analysis of repeat purchasing and buyer loyalty has revealed major differences between manufacturers which provide insights into the reasons for their differing market performances. The behavioural relations were different in the medium and heavy sectors of the truck market. Although having greater behavioural stability and greater buyer loyalty, manufacturer performance in the medium sector was not easily explained in terms of buyer loyalty or repeat purchasing behaviour. A possible explanation was found in the analysis of transport applications. The market performances in the medium sector appeared to be positively related to the manufacturer's ability to develop a product-market strategy that could successfully exploit the expanding application areas.

By contrast, high and increasing rates of repeat purchasing together with high buyer loyalty were associated with strong market performances in the heavy sector. The overall lower buyer loyalty in this sector seemed to have been caused by manufacturers undergoing dramatic changes in relative competitiveness. Consequently, the characteristics- or quality-adjusted price differentials exceeded the benefits gained by many buyers through remaining loyal to a given marque, including the fixed costs of switching marques.

The different market performances of truck manufacturers as regards this sample of 51 fleet operators would appear to be subject to major behavioural influences having an effect independent of market structure. There is considerable heterogeneity across manufacturers in terms of buyer behaviour reflecting the differing success rates of their different competitive product-market strategies. The results cast doubt on the usual assumption in industrial analysis of a homogeneity of behaviour of sellers and buyers within an industry.

NEIL DORWARD,
The Business School,
The Polytechnic of North London,
Holloway, London, N7 8DB

ACCEPTED FEBRUARY 1982

APPENDIX

TABLE AI
MARKET SHARES OF MAJOR MANUFACTURERS OF MEDIUM TRUCKS IN THE UK: 1976–79 (%)*

Manufacturer	*1976*	*1977*	*1978*	*1979*
Leyland	18.5	18.6	17.3	17.4
Ford	23.1	26.0	27.7	24.6
Chrysler	9.4	10.6	11.4	12.7
Bedford	39.7	35.0	30.7	29.7
Seddon-Atkinson	2.9	3.7	4.8	5.2
Other British	4.2	2.8	3.3	2.8
Foreign	2.2	3.2	4.8	7.6
Total Number of Trucks	25,982	24,926	26,196	27,968

TABLE AII
MARKET SHARES OF MAJOR MANUFACTURERS OF HEAVY TRUCKS IN THE UK: 1976–79 (%)*

Manufacturer	*1976*	*1977*	*1978*	*1979*
Leyland	27.0	25.4	21.5	19.4
Ford	6.0	6.8	6.2	5.9
Chrysler	2.2	1.1	1.7	1.2
Bedford	3.1	3.1	3.0	3.0
Foden	5.5	5.6	5.3	5.7
Seddon-Atkinson	11.1	11.1	11.2	12.5
ERF	9.9	10.5	11.4	11.6
Other British	0.2	0.0	0.0	0.1
Volvo	15.3	14.0	16.0	15.5
DAF	5.2	6.9	6.9	6.7
Other Foreign	14.5	15.5	16.8	18.4
Total Number of Trucks	16,939	19,565	22,887	25,864

* Tables compiled from Motorstat NR2 Data: by Courtesy of the Society of Motor Manufacturers and Traders.

REFERENCES

[1] CAVES, R. E. and PORTER, M. E., 'Market Structure, Oligopoly, and Stability of Market Shares', *Journal of Industrial Economics*, 26, (1978), pp. 289–313.

[2] *Transport Statistics: Great Britain, 1968–78*, (Department of Transport, Welsh Office, Scottish Development Department, HMSO, London, 1979).

[3] DORWARD, N. M. M., 'Market Structure and Buyer Loyalty: A Case Study of the West German Truck Market', *Journal of Industrial Economics*, 26, (1977), pp. 115–35.

[4] ———, 'Market Areas, Buyer Behaviour and Industrial Concentration in a Product Differentiated Market, *Applied Economics*, 10, (1978), pp. 141–60.

[5] *Freight Industry Yearbook*, (Transport and Distributed Press, Surbiton, 1978).

[6] HATTEN, K. J. and SCHENDEL, D. E., 'Heterogeneity within an Industry: Firm Conduct in the US Brewing Industry, 1952–71', *Journal of Industrial Economics*, 26, (1977), pp. 97–113.

[7] JACOBY, J., 'A Brand Loyalty Concept: Comments on a Comment', *Journal of Marketing Research*, 12, (1975), pp. 484–87.

[8] JACOBY, J. and KYNER, D. B., 'Brand Loyalty Vs. Repeat Purchasing Behaviour', *Journal of Marketing Research*, 10, (1973), pp. 1–9.

[9] RHYS, D. G., 'Heavy Commercial Vehicles: The Survival of the Small Firm', *Journal of Industrial Economics*, 20, (1972), pp. 230–52.

[10] TARPEY, L. X. Sr., 'A Brand Loyalty Concept—A Comment', *Journal of Marketing Research*, 11, (1974), pp. 214–17.

THE JOURNAL OF INDUSTRIAL ECONOMICS
Volume XXXII September 1983 No. 1

CONSISTENT VERSUS NON-CONSISTENT CONJECTURES IN DUOPOLY THEORY: SOME EXAMPLES*

MARCEL BOYER AND MICHEL MOREAUX

CONJECTURAL variations are at the root of duopoly theory. Cournot [5] was the first formally to study the problem of competition arising when only two firms are selling on a market for an homogenous good. In deriving his equilibrium concept for such a market situation, Cournot made the hypothesis that firm i would determine its production level q_i considering as *given* the production level of its competitor, firm j. Hence Cournot duopolists are said to have zero conjectural variations: each one is conjecturing that the competitor will not react to a change in one's production level. A Cournot equilibrium is reached when, considering both the production level of the competitor and its own production level and given the zero conjectural variations, none of the firms wants to change its own production level. As is well known, different solutions can be reached if non-zero conjectural variations are assumed. Kamien [9] suggests that any market configuration (q_i, q_j) can be accounted for by assuming appropriate conjectural variation coefficients for the duopolists. A major flaw of these models is that in all but very limited cases the conjectures one assumes to begin with are not validated at the equilibrium. Hence the models are inconsistent: the firms are assumed to hold conjectures which turn out to be different from the optimal reaction of the competitor, that is the reaction which restabilizes the competitor in a profit maximizing solution once the change in the firm's production level is made. A growing literature has developed recently to analyse the implications for duopoly theory of requiring that the conjectures held by the firms be consistent or rational. One may mention [1], [2], [3], [4], [10], [11], [12], and [15] for the partial equilibrium approach and [6], [7], [8], and [13] for a general equilibrium approach.

In this paper, we want to illustrate through examples that these consistency conditions do not restrict the wide diversity of *a priori* possible equilibria. As Boyer and Moreaux [1] have shown, extending Laitner's [11] previous results, practically any situation can be understood as a locally consistent conjectural equilibrium. Here, we work out three well known cases to demonstrate their rationality at equilibrium: *Cournot duopolists as well as*

* We are grateful to Louis Phlips for inciting us to work out the examples of this paper. It turns out that they provide useful insights for understanding the consistency problem in conjectural duopoly models. Financial assistance from CORE—Université de Louvain is gratefully acknowledged.

Stackelberg duopolists are thus seen to be correct when adopting apparently inconsistent conjectural variations! We also give an algorithm to compute, given any sustainable market situation (q_1, q_2), conjectural variations functions which make this market situation a locally rational conjectural equilibrium. The paper is organized as follows. In section I we first indicate why the traditional formulation of the conjectural variation duopoly models seems implausibly restrictive and we proceed to reformulate those models in a more acceptable framework. In section II we show in the simple framework of a linear model how some classical situations (Cournot [5], Stackelberg [14]) can appear as rational conjectural equilibria. In section III, the general algorithm is given. In the conclusion we discuss the implications of the results and give suggestions for future work.

I. CONSISTENT CONJECTURES

Let $p(Q)$ be the inverse demand function on some market, with two firms, $j = 1, 2$, whose cost functions are $C_j(q_j)$. The profits functions are $\pi_j(q_1, q_2) = P(q_1 + q_2)q_j - C_j(q_j)$. The first order conditions of profit maximization are then:

$$(1) \qquad \frac{d\pi_j}{dq_j} = P(q_1 + q_2) + q_j P'(q_1 + q_2)\left[1 + \left(\frac{dq_i}{dq_j}\right)^C\right] - C_j' = 0 \quad j = 1, 2 \quad i \neq j$$

where $(dq_i/dq_j)^C$ is the conjectural variation held by firm j.

Provided the higher order conditions are fulfilled, any pair (q_1^*, q_2^*), solution of this system, is a local equilibrium. In these first order conditions the term $(dq_i/dq_j)^C$ is the reaction of firm i, conjectured by firm j, to a variation of firm j's own production level. In the usual duopoly models these terms are assumed constant. Clearly, it is not a very plausible assumption but let us proceed with it and suppose that $(dq_i/dq_j)^C = \alpha_j$, and $(dq_j/dq_i)^C = \alpha_i$. One may wonder: what would firm j observe if it were to change slightly its production level from its equilibrium level? Firm i would react in order to reach a point of maximum profit given the new production level of firm j. This reaction must then satisfy:

$$(2) \qquad \frac{\partial}{\partial q_i}\left(\frac{d\pi_i}{dq_i}\right)dq_i + \frac{\partial}{\partial q_j}\left(\frac{d\pi_i}{dq_i}\right)dq_j = 0,$$

so that:

$$(3) \qquad \frac{dq_i}{dq_j} = -\frac{\dfrac{\partial}{\partial q_j}\left(\dfrac{d\pi_i}{dq_i}\right)}{\dfrac{\partial}{\partial q_i}\left(\dfrac{d\pi_i}{dq_i}\right)}$$

all the functions being evaluated at (q_1^*, q_2^*); if the conjectural variations are constant, it means that:

$$\frac{\partial}{\partial q_i}\left(\frac{d\pi_i}{dq_i}\right) = P' + P'[1 + \alpha_i] + q_i^* P''[1 + \alpha_i] - C_i''$$

$$\frac{\partial}{\partial q_j}\left(\frac{d\pi_i}{dq_i}\right) = P' + q_i^* P''[1 + \alpha_i]$$

hence:

$$(4) \qquad \frac{dq_i}{dq_j} = -\frac{P' + q_i^* P''[1 + \alpha_i]}{P'[2 + \alpha_i] + q_i^* P''[1 + \alpha_i] - C_i''}$$

The consistency of conjectures requires that the reaction of firm i, conjectured by firm j, be equal to the reaction which firm i will want to have; i.e., it requires that $(dq_i/dq_j)^C = (dq_i/dq_j)$; hence: from (4),

$$(5) \qquad \alpha_j = -\frac{P' + q_i^* P''[1 + \alpha_i]}{P'[2 + \alpha_i] + q_i^* P''[1 + \alpha_i] - C_i''} \qquad i \neq j$$

and symmetrically for the reaction of firm j conjectured by firm i. We have then two conditions for the two parameters α_i and α_j. Kamien and Schwartz [10], Perry [12] and Ulph [15] have shown that in particular situations these conditions may be very stringent.

But one may rightly ask why the conjectural variation should be a constant? It seems that the conjectures formed by the firms should take into account and depend on the characteristics of the situation including the production levels of the two firms, q_i and q_j. *A priori* many functional forms could be specified, but the simpler one is the linear form:

$$(6) \qquad \left(\frac{dq_i}{dq_j}\right)^C = \alpha_j + \beta_j q_j + \gamma_j q_i \qquad j = 1, 2 \quad i \neq j$$

It is difficult *a priori* to accept that the conjectural variation formed by firm i would be constant or independent of either its own production level q_i or its competitor's production level q_j. Since the linear form (6) is the simplest possible form, we propose to use it and see what it implies.

Assuming such a conjectural variation function, the first order conditions become:

$$(7) \qquad \frac{d\pi_j}{dq_j} = P(q_1 + q_2) + q_j P'(q_1 + q_2)$$

$$\times [1 + \alpha_j + \beta_j q_j + \gamma_j q_i] - C_j' = 0 \qquad j = 1, 2 \quad i \neq j$$

Let (q_1^*, q_2^*) be a solution of these two equations. What is firm i's reaction to a slight departure of firm j from q_j^*? Differentiating firm i's first order condition gives:

$$\frac{\partial}{\partial q_i}\left(\frac{d\pi_i}{dq_i}\right) = P' \cdot [2 + \alpha_i + 2\beta_i q_1^* + \gamma_i q_j^*]$$

$$+ q_i^* \cdot P'' \cdot [1 + \alpha_i + \beta_i q_i^* + \gamma_i q_j^*] - C_i''$$

$$= Z_i(\alpha_i, \beta_i, \gamma_i, q_i^*, q_j^*)$$

$$\frac{\partial}{\partial q_j}\left(\frac{d\pi_i}{dq_i}\right) = P' + q_i^*[P''[1 + \alpha_i + \beta_i q_i^* + \gamma_i q_j^*] + P'\gamma_i]$$

$$= Y_i(\alpha_i, \beta_i, \gamma_i, q_i^*, q_j^*)$$

Considering (3), conjectures (6) will be consistent if the following equation holds:

$$\left(\frac{dq_i}{dq_j}\right)^C = \alpha_j + \beta_j q_j^* + \gamma_j q_i^* = -\frac{Z_i(\alpha_i, \beta_i, \gamma_i, q_1^*, q_2^*)}{Y_i(\alpha_i, \beta_i, \gamma_i, q_1^*, q_2^*)} \qquad j = 1, 2 \quad i \neq j \tag{8}$$

Let us now consider the following problem: given a pair $(\hat{q}_1, \hat{q}_2) > 0$, is it possible to find linear conjectural variation functions such that this pair could be a consistent conjectural equilibrium? Clearly what is to be found are the six values $\alpha_i, \beta_i, \gamma_i, \alpha_j, \beta_j, \gamma_j$ of (6) satisfying a non linear system of four equations, the two first order equations (7) and the two consistent conjectures equations (8), and two inequalities stemming from the second order conditions. Once $(\hat{q}_1, \hat{q}_2)$ is given, all the elements of this system are taking given values except for α_1, β_1, γ_1 and α_2, γ_2, β_2. Boyer and Moreaux [1], and [2] have shown that such values exist, under very weak assumptions. In the next section we give three examples of classical duopoly models which are generally qualified as inconsistent but which can be seen to be locally consistent with proper linear conjectural variations functions. In the following section, we present an algorithm which can be used to generate any such case.

II. THREE EXAMPLES OF CONSISTENT CONJECTURAL EQUILIBRIA

Consider the following linear model where the inverse demand function is $P(Q) = \max[a - bQ, 0]$, $a, b > 0$, and the cost functions of the two firms $C_j(q_j) = cq_j$, $j = 1, 2$, $c > 0$, $a - c > 0$. It is well known that for this case, the competitive total output is $(a - c)/b$, and the collusive or monopoly total is $(a - c)/2b$. In this section we show how some classical duopoly configurations can be obtained as rational conjectural equilibria.

Example 1: *The Cournot solution*

With the above specification of the demand and cost functions, one can easily obtain that the Cournot solution will be

$$q_1 = q_2 = \frac{a-c}{3b}$$

giving a total output of

$$\frac{2}{3}\left(\frac{a-c}{b}\right).$$

This is the solution of Cournot's reaction functions obtained by assuming zero conjectural variations in (1) above. We obtain

$$(9) \qquad a - 2bq_j - bq_i - c = 0, \qquad i, j = 1, 2 \quad \text{and} \quad i \neq j$$

Hence the slope of this reaction function of firm j is

$$\frac{dq_j}{dq_i} = -\frac{1}{2}$$

showing that the conjectural variation held by firm i

$$\left(\frac{dq_j}{dq_i}\right)^C = 0$$

is inconsistent.

Now consider the following.

Suppose the conjectural variation functions have the following form:

$$(10.1) \qquad \text{Firm } \#1 \quad \left(\frac{dq_2}{dq_1}\right)^C = \frac{2}{3} + \left(\frac{b}{a-c}\right)q_1 + \left(\frac{3b}{c-a}\right)q_2$$

$$(10.2) \qquad \text{Firm } \#2 \quad \left(\frac{dq_1}{dq_2}\right)^C = \frac{1}{3} + \left(\frac{2b}{a-c}\right)q_2 + \left(\frac{3b}{c-a}\right)q_1$$

The conjectural variation functions are not symmetric, yet there exists a symmetric equilibrium. The first order conditions for profit maximisation are

$$(11) \qquad \begin{aligned} \frac{d\pi_1}{dq_1} &= \frac{a-c}{b} - \frac{8}{3}q_1 - \frac{b}{a-c}q_1^2 - q_2 + \frac{3b}{a-c}q_1q_2 = 0 \\ \frac{d\pi_2}{dq_2} &= \frac{a-c}{b} - \frac{7}{3}q_2 - \frac{2b}{a-c}q_2^2 - q_1 + \frac{3b}{a-c}q_1q_2 = 0 \end{aligned}$$

It can be easily checked that these equations have a symmetric solution

$$(q_1^*, q_2^*) = \left(\frac{a-c}{3b}, \frac{a-c}{3b}\right).$$

Furthermore the second order conditions for a conjectured maximum are satisfied. Indeed the second order condition is

$$\frac{d}{dq_j}\left(\frac{d\pi_j}{dq_j}\right) = 2P'\left[1 + \left(\frac{dq_i}{dq_j}\right)^C\right] + q_j P''\left[1 + \left(\frac{dq_i}{dq_j}\right)^C\right]^2$$
$$+ q_j^* P'\left[\frac{\partial}{\partial q_i}\left(\frac{dq_i}{dq_j}\right)^C \cdot \left(\frac{dq_i}{dq_j}\right)^C + \frac{\partial}{\partial q_j}\left(\frac{dq_i}{dq_j}\right)^C\right] - C_j'' < 0$$
$$j = 1, 2$$
$$i \neq j$$

so that at (q_1^*, q_2^*) we get after routine calculations:

$$\frac{d}{dq_1}\left(\frac{d\pi_1}{dq_1}\right) = -\frac{7}{3} < 0 \quad \text{and} \quad \frac{d}{dq_2}\left(\frac{d\pi_2}{dq_2}\right) = -\frac{8}{3} < 0$$

Hence (q_1^*, q_2^*) is an equilibrium, solving the two equations (11). To verify that this equilibrium is consistent, one must check that conditions (8) are satisfied. Indeed, one finds that at

$$(q_1^*, q_2^*) = \left(\frac{a-c}{3b}, \frac{a-c}{3b}\right)$$

the conjectural variation functions (10) take the values

$$\left(\frac{\partial q_2}{\partial q_1}\right)^C = \left(\frac{\partial q_1}{\partial q_2}\right)^C = 0$$

and differentiating implicitly the reaction functions (11) one gets for firm 2

$$\left[-\frac{7}{3} - \frac{4b}{a-c}q_2 + \frac{3b}{a-c}q_1\right]dq_2 - \left[1 - \frac{3b}{a-c}q_2\right]dq_1 = 0$$

hence at (q_1^*, q_2^*) the reaction of firm #2 to a slight modification of the production level of firm #1 is given by:

$$\frac{dq_2}{dq_1} = \frac{1-1}{1-(11/3)} = 0$$

which is precisely the *value* of conjectural variation function used by firm #1; and differentiating the first order condition of firm #1, we have:

$$\left[-\frac{8}{3} - \frac{2b}{a-c}q_1 + \frac{3b}{a-c}q_2\right]dq_2 - \left[1 - \frac{3b}{a-c}\right]dq_1 = 0$$

and at (q_1^*, q_2^*) the reaction of firm #1 to a slight modification of the output level of firm #2 is given by:

$$\frac{dq_1}{dq_2} = \frac{1-1}{1-(10/3)} = 0$$

which is precisely the *value* of the conjectural variation function used by firm #2. So the equilibrium appears as a rational conjectural equilibrium and the quantities are those of the Cournot equilibrium. Where is the problem? In the traditional Cournot model the conjectural variation functions are:

$$\left(\frac{dq_i}{dq_j}\right)^C = 0 \qquad \forall q_j, \forall q_i \qquad j = 1, 2; \qquad i \neq j$$

These functions do not generate a rational conjectural equilibrium because, as we saw above, with such conjectural variation functions, the effective reaction of firm $\# i$ to the production of firm $\# j$ gives:

$$\frac{dq_i}{dq_j} = -\frac{1}{2} \qquad j = 1, 2; \qquad i \neq j$$

It must be pointed out that other conjectural variations functions than those used here can generate a rational equilibrium with the Cournotian production levels. Symmetric functions are immediate candidates, as for example

$$(12) \qquad \left(\frac{dq_i}{dq_j}\right)^C = \frac{2}{3} + \left(\frac{b}{a-c}\right)q_j + \left(\frac{3b}{c-a}\right)q_i \qquad j = 1, 2; \qquad i \neq j$$

But many other functions, symmetric or not, could imply the same result. We give in section III an algorithm to compute the coefficients of the conjectural variation functions which permit one to obtain local rational conjectural equilibria. As the reader may then verify, infinitely many conjectural variation functions could give rise to a rational conjectural equilibrium with the Cournot output levels.

Example 2: *The weak Stackelberg solution*

The Stackelberg leader-follower model of duopoly is based on asymmetric behavior of the two firms. The leader is assumed to know the Cournotian reaction function of the follower. The latter behaves as a Cournot duopolist, that is with a zero conjectural variation. If, rather than assuming that the leader knows the follower's reaction function, we assume that the leader knows the follower's reaction slope only, which is $-\frac{1}{2}$ here as we noted before, then we have the weak Stackelberg solution. It is the same as the Stackelberg solution but allows us to define a reaction function for the leader as well. With the demand and cost functions specified above, one derives the weak Stackelberg solution with firm 1 as the leader as

$$q_1^* = \frac{a-c}{2b}$$

$$q_2^* = \frac{a-c}{4b} \qquad \text{giving a total output of } \frac{3}{4}\left(\frac{a-c}{b}\right).$$

The slope of the follower's reaction function is indeed $-\frac{1}{2}$ so that the leader's conjecture is consistent but the slope of the leader's reaction function—in the weak Stackelberg model—is $(-\frac{2}{3})$ and therefore the follower's conjecture is inconsistent.

Now consider the following. Assume that the conjectural variation functions are

$$\text{Firm } \#1 \qquad \left(\frac{dq_2}{dq_1}\right)^C = \frac{c-a}{2b} + q_1 + \frac{2b}{c-a}\, q_2$$

(13)

$$\text{Firm } \#2 \qquad \left(\frac{dq_1}{dq_2}\right)^C = \frac{c-a}{2b} + q_2 + \tfrac{1}{2} q_1$$

The first order conditions (1) now are:

$$\frac{d\pi_1}{dq_1} = \frac{a-c}{b} - \left(2 + \frac{c-a}{2b}\right) q_1 - q_2 - q_1^2 + \frac{2b}{a-c}\, q_1 q_2 = 0$$

(14)

$$\frac{d\pi_2}{dq_2} = \frac{a-c}{b} - \left(2 + \frac{c-a}{2b}\right) q_2 - q_1 - q_2^2 - \tfrac{1}{2} q_1 q_2 = 0$$

A solution is $(q_1^*, q_2^*) = \left(\frac{a-c}{2b}, \frac{a-c}{4b}\right)$, that is the Stackelberg quantities. The second order conditions are satisfied at (q_1^*, q_2^*), since then

$$\frac{d}{dq_1}\left(\frac{d\pi_1}{dq_1}\right) = -\left[2 + \frac{a-c}{b}\right] < 0, \quad \frac{d}{dq_2}\left(\frac{d\pi_2}{dq_2}\right) = -\left[2 + \frac{a-c}{4b}\right] < 0$$

hence (q_1^*, q_2^*) is a local equilibrium. The values of the conjectural variation functions are respectively

$$(15) \qquad \left(\frac{dq_2}{dq_1}\right)^C_{q^*} = -\frac{1}{2} \quad \text{and} \quad \left(\frac{dq_1}{dq_2}\right)^C_{q^*} = 0$$

To verify that the equilibrium is indeed consistent we have to verify that (8) are satisfied.

Differentiating firm #1 first order condition gives:

$$\left[-\left(2 + \frac{c-a}{2b}\right) - 2q_1 + \frac{2b}{a-c}\, q_2\right] dq_1 - \left[1 + \frac{2b}{c-a}\right] dq_2 = 0$$

so the first firm's reaction to output variations of firm #2, is, at (q_1^*, q_2^*),

$$\frac{dq_1}{dq_2} = \frac{0}{\frac{3}{2} + \frac{a-c}{2b}} = 0$$

and the second firm's conjecture is therefore consistent. Similary from differentiating firm #2 first order condition, it comes:

$$-\left[\left(2+\frac{c-a}{2b}\right)+2q_2+\tfrac{1}{2}q_1\right]dq_2-[1+\tfrac{1}{2}q_2]dq_1=0$$

so that the second firm's reaction to output changes by firm #1 is given, at (q_1^*, q_2^*), by:

$$\frac{dq_2}{dq_1}=-\frac{\left[1+\dfrac{a-c}{8b}\right]}{2\left[1+\dfrac{a-c}{8b}\right]}=-\frac{1}{2}$$

It follows that firm #1 conjecture is also correct.

But $\left(\dfrac{a-c}{2b}, \dfrac{a-c}{4b}\right)$ are the output levels of a Stackelberg equilibrium with #1 as leader and #2 as follower. As in the Cournot case many other conjectural variation functions could provide the same result.

With Stackelberg we got $\frac{3}{4}$ of the competitive output and with Cournot $\frac{2}{3}$. Other situations nearer the two extreme ones, competition or collusion, could also be obtained as rational conjectural equilibria. Example 3 shows how $\frac{5}{8}$ of the competitive output could appear.

Example 3: *The opposite weak Stackelberg case*

Suppose that the firms in this case hold conjectural variations respectively equal to $\frac{1}{2}$ for firm #1 and 0 for firm #2, from which the above name was given. For such conjectures, the equilibrium is

$$q_1^*=\frac{a-c}{4b} \quad \text{and} \quad q_2^*=\frac{3}{8}\left(\frac{a-c}{b}\right)$$

giving a total output of

$$\frac{5}{8}\left(\frac{a-c}{b}\right).$$

From the reaction functions of the duopolists, one can verify that the slopes are

$$\frac{dq_2}{dq_1}=-\frac{1}{2}$$

$$\frac{dq_1}{dq_2}=-\frac{2}{5}$$

which are different from the conjectures and so this equilibrium is also inconsistent.

Now consider the following.

Suppose the conjectural variation functions are:

$$\text{(16)}\quad \begin{aligned} &\text{Firm \#1} \quad \left(\frac{dq_2}{dq_1}\right)^C = \frac{7}{4} + \frac{b}{a-c} q_1 + \frac{4b}{c-a} q_2 \\ &\text{Firm \#2} \quad \left(\frac{dq_1}{dq_2}\right)^C = \frac{10}{12} + \frac{2b}{a-c} q_2 + \frac{19b}{3(c-a)} q_1 \end{aligned}$$

The system of first order conditions is:

$$\frac{d\pi_1}{dq_1} = \frac{a-c}{b} - \frac{15}{4} q_1 - q_2 - \frac{b}{a-c} q_1^2 + \frac{4b}{a-c} q_1 q_2 = 0$$

$$\frac{d\pi_2}{dq_2} = \frac{a-c}{b} - \frac{34}{12} q_2 - q_1 - \frac{2b}{a-c} q_2^2 + \frac{19b}{3(a-c)} q_1 q_2 = 0$$

A solution is $(q_1^*, q_2^*) = \left(\frac{a-c}{4b}, \frac{3(a-c)}{8b}\right)$. For (q_1^*, q_2^*):

$$\frac{d}{dq_1}\left(\frac{d\pi_1}{dq_1}\right) = -\frac{11}{4} < 0, \qquad \frac{d}{dq_2}\left(\frac{d\pi_2}{dq_2}\right) = -\frac{33}{12} < 0$$

hence (q_1^*, q_2^*) is a local equilibrium. And the *values* of the conjectural variation functions at the equilibrium are respectively

$$\left(\frac{dq_2}{dq_1}\right)^C_{q^*} = \frac{1}{2}\left(\frac{dq_1}{dq_2}\right)^C_{q^*} = 0 .$$

Following the now well established procedure, i.e., differentiating the first order conditions, it comes for firm #1:

$$-\left[\frac{15}{4} - \frac{2b}{a-c} q_1 + \frac{4b}{a-c} q_2\right] dq_1 - \left[1 + \frac{4b}{c-a} q_1\right] dq_2 = 0$$

and the slope of firm #1's reaction function is, at (q_1^*, q_2^*):

$$\frac{dq_1}{dq_2} = \frac{0}{-11/4} = 0 .$$

The conjecture of firm 2 is therefore consistent. For firm #2,

$$-\left[\frac{34}{12} - \frac{4b}{a-c} q_2 + \frac{19b}{a-c} q_1\right] dq_1 - \left[1 + \frac{19b}{3(c-a)}\right] dq_2 = 0$$

and so the slope of firm #2's reaction function at (q_1^*, q_2^*) is:

$$\frac{dq_2}{dq_1} = -\frac{11/8}{-33/12} = \frac{1}{2}$$

Examples could be multiplied. In the next section we present the algorithm by which one can compute the parameters of the conjectural variation functions making any sustainable output pair a rational conjectural equilibrium.

III. THE ALGORITHM

Although the examples of section II used linear demand and cost functions, the algorithm presented here uses general demand and cost functions. It is only required that they be twice differentiable. Also, the starting production levels must be sustainable, i.e., profits should be non-negative. Moreover, we need for the algorithm that $P'(Q) \neq 0$ and also that

$$(17) \qquad [C_1'(q_1) - P - q_1 P'][C_2'(q_2) - P - q_2 P'] \neq (P')^2 q_1 q_2$$

which is sufficient to make $F_1 F_2 \neq 1$ in the algorithm. Condition (17) rules out both the competitive equilibrium and the collusive equilibrium. If $B_i > 0$ for $i = 1, 2$ in step 3 of the algorithm, then one can drop condition (17); it is therefore not necessary for the existence of the desired conjectural variation functions.

We can now give the algorithm in 6 steps.

Step 1: Given $(q_1, q_2) > 0$, $P(Q)$, $C_1(q_1)$, $C_2(q_2)$ compute P, P', P'', C_1', C_1'', C_2', C_2'' and check that $P(Q)q_i \geq C_i(q_i)$ for $i = 1, 2$.

Step 2: Check if the following conditions are met

$$P' \neq 0$$

$$[C_1' - P - q_1 P'][C_2' - P - q_2 P'] \neq (P')^2 q_1 q_2 .$$

If not, the algorithm *may* not work.

Step 3: Compute sequentially

$$F_1 = [C_1' - P - q_1 P']/[q_1 P']$$

$$F_2 = [C_2' - P - q_2 P']/[q_2 P']$$

$$A_i = (q_i P')^{-1}[F_j[2P' + P'F_i + q_i P'' + q_i P''F_i - C_i''] + P' + q_i P''[1 + F_i]]$$

for $i = 1, 2$.

$$B_i = C_i'' - 2P'[1 + F_i] - q_i P''[1 + F_i]^2 + q_i P'F_i A_i$$

for $i = 1, 2$.

$$D_i = q_i P'[1 - F_1 F_2]$$

for $i = 1, 2$.

$$E_i = [-P'(2 + F_i) - q_i P''(1 + F_i) + C_i'']/(P' q_i)$$

for $i = 1, 2$.

Step 4: Choose any β_1, β_2 such that, for $i = 1, 2$

$$D_i \beta_i < B_i \text{ and } \beta_i \neq E_i .$$

Step 5: Compute

$$\left.\begin{aligned} \gamma_i &= -\beta_i F_j - A_i \\ \alpha_i &= -\beta_i q_i - \gamma_i q_j + F_i \end{aligned}\right\} \quad \text{for} \quad i = 1, 2 \quad \text{and} \quad j \neq i .$$

Step 6: Write the conjectural variation functions

$$\left(\frac{\partial q_j}{\partial q_i}\right)^C = \alpha_i + \beta_i q_i + \gamma_i q_j \qquad i, j = 1, 2 \quad \text{and} \quad i \neq j$$

which will make the pair (q_1, q_2) we started with a rational conjectural equilibrium.

The formal theorems and proofs on which the algorithm is based can be found in Boyer and Moreaux [2].

It is clear from step 4 that there exists a whole class of conjectural variation functions, one for each value of (β_1, β_2). Each pair of functions so obtained will give the same reaction function, they will lead to the same solution and the equilibrium will always be consistent.

IV. CONCLUSION

We have illustrated in this paper that any pair of production levels (q_1, q_2) which might or might not be the equilibrium solution to some duopoly model with constant conjectural variations can be obtained as a rational conjectural equilibrium for appropriately defined conjectural variation functions. We gave 3 examples and also a general procedure to generate such rational conjectural equilibria.

We also observed that, for the three examples given, a reinterpretation of the constant conjectural variation model was possible. For the case of the Cournot duopoly model with zero conjectural variations we noted that although this model is inconsistent—since at the equilibrium the conjectures are not validated by the best reply or reaction strategy of the duopolists—it is the case that the *values* of the duopolists' conjectural variation functions—which make the Cournot's quantities a rational conjectural equilibrium—are both 0 at the equilibrium. Therefore, the zero conjectural variation model of Cournot is in a sense a rational conjectural equilibrium since there exists a pair of conjectural variation functions making the

Cournot solution a rational conjectural equilibrium and whose values at the equilibrium are 0. Therefore, it is correct for the duopolists to use 0 as conjectural variations at the Cournot equilibrium. But in differentiating the necessary condition for profit maximization to find the slope of the reaction function, one must be careful not to consider that the conjectures are zero identically. In other words, by properly differentiating Cournot's reaction function it turns out that the slope of the reaction function is effectively 0 at the equilibrium. In that sense, Cournot's duopoly model is consistent and rational. A similar analysis holds for the other constant conjectures models.

It is worth noting also that restricting our attention to conjectural variation functions of the linear form (6) has no cost in terms of generality. Every model of duopoly based on conjectural variations can be rationalized through appropriately defined linear conjectural functions.

These results suggest that the requirement of consistency in conjectural models of duopoly allows a reinterpretation in terms of local conjectures which makes the usual constant conjectures consistent. It does not however restrict the duopoly solutions which can be theoretically sound. The restrictions obtained by Bresnahan, Perry, Kamien and Schwartz, Ulph and the others come from somewhat misspecified models whose basic elements are difficult to justify on rational grounds. It seems to us that the research effort should now deal with the origins, development and dynamics of the conjectures themselves to lift the arbitrariness which the consistency requirement has not eliminated.

ACCEPTED MARCH 1982

MARCEL BOYER,
Département de sciences économiques,
Université de Montréal,
Case postale 6128,
Montréal, H3C 3J7, Canada.

MICHEL MOREAUX
Faculté des sciences économiques (GREMAQ),
Université de Toulouse,
Place Anatole France,
31000 Toulouse, France.

REFERENCES

[1] Boyer, M. and M. Moreaux, "On 'Rational Conjectural Equilibrium'", Core, DP #8205, January 1982.

[2] Boyer, M. and M. Moreaux, "Conjectures, Rationality and Duopoly Theory", *International Journal of Industrial Organisation,* (forthcoming).

[3] BRAMNESS, G., "The General Conjectural Model of Oligopoly, Some Classical Points Revisited", Warwick Economic Research Paper 142, 1979.

[4] BRESNAHAN, T., "Duopoly Models with Consistent Conjectures", *American Economic Review*, 71, 5 (December 1981), pp. 934–45.

[5] COURNOT, A. A., *Recherches sur les principes mathématiques de la théorie des richesses* (Hachette, Paris, 1838).

[6] GALE, D., "A Note on Conjectural Equilibria", *Review of Economic Studies*, 45, 1 (February 1978), pp. 33–38.

[7] HAHN, F., "Exercises in Conjectural Equilibria", *Scandinavian Journal of Economics*, 79, 2, pp. 210–26.

[8] HAHN, F., "On Non-Walrasian Equilibria", *The Review of Economic Studies*, 45, 1 (February 1978), pp. 1–17.

[9] KAMIEN, M. I., "Review of 'Industrial Market Structure and Economic Performance' by F. M. Scherer", *Journal of Economic Literature*, XIII, 2 (June 1975), pp. 533–34.

[10] KAMIEN, M. I. and N. L. SCHWARTZ, "Conjectural Variations", *Canadian Journal of Economics*, 16, 2 (May 1983).

[11] LAITNER, J., "Rational Duopoly Equilibria", *Quarterly Journal of Economics*, XCV, 4 (December 1980), pp. 641–62.

[12] PERRY, M. K., "Oligopoly and Consistent Conjectural Variations", DP 179, Bell Laboratories, 1980.

[13] SILVESTRE, J., "A Model of General Equilibrium with Monopolistic Behavior", *Journal of Economic Theory*, 16, 2 (December 1977), pp. 425–42.

[14] STACKELBERG, H. VON, *Marktform und Gleichgewicht* (Springer, Berlin, 1934).

[15] ULPH, D., "Rational Conjectures in the Theory of Oligopoly", Mimeo, University College (London), 1981.

We are grateful to the following, in addition to our Associate Editors, for acting as referees over the past year:

J. A. Alexander,
University of Regina
G. J. Allen,
Trent University, Peterborough
James E. Anderson,
Boston College, Chestnut Hill
V. N. Balasubramanyam,
University of Lancaster
Randall Bartlett,
Smith College, Northampton
Donald Basch,
Simmons College, Boston
Lee Benham,
Washington University, St. Louis
J. I. Bernstein,
Carleton University, Ottawa
Charles H. Berry,
Princeton University
C. Blake,
University of Dundee
Ronald R. Braeutigam,
Northwestern University
Timothy Bresnahan,
Stanford University
Laurits R. Christensen,
University of Wisconsin
John H. Ciccolo,
Boston College, Chestnut Hill
Robert Crandall,
Brookings Institute, Washington D.C.
Neil Dorward,
Polytechnic of North London
Franklin Edwards,
Graduate School of Business,
Columbia University
David Elliot,
Monopolies and Mergers Commission
Robert Feinberg,
Federal Trade Commission
M. Therese Flaherty,
Harvard University
H. E. Frech, III,
University of California
Ann F. Friedlaender,
Massachusetts Institute of Technology
Pankaj Ghemawat,
London
Steven Globerman,
Simon Faser University, Burnaby

Frank M. Gollop,
Boston College, Chestnut Hill
Stanley L. Graham,
Federal Reserve Bank of Minneapolis
Jeffrey Harris,
Massachusetts Institute of Technology
John Hilke,
Federal Trade Commission
Ignatius Horstmann,
Western Ontario University
James A. Hurdle,
Federal Trade Commission
R. A. Jones
University of British Columbia
Stephen Karlson,
Wayne State University, Detroit
John E. King,
University of Lancaster
Marvin Kraus,
Boston College, Chestnut Hill
John Kwoka Jr.,
The George Washington University
George Lermer,
University of Lethbridge, Alberta
Albert N. Link,
Auburn University
S. C. Littlechild,
University of Birmingham
William Long,
Federal Trade Commission
C. Christopher Maxwell,
Boston College, Chestnut Hill
J. Huston McCulloch,
The Ohio State University, Columbus
James Meehan,
Colby College, Waterville
John Meisel,
University of Southern Illinois
S. Metcalfe,
University of Manchester
Herbert Mohring,
University of Minnesota
Douglas Needham,
Western Kentucky University
Jeffrey M. Netter,
The University of North Carolina
George Norman,
University of Reading

Bruce Owen,
Washington, D.C.
Keith Pavitt,
University of Sussex
Bohumir Pazderka,
Queen's University, Kingston
David W. Pearce,
University of Aberdeen
Joe Peek,
Boston College, Chestnut Hill
Martin Perry,
Bell Laboratories, Murray Hill
Harold Petersen,
Boston College, Chestnut Hill
David J. Ravenscraft,
Federal Bureau of Economics
Mark Roberts,
Pennsylvania State University
Arthur J. Rolnick,
Federal Reserve Bank of Minneapolis
David S. Salkever,
John Hopkins University

John T. Scott,
Dartmouth College, Hanover
Kenneth Small,
Princeton University
D. A. Smith,
Carleton University, Ottawa
John Grieve Smith,
Robinson College, Cambridge
Barbara Spencer,
Boston College, Chestnut Hill
John F. Stewart,
University of North Carolina
Robert S. Stillman,
Lexecon Inc., Chicago
J.Taylor,
University of Lancaster
John Vernon,
Duke University, Durham
C. W. R. Ward,
University of Lancaster
Bruce Yandle,
Federal Trade Comission

THE JOURNAL OF INDUSTRIAL ECONOMICS

Published first in October 1952, this Journal was founded to develop the analysis of the problems facing modern industry. It is concerned with the individual business and its relation to the economy—e.g. with outputs and prices and their behaviour in the market, and with the business decisions which affect these. It therefore aims to contribute both to economic theory and to practical public and private policies in the industrial field. The journal is naturally meant to interest business men as well as economists.

The Editors welcome contributions covering the fundamental categories in economics (such as prices, costs, investment, finance, location, wages and productivity) as well as the broader 'background' circumstances (such as the changing structure of industry, management policy and public monopoly policy). Preference is given to MSS bearing on these subjects from the standpoint of individual firms or industries. Theoretical discussion is welcome. Abstract theory is not barred, but authors in this case should provide an introduction and conclusion, so that non-specialist readers may see what the article is about. Alongside articles of more normal length, the Editors are willing to publish shorter notes, especially when these give interim results of important research studies. Books are not reviewed, although books received will be listed, sometimes with a short note; but substantial review articles will be considered. No payment is made to authors, but 25 free offprints are provided. Contributors are asked to send an Abstract, not exceeding 100 words, with their article.

Editorial Offices:

Manuscripts from North America should be sent to Professor H. Michael Mann, Department of Economics, Boston College, Chestnut Hill, Massachusetts, 02167, U.S.A.; manuscripts from all other countries to the General Editor, *The Journal of Industrial Economics*, The Institute of Economics and Statistics, The University of Oxford, St. Cross Building, Manor Road, Oxford, OX1 3UL, from whom detailed Information for Contributors is available.

Subscriptions, advertising, reprint enquiries, etc.

The journal is published by Basil Blackwell Publisher Ltd., 108 Cowley Road, Oxford OX4 1JF, England. US Mailing Agent, Expediters of the Printed Word Ltd., 527 Madison Avenue, Suite 1217, New York, NY 10022, U.S.A. Second Class postage paid at New York.

The journal is published four times a year in September, December, March and June. The subscription prices are as shown below.

All correspondence other than that dealing with contributions should be addressed to the publisher.

Price

Annual subscription for institutions: £24.00 (UK), £29.40 (overseas), $59.50 (USA), $72.90 (Canada)

Annual subscription for individuals: £14.95 (UK), £18.30 (overseas), $35.00 (USA), $43.25 (Canada)

Single issue price for institutions: £6.50 (UK), £7.75 (overseas), $16.00 (USA), $19.50 (Canada)

Single issue price for individuals: £4.75 (UK), £5.75 (overseas), $11.00 (USA), $13.50 (Canada)

Set by Santype International Ltd.,
Salisbury, Wilts. Printed and bound by
Whitstable Litho Ltd., Whitstable, Kent

CONTRIBUTORS TO THIS NUMBER

BO CARLSSON: Deputy Director of the Industrial Institute for Economic and Social Research, Stockholm, Associate Editor of *The Journal of Industrial Economics*, Member of the Swedish Government Committee on the Content of National Statistics, and of the Steering Committee of the European Association for Research in Industrial Economics.

R. DIXON: Senior Lecturer in Economics, University of Melbourne.

RAPHAEL KAPLINSKY: Fellow, The Institute of Development Studies, and Associate Fellow, Science Policy Research Unit, University of Sussex.

HIROYUKI ODAGIRI: Research Fellow, International Institute of Management, Berlin, and Lecturer, University of Tsukuba, Japan.

NEIL DORWARD: Head of the Business School, Polytechnic of North London.

MIKE POKORNY: Principal Lecturer in Economies, The Business School, Polytechnic of North London.

RAY BAYLDON: Research Assistant, The Business School, Polytechnic of North London.

MARCEL BOYER: Department of Economics, University of Montreal.

MICHEL MOREAUX: Université des Sciences Sociales de Toulouse et GREMAQ.

Contents of Volume XXXI, No. 4, June 1983, were:

An Empirical Analysis of Stockholder Injury Under §2 *of the Sherman Act,* by Malcolm R. Burns, Assistant Professor, Department of Economics, University of Kansas.

Regulation of 'Administered' Prices: An Empirical Analysis of the Microeconomics of Price Movement in Finland 1972–77, by Björn Wahlroos, Professor of Economics, Swedish School of Economics and Business Administration, Helsinki.

Joint Costs and Intra-Tariff Cross-Subsidies: The Case of Liner Shipping, by J. A. Zerby and R. M. Conlon, respectively Senior Lecturer, Department of Econometrics, and Senior Lecturer in Economics, University of New South Wales.

An International Comparison of the Fiscal Treatment of Shipping, by Bernard Gardner and Peter Marlow, respectively Senior Lecturer in Shipping and Economics, and Lecturer in Transport and Economics, UWIST.

An Analysis of Cost and Supply Conditions in the Liner Shipping Industry, by J. E. Davies, Assistant Professor of Economics, Acadia University, Nova Scotia.

Co-operative Agreements and the Organization of Industry, by P. Mariti and R. H. Smiley, respectively Associate Professor of Industrial Economics and Policy, University of Pisa, and Associate Dean for Academic Affairs, Graduate School of Business and Public Administration, Cornell University.

The Impact of Joint Ventures on the Market for OCS Oil and Gas Leases, by Alan Rockwood, Senior Economist, Texas Energy and Natural Resources Advisory Council.

Economic Effects of Non-Binding Constraints, by Rex L. Cottle and Myles S. Wallace, respectively Head of Department of Economics, and Associate Professor, Department of Economics, Clemson University.

THE JOURNAL OF INDUSTRIAL ECONOMICS

Volume XXXII DECEMBER 1983 No. 2

FRÉDÉRIC JENNY and ANDRÉ-PAUL WEBER
Aggregate Welfare Loss Due to Monopoly Power in the French Economy: Some Tentative Estimates 113

G. F. MATHEWSON
Information, Search and Price Variability of Individual Life Insurance Contracts 131

R. W. SHAW and S. A. SHAW
Excess Capacity and Rationalisation in the West European Synthetic Fibres Industry 149

R. K. TURNER and D. DEADMAN
The UK Wastepaper Industry and its Long Term Prospects 167

MANFRED NEUMANN, INGO BÖBEL and ALFRED HAID
Business Cycle and Industrial Market Power: An Empirical Investigation for West German Industries, 1965–77 187

C. W. L. HILL
Conglomerate Performance Over the Economic Cycle 197

MARC R. REINGANUM and JANET KIHOLM SMITH
Investor Preference for Large Firms: New Evidence on Economies of Size 213

JOHAN ARNDT and JULIAN L. SIMON
Advertising and Economies of Scale: Critical Comments on the Evidence 229

R. CLARKE and P. K. ELSE
Optimal Adjustments to Restrictions on Advertising: A Comment 243

MICHAEL R. BAYE
Optimal Adjustments to Restrictions on Advertising: Some Further Comments 249

ISSN 0022-1821
BASIL BLACKWELL OXFORD ENGLAND

ELIZABETH BRUNNER

WITH the death of Elizabeth Brunner on October 6th, 1983, the journal has lost a devoted former editor and industrial economics has lost one of those responsible for its resuscitation in the decade or so following the end of the Second World War. It is a loss that will be deeply felt by all who knew her as author and editor, as colleague and friend.

Elizabeth's distinguished career in economics did not start with an undergraduate training in that subject. Like many members of the generation of economists that was prior to her own, she began with a different subject, in her case, English Literature. The need to make good subsequently this lack of a previous training in economics imposed an additional burden when, in 1942, she became a member of the Nuffield College Post-War Reconstruction Survey. There may also have been some offsetting advantage. Her earlier training no doubt contributed to the development of her clear and graceful style of expression. Moreover her flexibility of mind had not been impaired by a rigorous drilling in the theory of imperfect competition with conclusions derived with geometrical inevitability from dubious premises. By the time Elizabeth came to direct her graduate's mind to this topic, the deficiencies in the pre-war orthodoxy were beginning to appear and she, for her part, was introduced almost simultaneously to new ways of thinking before she had been unduly conditioned by long familiarity with the old. One of the most determined critics and innovators was, of course, Phillip Andrews, and Elizabeth became his research assistant in 1944. It was the beginning of a partnership that was to last until his death in 1971.

In view of the importance of his influence on the development of Elizabeth's own thought, it is necessary to recall some of the main features of Andrews' work. He had already played an important role in the investigations carried out by the Oxford Economists Research Group and had been concerned in particular with the inquiry into business behaviour on which the famous piece by Hall and Hitch had been based. Although sympathetic towards their critical approach, he also saw that a number of questions were left unanswered. What determined the price at which the demand curve was said to be kinked? Were businessmen really so insensitive to market forces as to be content with crude full cost-pricing or with a conventional percentage mark-up? And so on. Thus he set about developing his theory of normal cost. As it happened, I saw a good deal of him at that time for he was secretary to the editorial board of *Oxford Economic Papers* and I was general editor. As I observed the development of his ideas, I did not form the impression that Elizabeth was making a large contribution at this early stage—which it would, after all, have been unreasonable to expect from a comparative newcomer to the subject. With the passage of time, however, her contribution clearly increased and its importance could not be concealed even by her self-effacing manner. Nor, for that matter, would Andrews have allowed it to be concealed for he was always generous in his attributions. Together they made a good team. Phillip was imaginative and creative, immensely vigorous but also impatient and unruly. Although by no means lacking—need it be said—in the the capacity for imaginative insight, Elizabeth had a more disciplined approach. Moreover she saw the need to compare the normal cost approach as clearly and explicitly as possible with approaches along more conventional lines and to translate, where appropriate, from one language into the other. Her article in *Economia Internazionale* (1952) was a beginning. Phillip was not prepared to do so. I often tried to persuade him that he was making a mistake, but in vain. It is only fair to add that Oxford, at that time, did not provide Elizabeth, any more than it had provided Phillip, with an interested and sympathetic audience, and both were to look increasingly elsewhere for such an audience.

I have said at the outset that Elizabeth was one of those responsible for the resuscitation of industrial economics which was in poor condition in those post-war years. Admittedly this remark may seem open to question for a good deal of attention was being directed by economists to the problems of particular industries, official working parties were being set up, and so on. The situation was, however, quite different in theoretical economics and, if the scepticism there expressed about the validity of the concept of an industry was justified, much of the empirical work also rested on insecure analytical foundations. It looked, at one time, as though this concept, already much damaged by the theories of imperfect competition, had received its *coup de grace* from Triffin. For if substitutability in consumption between different products is only a matter of degree, the drawing of industrial boundary lines would surely seem to be an arbitrary and rather pointless exercise. The answer given by Andrews and Brunner was that an industry should be regarded as a group of firms with similar productive processes and that this concept should be distinguished from that of the market for a product. It is my impression that Elizabeth contributed more to the evolution of this work on the industry than she had done to the initial work on normal-cost pricing, although the two lines of thought had always been related to each other and were to become part of an integrated theory. Subsequently Elizabeth presented a remarkably clear and succinct account of these developments in "Industrial Analysis Revisited" (*Studies in Pricing* by Andrews and Brunner, Macmillan, 1975). A number of fallacious assertions are incidentally disposed of in this paper, briefly but with unrhetorical firmness, in the process of presenting the proper theory as she saw it. Indeed one finds oneself wondering why some of these investigations should have received such widespread attention. An example is afforded by the study of new entry based on the assumption that this must come from newly created firms although the need for a wider and more realistic assumption had already been made clear by Andrews and Brunner.

Industrial economics, far from declining, has of course experienced a notable upsurge in modern times. Admittedly there may have been a greater concentration on econometric studies than would have been envisaged in those early days, but this is a queston of emphasis which must not be taken to imply hostility to that approach. Elizabeth, however, expressed some concern from time to time about the frequency with which the theory of the firm slips out of sight in some modern industrial studies. For her, firm and industry should as a general rule be viewed in relation to each other.

As specialised emphasis falls on particular branches of a subject, other branches may have to be restored to a place in the sun by giving them a new name. Business history is a case in point. Andrews and Brunner saw this as part of industrial economics and to it they made their own contributions: *Capital Development in Steel* (1951), *The Eagle Ironworkers, Oxford* (1965) and, of course, their biographical tribute to the founder of their college, *The Life of Lord Nuffield* (1955). Meanwhile the work of the Oxford Economists Research Group had continued with Roy Harrod in the chair and with Phillip and Elizabeth acting as organisers and rapporteurs. A long stream of businessmen came to Oxford to be interviewed and cross-questioned about their policies. In this way, a number of us who might not otherwise have done so at all, maintained at least some slight contact with managerial opinions. The group did not, however, embark upon large inquiries along earlier lines and did not produce well-known papers. Its educative influence was more indirect.

As the stream of publications on industrial economics increased and imposed a strain on existing periodicals—including *O.E.P.*—Andrews and Brunner decided that a new specialised periodical was necessary. It was thus that the *Journal of Industrial Economics* came into being in 1952 with Elizabeth as editorial assistant and then as assistant editor. In 1971 she became general editor and retained that position until her retirement, so soon to be followed by her illness and death.

In addition to her work, she did a good deal of consultancy, sometimes with Andrews. In particular, at the suggestion of the late Richard Blackwell, they acted as expert advisers when the case of the Publishers Association came before the Restrictive Practices Court in 1960. The following comment by G. R. Davies on their contribution might be said to apply to much of their work together: "Andrews was a talented academic and Elizabeth Brunner, no less expert in her grasp of economic theory, proved to be a brilliant expositor. She prepared a lucid account of industrial theory and law which was vital in convincing the Restrictive Practices Court of the special position of books in the nation's economic and social life." (*The Bookseller*, October 22, 1983).

Her interests in industrial economics were wide and extended to the holiday trades, the subject of her first publication. It was appropriate, therefore, that she should have been invited to join the English Tourist Board in 1978 and, in 1980, the Water Space Amenity Commission.

In a note of this kind, it is perhaps inevitable that attention should be concentrated on contributions to scholarship and to public policy, rather than to teaching. There is less that can be said in general terms about the contribution of a teacher, although the lesser volume is no indication of lesser importance. Elizabeth was an outstandingly good teacher. She was economics tutor at St. Hugh's from 1946 to 1957 and from 1957 onwards carried an important share of responsibility for teaching at the University of Lancaster. I cannot, of course, speak at first hand of this work at Lancaster any more than about her administrative achievements during two periods as Head of Department. I have, however, listened without surprise to the commendation of those who worked with her there. It seems in place to refer, however, to a notable aspect of the contribution she made. This is the fact that notwithstanding her many commitments, she madc sure that she was always available to her pupils or any young colleagues who were in search of guidance and advice.

It seems appropriate to conclude by referring to her contribution to the success of the *Journal of Industrial Economics*. Little, indeed, requires to be said for her achievement was apparent to all its readers. She was resolved that its reputaton as a learned journal of international standing should be firmly established and progressively extended. She was concerned to ensure that the board of editors and advisers should be distinguished and experienced in an appropriate range of different fields. With the invaluable assistance of Mrs. Doris Loft, she saw to it that the administration was smoothly efficient. The editorial meetings were well planned and well run, and when any troublesome matter arose it was handled effectively and with the least possible friction. For, in addition to her other gifts, Elizabeth had the rare quality of combining efficiency with good humour, firmness of purpose with unfailing patience, with cheerfulness and with tolerance.

T. Wilson
University of Glasgow

THE JOURNAL OF INDUSTRIAL ECONOMICS 0022–1821 $2.00
Volume XXXII December 1983 No. 2

AGGREGATE WELFARE LOSS DUE TO MONOPOLY POWER IN THE FRENCH ECONOMY: SOME TENTATIVE ESTIMATES

FRÉDÉRIC JENNY AND ANDRÉ-PAUL WEBER*

FOLLOWING the pioneering article of Harberger "Monopoly and Resource Allocation" [6], various authors have tried to assess the importance of the overall welfare loss accruing from the presence of monopolistic behavior of firms in the American economy. Those authors, using a partial equilibrium framework, have concerned themselves only with the static misallocations due to monopoly pricing. They have thus avoided more controversial questions such as estimating the effect of monopolies on the rate of technical progress. Yet as Bergson [1] aptly put it

> "If consequential welfare losses due to monopoly are not precluded in respect of consumption structure, they hardly are so more generally".

Despite the apparent simplicity of the theory underlying the idea that monopoly pricing on a particular market leads to a deadweight loss of consumer surplus, the attempt to measure the overall social cost of monopoly pricing is a difficult one both theoretically and empirically. The lack of consensus between the various authors on the best way to go about measuring the welfare losses and on the appropriate empirical assumptions to be made when the data were insufficient has led to widely different estimates of those losses for the U.S. economy. For example Harberger found that they amounted to less than one tenth of one percent of the G.N.P. whereas Kamerschen [13] thought that they could run as high as 8% of the G.N.P.

The purpose of this paper is twofold. First, we want to survey the literature and to present the main methodological and empirical controversies which have surrounded the computation of welfare losses in the US; second, we want to present estimates of those losses for the French economy. Before we get on with this task, however, it might be useful briefly to summarize Harberger's paper as most of the subsequent analysis used it as a starting point.

I. HARBERGER'S ANALYSIS

Harber explicitly refers himself to Hotelling's article "The General Welfare in Relation to Problems of Taxation and of Railway and Utility Rates" [8].

* The authors wish to thank an anonymous referee for his useful suggestions.

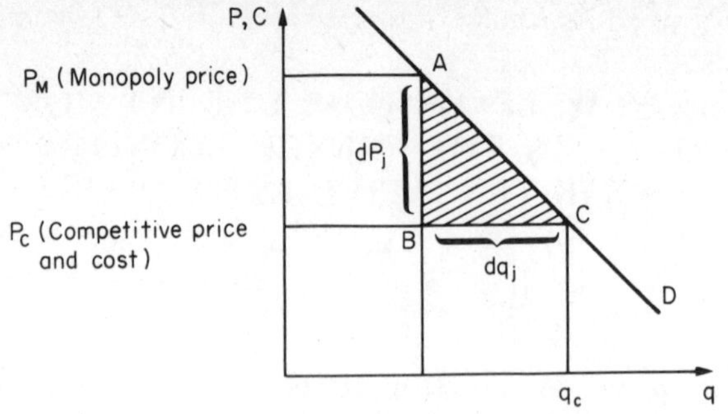

FIGURE 1

In this article Hotelling analyses the impact on a competitive economy of the replacement of an income tax by an excise tax (leading to the same amount of total revenue). He then shows that the total welfare loss for the community due to the imposition of the excise tax (which distorts the price structure and hence the allocation of resources) can be approximated by the expression $S = \frac{1}{2} \sum_j dp_j \, dx_j$ in which dx_j is the change in consumption of x_i that is induced by the general change in prices in the economy.

Harberger then remarks that for any particular industry (j) which is not in competitive equilibrium, the surface of the triangle of deadweight welfare loss (ie $\frac{1}{2}$ $dp_j \, dq_j$ on figure 1) can be expressed in terms of the profit rate and of the price elasticity of demand of that industry with some simplifying assumptions. More specifically, Harberger assumes that the supplier is just as efficient in production when he is in a monopoly situation as he would be in a competitive environment and that all firms in the economy face constant costs of production.

The deadweight loss in industry J due to monopoly power is

$$S_j \text{ (ABC)} = \tfrac{1}{2} \, dp_j \, dq_j$$

If η_j is the price elasticity of demand for good j and if $t_j = dp_j/p_j$ (that is the relative excess of price charged by the monopoly over that which would be charged in a competitive situation)

then by noting that $\quad dp_j = t_j p_j$

and that $\quad dq_j = q_j \eta_j t_j$

one can write $\quad S_j = \frac{1}{2} p_j q_j \eta_j t_j^2$

By summing across all industries, one gets an estimate of the overall welfare loss

$$S = \sum_j \tfrac{1}{2} p_j q_j \eta_j t_j^2$$

The interest of this reformulation for Harberger lies in the fact that, if one is willing to assume the value of the opportunity cost of capital and the price elasticities of demand, firm and industry data can be used to estimate the total welfare loss for the economy.

Indeed total sales are usually available on an industry basis and the t_j's can be computed using the observed profit rates and total sales of each industry as well as the assumed value of the opportunity cost of capital.

In his own empirical estimate Harberger uses a study by Epstein [5] of a sample of 2046 US corporations distributed in seventy three manufacturing industries and representing 45% of the total sales and capital of manufacturing for the period 1924–28. He assumes a price elasticity of one for all industries in the economy and takes the average rate of return in his sample as an estimate of the opportunity cost of capital. Computing the deadweight welfare losses for all the industries in his sample and adding them up, he then blows up the figure he gets to cover the whole economy and comes up with an estimated overall welfare loss of roughly one tenth of one percent of the yearly national income during the period under consideration.

II. CRITICISM OF HARBERGER'S ANALYSIS

Harberger's analysis led to various methodological and empirical criticisms and numerous reappraisals of the welfare losses for the American economy to which we now turn. We will center our discussion around four main points: the use of a partial equilibrium approach, the reference to Marshallian demand curves, the choice of unitary price elasticities, the calculation of excess profits.

a) *The use of a partial equilibrium approach*

Bergson [1] noted that there is a basic inconsistency in Harberger's approach. Indeed, throughout his paper, Harberger assumes that all the resources are employed even in the presence of monopolization and that the return to a long run competitive equilibrium could be obtained by a simple transfer of resources from industries having a lower than average profit rates into industries that have a higher than average profit rates. At the same time, Harberger uses the own price elasticity of the Marshallian demand curve of each industry (assumed to be equal to one in all cases) to compute the welfare loss associated with monopolization. However, Bergson points out that in the simple case of a two sector competitive economy in which one industry becomes monopolized and in which there is no change in the real income of the households, the new equilibrium point of the economy is below the production possibility frontier and the factors of production are not fully utilized. Hence the real income of the households has to be larger when one industry is monopolized than when they are both competitive if one is to assume that in both cases all factors are utilized. It follows that the quantities demanded for the product of an industry when the price is set at marginal cost and when it is set above marginal cost are not on the same

Marshallian demand curve (contrary to Harberger's assumption) since to go from one equilibrium to the other, and assuming full employment of resources in both cases, one has to vary the real income of consumers. Thus the variation in the quantity of a product demanded (*dq*) when the price of that product goes down from monopolistic to competitive level (and hence the estimate of the deadweight loss due to monopolization) depends not only on the price elasticity of the Marshallian demand curve (assumed to be 1 by Harberger) but also on the income elasticity of the good considered. Generalizing his analysis to a multi-sector economy in which several industries are monopolized, Bergson shows that to estimate the aggregate welfare loss one also has to take into consideration the cross price elasticities between all the goods since the setting of all prices at the level of marginal cost would alter the price structure which would in turn shift the Marshallian demand curves of all products. In short Bergson points out that Harberger, by assuming full employment of factors at all time, has carried out his empirical analysis as if all income elasticities and all cross elasticities were equal to zero.

Obviously unable to recompute the overall welfare loss for the US economy (due to a lack of data), Bergson then proceeds to compute the deadweight loss for various hypothetical economies under simplifying assumptions concerning the shape of the social utility function and that of the production function. The main interest of those computations is to show that the estimated welfare loss is heavily dependent on the value of various parameters (namely, the elasticity of substitution between any two consumer goods, the distribution of price cost ratios and the income share devoted to the consumption of each product).

Altogether Bergson's analysis leaves us with the distressing feeling that the sign and the relative importance of the bias incurred when one estimates the overall welfare loss accruing from monopoly through a partial equilibrium analysis rather than through the correct general equilibrium approach are unknown. At the same time, though, one would not necessarily be better off using the general equilibrium approach because of the arbitrary assumptions that one would have to make on the shape of the social utility function and because of the lack of data on the cross elasticities of substitution between goods.

However, we may take some comfort in a remark presented by Worcester [18] in a comment of Bergson's article. He points out that a comparison of the Harberger's estimate and of the Bergson's hypothetical computation lends credence to the idea that both approaches lead to welfare losses of the same order of magnitude when they start from roughly identical hypotheses. Indeed, on the one hand, when Bergson assumes an economy in which 50% of the economy is monopolized, in which the elasticity of substitution between any two goods equal 1 (which together with the assumption of a C.E.S. social utility function implies a price elasticity of 1 for each good) and in which the average price cost ratio in the non competitive sector is 10%, his estimate of the overall welfare loss ranges from 0.11% to 0.20% of the G.N.P. depending on whether he considers a two good economy or a multi good economy and on the assumed distribution of profit margins in the monopolized sector. On the other hand, Harberger's estimate of a welfare loss equal to 0.08% of the G.N.P. assumes that half the economy is monopolized, that, as a consequence, the average price cost ratio in the monopolized sector is 7.2%, and that the price elasticity of demand is equal to 1 for all goods.

b) *The reference to Marshallian demand curves*

Another issue raised in the literature concerns the appropriateness of using Marshallian demand curves to compute welfare losses due to non competitive pricing. As is well known, when a price is set above cost the surplus of the consumers decreases and the welfare loss incurred is part of this consumer surplus loss. The consumer surplus is the area above the price line and under the Hicksian compensated demand curve (i.e. the demand curve holding constant the utility of the consumers). The welfare loss computed from a Marshallian demand curve (along which the utility of the consumers is not constant) will thus not be equal to the correctly defined deadweight loss unless the marginal utility of income is constant. Willig [17] derives precise upper and lower bounds on the percentage errors incurred when one computes for an individual the variation in consumer surplus associated with a single price change using the observed demand curve instead of the compensated demand curve. He shows that those bounds depend on the income elasticity of demand for the good considered in the region of the price change and the proportion of the consumer's income spent on the good. Willig then concludes that "in most applications, the error of approximation will be very small. In fact, the error will often be overshadowed by the errors involved in estimating the demand curve". Hausman [7], however, in a recent paper, shows that if the observed (Marshallian) demand curve of an individual has been estimated, it is possible to derive his implicit utility function as well as his theoretically exact consumer surplus variation associated with a given price change. Hausman therefore notes that in principle one does not need to rely on a Marshallian approximation of this consumer surplus variation in empirical work. Besides, he points out that even when the Marshallian and Hicksian measures of consumer surplus variations associated with a price change are close, for example for goods on which the consumer spends but a small part of his budget, "the Marshallian deadweight loss can be a very poor approximation for the theoretically correct Hicksian measure of deadweight loss based on compensated demand curves". Indeed, given that the deadweight loss is usually a fraction of the total consumer surplus variation, a small percentage of error on the latter may be compatible with a large percentage of error on the deadweight loss.

c) *The estimate of price elasticities*

As we saw previously, Harberger carried out his computations with the assumption of a unitary price elasticity for all demand curves. Stigler, [16] however, pointed out that such an assumption implies that in monopolized industries the marginal revenue would be equal to zero. If that is the case, monopolists could increase their profits by cutting down on production and increasing their prices up to a point where the price elasticity of their demand curve is larger than one. Thus Stigler considers that by underestimating the value of the price elasticities, Harberger has introduced a downward bias in the estimate of the overall welfare loss. In the same vein, Bergson [1] notes that if a monopoly maximizes his profits, the Lerner formula [$\eta_i = p_i/(p_i - MC_i)$] can be applied. He then notes that assuming (as Harberger does) constant costs, an observable average price cost ratio of the magnitude of 10% in monopolized industries implies (if one assumes profit maximization) a price elasticity of demand of 11. Although, Bergson repeatedly points out that the Lerner formula probably does not apply for a wide range of non-competitive industries he, however, "doubts that an elasticity of unity or even of 2 can be nearly large enough to encompass the interesting range of possibilities for the purposes of a calculation such as in question". Cowling and Mueller [4] raise the same point when they point out that one of the flaws of Harberger's analysis is to have observed low price cost ratios (t) in monopolized industries (the average in his sample was 7.2%) and to have at the same time assumed unitary elasticities. They feel that to the extent that the price cost margin of a monopolist is a decision variable, its value must be dependent on the price elasticity of the demand curve that the monopolist faces.

As far as empirical estimates of the overall welfare loss for the American economy are concerned Kamerschen [13], using industry data, and Cowling and Mueller [4], using firm data, have taken into account the interdependency of the observed price cost ratios and of the value of the implicit price elasticity of demand. Those computations obviously lead to estimate of the aggregate social welfare loss much larger than Harberger's estimate. As an example, the figure most comparable to Harberger's estimate in the Kamerschen paper (but based on recomputed elasticities) is roughly equal to 2% of National Income. However, as Worcester [19] has pointed out, the use of the Lerner index to compute demand elasticities assumes that marginal revenue equals marginal costs. Then "serious errors arise if the 'monopolist' is only an oligopolist who fears entry, unfavorable publicity, government regulation or a weaker position at the bargaining table should profits be too high". Since Harberger published his article, one has witnessed a considerable development of Industrial Organization both at the conceptual and the empirical level. Various studies have lent credence of the idea that the Bain and Sylos-Labini model of limit pricing is, overall, a more accurate way to predict the behavior of firms which have market power but weak barriers to entry than the traditional monopoly model which assumes blockaded entry. Thus one cannot assume away as Kamerschen and Cowling and Mueller do (implicitly), the hypothesis that some monopolists facing a comparatively low elasticity of demand will nevertheless choose a low price-cost-margin. It is then possible that a more appropriate method to handle the problem at hand would be to gather data on barriers to entry (such as economies of scale, capital cost requirement and advertising) in industries which have a higher than competitive rate of return and to assume that in the industries in which the barriers are high the Lerner formula can be applied and in those industries in which the barriers to entry are low the Harberger assumption of a combination of low price cost margin and low elasticity can be used.

Further, one should add that Cowling and Mueller, trying to avoid an aggregation bias in their computations apply the Lerner formula at the firm level (rather than at the industry level). For sure, in measuring overall welfare loss, as in most empirical problems in Industrial Organization, a potential aggregation bias exists whenever the definition of industries is such that each one encompasses products which are not considered as close substitutes by consumers. However, by using the Lerner formula for each firm which has a profit rate greater than the assumed competitive rate, Cowling and Mueller assume away, among other things, the existence of oligopolistic industries in which the decisions of the various firms are interdependent. Yet, numerous industry studies focusing on cartels, price leadership, parallel pricing etc. . . . indicate that oligopolistic interdependence in pricing decisions among firms is a prevalent feature of the real world and that the purely neoclassical monopolistic pricing by individual firms, if it is to be found at all, is the exception rather than the rule. Thus their procedure does not seem to be acceptable on theoretical or empirical grounds.

d) *The debate on excess profits*

The estimate of the overall social loss associated with the monopoly pricing necessitates the computation of the excess profit rates in each industry. In carrying out his computation Harberger assumed the value of the competitive rate of return on capital and subtracted from the observed profits of each industry those that would have been registered had the rate of return in those industries been the opportunity cost of capital. The Harberger procedure has been criticized on two grounds: the observed profit rates in each industry are a poor indicator of actual profit rates and the particular assumed value of the competitive rate of return (i.e. the average rate of return for all industries in Harberger's sample) is a poor indicator of the opportunity cost of capital in theAmerican economy during the period under consideration. Deferring until the next section the discussion on the value of the competitive rate of return, let us, for the time being, focus our attention on the first question (i.e. the use of reported profit rates).

Stigler in "The Statistics of Monopoly and Merger" [16] notes that "if monopoly profits are capitalized, the capital of a monopolist grows in such a way that only competitive rates of return are being earned". Thus, according to Stigler, reported profit rates are poor indicators of the welfare losses accruing from monopolistic pricing since accounting practices allow reevaluation of assets in certain cases (such as a merger) but not in others (such as internal growth). The argument used by Stigler to criticize Harberger is a familiar one. Indeed, it has been used by the Chicago school to criticize the empirical work of various authors who have explored the relationship between concentration and profit rates at the industry or at the firm level. It has also been used to criticize the use of statistical cost curves to estimate the minimum efficient size of firms in an industry. As far as estimating the overall welfare loss in an economy, this argument is particularly distressing since, as Bergson [1] has shown, the estimate of this loss will be heavily dependent on (and positively related to) the dispersion of profit rates across (monopolized) industries. There is, thus, a downward bias in the estimates based on the Harberger's methodology.

Stigler's criticism is particularly relevant to the estimation of the social welfare loss due to monopoly pricing in France. Indeed, as we explained elsewhere [9], since 1965, French firms which merge can reevalutate part of their assets and France has experienced since then (most notably between 1965 and 1973) a very important merger wave. What is more, a study of mergers in France [10] supports the idea that one of the main gains from mergers in this country (perhaps even the only one) is the tax break due to the reevaluation of assets. We must thus keep in mind that estimations of the social welfare loss due to the monopoly pricing based on computations of reported excess profit rates will be biased downward in France. However the lack of systematic data on mergers (and on the subsequent reevaluation of assets) prevents us from eliminating this bias.

Stigler levels another criticism against Harberger when he states that "If there are monopoly gains in the payment of factors of production other than capital they are not detected by the procedure". As is clear from reading Schwartzman [15] analysis the failure of various authors to take into account the monopoly gains achieved by workers in non-competitive industries was originally due to the difficulty of showing empirically a positive and significant relationship between wage rates and concentration of industries. However recent studies both in the US and in France [11] support the idea that wages rates in concentrated industries are higher than in competitive ones (*ceteris paribus*).

A related but more general point is raised by Comanor and Leibenstein [3] when they note that in non-competitive markets inefficient producers are not necessarily forced out of the industry and that the general pressure on all firms to use their inputs efficiently is not as great as it is in competitive industries. Thus, the strengthening of competition in non-competitive industries would lead to a decrease in the average cost of those industries. To the extent that Harberger overlooked this factor, Comanor and Leibenstein feel that he underestimated the aggregate social welfare loss. Using a numerical example, they show that the Harberger computation leads to an estimated aggregate allocative welfare loss of approximately 0.18% of the net national product assuming that one half of the total output of the economy is produced in the monopolized sector, that the prices in the non-competitive sectors are on average 6 percent higher than costs and that the price elasticity of goods is equal to 2. If, however, they add the assumption of a cost-effective differential equal to 18% (which according to them "does not seem to be an impossible figure") the allocative welfare loss is nearly 3% of the net national product. Furthermore, in that case the pure X-inefficiency effect (distinct from the allocative effect) is 9% of the net national product.

While one may dispute in the numerical example of Comanor and Leibenstein the importance of the cost effect[1], it seems more difficult to argue that in the real world the level of competition in a particular market does not affect the unit cost of suppliers on this market. In France, at least, a favorite defence of firms investigated for having entered potentially illegal market sharing or price fixing agreements is that if competition prevailed in the industry a substantial portion of the firms would go bankrupt (and that as a consequence unemployment would increase!). The fact that, in the past at least, the antitrust authorities have not turned a deaf ear to such a defence of restrictive practices may, in any case, have induced firms with market power to keep underachievers alive (provided of course that in doing so they did not have to set price so high above the potential minimum average cost that they attracted entry).

It thus seems legitimate to take into account in the computations of overall aggregate social losses the fact that if competition prevailed in presently weakly competitive industries, the average unit costs would probably be lower than those observed.

III. EMPIRICAL ESTIMATES OF THE WELFARE LOSS DUE TO MONOPOLY IN FRANCE

We now present some estimates of the aggregate welfare loss due to monopoly in France. Those estimates, it should be emphasized, are highly tentative due to the methodological difficulties discussed above and to the poor quality of the data we had to use. The main interest of those computations, however,

[1] For a discussion of the importance of this cost-effect see Scherer [14, p. 405]. At the end of this discussion Scherer states: "My own feeling is that padding as high as 10 per cent of costs is not at all uncommon".

lies in the fact that they show, in the context of the French economy, the sensitivity of the measure of aggregate welfare loss to assumptions about the price elasticity of demand in each industry, the importance of X inefficiencies in non-competitive industries, and the value of the opportunity cost of capital.

The profits, sales, assets data used in those computations come from the annual income statements published by the Ministry of Economic Affairs for each industry for the years 1967 to 1974. Two main problems are worth mentioning with this data source. First, our knowledge of accounting practices aimed at evading taxes in France and previous empirical work on the relationship between concentration and profit rates in this country [12] lead us to believe that reported profits are a poor indicator of the economic performance of firms (and industries). A significant portion of profits seems to be hidden either as depreciation or as provisions. We therefore used as our indicator of profitability the net cash flow (i.e. after tax profits + depreciation + provisions). Second, the French economy is classified into 99 two digit industries in the data of the Ministry of Economic Affairs for the relevant years. It seems that industries are too loosely defined in this classification and that in a number of cases firms producing products that cannot be thought of as substitutes are grouped together in the same industry. However, in 1965 the Ministry of Economic Affairs published the income statements of industries both at the two-digit and at the three-digit level (the publication of the income statements of industries at the three-digit level was discontinued after that year). In the three-digit classification (roughly equivalent to the four digit S.I.C.), the French economy is divided into 601 industries. Casual observation suggests that the three-digit classification is more relevant to the computation of the aggregate welfare loss to the extent that, in this classification, products of firms grouped together seem to be reasonably close from the buyer's point of view (at least if we consider the formal definition of what those firms are supposed to be doing). To get an order of magnitude for the possible aggregation bias in our computations (using two-digit data) we used the 1965 income statements. For that year the estimated welfare loss computed at the two-digit level is equal to 76% of the estimated welfare loss computed at the three-digit level. Assuming this ratio constant over time we then multiplied our estimates of the welfare loss for the years 1967–74 (based on two-digit data) by 1.3 to correct for a possible aggregation bias.

The first estimate for the years 1967–70 (Table I, line a) is based on three assumptions: the price elasticity of demand is equal to one in all industries; non-competitive industries are as efficient in production as they would be if competition were forced upon them; the opportunity cost of capital is equal to the weighted average profit rate of all industries in the economy (with profits computed as we have indicated above) over the four years under consideration. The average yearly estimate (unadjusted for the

TABLE I

	Opportunity cost of capital	*Assumption about X-inefficiencies non-competitive industries*	*Sample (two-digit) (X 1000F)*	*Economy (two-digit) (X 1000F)*	*Possible aggregation bias*	*% of Gross Domestic Product*
		Period 1967–1970				
I $\eta = 1$ in all industries						
a)	9.39%[a]	no	—	659,396	×1.30	0.13%
b)	9.39%[a]	yes	1,651,598	×2.75	×1.30	0.85%
c)	12.00%	yes	1,069,445	×2.75	×1.30	0.57%
d)	8.00%	yes	2,206,348	×2.75	×1.30	1.18%
II η deducted from Lerner formula in concentrated industries with high barriers to entry; $\eta = 1$ otherwise						
a′)	9.39%[a]	no	2,360,701	×2.75	×1.30	1.26%
b′)	9.39%[a]	yes	13,755,211	×2.75	×1.30	7.39%
c′)	12.00%	yes	7,559,964	×2.75	×1.30	5.11%
d′)	8.00%	yes	16,489,972	×2.75	×1.30	8.85%
		Period 1971–1974				
$\eta = 1$	9.87%[b]	no	—	1,299,182	×1.30	0.21%

[a] Weighted average profit rate for the whole economy (period 1967–1970)
[b] Weighted average profit rate for the whole economy (period 1971–1974)

possible aggregation bias) is 0.1% of the average Gross Domestic Product. The value of the estimate is thus remarkably close to the Harberger estimate for the American economy.

The same computation was carried out for the period 1971–74. The weighted average profit rate for that period is 9.87% and the estimated yearly overall welfare loss is 0.16% of the Gross Domestic Product (unadjusted for the aggregation bias). Although it would be inappropriate to derive any firm conclusion from the simple comparison of the estimated welfare losses for 1967–70 and for the 1971–74 period, we cannot reject the hypothesis that the increase in the French industrial concentration in the 1960s may have resulted in an increase of the aggregate welfare loss.

As we saw previously, some authors have criticized Harberger for assuming unitary elasticities throughout although the combination of a unitary price elasticity of demand and a low positive price cost margin is not consistent with the neoclassical assumption of profit maximization. The same criticism can obviously be leveled against the above estimate. To try to meet partially this criticism, we feel that a distinction could be made among the concentrated industries registering above "normal" profits between those for which the barriers to entry are high and those for which these barriers are low. In the first case (high barriers to entry) the assumption of neoclassical profit maximization could be made as a first approximation. Then, for those industries, we could assume that the Lerner formula can be used to derive the price elasticity of demand. In the second case (low barriers to entry) we could assume that, rather than maximizing profits in the short run, firms choose to set price at a lower level so as to prevent entry. When the barriers to entry are low, then, one should not expect the Lerner Formula to hold and one cannot derive the magnitude of the price elasticity of demand from the value of the excess price cost margins. For those industries, therefore, we could keep (for lack of other data) the Harberger assumption of a unitary price elasticity.

With these assumptions in mind, we tried to identify the industries having higher than normal profits, high concentration and high barriers to entry. Unfortunately, data on concentration and barriers to entry are available only for a sample of 52 two-digit manufacturing industries accounting for 33.9% of the Gross Domestic Product between 1967 and 1970 and about 39% of the total welfare loss in the economy (when this loss is computed with the Harberger assumptions). We then carried out our computations on this sample. The index of concentration chosen is the share of the four largest firms in the total sales of each industry in 1965 (C_4). Concentration was considered to be high whenever C_4 was higher than 40%. For the highly concentrated industries exhibiting above normal profits we then computed an estimate of the height of barriers to entry. The indicator chosen was a measure of the cost disadvantage of small firms first used by Caves, Khalilzadeh-Shirazi and Porter [2]. This measure is the ratio of the value added per worker in the smallest firms accounting for 50% of the output of each industry to the value added per worker in the largest firms accounting for the other 50% of the output of the industry. Whenever this ratio, computed on the basis of data available in the census of industry in 1962, was lower than 0.90, the industry was considered to be characterized by important economies of scale and therefore high barriers to entry. For sure, other barriers to entry (such as differentiation) should have been examined. Unfortunately data on advertising are not available in France.

If one chooses the weighted average profit rate in the economy as the value of the opportunity cost of capital 13 industries (out of 52 in our sample) exhibit positive excess profits, high concentration and high barriers to entry. For those 13 industries we computed the price elasticity of demand using the Lerner formula and then the corresponding welfare loss. For all the other industries, the computations were carried out assuming a price elasticity equal to one. The total loss associated with the sample (Table I line a′) is equal to 2.360.701.000 F. Blowing up this figure (to account for the fact that the industries in the sample accounted for 39% of the total welfare loss in the previous computation) and correcting for the aggregation bias, we get an overall estimate equal to 1.26% of the Gross Domestic Product (roughly ten times the initial estimate).

Another criticism leveled against the type of estimate that we computed is based on the fact that it is likely that industries in which competition is weak or non-existent are not as efficient as they would be if competition prevailed. We also saw that, in the case of France, there seems to be some empirical support for the idea that unit costs of firms in concentrated industries are higher than they would be in a more competitive environment. Although we do not have any empirical estimates of the importance of X-inefficiencies in non-competitive industries, we computed the welfare loss assuming that in highly concentrated industries, characterized by high barriers to entry and positive excess profits, costs were 10% higher than they would be if competition prevailed. In all other industries we assumed no X-inefficiency. This means, in particular, that we assumed that whenever concentration was high but barriers to entry were low firms were coerced to be efficient if they wanted to enjoy some excess profits and prevent entry. Using the average rate of profit for the economy as the opportunity cost of capital and assuming unitary price elasticities throughout, the welfare loss associated with our sample is then equal to 1. 651,598,000 F (Table I, line b). Blowing up this figure to cover the whole economy and correcting for a possible aggregation bias, the overall estimate is equal to 0.85% of the Gross Domestic Product (6.5 times the original estimate). We also estimated the overall allocative welfare loss assuming that highly concentrated industries protected by high barriers to entry and exhibiting positive excess profits have unit costs 10% higher than those they would have if they were competitive and assuming that the price elasticity of those industries can be derived from the Lerner formula (Table I, line b′). Again, for purpose of comparison with the other estimates, the weighted average profit rate for the economy was considered to be the opportunity cost of capital. The overall allocative loss for the economy in that case (corrected for the aggregation bias) is equal to 7.39% of the Gross Domestic Product (nearly nine times the estimate when one assumes unitary elasticities throughout).

If one assumes that non-competitive industries are not as efficient as competitive ones and that price elasticities of demand are not necessarily equal to 1, there is no reason to assume that the opportunity cost of capital is equal to the weighted average profit rate in the economy even if the economy is characterized by full employment of the factors of production. However, it is not easy to find an indicator of what the opportunity cost of capital might be. Using the average rate of return on stocks between 1967 and 1970 might lead to biases for at least two reasons. First, as we mentioned previously, the 1967–70 period was characterized by a merger wave (among firms listed on the stock exchange) as many firms wanted to take advantage of the opportunity to reevaluate part of their assets. To the extent, then, that the discounted value of the tax break obtained through mergers is included in the rate of return of the relevant firms, the average rate of return on stocks over the period might be a biased estimate of the opportunity cost of capital. Second, as we showed elsewhere aggregate concentration increased during the late sixties and the average rate of return on stocks between 1967 and 1970 may include the discounted value of monopoly gains due to the increase of monopoly power. Rather than try to track down the value of the opportunity cost of capital we recomputed the allocative welfare losses assuming that the opportunity cost of capital was 12% and 8% (instead of the weighted average profit rate of 9.39%) to study the sensitivity of the measure to the value of the opportunity cost of capital. If one assumes that in industries in which firms are sheltered from competition, those firms are not as efficient in production as they would be if competition prevailed and if one assumes that all price elasticities are equal to one (Table I, lines c and d), the total allocative welfare loss for the economy (after correction for the aggregation bias) is equal to 0.57% of the Gross Domestic Product if the opportunity cost of capital is 12% (two thirds of the loss found using the weighted average rate of profit for the economy) and 1.8% of the Gross Domestic Product if the opportunity cost of capital is 8% (roughly 1.4 times the loss found using the weighted average rate of profit for the economy).

If we now add the assumption that the price elasticity of demand in industries with high concentration, high barriers to entry and positive excess profits can be derived from the Lerner formula (Table I, lines c′ and d′), the total allocative loss is 5.11% of the Gross Domestic Product with an opportunity cost of capital of 12% (69% of the estimated loss if we use the weighted average profit rate in the economy) and 8.85% of the Gross Domestic Product if we use an opportunity cost of capital of 8% (1.2 times the loss found when the opportunity cost of capital is 9.39%).

Three additional comments should be made to end this review of our findings.

First, the various estimates incorporating the possibility for some industries to have a price elasticity different from one and/or to have unit costs higher than they would be in a competitive situation were not computed for the 1971–74 period because of a lack of data on economies of scale. Indeed, the most recent industrial census in France covers the year 1962 and we felt that technological change might have significantly altered the magnitude of economies of scale in various industries between 1962 and 1971.

Second, when we assume that some industries have a price elasticity of demand different from one and also exhibit X-inefficiencies, the distribution of allocative welfare resources becomes very concentrated (which is not surprising). For example, in the case of the estimate shown in Table I line b′, the petroleum and the automobile industries account for 39% of the allocative welfare loss in our sample (or 11% of the overall allocative loss in the economy).

Third, it is interesting to note that when we assume the existence of X-inefficiencies in highly concentrated industries with high barriers to entry and positive excess profits, the amount of welfare loss due to X-inefficiency (distinct from the allocative loss) is quite important. For example, in the case of the estimates presented in Table I line b or b′, the welfare loss due to X-inefficiency in our sample is equal to 9.654.384.000 F. If we blow this figure to cover the whole economy and multiply by 1.30 to correct for the aggregation bias, we get an estimate equal to 5.18% of the Gross Domestic Product.

CONCLUSION

We must again emphasize that those estimates are very tentative. Some methodological problems have been ignored such as the vertical relationship of industries (implicitly all industries have been considered to be consumer goods industries) the effect of which is unclear on our measures. However, we have tried to incorporate in the Harberger methodology some reasonable assumptions, consistent with the theoretical and empirical works in the field of Industrial Organization, such as the fact that firms sheltered from competition are not as efficient as they would be in a more competitive environment and such as the fact that concentration and the height of barriers to entry should both be taken into consideration when one tries to anticipate the pricing strategies of the firms. Those crude assumptions led us to believe that in 13 cases in which entry in the industry seemed to be difficult and concentration was high, monopolistic pricing could be expected; as a consequence there had to be a relationship between the observed price cost margin and the elasticity of demand in those industries. Those assumptions, it turned out, changed the order of magnitude of the original estimate of allocative welfare loss (i.e. the estimate one gets assuming unitary elasticities throughout and no X-inefficiencies). Although one could argue that some of our estimates are biased upward because entry in the concentrated industries with high barriers is still possible (although difficult), one could also argue that our estimates are biased downward because in some of the concentrated industries in which barriers are low (according to our measure) X-inefficiencies are likely to be present. It is, of course, impossible to tell what the net effect of those two biases is. Our own feeling is that the allocative welfare loss for the French economy between 1967 and 1970 is probably somewhere between 0.85% and 7.39% of the Gross Domestic Product. This means that the allocative welfare losses are not negligible. What is more, as we noted, the welfare loss due to X-inefficiencies might well be as high as 5% of the Gross Domestic Product.

What, then, are the policy implications of those findings? On the one hand, if one relies on the assumption of unitary elasticities throughout and no X-inefficiencies in concentrated industries with high barriers to entry, the potential gains from the antitrust policy seem to be very small and those potential gains are scattered among a great many industries. This, of course, does not mean that no resources should be devoted to antitrust policy but it could mean that the attention of antitrust authorities should be focused on the behavior of firms rather than on the structure of industries. Unfortunately, the cost of examining the behavior of firms in a great many industries can undoubtedly be very high. To avoid devoting (at the margin) more resources to the prevention of anticompetitive practices than the social welfare loss they imply, it is likely that a combination of *per se* rules and an enforcement of those rules designed to be strongly dissuasive is called for. If, on the other hand, one believes (as we do) that firms in concentrated industries with high barriers to entry are a major source both of allocative welfare losses and of losses due to X-inefficiencies, the gains which can be expected from the enforcement of antitrust legislation are much more important and much more concentrated. In depth studies of a small number of industries both from the behavioral and structural point of view seem to be promising ways to tackle the problem of minimizing the social cost of monopoly and rules of reason seem preferable to *per se* rules.

In the case of France, the philosophy of the 1977 competition law seems to be consistent with the second approach. Indeed the law creates a merger control and contains a provision enabling deconcentration of firms which have acquired a dominant position through mergers whenever abuse of market power by those firms seems to be a direct consequence of those mergers. Also, anti-competitive practices are more severely condemned if they have also contributed to decreasing the efficiency of the firms involved. The enforcement of this law, however, leaves much to be desired. Cases seem to be referred to the "Commission de la Concurrence" (the administrative body hearing the cases) by the Minister of Economic Affairs not on the basis of the importance of the expected welfare losses to be found but rather on the basis of political considerations. The antitrust division of the Ministry of Economic Affairs seems to spend a disproportionate amount of resources examining the behavior of firms in scores of small industries in which neither concentration nor barriers to entry seem to be particularly high. When it investigates highly concentrated industries, it tends to focus its attention on the trade practices of the (often) independent retailers but it is very reluctant to investigate the structure and the strategies of the suppliers. As a result, and even if welfare losses are important in the economy, it is possible (some would even say likely) that our antitrust enforcement system, barking at the wrong tree, absorbs (at least at the margin) more resources than it saves.

Frédéric Jenny and André-Paul Weber,
E.S.S.E.C.,
Boite Postale 105,
95021 Cergy Pontoise, Cedex,
France

ACCEPTED MAY 1982

REFERENCES

[1] ABRAM BERGSON, "On Monopoly Welfare Losses", *American Economic Review,* Vol. 63, No. 5 (December 1973), pp. 853–70.

[2] R. CAVES, E. KHALILZADEH-SHIRAZI and M. PORTER, "Scale Economies in Statistical Analysis of Market Power", *The Review of Economics and Statistics,* Vol. 57, No. 2 (May 1975), pp. 133–41.

[3] WILLIAM S. COMANOR and HARVEY LEIBENSTEIN, "Allocative Efficiency, X-Efficiency and the Measurement of Welfare Losses", *Economica,* Vol. 36 (August 1969), pp. 304–9.

[4] K. COWLING and D. C. MUELLER, "The Social Costs of Monopoly Power", Mimeograph, April 1977.

[5] C. EPSTEIN, *Industrial Profits in the United States* (National Bureau of Economic Research, 1934).

[6] A. C. HARBERGER, "Monopoly and Resource Allocation", *American Economic Review,* Papers and Proceedings, Vol. 44 (May 1954), pp. 77–87.

[7] JERRY A. HAUSMAN, "Exact Consumer's Surplus and Dead Weight Loss", *American Economic Review,* Vol. 71 (September 1981), No. 4, pp. 662–73.

[8] HAROLD HOTELLING, "The General Welfare in Relation to Problems of Taxation and of Railway and Utility Rates", *Econometrica,* Vol. 6 (July 1938), pp. 242–69.

[9] F. JENNY and A. P. WEBER, "The Determinants of Concentration Trends in the French Manufacturing Sector", *The Journal of Industrial Economics,* Vol. XXVI, No. 3 (March 1978), pp. 193–207.

[10] F. JENNY and A. P. WEBER, "The Determinants and Effects of Mergers in France", in "*The Determinants and Effects of Mergers*", Dennis C. MUELLER ed., Oelgeschlager, Gunn and Hain 1980, pp. 133–63.

[11] F. JENNY and A. P. WEBER, "Wages Rates, Concentration and Unionization in French Manufacturing Industries", *The Journal of Industrial Economics,* Vol. 26 No. 4 (June 1978), pp. 315–27.

[12] F. JENNY and A. P. WEBER, "Profit Rates and Structural Variables in the French Manufacturing Sector", *European Economic Review,* No. 7 (1976), pp. 187–206.

[13] D. R. KAMERSCHEN, "An Estimation of the Welfare Losses from Monopoly in the American Economy", *Western Economic Journal*, Vol. 4 (Summer 1966), pp. 221–36.

[14] F. M. SCHERER "*Industrial Market Structure and Economic Performance*", Rand McNally, 1970.

[15] DAVID SCHWARTZMAN, "The Burden of Monopoly", *Journal of Political Economy*, Vol. 68, No. 6 (December 1960), pp. 627–30.

[16] G. J. STIGLER, "The Statistics of Monopoly and Merger", *Journal of Political Economy*, Vol. 64, No. 1 (February 1956), pp. 33–40.

[17] R. D. WILLIG, "Consumer's Surplus Without Apology", *American Economic Review*, Vol. 66, No. 4 (September 1976), pp. 589–97.

[18] D. A. WORCESTER Jr., "On Monopoly Welfare Losses: Comment", *American Economic Review*, Vol. 63 (December 1973), pp. 1015–23.

[19] DEAN A. WORCESTER Jr., "Innovations in the Calculation of Welfare Loss to Monopoly", *Western Economic Journal*, Vol. 7 (September 1969), pp. 234–43.

THE JOURNAL OF INDUSTRIAL ECONOMICS 0022–1821 $2.00
Volume XXXII December 1983 No. 2

INFORMATION, SEARCH, AND PRICE VARIABILITY OF INDIVIDUAL LIFE INSURANCE CONTRACTS

G. F. MATHEWSON*

I. INTRODUCTION

The objective of this paper is to explain the observed price variability of individual life insurance contracts. This market holds special interest because of the alleged strong informational asymmetries that favour life insurance firms over insurance consumers (Consumer's Union [4] and Federal Trade Commission [6]). Estimates indicate that the price variability of individual life insurance is substantial, so that the pay-off from additional consumer search is equally large. For example, term insurance contracts renewable to a specific age constitute a relatively simple and homogeneous class of products. Yet, a sample of 12 insurance firms issuing in 1979 to Canadian males aged 25, $100,000 term policies yearly renewable to age 70, indicates an annual price spread of $89 with an approximate 1979 present value price spread of $890 (using a 10% discount rate). A sample of 49 insurance firms issuing in 1977 to males in New York State aged 20, $50,000 term policies renewable every 5 years to age 70, indicates an annual price spread of $150 with an approximate 1979 present value price spread of $1500 (again using a 10% discount rate).[1]

There is more than one candidate explanation for retail price variability in any market. Pure price shopping models, where products are homogeneous, buyers and sellers are many, buyers with identical search costs search for sellers, and sellers with identical advertising costs advertise price to locate buyers, are sufficient to generate an equilibrium distribution of prices. However, such models do not appear to offer a consistent empirical explanation for the observed price variability in individual life insurance contracts.[2] The question is why not?

* I wish to thank Jeffrey Bernstein, Jack Carr, Yehuda Kotowitz, Herb Mohring, Ralph Winter and an anonymous referee of this journal for helpful comments on this material.

[1] These prices are taken from (respectively) Consumers' Association of Canada [3] and New York State Department of Insurance [5].

[2] Butters [2] provides a thorough analysis of such a pure price shopping, model. We take the Butters calculation for the equilibrium price variance and, for a set of Canadian life insurance prices for 1977, calculate the optimal consumer search for each category of insurance policy (where a category is defined by type of policy, age at which the policy is issued, sex of the purchaser, coverage in the policy) that yields the observed variance of prices. The implied optimal consumer search is not consistently reasonable. For example, if we estimate the per unit cost of life insurance firm advertising (including agents' fees) at 30% of the lowest-priced

(continued on p. 132)

There are several institutional features that differentiate the market for individual life insurance contracts from the markets that prevail in pure price-shopping models. First, life insurance contracts are not homogeneous products. There are important differences across contract types. Contracts are typically either term insurance (insurance of some specified amount renewable over a relatively short horizon (yearly or every five years)), or permanent insurance (insurance of some specified amount where there is an annual premium but the horizon for the contract is longer and the contract has savings and perhaps business investment (participating) components to it). Optional riders such as double indemnity, waiver of premium benefits, and guaranteed insurability are other possible contract features but these are usually restricted to permanent insurance.

Second, there are differences amongst underwriting insurance firms for any given contract type. For example, firms may have different medical criteria for additional benefits that are included in guaranteed insurability options, different loan rates where a cash value policy is used as collateral, different ages of consumers at which renewable term policies terminate, different service on policies, different dividend records or differing abilities to screen accurately consumer insurance risk.

Third, there are differences across insurance consumers in either the marginal cost of search or equivalently, the productivity of their search efforts. Commentators on the life insurance industry (e.g., Consumer's Union [4], Federal Trade Commission [6]) maintain that many (most?) consumers perceive only with error the real value of alternative contracts and, while consumers are aware of differences across underwriting firms, many (most?) can identify these firms only after extremely costly search. According to this view, this market is characterized by significant price distribution in equilibrium due to variability of consumer knowledge on the true value of life insurance contracts underwritten by alternative life insurance firms.

Finally, individual insurance contracts involve a negotiated bilateral exchange between the consumer and the life insurance agent where the agent identifies and "sells" the policy to the consumer and where the agent knows the educational and financial characteristics of the household, revealed by the consumer to facilitate a risk rating and a policy recommendation by the agent. Such knowledge on consumers plus information on the

firm in each category of insurance policy (an assumption which favours easy consumer search), 25 year old males buying $10,000 yearly renewable (to age 70) term insurance must find it optimal to search 6 hours over 7 underwriting firms. Fifty-five year-old women buying $50,000 of non-participating whole life insurance must find it optimal to search 110 hours over 29 under-writing firms. Obtaining price quotes over the telephone is *not* a particularly time-consuming activity per quote. If all consumers exhaustively search all possibilities, they are fully informed and the distribution of prices should collapse to a single competitive price. Therefore, 25 year old males and 55 year old females in the above example must be sufficiently unproductive in searching prices that in 6 and 110 hours respectively, they do not sample exhaustively. This is an unreasonable restriction.

true value of insurance contracts places the agent in a dominant informational position.

Ultimately, our objective is to estimate a reduced-form equation that explains and interprets those factors affecting the prices of individual life insurance contracts. To do this, we need to sketch a model of buyer choice and life insurance sales which incorporates the institutional features of this market. Our explanation of price levels and variability turns on the ability of life insurance firms through their agents to price discriminate against consumers who hold varying price elasticities of demand with respect to coverage from each contract underwritten by each life insurance firm. Therefore, our demand story is cast at the brand level and focuses on consumer ignorance. Variation in consumer price elasticities on brands of life insurance reflects variation in marginal search costs for rational but not fully informed consumers who, consequently, hold varying stocks of knowledge on alternative life insurance contracts and underwriting firms. Price discrimination across consumers by firms is possible as each individual contract sale is a negotiated bilateral exchange between a consumer and life insurance agent, and agents know consumer price elasticities through personal and financial information revealed by potential consumers to agents. Therefore, individual life insurance sales are a strong example of markets examined by Porter [12] where the institutional retail arrangements favour producers over consumers. Porter argues that similar explanations of price variability generalize to other markets characterized by retailer power due to asymmetric information between buyers and sellers, e.g., nonconvenience goods such as automobiles.

Section II sketches our model of buyer behaviour and retail sales of individual life insurance contracts. While the misperception and search specification is, by now, routine in the economics literature, its novelty lies in the empirical application to this industry. Section III tests the model over a wide collection of U.S. and Canadian data. The empirical results offer support to the model and lend themselves to reasonable interpretations. Finally, Section IV offers some summary comments and conclusions.

II. AN EQUILIBRIUM MODEL OF INSURANCE PRICES

Previous papers on insurance focus on the implication of adverse selection for a competitive equilibrium in insurance markets (Rothschild and Stiglitz [14]). Insurance firms cannot sort high and low risk consumers so that firms cannot sell more expensive coverage to high risk consumers. Information asymmetries favour consumers against firms. The result is that a zero-profit equilibrium does not exist. In this paper, our emphasis is on consumer misperception so that the information asymmetries are just the reverse.

Here, consumers are rational and engage in search across life insurance firms and policies. None of the basic uncertainty ideas in this paper is new. Based on research across policies, consumers form expectations on the value of competing forms of insurance. These expectations may involve misperceptions. They select the policy that maximizes expected surplus and prepare to search across agents representing alternative suppliers of the product. This search takes the form of a minimally acceptable value (reservation value) to the insurance package which consumers are prepared to seek. Different marginal opportunity costs of search for consumers leads to different reservation values for consumers. The assumption of zero marginal costs for at least some consumers means that these consumers are fully-informed.[3]

As Rothschild [13] points out, it is important that the supply side of search models guarantees that price dispersion is an equilibrium condition. In this model, it is the firms through their agents that locate consumers. Life insurance firms are assumed to know the attributes of their products and are capable of locating and differentiating consumers according not only to risk but, by assumption, the information held by consumers on the relative value of alternative life insurance schemes. Therefore, as life insurance sales are on an individual basis where resale is impossible, firms can price discriminate against consumers. The key to price discrimination is the life insurance agent. Successful agents have the capacity to find consumers and read perfectly the level of information on product quality held by these consumers by virtue of the complete personal and financial history of each household which is at the agent's disposal for purposes of risk rating and policy selection. The result is that the reservation values on product quality formulated by consumers in the definition of their optimal search rules are self-fulfilling. Life insurance firms through their agents are assumed to segment the retail market in individual life insurance contracts and to offer consumers in each segment a price-quality product package that they will just accept. Typically, agents identify appropriate consumers and then "sell" their insurance packages to these consumers. This identification of target consumer groups by firms and their agents facilitates market segmentation. Equilibrium prices emerge from the bilateral exchange between consumers and price discriminating life insurance firms. Out ultimate objective is to subject the set of equilibrium prices generated by our model to an empirical test.

[3] Butters [2] points out that strictly positive marginal search costs for all consumers in the context of Cournot-Nash reactive assumptions means that the only equilibrium price is the monopoly price as it always pays the lowest-price firm(s) to raise their price by an amount less than the marginal search cost.

II.1 *Consumer Model*

Consumers in our model are differentiated by the probability of death (risk), the marginal opportunity cost of search and their subjective evaluation of the alternative life insurance policies available. Within each risk class of consumers, we assume that there is an equal representation of consumers by search costs (which we treat as a continuum where convenient). Without loss of generality, but with a considerable reduction in the notational burden, this means that we may focus on the determination of equilibrium prices for a representative risk class of consumers. We impute to each consumer within this typical risk class a specific expected utility function linear in expected income and the perceived net benefits from holding life insurance policies. (This specific utility function eases the analytical burden.)

$$EU^j \equiv y + \sum_i \sum_l b^{ilj} \tag{1}$$

where $y \equiv Y - \Gamma L$; Y is the (common) income in the absence of death; Γ is the probability of death for consumers in this risk class; L is the (common) known loss of family income should death occur for the insurance; therefore, y is the expected income; b^{ilj} is the perceived expected benefits that accrue to the family (bequest motive) from holding insurance policy type l purchased from company i by the consumer j where consumers differ by search costs. All search and purchase decisions are assumed to be *ex-ante* for the consumer. We use perceived net benefits to measure expected utility as it is the perception of benefits that influences the decision to purchase.

The net benefits from the purchase of life insurance are equal to the gross benefits (defined as B^{ilj}) less all purchase and search costs. Gross benefits are assumed to be additively separable in three components of the contract. First, there are the death benefits of the policy, measured in multiple thousands of dollars as μ, that accrue to the heirs on death. The magnitude and circumstances for collection of these death benefits are known with certainty. The benefits accruing to the consumer from the policy are assumed to be diminishing in the payments to the beneficiaries upon the death of the insured. In other words, the rate of exchange for the family between income dollars while living and payments of the policy upon the death of the insured is less than one. This reflects the psychic loss to the household from the death of a family member. For subsequent empirical purposes, it is convenient to assume an iso-elastic evaluation of the face value of the contract.

The final two components reflect each consumer's evaluation of the relative merits of different insurance policies (policy evaluation) and competing suppliers of life insurance (firm evaluation). Policy evaluation is subject to possible consumer misperception; firm evaluation is characterized by consumer search without misperception. In our static model, consumer j's best estimate of the value of policy-specific attributes per dollar of death benefits is represented by a scalar u_l, policy "quality". As the data at our disposal do not afford tests on the nature of consumer research across contract types, we specify u_l as the consumer's best estimate of the value of contract l *after* policy-specific research net of any research expenses. Therefore, u_l for each consumer may contain evaluation errors in perceiving the quality of each policy. We assume that there is some distribution of u_l's across the set of consumers purchasing individual life insurance contracts.

h_i represents the value per dollar of death benefits to consumer j from a policy underwritten by firm i which we label as firm "quality". Differences in firm quality in the face of differing marginal costs of consumers search yield differing equilibrium prices for any policy. Consumers derive utility from these policy and firm attributes aside from death benefits even if they continue to survive. With this specification, gross insurance benefits in our model, net of policy-specific research costs, may be written as:

$$B^{ilj} \equiv \Gamma \mu^{\eta} + (h_i + u_l)\mu \tag{2}$$

where $\eta < 1$ because of our assumption that insurance benefits are diminishing in payments to beneficiaries upon the death of the insured.

We impute a simple search procedure to the selection of a firm by each consumer. We assume that consumers do know costlessly and perfectly the premium price for each policy underwritten by each firm but not the levels of policy or firm quality. Define P^{li} as the price per thousands of dollars of death benefits of policy l from firm i to consumer j. We assume that P^{li} is decomposable by all consumers into a policy component P^l and a firm component, P^i, i.e., $P^{li} \equiv P^l + P^i$. Therefore, consumers know the P^i's and P^l's but not the policy or firm quality level represented by alternative prices. For each policy l, each consumer knows that there is a distribution of firm quality described by $F(h_i; N)$ where N is the number of firms offering the contract of interest to the consumer. We define n as the number of searches for a typical consumer and α_j as the marginal opportunity cost of search for consumer j. σ_α^2 defines the variance of σ, assumed identical for each risk class of consumers. Variability of α across consumers reflects either varying opportunity costs to search or varying productivity in the search process.

Based on these assumptions and definitions, we may rewrite the expected utility for a typical consumer j in any risk class as:

$$EU^j \equiv y + \sum_i \sum_l [\Gamma \mu^{\eta} + (h_i + u_l)\mu - \alpha_j n - (P^l + P^i)\mu] \tag{3}$$

By assumption, consumer j has already carried out any research on the optimal contract to purchase. Therefore, consumers in our model must choose (i) the optimal contract l^*, (ii) the appropriate search rule over firms h^*, (iii) the optimal coverage μ^*.

As expected utility is linear in this choice of policy types, consumer j chooses l^* so that $(u_l - P^l)$ is maximized. By this, we mean that with knowledge on prices each consumer chooses to purchase the contract that maximizes expected surplus for quality dimensions related specifically to the contract based on the perception of policy quality gleaned from the research of this consumer across substitute contracts. Given the linearity of contract choice in the model, u_l and P^l may be defined to be net of the true value of the contract class. (Then, $u_l(>0,\ =0,\ <0)$ indicates that the consumer (over-values, exactly values, under-values respectively) these policy-specific elements of life insurance choice.) This characterization of contract choice facilitates our subsequent empirical analysis by permitting an identification of the variability of prices across firms within each class of contracts. We define u^* to be the level of consumer misperception for the chosen policy.

Within the chosen class of contracts, the appropriate rule for consumers to search across alternative suppliers is to define a reservation value h^* within the relevant distribution so that if the consumer encounters a firm whose quality level is $h_i \geq h^*$, then the consumer buys from firm i. Otherwise, the consumer continues to search. In a similar setting, Lippman and McCall [8] show that the solution to this standard search problem occurs when the expected marginal benefits from search equal the marginal cost of search for consumer j.

$$\mu H(h^*;\ N) = \alpha_j \tag{4}$$

where $H(h^*;\ n) = \int_{h^*}^{\infty} (h_i - h^*)\ dF(h_i;\ N)$ is a convex, non-negative strictly decreasing function with $\partial H/\partial h^* \equiv H_h = F(h^*;\ N) - 1$.

Lippman and McCall show that the expected quality gain from pursuing the optimal search strategy defined by (4) is the reservation search quality. Therefore, the optimal coverage for the best policy evaluated at the expected level of firm-specific quality net of search costs is given by:

$$\Gamma\eta\mu^{\eta-1} + h^*(\mu) + u^* = P^{li} \tag{5}$$

where, as we have defined it, P^{li} is the premium price per thousands of dollars of death benefits for consumer j from the perceived best policy and firm, net of true policy-quality values and $\mu < L$ (for reasons of moral hazard). This last constraint is assumed to be non-binding.[4]

Solving (4) and (5) for reservation values of firm quality as a function of price and other variables exogenous to these decisions for consumers is useful

[4] This specification yields sensible properties for the demand for individual insurance. From (5), $\partial\mu/\partial h^* = -1/[\Gamma\eta(\eta-1)\mu^{\eta-2}] > 0$, so that increased search across firms shifts the consumer's demand function for death benefits to the right, i.e., the identification of a better deal increases the desired coverage at a constant price. Further, if we define ε_P^μ to measure the price elasticity of coverage, then at a constant level of death benefits $(\hat{\mu})$, $\partial\varepsilon_P^\mu \partial h^*_{|\hat{\mu}} = \partial\varepsilon_P^\mu/\partial u^*_{|\hat{\mu}} = 1/[\Gamma\eta(\eta-1)\mu^{\eta-2}] < 0$. This says that increased search and an increased perception of the policy's quality at a given level of death benefits make consumers more price elastic. This result is consistent with the view that better-informed consumers are more price-elastic consumers.

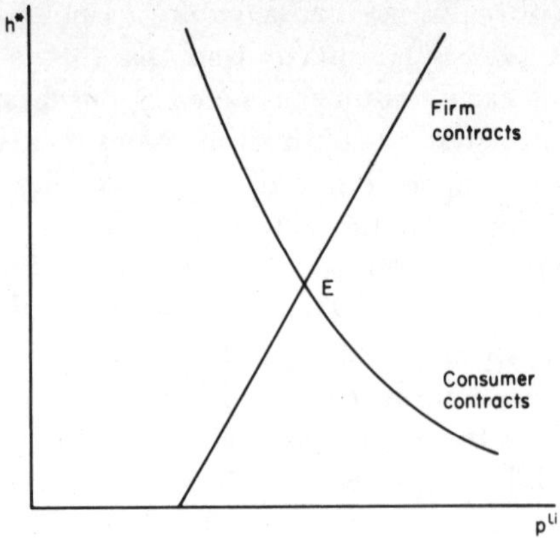

FIGURE 1

Consumer/Firm price—quality equilibrium for one policy and one segment of the life insurance retail market.

for our subsequent empirical analysis and yields:

(6) $$h^* = \xi_j(\alpha_j, \Gamma, N, P^{li}, u^*)$$

where by conventional comparative static techniques $\partial h^*/\partial P^j = -H/D < 0$ where $D \equiv \Gamma\eta(\eta - 1)\mu^{\eta-1}H_h - H > 0$ (by virtue of the concavity of the consumer's decision problem). (6) is illustrated in Figure 1. Therefore, as prices rise and consumers reduce their coverage, they reduce their search efforts. In a similar fashion, $\partial h^*/\partial\Gamma < 0$, $\partial h^*/\partial\alpha_j > 0$, $\partial h^*/\partial u^* 0$, $\partial h^*/\partial N < ? > 0$. At a given price, consumers facing either a greater risk of death, having a lower marginal opportunity cost of search (a higher marginal product of search) or imputing a larger value to the selected contract engage in greater research. The impact of additional firms on optimal search is uncertain, as we cannot forecast in general the effect of more sellers on the distribution of firm-specific quality.[5] These are intuitively reasonable results. These comparative static results will be interpreted further once the model is complete.

II.2 *Life Insurance Firm Model*

Define M to be the number of consumers in our typical risk class. Then, by assuming that firms servicing each risk class are alike, we may define

[5] More firms selling in any segment of the retail market may alter the optimal search patterns for rational consumers. This may shift the locus of optimal consumer contracts in Figure 1 but the direction of the change is unclear. The uncertainty stems from the uncertain impact on consumer search equilibrium of general changes in the distribution of offers from firms. For example, with a constant marginal cost of search, if more sellers shift the distribution to yield a higher marginal benefit to search at the old equilibrium, then both search and price are increased. This result turns on the sign of $H_N \equiv \int_{h^*}^{\infty} (h_i - h^*) f_N \, dh_i$ which, in general, is *not* known.

$m \equiv M/N$ as the number of contracts underwritten by each firm. This is our measure of a firm's output. We focus exclusively here on individual life insurance contracts. Further, we consider complete separability across contract classes (i.e., we view each firm as a single-product life insurance firm). Such separability eases the analytics by avoiding the difficulties in packaging that would emerge from multi-output firms.

Agents in our model discriminate across consumers in each risk class to measure with accuracy the reservation quality that this consumer would just accept. Given the extensive personal and financial information solicited in advance of a policy proposal by agents that would facilitate such discrimination, this is a reasonable assumption. Here, we assume that each life insurance firm underwrites only one level of quality in its contracts. Therefore, firms look across consumers in each risk and policy class and in the face of open entry, enter a segment of the retail market characterized by excess profits for existing firms and consumers with a common evaluation of the policy and a common cost to search (i.e., a common reservation value of firm quality).

Firm through their agents face each consumer in a bilateral exchange knowing they face a downward-sloping demand curve for death benefits, and knowing h^*, the consumer's reservation value on firm quality. For convenience, we permit firms to select coverage as a decision variable and use the inverse of the demand function. Therefore, (5) defines the individual demand curve faced by firms in their exchange with consumers.

Associated with each individual contract are certain expected costs: the expected death benefits and the costs of providing policy and firm quality known to the underwriting insurance firm. The cost of firm quality is the reservation value for consumers in that segment of the retail market serviced by each firm or h^*. (Here, there is uncertainty only on the location of firm quality not its value.) With the linearity of our model, the joint assumptions that life insurance salesmen measure h^* with accuracy and that the marginal costs of supplying h^* are constant and equal to one mean that the expected profits of the firm (and therefore its decision variables) are independent of h^*. As policy quality measures have been scaled as deviations from their true measures, the corresponding costs to the firm of misperceptions by consumers on the value of any contract are zero.

Next, there are the commissions to agents. Each agent screens consumers to select those appropriate for the policies underwritten by the agent's company.[6] Each sale requires a fixed number of hours of the agent's time which we define as $\bar{s}$. Although agents are paid a commission that is a portion of gross premium revenues, we assume an equilibrium number of salesmen. Therefore, in the face of open entry into the ranks of life

[6] In fact, agents not only screen consumers but by offering advice seek to affect consumer evaluations of alternative contracts. An examination of the welfare effects of this activity may be found in Mathewson [10].

insurance agents, and a homogeneous labour force, agents earn a competitive wage rate w.

As well, we assume that capital markets for the investment of each insurance firm's investment portfolio are competitive and in equilibrium. By this, we mean that life insurance firms neither outperform nor underperform either each other or other financial intermediaries in the construction of optimal investment portfolios. Therefore, expected revenues from investment just offset the opportunity costs for investment for each firm and may be ignored.

Finally, there are all other head-office and branch expenses for the firm which vary with the volume of contracts handled by the firm, the measure of the output of each firm.[7]

As all costs are now defined, they may be assembled into total costs: $(\Gamma + h^*)m$ represents expected pay-out and firm quality costs; agents' expenses are $wm\bar{s}$ which may be aggregated with all other expenses as $G(m, w) + C$ where $G', G'' > 0$, $G' > G(m, w)/m$ for all m and C is a positive constant.[8]

Given the exclusivity of choices of policy types by each consumer plus our cost specification of each firm with competitive capital markets in equilibrium, expected profits for each policy type (type of life insurance, risk category, firm specific quality) may be considered independently and, under Chamberlinian assumptions, are defined as:

$$E\Pi \equiv (\Gamma\eta\mu^{\eta} + u^*\mu - \Gamma\mu)m - G(m, w) - C$$

Expected profits for each firm are maximized with respect to insurance coverage (μ) and the number of policies underwritten (m). Expected profits are assumed to be concave in these decision variables. A firm equilibrium is given by:

$$\Gamma\eta^2\mu^{-1} + u^* = \Gamma \tag{7}$$

$$\mu[\Gamma(\eta\mu^{\eta-1} - 1) + u^*] = G' \tag{8}$$

Equations (7) and (8) are similar to the usual marginal conditions.[9] As each firm has the ability to discriminate across consumers, (7) and the average revenue from the sale of each contract in (8) are independent of firm size. These features facilitate our subsequent empirical tests. As well, as

[7] It is reasonable to expect that all head-office expenses should vary directly with the number of contracts underwritten, the physical volume of output. Fixed costs C arise as the set-up costs of establishing a head office and agency system for each policy type sold by each firm. These assumptions guarantee a unique firm size in an insurance industry equilibrium.

[8] Kellner and Mathewson [7] find no evidence of equilibrium scale economies for life insurance firms.

[9] The assumption that all M consumers buy a policy characterized by strictly positive coverage constrains the distribution of u^* across consumers to guarantee that the left-hand sides of (7) and (8) are strictly positive.

we indicated, our specification leaves (7) and (8) independent of h^*. Therefore, search decisions by consumers across firms do *not* affect the death benefit size of contract nor the number of contracts sold. This means that subject only to sufficient density of consumers to guarantee that $E\Pi \geq 0$ (in an industry equilibrium $E\Pi = 0$), life insurance firms are willing to supply any firm quality demanded. However, premium prices do depend on h^*. Using (5), we may define the optimal premium price per dollar of death benefits (corrected for true product quality) as:

$$P^{li} = [\Gamma - u^*(1 - \eta)]/\eta + h^* \tag{9}$$

where $\partial P^{li}/\partial h^* = 1$ (if h^* is treated as a parameter, then increases in h^* leave μ^*, defined by (7), unchanged but are passed along to consumers directly through increases in premium prices), $\partial P^{li}/\partial \Gamma > 0$, $\partial P^{li}/\partial u^* < 0$ and $P^{li} > 0$ requires $\Gamma + \eta h^* > u^*(1 - \eta)$. Increases in risk and decreases in policy evaluation because they reduce price elasticities, increase the premium price.

Equilibrium levels of premium price and firm-specific quality are determined by the simultaneous satisfaction of (6) and (9), the respective price/quality trade-offs for consumers and firm. Figure 1 illustrates such an equilibrium. The effects of changes in parameters on the equilibrium levels of h^* and P^{li} are essential for any empirical test. These are summarized as: $\partial h^*/\partial\alpha = \partial P^{li}/\partial\alpha < 0$; $\partial h^*/\partial\Gamma$, $\partial P^{li}/\partial\Gamma > 0$; $\partial h^*/\partial u^* > 0$; $\partial P^{li}/\partial u^* < ? > 0$; $\partial h^*/\partial N$, $\partial P^{li}/\partial N < ? > 0$. To illustrate these comparative statics, consider a change in the opportunity cost of search for the consumer (α) on the equilibrium in Figure 1. Changes in α leave the firm's contract locus unaffected. However, an increase in α means that the consumer will search less assiduously across competing firms at each price level so that the consumer's locus of equilibrium contract falls. Consequently, the observed equilibrium levels of both price and firm quality are reduced. Consumers are less willing to search and demand a lower minimum level of firm quality; firms supplying consumers with higher α's offer lower quality and require a lower price to cover the costs of such quality.

For any given risk category and price level, the distribution of firm-specific quality levels is determined by the joint distribution of the costs of search and policy evaluations across consumers. These are the firm-quality variations observed by consumers for each alternative type of policy.

III. EMPIRICAL ESTIMATION OF EQUILIBRIUM PRICE DISTRIBUTION

The test of our equilibrium model of information asymmetries in the life insurance industry is whether or not it is capable of explaining the observed variation and levels of prices of different life insurance companies for individual life insurance contracts. Specifically, we test the predictions generated by the model for the effects on relative price variability of changes in the age of the consumers group purchasing the contract, the number of companies underwriting the particular policy,[10] the sex of the consumer group, where the data include policies issued to both men and women and a set of variables that capture the characteristics of the policy.

The data available to test the model consist of five cross-sectional samples of life insurance prices from different geographical areas. Samples 1 and 2 are taken from the Consumers' Association of Canada, *Shopper's Guide to Canadian Life Insurance*, [3]. Sample 3 is from the New York State Department of Insurance, *Consumer's Shopping Guide for Life Insurance*, [5]. Sample 4 is from the State of Pennsylvania, Department of Insurance, *Shopper's Guide for Life Insurance*, pooled over 1972 and 1973 (in [17]). Sample 5 is from Belth, *Life Insurance; A Consumer's Handbook*, [1].

All samples except New York report interest-adjusted net-cost data over a horizon of 20 years, a standard method of price comparison in the insurance industry. This New York sample is interest-adjusted net-cost data over a horizon of 10 years.[11] This method of calculating the protection content of premium prices assumes that consumers of life insurance live with probability one for 20 years and then cash in the policy for the cash surrender value with probability one. For participating policies, dividends are forecasted over the period. Finally, all policies are evaluated at the end of the 20 year period by subtracting from the accumulated premiums, the cash-surrender value of the policy and the accumulated (forecasted) dividends. The result is present-valued as the pure insurance cost. The reported price is the pure insurance cost per thousand of dollars of coverage. Undoubtedly, the arbitrary assumptions on life expectancy, the horizon for holding the policy and the likelihood of surrender introduce biases but a systematic statement on the direction of the bias does not appear to be possible.[12]

Our data do not contain information on the search or income characteristics or insurance purchase decisions of individual households. The test of the model takes the form of explaining the relative price variability of individual life insurance contracts across firms for each contract type.

[10] We do not assume that the observation period for these measured prices is characterized by an industry equilibrium. Therefore, the number of underwriting companies is treated as an exogenous variable.

[11] For the New York Sample, policies are reported by ages 20, 35, 50 for issuing the contract. Many life insurance companies do not renew term insurance beyond 65 so that the sample of firms is greatly reduced for 20 year interest-adjusted cost data for policies issued to 50 year olds.

[12] For example, the Canadian data use interest rates of 6 per cent. These rates seem unduly low given inflationary expectations in excess of 6 per cent. This may overvalue savings and dividend elements and, therefore, underprice the cost of insurance elements. As well, the postponement of dividends involves a mortality factor as well as an interest factor as dividends are not paid when the insured dies and the death benefits are collected. Further, forecasted dividends policies are based on historical dividends. For these reasons, our attention is restricted to price variation across firms within each type of life insurance policy.

We use the comparative static predictions generated by the consumer and firm bilateral exchange equilibrium model under our assumptions. To develop the appropriate reduced-form equation from our model, we take logarithms of the firm's price-quality path, linearize the consumer's price-quality path, and calculate the corresponding relative price variances that arise due to variation in search costs for each category of policies.[13] Then, we derive

(10) $$[d \ln P^{il}]^2 = C[d\alpha_j]^2$$

where $C \equiv [\eta h^*_\alpha/(\Gamma + \eta h^* - u^*(1-\eta) - \eta h^*_{\ln P}]^2$.

Equation (10) may be re-interpreted with an error term as:

(11) $$\sigma^2_{\ln P} \simeq C\sigma^2_\alpha + \varepsilon_P$$

A linearization of C over the measurable variables (Γ, N, u^*) and substitution into (11) yields

(12) $$\sigma^2_{\ln P} \simeq (C^0 + C_\Gamma \Gamma + C_N N + C_u u^*)\sigma^2_\alpha + \varepsilon_P$$

Equation (12) is a reduced-form equation that tells us that the larger is the variance of consumer search costs, the greater is the observed variance of relative prices as discriminating life insurance firms accommodate perfectly the search patterns of consumers. Changes in the probability of death, the number of underwriting firms and misperceptions on product quality alter the relationship of relative price variability to search cost variability in either a predictable or an interpretable fashion *given our model*. For the equilibrium

[13] Taking logarithms of the firm's price-quality path permits us to evaluate relative price variability, a measure that is directly affected by the impact of the consumer insurance risk, the number of insurance firms and attributes of the products on price levels. Under these conditions, the firm and consumer paths become (respectively):

(i) $$\ln P^{il} = \ln[\Gamma + \eta h^* - u^*(1-\eta)] - \ln \eta$$

(ii) $$h^* = h^*_\alpha \alpha_j + h^*_\Gamma \Gamma + h^*_N N + h^*_u u + h^*_P P^{il}$$

(where $h^*_\alpha \equiv \partial h^*/\partial \alpha$ and so on).
For empirical purposes, we assume that u^* varies only across policies. Therefore, price variability is due to variability in consumer search costs so that (i) and (ii) yield:

(iii) $$d \ln P^{il} = \eta\, dh^*/[\Gamma + \eta h^* - u^*(1-\eta)]$$

(iv) $$dh^* = h^*_\alpha\, d\alpha + h^*_{\ln P}\, d \ln P^{il}$$

(where $h^*_P\, dP^{il} \equiv h^*_{\ln P} \cdot \partial \ln P^{il}/\partial P^{il} \cdot dP^{il}/d \ln P^{il} \cdot d \ln P^{il} \equiv h^*_{\ln P}\, d \ln P^{il}$).
Substituting (iv) into (iii), solving for $d \ln P^{il}$ and squaring both sides permits us to write (10) in the text. If logs were not used, (11) in the text would become:

$$\sigma^2_P \simeq c\sigma^2_\alpha + \varepsilon_P \qquad \text{where} \qquad c \equiv [h_\alpha/(1-h_P)]^2$$

Given our linearization, c is independent of (Γ, N, u^*) so that our model forecasts an approximately constant variance of prices across policy categories.

consumer-firm model developed here:

$C_\Gamma < 0$ as $\partial h^*/\partial\Gamma > 0$ from the consumer-firm equilibrium.[14]

$C_N < ? > 0$ as sign $C_N = -$sign H_N and the sign of H_N cannot be predicted uniquely from the consumer-firm equilibrium.

$C_u < ? > 0$ as sign $C_u = -$sign $\partial P^{li}/\partial u^*$ and the sign of C_u cannot be predicted uniquely from the consumer-firm equilibrium.

In the absence of differentials in consumer search costs and firm and policy quality, $\sigma_\alpha^2 = 0$ and $C_\Gamma = C_N = C_u = 0$. These differentials lie at the heart of the model in this paper.

Our price data do not include income information on consumers purchasing insurance contracts. Therefore, in our specification the consumer choice model leaves insurance demand independent of income. However, our empirical sense is that life insurance is a normal good so that we correct for the omission of incomes by calculating relative price variability for groups defined not only by risk and policy type but by the size of death benefits as well.

The measured characteristics of life insurance policies and their predicted effects are as follows:

(1) Age: Age is a measure of the probability of death. Therefore, based on our model, age should have a negative coefficient.
(2) Number of Companies Writing the Policies: For the Canadian data, the companies voluntarily reporting their prices to the Canadian Consumers Association do not constitute all companies underwriting the various policies in the Canadian market. As long as the sample of included companies is unbiased, there is no problem. The sign of C_N depends on the negative of the sign of $\partial h^*/\partial N$ which in the consumer-firm equilibrium depends on the sign of H_N. If C_N is positive (negative), then "on average" more sellers reduce (increase) the marginal benefit from search.

The next set of policy characteristics are measured by dummy variables. They do *not* measure the sign or magnitude of u^*, the value imputed to policy–specific quality iterms, but they do measure the relative values of u^*, i.e., they measure whether u^*'s held for one type of policy are higher or lower than u^*'s held for some reference type of policy. The discussion

[14] For example, C_Γ is defined as:

$$C_\Gamma \equiv -2[\eta h_\alpha^*]^2[1 + \eta h_\Gamma^*]/[\Gamma + \eta h^* - u^*(1-\eta) - h_{\ln P}^*]^3$$

As $h_{\ln P}^* < 0$, $P^{il} > 0$ (i.e., $\Gamma + \eta h^* > u^*(1-\eta)$) and $h_\Gamma^* > 0$, we predict that $C_\Gamma > 0$.

that follows assumes that $\partial P^{il}/\partial u^* > 0$ (i.e., increased perceived policy quality increases price) and therefore, that $C_u < 0$.

(3) Sex (relevant where a sample includes policies underwritten for both men and women): Sex differences are measured by a variable set equal to 0 if female, 1 if male. We cannot predict whether men or women systematically over-value or under-value life insurance. The decision for women to buy insurance may or may not be made independent of insurance decisions made by a husband if one exists. If women over-value policies relative to men, perhaps due to inexperience, or if men purchasing insurance for their wife over-value insurance relative to their own, then $C_u < 0$. Some firms have prices for women set equal to the prices for younger men due to a lower risk of death for any one age group. Therefore this sex variable may pick up a risk or an age effect.

(4) Type of insurance: Insurance policies are typically either term, permanent non-participating, or permanent participating. The three-way characterization of relative over or under-valuation of policy types requires two dummy variables, one variable equal to one if permanent insurance, (zero otherwise), and one variable equal to one participating permanent insurance (zero otherwise). Conventional wisdom on the insurance industry suggests that consumers over-value permanent insurance relative to term insurance.[15] Permanent insurance is considered an inferior commodity due to the low (negative real) rate of return on the savings component. If this is the case, then the coefficient on the first dummy variable should be negative. Conventional wisdom on the insurance industry suggests that in times of falling mortalities and growth in the demand for insurance, participating policies are better deals than non-participating policies for permanent insurance.[16] If participating insurance is under-valued relative to non-participating insurance, then the coefficient on the second dummy variable should be positive. The sum of these two coefficients indicates whether permanent participating insurance is under or over-valued relative to term insurance. There is no prediction on this magnitude by industry commentators.

Table I reports the estimated coefficients for the fitted equation. In general, F statistics for each regression (which are not reported in Table I) are sufficient to reject the hypothesis of no differences in consumer search costs or product quality. We may interpret the coefficients for each variable. As our model predicts, relative price variability falls with age in all samples.

[15] For example, Consumer's Union [4] reports that "except for families that need forced savings or a tax shelter, CU judges term insurance to be more likely to meet those (the family's) needs".

[16] For example, Consumer's Union [4] reports that "on balance, CU favours participating policies for those people buying cash value life insurance".

TABLE I
ESTIMATED REDUCED-FORM EQUATION FOR A MODEL OF CONSUMER SEARCH AND MISPERCEPTION FOR INDIVIDUAL LIFE INSURANCE CONTRACTS

Sample	*Constant*	*Age*	*No. of Companies*	*Sex Variable*	*Permanent Insurance Variable*	*Participating Variable*	*Permanent Participating Variable*	*Observations*	R^2
1	3.06*E*-02	−0.04*E*-02	0.03*E*-02	−0.85*E*-02	−0.74*E*-02	2.32*E*-02	1.58*E*-02	152	0.63
	(10.66)*	(−6.75)	(3.60)	(−6.33)	(−3.95)	(11.77)	(8.40)		
2	4.49*E*-02	−0.06*E*-02	0.03*E*-02	−1.19*E*-02	−0.24*E*-02	3.03*E*-02	2.79*E*-02	152	0.52
	(8.56)	(−5.32)	(2.07)	(−4.83)	(−0.68)	(7.99)	(5.57)		
3	−4.36*E*-02	−0.05*E*-02	0.20*E*-02	−1.44*E*-02	−0.52*E*-02	1.78*E*-02	1.26*E*-02	48	0.86
	(−3.26)	(−4.83)	(6.61)	(−5.21)	(−0.90)	(6.44)	(1.68)		
4	−1.30*E*-02	−0.05*E*-02	0.03*E*-02	—	−1.13*E*-02	1.86*E*-02	0.73*E*-02	24	0.82
	(−1.21)	(−5.83)	(3.02)		(−1.62)	(6.44)	(1.52)		
5	0.97*E*-02	−0.03*E*-02	0.04*E*-02	—	−0.05*E*-02	−0.65*E*-02	−0.70*E*-02	23	0.67
	(2.70)	(−2.90)	(3.59)		(−0.25)	(−3.09)	(−2.29)		

* *t*-statistics are reported in parentheses under each coefficient estimate.

Dependent Variable: Variance of the logarithms of the protection price of individual life insurance contracts by type of policy, coverage and age at which the policy is issued.

Our model traces this effect to both direct mortality effects and indirect search effects. More firms increase relative price dispersion. The interpretation of this result from our model is that more sellers by reducing the marginal benefit from search reduce the equilibrium search efforts and price for each consumer in each appropriate class. A reduction in price lowers relative price dispersion. In those samples which include policies underwritten for both men and women, women face greater relative price dispersion than men. For the most part, consumers appear to under-value participating relative to non-participating individual life insurance.

IV. CONCLUSIONS

The model in this paper attempts to explain the observed price variability for the pure protection elements of individual life insurance contracts. The key ingredients are uninformed but rational consumers capable of research into characteristics of policies and search across firm attributes and fully-informed life insurance firms capable of price discrimination across potential customers through life insurance agents. In the face of open entry into the ranks of agents and differences in the cost of consumer search and the evaluation of policies by consumers, the model yields an equilibrium distribution of life insurance prices.

The model is tested with the available price data whose construction permits comparisons across firms within policy categories (within-group comparisons) but forbids comparisons across policies (between-group comparisons). In general, a model based on product-quality uncertainty by consumers and price discrimination by life insurance firms appears to offer a consistent explanation of price levels and variance. In contrast, pure price-shopping models do not offer consistent explanations of price variability. While we cannot measure directly the productivity of individual consumer search effort, our empirical results are consistent with increased consumer search where the probability of death is greater, and where there are fewer sellers (i.e., more sellers reduce the need for consumers to search extensively). These are rational consumer responses. Further, our results indicate that consumers under-value participating relative to non-participating whole life insurance contracts but likely do not under-value term insurance relative to whole life insurance. Any under or over-valuation may be traced to consumer misperceptions.

G. Frank Mathewson,
Department of Economics,
University of Toronto,
150 St. George Street,
Toronto,
Canada M5S 1A1

ACCEPTED MARCH 1982

REFERENCES

[1] Belth, J., *Life Insurance, A Consumer's Handbook* (Bloomington: Indiana University Press, 1973).

[2] Butters, G., "Equilibrium Distributions of Sales and Advertising Prices", *Review of Economic Studies*, 44 (3), No. 138 (1977) pp. 465–92.

[3] Consumers' Association of Canada, *"Shopper's Guide to Canadian Life Insurance Prices"* (Toronto, 1978, 1979).

[4] Consumers' Union, *Report on Life Insurance*, (1977).

[5] Department of Insurance, State of New York, *"Consumer's Shopping Guide for Life Insurance"* (Albany, 1977).

[6] Federal Trade Commission, *Life Insurance Cost Disclosure*, (1979).

[7] Kellner, S. and Mathewson, G. F., "Entry, Size Distribution, Scale and Scope Economies in the Life Insurance Industry", *Journal of Business*, 56 (1), (1983), pp. 25–44.

[8] Lippman, S. A. and McCall, J. J., "The Economics of Job Search: A Survey", *Economic Inquiry*, 14 (2), (1976), pp. 155–89.

[9] MacMinn, R. D., "Search and Market Equilibrium", *Journal of Political Economy*, 88 (2), (1980), pp. 308–27.

[10] Mathewson, G. F., *Information, Entry and Regulation in Markets for Life Insurance*, Ontario Economic Council Research Studies, (University of Toronto Press, 1982).

[11] Mohring, H., "The Life Insurance Industry: A Study of Price Policy and Its Determinants", unpublished Ph.D. Dissertation, (Massachusetts Institute of Technology, 1959).

[12] Porter, M., *Interbrand Choice, Strategy and Market Power*, (Cambridge: Harvard University Press, 1976).

[13] Rothschild, M., "Models of Market Organization with Imperfect Information: A Survey", *Journal of Political Economy*, 81 (6), (1973), pp. 1283–308.

[14] Rothschild, M. and Stiglitz, J., "Equilibrium in Competitive Insurance Markets: An Essay on the Economics of Imperfect Information", *Quarterly Journal of Economics*, 90 (2), (1976), pp. 629–55.

[15] Spence, A. M., "Consumer Misperceptions, Product Failure and Producer Liability", *Review of Economic Studies*, 44 (3), No. 138, (1977), pp. 561–72.

[16] Stigler, G., "The Economics of Information", *Journal of Political Economy*, 69 (3), (1961), pp. 213–25.

[17] U.S. Senate Subcommittee on Antitrust and Monopoly of the Committee on the Judiciary, 93rd Congress, *"The Life Insurance Industry"*, Part 4, (1974).

THE JOURNAL OF INDUSTRIAL ECONOMICS 0022–1821 $2.00
Volume XXXII December 1983 No. 2

EXCESS CAPACITY AND RATIONALISATION IN THE WEST EUROPEAN SYNTHETIC FIBRES INDUSTRY*

R. W. Shaw and S. A. Shaw

This paper examines the process of rationalisation in an international oligopoly confronted by persistent excess capacity and losses. In particular it analyses the pattern of capacity reduction, plant closures and product area withdrawals as the firms strove to restore their profitability. It compares the actual pattern of rationalisation achieved between 1975 and 1981 with the predicted patterns of rationalisation based on theory, both under a cartel with government intervention and in a competitive solution free from such intervention.

The paper is divided into four sections. The first contains a brief outline of developments in the industry 1967–80. The second section examines the producer cartel and government intervention framework. The third section is devoted to the development of a predicted competitive pattern of rationalisation. Finally, the fourth section examines the actual pattern of rationalisation and compares this with both the cartel plus government intervention and the competitive pattern predictions.

I. WEST EUROPEAN SYNTHETIC FIBRES INDUSTRY 1967–80

The late 1960s and early 1970s were periods of rapid growth in the industry. Output of both acrylic and polyester fibres more than trebled between 1967 and 1973 while output of nylon virtually doubled. The same period also witnessed the development of an integrated Western European market following the expiry of the major nylon (or polyamide) and polyester patents in the early and mid 1960s [4], [6]. As a consequence the major European producers interpenetrated each others' national markets both through exports and the setting up of overseas manufacturing subsidiaries. At the same time major US producers were also developing their interests in Europe. Within this market by the end of 1974 ten firms controlled over 90 percent of production capacity. Although the distribution among these firms varied between the three fibres, in each case the largest four firms controlled at least 56 per cent of total capacity (see Table I).

* This paper was written while the authors were on sabbatical leave at the Department of Economics, University of Newcastle, Australia. The authors are grateful to the University of Newcastle for its support.

TABLE I
PERCENTAGE SHARE OF CAPACITY, NUMBER OF PLANTS AND AVERAGE CAPACITY PER PLANT[a]

Group	Acrylic			Nylon				Polyester		
	Percentage share of capacity	Number of plants	Average capacity per plant '000 tonnes	Percentage share of capacity	Number of plants	Average capacity per plant '000 tonnes	Nylon type[e]	Percentage share of capacity	Number of plants	Average capacity per plant '000 tonnes
AKZO[b]	4.5	1	39.0	18.0	8	21.5	6 & 66	22.0	8	32.0
Bayer	14.5	1	123.5	6.0	2	27.5	6	4.5	1	42.5
Courtaulds	20.0	3	62.0	5.5	4	13.0	6	1.5	1	16.0
Du Pont	7.5	2	35.0	6.0	1	69.0	66	6.5	1	67.5
Fabelta[b]	3.0	1	24.0	0.5	1	7.0	66	—	—	—
Hoechst	9.5	1	80.0	0.5	1	4.0	6	22.0	5	46.0
ICI	—	—	—	19.0	6	32.5	66	14.0	7	21.5
Monsanto	8.0	2	40.0	4.0	2	18.5	66	—	—	—
Montefibre	12.5	2.5	50.0[d]	5.5	4	13.0	6 & 66	6.0	4.5	15.5[d]
Rhone Poulenc	6.5	1	52.5	16.5	12	14.0	66	13.5	8	20.5
Snia Viscosa	5.0	2	21.5	9.5	7	14.0	6	2.5	3	8.5
ANIC	5.5	1.5	41.5[d]	1.5	1	13.0	6	3.0	1.5	22.0[d]
SIR	1.0	1	10.0	—	—	—	—	2.0	1	23.0
Other	2.5	—	—	7.5	—	—	—	2.5	—	—
Totals[c]	100.0	19	47.0	100.0	49	17.0 } 20.5 }	6 66	100.0	41	26.0

Sources: Montedison (parent company of Montefibre) estimates reported in European Chemical News, 10 October 1975. Textile Organon, World Man-Made Fiber Surveys 1975 and 1976. Trade press and industry sources.

[a] Capacity data are based on the Montedison estimates for end 1974 adjusted to 1975 to allow for new capacity in the course of construction. Average capacity per plant has been adjusted upwards where new capacity was in operation by 1976 to give a more respresentative picture of average plant sizes during the early years (1975–78) of the industry crisis. The number of plants refers to the number of production sites at which each of the three types of synthetic fibre were made. Thus, if acrylic, nylon and polyester fibres were produced at a single site, e.g. Bayer's complex at Dormagen in West Germany this would count as 3 plants, one for each type of fibre.

[b] Fabelta was a subsidiary in the AKZO Group until February 1976. It has been listed separately as it operated independently for most of the crisis period.

[c] The number of plants and average plant capacities in the totals row are for the 13 major producers only.

[d] ANIC and Montefibre shared acrylic and polyester plants at Ottana.

[e] AKZO's nylon plant was mainly of the nylon 6 type; Montefibre's capacity was split approximately evenly between nylon 6 and 66. Virtually the [illegible] to Nurel in Spain produced nylon 6.

The rapid growth phase, however, came to a halt after 1973. Output of all three fibres declined in 1974 and 1975 and, although there were recoveries in 1976, 1978 and 1979, the overall level of output was only 3 per cent higher in 1979 than it had been in 1973. In 1980 output declined once again to below the 1973 level. While stagnation, or even absolute decline (particularly for nylon), replaced rapid growth in output, capacity continued to expand at least in the mid 1970s. Expectations of continuing growth, together with competitive aspirations for increasing market share which led to these increases in capacity, thus exacerbated the deteriorating competitive environment.

There were a number of contributory factors to the changed conditions. These included the world recession, sharply increased feedstock costs, a change in fashion from some synthetic fibres back towards natural fibres and increasing competition from outside Western Europe.

In the changed situation severe excess capacity emerged and the Western European synthetic fibres industry became heavily unprofitable. In the seven years between 1974 and 1980 the average capacity utilization of all synthetic fibres plants in Western Europe was only 68 per cent. One producer estimated losses of $4.3 billion by the man-made fibre producers between mid-1974 and 1979 [7]. It is the reaction to these developments that is the subject matter of the remainder of this paper.

Two alternative rationalisation patterns are examined: firstly the pattern resulting from the mixture of government intervention and the producer cartel that actually existed; and secondly, a predicted pattern if a competitive environment had existed. The frameworks and the resulting predictions are discussed in turn.

II. THE PRODUCER CARTEL AND GOVERNMENT INTERVENTION FRAMEWORK

While excess capacity, low prices and heavy losses made some rationalisation necessary it was soon apparent that competitive forces would not be allowed to operate freely. For example, early in 1976 Fabelta, the loss-making subsidiary of the AKZO Group, was taken into public ownership as an alternative to the closure of some of its fibre activities. Similarly, in March 1977 the Italian Government threatened to suspend its subsidies to Montedison if that company's fibres subsidiary Montefibre closed its obsolete plants in Piedmont and ceased co-operation in the development of a major fibres complex at Ottana in Sardinia. The plants stayed open and government aid continued, including the payment of wages by the state for 6,000 Montefibre workers. In the same year Montefibre also sought permission to close its nylon plant in France but once again ran into trade union and government objections and with help from a government-supported debt moratorium the plant stayed open. At the same time as plant closures were being prevented or impeded by such government interventions, state assistance was also being used to extend synthetic fibres capacity in the case of the Italian industry.

Since the competitive process was not going to be allowed to operate without national government intervention, the major EEC fibre producers asked the EEC Commission for assistance in achieving an orderly reduction in industry capacity. The non-Italian companies were particularly anxious that any capacity reduction by them should not be matched by new capacity installations in Italy and the raising of the Italian market share based on state aid. As a first stage in the summer of 1977 the EEC asked the governments of member countries to stop giving aid towards creating additional production facilities for two years and asked the European Investment Bank not to grant any new loans to finance capacity increases. However, the non-Italian producers wanted to go further than this and establish a collaborative scheme for reducing capacity. The ban on capacity increases was regarded as ineffectual as it excluded schemes such as the Italian ones that were already in progress. After long delays the EEC Industry Commissioner Viscount Davignon negotiated a coordinated plan with the industry designed both to reduce overall capacity and to meet some of the Italian aspirations for modernising and developing its industry. A provisional agreement on what was effectively a cartel plan was finally reached in June 1978.

Under the cartel plan the seven major European non-Italian producers agreed to reduce their combined capacity for six major fibre types[1] by 16.5 per cent between 1977 and mid 1979 and hold capacity at the new lower level until 1981. The four major Italian producers agreed to reduce their capacity by 16 per cent by the end of 1978 but they would then be allowed to increase capacity again. The effect of this compromise was that the Italians, like the other EEC producers, would have to eliminate some of their existing capacity, but they would at the same time be able to modernise their industry. A second part of the agreement involved market sharing. The producers were expected to maintain their 1976 supply patterns but the Italians were to be allowed to increase their market share from 17 per cent to 21 per cent by 1981. The two American firms, Du Pont and Monsanto, which were excluded from the agreement because of the US anti-trust laws, were nevertheless stated to be sympathetic.

While the capacity reduction part of the cartel plan was reluctantly accepted, or at least not outlawed, by the EEC Commission, the market sharing part was strongly contested as being contrary to EEC competition

[1] Nylon textile filament; nylon carpet yarn; nylon staple; polyester filament yarn; polyester staple; and acrylic fibres. The percentage reduction varied between these fibre types with nylon filament taking the largest cut of 34 per cent.

policy and in particular to contravene Article 85 of the Treaty of Rome.[2] As a result of this objection the producers were unable to implement the market sharing part of the agreement, though it was not formally abandoned until early 1980.

The ambiguous legal status of the cartel, the exclusion of the two major American producers in Europe, as well as the exclusion of minor producers, non-EEC Western producers and imports, in addition to potential intervention by individual national governments, made the success of the cartel in unfavourable economic conditions at best uncertain. However, the combination of the market sharing intention and the reluctance of some national governments to allow the closure of inefficient plant make it possible to make three predictions of the outcome intended by the cartel. Firstly, as the price of their agreement to participate, the weaker competitors would at least retain their position in the market and, in the case of the Italians, would increase their overall market share. Secondly, the relative market positions of individual non-Italian producers would be unchanged. Finally some inefficient plant would tend to remain in operation rather than be eliminated as part of the rationalisation.

III. THE 'COUNTER-FACTUAL' OR COMPETITIVE SOLUTION

Although it is notoriously difficult to predict what would have happened in a different environment from that which existed, it is important to obtain benchmarks against which the actual rationalisation pattern can be assessed. In an oligopolistic industry at least two such benchmarks may be envisaged: firstly, the predicted outcome of an aggressive competitive process where the latter remained free of government or EEC intervention; and secondly, the predicted outcome where oligopolistic restraint, due to the recognition of mutual interdependance, was practised but without any cartel or any government or EEC intervention. Initially the predicted outcome in the agressive competition solution is considered. The basis for prediction is obviously relative competitive strength and it is to this that we now turn. However, three complications must be noted immediately: firstly, the major

[2] Article 85(1) prohibits agreements between firms involving 'market-sharing' and 'the limiting or controlling of production, markets, technical development or capital investment'. A possible loophole in Article 85(3) allows 'concerted practices . . . which contribute to the improvement of the production or distribution of goods or to the promotion of technical or economic progress while reserving to users an equitable share in the profit resulting therefrom, and which:

'(a) neither impose on the enterprises concerned any restrictions indispensable to the attainment of the above objectives
(b) nor enable such enterprises to eliminate competition in respect of a substantial portion of the goods concerned.'

The market sharing scheme in particular seemed to directly contravene Article 85(1) while at the same time eliminating competition in a considerable sector of the industry. If the cartel was successful it would also raise prices in the short term and hence offer no benefit to users, at least initially.

producers each participated in at least two of the three synthetic fibre markets and hence competitive strength may be assessed in relation both to each individual market and to synthetic fibres in general; secondly, most of the major producers had substantial interests either outside the synthetic fibres market or outside the Western European market; and thirdly, some of the producers were vertically integrated either backwards into the production of synthetic fibres raw materials or forwards into the textile industry. While it is not clear that firms protected by cash flow in other product areas or by being vertically integrated would necessarily strive to stay in the synthetic fibres industry, their ability to do so might affect both their own and other firms' commercial decisions. Therefore the procedure adopted is to develop predictions based on previous relative competitive strengths in the three synthetic fibre markets taken separately and subsequently to suggest modifications to these based on the other factors outlined above.

From the limited data available,[3] the measures of competitive strength are based on evidence of relative market shares, plant sizes and output per employee at the beginning of the crisis in 1975.

Table I shows the percentage share of capacity, number of plants, and average capacity per plant for the major synthetic fibre producers for acrylic, nylon and polyester fibres. Percentage share of capacity is used as a proxy for market share.[4] This gives two clues to market strength. Firstly, firms with large market shares have clearly obtained substantial customer acceptance while firms with relatively small shares have at best obtained acceptance from only a small fraction of the market. Secondly, in a technologically progressive industry research and development are needed to develop new products and production processes. The cost of such research and development in any given product area is partly independent of the subsequent output by the firm and hence will form a larger percentage of unit costs for firms with relatively low levels of output. Thus firms with low levels of output (or low market share) will either have to bear the cost disadvantage resulting from their research and development or risk becoming technically outdated in their products and production processes. For both reasons, customer acceptance and unit costs of research and development, it is concluded that market share is positively correlated with market strength.

A second indicator of market strength is provided by average production capacity per plant. The existence of economies of scale in production will tend to mean that firms with small plants will be at a cost disadvantage

[3] Profitability figures for synthetic fibres in Western Europe by company are not available.

[4] Market share data are unavailable. However individual company statements on short time working and capacity utilization together with industry data on capacity utilization in the various countries indicate that market shares can be approximated by share of capacity. Average capacity utilization for the three synthetic fibres for 1975–77 for the main Western European countries varied between 69.6 per cent for West Germany and 59.2 per cent for Italy, and averaged 63.7 per cent. The relatively low figure for Italy probably reflects capacity increases which were not fully operational at the reporting dates.

TABLE II
AVERAGE PLANT SIZE 1975 AND ESTIMATED MINIMUM SIZE TO AVOID PRODUCTION COST DISADVANTAGE

Fibre type	*Average plant size*[a]	*Minimum size*[b]
	'000 tonnes	*'000 tonnes*
Acrylic	47.0	40.0
Nylon 6	17.0	20.0
Nylon 66	20.5	50.0
Polyester	26.0	40.0

[a] Average size for plants operated by the thirteen major producers listed in Table I.
[b] *Sources:* Acrylic (Pratten [5]); Nylon 6 and 66 (Cameron [1], see also Pratten [5]); Polyester (Pratten [5], Shaw and Shaw [6]).

compared with firms with larger plants. For instance, Shaw and Shaw [6] reported on estimated economies of scale for polyester staple plant in the late 1970s. Even a 20,000 tonne per year plant would enjoy a 4 per cent cost advantage over a plant half its size while a 100,000 tonne per year plant would enjoy a 10 per cent advantage. Similarly, with a reported minimum economic scale of 50,000 tonnes per year for nylon 66, Monsanto gave the small size of its two 16,000–20,000 tonne per year plants as one reason for its decision to cease nylon production in Europe [1].

In the absence of detailed estimates of the cost functions for the different types of fibre, two measures are used to indicate the existence of competitive disadvantage arising from suboptimal scale plant. A firm that has both an average plant size for a particular fibre that is below the average for all plants for the thirteen major producers,[5] and below the reported minimum economic size, is classified as suffering from a production cost disadvantage (see Table II).

A third indicator of market strength, this time on a country basis, is given by the output per man achieved in all man-made fibres including cellulosics (see Table III). The outstanding feature is the large gap between output per man in Italy compared with other major Western European fibre producing countries. At the other extreme the relative strength of the West German industry is apparent.[6]

While the labour productivity figures give a good indication of relative

[5] Data on both the size distribution of plants and their ages are unavailable.

[6] Nearly 90 per cent of the combined Montefibre, Snia Viscosa, Anic and SIR synthetic fibre capacity was concentrated in Italy. Further, these four companies accounted for almost 90 per cent of Italian synthetic fibre capacity. Similarly 90 per cent of Hoechst's capacity and 96 per cent of Bayer's capacity was concentrated in West Germany. The two companies accounted for nearly 50 per cent of West German capacity. The two other major contributors to West German capacity were AKZO and Du Pont with a combined capacity of 32 per cent. Synthetic fibre capacity in France was dominated by Rhone Poulenc (nearly 70 per cent) and Courtaulds (20 per cent); in the UK by ICI (38 per cent) and Courtaulds (31 per cent); and in the Benelux countries by AKZO (57 per cent), Fabelta and Du Pont (13 per cent each).

TABLE III
EMPLOYMENT AND OUTPUT PER MAN IN MAN-MADE FIBRES

Country	1975		1977		1979		Synthetic Fibre Output as a Percentage of Man-Made Fibre Output Average for 1975, 1977 and 1979
	Employment '000s	*Output per man tonnes*	*Employment '000s*	*Output per man tonnes*	*Employment '000s*	*Output per man tonnes*	
Benelux	n.a.	n.a.	n.a.	n.a.	10.4	19.1	68.3
France	20.4	14.1	16.5	19.7	13.1	23.0	73.4
W. Germany	43.1	16.7	36.0	22.2	30.7	28.3	87.0
Italy	41.8	8.7	33.7	13.0	30.8	14.2	78.0
U.K.	37.0	14.9	33.0	16.2	27.4	21.1	66.2
Spain	12.7	13.5	11.0	19.8	11.0	24.6	73.8

Sources: Textile Organon, CIRFS—International Rayon and Synthetic Fibres Committee.
n.a. = not available.

technical efficiency it should be noted that differences in wage costs together with exchange rate changes would modify this result when comparing economic efficiency [3]. Nevertheless, the Italian producers themselves acknowledged that much of their old and small plant was inefficient and internationally uncompetitive [2] and indeed Montefibre was continually trying to persuade the Italian Government to let it close some of this plant.

Thus the evidence of small market shares, together with that of uneconomic plant sizes, leads to the predicted product area withdrawals listed in Table IV in the case of the predatory mode of competitive rationalisation. The withdrawals are shown in descending order of likelihood on the basis of the two criteria. The relatively weak competitors in each fibre sector fall conveniently into two groups: firstly, those with a market share of under 5 per cent combined with uneconomic plant size; and secondly those with either a market share of between 5 and 7.5 per cent combined with uneconomic plant size or a market share of under 7.5 per cent and an economic plant size. The second group is stronger than the first on either or both market share and plant size criteria. For predictive purposes it is assumed that firms with market shares of over 7.5 per cent are sufficiently large to be committed to that fibre market and to be able to reorganise their own productive capacity so as to eliminate uneconomic plant without withdrawing from the market. Indeed, with the elimination of weaker competitors and product area withdrawal by others the market shares of the remaining producers in each product area would have increased. It is noteworthy that, in Table IV, 5 of the 11 category 1 predicted withdrawals were by the four Italian groups—ANIC, Montefibre, SIR and Snia Viscosa. These groups also provided 4 of 11 category 2 predicted withdrawals. These results are consistent with the low labour productivity figures for Italy quoted in Table III.

The effect of allowing for aspects of competitive strength beyond individual

TABLE IV

PREDICTED PRODUCT AREA WITHDRAWALS IN A COMPETITIVE SOLUTION[a]

Withdrawal Category	Acrylic		Nylon		Polyester	
	Group	Market Share %	Group	Market Share %	Group	Market Share %
1. Market share <5% and uneconomic plant size.	SIR	1.0	Hoechst	0.5	Courtaulds	1.5
	Fabelta	3.0	Fabelta	0.5	SIR	2.0
	AKZO	4.5	ANIC	1.5	Snia Visc.	2.5
			Monsanto	4.0	ANIC	3.0
2a Market share $5 \gtreqless 7.5\%$ and uneconomic plant size	Snia Visc.	5.0	Montefibre	5.5	Montefibre	6.0
	ANIC	5.5	Courtaulds	5.5		
	Du Pont	7.5				
2b Market share $\leq 7.5\%$ and economic plant size.	Rhone Poulenc	6.5	Bayer	6.0	Bayer	4.5
			Du Pont	6.0	Du Pont	6.5

[a] This table does not take into account the effects of vertical integration, fibre interests outside Western Europe, or the financial strength of the companies. These factors would have reduced the apparent vulnerability of Du Pont considerably and to a lesser extent Courtaulds and Snia Viscosa.

fibre markets taken separately is difficult to predict. However, the predictions in Table IV concerning ANIC, Fabelta and SIR would be unaffected so long as government assistance was excluded. ANIC, Fabelta and SIR were financially weak and all would have left the industry without government assistance. ANIC and SIR had to be supported by the Italian government and Fabelta was in continuing financial difficulties both before and after it was taken into public ownership by the Belgian Government in 1976. For all the other producers identified in Table IV, the effects of vertical integration and fibre interests outside Western Europe on the financial strength of the firms concerned would have reduced their apparent vulnerability to a process of competitive attrition. This would have been particularly true of Du Pont, the leading synthetic fibres producer in the USA, with its large total output base over which to spread research and development costs. Indeed for all these firms much would depend on their attitude to the advantages of maintaining a full product line in synthetic fibres compared to the disadvantage of having to spread their research and development and promotion efforts over a wider area. However it seems reasonable to suggest that the net benefit of maintaining an interest in a particular type of fibre will be positively related to market share and the expected growth prospects for that fibre. The former factor leaves the predictions in Table IV unaltered while the latter indicates that firms would be more likely to withdraw from the nylon market, other things being equal. This market declined the most during the period 1975 to 1980 and its expected growth prospects in the longer term were less favourable than for the other two types of fibre.

Finally, the alternate predicted outcome with oligopolistic restraint and informal recognition of interdependence must be considered, although prediction here is even more difficult. The outcome of any implicit or explicit bargaining would mainly depend on two factors. The stronger competitors would have the threat of predatory competition to use against weaker competitors. This threat suggests that the latter might be prepared to concede market share to the stronger competitors rather than run the risk of a trial of strength. However, the stronger competitors may incur greater losses by engaging in such predatory competition than they would incur by conceding market share. This detracts from the credibility of their threat of predatory competition. Thus the outcome cannot be predicted exactly. However, given its small plants, small market share and financial weakness indicated above, Fabelta would probably have been eliminated. Similarly, some form of reorganisation of the Italian companies would also have been necessary and it is unlikely that the other members of the oligopoly would have allowed the Italian market share to be increased. Given that constraint, and depending on the form of reorganisation, it is probable that some of the older and smaller plants operated by all four Italian firms would have been closed. In these circumstances the market shares of the leading firms in each fibre would have been at least maintained and perhaps increased due to strategic product area withdrawals as firms concentrated on their stronger product areas and sought to reduce the points of competitive conflict.

IV. THE ACTUAL PATTERN OF RATIONALISATION

The actual pattern of rationalisation was strongly influenced by government intervention both in the form of preventing or delaying plant closures and redundancies and in providing assistance for the development and modernisation of the Italian industry. As a consequence the pattern of rationalisation was influenced by the international location of plants as well as by the desires of the companies involved.

Three features of the rationalisation process are examined: the pattern of plant closures; changes in the shares of industry capacity (a proxy for market share changes), and the pattern of product withdrawals.

Firstly, with regard to plant closures the overall period splits into two distinct parts 1975 to 1979 and 1979 to 1981. Between 1975 and 1979 there were very few complete plant closures: the thirteen major companies operated 104 plants in 1979 as against 109 in 1975. The only notable changes occurred in West Germany where AKZO, Bayer, Hoechst and ICI all closed plant in 1977/78 though in Bayer's case some of the polyester facilities at its associate Huls plant were transferred to another site. The small number of plant closures among the Italian firms in this period was largely offset in capacity terms by the opening and development of other larger plants. As a result of these relatively minor changes most of the companies with average plant sizes that were classified as being uneconomic in 1975 (see Tables I and II) were still in that position five years later in 1980 (see Table V). It was only in the second period 1979–81 that the position changed significantly with 17 further plant closures reducing the total number of plants to 87. Prominent among the groups reducing their plant numbers in this period was Rhone Poulenc which had been frustrated by the French Government in earlier attempts at rationalisation.

The second feature, capacity or market share changes between 1975 and 1980, reflects the relatively minor changes in plant rationalisation up to that time as well as the implementation of the Davignon Plan cartel. Taking each of the 13 major groups' participation in each of the three fibres gives 35 observations for 1975. Between then and 1980 in only five cases did a group have a percentage point change in market share in excess of two per cent. In four of those cases the group concerned had either left that market (e.g. Monsanto stopped producing nylon in Western Europe) or was in the process of so doing. In a fifth case an Italian group, ANIC had achieved a five percentage point increase in share. This change was consistent with the Davignon Plan cartel agreement allowing for an increase in share for the Italian companies. Similarly, apart from the changes consequent on ANIC's expansion and the withdrawals of the other four groups, there were only minor

TABLE V
PERCENTAGE SHARE OF CAPACITY, NUMBER OF PLANTS AND AVERAGE CAPACITY PER PLANT 1980[a]

	Acrylic			Nylon				Polyester		
Group	Percentage share of capacity	Number of plants	Average capacity per plant '000 tonnes	Percentage share of capacity	Number of plants	Average capacity per plant '000 tonnes	Nylon type	Percentage share of capacity	Number of plants	Average capacity per plant '000 tonnes
AKZO	6.0	1	60.0	16.0	6	24.0	6 & 66	23.0	8	29.0
Bayer	13.5	1	140.0	5.0	2	23.0	6	0.5	1	5.0
Courtaulds	18.0	3	62.0	4.0	4	9.0	6	2.0	1	20.0
Du Pont	4.0	1	40.0	6.5	1	60.0	66	7.5	1	75.0
Fabelta	3.0	1	30.0	1.0	1	10.0	66	—	—	—
Hoechst	7.5	1	75.0	—	—	—	—	20.0	5	40.0
ICI	—	—	—	21.0	5	38.0	66	14.0	4	35.0
Monsanto	8.0	2	40.0	—	—	—	—	—	—	—
Montefibre	12.0	2.5[c]	50.0	4.5	3	14.0	6 & 66	4.0	3[c]	14.0
Rhone Poulenc	3.5	1	35.0	17.5	12	13.0	66	14.0	8	18.0
Snia Viscosa	6.0	2	30.0	11.0	7	14.0	6	2.5	3.5[c]	7.0
ANIC	10.5	1.5[c]	73.0	2.5	1	21.0	6	5.0	1.5[c]	34.0
SIR	3.0	1	30.0	—	—	—	—	2.0	1	20.0
Other	5.0	—	—	11.0	—	—	—	5.5	—	—
Totals[b]	100.0	18	54.0	100.0	42	19.0		100.0	37	26.0

[a] See Footnote a, Table I.
[b] The number of plants and average plant capacities in the totals row are for the 13 major producers only.
[c] ANIC and Montefibre shared acrylic and polyester plants at Ottana; Montefibre and Snia Viscosa shared a polyester plant at Acerra.
Sources: Textile Organon, World Man-Made Fibre Survey 1980. Trade press and industry sources.

adjustments in rank order of market shares. The details can be seen by a comparison of capacity shares between Tables I and V. However, for convenience a simplified list of the four market leaders in each sector is shown in Table VI.

In essence the market positions of firms were largely frozen in their mid 1970s pattern and relatively small and inefficient plants and firms (in each fibre) were not eliminated. Compared with the predictions in Table IV based on a competitive solution, the Davignon Plan cartel combined with state support and other interventions to prevent plant closures led to a very different result, at least up to 1980. Of the 11 category 1 (market share <5% and uneconomic plant size) predicted withdrawals only two had taken place. Hoechst and Monsanto had both withdrawn from the nylon market. Similarly, of the eleven category 2 predicted withdrawals none had occurred though there were indications that withdrawals were beginning (e.g. Du Pont had closed one of its two acrylic plants and Rhone Poulenc had indicated that its continuance in that market was under review).

As indicated in the data on plant closures the position began to change significantly around 1980 with a further deterioration in market conditions.[7] It was at this stage, after the formal abandonment of the Davignon Plan cartel,[8] that both plant closures and product withdrawals occurred in significant proportions. The key question from the point of view of competitive processes is whether firms with small market shares and/or uneconomic plant sizes were the firms to withdraw. The evidence is summarized in Table VII which compares the manufacturing involvements of the thirteen major producers at the end of 1981 with the predicted withdrawals taken from Table IV.

Two firms, Fabelta and SIR, at the end of 1981 appeared to be being forced into closure. Both were shown in the 1975 predictions as having uneconomic plant sizes and a small market share in both of their product areas. Among the other category 1 (strong) withdrawal predictions: Hoechst and Monsanto had withdrawn from all sectors of the nylon market; ANIC was probably withdrawing into specialised sectors of the nylon market; Snia Viscosa had withdrawn from the polyester staple market and into specialised sectors of the polyester filament market; and Courtaulds had abandoned a plan to produce polyester staple at its new plant in the Republic of Ireland. Thus of the 11 predicted withdrawals nine had been either fully or partially fulfilled. In the remaining cases AKZO had increased the capacity of the

[7] Market penetration by imports had risen sharply in some areas, e.g. the US market share for polyester yarn in the UK market had risen from 7 per cent in the third quarter of 1978 to 25 per cent a year later. Despite capacity reductions the level of capacity utilization in Western Europe as a whole in 1980 was only 64 per cent.

[8] The plan, on which the cartel was based, was agreed to in June 1978 but was neither ratified nor legally condemned by the European Commission until August 1979 when the Commission demanded the cartel's abolition. The producers complied with the EEC decision in January 1980.

TABLE VI
PRODUCTION CAPACITY SHARES OF MARKET LEADERS 1975 AND 1980

Acrylic				Nylon				Polyester			
1975		*1980*		*1975*		*1980*		*1975*		*1980*	
Group	*% share*	*Group*	*% share*	*Group*	*% share*	*Group*	*% share*	*Group*	*% share*	*Group*	*% share*
Courtaulds	20.0	Courtaulds	18.0	ICI	19.0	ICI	21.0	AKZO	22.0	AKZO	23.0
Bayer	14.5	Bayer	13.5	AKZO	18.0	Rh. Poulenc	17.5	Hoechst	22.0	Hoechst	20.0
Montefibre	12.5	Montefibre	12.0	Rh. Poulenc	16.5	AKZO	16.0	ICI	14.0	ICI	14.0
Hoechst	9.5	ANIC	10.5	Snia Visco.	9.5	Snia Visco.	11.0	Rh. Poulenc	13.5	Rh. Poulenc	14.0

TABLE VII

COMPARISON OF WITHDRAWAL PREDICTIONS WITH MANUFACTURING INVOLVEMENTS IN SYNTHETIC FIBRES IN WESTERN EUROPE AT THE END OF 1981[a]

	Acrylic			Nylon			Polyester		
Involvement	*Firm*	*Market Share 1975 %*	*Withdrawal Category*	*Firm*	*Market Share 1975 %*	*Withdrawal Category*	*Firm*	*Market Share 1975 %*	*Withdrawal Category*
Continuing major involvement	Courtaulds	20.0		ICI	19.0		AKZO	22.0	
	Bayer	14.5		Snia Viscosa	9.5		Hoechst	22.0	
	Montefibre	12.5		Du Pont	6.0	2b	Montefibre	6.0	2a
	Hoechst	9.5					ANIC	3.0	1
	Monsanto	8.0							
	ANIC	5.5	2a						
	Snia Viscosa	5.0	2a						
	AKZO[b]	4.5	1						
Scaled down to speciality end uses or withdrawn from some major market segments				AKZO	18.0		ICI	14.0	
				Rhone Poulenc	16.5		Rhone Poulenc	13.5	
				Bayer	6.0	2b	Du Pont	6.5	2b
				Montefibre	5.5	2a	Snia Viscosa	2.5	1
				ANIC	1.5	1	Courtaulds	1.5	1
Completely withdrawn or withdrawal announced	Du Pont	7.5	2a	Courtaulds	5.5	2a	Bayer	4.5	2b
	Rhone Poulenc	6.5	2b	Monsanto	4.0	1	SIR	2.0	1
	Fabelta	3.0	1	Hoechst	0.5	1			
	SIR	1.0	1	Fabelta	0.5	1			

[a] The pattern of involvement and withdrawals by the four major Italian groups, ANIC, Montefibre, SIR and Snia Viscosa may change in the reorganisation of the Italian chemical industry following the financial collapse of SIR.

[b] Remaining involvement only through minority shareholding in Cyanenka of Spain. Other acrylic interests divested when Fabelta sold in 1976.

acrylic plant of its partly owned subsidiary to an economic scale and ANIC had similarly increased its plant sizes in the polyester sector.

Among the category 2 withdrawal predictions both Du Pont and Rhone Poulenc were withdrawing from the acrylic sector while ANIC had substantially increased its plant capacity and market share. It is important to remember however that ANIC had been a significant recipient of state aid to build these plants. On the evidence of both the 1975 and 1980 relative plant sizes and market shares, however, Du Pont appeared a stronger competitor than Snia Viscosa which was continuing its major involvement in acrylics. Rhone Poulenc also appeared stronger than Snia Viscosa on both criteria in 1975 though only in terms of plant size in 1980. All four market leaders listed in Table VI were continuing their major involvement in acrylics as was Monsanto, the fifth ranked firm in both years.

In the nylon sector, among the category 2 withdrawal predictions, Courtaulds had withdrawn completely, and both Montefibre and Bayer had withdrawn from some areas. Only Du Pont was continuing its major involvement though it had always concentrated on specialist end uses such as carpet fibres. Its plant was also large and the European division had the backing of the product leader in the USA. Among the four market leaders listed in Table VI only ICI (ranked number 1) and Snia Viscosa (ranked number 4) were continuing with a full involvement in all the nylon sectors. Both AKZO and Rhone Poulenc had decided to specialise on some segments—in Rhone Poulenc's case mainly on nylon for textile uses. The relatively heavy incidence of withdrawals from the nylon sector compared with either the acrylic or polyester sector reflected both nylon's sharp decline in the 1970s and its poorer expected growth prospects in the 1980s.

In the polyester sector, of the three category 2 withdrawal predictions, Bayer was withdrawing completely, Du Pont was largely withdrawing from the polyester filament area while Montefibre was continuing its major interests in all sectors. Among the four market leaders, the top two, AKZO and Hoechst, were continuing their major involvement, while ICI and Rhone Poulenc were concentrating their activities on specialist segments while withdrawing from others. Once again there is an element of surprise in that one apparently weaker competitor, Montefibre, was retaining its major interest while ICI and Rhone Poulenc were partially withdrawing. State aid in helping Montefibre and its associate ANIC to develop new plant was undoubtedly a major factor in this apparently perverse result.

One final characteristic of the withdrawal process was the pattern of product withdrawal within each firm. Among the surviving firms there was a strong and natural tendency for each to retain its strongest product areas and withdraw from others. The effect of these moves was to strengthen the position of the leading firms in each market and to reduce the points of competition between the major fibre producers. For instance, among the market leaders listed in Table VI AKZO decided to concentrate on polyester and withdraw from some areas of the nylon market; ICI conversely decided to concentrate on nylon and withdraw from some sectors of the polyester market; and finally Rhone Poulenc decided to concentrate mainly on textile end uses for both polyester and nylon. All three firms were among the leading four in both fibres in 1975 and 1980 so the pattern of mutual withdrawal significantly reduced the degree of competitive conflict. Perhaps less significantly, among the other competitors Du Pont withdrew from acrylics while retaining its major nylon interest while Monsanto withdrew from nylon but retained its acrylics activities.

Taking the end of 1981 as the benchmark it appears therefore that the outcome is fairly close to that predicted in an aggressive competitive solution. Most of the withdrawals were by weaker competitors with uneconomic plants and most of the market leaders that had economic sized plants retained their leadership position. The end-1981 position however differs markedly from that up to 1980 when there was little evidence of the competitive process penalising the relatively weak. Up till then state intervention coupled with the cartel solution of freezing market shares had prevented any such development. Finally, there is some evidence of a pattern of mutual withdrawals by major firms thus reducing the points of competitive conflict between them.

V. CONCLUSIONS

The process of rationalisation in the industry contained two distinct phases. The first period from 1975 until 1979–80, which included the Davignon Plan cartel, consisted of the virtual freezing of market shares of most firms and the preservation of both weak competitors and some uneconomic plants. Indeed, the main changes were in the improved market share of the four main Italian companies taken together despite their relative inefficiency and continuing state of near financial collapse. These results are consistent with the predictions for a cartel where the weak companies are protected by state aid.

The second period from 1979–80 until the end of 1981 covered the period after the formal abandonment of the cartel. In this period the rationalisation pattern followed closely on predictions based on the operation of the competitive process. Many small and uneconomic plants were closed and weaker competitors in each of the three synthetic fibres were forced out of the market. The exceptions to this pattern were mainly Italian companies dependent on state aid for their survival and development. In addition, most competitors chose to withdraw from their weaker market areas and concentrate their efforts on narrower product ranges. While this was predictable in an industry in continuing crisis, the product withdrawals also showed some tendency for major firms to reduce competition between themselves.

Economic theory suggests two distinct response patterns for either a collusive or restrained group of oligopolists: they might reduce capacity proportionately and maintain markets in each sector, or they might individually withdraw from sectors in which they were weak thus reducing the points of competition between them. It is perhaps significant that in the earlier period when a formal cartel plan existed the response should have been of the first type while after the plan's abandonment and in deteriorating competitive conditions the response led to results close to those predicted as the outcome of the competitive process, though of course this process also reduced the number of competitors.

R. W. and S. A. Shaw,
University of Stirling,
Stirling,
FK9 4LA.

ACCEPTED OCTOBER 1982

REFERENCES

[1] Cameron, S., 'Why Small is Not Beautiful for Monsanto's Nylon', *Financial Times* (10 May 1979).

[2] *European Chemical News*, 10 October 1975, p. 15.

[3] Lossius, T., 'A Case Study of International Efficiency Comparisons—ICI's Synthetic Fibres Business', in C. Bowe, ed., *Industrial Efficiency and the Role of Government* (H.M.S.O., London, 1977).

[4] O'Brien, D. P., 'Patent Protection and Competition in Polyamide and Polyester Fibre Manufacture', *Journal of Industrial Economics* XII, 3 (July 1964), pp. 224–35.

[5] Pratten, C. F., *Economies of Scale in Manufacturing Industry* (Cambridge University Press, Cambridge, 1971).

[6] Shaw, R. W. and Shaw, S. A., 'Synthetic Fibres' in P. S. Johnson, ed., *The Structure of British Industry* (Granada, London, 1980).

[7] United Nations Conference on Trade and Development (UNCTAD) *Fibres and Textiles: Dimensions of Corporate Marketing Structures* (United Nations, 1980), p. 122.

THE JOURNAL OF INDUSTRIAL ECONOMICS 0022-1821 $2.00
Volume XXXII December 1983 No. 2

THE UK WASTEPAPER INDUSTRY AND ITS LONG TERM PROSPECTS*

R. K. TURNER AND D. DEADMAN

STRUCTURE OF THE UK PAPER AND BOARD INDUSTRY

IT has been suggested that of all the secondary materials presently discarded as waste, recovery of paper and board residuals (wastepaper or paper-stock) can offer the greatest economic savings [2]. This article examines the market facing the UK wastepaper supply industry and presents some forecasts of the demand for its products up to the year 2000. UK paper and board mills have been utilising wastepaper as a raw material production input on a significant scale for many decades. In 1980 and 1981 wastepaper accounted for about 53% of the total fibre input in the mills' furnish (see Table I).

TABLE I
UK WASTEPAPER RECOVERY AND UTILISATION RATES

	1960	*1963*	*1965*	*1966*	*1967*	*1968*	*1969*	*1970*	*1971*	*1972*
Recovery[a] Rate	27.8	27.5	28.6	27.1	26.5	27.0	27.0	28.7	28.7	27.0
Utilisation[b] Rate	32.3	34.1	35.7	34.4	35.7	36.0	37.9	38.2	43.2	41.8

	1973	*1974*	*1975*	*1976*	*1977*	*1978*	*1979*	*1980*	*1981*
Recovery Rate	27.5	27.6	28.8	28.9	29.2	28.8	30	32	n/a
Utilisation Rate	44.3	45.8	46.8	49.5	51.4	50.7	51.9	53	52

Notes:
[a] Recovery rate = ratio of wastepaper collected to paper and board apparent consumption. Apparent consumption = production plus imports minus exports.
[b] Utilisation rate = ratio of apparent consumption of waste paper to total fibre usage (equivalent to paper and board production assuming no conversion losses).
Source: OECD Pulp and Paper Statistics, Paris.

UK production of paper and board reached a peak of around 4.9 m tonnes in 1969/70 since when there has been a prolonged decline (see Table II). Faced with severe competition from imports, and from products made with

* The authors thank the staff at PIRA, other trade sources and a referee for their help and information. Responsibility for the analyses and remaining errors is entirely the authors'.

TABLE II
UK PRODUCTION OF PAPER AND BOARD
(000's tonnes p.a.)

Product Category	*1964* (%) of total[a]	*1974* (%)	*1978* (%)	*1979* (%)	*1980* (%)	*1981*	*1982 (Jan–Nov)*
Newsprint	761.9 (17.4)	382.5 (8.4)	318.8 (7.7)	364.1 (8.7)	361.4 (9.5)	—	—
Printing and Writing Papers and Boards	1053.9 (24)	1207.7 (26.5)	1058.7 (25.5)	1056.5 (25.2)	963.1 (25.4)	—	—
Corrugated Case Material	392.0 (80)	879.1 (19.3)	940.1 (22.6)	955.9 (22.8)	883.2 (23.3)	—	—
Packaging Papers	534.1 (12.2)	333.3 (7.3)	245.0 (5.9)	242.3 (5.8)	210.7 (5.6)	—	—
Packaging Boards	951.7 (21.7)	888.3 (19.5)	758.1 (18.3)	743.9 (17.7)	590.3 (15.6)	—	—
Household, Toilet Papers and Tissues	186.0 (4.2)	367.9 (8.1)	403.1 (9.7)	417.4 (9.9)	434.8 (11.5)	—	—
Industrial and Special Purpose Papers and Boards	508.1 (11.6)	496.5 (10.9)	429.7 (10.3)	418.2 (10.0)	349.8 (9.1)	—	—
Total	4387.7 (100)	4555.3 (100)	4153.5 (100)	4198.3 (100)	3793.8 (100)	3381.5	3120.4

Source: British Paper and Board Industry Federation.
Notes: [a] = Errors due to rounding.

alternative materials such as plastics, the UK industry has been forced into a long period of rationalisation with a large number of smaller mills being phased out. Between 1967 and 1975 some 47 mills were closed or partly closed and over 100 paper making machines ceased production. Production has been concentrated in larger units and the industry as a whole has sought to specialise in a limited range of end-products, many of which (e.g. newsprint, packaging papers and boards and tissues) are based on substantial inputs of recycled fibre. Of the 141 mills in production in 1977 the 10 mills in the largest size category (> 100,000 tonnes output per annum) produced 37% of the industry's total output and the 30 mills in the 25,000–50,000 tpa size category produced 27% of total output. By the end of the 1970s five major producers, Bowater, Reed International, Wiggins Teape, Dickinson Robinson and Thames Board controlled over 50% of the industry's total output. All of these 'majors', with the exception of Wiggins Teape, were heavy users of recycled fibre inputs. In 1980 Reed, for example, produced 1/6th of the total UK output of paper and board and 70% of its raw material inputs into its nine UK mills were recycled fibres [18].

The current recession in the international economy has hit the UK industry severely. During 1980 some 16 mills and 44 machines were closed down. In total the industry lost some 20% of its production capacity, including 500,000 tonnes of recycled fibre using capacity. Output of paper and board and wastepaper consumption by the mills, however, fell by only 9.6% and 7.8% respectively between 1979–80. In the period 1980–81 paper and board output fell by 10.9% but wastepaper consumption declined by only 2.7% (down from just over 2 mt to 1.95 mt) despite the fact that the sectors most severely hit, newsprint and kraft wrappings, are both heavily dependent on recycled fibre [1]. The recycled fibres released have probably been absorbed by the market in corrugated medium and boards for packaging. The rate of growth of the UK packaging industry as a whole is likely to be slower in the next decade than in the last three. Nevertheless it is forecast to exceed, by around 1% per annum, the growth of manufacturing industry generally. The fibre board containers market is the second largest sector in the packaging products industry and corrugated cases, which now occupy 95% of this market, can contain up to 65% recycled fibre. Both the case and corrugated board products face competition, however, from products such as shrink wrapped pallets and trays, flexible packaging, expanded polystyrene and returnable plastic crates. The major growth sector in the UK paper industry is tissues production. Sales of tissues have been growing by 3% per annum in recent years. Transport costs on what is a relatively cheap and bulky product offer some protection to UK producers in a market where consumption per head is still well below US levels. Bowater-Scott controls about 40% of the UK disposable tissues market and currently uses an average of 20% waste paper in its furnish [4]. Both paper and board production and waste paper consumption continued to decline in the period

1981–82. On a January to November basis the former category fell by 7.7% and the latter by 3.9%.

WASTEPAPER SUPPLY

The wastepaper supply enterprises have sought to meet the mills' requirements by recycling residuals from a range of generation sources—industrial, commercial and residential. There is also a significant international trade in secondary paper and board [9]. The supply side of the market is composed of four types of enterprises—mill integrated merchants, independent merchants, local authorities and voluntary/charity organisations (see Figure 1). Around 70% of the wastepaper supplied to the mills is now handled by their own integrated merchant network. These merchant enterprises typically acquire over 60% of their supply via 'factoring' i.e. purchasing supplies from smaller independent merchants rather than through collections at the sources of waste arisings. The independent merchants acquire a far smaller proportion of their supplies via 'factoring', typically around 28% [16]. The importance of the local authority collection system has been declining over time, due mainly to the relatively high collection costs involved in municipal operations. The number of municipalities collecting wastepaper fell from 450 in 1945 to about 150 by the end of the 1970s and the trend has continued into the 1980s. Local authorities accounted for some 17% of the wastepaper consumed by mills in 1970, but this had fallen to 14% by 1975. They currently collect less than 10% of the total UK supply. While charity groups have in the past collected as much as 12% to 15% of supplies this level has rarely been sustained for any length of time. The voluntary/charity group supply contribution is now around 5% of the total supply.

Wastepaper is not an homogeneous product and there are a number of sub-markets in existence based on the quality or grade of the paper and board residuals concerned (see Table III). Of the ten general UK grade categories the first four contain high quality residuals which, together with grade six, can readily substitute for primary woodpulp in the furnish required for the production of some papers and tissues. The other middle and lower grade residuals have a more restricted use and in fact the utility of the residuals declines as the grade level falls unless upgrading processes are applied such as, for example, de-inking and/or cooking and bleaching. Packaging products and newsprint can tolerate significant quantities of middle and lower grade recycled fibres in their furnish makeup. The 'pulp substitute' paper making and tissues market is relatively stable and wastepaper prices do not fluctuate excessively. The board making sub-market has by contrast become more unstable in recent years.

Overall, on the demand side of this factor market there is imperfect competition with four major mill enterprises dominating. Three of the four mill groups, Reed, Bowater and Thames Board, are themselves part of highly

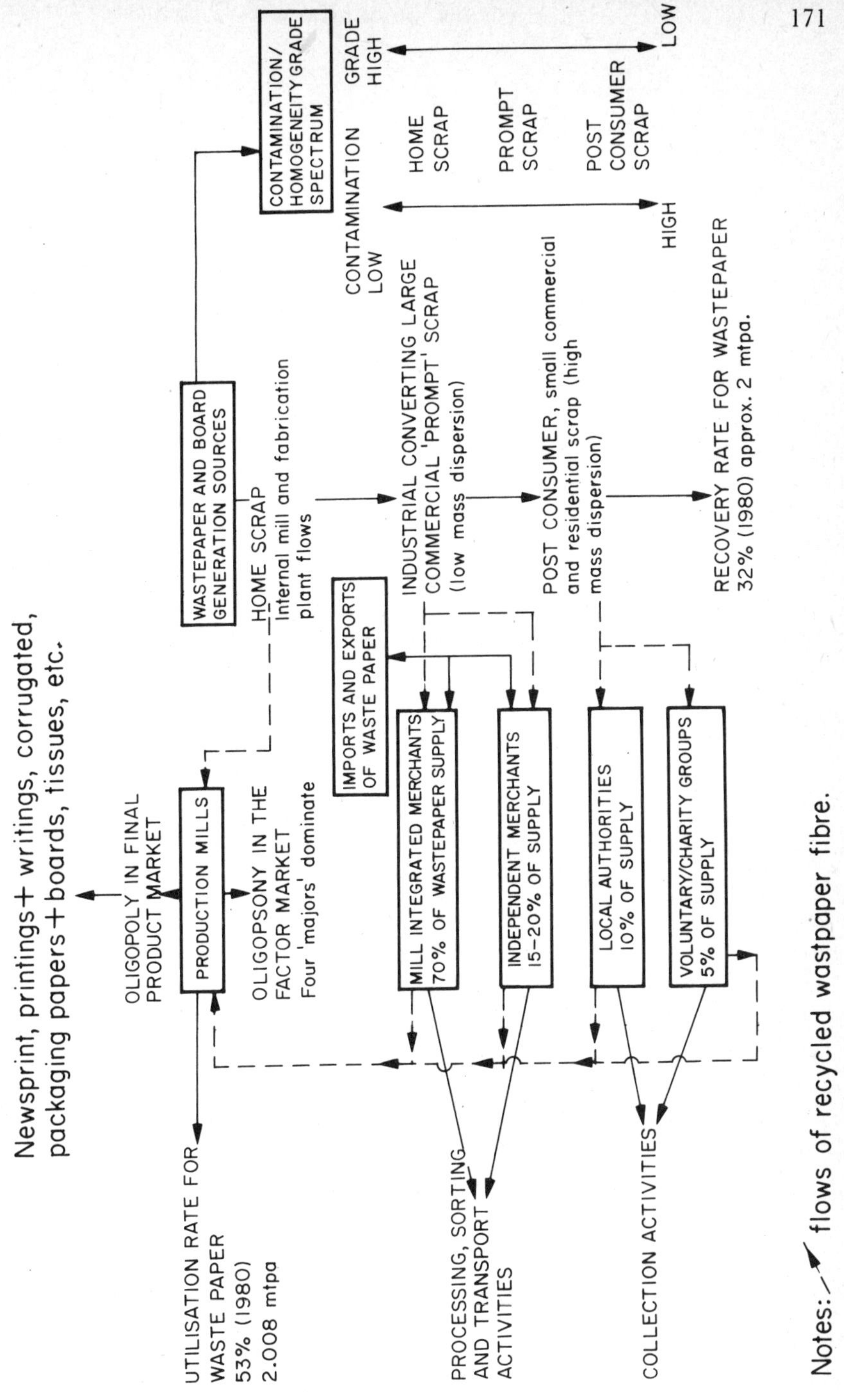

FIGURE 1.
UK Wastepaper Supply Network.

TABLE III
WASTE PAPER GRADES, SELECTED END USES AND GENERATION SOURCES

Type of Secondary Material	*UK Grade Higher (Papermaking) Grades*	*End Use*	*Generation Source*
Wastepaper (paperstock), clean unprinted papers, printers' waste, paper converters' waste, stationers' and book binders' waste etc.	1 + 2	Liners for board, printing and writing papers, tissues.	INDUSTRIAL/CONVERTING SOURCES, printers, converters, newspaper publishers.
Envelope shavings, tabulating cards and listings, ledgers, carbonless copy paper waste, forms, etc.	3 + 4	Tissues, wrapping paper, liners and envelope papers, de-inked office papers can also be used for printing and writing papers and tissues.	Large industrial/commercial sources, institutional sources.
	BULK (BOARD-MAKING) GRADES		
Over-issue newspapers, brochures and directories, returns and used newspapers from householders.	5	Liners for board, after de-inking newsprint and tissues, cellulose insulation animal bedding.	Magazine and newspaper printers, households.
Kraft papers.	6	Kraft paper, packaging boards, boxes, cartons and cardboard.	Industrial sources, sack, bag and box manufacturers, shops.
New Kraft lined corrugated paperboard waste.	7	Backs and liners for board, fluting medium and test liner, corrugating medium, building board.	Shops, board converters, schools, offices and households.
Container waste.	8		
Mixed paper, coloured card, and all other types.	9 + 10		

diversified transnational conglomerates. Since the 1960s these mill groups have sought to secure stability of input supply by integrating upstream into merchanting and have simultaneously themselves been linked to other downstream end product operations through group interests in, among others, publishing, newspaper production, packaging products manufacture and tissues manufacture. On the supply side, while some of the merchant enterprises are large firms in their own right, and at least one has begun to diversify into aluminium can recovery, the enterprises are characteristically small scale and numerous.

THE INTERNATIONAL PULP AND WASTEPAPER MARKETS

Before going on to present new forecasts we need to analyse in more detail the relative nature of the UK paper and board and wastepaper industries as well as their significance in the world pulp, wastepaper and final goods markets. Probable future trends in these markets are highlighted and form the basis for the assumptions underlying our new forecasts.

Whilst paper and board production in the UK (a pulp deficit economy) has been undergoing a prolonged decline (output in 1981 was 30% below the level achieved in 1964 and 26% below the last most recent record output level achieved in 1974) wastepaper consumption has held up extremely well. Over the period 1973–80 waste paper consumption remained within a range of 2 m tonnes to 2.2 m tonnes per annum, although in 1981 consumption did fall to 1.9 m tonnes. Both the nature of the raw material base the UK paper and board industry has available to it and the end product mix that has evolved over the last two decades are primarily responsible for the significant levels of recovery and utilisation of wastepaper. There is also an international market in waste paper linking UK suppliers to buyers in both pulp deficit and surplus countries.

Progress in de-inking technology has been affecting the world market for wastepaper since the late 1970s and could lead to substantial increases in demand for certain grades. By 1980 worldwide de-inking capacity (flotation plus washing process) was variously estimated to be between 3.8 m tonnes and 5 m tonnes. In 1976 world flotation de-inking capacity had been below 1 m tonnes. Newsprint de-inking capacity has been considerably expanded in the eastern USA and Canada since the late 1970s. Sweden has been importing around 100,000 tonnes of wastepaper per annum since 1980 in order to meet her de-inking requirements. FAO estimate that world newsprint capacity may have increased by 6% in 1981 and will increase by another 5% in 1982. Whether there is a sufficiently high level of demand for this increased supply of newsprint is, however, open to question. World demand for newsprint has been growing at an average of only 2% per annum in recent years. More optimistic forecasters point to the impact of increasing literacy in developing economies, as well as a general improvement in living standards which are possible in the future. Both trends, if they materialise and are sustained, could lead to a major expansion in world paper markets. The potential is certainly there, since annual paper consumption in 1980 averaged 274 kilograms per person in the USA, 73 k per person in Europe and only 14 k per person in Asia. On a more pessimistic note, recession in the international economy is affecting growth rates in both developed and developing economies, and a number of the paper and board products consumed in the former economies face stiff competition from plastic and metal based products.

Further, not all technological advances are benign as far as the paper industry is concerned. Advances in electronics and associated procedures such as, for example, visual display, personal microcomputers, computerised record keeping and mail services, may perhaps reduce the aggregate demand for paper in the future. The precise impact of this type of technological advance on the future demand for paper products is very difficult to predict. Ross and Purcell [14] conclude that "while some futurists foresee the not-too-distant era of the 'paperless office' . . . others argue that as information processing is made easier by electronic technology, the demand for printed reports from this information explosion will be greater than ever". According to the authors, despite the uncertainty, two facts are emerging—"technological advances continue and are increasing the viability of the 'paperless office' concept. Microcomputers are rapidly decreasing in cost, and fibre optics systems which could bring in as many as 10,000 separate channels to the home and office are in the offing. The second factor is that, despite these technological advances, a number of considerations dictate that large scale adoption of electronic media systems of the kind that reduce absolute paper use may take decades; we may be well into the next century before we see large scale competition between printing paper and and the electronic media".

A number of new markets for waste paper have begun to expand in the last few years. These new outlets range from plants designed to capture the energy potential of waste papers, through animal bedding products and cellulose fibre insulation products, to moulded paper products for disposable egg and fruit packaging. None of these non-paper markets in the UK has as yet expanded to any significant scale but the combined market probably absorbed around 100,000 tonnes of waste paper in 1981. Future prospects are difficult to estimate but the market could double by 1990. If the refuse derived fuel plants currently under test prove viable then large tonnages of wastepaper could be diverted away from the recycling industry.

There is no doubt that the rate of increase in world paper consumption did slow down during the 1970s from an average annual rate of increase of 4.8% over the period 1950–78 to around 2.9% per annum in the period 1970–78. The fact that paper consumption increased more slowly than GDP in the USA can also possibly be interpreted as an ominous precedent for consumption patterns in other regions from the late 1980s onwards.

The paper and board industries of Western Europe as a whole do not have access to domestic woodpulp supplies on anything like the scale available to North American and Scandinavian producers. They therefore rely to a significant extent on 'market pulp' for their virgin material inputs. Sweden and Canada between them supply over 40% of this 'market pulp' requirement in Europe. During the period 1965–80 the proportion of primary pulp used in western Europe paper and board mills declined to an average level just below 70% by 1980. At the same time the amount of waste paper used to produce 1,000 Kg of paper and board increased by 5%. The UK's indigenous timber resources only provide between 8% to 12% of the paper and board industry's fibre requirements and this contribution is unlikely to rise above 15% even by the year 2000. Waste paper utilisation rates are currently around 52% so the residual 30% to 40% of fibre requirement has to be met by importing 'market pulp'. Although woodpulp is an internationally traded commodity, 'market pulp'—the surplus output of the integrated mills plus the output of the nonintegrated mills in North America, Scandinavia and increasingly Brazil—is only a relatively small fraction of total world pulp production (12%–15%).

A number of forecasting organisations have also warned that by the year 2000 there may be a world shortage of timber. One such group predicts that world demand for timber will be 86% higher in the year 2000 than it was in 1976 and expresses some concern about future supplies and price levels [7]. Another organisation states that "taking world demand and supply together by the year 2000 . . . there will be at least 40 mm^3 of unsatisfied demand at fixed prices i.e. 8% of total demand. By 2025, the gap will have widened to 3000 mm^3, with supply falling short of demand by 32% at fixed prices" [17]. There is a considerable amount of conjecture, however, about the subject of future world timber supplies and related pulp outputs. A number of new producers in the less developed world, especially Brazil, have been rapidly increasing their production of market pulp, and low cost wood from the southern states of the USA is making a significant difference to the US indigenous supply position. Further, the forecasts quoted above depend on assumed future GNP growth rates which may or may not be constrained by other material and energy supply difficulties.

Any country importing 'market pulp' has to incur the additional cost of drying, transporting and repulping. Because of this and the relatively small average scale of production in the UK and elsewhere in Europe, the narrow margin between the price of imported pulp and the selling price of finished products from North America and Scandinavia makes it difficult for many European mills to rely entirely on imported pulp. UK mills have therefore been forced to concentrate on two main areas of production—high-quality, low-volume speciality paper, mainly utilising wood pulp and small amounts of high-quality recycled fibres, or high-volume, wastepaper-based packaging products incorporating only small pulp inputs. In direct contrast to the USA, for example, wastepaper in the UK and Europe is in no sense an 'input of the last resort'. In principle, the price of imported pulp effectively sets a ceiling for the price of wastepaper in the UK [10]. In practice, UK mills generally use wastepaper inputs as long as they are available, provided that they have sufficient fibre cleaning equipment installed and if prices are less than 60 to 70% of the price of the substituted virgin fibre. UK wastepaper based final products have traditionally been sold at a discount of up to 10% below the price of imported virgin fibre-based products.

The UK mills' trading situation is further complicated by the fact that woodpulp is priced in terms of US dollars so that mill costs are heavily dependent on the sterling exchange rate. Woodpulp prices over the last decade or so peaked in the period 1975–77, fell back during 1977 to 1978 to a level 25% below the average price for 1975; only to increase again from mid 1978, surpassing the previous peak in June 1979. The potential cost advantages accruing to UK recycled fibre based products because of the sustained rise in woodpulp dollar prices have, however, been modified by the strength of sterling and weakness of the dollar during much of the period 1979–81.

Paper and board products import penetration by North American and Scandinavian producers has been growing steadily throughout Europe. In the UK imports now account for over 50% of the total consumption of paper and board. To add to the competitive pressure, in 1984 the EEC tariffs on Scandinavian paper and board products are due to be eliminated. EFTA and the EEC will then share a common external tariff of 9% for paper products, 5% for newsprint and 6% for packaging papers. In the face of such sustained competition from low cost producers it is in the interests of European mills to attempt to turn wastepaper into the kind of stable, guaranteed input that woodpulp is to the integrated producers in pulp surplus regions. Vertical integration into merchanting, and the degree of stability this imparts to wastepaper prices, is a move in this direction, although the very nature of secondary paper and board materials makes this move an incomplete one. We indicated earlier that some 70% of the wastepaper supply is now controlled by mill integrated merchants in the UK. In the Netherlands and Germany 50% and 25% respectively of the supply is similarly controlled. Wastepaper prices are generally less stable in Europe than they are in the UK where levels of integration are highest and where, until the mid 1970s, local authority collections, tied by guaranteed contracts to mill-merchant groups, were widespread.

FORECASTING THE FUTURE DEMAND FOR WASTE PAPER

The crucial importance of the state of the UK economy to the wastepaper industry is generally accepted. In particular the output of recycled fibre based packaging papers and boards and corrugated case materials are very sensitive to changes in manufacturing output. The connection is demonstrated in the performance of models developed for the short run forecasting of the consumption of wastepaper both for the UK and the USA [3] [5] [8]. The long run situation need not be so closely tied to aggregate output because of the existence of technological change which may open up new outlets for the financially profitable utilisation of recycled fibres. Further, government intervention on grounds of potential social benefits from extra recycling can also alter the long run relationship between wastepaper recovery and utilisation rates and the state of the economy [13]. Despite a Green Paper on waste recycling in 1974 [15] and some, as yet unimplemented, sections in the 1974 Control of Pollution Act designed to require local authorities to promote waste reclamation, the UK government has not yet intervened in any widespread fashion. This 'voluntary' approach to recycling is exemplified by government statements to the effect that consumer choice would be adversely affected by any mandatory use of recycled paper in government offices. Action has been limited to a £23 m grant aid scheme initiated in 1976, to stimulate increased waste paper utilisation by mills and processors. There has also been some provision of research initiatives and funding for a limited number of demonstration plants for the mechanical recovery of components of the municipal waste stream and the production of refuse derived fuel pellets (mixture of paper and plastics). The long term compatability of these latter plants, if widely adopted, with the wastepaper industry is somewhat questionable. Any government initiatives leading to a reduction in end product 'quality' standards, for example, the 'brightness' of paper, could produce a major stimulus to wastepaper utilisation. Currently only 10% of the UK paper supplied to HMSO contains recycled fibres (equivalent to 5% of the Office's total intake).

FORECAST UK CONSUMPTION OF WASTEPAPER: NO TECHNICAL CHANGE

Forecasts for GDP growth up to the year 2000 have been derived, on the basis of a 5-year moving-average trend, by Resources for the Future Inc. (see Table IV) [6]. If these forecasts are taken as reasonable growth rates for wastepaper consumption from a base year of 1981 then the peak wastepaper consumption figure of 2.2 m tonnes achieved in 1979 will not be matched again until well into the 1990s (see Table V, column A). This result is conditional on there being no technological change during the relevant period.

TABLE IV
PROJECTED ANNUAL PERCENTAGE GROWTH (PER CAPITA) OF UK GDP

1980–85	*1985–90*	*1990–95*	*1995–2000*
1.7	1.5	1.3	1.3

Source: Fischman [6].

TABLE V
FORECAST UK WASTE PAPER CONSUMPTION

	m tonnes A[a]	m tonnes B[b]
1985	1.99	2.06
1990	2.14	2.23
1995	2.28	2.38
2000	2.44	2.54

[a] Assuming base figure of 1.9 m tonnes for wastepaper consumption in 1981.
[b] Assuming base figure of 2.0 m tonnes for wastepaper consumption in 1983.

On a more optimistic basis it is not unreasonable to expect industrial output to pick up more quickly than GNP or GDP in the initial stages of a recovery cycle. In this case wastepaper consumption could be rapidly restored to the 2 million tonnes target level by the end of 1983. Once the economy as a whole was operating at a level of output comparable to the pre-recession output achieved in the 1970s then the basic relationship observed between GDP growth and wastepaper consumption (see Table VI) would be restored. Column B in Table V presents the more optimistic wastepaper consumption estimates. Nevertheless, unless a case can be made for wastepaper consumption growth rates above those for the economy as a whole, or for new market opportunities stimulated by technological change, the prospects for a major expansion in the use of recycled paper do not appear encouraging.

TABLE VI
UK GDP AND WASTE PAPER CONSUMPTION GROWTH RATES

Period	GPD Growth (% change over period)	Waste Paper Consumption (% change over period)
1960–64	14.62	10.27
1965–69	11.33	11.55
1970–74	10.68	9.70
1976–80	3.15	2.14

FORECAST UK CONSUMPTION OF WASTEPAPER: INPUT-OUTPUT APPROACH

In order better to take into account technical change we adopt an input-output approach to forecasting. The initial step in the analysis is to define the relationship between outputs of paper and board products and the required inputs of wastepaper. A matrix of utilisation coefficients can then be constructed. Table VII presents a range of estimated coefficients con-

TABLE VII
UK WASTEPAPER UTILISATION COEFFICIENTS
(in per cent)

Product Category	*Mixed Paper* Massus 1973 (*A*)	*Mixed Paper* Late 1970s (*B*)	*Mixed Paper* Early 1980s (*C*)	*Mixed Paper* 1990s (*D*)	*Corrugated* (*A*)	*Corrugated* (*B*)	*Corrugated* (*C*)	*Corrugated* (*D*)	*Old News* (*A*)	*Old News* (*B*)	*Old News* (*C*)	*Old News* (*D*)	*Printers' Waste* (*A*)	*Printers' Waste* (*B*)	*Printers' Waste* (*C*)	*Printers' Waste* (*D*)	*Kraft* (*A*)	*Kraft* (*B*)	*Kraft* (*C*)	*Kraft* (*D*)
Printing and Writing Papers	4	0	0	0	0	0	0	0	45	61	45	50	40	37	52	47	11	2	3	3
Corrugated Medium	69	50	40	45	27	50	55	55	4	0	5	0	0	0	0	0	0	0	0	0
Other Packaging Paper	15	11	10	10	46	50	55	45	9	0	2	5	31	13	15	20	6	25	18	20
Boards	72	53	40	45	16	40	45	45	10	4	10	5	2	1	3	0	3	2	2	5
Other Papers and Boards (including tissues)	32	7	12	26	8	20	25	22	10	27	32	20	32	47	31	30	17	0	0	2

Source: Massus [11] and private communication, D. Guest, PIRA.

structed after consultations with a number of trade and research organisation sources. The coefficients estimated to be indicative of the main outlets for wastepaper in the UK in the latter half of the 1970s (column B) are broadly in line, in proportional terms, with those estimated by Massus in 1974 and which related to the early 1970s (column A) [11]. There are, however, a number of significant exceptions. The Massus coefficients relating inputs of printers' waste and kraft waste to the packaging papers sectors are respectively too high and too low. Another apparently major discrepancy concerns the relative proportions of corrugated and kraft waste being channelled into the other papers and boards sector. Possibly the relatively high Massus coefficient for kraft includes new kraft lined corrugated waste which is defined as kraft in Europe but as corrugated in the UK. Finally, the Massus coefficient for mixed paper and old news inputs into the other papers and boards sector are respectively too high and too low.

Because of the severe recession in the UK the paper and board industry is now much smaller than it was at the beginning of the 1970s and some wastepaper utilisation practices and trends have been altered. Newsprint production has been reduced by around 70% and although recycled fibre inputs in this sector are high, around 60%, some old news waste has had to be reabsorbed in the corrugated medium and board sectors. There has also been an increased use of corrugated waste relative to mixed papers in boards and corrugated medium. Some middle grade corrugated waste has also been used in increasing proportions in paper towelling product furnishes (part of other papers and boards sector). The coefficients in column (C) reflect these changes.

The estimated coefficients for 1990 (column D) are meant to reflect a number of likely technical changes and utilisation trends. Advances in de-inking technology will reduce the cost of producing de-inked fibre and increase the amount of high and some middle grade wastepaper inputs into printing and writing papers and in tissues. Thus, for example, high grade residuals such as computer printout papers will form an increasing fraction of the furnish for coloured tissues. De-inked middle grade residuals such as journals and magazines may also find an increasing outlet in tissue production along with some low grade mixed papers if bleaching techniques improve sufficiently.

The physical availability of suitable supplies of high and middle 'pulp substitute' grades may ultimately prove to be more of an obstacle than technical advances. These 'captive' grades are periodically under heavy pressure even with current practices and the low newsprint output now being produced by UK mills. It is the lower grade paper and board residuals discarded to the municipal waste-stream that offer a large future supply of recycled fibre. Table VIII presents some crude estimates of the magnitude of the potentially available supply of wastepaper. A materials balance calculation is made for the UK as a whole and an estimate derived from published

TABLE VIII
POTENTIAL SECONDARY MATERIALS SUPPLY IN THE MUNICIPAL WASTESTREAM (1979/80)
MATERIALS BALANCE METHOD

Area	Apparent consumption of paper and board[a]	Estimated non-recoverable[b]	Current paper recovery	Physical availability[c]	Potential availability[d]: Estimated 35% loss	Potential availability[d]: 50% loss
		(million tonnes)				
United Kingdom	7.3	1.09	2.1	4.11	2.7	2.1

REFUSE COLLECTION METHOD

Area	Domestic and commercial waste stream estimated tonnages per annum[e]	Waste composition breakdown: av % by weight	Physical availability	Estimated paper recovery	Potential availability: 35% loss	Potential availability: 50% loss
England and Wales	14–16	paper = 30%	4.2–4.8	0.137[f]	2.6–3.0	2.0–2.3

Notes:

[a] Apparent consumption = production of paper and board minus exports plus imports.

[b] Average 15% loss to cover dissipative uses and residuals locked into -long-life products.

[c] Assumed equivalent to tonnage of paper in the municipal wastestream—this is likely to overestimate the actual tonnage depending on the tonnages of paper and board disposed of by industrial and commercial enterprises i.e. private disposal.

[d] Technical, handling and processing losses.

[e] Waste collection authority returns 1979/80, Cipfa (1981) Waste Collection Statistics, 1979–80, Chartered Institute of Public Finance and Accountancy, London.

[f] Estimated average annual tonnage recovered by waste collection and disposal authorities 1977/78–1979/80—sources Cipfa (1981) and DOE (1979) Waste Management Paper No. 22, HMSO, London.

municipal refuse collection tonnages in England and Wales is also presented. The results confirm the hypothesis that refuse collection estimates tend to overestimate the true magnitude of the solid waste stream [12]. Despite the inevitable uncertainties associated with such estimates there seems to be no doubt that substantial potential supplies of fibre are available.

By the 1990s methods for the complete removal of difficult contamination problems such as adhesives, and cleaning techniques able to deal with contaminants like hot melt glues and plastic laminates may be operational. This could lead to a much greater use of these lower grades of wastepaper in products such as corrugated medium, tissues and certain packaging papers.

In order to derive forecasts of wastepaper consumption the utilisation coefficients matrix (Table VII) is multiplied by independent forecasts of the output of paper and board in the UK. These forecasts can be derived from either a simple regression relating paper and board output to GDP, or from a time trend extrapolation. Both methods yield consistent forecasts of a

TABLE IX
FORECAST PAPER AND BOARD PRODUCTION

	m tonnes
1985	3809
1990	3597
1995	3347
2000	3144

TABLE X
SECTORAL BREAKDOWN OF TOTAL PAPER AND BOARD OUTPUT

	% of Paper and Board Output			
Sectors	*1973*	*1976*	*1978*	*1979*
Printing and Writing	36.16	33.07	42.49	35.36
Corrugated	14.88	16.91	19.86	18.50
Other Packaging	5.22	5.03	5.00	4.36
Boards	31.56	39.69	23.45	28.04
Other	12.18	13.30	9.20	13.74

TABLE XI
WASTE PAPER INPUTS INTO PAPER AND BOARD PRODUCTS
(% by weight)

	Hypothesis "A"	*Hypothesis "B"*
Printing and Writing	0.07	0.33
Corrugated	0.85	0.86
Other Packaging	0.40	0.60
Boards	0.79	0.81
Other	0.31	0.52

Source: Massus [11].

reduction in total output of about 800 to 900 m tonnes by the year 2000. Table IX presents our forecasts of UK paper and board production levels in the period up to the year 2000.

Forecasts of paper and board output by main categories and the required disaggregated wastepaper inputs are also required. Generally, the proportions of final output in each category of paper and board (and particularly in the wastepaper dominated 'corrugated' and 'boards' categories) have remained fairly constant over time (see Table X). Table XI presents estimates of the percentage (by weight) of wastepaper utilised in each paper and board output category [11]. The hypothesis 'A' column in Table XI relates to the actual situation in the mid 1970s, while the hypothesis 'B' column is an optimistic forecast based on expected technological advances. In particular, progress in

TABLE XII
FORECAST TOTAL WASTE PAPER USAGE

	1978 Paper and Board Breakdown		*1979 Paper and Board Breakdown*	
	Hypothesis "A"	*"B"*	*Hypothesis "A"*	*"B"*
1985	1646	2205	1766	2287
1990	1555	2081	1667	2159
1995	1447	1937	1551	2010
2000	1358	1820	1457	1888

TABLE XIII
FORECAST WASTE PAPER USAGE BY GRADE
(000's tonnes)

	Paper and Board Breakdown 1978		*Paper and Board Breakdown 1979*	
Waste Paper Grade	*"A"*	*"B"*	*"A"*	*"B"*
	1985			
Mixed	643	677	698	743
Corrugated	729	775	775	827
Old News	117	345	125	325
Printers' Waste	101	329	106	310
Kraft	56	79	62	82
	1990			
Mixed	607	638	659	701
Corrugated	689	732	732	781
Old News	111	326	118	307
Printers' Waste	95	310	100	293
Kraft	53	74	58	77
	1995			
Mixed	·565	595	613	653
Corrugated	602	640	639	683
Old News	97	285	103	268
Printers' Waste	83	271	88	256
Kraft	46	65	51	68

de-inking technology was expected to lead to a large increase in middle grade wastepaper inputs into the printing and writing output sector. In the light of the current economic recession hypothesis 'B' must be rated as highly optimistic. Table XII illustrates the forecast total wastepaper usage up to the year 2000 based on the data displayed in Tables IX, X and XI. The results are consistently below the 2.4 m tonnes level predicted by the trend extrapolation method outlined earlier.

The input-output coefficients in Table VII, column D can now be combined with the total wastepaper consumption forecasts in Table XII to give estimated wastepaper usage by grade up to the year 2000 (see Table XIII).

CONCLUSIONS

The future economic fortunes of the UK wastepaper industry will continue to be primarily (though not exclusively) dependent on the general economic health of the UK paper and board industry and in particular on the packaging sector's prospects. Any technological changes likely to stimulate extra demands for wastepaper are unlikely to outweigh the long term effects of the established decline in UK paper and board output, although they may enable the wastepaper industry at least to avoid a significant contraction. Technological advances will allow a certain degree of substitution of input requirements. Some middle and lower grade wastepapers will supplement inputs of higher grade recycled fibres in certain end products. The bulk of the currently unexploited wastepaper resources are to be found in those residuals disposed of via the municipal waste stream. Advances in treatment processes to ameliorate various contamination problems as well as an economic collection system are required before such resources can be fully exploited. Adhesive contaminants remain a difficult problem across many grades of wastepaper. Collection systems involving cooperation between merchants and voluntary groups deserve further experimentation and scrutiny.

Outside the traditional market for wastepaper a wide diversity of potential new outlets for recycled fibres have emerged. The combined capacity of these alternative markets is not very large at the moment. Future growth rates are difficult to predict and paradoxically one promising outlet, refuse derived fuel (RDF) production, might severely hamper the wastepaper industry's traditional business if an extensive network of RDF plants were constructed.

ACCEPTED DECEMBER 1982

R. K. Turner,
University of East Anglia,
School of Environmental Sciences,
University of East Anglia,
Norwich NR4 7.

D. Deadman,
University of Leicester,
Leicester.

REFERENCES

[1] Anon, 'Paper Reclamation Review', *Materials Reclamation* (June 1982) pp. 20–23.

[2] Bridgewater, A. V. and Mumford, C. J., *Waste Recycling and Pollution Control Handbook* (George Godwin Press, London, 1979).

[3] Deadman, D., Grace, R. and Turner, R. K., 'Modelling the UK Wastepaper Market', *Resource Recovery and Conservation*, 3, 4 (December 1978), pp. 237–47.

[4] Economist Intelligence Unit, *The UK Packaging Industry: Its Structure and Suppliers* (Economist Intelligence Unit Ltd., London, 1980).

[5] Edwards, R., 'Price Expectations and the Supply of Wastepaper', *Journal of Environmental Economics and Management*, 6, 4 (December 1970), pp. 332–40.

[6] Fischman, L., *World Mineral Trends and US Supply Problems* (Resources for the Future, Washington, 1980).

[7] Gammie, J. I., *World Timber to the Year 2000*, (Economist Intelligence Unit Ltd., London, 1981).

[8] Gill, G. and Lahiri, K., 'An Econometric Model of Wastepaper Recycling in the USA', *Resources Policy*, 6, 4 (December 1980), pp. 320–25.

[9] Grace, R., Turner, R. K. and Walter, I., 'Secondary Materials and International Trade', *Journal of Environmental Economics and Management*, 5, 2 (June 1978), pp. 172–86.

[10] Grace, R., Turner, R. K. and Walter, I., 'Secondary Materials and International Trade: Reply', *Journal of Environmental Economics and Management*, 6, 3 (September 1979), pp. 204–7.

[11] Massus, M., *Waste Paper in the EEC* (EEC, Brussels, 1974).

[12] OECD, *Waste Paper Recovery: Economic Aspects and Environmental Impacts* (OECD, Paris, 1979).

[13] Pearce, D. W. and Nash, C. A., *The Social Appraisal of Projects* (Macmillan, London, 1981).

[14] Ross, M. and Purcell, A. H., 'Decline of Materials Intensiveness: The US Pulp and Paper Industry', *Resources Policy*, 7, 4 (December 1981), pp. 235–50.

[15] UK Department of the Environment, *War on Waste: A Policy for Reclamation* (HMSO, London, 1974).

[16] UK Department of Industry, *Report of the Committee on Waste Paper Supply* (HMSO, London, 1980).

[17] University of Reading, Centre of Agricultural Strategy, *Strategy for the UK Forest Industry* (University of Reading, Reading, 1980).

[18] Wray, M., *The British Paper Industry: A Study in Structural and Technological Change* (The British Paper and Board Industry Federation, London, 1979).

THE JOURNAL OF INDUSTRIAL ECONOMICS 0022–1821 $2.00
Volume XXXII December 1983 No. 2

BUSINESS CYCLE AND INDUSTRIAL MARKET POWER: AN EMPIRICAL INVESTIGATION FOR WEST GERMAN INDUSTRIES, 1965–1977*

MANFRED NEUMANN, INGO BÖBEL AND ALFRED HAID

I. INTRODUCTION

As implied by the notion of sellers' and buyers' markets, respectively, the effective industrial market power is, to a large extent, determined by the business cycle situation. Sellers are holding a relatively strong position during business cycle upswings and their market power is weakened by recessions. This reasoning suggests that the price-cost margin is apt to rise in response to business cycle upswings in concentrated industries when it may remain constant elsewhere. Conversely, in business cycle downturns the price-cost margin should be expected to decrease in concentrated industries to a larger extent than in less concentrated industries.

The previous literature, however, has been dominated by the view that price-cost margins of highly concentrated industries are less flexible in response to the business cycle compared to those of less concentrated industries. Only recently this view, which is closely connected with G. Means' [7] "administered prices hypothesis", has been challenged by Qualls [12]. He suggested that high concentration facilitates an exchange of information, so that pricing can be more finely tuned to cyclical demand changes and, therefore, that the price-cost margin is more responsive to demand fluctuations. Qualls was able to adduce evidence from the U.S. economy to corroborate his hypothesis.

Concurring with the Qualls hypothesis is the notion that business cycle fluctuations of demand entail shifts of demand giving rise to changes of elasticities relevant for the firms' pricing decisions. Thus a business cycle upswing is deemed to lower the elasticity prevailing at the previous price and consequently gives rise to a higher price-cost margin and vice versa.[1]

To throw some further light on the competing hypotheses and on the related problem of whether concentration conveys monopolistic market power or not, in this paper, the impact of various market structure variables on the price-cost

* We gratefully acknowledge helpful comments on an earlier draft from participants of seminars at the International Institute of Management, Berlin and at the Graduate School of Management, Rutgers University, Newark, New Jersey.

[1] In the framework of an extended Cournot model, for example, the price-cost margin of an industry is given by $m = [(1-\zeta)H + \zeta]/\varepsilon$ where H = Herfindahl index of concentration, ζ = elasticity of conjectural quantity reaction of rivals to a change of the quantity sold by an individual firm, ε = price elasticity of demand of the market. One obtains $\partial m/\partial\varepsilon = -[(1-\zeta)H + \zeta]/\varepsilon^2$. Hence, the impact of a decrease of ε on m is the larger, the higher H.

margin during the business cycle shall be investigated for West German manufacturing industries during the thirteen years period 1965–77. This time-span comprises three recessions (1967, 1971, 1975) and four business cycle upswings (1965, 1970, 1973, 1976).

Of particular interest will be the possibility of analyzing the interaction of international influences on competition in national markets (for a literature survey see Caves [2]). Hereby we address the question first investigated by Schwartzman [13] and the Espositos [5]—how effectively does import competition influence the exercise of market power. To isolate the explanatory power of domestic market power variables we also investigate the influence of export opportunities on profitability during the business cycle.

In section II we shall outline the basic model which is an extended version of our previous work [8]. Finally, in section III, the basic model is applied year by year in order to investigate the impact of the respective business cycle situation (boom vs. recession) on the various coefficients of regression.

II. THE BASIC MODEL

In the empirical analysis we start out with the standard structure-performance model in order to identify the determinants of profitability over the time-span 1965–77. Because of our theoretical considerations we expect a positive relationship between the price-cost margin and the degree of sellers' concentration.

The study pertains to 283 joint stock companies of West German manufacturing industry. The total number of firms was determined by the availability of data for the entire time-span under consideration.

Let the price-cost margin be the difference between total revenue and current expenses for labour and raw material inputs divided by equity capital. The dependent variable (P) can then be considered as an approximation to the "Lerner-index" of monopoly power normalized by the ratio of sales to equity.

The basic profit equation is given by

$$P = f(C3, EX, IM, VI, CART, PD, RISK, S, G, LEV)$$

where C3 = three-firm concentration ratio

EX = export ratio

IM = import ratio

VI = degree of vertical integration

CART = cartelization

PD = product differentiation

RISK = risk bearing

S = size of the firm

G = rate of growth of sales

LEV = leverage.

Detailed definitions are given in the appendix.

The regression coefficients, according to an OLS-estimation, and the respective t-ratios pertaining to the entire time span are given in Table I. More than 50% of the variance of the price-cost margin can be accounted for by the explanatory variables. The results generally confirm the findings of our previous study [8] covering the time period 1965–72. In particular, the domestic degree of concentration exerts a fairly strong favourable influence on profitability. The same obtains for vertical integration and cartelization although the impact of cartels does not, appear to be statistically significant over the entire span.[2] The positive influence of the rate of growth of the sales variable on the price-cost margin which can be interpreted as the rate of growth of demand means that it is easier for firms with high growth to utilize economies of size and therefore profits increase.

The size variable bears a negative sign. This is probably not surprising as firms with increasing size typically try to increase the degree of diversification to reduce risk. As a result the expected value of profits of larger firms could be lower. Larger firms usually pay higher wages compared to

TABLE I
DETERMINANTS OF THE PRICE-COST MARGIN IN WEST GERMAN INDUSTRIES 1965–1977

Explanatory Variables		*Regression Coefficient (OLS)*	*t-Ratio*
3-Firm Concentration		0.6451×10^{-2}	2.90
Export Ratio		−1.216	5.05
Import Ratio		−0.4866	2.29
Vertical Integration		0.6084	7.32
Cartelization		0.2071×10^{-4}	0.22
Product Differentiation		0.2678	2.31
Risk[a]	Variance	0.1896	4.69
	Covariance	11.77	2.89
Size of Firm		−0.0465	2.57
Rate of Growth of Sales of the Firm		1.745	3.21
Leverage		1.632	8.57
Coefficient of Determination (R^2) 0.5293			

[a] Variance in the case of 72 big firms, covariance in the case of 211 smaller firms (for an explanation see Neumann, Böbel, Haid [8]).

[2] Cartelization, however, exerted a statistically significant influence in some single years.

smaller or medium sized firms. This could also reduce firms' profitability. Finally, increasing firm size might be a sign of a higher degree of X-inefficiency which in turn reduces profits.

On the other hand, the price-cost margin is adversely affected by exports and imports. Both variables are considered as indicators of foreign competition. This interpretation is obvious in the case of imports (for a theoretical discussion see White, [14] for an interpretation of the empirical results see Neumann, Böbel and Haid [8]; Caves [1]; Jacquemin, de Ghellinck and Huveneers [6]; Pugel [11]; Caves, Porter and Spence [4]). The higher the import ratio of an industry the higher—*ceteris paribus*—the degree of competition in that industry and the lower profitability. The influence of export opportunities on the price-cost margin is much less straightforward than that of import competition and therefore a few interpreting remarks are in order. First, domestic firms may have been supplanted from their traditional markets by increased foreign competition entailed by the enlargement of markets, especially during the more recent development of the EEC. The necessity of survival forced domestic firms to increase their export activities.[3] So, upon this interpretation, export ratios reflect the intensity of foreign competition.[4] Second, German firms may have autonomously intensified their export activities in order to exploit profit opportunities entailed by a technical lead and other comparative advantages. The single firm does not normally expect that its own activities will considerably affect world market prices. Since generally, however, many firms and not only firms from one country act in response to perceived profit opportunities, actual profits may be lower than those envisaged initially. In this case, too, the export ratio reflects the degree of competition. Finally, it should be noticed that the adverse influence of exports on actual profitability does not imply that exporting firms are incurring losses. Exports can be profitable although the ratio of profits to equity is lower in competitive sectors than in those sectors which are more protected from outside competition (see Caves [1]; Caves and Khalilzadeh-Shirazi [3]; Jacquemin, de Ghellinck and Huveneers [6]; Neumann, Böbel and Haid [8]; Pugel [10]).[5]

III. CONCENTRATION AND BUSINESS CYCLE

In order to delineate how the impact of the various explanatory variables on the price-cost margin are affected by the business cycle, we applied the basic model year by year to the respective data. In doing that we encountered several problems. First, for the concentration variable, only data for selected

[3] The export ratio increased from 17% in 1965 to approximately 30% in 1977.

[4] If one compares columns 9 and 10 in Table II it seems that the increase of the export ratios is leading against the increase of the import ratios over the entire time span.

[5] A comparison of the development of the concentration ratio (column 10) and foreign trade (columns 11 and 12) seems to indicate that the intensity of competition during the 13 years period has rather increased than decreased.

years were available. We therefore had to adjoin the published data to the subsequent years until new data came up. Second, some of the variables, i.e. risk and the rate of growth of sales, have been defined in such a way that only a figure covering the whole time span makes sense. Thus, these variables entered the regression with a single value for all years. Third, the basic model, as outlined in Section II, pertained to averages over 1965–77. Averaging was done in order to eliminate a lot of accidental facts. If we now return to a year by year analysis a considerable amount of noise is coming back which will lower the explanatory power of the model for the individual years.

The result was that a clear business cycle pattern only emerged for concentration, exports, imports, vertical integration, and size. The annual coefficients for these variables are listed in Table II where also the coefficients of determination are given. In order to depict the business cycle in West Germany annual rates of change of Gross National Product in constant prices and rates of change of the index of domestic prices of manufacturing industry are given. The phasing of the business cycle would be the same if instead of GNP the rates of change of production of manufacturing industry had been used. In Table II, additionally, the average rates of domestic concentration (unweighted) and average (across industries) export and import ratios are listed.

As can be seen from Table II, concentration has a particularly favourable impact on the price-cost margin during business cycle upswings which occurred during 1965, 1970, 1973 and 1976. Its influence is less favourable during recessions, i.e., in 1967, 1971 and 1975. Notice, moreover, that, with the exception of 1976, the coefficient of regression of concentration attained its respective maximum value only in the second or even a later year of business cycle expansion when normally price increases tend to dominate expansion of output.

To test whether or not the impact of concentration on the price-cost margin is significantly related to the business cycle we computed correlation coefficients which are given in Table III. Apparently, the *t*-test ratios of the regression coefficients of C3 are significantly related to the rate of change of GNP and also to the rate of change of the price index, provided the extremely inflationary year 1974 is excluded. On the other hand, the size of the regression coefficient of C3, although positively associated with the business cycle situation, does not seem to be significantly determined by the business cycle. Hence we may conclude that concentration does appear to convey monopolistic market power. It remains open, however, to what extent that is the case.

Imports exerted a significantly adverse influence on the price-cost margin primarily during recessions. The impact of imports was less significant during boom periods. Since the import ratio itself did not display a clear cyclical pattern the following inference appears to be obvious: During business cycle upswings concentration of domestic production enabled producers to exercise

TABLE II
MARKET POWER DURING THE BUSINESS CYCLE

Year	Coefficients of Regression[a]						Annual Percentage Rates of Change of		Average Values		
	C3[b]	EX	IM	VI	S	R^b	GNP[c]	Price[d]	C3	EX	IM
1965	1.12	−0.64	−0.21	0.90	−0.06	0.56	5.5	2.4	22.4	0.174	0.128
	(3.3)	(1.6)	(0.7)	(7.9)	(2.4)						
1966	0.71	−0.84	−0.23	0.81	−0.05	0.73	2.5	1.8		0.188	0.129
	(2.2)	(2.3)	(0.8)	(7.5)	(2.1)						
1967	0.23	−0.76	−0.56	0.90	−0.03	0.43	−0.1	−1.1	21.7	0.207	0.127
	(0.7)	(2.2)	(1.8)	(8.2)	(1.1)						
1968	0.53	−0.79	−0.21	0.78	−0.08	0.54	6.5	−0.9		0.226	0.148
	(2.3)	(3.1)	(1.0)	(9.8)	(0.4)						
1969	0.69	−1.03	−0.45	0.64	−0.02	0.52	7.9	2.0	23.5	0.223	0.157
	(3.0)	(3.9)	(2.0)	(7.8)	(0.9)						
1970	0.76	−1.04	−0.31	0.80	−0.06	0.48	5.9	5.0		0.215	0.158
	(2.5)	(3.2)	(1.0)	(8.5)	(2.6)						
1971	0.73	−1.06	−0.80	0.92	−0.04	0.47	3.3	4.2	24.2	0.220	0.160
	(2.5)	(3.3)	(2.2)	(9.2)	(1.8)						
1972	0.55	−0.79	−1.01	0.79	−1.0	0.45	3.6	2.3		0.228	0.166
	(1.8)	(2.6)	(2.7)	(7.5)	(4.0)						
1973	1.01	−1.39	−0.58	0.74	−0.03	0.42	4.9	6.8	23.2	0.246	0.167
	(3.7)	(4.5)	(1.7)	(6.9)	(1.4)						
1974	0.68	−1.05	0.01	0.51	−0.10	0.24	0.4	13.3		0.281	0.184
	(1.9)	(2.7)	(0.0)	(3.6)	(3.2)						
1975	0.53	−1.30	−0.69	0.73	−0.04	0.34	−1.8	3.3	23.2	0.268	0.187
	(1.8)	(3.7)	(2.5)	(6.2)	(1.6)						
1976	0.99	−0.45	−0.39	0.71	−0.04	0.32	5.3	3.5		0.321	0.234
	(3.6)	(1.6)	(1.9)	(6.5)	(1.6)						
1977	0.55	−1.96	−0.32	0.52	−0.01	0.67	2.6	2.8		0.287	0.211
	(1.2)	(3.5)	(0.9)	(2.8)	(0.2)						

[a] Legend: C3 = concentration, Ex = export ratio, IM = import ratio, VI = vertical integration, S = firm size.
[b] Times 10^{-2}. [c] GNP at prices of 1970. [d] Index of domestic prices of manufacturing industries.

TABLE III
IMPACT OF CONCENTRATION ON THE PRICE-COST MARGIN AS RELATED TO THE BUSINESS CYCLE: CORRELATION MATRIX FOR 1965–1977 (*t*-ratios in parentheses)

	Rate of change of		
	GNP	*Price Index*	*excluding* 1974
Regression coefficient of C3	0.246 (0.85)	0.125 (0.43)	0.322 (1.07)
t-ratio of regression coefficient of C3	0.674 (2.33)	0.205 (0.70)	0.563 (1.87)

market power because excess demand is giving rise to sellers' markets. Imports did not rise to such an extent that domestic market power could have been checked. In recessions, however, imports contributed to excess supply and thus effectively diluted market power entailed by domestic concentration. This finding supports the hypothesis that concentration reflects market power. Concentration seems to have to no small extent engendered price increases in the more concentrated sectors during business cycle upswings. Generally an increase of the import ratio entailed an adverse impact on the price-cost margin (1969, 1972, 1973).

Exports appear as leading against imports. Exports rose in 1967/68 and again in 1973/74 followed by imports in 1968/69 and in 1974/75, respectively. In both cases the adverse impact of exports increased and became quite pronounced after imports had caught up. In the most recent business cycle upturn considered in the present investigation, export and import ratios increased simultaneously. The adverse influence of exports on the price-cost margin became visible only after the rate of expansion began slowing down in 1977.[6]

Vertical integration appears to exert the most favourable influence on the price-cost margin in recessions. This finding contradicts the hypothesis that vertical integration is a means of securing supplies of inputs at reasonable prices when shortages of inputs are arising and monopoly power of suppliers is most effective. In view of the present findings vertical integration seems primarily to be used, first, to secure a higher degree of utilization of plants in the case of backward integration, and, second, to exploit vertical integration as a means to lower risk insofar as it simultaneously constitutes a diversification of operations.

[6] A similar interpretation of the inverse relationship between price-cost margins and export ratios (as well as import ratios) for a sample of European countries has been put forward by Pagoulatos and Sorensen [9].

This interpretation seems to be confirmed by the varying impact of size on the price-cost margin. Size generally exerts an unfavourable influence on profitability. The impact is, however, relatively weak during recessions. Since large firms are usually more diversified than smaller ones the influence of size on the price-cost margin can, at least to some extent, be taken to reflect the superior capability of diversified firms to stand the strains entailed by recessions.

IV. SUMMARY

In our study we come up with two interesting results:

(1) In contrast to the conventional view that the price-cost margin is less responsive to cyclical demand variability in high concentrated industries we found that price-cost margins increased during business cycle upswings and decreased during recessions.

(2) A given degree of domestic concentration brings about a higher degree of market power during business cycle upswings (= sellers' market) compared to times of lower economic activity (buyers' market) when market power is reduced in particular by increased import competition.

Manfred Neumann,
Volkswirtschaftliches Institut,
Universität Erlangen-Nürnberg,
P.O. Box 3931,
D-8500 Nürnberg 1,
West Germany.

ACCEPTED JUNE 1982

APPENDIX

Definition of Variables:

Price-cost margin: (Total revenue—current expenses for labour and raw materials) over equity capital (including reserves).

Concentration: Three-firm concentration ratio.

Export ratio: Exports of commodities of the industry over total sales of the industry.

Import ratio: Imports of commodities of the industry over total sales of the industry.

Vertical integration: Ratio of value added over sales of the firm divided by the ratio of value added over sales of the respective industry.

Cartelization: Number of cartels (excluding pure export cartels) registered with the Federal Cartel Office over sales of the industry (times 1 mio. DM for normalization).

Product differentiation: Number of trade marks registered by the firm with the German Patent Office over equity capital.

Risk: Trend free variance and covariance (with profits of all West German firms) of profits as defined above.

Size of the firm: Natural logarithm of total value of assets.

Rate of growth of sales of the firm: Slope of exponential time trend of sales of the firm for 1965–1977.

Leverage: Debt/equity plus debt ratio.

REFERENCES

[1] CAVES, R. E., "International Trade and Industrial Organization: Introduction. Symposium on International Trade and Industrial Organization", *Journal of Industrial Economics*, 29, 2 (December 1980), pp. 113–18.

[2] CAVES, R. E., "International Cartels and Monopolies in International Trade", in: *International Economic Policy: Theory and Evidence*, ed. R. Dornbusch and J. A. Frenkel (Johns Hopkins University Press, Baltimore and London, 1979) pp. 39–73.

[3] CAVES, R. E., and KHALILZADEH-SHIRAZI, J., "International Trade and Industrial Organization: Some Statistical Evidence", in *Welfare Aspects of Industrial Markets*, ed. A. Jacquemin and H. W. de Jong (Martinus Nijhoff Social Sciences Division, Leiden, 1977), pp. 111–28.

[4] CAVES, R. E., PORTER, M. E., and SPENCE, M. A., *Competition in the Open Economy: A Model Applied to Canada*. (Harvard University Press, Cambridge, 1980).

[5] ESPOSITO, L., and ESPOSITO, F. F., "Foreign Competition and Domestic Industry Profitability", *Review of Economics and Statistics 53*, 4 (November 1971), pp. 343–53.

[6] JACQUEMIN, A., DE GHELLINCK, E., and HUVENEERS, CH., "Concentration and Profitability in a Small Open Economy", *Journal of Industrial Economics*, 29, 2 (December 1980), pp. 131–44.

[7] MEANS, G., U. S. Congress, Senate, "Subcommittee on Antitrust and Monopoly Hearings, Economic Concentration, Part I", 89th Congress, Ist Session (1964).

[8] NEUMANN, M., BÖBEL, I., and HAID, A., "Profitability, Risk and Market Structure in West German Industries", *Journal of Industrial Economics*, 27, 3 (March 1979), pp. 227–42.

[9] PAGOULATOS, E., and SORENSEN, R., "Foreign Trade, Concentration and Profitability in Open Economies", *European Economic Review* 8 (1976), pp. 255–67.

[10] PUGEL, T. A., *International Market Linkages and U.S. Manufacturing* (Ballinger, Cambridge MA, 1978).

[11] PUGEL, T. A., "Foreign Trade and U.S. Market Performance", *Journal of Industrial Economics*, 29, 2 (December 1980), pp. 119–30.

[12] QUALLS, P. D., "Market Structure and the Cyclical Flexibility of Price-Cost Margins", *Journal of Business*, 52, 2 (April 1979), pp. 305–25.

[13] SCHWARTZMAN, D., "The Effect of Monopoly on Price", *Journal of Political Economy*, 67, 4 (August 1959), pp. 352–62.

[14] WHITE, L. J., "Industrial Organization and International Trade: Some Theoretical Considerations", *American Economic Review*, 64, 6 (December 1974), pp. 1013–20.

DATA SOURCES

1. Bayerische Hypotheken-und Wechselbank (Hrsg.), Wegweiser durch dutsche Aktiengesellschaften, versch. Jahrgänge 1965–1978, München (1966–1979).
2. Bundeskartellamt, Bericht des Bundeskartellamtes über seine Tätigkeit im Jahr 1973 sowie über die Lage und Entwicklung auf seinem Arbeitsgebiet (§ 50 GWB), Bundestagsdrucksache 7/2250, Bonn (1974).
3. Monopolkommission, Hauptgutachten 1976/77, Fortschreitende Konzentration bei Großunternehmen, Baden-Baden (1978); darin: Gutachten im Auftrage der Monopolkommission erstellt vom Deutschen Institut für Wirtschaftsforschung (DIW), Konzentration und industrielle Entwicklung, S. 579–659.
4. Verlag Hoppenstedt (ed.), Börsenführer—Stock Guide, Darmstadt (1976 bzw. 1977).

THE JOURNAL OF INDUSTRIAL ECONOMICS 0022–1821 $2.00
Volume XXXII December 1983 No. 2

CONGLOMERATE PERFORMANCE OVER THE ECONOMIC CYCLE

C. W. L. HILL*

I. INTRODUCTION

THE economic efficiency aspects of conglomerate mergers have taken on a degree of importance which is not attached to the economic efficiency aspects of non-conglomerate mergers. As the Monopolies Commission noted in its "General Observations on Mergers" [9], this is because a "pure" conglomerate merger, which by definition does not have any immediately observable effect on industry structure, cannot be assessed with respect to its effects on competitive markets in the same way as other types of merger can. There have been several attempts to assess the long term effects of conglomerate entry on industry structure, notably by Utton [15] and Kelly [5] in the UK, and by Goldberg [4], Rhodes [12], and Berry [1] in the USA, but, as these authors would be the first to admit, their conclusions are both tenuous, given the paucity of the data with which they have had to work, and somewhat contradictory between studies.

However, all is not lost, for it is possible to assess a "pure" conglomerate merger with respect to its expected effects on the efficiency with which resources will be used. A number of studies have looked at the comparative performance of conglomerate and non-conglomerate concerns in an attempt to establish just what the effects of conglomeration are on enterprise performance and, by extension, economic efficiency. In the UK, studies by Utton [14], Econtel [3] and Kumps [6] have all compared the performance of conglomerate and non-conglomerate concerns over a given time period. While Utton found no difference between the performance of two such groups, both Econtel and Kumps did find significant evidence that conglomerates outperformed non-conglomerates. So in the UK the balance of the evidence to date would seem to indicate that conglomerates perform at least as well, if not a little better, than non-conglomerate concerns.

In the USA too, a number of studies have come out in favour of conglomerate firms. Most important of these studies are those by Weston and Mansinghka [16] and Weston, Smith and Shrieves [17]. But as Mueller [10] has argued, these analyses may be flawed given that they focus on the performance of conglomerate firms during the boom period of the 1960s. Mueller believes that the real test of conglomerate performance is not how

* Acknowledgements: Thanks to my supervisor Professor John Pickering for careful guidance and helpful comments.

they perform during the upswing of an economic cycle, when they may be engaged in making frequent acquisitions, but how they perform over the whole economic cycle.

Some preliminary American evidence on this point has been reported by Reid [11] and Melicher and Rush [8]. Reid found that the stocks of a sample of American conglomerates performed less well than the stocks of an equivalent sample of non-conglomerate concerns during the initial phase of the collapse of the 1960s American stock market boom. Melicher and Rush found that the rate of return on conglomerate stocks was significantly higher than that earned on a group of non-conglomerate stocks for the boom period of June 1966 to February 1969, but for the slump period of March 1969 to December 1971 the conglomerates rate of return was significantly lower. Over the entire period the return earned on the two sets of stocks was nearly equal.

There is a suggestion in Melicher and Rush's work then that the performance of conglomerate firms is more volatile than that of non-conglomerates over the whole of the economic cycle. The aim of this study is to try to determine if this was also the case for a sample of British conglomerates over a well defined economic cycle. Below we examine the performance of a sample of conglomerates over the British economic cycle of the early 1970s and compare this against the performance of two different categories of non-conglomerate firms over the same period.

II. HYPOTHESES

There are a number of theories that can be advanced as to why the performances of conglomerate firms may be more volatile than that of non-conglomerate firms over the whole of an economic cycle. They are as follows:

(1) As Lintner [7] has pointed out, a somewhat suspect type of financial synergy occurs when a conglomerate acquires a firm with a lower price/earnings ratio than its own. In such cases the market often evaluates the combined earnings of the two firms at the higher P/E ratio of the conglomerate, rather than applying the weighted average of the two P/E ratios, thus producing an instantaneous capital gain and an over-valuation of the shares of the company involved. It therefore follows that conglomerate growth, based upon acquisitions, and utilizing the tool of different P/E ratios to obtain this end, necessitates, in the absence of any tangible "organic growth", further acquisitions in order to maintain the illusion of steady earnings growth. Once a firm embarks upon such a strategy it can become dependent upon acquisitions to keep its P/E ratio high. In times of general stock market advance a firm can happily pursue such a strategy, but this will not be the case during the downturn when its declining P/E ratio will make acquisitions more

difficult. Given that it is the conglomerate's rate of growth which gives the impression of earnings growth in the first place, clearly the earnings of the conglomerates will appear to decline further than those of non-conglomerates during the downturn, thus producing a more volatile pattern over the whole cycle.

(2) Conversely, it is possible that the conglomerate may fund its acquisitions by borrowings rather than, or in addition to, issuing its own paper. This is important as in the early 1970s the economic downturn was accompanied by a sharp increase in interest rates leading to an increase in the level of interest payments, both in absolute terms, and in relation to profits as they turned down in the slump. Hence if conglomerates were more dependent upon borrowings than non-conglomerates, then their performance may have declined more rapidly during the downturn due to their extra burden of interest payments.

(3) A further possibility is that during the upswing of the cycle, when the conglomerate is making frequent acquisitions, it may be able to maintain the illusion of good performance by indulging in "window dressing", (i.e. by selling or rearranging recently acquired assets to show extra paper profits). During the downswing of course, a fall in the rate of new acquisitions will result in a reduction in the opportunities for selling off or rearranging assets to boost profit figures.

(4) Finally, the conglomerates' lack of any obvious "industrial logic' may adversely affect their performance. Now it may be a relatively easy matter to manage a number of unrelated activities during boom conditions. In such circumstances the philosophy of management by exception could successfully be put into practice by a small central management team. However, during a general downturn in economic activity of the scale that occurred in the UK after 1973 for example, a small central management team may find itself unable to deal effectively with the problems that may simultaneously occur in a large proportion of its unrelated activities. Thus for managerial reasons too, the performance of conglomerates may deteriorate further, relative to the performance of non-conglomerates, during the downswing.

What then would we expect of the performance of non-conglomerates over the economic cycle? Here we must recognize that "non-conglomerate firms" are by no means a homogeneous set of enterprises. On the contrary, as Channon [2] has shown, there are a number of different strategic postures which large firms may adopt with respect to diversification and, as Rumlet [13] has demonstrated for large American firms, these differences in strategy are related to differences in enterprise performance. In this study the non-conglomerate firms have been divided into two categories. First, the concentric diversifiers and secondly, single industry and closely related firms.

The difference between conglomerate and concentric diversifiers is to be found in the logic of the diversification move. Whereas conglomerates have diversified into unrelated areas, concentric firms have diversified into areas which are related to each other by either marketing or technological links. This difference of approach may affect performance in two ways. First, because the concentric firms knows something about the industry into which it is diversifying it may make better judged diversification moves than a conglomerate, giving such a move a subsequently greater chance of success. Secondly, the thread of industrial logic which runs through the activities of a concentric firm may mean that the central management of such an organisation is better able to understand, anticipate and cope with the problems which may be faced by diversified subsidiaries in a slump. Thus for the above reasons the performance of concentric firms may be more stable over the slump.

Closely related firms are those which have diversified primarily into areas which are related to each other by both marketing and technological links. Together with single industry firms the performance of such enterprises is more difficult to predict over the whole cycle precisely because their fortunes are linked to the fortunes of a number of closely related activities or a single activity. Other things being equal, such firms are more likely to have market power than similar sized concentric or conglomerate firms. But whereas such market power may mean greater profits during the upswing of an economic cycle, this may or may not be the case during the downturn depending upon the vulnerability of the narrow industrial base upon which such firms are dependent in a recession.

III. THE PERIOD OF ANALYSIS

The time period on which we are focusing here is 1970 to 1976. As Table I shows, during this period the British economy went through a well defined

TABLE I
INDEX OF INDUSTRIAL PRODUCTION, FT INDEX AND NO. OF MERGERS PER YEAR, 1970–76

Year	*Index of Industrial Production*	*FT Index*	*No. of Mergers*
1970	99.7	361.0	793
1971	99.8	386.2	884
1972	102.0	503.8	1210
1973	109.5	435.6	1205
1974	105.1	251.2	503
1975	100.0	311.0	315
1976	102.0	368.0	353

Sources: Index of Industrial Production, Economic Trends, Annual Supplement, 1979 Edition, HMSO: FT Index, Financial Statistics, CSO, HMSO: No. of Mergers, Business Monitor NQ7, Acquisitions and Mergers of Industrial and Commercial Companies, HMSO.

economic cycle, with boom conditions from 1970–73 and slump conditions thereafter with a small recovery beginning in 1976.

It is of some interest to note that the stock market boom, according to the FT Index, peaked in 1972, while the index of industrial production, which is a more suitable indicator of the general economic cycle, did not peak until 1973. Furthermore, while the FT Index bottomed out in 1974, the index of industrial production shows that the more general slump in the economy reached its lowest point in 1975. Whatever the reason for this difference, and one could argue that the pattern shows that the stock market was merely anticipating future changes in economic activity, it would be as well to keep it in mind although it does not unduly complicate the analysis.

IV. THE SAMPLE

The sample consists of 60 firms selected from the top 300 firms ranked by turnover as listed in the Times 1000 for 1974/75, (which is based upon 1973/74 company figures, the middle years of the sample period). The 60 firms comprise 20 conglomerates, 20 concentric diversifiers and 20 single industry and closely related firms. The sample size was determined by the fact that it was possible to identify with absolute certainty only 20 conglomerates amongst the top 300. Two equally sized samples of the other two categories were then selected at random from the remaining firms in the population that could be classified. A list of firms in each category is given in Appendix I. There is, it should be noted, no industry basis to these groupings. Indeed, to use an industry classification here would have been inappropriate given both the diversity of the conglomerates and of many of the concentric firms which, in spite of the logic behind their diversification moves, are often active in several different end markets. Furthermore, to compare conglomerates, which by definition are active in a number of industries, with single and closely related firms drawn from a particular industry would be incorrect in so far as it would not be comparing like with like.

The firms in the population were classified into one of the above categories on the basis of an analysis of the breakdown of company sales, published in company annual accounts and summarized on EXTEL record cards. The first step in this process was to calculate the following ratios for each of the firms in 1973.

LSBR – The largest single business ratio, defined as the proportion of sales concentrated in the largest single identifiable area of the firm's activities.

RR – The related ratio, defined as the proportion of the firm's total sales concentrated in activities which are related to the LSBR of the firm by *both* marketing and technological links. Vertically integrated operations were also included here.

CR — The concentric ratio, defined as the proportion of a firm's activities related to the largest single business or related activities of the firm by *either* marketing *or* technological links.

UR — The unrelated ratio, defined as the proportion of a firm's total sales which are unrelated to either the largest single business or related activities of the firm by either marketing or technological links.

The next step was to classify those firms for which the above ratios would be worked out into one of the three categories given below on the basis of the following decision rules.

Conglomerates—firms for which the LSBR + RR is less than 0.4 and UR is greater than 0.4.

Concentric Diversifiers—firms for which LSBR + RR is less than 0.6 and UR is less than 0.2., so CR is greater than 0.2.

Closely Related and Single Industry Firms—firms for which LSBR is greater than 0.8 or LSBR + RR is greater than 0.9.

As Table II shows, the effect of these decision rules was to isolate three distinct categories with respect to diversification. The decision rules also had

TABLE II
THE AVERAGE PROPORTION OF TURNOVER IN EACH OF THE SPECIFIC RATIOS FOR EACH OF THE STRATEGIC CATEGORIES

Type of Firm	*LSBR + RR*	*CR*	*UR*	*Number*
Conglomerates	0.37	0.09	0.5	20
Concentric Diversifiers	0.49	0.42	0.09	20
Single and Closely Related	0.94	0.04	0.02	20

the additional effect of eliminating those firms whose position with respect to the above categories was somewhat questionable. The Imperial Group for example, had an LSBR + RR value of 0.65 and a UR value of 0.35 in 1973 and was thus still clearly dependent upon one business, the tobacco business, while at the same time having adopted a strategy of conglomerate diversification. Imperial is thus an example of a firm in the process of strategic change and given that it was neither a conglomerate, nor a single industry firm, it was eliminated from the analysis on the basis of the above decision rules. The end result of this screening process is that the firms which remained in the sample were all "pure" examples of their types.

V. THE FINANCIAL VARIABLES

The following variables were included in the analysis.

ROS — Return on sales, defined as gross profit over sales.

ROK	–	Return on capital employed, defined as profit before tax, but after interest payments, over capital employed at the beginning of the year.
GSALES	–	Growth of sales, estimated as the percentage change in sales for the period under examination.
GINCOME	–	Growth of income, estimated as the percentage change in income for the period under examination.
TC	–	Ratio of times interest payments are covered, defined as gross profit over interest payments.
PHi	–	Highest stock market share price in calendar year "i".
PLi	–	Lowest stock market share price in calendar year "i".
PAi	–	Average stock market price in calendar year "i", defined as (PHi + PLi)/2.
EPSi	–	Earnings per share in calendar year "i".
Pi/Ei	–	Price/earnings ratio for year "i", defined as PAi/EPSi.

The source of all the financial information was EXTEL. The problem of different accounting periods was dealt with by classifying financial information into the calendar year covered by the bulk of the accounting period. In practice most accounting periods ended in either the fourth quarter of the year or the first quarter, so the distortion introduced into the analysis by different accounting periods should not have been too great.

VI. THE ANALYSIS

i. *The volatility of conglomerate and non-conglomerate performance* A glance at Figure 1, which illustrates the mean return on sales earned by each of the

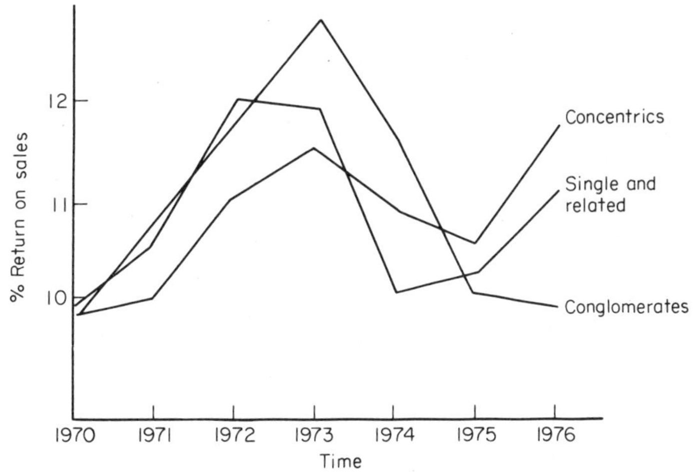

FIGURE 1
Return on sales 1970–76

three categories for the seven year period under observation, bears out, in an unsophisticated sense, the prediction that the performance of conglomerate firms will be more volatile over the whole economic cycle than that of non-conglomerates.

Starting with similar profit margins of around 10% in 1970, the position changed during the boom years so that by 1973 the conglomerates were getting an average return on sales of around 12.8%, as against 12% earned by single and closely related firms and the 11.6% earned by concentric diversifiers. Three years and a slump later however, in 1976, the situation had been effectively reversed, with the conglomerates getting a 10.1% return on sales, as against 11.2% earned by single industry and closely related firms and the 11.8% earned by concentric diversifiers.

In no one year however were the observable differences between the average returns on sales statistically significant. This is hardly surprising given the variance of earnings within such small groups. Nevertheless, the results are indicative of a trend and if we look at the relative changes in the returns earned on sales by the different categories over this period, rather than the absolute values registered, which is after all the real test of volatility, then we do get statistically significant results, which are summarised in Table III.

Table III shows that by 1973 the margins with which the conglomerates were operating were, on average, 38.7% higher than they had been in 1970, whereas single industry and closely related firms only managed to widen their margins by 20.3% and concentric firms by only 17.6%. The differences were significant at the 10% level. During the slump period of 1973–75 however, the size of conglomerate margins fell, so that by 1975 they were achieving an average return on sales of 20.5% less than the return earned in 1973. For the other two groups, and especially the concentric diversifiers the falls were much less and the differences between the group means are

Table III
The Mean Percentage Change in ROS and ROK 1970–73, 1973–75, 1973–76

% change ROS(ii)	*Single and Closely Related*	*Concentric*	*Conglomerate*	*F-Ratio*(i)
1970–73	+20.3%	+17.6%	+38.7%	3.09*
1973–75	−13.1%	−5.3%	−20.5%	4.46**
1973–76	−10.1%	+9.0%	−19.2%	9.29***
% change ROK(iii)				
1970–73	+39.4%	+29.2%	+24.0%	0.54 n/s
1973–75	−5.1%	+5.9%	−19.1%	3.31**
1973–76	+5.2%	+20.8%	−5.0%	2.64*

Notes: (i) Significance level * = 10%, ** = 5%, *** = 1%, n/s = not significant (ii) % change ROS for 19800-73 calculated as ROS73/ROS70 × 100, for 19733-75 as ROS75/ROS73 × 100, 19733-76 as ROS76/ROS73 × 100 (iii) % change ROK calculated in same manner as percentage change ROS.

significant at the 5% level. It is also of considerable interest to note that during the third time period, 1973–76, which included the initial phase of recovery in 1976, the performance of the concentric diversifiers improved so much as to give them a positive rating for the period as a whole, while the margins of the conglomerates were still, on average, 19.2% lower than they had been in 1973. The inter-group differences for 1973–76 were significant at the 1% level.

A similar analysis was also carried out on the return on capital employed earned by the three categories for the period in question. The results of this analysis are also given in Table III. This time the results are statistically significant only for the slump periods of 1973–75 and 1973–76. Nevertheless, these significant results do reinforce the conclusion of the ROS analysis that during the slump the earnings of the conglomerates deteriorated further, relative to those of other categories, and that the conglomerates also appeared to suffer from the effects of the slump for a longer period. Thus by 1975 the return on capital employed earned by the conglomerates was 19% lower than that earned in 1973, while the single industry firms had experienced a fall of only 5% and the concentric diversifiers had actually increased the return they earned on capital employed by 6%. Furthermore, by 1976 the ROK earned by the conglomerates was still below its 1973 value, while the returns earned by the non-conglomerate categories were above their 1973 values. A word of caution though, the ROK figures may be distorted by the continued use during this period of historic accounting methods to value capital employed despite high inflation. Thus there would have been a nominal increase in ROK in any event. In addition, it may be that conglomerates, being more of a financial phenomenon, revalue their assets more frequently. This might explain why, for example, the conglomerates' performance was relatively poor on the capital employed measure for 1970–73, while it was relatively good on the ROS measure during the same period.

Similar analyses to the above were also undertaken with respect to GSALES and GINCOME, but no significant differences were found. The finding of no significant difference between the growth of conglomerate and non-conglomerate sales during the boom period of 1970–73 is one that goes against the common expectation that conglomerates will have a greater merger rate than non-conglomerates and therefore grow faster. On the other hand, between 1971–72, when the merger boom was racing towards its peak, a significant difference was observed. Between these two years the conglomerates' sales grew by 29%, those of the single and closely related firms by 19% and those of the concentric diversifiers by 15%. With an F-Ratio of 3.37 the differences were significant at the 5% level. Thus the evidence as to whether conglomerates grow somewhat faster than non-conglomerates during the upswing is somewhat ambiguous.

Overall however, on the basis of the evidence reviewed so far, it would

TABLE IV
MEAN PERFORMANCE 1970 TO 1976

Measure	*Single and Closely Related*	*Concentric*	*Conglomerate*	*F-Ratio*[(i)]
ROS	11.0	10.9	11.1	0.004 n/s
ROK	16.0	14.8	14.4	0.57 n/s
GSALES	+339%	+304%	+339%	0.56 n/s
GINCOME	+361%	+392%	+378%	0.13 n/s

Notes: (i) n/s = not significant.

seem that the performance of conglomerate firms is more volatile over the whole cycle, with the significant evidence being that the return on sales earned by the conglomerates is subject to greater improvement during the upswing, but that during the downswing the return earned by the conglomerates on both sales and capital employed deteriorates further relative to the returns earned by non-conglomerate concerns. Furthermore, on both the ROS and ROK measures the performance of the concentric diversifiers was the least volatile of all.

ii. *Comparative performance over the whole cycle* Given that the above analysis presents strong evidence in support of the proposition that the performance of conglomerate firms is more volatile over the whole cycle, the question now arises as to whether there is any difference between the performance of the various categories averaged out over the whole period. Table IV, which gives the results of such an analysis, shows that this was not the case.

This conclusion is in agreement with the work of Melicher and Rush [8] who also examined performance over the whole cycle.

iii. *The burden of interest payments* It was argued earlier that conglomerate performance may be more volatile over the whole cycle because they have to shoulder a greater burden of debt during the downturn as interest rates rise. Figure 2 shows how the measure of interest payment cover varies for each of the three categories between 1970 and 1976. In every year the interest payment cover for the conglomerates appears to be below that of the single and closely related firms. There appears to be very little difference though between the times covered positions of the conglomerate and concentric diversifiers, although one might note that between 1972 and 1975 the times covered position of the conglomerates deteriorated from a relatively healthy 10 to a low of 4.8, while the times covered position of the concentric diversifiers was fairly constant at around 7.5.

Unfortunately, the difference between the three categories is significant only in 1970, when an F-Ratio of 2.6 means that the observable differences are statistically significant at the 10% level. This is due in part to the small differences between the interest payment covered positions of the conglomerates and the concentric diversifiers and if we group these two

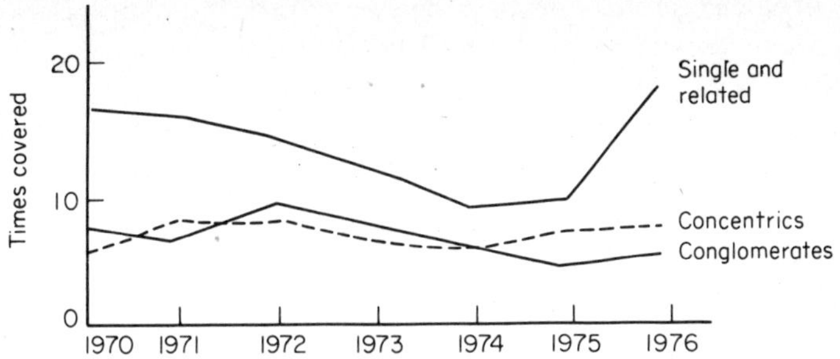

FIGURE 2
The times covered positions of the three categories 1970–76

categories together, then we get a set of results which are often significant. See Table V.

The difference which now emerges is between the expansion oriented strategies of the conglomerates and concentric diversifiers on the one hand, which rely in part upon borrowed money to finance acquisitions, and the less aggressive strategies of the single and closely related firms on the other. The significance of this observation lies in the fact that while conglomerates and concentric diversifiers both have to face a similar pattern of high interest payments as part of the price of expansion, over the economic cycle it is the earnings of the conglomerates which are volatile, not those of the concentric diversifiers. Thus an explanation of the differences between the performance of conglomerates and concentric diversifiers must include factors other than the burden of interest payments.

iv. *The stock market's valuation of conglomerates* It was implicit in the theory set out earlier, which sought to explain the more volatile nature of conglomerate performance, that the stock market may price conglomerate shares at a premium during boom periods, thus enabling the conglomerate to work with a high price/earnings ratio, which in turn facilitates acquisitions. If conglomerates are to gain an advantage in this respect one would expect the

TABLE V
THE TIMES COVERED POSITION OF SINGLE AND CLOSELY RELATED FIRMS AND A JOINT CONGLOMERATE/CONCENTRIC GATEGORY

Category	*1970*	*1971*	*1972*	*1973*	*1974*	*1975*	1976
Single and Closely Related	16.3	16.6	14.5	10.8	8.9	9.4	24.7
Conglomerates and Concentrics	6.5	6.9	8.8	7.5	5.9	5.9	7.3
F-Ratio(i)	5.1**	3.5*	3.2*	2.1 n/s	2.5 n/s	2.5 n/s	2.8*

Notes: (i) Significance level, *** = 1%, ** = 5%, * = 10%. n/s = not significant.

rise in conglomerate share prices to be greater than the rise experienced by non-conglomerate concerns. Table VI below looks at the percentage rise in the share price of the three categories from their low point in 1970 to their high point in 1972 and their corresponding fall from that peak to their low point in early 1975.

TABLE VI
THE PERCENTAGE CHANGE IN SHARE PRICES 1970–72 AND 1972–75

Category	*low 1970 to high 1972*	*high 1972 to low 1975*
Single and Closely Related	+319%	−535%
Concentric	+221%	−513%
Conglomerate	+316%	−541%
F-Ratio(i)	6.47***	0.06 n/s

Notes: (i) significance level *** = 1%, n/s = not significant.

The interesting points that come out of Table VI are, first, that during the stock market boom, the statistically significant evidence is that the shares of both the conglomerates and the single and closely related firms were priced at a premium, and secondly, that during the slump all were sold with equal enthusiasm. The high demand for the shares of the firms in the single and closely related category may be linked with the possibility that, other things being equal, these firms are more likely to have substantial market power and are therefore more likely to earn monopoly profits during the upswing. Thus their shares would be an attractive proposition. The rise in conglomerate share prices is consistent with expectations, but the near identical fall in the share prices of all three categories during the slump is not. It will be remembered that Reid [11] found that the fall in conglomerate stock prices in the USA was greater than the fall in the price of non-conglomerate stocks. The fact that such a phenomenon does not seem to have occurred in the UK may be due to the altogether more severe nature of the British stock market slump during the period under observation.

The question now arises as to whether the observable preference for conglomerate shares (and single and closely related shares), which Table VI suggests that the stock market had in the 1970 to 1972 period, was converted into a relatively high price/earnings ratio which would have facilitated conglomerate acquisitions. Table VII gives a comparison of the price/earnings ratios for the three categories in the peak year of the stock market boom, 1972, and in the worst year of 1974.

Now if conglomerates do operate with higher price/earnings ratios during a stock market and merger boom then one would expect to find, in 1972 at least, which was the peak year of the stock market and merger boom, some indication of this. However, as a glance at Table VII will verify, this was clearly not the case. The results for 1974, which are given for com-

TABLE VII
PRICE/EARNINGS RATIOS FOR 1972 AND 1974(i)

Category	*P/E* 1972	*P/E 1974*
Single and Closely Related	13.2	7.7
Concentric	13.5	6.2
Conglomerate	12.7	6.8
F-Ratio(ii)	0.1 n/s	0.65 n/s

Notes: (i) Figures for other years were also insignificant
(ii) Significance level n/s = not significant.

parison, tell a similar tale, for although the price/earnings ratios are generally lower, which is what one would expect during a slump, there is still no significant difference between the means.

The implication of the above results is that the role sometimes assigned to the stock market in promoting conglomerates may have been overstated. This does not mean however, that the more rapid increase in conglomerate margins, which was observed during the 1970–73 period, was due to more tangible factors than those which have been suggested to date. If this had been the case, then the mean performance of the conglomerates in the sample would not have deteriorated in the manner that it did from 1973 onwards. That we have found no evidence to suggest that the conglomerates were given a helping hand by the stock market in their acquisitions does not mean that they did not then rearrange the assets of acquired companies so as to given an illusion of improving performance.

VII. CONCLUSION

In this paper we have examined the possibility that the performance of conglomerate firms may be more volatile than that of non-conglomerate firms over the economic cycle. It has been shown that this hypothesis is basically correct in so far as the performance of the conglomerates was found to have improved significantly more than the performance of the two non-conglomerate categories during the upswing on the return on sales measure, and that during the downswing the performance of the conglomerate concerns deteriorated significantly more rapidly than that of the two non-conglomerate categories on both of the performance measures used.

However the attempts to explain these differences in terms of the interest structures of the different categories and their price/earnings ratios have met with little success. In retrospect it may be that the failure of these factors to explain the observed differences in performance could be due to a limitation of the study. This is that the lumping together of firms into categories on the basis of 1973 sales figures tends to ignore the individual past history of each of the firms. Now, although many of the firms included in the sample did expand via acquisitions during the merger wave of the early 1970s, for some firms at least, particular phases of rapid growth could have occurred outside the sample period. This implies that the acquisition related hypotheses, advanced earlier to explain the more volatile performance of the conglomerates, may not have been applicable in this instance given that some firms within the same category may have been growing at a much faster rate than others via acquisitions.

However, that an observable difference in performance between the categories did occur suggests that other factors are also of importance here. In particular, the approach of top management towards the acquisition process and the ability of top management to deal with a general slump in economic activity may explain the differences in performance. Thus, although conglomerate and concentric firms have often diversified to a similar degree, it is the concentric diversifiers which register the more consistent performance. It may well be that the difference in performance can be attributed to the fact that whereas the top management of a concentrically diversified firm understands the nature of the businesses in which it is involved, the top management of a conglomerate firm does not. The resolution of this problem however, clearly requires further research.

ACCEPTED MAY 1982

Charles Hill,
Department of Management Sciences,
The University of Manchester
Institute of Science and Technology,
P.O. Box 88,
Manchester M60 1QD

APPENDIX: FIRMS INCLUDED IN THE ANALYSIS

Conglomerates	*Concentric*	*Related and Single*
Thomas Tillings	ICI	BICC
Sears Holdings	GEC	Tate and Lyle
Rank Organization	Dunlop	Boots
Lonhro	Thorn	GUS
British Electric Traction	Metal Box	Rank Hovis Macdougal
Grand Metropolitan	EMI	Distillers
S. Pearson & Sons	Glynwed	Arthur Guinness
Powell Duffryn	Fisons	Debenhams
Trafalgar House	Stonne Platt	Associated Portland Cement
Harrisons and Crosfields	Turner and Newall	Rowntree Mackintosh
Charterhouse Group	Simon Engineering	FMC
Cope Allman	Northern Foods	Pilkingtons
Wikinson Match	English China Clays	United Biscuits
	Hepworth	
	BPB	

Hanson Trust	Smith and Nephew	Chloride
Hargreaves Group	Chubb	Redland
Norcros	Dowty Group	Blackwood Hodge
Laird Group	BTR	Gestetner
Reckitt and Coleman	BOC	Associated Biscuits
De La Rue		BSR
Granada Group		Westland Aircraft

REFERENCES

[1] Berry, C. H., *Corporate Growth and Diversification* (Princeton University Press, Priceton 1975).

[2] Channon, D. F., *The Strategy and Structure of British Enterprise* (Macmillan, London, 1973).

[3] Econtel Research., *Conglomerates* (British Industry Series, London, 1969).

[4] Goldberg, L. G., "Effect of Conglomerate Mergers on Competition", *Journal of Law and Economics*, Vol. 16, (April 1973), pp. 137–58.

[5] Kelly, M., "Mergers and Economic Performance", in Cowling, K., Stoneman, P., Cubbin, J. *et al.* (Cambridge University Press, London 1980).

[6] Kumps, A. M., "Conglomerate Mergers: the Case of Great Britain", (Document de Travail, CRIDE, No. 751, Brussels, 1975).

[7] Lintner, J., "Expectations, Mergers and Equilibrium in Purely Competitive Securities Markets", *American Economic Review*, Vol. 61, (May 1971), pp. 101–11.

[8] Melicher, R. M. and Rush, D. F., "The Performance of Conglomerate Firms: Recent Risk and Return Experience", *Journal of Finance*, Vol. 29, (May 1973), pp. 141–49.

[9] Monopolies Commission., *General Observations On Mergers*, Annix to Unilever Limited and Allied Breweries Limited—A Report on the Proposed Merger (HMSO, London, 1969).

[10] Mueller, D. C., "The Effects of Conglomerate Mergers: A Survey of the Empirical Evidence", *IIM*, Berlin, 1977, (mimeo).

[11] Reid, S. R., "A Reply to the Weston and Mansinghka Criticisms Dealing with Conglomerate Mergers", *Journal of Finance*, Vol. 26, (September 1971), pp. 937–40.

[12] Rhodes, S. R., "The Effects of Diversification on Industry Profit Performance in 241 Manufacturing Industries", *Review of Economics and Statistics*, Vol. 55, (May 1975), pp. 146–55.

[13] Rumlet, R. P., *Strategy, Structure and Economic Performance* (Division of Research, Graduate School of Business Administration, Harvard, Boston 1974).

[14] Utton, M. A., "The Performance of Conglomerate Firms", *Business Ratios*, Vol. 3, No. 1., (1969), pp. 24–28.

[15] Utton, M. A., *Diversification and Competition*, (NIESR, Cambridge University Press, London 1979).

[16] Weston, J. F., and Mansinghka, S. K., "Tests of the Efficiency Performance in Conglomerate Firms", *Journal of Finance*, Vol. 26, (September 1971), pp. 919–36.

[17] Weston, J. F., Smith, K. V., and Shrieves, R. E., "Conglomerate Performance Using the Capital Asset Pricing Model", *Review of Economics and Statistics*, Vol. 54, (November 1972), pp. 357–63.

THE JOURNAL OF INDUSTRIAL ECONOMICS 0022–1821 $2.00
Volume XXXII December 1983 No. 2

INVESTOR PREFERENCE FOR LARGE FIRMS: NEW EVIDENCE ON ECONOMIES OF SIZE

Marc R. Reinganum and Janet Kiholm Smith*

I. INTRODUCTION

In the last several decades, industrial organization literature has been replete with studies demonstrating a systematic relationship between accounting rates of return and firm size in the direction of greater (and more stable) accounting profits for larger firms.[1] These studies have been subject to criticism for an alarming number of statistical and conceptual problems, the most important of which alleges a serious bias in accounting profit measures as proxies for economic profit.[2] The criticisms have resulted in a stalemate in the interpretation of empirical evidence on firm size and performance. Nevertheless, there is continued interest in the area, ostensibly resulting from policy concerns with large firm advantages in both product and capital markets.

This paper provides new evidence concerning the industrial organization literature controversy of the connection between firm size and performance. Stock market data are used to examine the relationship between capital market returns, risk, and firm size. The findings suggest that even if there were no advantages of large size in the product market (equal rates of operating profit), large firms would still have a substantial capital-raising advantage over small firms. This advantage is unrelated to the widely recognized floatation cost economies. Even after controlling for nondiversifiable risk using the Capital Asset Pricing Model (CAPM), investors still demonstrate a statistically significant and economically important preference for the securities of larger firms. Investors apparently place a premium on large firms which is not attributable to large firms' observed lower risk as captured by the widely used measure of nondiversifiable risk (beta risk). This finding, a fresh contribution to the

* We would like to thank Victor Canto, Chap Findlay, Doug Joines, Terry Langetieg, Richard Smith, and an anonymous referee for their comments and suggestions. Naturally, any remaining errors are our own doing.

[1] There are a few studies which have revealed such a positive relationship between accounting profitability and firm size over only a limited range of firm size. Still others have revealed no such relationship. The major industrial organization studies in the area of accounting profitability and firm size include: Stekler [31]; Collins and Preston [6]; Hall and Weiss [13]; Shepherd [28]; Blair [5]; Demsetz [7].

[2] A review of primary criticisms surrounding these studies is found in Goldschmid, Mann, and Weston [12]. The bias in the accounting profitability measure is said to arise due to variations in accounting procedures for depreciation, advertising, R&D expenditures, and the like. Also, if owners of small companies reduce reported profits by withdrawing inflated salaries, an error in variables problem arises.

firm size and performance literature, is generated based on a model of capital market efficiency.

In Section II the CAPM is discussed as a tool for estimating cost of capital and its use and shortcomings for measuring abnormal returns are described. The model is used to measure stock market returns for portfolios grouped by firm size (defined as market value of common stock). The analysis demonstrates that smaller firms earn returns which are systematically above the required return estimated by the CAPM. This translates into significantly higher costs of capital for small firms. The section further demonstrates that these reults are not attributable to such factors as infrequent trading, bankruptcy, or a size-related listing effect. In Section III we discuss the economic meaning of the results and offer some possible explanations for the findings.

II. EMPIRICAL TESTS FOR SIZE EFFECTS USING THE CAPM

The Capital Asset Pricing Model developed by Sharpe [27], Lintner [18], and Mossin [20] provides a framework in which to measure the performance of small and large firms after controlling their returns for risk. The economic reasoning behind this theory is that the market will not reward investors for bearing unnecessary risk. Investors can diversify the risk of any one risky asset by combining it with other risky assets in a portfolio. An asset will earn a risk premium only to the extent that it affects the uncertainty of the overall portfolio return. In the limit, the gains from diversification are maximized by holding a portfolio consisting of all risky assets in the economy, i.e. the "market portfolio". Hence, the risk premium for an asset will be proportional to the covariance of its return with the return of the market portfolio.

Given the assumptions of the CAPM,[3] one can derive a simple relationship between risk and expected return. That is,

$$E(\tilde{R}_i) = R_f + \beta_i[E(\tilde{R}_m) - R_f] \tag{1}$$

where

$E(\tilde{R}_i)$ = expected return on asset i

$E(\tilde{R}_m)$ = expected return on the market portfolio

R_f = risk-free rate of interest

$\beta_i = \mathrm{cov}(\tilde{R}_i, \tilde{R}_m)/\mathrm{var}(\tilde{R}_m)$, the beta of asset i.

[3] The simplest version of the model assumes that: (1) asset returns are multivariate normally distributed, (2) risk-averse investors make investment decisions in period 1 to maximize their expected utility of period 1 and period 2 consumption, (3) capital markets are perfect in the sense that there are no transaction costs or other barriers to entry or exit, (4) investors completely agree upon the values of the parameters of the joint distribution of asset returns, and (5) investors can borrow and lend at the risk-free rate of interest.

Equation (1) states that the expected return on a risky asset equals the risk-free rate of interest plus a risk premium, where the risk premium is proportional to the covariance of the asset's returns with market returns divided by the variance of market returns, i.e. the asset's "beta". Different assets earn different rates of return only if their betas differ. Hence, beta is a measure of security risk within this model, and investors are only compensated for bearing beta (nondiversifiable) risk. The expected return for any asset in excess of the risk-free rate of interest is that asset's risk premium. Thus, the risk risk-adjusted expected return for all assets should equal the risk-free rate of interest. That is, rearranging (1):

$$E(\tilde{R}_i) - \beta_i[E(\tilde{R}_m) - R_f] = R_f \quad (2)$$

By (2), the risk-adjusted expected return for any asset in excess of the risk-free rate of interest should be zero. This implication of the CAPM will form the basis upon which the statistical tests for size effects are designed.

To test for firm size effects, a simple two-step technique is employed. First, at the end of year Y-1, the market values of all common stocks that trade on the New York and American Stock Exchanges are calculated. Securities are ranked on the basis of their market values and placed into one of ten portfolios based upon their relative size rankings. Hence, a small firm, a large firm, and eight intermediate firm portfolios are created. Second, in year Y, the daily returns of firms within each portfolio are combined with equal-weights $(1/n)$ to create the daily return of the portfolio. Statistical tests based on the CAPM are performed using these returns of the ten market-value portfolios to detect any size effects. Each year new rankings are calculated and the process is repeated.

The securities selected for analysis in this study are a subset of the stocks contained in the December 1978 version of the University of Chicago's Center for Research in Security Prices (CRSP) daily tape files. The CRSP daily stock return file includes all securities that have traded on the New York and American Stock Exchanges since July of 1962. The sample of firms analyzed in this study changes yearly. To qualify for inclusion in a given year, the data for number of common shares and price per share had to be available in order to compute the market value of the common stock. No survivorship requirements were imposed upon the data. The number of firms which satisfied the data requirements ranged from about 1500 in 1963 to over 2500 in the mid-1970s.

If one possessed the true beta of each portfolio, then the following time series could be constructed for each of the ten market-value portfolios using realized returns:

$$R_{p,t} - \beta_p[R_{m,t} - R_{f,t}] - R_{f,t} \quad (3)$$

If the data are consistent with the CAPM, then the mean of the above time series should be indistinguishable from zero according to equation (2). That is, the mean risk-adjusted excess returns for all portfolios should equal zero under the null hypothesis. Since portfolios are grouped on the basis of the market values of common stock, any systematic departures from zero would be indicative of a firm-size effect.

The direct implementation of (3) is hindered by several factors. First, true betas are not known and must be estimated. In this study, the estimation procedure suggested by Dimson [8] is employed. Dimson argued that with daily return data, infrequent trading could yield OLS beta estimates that are biased and inconsistent. Since trading frequency is related to firm size, it is necessary to correct for this potential systematic bias. To obtain consistent beta estimates Dimson suggested that one regress contemporaneous, leading, and lagged market returns on a portfolio's return. The estimated beta of the portfolio would be the sum of the slope coefficients from this regression. To estimate the betas of the ten market-value portfolios analyzed in this paper, a procedure similar to the ones followed by Roll [25] and Reinganum [22] is used. Namely, the contemporaneous, twenty lagged, and five leading CRSP value-weighted market returns serve as the independent variables. That is,

$$(4) \qquad R_{p,t} = \alpha_p + \sum_{l=-20}^{+5} b_{p,t+l} \cdot R_{m,t+l} + e_{p,t}$$

The estimated portfolio beta is the aggregate value of the twenty-six slope coefficients:

$$(5) \qquad \hat{\beta}_p = \sum_{l=-20}^{+5} \hat{b}_{p,t+l}.$$

The implementation of (3) is also hindered because one-day returns for the risk-free rate surrogate, U.S. Government Treasury Bills, are not available on a daily basis. However, one-month returns for T-Bills can be obtained from the CRSP U.S. Government Bond Tape File.[4] Hence, the time series proposed in (3) is constructed with one-month T-Bills rates, monthly portfolio returns calculated by compounding the daily portfolio returns, and portfolio betas estimated by Dimson's aggregated coefficients technique.[5] The excess returns are calculated using annually updated beta statistics.

Table I presents the mean monthly returns, mean risk-adjusted excess returns, and geometric mean risk-adjusted excess returns for each of the ten market portfolios during the period from 1964 through 1978. The smallest-market-value portfolio, MV1, on average earned a monthly return of 3.36%. The largest-market-value portfolio, MV10, experienced an average monthly

[4] Treasury Bills do not always mature exactly on the last day of the month. To compute the one-month returns, the maturity date nearest the end of the month is chosen. This is typically not more than a couple of days away from the last day of the month.

[5] Dimson betas are more likely to account for the size effect than OLS betas estimated with monthly returns. The reason is that the Dimson betas of the small firm portfolios are actually greater than the betas of these portfolios computed using the OLS estimator with monthly returns.

TABLE I

MEAN RETURNS AND RISK ADJUSTED EXCESS RETURNS FOR THE TEN MARKET-VALUE PORTFOLIOS

Portfolio	Mean[a] Monthly Return	Mean Risk-[b] Adjusted Excess Return	Geometric[c] Mean Risk-Adjusted Excess Return	Average[d] Median Stock Market Value	Average[e] Estimated Portfolio Beta	Average[f] Percent on AMEX
MV1	3.36	2.71	2.40	4.7	1.69	92.41
	(4.48)	(4.64)	(4.45)			
MV2	2.18	1.53	1.38	11.1	1.64	72.12
	(3.52)	(3.74)	(3.49)			
MV3	1.84	1.21	1.10	19.8	1.55	49.77
	(3.28)	(3.53)	(3.32)			
MV4	1.50	0.87	0.80	31.5	1.50	32.15
	(2.83)	(2.99)	(2.79)			
MV5	1.37	0.74	0.68	48.3	1.46	20.50
	(2.70)	(2.84)	(2.65)			
MV6	1.24	0.62	0.58	75.4	1.39	12.63
	(2.65)	(2.91)	(2.74)			
MV7	1.06	0.46	0.43	120.4	1.31	7.81
	(2.46)	(2.59)	(2.44)			
MV8	0.97	0.37	0.36	213.4	1.24	4.09
	(2.35)	(2.74)	(2.64)			
MV9	0.81	0.23	0.22	436.3	1.13	3.29
	(2.13)	(2.20)	(2.13)			
MV10	0.54	−0.02	−0.02	1086.0	0.97	2.27
	(1.66)	(−0.36)	(−0.41)			

[a] A mean monthly return is calculated with 180 months of portfolio returns. Mean returns are reported in percentages. T-values under the null hypothesis of a zero mean return are reported in parentheses. MV1 is the smallest market-value portfolio. MV10 is the largest market-value portfolio.

[b] The calculation of risk-adjusted excess returns is reported in quation (3) of the text. The autocorrelations of these returns are not very great. Typically, they hover near 0.1 in absolute value.

[c] The geometric mean is computed by taking the arithmetic average of $\ln(1 + R_i)$ where R_i is the monthly risk-adjusted excess return.

[d] The median value of the common stock (in millions of dollars) for firms within each portfolio averaged over the fifteen years of the study.

[e] The fifteen year average of the annually computed Dimson beta statistic.

[f] The percentage of firms within each portfolio that are listed on the American Stock Exchange averaged over the fifteen years of the study.

return of only .54%. One also observes that mean monthly portfolio returns and firm size are monotonically related. That is, mean returns increase as one moves to portfolios with smaller firms. Column 5 of Table I shows the size distribution for the ten portfolios. The median market values for common stocks within a portfolio range from 4.7 *million* dollars for portfolio MV1 to 1.086 *billion* dollars for portfolio MV10.

While small firms earn higher returns than large firms, small firms are also riskier as measured by their betas. Column 6 shows that the fifteen year average of the annually estimated beta of the small-firm portfolio is 1.69 whereas the average annual estimated beta of the large-firm portfolio is only 0.97. Estimated betas and firm size are monotonically related. Higher betas are associated with smaller firms. The real issue, though, is whether any differences in mean returns persist after adjusting the portfolio returns for risk. The evidence in Table I demonstrates that differences exist even after the beta risk-adjustment. The mean risk-adjusted excess return of the small-firm portfolio is 2.71% per month, which is more than four standard errors from zero. The mean risk-adjusted excess return of the largest-firm portfolio is indistinguishable from zero as the CAPM would predict. Thus, to the extent that estimated betas accurately measure risk, small firms experience substantially higher average returns than large firms on a risk-adjusted basis. Departures from the predictions of the CAPM are systematically related to firm size. The magnitude of average returns not explained by beta risk is monotonically related to the size of firms within the portfolios. Small firms are apparently required to earn much higher rates of return than large firms even after controlling for beta risk differentials.[6]

Although the specification used above is standard in securities market research,[7] a potential bias arises if one uses mean monthly returns to impute an annualized effect. The bias will be greater the larger the variance of monthly returns. Hence, it is expected the bias will be greater for the smallest firm portfolios. To provide a more precise way to interpret the performance results in Column 3 over longer time intervals (e.g. compounded annual returns), the geometric mean risk-adjusted excess returns were estimated for the portfolios and appear in Column 4. As expected, the estimated returns are slightly lower, especially for the smallest portfolios. However, the results are not materially different in that both series in Columns 3 and 4 exhibit the same pattern of decreasing risk-adjusted excess returns as firm size increases.

The evidence in Column 7 indicates that the smallest-firm portfolios are comprised mostly of companies that trade on the American Stock Exchange, and that companies within the largest-firm portfolios trade almost exclusively on the New York Stock Exchange. This result should not be surprising, since the listing requirements of the two exchanges differ.

One potential concern in working with the stock returns of small firms is whether bankruptcies are properly recorded. This is a concern since it is reasonable to expect that bankruptcy may be related to firm size. While CRSP attempts to determine the price of a security after delisting so that a final return can be calculated, errors and oversights might still remain in the data base. In order to assess the potential impact of bankruptcies on the results in Table I, a worst case scenario is created. That is, whenever a firm is delisted its last return is recorded as −100%, regardless of what CRSP reports. Hence, in this scenario, delisting and total bankruptcy are identical

[6] This result does not hinge upon the Sharpe-Lintner version of the CAPM with a risk-free rate of interest (see Reinganum [22]).

[7] The finance literature traditionally uses simple monthly returns rather than continually compounded returns. See, for example, the classic article by Fama and MacBeth [9]. There are several studies which have explored the bias created in estimating returns in the standard manner. In a different application the bias is found to be statistically unimportant for short trading periods, i.e. 32 days or less. See Schwartz and Whitcomb [26]).

events. Of course, this scenario is unrealistic in the sense that delistings are not necessarily associated with "bad" events such as bankruptcy but can be associated with events such as mergers. None-the-less, this scenario bounds the effect that bankruptcies can have on the firm-size effect.

Table II contains monthly mean returns, risk-adjusted excess returns, and geometric mean risk-adjusted excess returns for the ten market-value portfolios, where portfolio returns have been altered to reflect the assumption that delisting implies total bankruptcy. The biggest impact of this assumption is found in portfolio MV1, the smallest-firm portfolio. This is because small firms are delisted more often than large firms for whatever the reason. Of particular interest are the columns with mean risk-adjusted excess returns

Table II

Mean Returns and Risk Adjusted Excess Returns for the Ten Market-Value Portfolios Assuming Delisting Implies Total Bankrupcy

Portfolio	*Mean[a] Monthly Return*	*Mean Risk-[b] Adjusted Excess Return*	*Geometric[c] Mean Risk-Adjusted Excess Return*	*Average[d] Median Stock Market Value*	*Average[e] Estimated Portfolio Beta*	*Average[f] Percent on AMEX*
MV1	2.69	2.04	1.76	4.7	1.63	92.41
	(3.70)	(3.59)	(3.32)			
MV2	1.71	1.07	0.93	11.1	1.59	72.12
	(2.84)	(2.69)	(2.42)			
MV3	1.41	0.77	0.68	19.8	1.52	49.77
	(2.55)	(2.31)	(2.07)			
MV4	1.09	0.47	0.40	31.5	1.47	32.15
	(2.12)	(1.64)	(1.41)			
MV5	0.99	0.37	0.32	48.3	1.43	20.50
	(2.00)	(1.45)	(1.24)			
MV6	0.85	0.25	0.21	75.4	1.36	12.63
	(1.85)	(1.17)	(1.00)			
MV7	0.79	0.19	0.16	120.4	1.29	7.81
	(1.85)	(1.05)	(0.90)			
MV8	0.74	0.15	0.14	213.4	1.23	4.09
	(1.84)	(1.13)	(1.01)			
MV9	0.71	0.13	0.12	436.3	1.13	3.29
	(1.88)	(1.24)	(1.15)			
MV10	0.51	−0.05	−0.05	1086.0	0.97	2.27
	(1.57)	(−0.94)	(−0.98)			

[a] A mean monthly return is calculated with 180 months of portfolio returns. Mean returns are reported in percentages. T-values under the null hypothesis of a zero mean return are reported in parentheses. MV1 is the smallest market-value portfolio. MV10 is the largest market-value portfolio.

[b] The calculation of risk-adjusted excess returns is reported in equation (3) of the text. The autocorrelations of these returns are not very great. Typically, they hover near 0.1 in absolute value.

[c] The geometric mean is computed by taking the arithmetic average of $\ln(1 + R_i)$ where R_i is the monthly risk-adjusted excess return.

[d] The median value of the common stock (in millions of dollars) for firms within each portfolio averaged over the fifteen years of the study.

[e] The fifteen year average of the annually computed Dimson beta statistic.

[f] The percentage of firms within each portfolio that are listed on the American Stock Exchange averaged over the fifteen years of the study.

(Columns 3 and 4). One observes in Table II that these means for portfolios MV4 through MV10 are within two standard errors of zero. In contrast, in Table I, only the mean risk-adjusted excess return for portfolio MV10 is within two standard errors of zero. Thus, assuming delisting implies total bankruptcy, induces the return behaviors of six other portfolios to be consistent with the predictions of the CAPM. However, the smallest-market-value portfolios, MV1, MV2, and MV3, still experience mean risk-adjusted excess returns more than two standard errors greater than zero. Furthermore, the monotonocity of the pattern of returns remains stable. Thus, even with the drastic bankruptcy assumption, an economically and statistically significant size effect still remains.

In order to evaluate the persistence of the size effect over time, mean monthly risk-adjusted excess returns for the market value in three five-year subperiods were compiled. The evidence presented in Table III shows that

TABLE III
MEAN RISK-ADJUSTED EXCESS MONTHLY RETURNS FOR THE TEN MARKET VALUE PORTFOLIOS IN EACH OF THE THREE FIVE-YEAR SUBPERIODS WITH AND WITHOUT TOTAL BANKRUPTCY CORRECTION

	Mean Returns for Portfolios without Bankruptcy Correction[a]			*Mean Returns for Portfolios with Bankruptcy Correction*[b]		
Portfolio	*6468*	*697η*	*7478*	*6468*	*697η*	*7478*
MV1	3.11	0.08	4.94	2.67	−0.40	3.86
	(4.83)	(9.11)	(3.57)	(4.13)	(−0.54)	(2.87)
MV2	2.01	−0.40	2.98	1.50	−0.73	2.45
	(4.41)	(−0.76)	(3.07)	(3.43)	(−1.42)	(2.57)
MV3	1.40	−0.33	2.55	0.90	−0.64	2.06
	(3.93)	(−0.77)	(3.07)	(2.49)	(−1.59)	(2.52)
MV4	1.08	−0.51	2.05	0.61	−0.79	1.60
	(3.48)	(−1.42)	(2.93)	(1.96)	(−2.18)	(2.32)
MV5	1.03	−0.42	1.62	0.65	−0.75	1.22
	(3.55)	(−1.38)	(2.54)	(2.27)	(−2.52)	(1.92)
MV6	0.72	−0.32	1.47	0.21	−0.57	1.10
	(3.29)	(−1.23)	(2.79)	(1.11)	(−2.30)	(2.09)
MV7	0.59	−0.33	1.13	0.19	−0.50	0.88
	(3.08)	(−1.40)	(2.68)	(0.96)	(−2.14)	(2.08)
MV8	0.32	−0.08	0.87	0.07	−0.29	0.68
	(2.38)	(−0.37)	(2.76)	(0.48)	(−1.45)	(2.16)
MV9	0.24	−0.15	0.60	0.11	−0.23	0.52
	(2.18)	(−0.78)	(2.88)	(0.90)	(−1.17)	(2.48)
MV10	−0.16	0.15	−0.04	−0.19	0.12	−0.07
	(−1.88)	(1.70)	(−0.51)	(−2.12)	(1.35)	(−0.84)

[a] These portfolio returns are based upon the unaltered security returns collected and reported by the University of Chicago's Center for Research in Security Prices (CRSP). Mean monthly returns are reported in percentages. T-values under the null hypothesis of zero mean risk-adjusted excess returns are in parentheses. MV1 is the smallest-market-value portfolio. MV10 is the largest-market-value portfolio.

[b] These portfolio returns are created assuming that delisting of a security implies total bankruptcy. Hence the final return for a security that is delisted is recorded as −100%, regardless of what CRSP reports.

in two of the three subperiods a very strong size effect existed. For example, during 1974–78, portfolio MV1 earned mean excess returns nearly 5% more per month than predicted by the CAPM. Similarly, during 1964–68, the CAPM underestimated the monthly return on this portfolio by 3.11% on average. However, during 1969–73, the return behaviors of the ten market-value portfolios were consistent with the mean returns implied by the CAPM. During this subperiod, size effects did not appear in the data. Thus, while small firms outperform large firms on average, the superior returns are not assured every period but only over long periods of time. Unfortunately, these data cannot be extended back beyond the early 1960s because market capitalization information for firms traded on the American Stock Exchange is not kept by CRSP in computer-readable form. However, Banz [3] detected size effects in NYSE company stock returns dating back to 1930. The advantage of including AMEX companies is that small firms are analyzed and a larger size effect can be measured. Banz's work, though, should partially allay any suspicion that the firm-size effect is actually an exchange-listing effect or the result of short-run disequilibrium.

The issue of disequilibrium is of concern since it would be incorrect to interpret a finding of excess returns to small firms as a higher cost of capital if, over the period of study, small firms became less risky or more profitable relative to large firms. To control for the former possibility, the excess returns reported above were estimated using beta statistics which were claculated annually.[8] Furthermore, there does not appear to have been a systematic shift in profitability of small versus large firms over the relevant time period. This is evidenced by a positive and stable differential in accounting profitability across firm sizes.[9,10]

[8] See Whittington [35], Hurdle [14], Winn [35], Smyth, Boyes, and Peseau [29] for evidence on the intertemporal relationship between firm size and profit variability. These studies, which cover several different time periods, generally report a significant and inverse relationship across firm size classifications.

[9] AFTER TAX RETURN ON EQUITY FOR MANUFACTURING FIRMS BY ASSET SIZE* 1965–79

Corporations with Assets of:	*1965–69*	*1970–74*	*1975–79*
1 Billion+	12.8	11.8	14.2
250–1000 Million	12.1	11.5	13.9
100–250 Million	12.1	10.6	13.1
50–100 Million	11.2	10.2	13.1
25–50 Million	11.3	9.7	13.0

* Returns are unweighted averages of quarterly rates of return.

Source: Federal Trade Commission, Quarterly Financial Report for Manufacturing Corporations, Washington, D.C.: Government Printing Office, various issues.

[10] Related to the issue of disequilibrium is the nature of the intertemporal relationship between price-earnings ratios and excess returns. Reinganum [23] has considered this issue and finds that when controlling for changes over time in earnings-price ratios (calculated annually), a large and persistent firm size effect is still detected. The findings do reveal a close and stable correlation between firm size and price-earnings ratios, yielding additional support for our finding of a capital cost advantage for large firms.

In short, evidence in this section indicates that investors require small firms to earn substantially higher average returns than large firms even after controlling returns for risk where risk is measured by an asset's beta, a measure proposed by the CAPM. While recent empirical research suggests that the CAPM may be misspecified (for example, see Gibbons [11], Marsh [19], and Reinganum [23]), no other model of capital market equilibrium is generally agreed to be empirically superior to the CAPM at this time. Thus, even though beta may not be the perfect measure of risk, no other measure has been shown to be demonstrably better.[11] However, even in the event of misspecification (which the results here indicate must be the case), an interesting economic question still remains; namely, what is the nature of the omitted risk-related variable which leads to the observed higher required returns for smaller firms? In the next section, we discuss some economic ramifications of this firm size effect.[12]

III. DISCUSSION OF RESULTS

In efficient capital markets, new information regarding expected changes in quasi-rents due to changes in a firm's product market monopoly power or relative efficiency is capitalized in the secondary capital market. Thus, secondary capital market return data, such as those presented in Section II, are unable to shed new light on the issue of whether large firms have more *product market* monopoly power as evidenced by abnormal *economic* profits. Rather, the results contribute a new piece to the empirical puzzle concerning firm size and performance; namely, that after controlling for risk as measured by beta, capital market investors *value* the earnings of large firms more than they do earnings of small firms. This translates into a higher required rate of return for smaller firms and constitutes a substantial capital-raising economy for large firms. The finding is consistent with a finding that the CAPM is misspecified since the market evidently finds some factor other than systematic risk relevant for capital asset (firm) valuation. We are compelled to ask what is the source of the factor which is correlated with firm size and generates this capital raising advantage? While the purpose of the study is not to solve the puzzle, it is possible to identify what the size advantage is *not* attributable to and to offer some possible explanations for it.

[11] If small firms tend to be held in undiversified portfolios, this may suggest variance of returns is a more appropriate measure of risk than beta. See Levy [17]. A study of Banz [2], however, finds firm size has additional and significant explanatory power if variance is used rather than beta in estimating excess returns. Further, arbitrage pricing model results indicate the firm size effect does not disappear in up to a five factor market model, suggesting that use of variance as a measure of risk will not explain the firm size effect. The divergence in the magnitude of returns for small versus large firms cannot be explained by factors associated with variance, even when factors accounting for a substantial fraction of the variance are included. See Reinganum [24].

[12] For evidence on the relationship of rate of return and firm size using book value as a measure of size, see Stattman [30] and Keim [16].

First, the existence (if any) of product market power will not explain the result. With efficient capital markets, any expectation of a change in product market power (as indicated by expected abnormal economic profits) will be capitalized in the price of the stock. Also, the stock price will incorporate the capitalized value of the existing level of production scale economies or any existing differential market power for larger firms. Therefore, any size-related excess return must reflect the net impact of capital market considerations only.

The economic implications of the finding of higher cost of equity capital for small firms are far-reaching. It suggests that a small firm might reject a risky project as a negative net present value (NPV) project, whereas a larger firm would accept the project as a positive NPV project. Further, an equally risky larger firm could raise more equity capital per unit of productive capacity than could a smaller firm. The finding also implies that a purely financial conglomerate merger of two small firms might be economical since, by way of merger, the combined larger firm would reduce its equity cost of capital. In support of the latter argument, the periods of abnormal required returns for small firms presented in Table III are contemporaneous with the conglomerate merger waves of the late '60s and mid-to-late '70s. Perhaps the small-firm effect may contribute to the not well understood pattern of aggregate merger behavior.

To the extent the tests in Section II control for nondiversifiable or systematic risk, as measured by beta, it is possible to rule out a number of explanations for the capital-raising economy of large firm size. Factors affecting a firm's beta, such as operating leverage, the degree of cyclicality of firm revenues, or sensitivity to macroeconomic changes, will not explain the difference in required returns.[13] Capital asset pricing theory maintains the only risk which stockholders will be compensated to bear (in the form of a higher required rate of return) is systematic or market risk, which is controlled for in the model. Accordingly, characteristics unique to a firm (which again may be size related), such as probability of bankruptcy, variability of managerial incentives for sacrificing higher expected profits for security, and ability to stabilize earnings and pricing policies, all relate to a component of risk that can be eliminated by holding a well-diversified portfolio of firms.

Whether large or small, firms will not be paid to bear a risk investors can eliminate for themselves. For example, information about small firms may not be as complete or as accurate as large firm information for a variety of reasons. But, to the extent this risk is idiosyncratic rather than systematic, it is diversifiable. Diversification can be achieved simply by holding small firms within a large portfolio.

Nevertheless, in one respect, imperfect information may be a contributing

[13] Recent research suggests a variety of other factors which may affect a firm's beta. See, for example, Thompson [33] and Foster [10].

factor to the larger required market returns of small firms. If information about the future performance of a firm is asymetrically held by stock market investors, then insiders (corporate officers, directors, and large stockholders) may exploit this advantage to the detriment of outsiders. In any trade, the outsider knows there is some probability that he will be engaged in an exchange with an insider who possesses superior information. The result is that outsiders may require a return premium which depends on the probability that the investor is betting against an insider. If the magnitude of insider trading is greater for small firms, then under some conditions the premium required by outsiders for bearing this risk would be greater when investing in small firms.[14]

Other potential sources of the divergence in required returns are the numerous regulatory and institutional constraints on the capital market, which may render the abnormally large returns to small firms impossible to successfully arbitrage away. The "prudent man rule" and related state and federal legislation inhibit creation of small-firm mutual fund shares and trustees' investments in small firms. The investment powers of trustees, like banks, pension funds, and investment managers in general, are governed by common law and state and federal legislation. The prudent man rule limits investments of fiduciaries to those a "prudent man would make, having due regard to preservation of principal and regularity of income".[15] Typically this rule has been interpreted as restricting fiduciary investments in bonds to "Baa or better" and to "blue chip" stocks.[16] The trustee is liable if the portfolio does not perform well and the prescribed rules of prudence have not been followed. The burden of proof of investment mismanagement lies with the principal, provided the trustee has made portfolio investments in assets generally established by case law or legislation as being reasonable and prudent. However, the burden of proof shifts to the fiduciary to prove prudence whenever the trustee selects investments outside of this narrow boundary of acceptable investments.[17] The regulatory effect of the statutes

[14] The hypothesis that the capital market premium to size is attributable to asymmetric information finds limited support in a tangential study by Jaffe [15]. Jaffe investigates the profitability of insider trades by examining the performance of a security subsequent to specific types of insider trades in the security. The findings do indicate that insiders possess special information and that trading by insiders is generally profitable, especially for large transactions. However, the results do not test for the relative profitability of insider trading in small versus large firms. Future research may clarify the relationship between special information, insider trading, and firm size.

[15] This principle was first enunciated by the Supreme Judicial Court of Massachusetts in 1830 in *Harvard College v. Amory* 26 Mass 446, 1830. Federal legislation of prudence and reasonable care in investment management of pensions has also been enacted. See Employee Retirement Income Security Act of 1974, 29 USC. For a discussion of ERISA's investment management regulation, see Bines [4].

[16] The official American Bar Association position is that investments in options, indexed accounts, and new small companies are highly doubtful investments for fiduciaries. The analysis is that these investments are difficult to execute competently and with respect to small companies inherently risky. See: American Bar Association, The Committee on Investments by Fiduciaries [1].

[17] See Bines [4] for a complete statement and interpretation of the law.

and common law may be to systematically eliminate one large class of potential investors in small firm securities. For example, Reilly [21] documented that during the 1970s, large institutions concentrated their attention on a universe of less than 700 stocks of large firms, while the number of public companies that did not qualify for investments by institutions likely exceeded 8000.

To complete the argument above, one must posit that there are significant costs associated with nonfiduciaries (individual traders) arbitraging away the gains to small firm portfolios. There are no explicit sanctions against individuals' KEOGH, IRA and similar portfolios containing primarily small firm securities. Nevertheless, the transactions costs associated with *maintenance* of a well diversified small firm portfolio may be significantly greater than those associated with maintenance of a large firm portfolio. Since a greater proportion of small firm securities are delisted, maintenance of a small portfolio will necessarily involve more transactions (more commissions). Future research may generate evidence as to the empirical impact of regulations on institutional trading and on required rates of return associated with firms of various sizes.

ACCEPTED JULY 1982

Marc R. Reinganum,
Graduate School of Business,
University of Southern California,
Los Angeles,
California 90007

Janet Kiholm Smith,
Department of Economics,
Arizona State University,
Tempe,
Arizona 85287

REFERENCES

[1] AMERICAN BAR ASSOCIATION, Report of the Committee on Investments by Fiduciaries, "Current Investment Questions and the Prudent Person Rule", 13 *Real Property, Probate and Trusts Journal*, 650 (1978).

[2] BANZ, ROLF W., "Limited Diversification and Market Equilibrium: An Empirical Approach", unpublished Ph.D. dissertation, University of Chicago (1978).

[3] ———, "The Relationship Between Return and Market Value of Common Stocks", *Journal of Financial Economics*, 9, 1 (March 1981) pp. 3–18.

[4] BINES, HARVEY E., *The Law of Investment Management* (Boston: Warran, Gorham and Lamong, Inc., 1978) (1980 supplement).

[5] BLAIR, JOHN M., *Economic Concentration* (New York: Harcourt Brace Jovanovich 1972) pp. 177–85.

[6] COLLINS, N., and L. PRESTON, "Price-Cost Margins and Industry Structure", *Review of Economics and Statistics*, 51, 3 (August 1969) pp. 271–86.

[7] DEMSETZ, HAROLD, "Industry Structure, Market Rivalry, and Public Policy", *Journal of Law and Economics*, 16 (April 1973) pp. 1–10.

[8] DIMSON, ELROY, "Risk Measurement When Shares Are Subject to Infrequent Trading", *Journal of Financial Economics*, 7, 2 (June 1979) pp. 197–226.

[9] FAMA, E. F., and J. D. MACBETH, "Risk, Return and Equilibrium: Empirical Tests", *Journal of Political Economy*, 81, 3 (May 1973) pp. 607–38.

[10] FOSTER, G., *Financial Statement Analysis* (Englewood Cliffs, N.J.: Prentice-Hall, Inc., 1978), Chapter 9.

[11] GIBBONS, MICHAEL R., "Multivariate Tests of Financial Models: A New Approach", *Journal of Financial Economics*, 10, 1 (March 1982) pp. 3–27.

[12] GOLDSCHMID, H., H. M. MANN, and J. FRED WESTON (eds.), *Industrial Concentration: The New Learning* (Boston: Little, Brown, and Company, 1974).

[13] HALL, M. and L. WEISS, "Firm Size and Profitability", *Review of Economics and Statistics*, 49, 3 (August 1967) pp. 319–31.

[14] HURDLE, GLORIA J., "Leverage, Risk, Market Structure and Profitability", *Review of Economics and Statistics*, 56, 4 (November 1974) pp. 481–82.

[15] JAFFE, JEFFREY F., "Special Information and Insider Trading", *Journal of Business*, 47, 3 (1974) pp. 410–78.

[16] KEIM, DONALD B., "Accounting Book Value and Stock Returns: An Empirical Analysis", unpublished manuscript, Graduate School of Business, University of Chicago, 1981.

[17] LEVY, HAIM, "Equilibrium in an Imperfect Market: A Constraint on the Number of Securities in the Portfolio", *American Economic Review* 68, 4 (September 1978) pp. 643–58.

[18] LINTNER, JOHN, "The Valuation of Risk Assets and the Selection of Risky Investments in Stock Portfolios and Capital Budgets", *The Review of Economics and Statistics*, 47, 1 (February 1965) pp. 13–37.

[19] MARSH, TERRY, "Intertemporal Capital Asset Pricing and the Term Structure of Interest Rates", Working Paper, Sloan School of Management, Massachusetts Institute of Technology, September 1980.

[20] MOSSIN, JAN, "Equilibrium in a Capital Asset Market", *Econometrica*, 34, 4 (October 1966) pp. 768–83.

[21] REILLY, FRANK F., "A Three Tier Stock Market and Corporate Financing", *Financial Management*, 4, 1 (Autumn 1975) pp. 7–15.

[22] REINGANUM, MARC R., "A Direct Test of Roll's Conjecture on the Firm Size Effect", *Journal of Finance*, 37, 2 (March 1982) pp. 27–36.

[23] ———, "Misspecification of Capital Asset Pricing: Empirical Anomalies Based on Earnings' Yields and Market Values", *Journal of Financial Economics*, 9, 1 (March 1981) pp. 19–46.

[24] ———, "The Arbitrage Pricing Theory: Some Empirical Results", *Journal of Finance*, 36, 2 (May 1981) pp. 313–21.

[25] ROLL, RICHARD, "A Possible Explanation of the Small Firm Effect", *Journal of Finance*, 36, 4 (September 1981) pp. 879–88.

[26] SCHWARTZ, ROBERT A. and DAVID K. WHITCOMB, "Evidence on the Presence and Causes of Serial Correlation in Market Model Residuals", *Journal of Financial and Quantitative Analysis*, 12, 2 (June 1977) pp. 291–311.

[27] SHARPE, WILLIAM F., "Capital Asset Prices: A Theory of Market Equilibrium Under Conditions of Risk", *Journal of Finance*, 19, 3 (September 1964) pp. 425–42.

[28] SHEPHERD, WILLIAM G., *Market Power and Economic Welfare* (New York City: Random House, 1970).

[29] SMYTH, D., W. BOYES and D. PESEAU, *Size, Growth, Profits and Executive Compensation in the Large Corporation* (New York: MacMillan Press, 1975).

[30] STATTMAN, DENNIS, "The Book Values and Stock Returns", *The Chicago MBA* (Spring 1980) pp. 25–45.

[31] STEKLER, HERMAN O., *Profitability and Size of Firm*, Berkeley: University of California Institute of Business and Economic Research (1963).

[32] SULLIVAN, TIMOTHY G., "The Cost of Capital and Market Power of Firms", *Review of Economics and Statistics*, 60, 2 (May 1978) pp. 209–17.

[33] THOMPSON, DONALD J., "Sources of Systematic Risk in Common Stocks", *Journal of Business*, 49, 2 (April 1976) pp. 173–88.

[34] WHITTINGTON, *The Prediction of Profitability* (Cambridge: Cambridge University Press, 1971).

[35] WINN, DARYL N., "On the Relations Between Rates of Return, Risk, and Market Structure", *Quarterly Journal of Economics*, 91, 1 (February 1977) pp. 157–63.

THE JOURNAL OF INDUSTRIAL ECONOMICS 0022–1821 $2.00
Volume XXXII December 1983 No. 2

ADVERTISING AND ECONOMIES OF SCALE: CRITICAL COMMENTS ON THE EVIDENCE

JOHAN ARNDT AND JULIAN L. SIMON

> Advertising is a subject about which the ratio of poetic opinion to systematic analytics approaches infinity. Like romance, advertising is an activity to which most people have been exposed and about which little is known.
> Harold Demsetz

I. INTRODUCTION

THE general issue to be discussed in this review article is: Does the advertising cost per dollar of sales increase as increases in total advertising expenditures occur? Stated in this fashion, however, the question of economies of scale and increasing returns to advertising is vague and equivocal. The difficulty of formulating the question in a rigorous enough fashion is the root cause of much of the controversy and confusion about the efficiency of advertising at various levels of advertising expenditures or other forms of advertising input.

Regardless of the formidable theoretical and methodological problems involved, the economies of scale in advertising remain an important issue. More often than not, antitrust measures and public regulation of the marketplace are based on (or legitimized by) assumptions of substantial scale economies enabling established large corporations to maintain market power keeping competitors out and prices up.

The purpose of this article is critically to review the most important empirical evidence relating to economies of scale in advertising. The article is organized as follows:

Economies of scale vs. the response function of advertising.
The shape of the advertising response function.
Sources of economies of scale in advertising.
The problems of conceptualizing economies of scale.
Studies using the A/S ratio.
Advertising and prices.
Cost advantages due to media rate structures.
The tricky issue of multibrand economies.
Dynamic barrier effects—"stay-out advertising".

II. ECONOMIES OF SCALE VS. THE RESPONSE FUNCTION OF ADVERTISING

In the literature as well as in the public debate, the notion of economies of scale in advertising is often confused with the advertising response function.

The advertising response function refers to the relationships between sales, or some other effect indicator, and advertising input, holding other inputs constant. Hence, it positions the advertising-sales linkage as a stimulus-response relationship. Formally, the advertising response function may be expressed in terms of the advertising elasticity, defined as the proportionate rate of change in sales (S) with respect to advertising (A):

$$\frac{\partial S}{\partial A}\frac{A}{S}$$

While the advertising response function is concerned with the *short term* relationship between sales and advertising, the economies of scale concept refers to the relationship between sales and advertising or other inputs in the *long run,* when the individual firm has complete flexibility in determining the character of the productive process [17, Chapter 6]. Generally, the concept of economies of scale refers to the case when the proportions of all productive inputs remain the same as the scale or size of the firm changes.[1]

This article focuses on the latter concept, economies of scale in advertising. First, however, a few words on the evidence relating to the advertising response function would seem in order.

III. THE SHAPE OF THE ADVERTISING RESPONSE FUNCTION

Many theoreticians and practitioners of marketing believe that there is a threshold effect in that the advertising response curve is S-shaped, which implies initial increasing returns. Advertising campaigns involving high degrees of domination, concentration, and repetition would be unlikely if there were not widespread belief in some kind of S-shaped curve.

To evaluate the empirical evidence, the present authors recently conducted a comprehensive review of the literature [32]. The studies reviewed covered a wide range of designs, from laboratory and field experiments to econometric analyses of cross-sectional or time-series data. The independent variable, advertising input, was measured by advertising expenditures as

[1] In formal terms, economies of scale may be expressed by the so-called *passus coefficient* which in this case is defined as the elasticity of sales with respect to advertising when advertising and all other factors are varied proportionately [13, pp. 78–80]:

$$\frac{d^{pr}S}{d^{pr}A}\frac{A}{S}$$

where $d^{pr}A$ denotes the infinitesimal *proportionate* change in advertising (the relative magnitude of advertising to other input factors remains the same), and $d^{pr}S$ denotes the corresponding change in sales.

well as by quantity in terms of size (size of print advertisements, length of TV commercials, etc.) or number of repetitions. The dependent variable indicators included sales or "intermediate" effect measures such as intentions to buy, attitudes, or awareness.

After a critical review of both the substantive findings and the methodologies, only *one* study was found to present clear evidence of initial returns to scale to advertising, McNiven's field experiment concerning Du Pont's Teflon product [21]. Several studies purporting to show threshold effects were found questionable. In some cases, such as the Stewart [33] study, the analysis was flawed, and a reanalysis gave evidence against increasing results. Other reports, had dubious validity because of *ex post* designs and inadequate controls for potentially confounding factors.[2] The majority of the econometric studies based on aggregate data assumed a given form of the advertising response curve by entering the advertising variable in a pre-specified form, such as the logarithmic form. Hence, such analyses could not be expected to reveal an S-shaped response curve, even if such a relationship existed.[3]

The remainder of the studies showed a negatively accelerated curve over the range of the observations and no threshold effects. Hence, this review supports the position of Little that "the S-shaped curve is still on shaky ground" [19, p. 662].

But even if the advertising response function is downward-concave, advertising could give an advantage to the big spender over the smaller spender. This could happen if there is an interaction between the various levels of advertising and various other factors of production, for example in a multiplicative way. This is the issue which is explored in this article.

IV. SOURCES OF ECONOMIES OF SCALE IN ADVERTISING

In general, economies of scale may be traced to two broad classes of factors, "real" factors and "pecuniary" factors. "Real" economies of scale refer to higher efficiency because larger firms may benefit from specialization and division of labor, indivisibilities of input factors (less excess capacity as the scale increases), better administration, and less uncertainty. Larger firms may also be able to take the advantage of "pecuniary" economies by utilizing monopoly or monopsony power to squeeze customers or suppliers [17, pp. 109–23].

Though there are ideological issues involved and the empirical evidence is somewhat mixed, it is fair to conclude that the literature has convincingly documented the existence of economies of scale, at least at the lower end of the scale. Similarly, at the high end, there are diseconomies owing to the difficulties of managing very large enterprises [17, Chapter 6].

The issue of interest in this article, however, is not whether there are general returns to scale, but whether there are advantages of size in *advertising*. Several

[2] Examples include McDonald [20], Geiger and Ernst [15], and Rao and Miller [28].
[3] See Little [19].

writers suggest that advertising economies of scale result from media advertising rates (which tend to increase less than proportionately with audience size—large advertisers can then use national media with lower contact costs per customer), special volume discounts, better organization of advertising expenditures, and indivisibilities (large advertisers may use high grade copy and art work).[4]

V. THE PROBLEMS OF CONCEPTUALIZING ECONOMIES OF SCALE

At first look, the notion of economies of scale appears deceptively simple. However, when it comes to research, it is difficult to make sense out of the concept of economies of scale with respect to advertising—or with respect to any other single input factor, for that matter. The difficulty is that, as earlier pointed out, the concept of economies of *scale* refers to differences in just that, the scale of the enterprise with *all* factors taken together, including their interaction. As the economies of scale concept assumes that *all* inputs in the productive process are variable in nature, it would seem to be empirically and conceptually meaningless to attempt to isolate the role of advertising. The concept was not designed to throw light on the operation of a single factor alone. Hence the criticism below of empirical research on scale economies in advertising really applies also to the research in the economic literature on other input factors [17, Chapter 6].

True economies of scale would be shown if a firm that has been operating in one market moves into a second *identical* market, uses the same amounts of inputs in the second market that it did in the first market, and obtains more than double the total sales.

Within a given market, it is clear that the larger firm will not employ all factors in the same proportion as the smaller firms. And geographic expansions of the sort demanded for a pure test of economies of scale are seldom, if ever, available. But even if such a test were available in practice, it would not tell anything definite about *advertising's* role in economies of scale. One would never know it is advertising that has a role in the interactive combination of factors that leads to the economies of scale, whether advertising operates independently or whether it even exerts a drag effect. So it is impossible in principle to know that advertising is responsible for economies of scale, given that there are not increasing returns to advertising when other factors are held constant—as the empirical evidence suggests [32].

Another way of looking at economies of scale is to ask whether twice as much output can be produced with twice as much of some inputs and less than twice as much of other inputs. But because a larger firm in a given market usually does not employ factors in the same proportion as the smaller firm, empirically it is customary to consider the results achieved by firms of different *total* size;

[4] See Chamberlin [6, pp. 133–34], Comanor and Wilson [8, pp. 49–53], and Ferguson [12, pp. 73–75].

that is, "bigger" and "smaller" are now one-dimensional concepts for which the total inputs are reduced to a common dimension—money. Such a study then considers physical output as a function of a total expenditure. Such an investigation is commonly referred to as a study of "economies of scale",[5] though it would be clearer to speak of "economies of size". Furthermore, such studies usually measure the total assets rather than expenditures, but this last deviation from theory (unlike the others) is not serious.

The difficulty of empirically pinning down the concept of economies of scale is illuminated by the study by Peles [24], in which he estimated regression equations for beer that are variants of the following:

$$\begin{aligned}\text{Market Share}_t = {} & a_1 \text{ Advertising Share}_t + \\ & a_2 \text{ Advertising Share}_{t-1} + \\ & a_3 \text{ Advertising Share}_{t-2} + \\ & a_4 \text{ National or local firm}\end{aligned}$$

Peles found negative coefficients for a_4, a dummy variable equal to one for local firms and zero for national firms, which may be considered a proxy for size of firm. And Peles concluded: "The minus sign means that a dollar spent for advertising will increase the demand for the product of a big firm more than that of a small firm. In other words, it is plausible to interpret the above finding as evidence of economies of scale in the advertising of the beer industry ..." [24, p. 35].

A more valid interpretation of Peles' linear regression, however, is simply that a national firm obtains more sales than a local firm, perhaps because of its distribution network and without regard to advertising. The additive linear form does not permit a test of the interaction between advertising and size. Moreover, to get closer to showing that advertising is more effective for large firms, a slope dummy rather than an intercept dummy should have been used.[6]

Lambin's [18] ambitious and exhaustive study may be considered the centerpiece investigation of the advertising-sales relationship. His sample covered 107 brands of 16 product classes in 8 European countries. First, in his time-series analysis, each individual response function was best described by a concave-downward diminishing returns equation.

Second, Lambin examined the relationship of each brand's advertising share to its market share. The results showed that brands with relatively small market shares had advertising shares larger than their market shares. This Lambin interpreted as indicating that there is a threshold for advertising effectiveness below which advertising expenditures have no effect. Such a threshold constitutes an inflection point, the lower boundary of a region of increasing returns. In the words of Lambin: "Therefore, to reach the level of

[5] E.g. Stigler [34].

[6] Similar interpretations of the Peles study can be found in Schmalensee [29, p. 231] and Ferguson [12, p. 78].

communication effectiveness, small brands have to keep their advertising share higher than their market shares" [18, p. 128].

These data need not indicate a threshold, however, as will be explained below. In essence, the data involve a comparison of the response functions *from one brand to another*, with *nothing held constant*.[7] That is, it is reasonable and likely that a larger firm has a much more extensive distribution network and a larger sales force than does a smaller one. That would explain *both* why the larger firm has a higher response function *and* why it advertises more in total than does its smaller competitor.

Many of the economies-of-scale studies focusing on advertising have used the advertising-to-sales (*A*/*S*) ratio as a central variable. In a sense, the *A*/*S* ratio may be viewed as a rough indicator of the unit cost of advertising.

VI. STUDIES USING THE *A*/*S* RATIO

Like the other data reviewed above, *A*/*S* ratio data by themselves are flawed for the purpose of examining the role of advertising in economies of scale because there are many other policies and strategies that may be systematically different between larger and smaller firms.

Many economists have found evidence that higher output levels are associated with lower unit advertising costs (lower *A*/*S* ratios). Therefore, the argument is that smaller firms, including most potential entrants, are placed at a substantial disadvantage. For instance, in the automotive industry in the 1950s, the two smaller firms—Studebaker and American Motors—spent more than twice as much on advertising per car than did General Motors and Ford. This fact has been interpreted as evidence of a threshold volume for advertising out of reach for the smaller firms.[8]

Several studies have linked the *A*/*S* ratio to differences in profitability among firms and industries. Imel and Helmberger [16] related the profitability of food processing firms to the *A*/*S* ratio (allowing for concentration ratio, R&D expenditures, assets, and other variables) and found a positive relationship. Similar results were reported by Vernon and Nourse [36], who added that "the association should be interpreted as advertising barriers causing high profits". But the sensible firm will increase its advertising well into the region of diminishing returns, the profit-maximizing criterion being that advertising expenditures should be increased to the point where marginal revenue equals marginal cost. Hence no conclusions about *increasing* returns can be drawn from such a relationship, even if it exists, and it may imply diminishing returns.

Comanor and Wilson [8] have studied at book length the dependence of profits and optimal firm size on the *A*/*S* ratio and firm size in cross-sections of

[7] The first set of Lambin's analyses related to the separate advertising function for each firm, showing the returns to advertising with all other (empirically controllable) factors *held constant*.

[8] See Comanor and Wilson [8, pp. 52–53].

industries and size-classes of firms within industries. They concluded flatly that, "The findings provide empirical support for the view that there are advantages to size that are related to the level of advertising intensity in an industry" [8, p. 234]. The main warrant for this conclusion is that there is a positive relationship between the profit rate and an interactive term (assets per size class of firms *x* industry advertising/sales ratio), whereas the asset term by itself had no principal effect [8, p. 220]. Additionally, they found that "advertising outlays interact with scale economies at the plant level to influence the minimum size of an efficient firm. Particularly where scale economies are small in relation to the market, heavy advertising outlays may increase the minimum share of the market accounted for by an efficient firm" [8, p. 228].

It would require an entire article to consider the Comanor-Wilson method and findings in satisfactory detail. It is fair to say in brief that whatever they do show, the Comanor-Wilson findings do not throw light on whether any particular seller of a given product has an advantage over another seller of the same product by virtue of using more advertising than the other firm. A long chain of logic would be needed to connect the behavior of competing sellers of a given specific product and the Comanor-Wilson findings. One would need to assume that larger and smaller firms in various industries have the same product mix. This is most unlikely. Moreover, the product mix is likely to be related to the extent to which the various specific products are advertised, which would invalidate the Comanor-Wilson conclusion. Furthermore, if smaller sellers of a given product do choose a different marketing strategy than do larger sellers, emphasizing low price rather than heavy advertising—because smaller firms can cut prices more flexibly than can large firms—this also would invalidate the conclusion of Comanor and Wilson.

Even in their own context, the Comanor-Wilson findings present some puzzles. For example, they found that firm size *is* positively related to the advertising/sales ratio, "larger firms spend proportionately more on advertising than their rivals" [8, p. 215]. The simplest interpretation of this finding is that there are diseconomies of scale with respect to advertising, though there are many other possible interpretations too.

Comanor and Wilson's results would seem to tell more about the *structure of markets*, such as which size class of firms choose products which they then advertise heavily, and which size classes of firms emphasize advertising rather than price within the marketing mix, than they do about economies of scale related to advertising.

Studies such as Comanor and Wilson may also be questioned because of their use of current profits as the criterion. Since advertising generally has been found to have lagged effects,[9] it would seem inappropriate to treat advertising as a current expense [10], [12, Chapter 9].

[9] For a comprehensive review of the literature, see Clarke [7].

Bloch [5] has recomputed regressions like those of Comanor and Wilson's on a set of data from food firms, trying out as the dependent variable both (a) current profits, and (b) profits allowing for lagged advertising effects. The regressions making allowance for lagged advertising effects showed no effect of the A/S ratio on profits, though the unadjusted current-profits regressions agreed with the Comanor-Wilson results. This suggests that the Comanor-Wilson result may be an artifact resulting from improper definition of the dependent variable.

All in all, the Comanor-Wilson study does not seem relevant to the question being addressed here, though the results may be illuminating and useful for other purposes.

Porter [26] reported that the A/S ratio had a positive effect on profits for "convenience goods" industries, but not in the "shopping goods" industries. This well-documented finding suggests that the relationship between profitability and advertising intensity is not homogeneous across industry groups or even across firms. It implies that there are dangers of uncritical pooling of observations across potentially heterogeneous firm and industry groups. The issue of homogeneity has also been addressed by Bass and his associates. They found that when firms were clustered into homogeneous groups, the relationship between profits and advertising evaporated in some cases.[10] This suggests again that effects of advertising in ordinary cross-sectional studies may be confounded with effects of structural variables.

In brief, studies of the relationship between size of profitability and the A/S ratio may be useful as evidence on the role of the *structure* of markets, but tell little or nothing about *economies of scale* related to advertising.

The review so far leads us to the conclusion that is has been convincingly demonstrated that large firms may be more efficient than smaller firms. On the other hand, it has not been possible to relate the higher efficiency of the larger firms to the volume or quality of their advertising.

Though it appears that a total and *direct* test of economies of scale in advertising is futile and meaningless, the matter may be approached by partial, *indirect* tests. Below the following indirect tests of the scale issue will be briefly addressed: advertising and prices, cost advantages due to media rates, multibrand economies, and the use of "stay-out advertising".

VII. ADVERTISING AND PRICES

Economies of scale might be involved if large advertisers were found to have lower prices than their smaller competitors (though the relationship could also be explained by other factors).

In the formulation of Farris and Albion [11], there appear to be two main schools of thought among economists concerned with the advertising-prices

[10] See [3] and [4].

issue. The first school adheres to the Advertising = Market Power model and maintains that advertising results in weakened competition and higher prices. In contrast, the Advertising = Information school argues that advertising strengthens competition and decreases industry prices.

Instead of reviewing the many studies here in detail, we will build on the review of Farris and Albion [11]. Not surprisingly, Farris and Albion concluded that the evidence connecting manufacturer advertising and prices was neither complete nor definitive [11, p. 30]. However, as far as the data went there were two strong tendencies. At the *factory* level advertising was found in most cases to decrease price sensitivity and to increase relative manufacturer prices. However, at the *retail* (consumer) level there was an opposite relationship as advertising was found to increase price sensitivity and to lower absolute prices. In this way, Farris and Albion called a draw for the two opposing schools of thought. The two effects appeared to neutralize one another.

VIII. COST ADVANTAGES DUE TO MEDIA RATE STRUCTURES

Increasing returns to advertising expenditures may result from volume discounts in media rates structures. It has been suggested that such discounts are important in national magazines, network radio, and specially network television.[11] Comanor and Wilson who investigated price structure for the three American networks,[12] reported that the principal source of cost advantages of large-scale advertisers was quantity discounts on individual programs (but not on aggregate firm purchases from the network) [8, pp. 53–61].

Another potential advantage of large advertisers is the access to essentially indivisible nation-wide media such as television networks. Though the evidence is mixed, such economies have been pointed out. For instance, Porter [27] found that network rates ranged from approximately 10 to 70 per cent of the sum of the individual station (spot) rates, with the discount varying by time of day and season. Moreover, in regression estimates of profit rates across 39 consumer goods industries significant positive results were obtained for a variable relating to network advertising as per cent of sales. However, a newer analysis using improved methodology showed that the differences between network and spot rates in television was much smaller than the range suggested by Porter.[13]

In conclusion, the evidence available is suggestive rather than conclusive. Obviously more work is needed before firm conclusions may be made regarding the cost advantages due to media rates. However, as far as the results go, there appear to be *some* scale economies relating to network television.

[11] See for instance Ferguson [12, pp. 74–75].
[12] Admittedly, the evidence relating to networking has less relevance outside the U.S.
[13] See Peterman [25].

IX. THE TRICKY ISSUE OF MULTIBRAND ECONOMIES

Multibrand economies of size stemming from advertising are logically similar to geographical economies. One might speculate that a merger of two related-product brands, or the development of a related-product brand by a going firm, might produce both volume discounts in advertising and communication economies such as the use of a common trademark. And the increase in the number of advertised brands in a majority of consumer categories [31, pp. 232–34] is consistent with this speculation. (This also represents lessened industrial concentration at the brand level, by the way, an important phenomenon in its own right.)

But a trend toward a larger number of brands sold per firm might also stem from economies of distribution, production, and purchasing (e.g., packing materials). Hence, this is certainly not strong evidence for multibrand economies of size flowing from advertising. Nor is there other relevant evidence. And it is difficult to think of a sound design to test for this effect.

X. DYNAMIC BARRIER EFFECTS—"STAY-OUT ADVERTISING"

Advertising might be used as a barrier against potential entrants into the market, just as "stay-out pricing" might be used. The latter has been discussed under the title of "limit pricing", analysed in a static manner by Bain [1], Modigliani [22], and Sylos-Labini [35], and in a more dynamic content by Gaskins [14].

It appears that the dynamic theory of advertising barriers effects has yet to be spelled out in a rigorous enough fashion.[14] Cubbin [9] argues persuasively that the positive associations often found between advertising intensity and profitability[15] does not mean that advertising acts as an entry barrier. The relationship may be a spurious one, as the studies have not controlled for the monopoly power effect.

It is not immediately obvious how one would formalize for a mature market the ideas vaguely expressed by the literary concept. For a new product, it seems rather straightforward that a firm making high profits from an innovation might buy advertising beyond what a monopolist would, in order to bind customers more closely for the future. And in this way, as well as by simply lowering the prospective profits because of advertising expenditures, a firm with a new product might render entry less attractive. That is, more advertising in period t might mean relatively fewer sales in period $t+1$ for a potential entrant with given levels of price and advertising.[16]

Why would one set up a barrier with advertising instead of price? It may be

[14] For a promising start see Schupack [30], and Cubbin [9].

[15] Some of these studies were reviewed above in section VI.

[16] See Cubbin [9, p. 296].

that advertising is a better barrier because advertising in t results in a *real* change in the entry conditions in $t+1$, whereas a stay-out price in t is only a signal of *intentions* about behavior in $t+1$ and can be interpreted only as a bluff.

Working in the other direction is advertising's role as a competitive tool that makes it easier for potential entrants actually to enter successfully. If one could not advertise, it would be much harder for a potential entrant with a product improvement—a ball-point pen or a rotary engine—or even a potential entrant without a product improvement, to enter the market. In this way advertising has a procompetitive dynamic effect.

Unfortunately, no body of empirical work could be found to determine whether the net outcome of advertising is to increase or decrease the rate of market entrance. And it will not be an easy task to design sound research to answer this question. One research possibility is to investigate changes in industrial structure in countries that have banned advertising for a product group such as tobacco, alcoholic beverages, etc.

This question must be distinguished from the advertising-and-competition question that has so much interested economists in recent years. In practice, the latter has reduced to the question whether industries that, for one reason or other, spend a relatively high proportion of sales on advertising also have a relatively high concentration ratio. But the logical links between this question and questions about the effects of more or less advertising, whether or not in conjunction with controlled changes in other variables, are tenuous indeed. Furthermore, the material on advertising and competition has been treated at great length, and would not benefit from further discussion in this context.[17] The *ex cathedra* reaction is that is does not matter much whether after a great deal of sophisticated econometrics and controversy there is seen to be a significant-but-slight effect or none at all. An effect that can be seen only so elusively and only with such a fine measuring instrument is not likely to be economically important.

XI. CONCLUSION

This review has supported the contention by Bass that "there is no more difficult, complex, or controversial problem in marketing than measuring the influence of advertising on sales" [2, p. 291].

It seems well established that there are general returns to scale in the sense that large firms are often more efficient than smaller ones. However, whether advertising is directly implicated in any economies of scale has never been subjected to a satisfactory test. Since the economies of scale concept refers to the simultaneous variation of all factor inputs, the issue even appears to be meaningless from a conceptual point of view.

[17] See Comanor and Wilson [8], Ferguson [12], Lambin [18], and Ornstein [23].

There is, however, some indirect evidence of scale economies for large advertiser in terms of media discounts and opportunities to use network television, which seems to be more cost efficient.

There was no conclusive evidence on the relationship between advertising and prices. Nor was there any evidence on multibrand economies. It was not possible to find conclusive studies of the use of advertising as a barrier to entry, or evidence that shows whether on balance the existence of advertising as a competitive weapon is pro-competitive or anti-competitive.

To conclude, there is little conceptual or empirical evidence supporting the myth of substantial returns to scale for advertising.

ACCEPTED APRIL 1982

Johan Arndt,
Professor of Business Administration,
Norwegian School of Economics and Business Administration,
Hellevien 30,
N-5035 Bergen-Sandviken, Norway

Julian L. Simon,
College of Commerce and Business Administration,
University of Illinois at Urbana—Champaign,
350 Commerce Building (West),
1206 S. Sixth Street,
Champaign, Illinois 61820

REFERENCES

[1] BAIN, JOE S., *Barriers to New Competition* (Harvard University Press, Cambridge, 1956).

[2] BASS, FRANK M., Simultaneous Equation Regression Study of Advertising and Sales of Cigarettes," *Journal of Marketing Research, 4,* (August 1969), pp. 291–300.

[3] ———, "Profit and the *A/S* Ratio," *Journal of Advertising Research, 14,* (December 1974), pp. 9–19.

[4] BASS, FRANK M., CATTIN, PHILIPPE, and WITTINK, DICK R., "Firm Effects and Industry Effects in the Analysis of Market Structure and Profitability," *Journal of Marketing Research, 15,* (February 1978), pp. 3–10.

[5] BLOCH, HARRY, "Advertising and Profitability: A Reappraisal," *Journal of Political Economy, 82,* (March–April 1974), pp. 267–86.

[6] CHAMBERLIN, EDWARD H. *The Theory of Monopolistic Competition* (Harvard University Press, Cambridge, 1962).

[7] CLARKE, DARRAL G., "Econometric Measurement of the Duration of Advertising Effect of Sales," *Journal of Marketing Research, 13,* (November 1967), pp. 345–57.

[8] COMANOR, WILLIAM S. and WILSON, THOMAS A. *Advertising and Market Power* (Harvard University Press, Cambridge, 1974).

[9] CUBBIN, JOHN, "Advertising and the Theory of Entry Barriers", *Economica, 48,* (1981), pp. 289–98.

[10] DEMSETZ, HAROLD, "Accounting for Advertising as Barrier to Entry," *Journal of Business, 52,* (July 1979), pp. 345–60.

[11] FARRIS, PAUL W., and ALBION, MARK S., "The Impact of Advertising on the Price of Consumer Products," *Journal of Marketing, 44*, (Summer 1980), pp. 17–35.

[12] FERGUSON, JAMES M., *Advertising and Competition: Theory, Measurement, Fact* Ballinger, Cambridge, 1974).

[13] FRISCH, RAGNAR, *Innledning til produksjonsteorien* (Universitetsforlaget, Oslo, 1971).

[14] GASKINS, DARIUS W., "Dynamic Limit Pricing: Optimal Pricing under Threat of Entry," *Journal of Economic Theory, 3*, (September 1971), pp. 306–22.

[15] GEIGER, S. and ERNST, O., "Advertising Pressure: Advertising Response Differentiations of Response Functions According to Target Groups and Media Consumption Groups," ESOMAR/Wapor Conference, (Part II), 1971, pp. 401–55.

[16] IMEL, J. BLAKE and HELMBERGER, PETER, "Estimation of Structure-Profit Relationships with Applications to The Food Processing Sector," *American Economic Review, 61*, (September 1971), pp. 614–27.

[17] KOCH, JAMES V., *Industrial Organization and Prices*, 2nd ed. (Prentice-Hall, Englewood Cliffs, New Jersey, 1980).

[18] LAMBIN, JEAN-JACQUES, *Advertising, Competition and Market Conduct in Oligopoly over Time* (North-Holland, Amsterdam, 1976).

[19] LITTLE, JOHN D. C., Aggregate Advertising Models: The State of the Art," *Operations Research, 17*, (1979), pp. 629–67.

[20] MCDONALD, COLIN, "What is the Short-Term Effect of Advertising?" *Proceedings of the 1970 ESOMAR Conference*, Barcelona, 1970.

[21] MCNIVEN, MALCOLM, ed., *How much to Spend for Advertising?* (Association for National Advertisers, New York, 1969).

[22] MODIGLIANI, FRANCO, "New Developments on the Oligopoly Front," *Journal of Political Economy, 66*, (June 1958), pp. 215–32.

[23] ORNSTEIN, STANLEY I., *Industrial Concentration and Advertising Intensity* (American Enterprise Institute, Washington, 1977).

[24] PELES, YORAM, Economies of Scale in Advertising Beer and Cigarettes, *Journal of Business, 44*, (1971), pp. 32–7.

[25] PETERMAN, JOHN L., Differences Between the Levels of Spot and Network Television Advertising Rates," *Journal of Business, 52*, (1979), pp. 549–61.

[26] PORTER, MICHAEL E. *Interbrand Choice, Strategy and Bilateral Market Power* (Harvard University Press, Cambridge, 1976).

[27] ———, Interbrand Choice, Media Mix and Market Power, *American Economic Review, 66*, (1976), pp. 398–406.

[28] RAO, ANBAR G. and MILLER, PETER B., "Advertising/Sales Response Functions," *Journal of Advertising Research, 15*, (April 1975), pp. 7–15.

[29] SCHMALENSEE, RICHARD, *The Economics of Advertising* (North Holland, Amsterdam, 1972).

[30] SCHUPACK, M. B., *Dynamic Limit Pricing with Advertising*. Brown University, Mimeo, 1972.

[31] SIMON, JULIAN L., *Issues in the Economics of Advertising* (University of Illinois Press, Urbana 1970).

[32] ———, and ARNDT, JOHAN, "The Shape of Advertising Response Function," *Journal of Advertising Research, 20*, (August 1980), pp. 11–28.

[33] STEWART, JOHN B., *Repetitive Advertising in Newspapers: A Study of Two New Products* (Harvard University, Graduate School of Business Administration, Division of Research, Cambridge, 1964).

[34] STIGLER, GEORGE J., "The Economies of Scale," *Journal of Law and Economics, 1*, (October 1958), pp. 54–71.

[35] Sylos-Labini, Paolo, *Oligopoly in Technical Progress* (Harvard University Press, Cambridge, 1962).

[36] Vernon, John M. and Nourse, Robert E. M., "Profit Rates and Market Structure of Advertising Intensive Firms," *Journal of Industrial Economics*, *22*, (September 1973), pp. 1–20.

THE JOURNAL OF INDUSTRIAL ECONOMICS 0022–1821 $2.00
Volume XXXII December 1983 No. 2

OPTIMAL ADJUSTMENTS TO RESTRICTIONS ON ADVERTISING: A COMMENT*

R. CLARKE AND P. K. ELSE

I. INTRODUCTION

In a recent paper in this journal, Baye[1] has argued that restrictions on the volume of advertising on products considered to have harmful effects need not lead to less of the products being consumed and could lead to more.[2] His analysis is based on the supposition that such a restriction will lead to an increase in the price of advertising messages and he shows, using standard comparative static techniques, that the effects of such an increase on the quantity produced and sold by a profit maximising firm are indeterminate. It is our contention that restrictions on the volume of advertising need not necessarily lead to an increase in the cost of advertising but we also argue that similar effects on consumption of the product will be observed from an advertising restriction regardless of whether the cost of advertising rises or falls. Moreover, we suggest that restrictions on advertising would lead to an increase in the quantity of the product sold only in rather exceptional circumstances.

II. EFFECTS OF RESTRICTION ON THE VOLUME OF ADVERTISING ON THE PRICE OF ADVERTISING MESSAGES

Baye assumes a competitive market for television time with an equilibrium price and quantity determined where demand is equal to supply. He then suggests that if the volume of advertising is restricted to something less than the equilibrium level, the price of advertising will be bid up until demand is equal to the restricted supply. However, this implies that the restrictions apply to all advertised commodities. If the restrictions applied only to the advertising of specific types of product (e.g. sweets and tobacco) the effect could be rather different. In that case the demand curve for advertising messages would be pushed to the left for all prices at which the affected firms' demand exceeded the limit allowed—as indicated by the dashed curve DD_R in Figure 1 (where DD_1 indicates the unrestricted demand curve). Thus

* We would like to thank the referee for helpful comments. Responsibility for errors lies with the authors.

[1] M. R. Baye, 'Optimal Adjustments to Changes in the Price of Advertising', *Journal of Industrial Economics*, 30, no. 1 (September 1981), pp. 95–103.

[2] Baye also notes that such restrictions will have an indeterminate effect on price. We do not pursue this particular aspect of his analysis here.

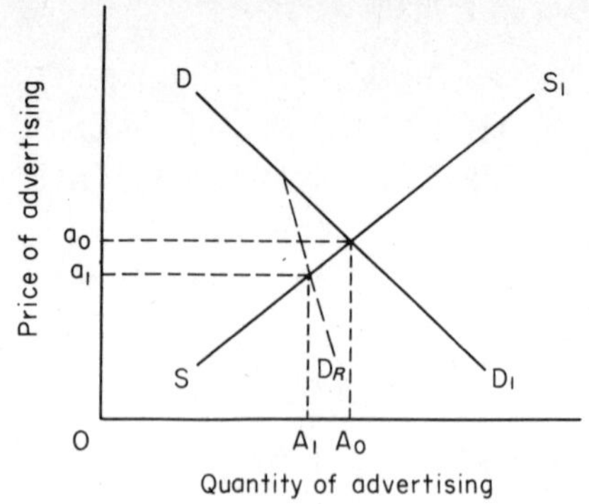

FIGURE 1

the equilibrium price of advertising space would *fall* as suppliers attempted to attract new advertising to replace that lost by the controls.

If the market for television advertising is non-competitive, the effect of advertising restrictions on the cost of advertising may be sensitive to the market structure assumed. For example, with a non-discriminating monopolistic seller of advertising space and competitive buyers, the effect of the restriction on the price of advertising is indeterminate—as is normally the case with an unspecified shift in the demand curve. In fact, depending on circumstances, a restriction on the volume of advertising may give rise either to a rise or fall in the cost of advertising.

In what follows we consider Baye's case in which the price of advertising rises and an alternative case in which other rationing procedures may be used. In the latter case the price of advertising may rise or fall, but we shall argue that this is not relevant to the matter at issue here.

III. EFFECTS ON THE FIRM—INDEPENDENT FIRM CASE

Consider first the analysis of Baye. He assumes a demand function $P = F(QA)$ in which A is the quantity of advertising, and a cost function $C(Q) + Aa_0$ where a_0 is the (given) cost per unit of advertising.

The profits function can be expressed as

$$(1) \qquad \pi = F(A, Q) \cdot Q - c(Q) - Aa_0$$

and profits are maximised where

$$(2) \qquad \pi_Q = F_Q \cdot Q + F(A, Q) - c'(Q) = 0$$

$$(3) \qquad \pi_A = F_A \cdot Q - a_0 = 0$$

$$(4) \qquad \pi_{QQ} = F_{QQ} \cdot Q + 2F_Q - c''(Q) < 0$$

and

$$(5)\qquad \begin{aligned} |H| &= \pi_{QQ} \cdot \pi_{AA} - (\pi_{AQ})^2 \\ &= F_{AA} \cdot Q[F_{QQ} \cdot Q + 2F_Q - c''(Q)] - [F_{AQ} \cdot Q + F_A]^2 > 0 \end{aligned}$$

Also of course (4) and (5) together require

$$(4a)\qquad \pi_{AA} = F_{AA} \cdot Q < 0$$

The effect of a change in a_0 can then be found by differentating (2) and (3) with respect to a_0 and solving, which yields Baye's result that

$$(6)\qquad \frac{dQ}{da_0} = -\frac{[F_{QA} \cdot Q + F_A]}{|H|} \gtrless 0 \quad \text{as} \quad F_{QA} \cdot Q + F_A \lesseqgtr 0$$

(6) was the source of Baye's conclusion that the quantity sold of a commodity subject to restrictions in advertising might actually increase rather than fall, but the question is whether it is a likely result.

Before addressing this issue consider the alternative case where, irrespective of the effect on the price of advertising, there is an absolute restriction on advertising. If the firm's advertising is restricted to be equal to or less than A^*, and the constraint is binding, then maximisation of (1) with respect to output gives (2) with $A = A^*$. Totally differentiating (2) with respect to A^* and re-arranging gives

$$(7)\qquad \frac{dQ}{dA^*} = -\frac{[F_{QA} \cdot Q + F_A]}{\pi_{QQ}} \lesseqgtr 0 \quad \text{as} \quad F_{QA} \cdot Q + F_A \lesseqgtr 0$$

where $\pi_{QQ} < 0$ by the second order conditions. Thus, the condition for a rise in consumption following a relaxation of an advertising quota (i.e. $F_{QA} \cdot Q + F_A > 0$) is precisely the same as that derived by Baye for a rise in consumption following a fall in the price of advertising (in equation (6) above). The effect of the advertising restriction on the price of advertising is therefore irrelevant as far as qualitative predictions are concerned.

This point may be usefully demonstrated in a diagram. The first order condition for maximum profits expressed in equation (2) can be represented by a curve (QQ' in Figure 2) whose slope is

$$(8)\qquad \left(\frac{dQ}{dA}\right)_{QQ'} = \frac{-[F_{QA} \cdot Q + F_A]}{F_{QQ} \cdot Q + 2F_Q - c''(Q)}$$

whilst the other first order condition expressed in equation (3) can be represented by a curve (AA') whose slope is

$$(9)\qquad \left(\frac{dQ}{dA}\right)_{AA'} = \frac{-F_{AA} \cdot Q}{F_{QA} \cdot Q + F_A}$$

Given the direct second order conditions (4) and (4a), if as argued below $F_{QA} \cdot Q + F_A > 0$, both those curves will be positively sloped. The uncon-

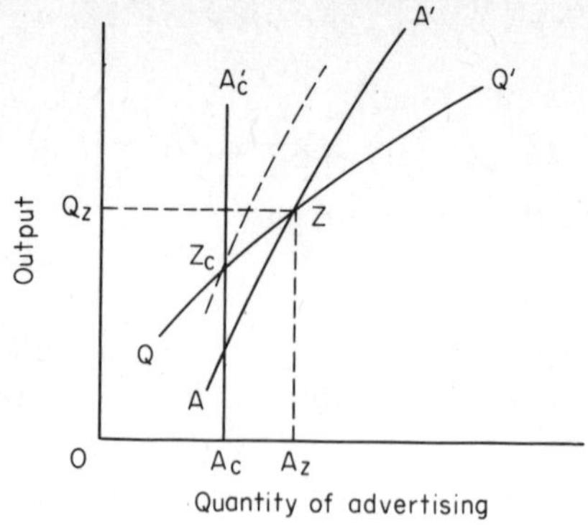

FIGURE 2

strained profit maximising position is at the point of intersection of these curves provided that (using (5)) AA' is steeper than QQ'—as at Z in Figure 2.

An increase in the cost of advertising will simply push AA' to the left, thus reducing the equilibrium values of both A and Q (as long as the curves are positively sloped or $F_{QA} \cdot Q + F_A > 0$). Hence if it was required to restrict total advertising to A_c a suitable increase in price would move the profit maximising position to Z_c, at which the firms demand for advertising would have been reduced to the desired level in line with the previous analysis.

However, if the volume of advertising is restricted by non-price methods where the price change is other than that required to limit demand to A_c, the firm would still produce at Z_c, because that point, since it lies on QQ', indicates the optimum level of Q for the constrained volume of advertising whatever the cost of advertising.

What happens to the price of advertising therefore would appear to be irrelevant as far as determining the effect of advertising restrictions on the quantity sold is concerned. The price of advertising mainly determines the effects on the profits of the parties involved. But whatever happens to that price the quantity of the advertised commodity sold will fall as long as $F_{QA} \cdot Q + F_A > 0$.

Whether this condition is satisfied or not is, of course, an empirical question. But on an *a priori* basis there seem to be good reasons for suggesting that it is likely to be satisfied particularly if appropriate restrictions are put on the demand function.

Baye discussed the sign of $F_{QA} \cdot Q + F_A$ in terms of the relationship between the elasticity of demand with respect to advertising and what he referred to as the 'slope elasticity of advertising' ($= \partial F_Q/dA \cdot A/F_Q$). It is perhaps more straightforward to note that

$$F_{QA} \cdot Q + F_A = F_A \cdot \left(\frac{F_{QA}}{F_A} \cdot Q + 1\right) < 0 \quad \text{if} \quad \frac{F_{QA} \cdot Q}{F_A} < -1$$

Now $(F_{QA} \cdot Q)/F_A = \partial F_A/\partial Q \cdot Q/F_A$, which is the elasticity of F_A with respect to Q, and thus measures the responsiveness of the increase in price consumers are induced to pay for a given quantity as a result of advertising to changes in quantity. A negative dQ/da_0 thus requires an increase in Q to be associated with a more than proportionate reduction in F_A, or in other words it requires advertising to be proportionately much less effective in inducing people to pay higher prices when prices are initially low (and quantity relatively high) than when prices are initially high. It is not intuitively obvious why this should be the case, but there are also other more specific reasons for suggesting why it might not occur.

With $F_A > 0$ a necessary condition for $F_{QA} \cdot Q + F_A < 0$ is $F_{QA} < 0$, or in other words increases in advertising make the demand curve steeper. If this happens whilst an increase in advertising pushes the demand curve upwards in the region in which the firm is operating (making $F_A > 0$) there may be some range of prices over which the new demand curve lies below the old one. In these circumstances the firm may find that an increase in advertising, whilst allowing it to charge more for its existing output (or sell more at its current price) actually reduces its optimum level of output (where $MC = MR$). This in fact is precisely the kind of situation in which $F_{QA} \cdot Q + F_A < 0$.

However, it would seem reasonable to suppose that if advertising had a positive effect on demand at some prices it would have a positive effect at all non-negative prices, or alternatively $F_A > 0$ for $P \geq 0$.

With this restriction the chances of $F_{QA} \cdot Q + F_A$ being negative are much reduced. Indeed with a demand function of the form

$$P = f(A) - g(A) \cdot Q \tag{10}$$

(where the demand curve is a straight line whose slope and intercept are influenced by A) it can be shown that the restriction implies that $F_{QA} \cdot Q + F_A$ must be positive even when F_{QA} $(= -g'(A))$ is negative.[3]

With non-linear demand curves the possibility of the opposite result is not entirely ruled out but it is considerably reduced.[4] All this suggests therefore that the case where more is sold as a result of an increase in the cost of advertising is likely to be rather unusual.

[3] In this linear case it can be shown using (10) that the restriction that $F_A > 0$ for all $P \geq 0$ requires (when $g'(A) > 0$)

$$f'(A)g(A) - g'(A)f(A) > 0$$

It can then be shown using condition (2) that if this holds

$$F_{QA} \cdot Q + F_A = f'(A) - 2g'(A)Q > 0.$$

[4] Note also that with a constant elasticity demand function of the form $P = B \cdot Q^{-1/\alpha} \cdot A^{\beta}$ $(\alpha, \beta > 0)$, the possibility that $dQ/da_0 > 0$ is ruled out *in general.* In this case $F_{QA} \cdot Q + F_A = \beta(P/A) \cdot [(\alpha - 1)/\alpha]$ which is strictly positive given that marginal revenues $= P \cdot [(\alpha - 1)/\alpha] > 0$.

IV. EFFECTS ON THE FIRM—INTERDEPENDENT FIRM CASE

Finally, with obvious notational adjustments, the above analysis generalises to Baye's interdependent firm case. In particular, for firm i, $(dQ^i/da_0) > 0$ implies the (perceived) elasticity

$$\frac{F^i_{Q^iA}}{F^i_A} Q^i$$

is less than minus one which as in the single firm case lacks intuitively plausibility. Also the analysis of Figure 2 carries through to the interdependent firm case, with appropriate notational adjustments, implying in this case also that what happens to the price of advertising is not relevant to the effect of advertising restrictions on the quantity sold. Thus we would argue that recognition of firm interdependence does not materially alter our analysis of Section III.

However, we may note that in the event that $F^i_{QA} < 0$, more collusive conjectural variations (i.e. $\sum_{j \neq i} dQ_j/dQ^i > 0$) relative to the Cournot case, will give more weight to the possibility of an output increasing effect. This finding we would regard as of only minor interest given our above comments however.

V. CONCLUSIONS

In this paper we have argued that Baye's[5] earlier formulation of the problem of restrictions on the volume of advertising on products in terms of the price of advertising messages is neither firmly based nor necessary to the analysis. Further, we have argued that such restrictions will usually lead to a reduction in the consumption of products and that the possibility of "perverse" increases in consumption must be considered unlikely.

From a policy point of view, we would argue that restrictions on advertising of products considered to have harmful effects, such as sweets and tobacco, are very likely to reduce their consumption. Whilst this must ultimately be decided by empirical means, in our view the possibility of 'perverse' results seems small enough to be ignored by policy makers in normal circumstances.

R. Clarke and P. K. Else,
Department of Economics,
University of Sheffield,
Crookesmoor Building,
Conduit Road,
Sheffield S10 1FL.

ACCEPTED MARCH 1983

[5] *Op. cit.*

THE JOURNAL OF INDUSTRIAL ECONOMICS 0022–1821 $2.00
Volume XXXII December 1983 No. 2

OPTIMAL ADJUSTMENTS TO RESTRICTIONS ON ADVERTISING: SOME FURTHER COMMENTS*

MICHAEL R. BAYE

CLARKE and Else correctly point out that in some instances advertising restrictions may not lead to increases in the price of advertising. However, by ignoring any effect on the price of advertising Clarke and Else have merely reproduced the results derived by Samuelson in *Foundations of Economic Analysis* [4, pp. 41–42].

In my original paper I examine the type of advertising restrictions which were imposed on children's programming in the United States in the early 1970s. With respect to these restrictions Alan Pearce reports:

> "Although minutes available and minutes sold are down, due mainly to the enforced reduction beginning January 1, 1973, the average price per minute is 14% higher—$6,900 for the first four months of 1972 as against $7,900 for the first four months of 1974".[1] [3, pp. 11–12].

It is this fact which intially motivated me to extend Samuelson's model by examining the profit-maximizing firm's response to changes in the price of advertising, and therefore, to examine the effects of market specific advertising restrictions.

Regardless of whether advertising restrictions are firm or market specific, the effect on product output depends on the sign of $F_{QA} \cdot Q + F_A$, which is nothing more than the change in the marginal revenue of output due to a change in a unit of advertising. The question of its sign is an empirical one. This point is also made by Samuelson:

> "Thus, the direction of change in output depends upon the direction of shift in the marginal revenue schedule (upwards or downwards) as advertising changes. Now there is nothing in the formulation of the problem which requires that this shift be of any particular direction. Hence, short of quantitive empirical investigation of sales response to advertising, no presumption is possible". [4, p. 42].

Although Clarke and Else also admit this to be an empirical question, they

* I wish to thank Dub Lane, Chuck Maurice, and Steve Wiggins for helpful discussions, and Purdue and Texas A&M Universities for research support. Any remaining inadequacies in this paper are my own.

[1] Adjusting Pearce's figures for inflation during the period leads to a price increase of 3%.

attempt to convince readers that the "perverse" case can be ignored. The basis for their argument is that two special functional forms imply no "perverse" effect. I will respond to this below, but first address another issue.

The authors point out that the 'perverse effect' "requires advertising to be proportionately much less effective in inducing people to pay higher prices when prices are initially low than when prices are high" [2, p. 247]. I commend the authors for providing this economic interpretation. However, the authors add "It is not intuitively obvious why this should be the case . . ." [2, p. 247]. Not withstanding my previous comments concerning the empirical nature of the question, the following type of advertising may satisfy the conditions necessary for the 'perverse case' to occur.

A common advertising strategy is to emphasize the characteristics of the product being sold. For example, Seven Up, a soft drink producer, recently began an advertising campaign which states "Seven Up is caffeine free—Coke and Pepsi are not". Consider the effect of this information on two types of consumers: those who prefer caffeine free drinks to ones with caffeine, and those who prefer drinks with caffeine to drinks without caffeine. As a result of the information conveyed in Seven Up's advertising message, one would expect the consumers who prefer caffeine free drinks to increase their reservation price for Seven Up, and the consumers who prefer drinks with caffeine to decrease their reservation price for Seven Up. The effect of these changes on the market demand for Seven Up is illustrated in Figure 1. $D_C(A_0)$ and $D_N(A_0)$ represent hypothetical pre-advertising demands for Seven Up by the two groups. Even if, as in Figure 1, the advertising message leads to offsetting parallel shifts to $D_C(A_1)$ and $D_N(A_1)$, only the top portion of the market demand schedule shifts outward. Thus, when viewing the effect of advertising on *market demand*, advertising appears relatively more effective at inducing people to pay a higher price when prices are initially high. Thus the conditions under which the "perverse effect" would occur

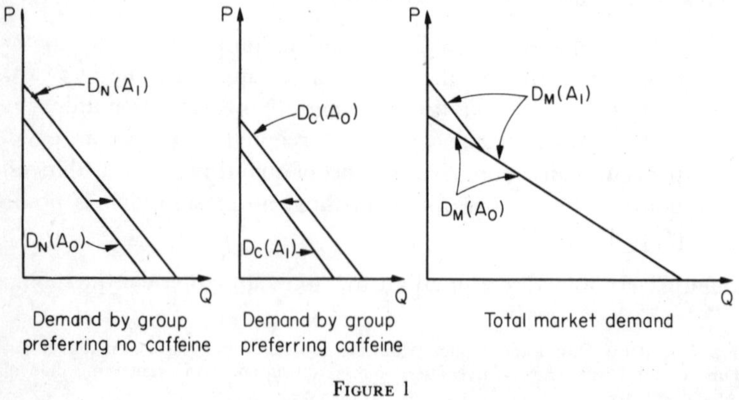

FIGURE 1
The effect of advertising on market demand.

appear to me to be intuitively plausible, but remain an empirical issue. As an aside, it should be pointed out that the relative shifts in $D_N(A_0)$ and $D_C(A_0)$ in Figure 1 and the subsequent effect of advertising on market demand depends on many factors, including the number of consumers of each type, the "strength" of their preferences for or against caffeine as well as the number and behavior of firms selling substitutes for Seven Up.

Finally, let me briefly respond to Clarke and Else's special functional forms (their equation (10) and footnote 4). The fact that these functional forms imply $F_{QA} \cdot Q + F_A > 0$ merely suggests that the functions are *not* flexible enough to answer the empirical question alluded to by Samuelson and myself. Despite the claims of the authors, these forms do *not* imply that the "possibility of 'perverse' results seems small enough to be ignored by policy makers in normal circumstances" [2, p. 248]. Using the author's reasoning, we would ignore inferior goods in consumer theory since Cobb-Douglas (and other homothetic) preferences rule them out.

Michael R. Baye,
Department of Economics,
University of Kentucky,
Lexington,
KY 40506–0034.

ACCEPTED MARCH 1983

REFERENCES

[1] BAYE, MICHAEL R., "Optimal Adjustments to Changes in the Price of Advertising", *The Journal of Industrial Economics,* XXX, 2 (September 1981), pp. 95–103.
[2] CLARKE, R. and ELSE, P. K., "Optimal Adjustments to Restrictions on Advertising: A Comment", this issue.
[3] PEARCE, ALAN, *The Economics of Children's Television: An Assessment of the Impact of a Reduction in the Amount of Advertising* (Office of Plans and Policy, FCC, June 1974).
[4] SAMUELSON, PAUL A., *Foundations of Economic Analysis* (Eighth Printing) (Atheneum, New York, 1976).

STATISTICS USERS' CONFERENCE

Publication of proceedings now available from NEDO.

Session 1 Official statistics on the distributive trades

Chairman Sir John Boreham. KCB, Director and Head of the Government Statistical Service

Papers Statistics of the distributive trades
Mr L S Berman, CB, Director of Statistics for the Departments of Industry and Trade

Statistics for the distributive trades: employment and earnings Mr A G Carruthers, Director of Statistics, Department of Employment

The National Food Survey
Dr P J Lund, Senior Economic Adviser, Ministry of Agriculture, Fisheries and Food

Statistics on the distributive trades: notes on the papers Lady Hall, Honorary Fellow of Somerville College, Oxford, Consultant to the Distributive Trades EDC

Discussion led by Lady Hall

Session 2 Measurement of distributive trades' performance

Chairman Professor W G McClelland, Chairman, Distributive Trades EDC

Papers The measurement of distributive performance: a stockbroker's view
Mr J Hewitt, Scrimgeour, Kemp-Gee & Co

Distributive statistics: a trade union view of their use in an industrial relations context
Mrs D Jeuda, Research Officer, USDAW

Measurement of distributive trades' performance: use of employment statistics Mr C B Moir, NEDO

Outlet planning by shopping centre within C & J Clark Ltd
Mr J Gill, Market Researcher, C & J Clark Ltd

The measurement of company retail performance
Mr J Butler, Special Duties, The Littlewoods Organisation plc

Discussion Led by Professor C Winsten, Professor of Mathematics, University of Essex

Session 3 Statistics and retail planning policy

Chairman Professor W G McClelland, Chairman, Distributive Trades EDC

Papers Retail planning and urban policy
Sir Wilfred Burns, CB, CBE, formerly Chief Planner, Department of the Environment

Retail planning statistical requirements – the local authority view Mr W A K Struthers, Deputy Chief Planning Officer, West Midlands

Statistical requirements at a planning appeal – a consultant's view on the information required
Mr R W Evely, Managing Director, Development Analysts Ltd

Statistical requirements for planning inquiries into shopping proposals
Mr E Booth, Assistant Chief Planning Inspector, Department of the Environment

Statistics and retail planning policy: notes on the papers Dr D Thorpe, Head of Research, John Lewis Partnership

Discussion led by Dr D Thorpe, Head of Research, John Lewis Partnership

Session 4 Documentation of wholesaling activity

Chairman Professor W G McClelland, Chairman, Distributive Trades EDC

Papers Wholesaling – size and classification
Mr C B Moir, NEDO

A wholesaler's view of the need for information
Mr A Niner, Chairman, Textile Distributors Association

My need for distribution statistics
Mr D Corbett, Managing Director, Produce Studies Ltd

Discussion led by Dr P Chisnall, Senior Lecturer in Marketing, Manchester Business School

The conference proceedings have been published in four parts (sessions) as above. Each part can be purchased separately at a price of £5 or all four parts are available at £12. Please use this coupon to obtain copies.

To: NEDO Books, Millbank Tower, Millbank, London SW1 4QX.
Please send copies as shown. My remittance for £. . . . . is enclosed.

. . . . copies of Part 1 Name . . . .
. . . . copies of Part 2 Address . . . .
. . . . copies of Part 3 . . . .
. . . . copies of Part 4 . . . .
. . . . copies of Parts 1,2,3 & 4. . . . .

THE JOURNAL OF INDUSTRIAL ECONOMICS

Published first in October 1952, this Journal was founded to develop the analysis of the problems facing modern industry. It is concerned with the individual business and its relation to the economy—e.g. with outputs and prices and their behaviour in the market, and with the business decisions which affect these. It therefore aims to contribute both to economic theory and to practical public and private policies in the industrial field. The journal is naturally meant to interest business men as well as economists.

The Editors welcome contributions covering the fundamental categories in economics (such as prices, costs, investment, finance, location, wages and productivity) as well as the broader 'background' circumstances (such as the changing structure of industry, management policy and public monopoly policy). Preference is given to MSS bearing on these subjects from the standpoint of individual firms or industries. Theoretical discussion is welcome. Abstract theory is not barred, but authors in this case should provide an introduction and conclusion, so that non-specialist readers may see what the article is about. Alongside articles of more normal length, the Editors are willing to publish shorter notes, especially when these give interim results of important research studies. Books are not reviewed, although books received will be listed, sometimes with a short note; but substantial review articles will be considered. No payment is made to authors, but 25 free offprints are provided. Contributors are asked to send an Abstract, not exceeding 100 words, with their article.

Editorial Offices:

Manuscripts from North America should be sent to Professor H. Michael Mann, Department of Economics, Boston College, Chestnut Hill, Massachusetts, 02167, U.S.A.; manuscripts from all other countries to the General Editor, *The Journal of Industrial Economics*, The Institute of Economics and Statistics, The University of Oxford, St. Cross Building, Manor Road, Oxford, OX1 3UL, from whom detailed Information for Contributors is available.

Information for subscribers

The journal is published four times a year, in September, December, March and June, by Basil Blackwell Publisher Ltd., 108 Cowley Road, Oxford OX4 1JF, England. Prices are as follows:

	UK	Overseas	USA	Canada
Institutions	£24.00	£29.40	$59.50	$72.90
Individuals	£14.95	£18.30	$35.00	$43.25
Single issue prices for:				
Institutions	£6.50	£7.75	$16.00	$19.50
Individuals	£4.75	£5.75	$11.00	$13.50

CONTRIBUTORS TO THIS NUMBER

FRÉDÉRIC JENNY: Professor of Economics, Ecole Supérieure des Sciences Economiques et Commerciales, (ESSEC), Cergy Pontoise, Cédex, and Associate Editor of this Journal.

ANDRÉ-PAUL WEBER: Professor of Economics, Ecole Supérieure des Sciences Economiques et Commerciales, (ESSEC), Cergy Pontoise, Cédex.

G. F. MATHEWSON: Professor of Economics, University of Toronto.

R. W. SHAW: Senior Lecturer in Economics, University of Stirling.

S. A. SHAW: Lecturer in Business Studies, University of Stirling.

R. K. TURNER: Lecturer, University of East Anglia, and Consultant to OECD (Paris).

D. DEADMAN: Lecturer, University of Leicester.

MANFRED NEUMANN: Professor of Economics, University Erlangen-Nürnberg.

INGO BÖBEL: Associate Professor, Rutgers University, Graduate School of Management, Newark, NJ.

ALFRED HAID: Wissenschaftlicher Assistant, University of Erlangen-Nürnberg.

C. W. L. HILL: Lecturer in Managerial Economics, Department of Management Sciences, UMIST.

MARC R. REINGANUM: Associate Professor of Finance, Graduate School of Business, University of Southern California.

JANET KIHOLM SMITH: Assistant Professor of Economics, Arizona State University, Tempe.

JOHAN ARNDT: Professor of Business Administration, Norwegian School of Economics and Business Administration.

JULIAN L. SIMON: Professor, College of Commerce and Business Administration, University of Illinois at Urbana-Champaign.

R. CLARKE: Lecturer, University of Sheffield.

P. K. ELSE: Senior Lecturer, University of Sheffield.

MICHAEL R. BAYE: Assistant Professor of Economics, University of Kentucky.

US Mailing: Second class postage paid at New York. Postmaster: Send address corrections to : Journal of Industrial Economics, c/o Expediters of the Printed Word Ltd., 527 Madison Avenue, Suite 1217, New York, NY 10022 (US Mailing Agent).

Set by Santype International Ltd., Salisbury, Wilts.
Printed and bound by Whitstable Litho Ltd., Whitstable, Kent

THE JOURNAL OF INDUSTRIAL ECONOMICS

Volume XXXII MARCH 1984 No. 3

W. H. DAVIDSON and DONALD G. McFETRIDGE
International Technology Transactions and the Theory of the Firm 253

STEVEN SCHWARTZ
An Empirical Test of a Managerial, Life-Cycle, and Cost of Capital Model of Merger Activity 265

MICHAEL L. LAWRIWSKY
Some Tests of the Influence of Control Type on the Market for Corporate Control in Australia 277

JOHN F. STEWART, ROBERT S. HARRIS and WILLARD T. CARLETON
The Role of Market Structure in Merger Behavior 293

MARTIN K. PERRY
Scale Economies, Imperfect Competition and Public Policy 313

ELI NOAM
Market Power and Regulation: A Simultaneous Approach 335

SHERRILL SHAFFER
Regulation and Risk Preference 349

BRUCE YANDLE
Polluters' Profits: An Empirical Note 359

W. J. BOYES and DALE BECK FURNISH
A Note on the Use of Incorporation as an Escape from Usury Ceilings 367

JAN J. P. VAN HEEMST
Subcontracting Between Small-Scale Enterprises in Developing Countries: A Note 373

DAVID LEVY
Testing Stigler's Interpretation of 'The Division of Labor is Limited by the Extent of the Market' 377

RONALD P. WILDER and IRVIN B. TUCKER
Trends in Vertical Integration: Reply 391

ISSN 0022-1821
BASIL BLACKWELL OXFORD ENGLAND

THE JOURNAL OF INDUSTRIAL ECONOMICS 0022-1821 $2.00
Volume XXXII March 1984 No. 3

INTERNATIONAL TECHNOLOGY TRANSACTIONS AND THE THEORY OF THE FIRM*

W. H. DAVIDSON AND DONALD G. MCFETRIDGE

I. INTRODUCTION

THE THEORY of the firm, as conceived by Coase [6] and developed by Williamson ([23], [24], [25], [26]), holds that the firm and the market are alternative methods of organizing exchange and that the choice between intrafirm and market exchange will be based on their relative costs. Arrow [2] has argued that market exchanges of information will be particularly costly relative to intrafirm exchanges. This insight has been cited by a number of authors to explain the prominence of multinational firms in high-technology industries (Caves [5]; Vernon [20]; Teece [17], [18]; Buckley and Casson [3]; Magee [12]; Casson [4]; and Dunning [8]).

This paper employs the theory of the firm in an attempt to define more precisely the circumstances under which it is advantageous to internalize international transactions involving technology. The hypotheses which emerge from our analysis are tested using a sample of 1,376 internal and arm's-length (market) transactions involving high-technology products carried out by 32 U.S.-based multinational enterprises between 1945 and 1975.[1] We find that there are systematic differences in the characteristics of intrafirm and market technology transactions. These differences are largely consistent with those implied by the theory of the firm.

II. THE CHOICE OF TRANSACTION MODE: IMPLICATION OF THE THEORY OF THE FIRM

Differences in the respective costs of intrafirm and market transactions are the result of differences in the incentives of the transacting parties (Williamson [23, p. 113], [24, p. 29]; McKean [15, p. 124]; McManus [16, p. 344]). Each party in a market transaction has an incentive to attempt to appropriate a larger fraction of the gain from trade. Each party will expect the other to use whatever opportunities are available to turn the terms of trade in their favour.

* This paper is based on research supported by the National Science Foundation and the Harvard Multinational Enterprise Project. The authors wish to thank Greg Hammett and Luis Leigh for research assistance and Keith Acheson, Steven Ferris and Ed Hughes for their advice and comments.

[1] In this paper all transactions between unaffiliated firms are regarded as market transactions. Two firms are unaffiliated if neither holds more than five per cent of the equity of the other. A transaction is defined as internal if one of the firms involved holds at least 95 per cent of the equity of the other. Transactions between firms, one of which holds between 5 and 95 per cent of the equity of the other are not analyzed in this paper. A full description of the data can be found in Vernon and Davidson [22] or in Davidson [7].

The participants in an intrafirm transaction have different incentives. The incomes of firm members will not, in general, depend on the outcomes of transactions carried out within the firm. As a consequence, the parties in an intrafirm transaction will have less incentive to engage in activities designed to redistribute the gains from trade.

While firm membership weakens the relationship between an individual's income and the outcome of the intrafirm transactions in which he participates, it also weakens the relationship between his income and his productive activity. Individual firm members will therefore find the consumption of leisure (shirking) and other non-pecuniary benefits less costly in terms of income foregone than would participants in a market transaction (Alchian and Demsetz [1, pp. 778–81]; McManus [16, pp. 343–45]).

Behaviour of this nature can be reduced by the expenditure of resources to monitor the activities of firm members. Monitoring will be carried to the point at which its marginal cost is equal to the marginal output loss it prevents. Intrafirm exchange will be less costly than market exchange whenever the value of resources saved by reducing redistributive activity exceeds the sum of the values of output lost due to shirking (given optimal monitoring) and the resources devoted to monitoring.

Williamson [24, pp. 21–27]; [25, pp. 248–54] suggests that the extent to which redistributive activity can be reduced by the internalization of exchange will be greater: (a) the more costly it is to measure the qualities of the goods or services involved; (b) the greater is the degree of uncertainty regarding the environment within which the transaction is to take place; and (c) the greater is the extent to which the transaction is supported by durable transaction-specific assets.[2]

In addition, the net advantage of internalization will decline with the value of the intrafirm transactions contemplated. The formation of a firm will involve shirking and monitoring costs regardless of the amount of intrafirm exchange it facilitates. The smaller are the potential gains from intrafirm trade, the less likely it is that savings from reduced redistributive activity will offset losses in output due to shirking and the diversion of resources to monitoring.[3]

III. DETERMINANTS OF THE MODE OF TECHNOLOGY TRANSFER

The extent to which a technology transaction is likely to be burdened by high measurement (verification) costs, uncertainty and the need to make transaction-specific investments will be greater: (a) for newer technologies;

[2] In an earlier version of this paper we used the term "irreversible commitments" to describe a situation in which it is costly for either or both parties to turn to alternative traders should their arrangements prove unsatisfactory. For further discussion see Klein, Crawford and Alchian [10, p. 307] and Williamson [26, pp. 10–12].

[3] McManus [16, p. 346] deals with the limiting case in which there is no interdependence among firm members and thus no intrafirm exchange. The formation of a firm will involve shirking and monitoring costs with no offsetting benefits and will thus be wealth-reducing.

(b) for technologies which represent a more significant advance on the state of the art; (c) for technologies with fewer previous transfers; (d) for technologies with fewer and more distant substitutes; and (e) the smaller is the amount of past transfer activity of the parties involved.

For widely used technologies which are close to "existing practice" it is less costly to verify assertions regarding their characteristics and there will be less uncertainty surrounding their application.[4] Verification costs and uncertainty will also be lower if the technology involved is an imitation rather than an innovation and if either or both parties have a record of past transfer activity from which inferences of reliability can be drawn.

The extent to which one or both of the transacting parties must make investments which are specialized to the transaction, and is therefore vulnerable to the opportunism of the other party, will be greater the newer, more radical and less widely used is the technology involved.

The advantages of internalization will be less likely to outweigh its costs the smaller in value and/or the less frequent are the transactions contemplated.[5] The transacting parties are less likely to expect the repetition of transfers of technologies which are distantly related to the transferor's principal line of business.

The number of transfers which are expected to occur in the future will increase with the amount of new technology the transferor is expected to produce. The anticipated flow of new technology should, in turn, be greater the larger is the fraction of the transferor's resources devoted to scientific research and development.

The value of a technology, that is, the stream of rents it can command, will be smaller the closer and the greater in number are the substitutes for it. The smaller is the value of the stream of rents involved, the less there is to be gained by reducing the incentive of the transacting parties to redistribute them, that is, by internalizing the transaction.

Vernon [21, p. 81] has argued that the post-war period has been characterized by increasing international competition in the development of new technologies. If this were the only secular factor in operation we should observe that, other things being equal, there is a trend toward market technology transactions over the sample period.

The relative cost of an intrafirm transfer will also depend on the mode of transfer which has been adopted in the past. If the transferor already has an affiliate in the receiving country, the fixed cost of internalization is a sunk cost. Since it is with the small incremental cost of the internal transfer with which the market alternative is then compared, the presence of an affiliate increases the likelihood that subsequent transfers will be internal.

[4] See Magee [12, pp. 328–29]. Williamson [25, p. 254] has also suggested that the uncertainty surrounding a transaction will decline as the industry in which the transacting parties are located matures.

[5] This point has also been made by Caves [5, p. 7].

Finally, the mode of transfer chosen will also depend on the characteristics of the receiving country. We do not discuss these characteristics or test for their effect in this paper. Instead, we examine and report on a number of alternative means of holding country effects constant. There include: (1) employing the past relative frequency of internal transfers to each receiving country as an additional variable in the model; (2) allowing the intercept term to vary across countries or groups of countries; and (3) estimating the model for individual countries, or relatively homogeneous groups of countries.

IV. THE MODEL: ITS SPECIFICATION AND ESTIMATION

The determinants of the probability of internal transfer suggested by the discussion of Section III are summarized in equation (1). Variable definitions together with the expected signs of the partial derivative of the dependent variable with respect to each independent variable follow.

$$P_i = f(t_i, C_i, A_i, T_i, N_i, M_i, B_i, E_i, R_i, F_i) \tag{1}$$

where P_i = probability that the ith transfer will be internal;

t_i = year in which the ith transfer is made;

C_i = proportion of transfers to the country receiving the ith transfer during the preceding five years which have been internal, $f_C > 0$;

A_i = age of the technology, in terms of number of years since its U.S. introduction, at the time of the ith transfer, $f_A < 0$;

T_i = number of transfers of the technology prior to the ith transfer, $f_T < 0$;

N_i = dummy variable equal to one if the ith transfer is of a technology which is a radical advance on the state of the art, zero if it is an incremental advance, $f_N > 0$;

M_i = dummy variable equal to one if the ith transfer is of an innovation, zero if it is of an imitation, $f_M > 0$;

B_i = dummy variable equal to one if the ith transfer is of a technology assigned to the same U.S. three digit SIC code as the transferor, $f_B > 0$;

E_i = number of prior transfers made by the firm making the ith transfer, $f_E < 0$;

R_i = R&D: Sales ratio of the form making the ith transfer, $f_R > 0$;

F_i = dummy variable equal to one if the firm making the ith transfer had an affiliate in the receiving country in the year prior to the transfer, zero otherwise, $f_F > 0$.

Since each transaction must fall into either the market or the intrafirm category, the dependent variable in this model is a binominal random variable, Y, which takes on values of zero and one for market and intrafirm transactions respectively. The probability P_i in equation (1) is thus the expectation of Y conditional on the values of the independent variables. If (1) is written as a linear function and the ith value of the jth independent variable is written as X_{ij}, the population regression model is:

$$(2) \qquad Y_i = E(Y_i) + \varepsilon_i = P_i + \varepsilon_i = \sum_{j=1}^{J} b_j X_{ij} + \varepsilon_i$$

As Goldberger [9, p. 249] and others have noted, (2) does not constrain P_i to lie between zero and one. It is also characterized by heteroskedastic residuals.

An alternative which constrains P_i to lie between zero and one and which stabilizes the variance of ε_i is to write (2) as a logistic function. Thus

$$(3) \qquad E(Y_i) = P_i = 1 \Big/ \left[1 + \exp\left(- \sum_{j=1}^{J} c_j X_{ij} \right) \right]$$

The $\hat{c}_j$ values are then obtained by the maximum likelihood method. To assist in the interpretation of the $\hat{c}_j$ reported in Section V, we note that by differentiating (3) with respect to X_j and substituting we obtain

$$(4) \qquad \frac{dP}{dX_j} = c_j P(1 - P)$$

The change in the probability of an internal transfer resulting from a given change in X_j is a function of c_j and the probability of internal transfer itself. The marginal effect of X_j on P can be calculated for any given P. It reaches its maximum value at $P = 0.5$.

If, as is often the case in this study, the X_j are in logarithmic form, differentiating (3) with respect to X_j and substituting yields

$$(5) \qquad X_j \frac{dP}{dX_j} = c_j P(1 - P)$$

In this case the change in P resulting from a given percentage change in X_j is a function of P and reaches its maximum at $P = 0.5$. A measure of the maximum effect on P of a given percentage change in X_j can be obtained by multiplying reported $\hat{c}_j$ values by 0.25.

Finally, the likely changes (or percentage changes) in the X_j will differ for $j = 1, \ldots, J$. To indicate the effect on P of equally likely changes in the X_j we report estimates of the standardized coefficients of the X_j which we refer to as d_j coefficients. The coefficient $d_j, j = 1, \ldots, J$ can be interpreted as the effect on P of a one standard deviation change in X_j, $j = 1, \ldots, J$ evaluated at $P = 0.5$.

Logit estimates of the c_j were obtained from a sample of 1,376 international transfers of 221 significant new product innovations and 359 imitations undertaken subsequent to U.S. introduction by 32 U.S.-based multinationals during the period 1945–75.[6] The 32 firms from which new product transfer information was obtained are listed in Vernon and Davidson [22, pp. 83–86] and in Davidson [7, pp. 206–7]. Significant innovations and imitations are those which met the minimum standards for technological novelty and accumulated U.S. sales described in Davidson [7, p. 16].

V. EMPIRICAL RESULTS AND THEIR INTERPRETATION

Five sets of estimates of the c_j in equation (3) are reported in Table I. The first set is based on the full sample with all continuous independent variables in logarithmic form and employs the fraction of internal transfers during the preceding five years to the country receiving the *i*th transfer to standardize for country effects.

The second set differs from the first only in that there is no logarithmic transformation of any of the independent variables. The third set is the same as the first except that the existing affiliate variable, B, is omitted.

The fourth set differs from the first in the manner in which country characteristics are held constant. In this case estimates are based on a subsample which includes only transfers to Canada and western Europe. The intercept is allowed to differ between Canada and western Europe and this difference is reflected in the coefficient of the Canada dummy, CDA.

The fifth set differs from the fourth in that it is estimated using a subsample which includes all transfers to non-communist countries. In this case the intercept term is allowed to take on a different value for each of three countries or groups of countries, Canada, western Europe and the balance of the non-communist world. The differences between the Canada and western Europe intercepts is given by the coefficient of the Canada dummy, CDA, while the difference between the respective intercepts of western Europe and the balance of the non-communist world is given by the coefficient of the rest of the world dummy, ROW.

The results are generally robust with respect to changes in specification and sample size.[7] Only one variable, the innovation/imitation dummy, M, takes on a sign which is not in accord with our theoretical expectations. All other

[6] Estimates of the parameters of the logit model were obtained using the AQD package at Harvard Business School. See Schlaifer [19, pp. 232–36].

[7] The results of a classification analysis performed using Equation (1), Table I are:

		Predicted	
Actual	*Market*	*Intrafirm*	*Total*
Market	293	179	472
Intrafirm	107	797	904
Total	400	976	1376

Percentage correctly classified = 79.2
A transaction is assigned to the "intrafirm" category if $\hat{P} > 0.5$

coefficient estimates are not only of the expected sign but, with the exception of the coefficients of age and the radical/incremental dummy in equation (4), also are different from zero at significance levels under 5 per cent (one tail test).

The results imply, first, that the possibility that a given transaction will be internal depends on the characteristics of the receiving country. Specifically, equations (1) ··· (3) imply that the probability that the ith transfer will be internal increases with the fraction of previous transfers by all sample firms to the receiving country which were internal. Equations (4) and (5) imply that, other things being equal, the probability of an internal transfer is greater in the case of Canada than Western Europe and greater in the case of Western Europe than in the balance of the non-communist world.

Second, the probability of an internal transfer is greater if the transferor had an affiliate in the receiving country in the year prior to the transfer. When the existing affiliate variable is omitted (column 3, Table I), explained variation falls but remains statistically significant. Inferences regarding the other parameters of the model remain unchanged. Thus, while the existing affiliate variable is clearly important to the model, it does not appear to be the source of any misleading inferences as to the marginal effects of the other independent variables.[8]

Third, the probability of internal transfer is higher the newer and more radical is a technology and the fewer the occasions upon which it has been transferred. These results confirm those obtained in other investigations of the technology transfer process. A negative relationship between the age of a technology and the probability of internal transfer has been observed in a bivariate context by Mansfield and Romeo [13, pp. 738–39].[9] Wilson [27, p. 177] found a negative relationship between product complexity and the propensity to engage in arm's-length licensing arrangements. Finally, Teece [17, p. 84] found that the cost advantage of an internal over a market transaction was greater for technologies which had no prior commercial application.

Changes in prior transfer activity have a greater effect on the probability of internal transfer than do changes in the age of a technology. In the case of equation (1), Table I, for example, the d estimates imply that, beginning from $P = 0.5$, a one standard deviation increase in the logarithm of age reduced P by 0.09 while a one standard deviation increase in the logarithm of the number of prior transfers reduced P by 0.14.

A fourth inference which may be drawn from our results is that, although the relationship is statistically weak, an imitation is more likely than an innovation to be transferred internally. The argument that verification costs will be lowered and that there will be less scope for opportunistic behaviour during the transfer of imitations is not supported by these results.

Fifth, the probability that a transfer will be internalized is greater the larger

[8] The percentage of transactions classified correctly falls to 76.2.
[9] A similar finding is reported by Mansfield, Romeo and Wagner [14, pp. 54–55].

TABLE I
ESTIMATES OF EQUATION (3)

Variable	Equation 1 $\hat{c}$	Equation 1 $\hat{d}$	Equation $\hat{c}$	Equation $\hat{d}$	Equation 3 $\hat{c}$	Equation 3 $\hat{d}$	Equation 4 $\hat{c}$	Equation 4 $\hat{d}$	Equation 5 $\hat{c}$	Equation 5 $\hat{d}$
const.	−0.1824	—	−3.365	—	0.4332	—	1.810	—	0.3156	—
	(0.7912)		(0.600)		(0.7529)		(1.110)		(0.7853)	
t	0.2246	0.587	0.1925	0.503	0.1910	0.534	0.2667	0.681	0.2560	0.664
	(0.0574)		(0.0559)		(0.0551)		(0.0779)		(0.0569)	
t^2	−0.0042	−0.460	−0.0034	−0.373	−0.0030	−0.351	−0.0046	−0.477	−0.0041	−0.443
	(0.0013)		(0.0014)		(0.0012)		(0.0019)		(0.0013)	
C	—	—	1.679	0.209	—	—	—	—	—	—
	—	—	(0.226)		—	—	—	—	—	—
ln C	2.528	0.224	—	—	3.458	0.327	—	—	—	—
	(0.316)		—	—	(0.295)		—	—	—	—
A	—	—	−0.0267	−0.078	—	—	—	—	—	—
	—	—	(0.0147)		—	—	—	—	—	—
ln $(A + 1)$	−0.2641	−0.091	—	—	−0.3268	−0.120	−0.2048	−0.071	−0.3029	−0.104
	(0.1364)		—	—	(0.1303)		(0.1918)		(0.1371)	
T	—		−0.1023	0.172	—	—	—	—	—	—
	—		(0.0209)		—	—	—	—	—	—
ln T	0.4235	−0.143	—	—	−0.4882	−0.177	−0.5282	−0.166	−0.4083	−0.133
	(0.0993)		—	—	(0.0950)		(0.1420)		(0.0998)	

N	0.3131	0.060	0.4154	0.079	0.1754	0.036	0.3932	0.071	0.2840	0.054
	(0.1565)		(0.1546)		(0.1483)		(0.2237)		(0.1556)	
M	−0.2017	−0.041	−0.1675	−0.034	−0.1644	−0.036	−0.4762	−0.094	−0.2537	−0.051
	(0.1466)		(0.1473)		(0.1397)		(0.2078)		(0.1461)	
B	1.196	0.237	1.185	0.235	1.061	0.225	1.375	0.266	1.256	0.249
	(0.160)		(0.158)		(0.154)		(0.249)		(0.160)	
E	—	—	−0.0122	−0.150	—	—	—	—	—	—
	—	—	(0.0033)		—	—	—	—	—	—
ln (E + 1)	−0.3321	−0.171	—	—	−0.3007	−0.165	−0.2705	−0.134	−0.3625	−0.187
	(0.0860)				(0.0819)		(0.1249)		(0.0862)	
R	—	—	18.25	0.123	—	—	—	—	—	—
	—	—	(4.90)		—	—	—	—	—	—
ln R	0.5790	0.135	—	—	0.5828	0.145	1.038	0.231	0.5771	0.135
	(0.1284)		—	—	(0.1212)		(0.186)		(0.1264)	
F	1.587	0.298	1.585	0.298	—	—	1.455	0.279	1.685	0.319
	(0.167)		(0.168)		—	—	(0.232)		(0.164)	
CDA	—	—	—	—	—	—	1.467	0.234	1.380	0.181
	—	—	—	—	—	—	(0.373)		(0.362)	
ROW	—	—	—	—	—	—	—	—	−0.4830	−0.097
	—	—	—	—	—	—	—	—	(0.1454)	
R^2	0.444		0.443		0.363		0.478		0.441	
n	1376		1376		1376		776		1357	

is the fraction of the transferor's resources devoted to scientific R&D and if the technology involved lies within the transferor's principal line of business.

Sixth, the greater is the number of prior transfers of all technologies conducted by the transferor, the lower is the probability that a subsequent transfer will be conducted internally.

Seventh, given the characteristics of the technology and of the parties to the transfer, the probability of an internal transfer has changed over time. The quadratic specification reported in Table I implies that the probability of an internal transfer rose until 1970 and fell thereafter. This is consistent with the contention that there has been an increase in international competition in high technology industries in recent years.[10]

VI. CONCLUSIONS AND SUGGESTIONS FOR FUTURE RESEARCH

In this paper we have analyzed the factors which determine whether a technology will be transferred internally between affiliated firms, or through an arm's length licensing arrangement. While we have had some success in isolating the factors which influence this decision, much remains to be done.

First, technology transfer joint ventures, in which the transferor holds between 5 and 95 per cent of the equity of the receiving firm have yet to be analyzed. The theory of the firm can assist in explaining both when joint ventures will be used and the form they will take.[11]

Second, Williamson [25, p. 253] has noted that what we have called transactions may be carried out under any one of a number of distinct types of contractual arrangements. Other investigators have noted that, given explicit contractual provisions, so-called market arrangements vary widely in duration and in the implicit standards of co-operation (MacMillan and Farmer [11, pp. 280–82]). A complete analysis would establish the circumstances under which each of the possible arm's length technology transfer arrangements is chosen.

Third, there are other methods by which the characteristics of technology receiving countries might be taken into account. Both the economic and social characteristics of receiving countries and the policies of their governments

[10] This increase in international competition has reduced the relative cost of market transactions, first, by increasing the ease with which the qualities of a given technology can be verified. Second, it has reduced the extent to which either party in a technology transaction will be "locked in" and thus vulnerable to the opportunism of the other. Third, it has resulted in a more rapid bidding down of the rents to new technologies thereby reducing the incentive to engage in redistributive behaviour. The finding of Mansfield, Romeo and Wagner [14, p. 55] that "marginally profitable" technologies are less likely to be transferred on an intrafirm basis is consistent with this line of reasoning.

[11] We have something under 400 additional observations on transfers in which the transferor owns between 5 and 95 per cent of the receiving firm. Most of these observations involve ownership percentages between 48 and 52 per cent. (Davidson [7, p. 80]. While the theory of the firm should be of assistance in predicting when joint ventures will be observed and what form they will take, our view is that the joint venture decision can and should be analyzed separately from the choice between purely intrafirm and purely market transactions.

toward technology transfer are potentially measurable. In subsequent papers we hope to examine their impact on the mode of transfer adopted.

ACCEPTED NOVEMBER 1982

W. H. Davidson,
The Colgate Darden School of Business Administration,
The University of Virginia,
Charlottesville, Virginia,
22906, U.S.A.

D. G. McFetridge,
Faculty of Social Sciences,
Department of Economics,
Carleton Unviersity,
Loeb Building,
Ottawa,
Canada, K1S 5B6

REFERENCES

[1] ALCHIAN, ARMEN A. and HAROLD DEMSETZ, "Production, Information Costs and Economic Organization", *American Economic Review*, 62, No. 5 (December 1972), pp. 777–95.

[2] ARROW, K. J., "Economic Welfare and the Allocation of Resources for Invention" in *The Rate and Direction of Inventive Activity: Economic and Social Factors* (NBER, Princeton, Princeton U. Press, 1962), pp. 609–26.

[3] BUCKLEY, P. J. and MARK CASSON, *The Future of the Multinational Enterprise* (London, MacMillan, 1976).

[4] CASSON, MARK, *Alternatives to the Multinational Enterprise* (London, MacMillan, 1979).

[5] CAVES, R. E., "The International Corporation: The Industrial Economics of Foreign Investment", *Economica* 38, No. 149 (February 1971), pp. 1–27.

[6] COASE, RONALD, "The Nature of the Firm", *Economica*, 4, No. 16, 1937, pp. 386–405; reprinted in G. J. Stigler and K. S. Boulding, eds., *Readings in Price Theory* (Homewood, Irwin, 1952), pp. 331–51.

[7] DAVIDSON, W. H., *Experience Effects in International Investment and Technology Transfer* (Ann Arbor: UMI Research Press, 1980).

[8] DUNNING, JOHN H., "Alternative Channels and Modes of International Resource Transmission", in Tagi Sagafi-nejad, Richard W. Moxon and Howard V. Perlmutter, eds., *Controlling International Techology Transfer: Issues, Perspectives and Policy Implications* (New York, Pergamon, 1981).

[9] GOLDBERGER, ARTHUR S., *Econometric Theory* (New York, Wiley, 1964).

[10] KLEIN, B., R. G. CRAWFORD and A. A. ALCHIAN, "Vertical Integration, Appropriable Rents and the Competitive Contracting Process", *Journal of Law and Economics*, 21, No. 2, (October 1978), pp. 297–326.

[11] MACMILLAN, KEITH and DAVID FARMER, "Redefining the Boundaries of the Firm", *The Journal of Industrial Economics*, 27, No. 3, (March 1979), pp. 277–85.

[12] MAGEE, STEPHEN P., "Information and the Multinational Corporation: An Appropriability Theory of Foreign Direct Investment", in J. N. Bhagwati, ed.,

The New International Economic Order: The North–South Debate (Cambridge, MIT Press, 1977).

[13] MANSFIELD, EDWIN and ANTHONY ROMEO, "Technology Transfer to Overseas Subsidiaries by U.S.-Based Firms", *Quarterly Journal of Economics*, 94, No. 4 (December 1980), pp. 737–50.

[14] MANSFIELD, EDWIN, ANTHONY ROMEO and SAMUEL WAGNER, "Foreign Trade and U.S. Research Development", *Review of Economics and Statistics*, 61, No. 1 (February 1979), pp. 49–57.

[15] MCKEAN, ROLAND N., "Discussion", *American Economic Review*, 61, No. 2, (May 1971), pp. 124–25.

[16] MCMANUS, J. C., "The Costs of Alternative Economic Organizations", *Canadian Journal of Economics*, 8, No. 3 (1975), pp. 334–50.

[17] TEECE, D. J., *The Multinational Corporation and the Resource Cost of International Technology Transfer* (Cambridge, Ballinger, 1976).

[18] TEECE, D. J., "The Multinational Enterprise: Market Failure and Market Power Considerations", *Sloan Management Review*, 22, No. 3 (Spring 1981), pp. 3–17.

[19] SCHLAIFER, ROBERT, *User's Guide to the AQD Collection* (Boston, Harvard Business School, 1978).

[20] VERNON, R., *Sovereignty at Bay: The Multinational Spread of U.S. Enterprises* (New York, Basic, 1971).

[21] VERNON, R., *Storm Over the Multinationals* (Cambridge, Harvard University Press, 1977).

[22] VERNON, R. and W. H. DAVIDSON, "Foreign Production of Technology-Intensive Products by U.S.-Based Multinational Enterprises" (Working Paper, Graduate School of Business Administration, Harvard University, Boston, 1977).

[23] WILLIAMSON, O. E., "Vertical Integration of Production: Market Failure Considerations", *American Economic Review*, 61, No. 2 (May 1971), pp. 112–23.

[24] WILLIAMSON, O. E., *Markets and Hierarchies: Analysis and Antitrust Implications* (New York, The Free Press, 1975).

[25] WILLIAMSON, O. E., "Transaction-cost Economics: The Government of Contractual Relations", *The Journal of Law and Economics*, 22, No. 2 (October 1979), pp. 233–61.

[26] WILLIAMSON, O. E., "Vertical Integration and Related Variations on a Transaction Cost Economics Theme" (Paper prepared for presentation at an International Economics Association Conference on "New Developments in Market Structure", Ottawa, Canada, May 10–14, 1982.

[27] WILSON, ROBERT W., "The Effect of Technological Environment and Product Rivalry on R&D Effort and Licensing of Inventories", *Review of Economics and Statistics*, 59, No. 2 (May 1977), pp. 171–78.

THE JOURNAL OF INDUSTRIAL ECONOMICS 0022-1821 $2.00
Volume XXXII March 1984 No. 3

AN EMPIRICAL TEST OF A MANAGERIAL, LIFE-CYCLE, AND COST OF CAPITAL MODEL OF MERGER ACTIVITY

STEVEN SCHWARTZ*

INTRODUCTION

THE MERGERS literature is full of attempts to explain merger activity by invoking a "single cause" explanation. These studies, which include Lintner [7], Levy and Sarnat [5], Mead [10], Manne [8], and Gort [2], suggest some (financial) economy which accrues to acquiring firms as a *primary* determinant of mergers. Steiner [15], while noting that each of the (financial) variables may explain some mergers, argues no "single cause" exists to explain all (or even most) merger activity. Steiner, instead, offers an eclectic theory in which a variety of motives are used to explain the merger decision.

Mueller [11], [12] goes a step beyond Steiner by arguing that the inability of any of the motives suggested in the above studies to lead to a "single cause" theory is rooted in their reliance on the assumption of profit maximization by firms.[1] He argues that the evidence on the success of mergers implies that mergers are not, in general, profitable and that the level of merger activity in recent years is not consistent with profit maximizing behavior. Mueller suggests that an explanation for mergers can be found in the Marris growth maximizing hypothesis [9], the Mueller life-cycle hypothesis [13], and in a cost of capital/cash flow hypothesis. However, he offers no rigorous empirical procedure to test his assertions. In this paper, a model of firm level merger activity which incorporates the growth maximizing paradigm, the life-cycle hypothesis, and a cost of capital/cash flow motivation is developed and tested to see if these hypotheses lead to results sufficiently robust to claim any (or all) of them as single cause explanations for merger activity.

THE EMPIRICAL MODEL

In the Marris framework, managerial utility is a positive function of growth and security. Growth (G) is hypothesized as being a function of investment (I), broadly defined to include capital expenditures and/or acquisitions, dividends (D), and acquisitions (M). Security is a positive function of dividends alone. Thus, managerial utility can be expressed as $U = k(I, D, M)$.

* Helpful comments were provided by Dennis Mueller and William J. Moore, and an anonymous referee. Of course, any remaining errors are the responsibility of the author alone.

[1] Steiner does not see growth maximization as a "single cause" explanation of mergers. However, he has no empirical evidence on which to base this conclusion.

Utility maximization requires managers to equate the marginal rate of return from each use of funds to the marginal cost of finance ($MRR_j = MCF$), where both are measured in utility units. The expressions for the marginal rates of return and marginal cost of finance can be approximated by linear equations since such expressions are convenient, are analytically tractable, and are equally compatible with the theory as more complicated expressions. Assume these expressions have the following form:

(1a) $$MRR_I = a_I + b_I I + c_I D + d_I M + e_I X_I$$

(1b) $$MRR_D = a_D + b_D I + c_D D + d_D M + e_D X_D$$

(1c) $$MRR_M = a_M + b_M I + c_M D + d_M M + e_M X_M$$

(1d) $$MCF = g * (I + D + M) + hZ$$

(with the X_i vectors containing exogenous elements specific to the ith expenditure and the Z vector containing exogenous variables determining the cost of capital). Such marginal expressions yield the following simultaneous model of firm expenditures.

(2a) $$I = \frac{1}{b_I - g}((g - c_I)D + (g - d_I)M + hZ - e_I X_I - a_I)$$

(2b) $$D = \frac{1}{c_D - g}((g - b_D)I + (g - d_D)M + hZ - e_D X_D - a_D)$$

(2c) $$M = \frac{1}{d_M - g}((g - b_M)I + (g - c_M)D + hZ - e_M X_M - a_M)$$

Equations (2a)–(2c) represent the general form of the simultaneous model to be estimated.[2] The investment and dividend equations are taken directly from Grabowski and Mueller [4]. The empirical form of the first two of these equations is:

(2a′) $I = g$(Dividends, Mergers, Cash Flow, Price/Earnings, Debt/Equity, Depreciation, Change in Sales)

(2b′) $D = f$(Investment, Mergers, Cash Flow, Price/Earnings, Debt/Equity, Change in Earnings/Share, Standard Deviation of Earnings/Share)

The dividend equation is based on Lintner's suggested cross-sectional determinants of the payout ratio [6]. There are two key variables: a measure of firm growth and a measure of the variability of profits. Here we follow Grabowski and Mueller closely and use growth in earnings/share as the growth

[2] The simultaneous approach to analyzing firm expenditures has been employed with success by Dhrymes and Kurz [1], Mueller [11], and Grabowski and Mueller [4] in their cross-sectional analyses. None of these studies incorporated mergers; however, the extension of the simultaneous equations approach to include a merger equation seems obvious.

variable and the standard deviation of earnings/share as the variability measure. The growth variable should have a positive coefficient; however, the coefficient of the profit variability measure is less certain. In the Lintner framework, this variable would have a negative coefficient. However, a positive coefficient is consistent with the managerial framework. The more earnings fluctuate, the lower will be stock prices. *Ceteris paribus*, lower stock prices tend to threaten managerial security by lowering the valuation ratio (the key variable in Marris' security constraint). This depressing effect on stock prices and the threat to security can be (partially) offset by paying dividends. The cash flow variable should have a positive coefficient. The coefficeint P/E is uncertain, while the leverage ratio should be negative.

In the investment equation, change in sales is included as an accelerator type variable which should be positvely related to the level of capital expenditures. Depreciation is included as a measure of replacement demand. If we assume firms will not disinvest, the level of depreciation should be positively related to capital expenditures. Cash flow and the price/earnings ratio should be positively related to capital expenditures.

The expression of the empirical form of the merger equation is somewhat more complex because the managerial theory does not identify specific variables as being related to merger activity. Rather, the Marris theory suggests that the separation of ownership and control and life-cycle[3] factors are related to merger activity. Thus, the difficulty faced in testing the theory is identifying appropriate empirical proxies for the general variables suggested by Marris' theory. Further, our equation must include variables to account for the cost of capital/cash flow factors which (may) influence merger activity. We can write the merger equation as follows:

(2c′) $M = h$(Investment, Dividends, Owner/Manager Control Variables, Life-Cycle Variables, Cost of Capital Variables)

where the owner/manager control variables are the average number of shares/ stockholder and the overlap between the corporate officers and corporate directors; the life-cycle variables are firm age, technology age, patents/sales, the ratio of past internal growth in assets; and the cost of capital. Cash flow variables are cash flow, price/earnings, and debt/equity.

a. *Owner/Manager Control Variables*

Within the context of the Marris model, the ability of managers to pursue growth producing mergers, irrespective of their profitability (subject to a security constraint), depends on the extent to which managers are insulated from shareholders; that is, on the extent of the separation of ownership and

[3] The life-cycle variables which are included here also provide a test of the life-cycle theory of mergers. Thus, support for the life-cycle theory would also constitute support for the managerial theory.

control. The average number of shares held/stockholder, adjusted for stock splits, measures the dispersion of stock ownership. The more highly dispersed the stock ownership, the higher the transactions costs of shareholders challenging management. Managerial discretion is increased and managers have more freedom to pursue managers' interests. A negative coefficient is expected.[4]

A second variable is the overlap between the corporate officers and the corporate directors and measures the extent to which managers are part of the ultimate decision-making process. If the managerial model is correct, the sign of the coefficient should be positive.

b. *Life-Cycle Variables*

The life-cycle variables are particularly important variables because the industrial life-cycle model predicts a clear link between life-cycle position and the merger activity of firms within an industry [14]. Further, the managerial model predicts that growth seeking firms will vary in their propensity to grow externally depending on the internal growth opportunities available to them; that is, on their life-cycle position.

Age of the firm is a first approximation of maturity. While old-age is neither necessary nor sufficient for maturity, age (measured as years since initial incorporation) is correlated with "technology age" and is therefore a reasonable proxy. An alternative measure is the age of the firm's technology such as the one used by Grabowski and Mueller.[5] The variable is specified as a 0/1 dummy, with the value equal to one if the firm has a young technology. Both age variables should have positive coefficients.

Another way to measure position in the life-cycle is with some measure of technological advance or innovation. If firms are innovating, they are creating some internal growth opportunities (growth opportunities within the major industry in which the firm operates), *ceteris paribus*. Mergers are less likely to occur since growth maximizing managers prefer internal to external growth [14]. Patents are used as a proxy for the technological opportunities available to a firm, and, therefore, the internal growth opportunities available to the firm. The variable coefficient should be negative. Firms with high patents/sales ratios have opportunities for internal expansion and are likely to do less acquiring.[6]

[4] Since the distribution of stock ownership is not known, we must use a simple unweighted average as opposed to a weighted average. As a result, there is a possibility of misrepresenting the diffusion of stock ownership. Consider the following. Suppose firm A has 1 million shares outstanding and 1,000 stockholders. The average stockholding is 1,000 shares. Suppose that firm B also has 1 million shares outstanding and 1,000 stockholders, but the Mr. B, the founder of firm B owns 500,000 shares. The calculated average shareholding is 1,000 shares for firm B and firm B appears to have stock ownership as diffuse as Firm A. This is clearly not the case since Mr. B owns 1/2 of the shares outstanding. A weighted diffusion measure would solve this problem.

[5] See Grabowski and Mueller [4]. Dennis Mueller graciously provided the author with the technology age data.

[6] This variable was used by Grabowski and Mueller in their study of alternative models of firm expenditure [4].

A direct measure of the effect of internal growth on merger activity is included. This variable is the ratio of past internal growth in assets (growth in assets are due to acquisitions) to past total growth in assets. *Ceteris paribus*, the greater the percentage of past growth that is accomplished internally, the greater the current internal growth opportunities and the less likely the firm is to engage in acquisition activity.[7]

c. *Cost of Capital/Cash Flow Variables*

The cost of capital/cash flow variables are important in this model since changes in the cost of capital variables and the amount of cash firms have "on hand" are important independent determinants of merger activity and may be important in a managerial context (and a profit maximizing one, as well). The cost of capital to a growth maximizing manager is different than for a profit maximizing manager. Rather than being some measure of shareholder opportunity cost, the managerial cost of capital is some measure of managerial opportunity cost. This distinction has important implications.

For a managerial firm internal capital is presumed to be cheaper than external capital. External funds are relatively more expensive to managers for several reasons. New stock or bond issues necessarily attract market attention to a firm's investment and dividend policies and market imposed constraints can be tighter than shareholder constraints. Second, risks associated with borrowing may raise the possibility of firm failure and, *ceteris paribus*, reduce managerial security (although these changes may be very small). Finally, while transactions costs for using internal funds are essentially zero, they are positive and (may be) substantial for external funds.

An important measure of the availability of internal funds is cash flow. As cash flow increases, the internal funds constraint is less severe and *ceteris paribus*, expenditure on *all* uses of internal funds should increase. In particular, one would expect investment spending, be it capital expenditures or acquisitions, to increase.[8] In addition, it has been suggested that the presence of substantial amounts of cash has a direct effect on the likelihood of a firm making an acquisition (effects over and above the cash flow effects described above) [14].

Two measures of the cost of externally raised capital will be used since external funds can be generated in two ways: equity issues or borrowing. One measure is price/earnings. The P/E ratio is a cost of capital measure in that it reflects how the market evaluates firm performance. A high P/E ratio implies that the market places a higher value on the firm's earnings performance;

[7] An alternative interpretation of this variable would be that internal growth may be subject to diminishing returns. Thus, without *a priori* knowledge of the stream of returns from internal growth, predictions about future growth policies may be inappropriate. Thanks to the referee for making this point.

[8] See Grabowski and Mueller [4].

hence, it will be more receptive to equity issued by that firm and the cost of raising equity capital will be reduced.

An alternative measure of the cost of equity capital, similar to a measure employed by Grabowski and Mueller, is used. The rate of return for Company A is calculated by figuring the interest return a shareholder in Company A would have received had he bought the stock on January 1, sold it on December 31, and collected all cash dividends paid by the firm. (This calculation fails to account for taxes and transactions costs, thus overestimating the rate of return.) The firms in the sample are then ranked by the variance in this rate of return. The cost of capital measure for Company A is then calculated as the simple average rate of return for the fifteen firms ranked above and below Company A.[9] This approximates the returns from holding stock of comparable risk and measures shareholder opportunity cost. As shareholder opportunity cost rises, fewer investment opportunities will exceed opportunity cost (that is, the rates of return on those investment opportunities) and, *ceteris paribus*, one would expect less investment to occur.

The second external cost measure is firm leverage, measured by the debt/equity ratio. One difficulty in interpreting the coefficient of the ratio is that it reflects several things. On the one hand, highly levered firms are more risky and riskier firms pay a higher return on the debt they issue. This suggests a negative coefficient would be expected. On the other hand, conglomerates tend to be more highly levered. Thus, a high debt/equity ratio may be positively related to conglomerate merger activity. *Ex ante*, the sign of the coefficient is uncertain.[10]

DATA AND ECONOMETRIC METHODOLOGY

The simultaneous form of the model and the dichotomous nature of the dependent variable of the merger equation means that simultaneous probit must be used. In a simultaneous model where one equation has a binary dependent variable and the other equations have continuous dependent variables, the conditions for identification are identical to that of a system estimated with 2SLS.

One statistical issue is the method of incorporating the lag between the time a decision is made to acquire another firm and the time the merger is consummated. Current merger activity depends on past values of the independent variables. A lag of three years was chosen because casual reviews of merger negotiations indicate that very few acquisitions take longer than three years to

[9] If Company A was ranked in the top (bottom) 15, the rate of return was calculated as the simple average of the rates of the 15 firms ranked below (above) Company A and all firms ranked above (below).

[10] Variables which measured diversification at the 2 and 3 digit SIC level were included as measures of the extent of previous conglomeration. When each was included separately and when they were included together, the variable coefficients were not significant and were dropped from the model.

complete. To err by making the lag too long is viewed as less serious than making the lag too short. Since the model is estimated on a cross-section basis and since no estimates of the relative importance of the values of the three years preceding the year for which the firm is chosen (see below) can be made on other than an *ad hoc* basis, it was decided to measure the value of all exogenous variables as average values of the three preceding years.

The time period covered in this study is 1962–77. This period was divided into four sub-periods, each of which corresponds to a particular part of the merger cycle:

1962–66	average merger activity
1967–70	more rapid activity (including peak of cycle)
1971–75	declining merger activity (including trough of cycle)
1976–77	more rapid activity

The sample used for each period was drawn randomly. Each firm on the Primary Industrial File of the Compustat tape was randomly assigned an identification number. Next a random number table was used to choose firms for the sample for each year between 1962–77. Approximately 100 numbers were drawn for each year; however, the exact number of firms per year is less than 100 because a) firms whose numbers were drawn more than once in a given year were counted only once and b) firms for which *any* data were missing or incomplete were dropped from the sample. Thus, the sample includes only those firms for which a complete data set was available. The sample sizes are as follows:

1962–66	287 firms
1967–70	298 firms
1971–75	382 firms
1976–77	164 firms

RESULTS

A careful perusal of Table II leads one to conclude that the support for the three hypotheses which are included in the merger equation is partial, at best. (See Table I for variable definitions). Among the life-cycle variables, the internal growth ratio coefficient is significant with the correct sign in the last three periods; however, no other life-cycle variable is statistically significant. Thus, the data fail to support strongly the notion that either technologically or chronologically old firms are more likely to merge.

The owner/manager control variables' performance is ambiguous. The stock diffusion measure's coefficent is significant with the correct sign in 1967–70 and 1976–77; however, in 1971–75, there is a perverse (and unexplainable) sign change. The overlap variable coefficent is significant with the "wrong" sign in 1962–66.

TABLE I
VARIABLE NAMES

ACQYES—0/1 dummy, with value = 1 if firm made an acquisition in year of analysis
DIV—dividends/sales
INV—investment/sales
STKSHR—# of shares per stockholder
OVER—% of officers of corporation who are members of board of directors
AGE—age of firm, measured by date of incorporation
PATSAL—ratio of patents to sales
IGR—ratio of internal growth in assets to total growth in assets
CFL—cash flow in dollars
DETEQ—debt/equity ratio
PE—price/earnings ratio
DEPR—depreciation (average value of three previous years)
CHGSAL—change is sales (percentage) over three previous years
CHGEES—changes in earnings/share (percentage) over three previous years
STDEES—standard deviation of earnings/share

TABLE II
MERGERS EQUATION

Dependent Variable: ACQYES

Independent Variable	*1962–66*	*1967–70*	*1971–75*	*1976–77*
AGE	0.0073[c]	0.0011	0.0047	−0.0099
	(1.469)	(0.224)	(1.057)	(−1.13)
OVER	−1.298[b]	−0.7702	−0.0569	0.5413
	(−2.00)	(−1.28)	(−0.10)	(0.444)
DETEQ	0.4952	0.1085[b]	0.0200	0.2856
	(1.421)	(1.861)	(−0.11)	(0.756)
IGR	−0.0436	−0.3772[c]	−0.3621[b]	−0.9714[b]
	(−0.33)	(−1.34)	(−2.12)	(−2.22)
PE	−0.0024	0.0043	−0.0004	−0.0051
	(−1.08)	(1.109)	(−0.18)	(−0.25)
PATSAL	0.3187	0.6462	−2.124	0.6920
	(−1.08)	(1.109)	(−0.18)	(−0.25)
STKSHR	−0.0001[c]	−0.0003[a]	0.0001[b]	−0.0002[a]
	(−1.22)	(−2.50)	(2.000)	(−1.30)
CFL	−1.865	1.3887	−0.5802	7.3026[a]
	(−0.69)	(0.978)	(−0.34)	(2.073)
INV	5.8052	−1.569	1.2599	−0.3246
	(1.546)	(−0.50)	(0.556)	(−0.07)
DIV	−5.318[a]	−8.852[a]	−2.519[c]	−0.0013[c]
	(−3.98)	(−4.05)	(−1.53)	(−1.59)
CONSTANT	−0.4299	0.3112	−1.471	−0.6834
	(−0.88)	(0.560)	(−2.84)	(−0.74)
Log of Likelihood Fn.	66.79	106.03	18.07	14.26

(*t*-statistics in parentheses)
[a] significant at 1% level in appropriate (one or two tail) test
[b] significant at 5% level in appropriate (one or two tail) test
[c] significant at 10% level in appropriate (one or two tail) test

This may result if a position on the board of directors changes managerial behavior. Since a position on a board of directors is a visible one, managerial actions are more apparent to the public and subject to greater scrutiny. If the threat of public scrutiny represents a threat (potential or real) to managerial security, utility maximizing managers who dominate boards may act to secure their positions.[11] This result may also indicate that managerial control is not correctly measured by the overlap variable.

Among the cost of capital/cash flow variables, only the cash flow variable is ever significant. While it is significant in the period (1976–77) when a larger proportion of mergers were cash financed, the failure to observe significant coefficients in other periods mitigates against claiming strong support for the cost of capital/cash flow hypothesis.

Thus, the data send us mixed signals about the efficacy of our managerial, life-cycle, and cost of capital theories of mergers. The data seem to say that while we may have identified general classes of variables which, from time to time, may help explain the merger decision by firms and merger activity in general, the case is overstated if we claim for any of our theories of merger activity the capability to explain merger activity as a "single cause" model. This result is consistent with Steiner's conclusions vis-a-vis the determinants of mergers. It has been shown that these models, like many others, can make some contribution to an understanding of the merger process and can probably explain some particular mergers. However, we have not demonstrated that any of the alternative merger models is anything more than a part of Steiner's "eclectic theory" of mergers. Indeed, we conclude that Steiner's belief that no single cause explanation of merger activity exists is correct.

THE INVESTMENT AND DIVIDEND EQUATIONS

The results of the estimation of these two equations (see Table III) are consistent with those of Grabowski and Mueller [3]. The depreciation variable in the investment equation is small and significant. One can reasonably conclude that while replacement demand has a statistically significant causal relationship to investment, the "marginal importance" is small. The accelerator view of firm investment receives incomplete support. The results are similar to those in Mueller's study. There are two explanations offered for this. The first is that the cash flow variable captures a portion of the explanatory power of the accelerator variable. The second explanation notes that the presence of excess capacity would reduce the explanatory power of the accelerator variable. If there is excess capacity, increases in sales signal the need for increased utilization of existing plant and equipment rather than the need for additions to capacity. The periods in which the accelerator variable is not significant are

[11] This result calls into question the need for S.E.C. rules increasing the proportion of outside directors on corporate Boards. If these results reflect consistent behavior by officers/directors, it appears that shareholder interests *can* be adequately represented by inside directors.

TABLE III
INVESTMENT AND DIVIDEND EQUATIONS

Dependent Variable: Investment				
	1962–66	*1967–70*	*1971–75*	*1976–77*
CONSTANT	0.0304	0.0430	0.0069	−0.0641
	(8.5700)[a]	(9.4800)[a]	(0.9200)	(−3.520)
DEPR	0.0001	0.00005	0.000045	0.00005
	(2.8900)[a]	(3.3600)[a]	(2.6600)[a]	(2.1600)[b]
CHGSAL	−0.000002	0.0004	−0.0000027	0.00006
	(−0.100)	(8.0000)[a]	(−0.130)	(2.2000)[b]
DETEQ	0.0099	0.0027	0.0155	0.104
	(2.6600)[a]	(0.8900)	(1.2700)	(1.0900)
PE	0.00006	0.0001	0.00001	−0.0004
	(1.0800)	(−0.020)	(0.1200)	(−0.620)
CFL	0.3945	0.2270	0.4315	0.9758
	(18.570)[a]	(9.9100)[a]	(15.700)[a]	(8.2300)[a]
TAC	0.1121	0.0817	0.0019	0.9425
	(8.6400)[a]	(4.9200)[a]	(0.8400)	(26.720)[a]
DIV	0.1820	0.2900	0.5788	0.0092
	(18.550)[a]	(9.0100)[a]	(26.620)[a]	(0.6300)
R^2	0.889	0.665	0.812	0.868
F-Value	313.290	82.380	224.690	139.090
Dependent Variable: Dividends				
CONSTANT	−0.1769[a]	−0.0780[a]	−0.0580[a]	−0.2543[b]
	(−13.37)	(−10.70)	(−6.01)	(−2.09)
CHGEES	−0.0047	−0.0051	−0.0003	−0.0063)
	(−0.72)	(−1.22)	(−0.23)	(−0.16)
STDEES	0.0146	−0.0111[b]	−0.0122[b]	−0.2316[a]
	(0.72)	(−1.65)	(−2.45)	(−3.06)
DETEQ	−0.0069	0.0313[a]	0.0235[a]	0.6057[a]
	(−0.44)	(7.11)	(4.42)	(12.62)
PE	−0.0004[a]	−0.0002[a]	−0.0001	−0.0007
	(−6.50)	(−3.09)	(−1.52)	(−0.15)
CFL	0.7920[a]	0.0662	−0.4228[a]	2.1498[b]
	(6.33)	(1.47)	(−9.33)	(2.05)
TAC	−0.8303	−0.4431[a]	−0.0279[a]	−1.425[b]
	(−25.52)[a]	(−45.07)	(−9.54)	(−2.25)
INV	3.0261[a]	0.6398[a]	1.1419[a]	−0.8356
	(17.78)	(7.69)	(26.13)	(−1.34)
R^2	0.898	0.922	0.814	0.542
F-Value	343.25	489.60	231.78	25.19

[a] significant at 1% level in appropriate (one or two tail) test
[b] significant at 5% level in appropriate (one or two tail) test

ones in which substantial excess capacity existed for at least a portion of those periods.[12]

In the dividends equation, the profit variability measure has negative and significant coefficients in the last three periods. This is consistent with the Lintner view, but is contrary to the managerial theory's prediction. This

[12] Ideally, *firm level* capacity utilization measures would be included; however, no firm level measures are available.

seems to suggest that the security threat is better measured through some other variable (variation in share price, perhaps) than by fluctuations in earnings per share.

The cash/flow investment relationship is confirmed by the data. Cash flow is a highly significant variable (with the correct sign) in the investment equation. Further, cash flow is positively and significantly related to dividends, as would be expected, with the exception of one period (1971–75). The result for 1971–75 is unexpected. A possible explanation for this is that the presence of wage and price controls distorted firm behavior.[13] This is uncertain, however. In three of the four periods studied, leverage is negatively related to dividends, as would be anticipated.

CONCLUSIONS

The estimation of a merger model accounting for managerial (growth maximizing), life-cycle, and cost of capital/cash flow factors does not support the contention that any of the suggested models can serve as a "single cause" model of merger activity. The results are not sufficiently strong. The results do indicate that these factors should be included as part of Steiner's eclectic theory. These results, combined with the other results on determinants of mergers, strongly suggest that no single cause model can be specified. Thus, in explaining merger activity, we are left with a hodge podge of potential explanations and no single coherent theory of mergers.

Steven Schwartz,
Miami University,
Department of Economics,
School of Business Administration,
208 Laws Hall,
Oxford, Ohio 45056,
U.S.A.

ACCEPTED FEBRUARY 1983

REFERENCES

[1] DHRYMES, P. J. and KURZ, M., "Investment, Dividend, and External Behavior of Firms." *Determinants of Investment Behavior*, Robert Ferber, ed., (New York: National Bureau of Economic Research, 1967).

[2] GORT, MICHAEL, "An Economic Disturbance Theory of Mergers." *Quarterly Journal of Economics*, 83 (November, 1969), pp. 624–42.

[3] GRABOWSKI, H. G. and MUELLER, D. C., "Life Cycle Effects on Corporate Returns on Retentions." *Review of Economics and Statistics*, (November, 1975), pp. 400–409.

[4] GRABOWSKI, H. G. and MUELLER, D. C., "Managerial and Stockholder Welfare Models of Firm Expenditure." *Review of Economics and Statistics*, 54 (November, 1972), pp. 9–24.

[13] Thanks to the referee for suggesting this point.

[5] LEVY, H. and SARNAT, M., "Diversification, Portfolio Analysis and the Uneasy Case for Conglomerate Mergers." *Journal of Finance*, 25 (September, 1970), pp. 795–802.

[6] LINTNER, JOHN, "Distribution of Income of Corporations Among Dividends, Retained Earnings, and Taxes." *American Economic Review*, 46 (May, 1956), pp. 97–113.

[7] LINTNER, JOHN, "Expectations, Mergers, and Equilibrium in Perfectly Competitive Securities Markets." *American Economic Review*, 61 (Spring, 1971), pp. 101–11.

[8] MANNE, H., "Mergers and the Market for Corporate Control." *Journal of Political Economy*, 73 (April, 1965), pp. 110–20.

[9] MARRIS, ROBIN, *The Economics of 'Managerial' Capitalism.* (New York: Free Press of Glencoe, 1964).

[10] MEAD, W. J., "Instantaneous Merger Profit as a Conglomerate Merger Motive." *Western Economic Journal*, 7 (December, 1069), pp. 295–306.

[11] MUELLER, DENNIS C'. "The Firm Decision Process: An Econometric Investigation." *Quarterly Journal of Economics* (February, 1969), pp. 643–59.

[12] MUELLER, DENNIS C., "The Effects of Conglomerate Mergers." *Journal of Banking and Finance*, 1 (December, 1977), pp. 315–47.

[13] MUELLER, DENNIS C., "A Life-Cycle Theory of the Firm." *Journal of Industrial Economics*, 21 (July, 1972), pp. 199–219.

[14] MUELLER, DENNIS C., Testimony before the Senate Subcommittee on Antitrust, Monopoly, and Business' Rights, 1979.

[15] STEINER, P. O., *Mergers.* (Ann Arbor: University of Michigan Press, 1975).

THE JOURNAL OF INDUSTRIAL ECONOMICS 0022-1821 $2.00
Volume XXXII March 1984 No. 3

SOME TESTS OF THE INFLUENCE OF CONTROL TYPE ON THE MARKET FOR CORPORATE CONTROL IN AUSTRALIA

MICHAEL L. LAWRIWSKY*

WHILE Bearle and Means [1, pp. 82–83] dismissed the effectiveness of a market for corporate control, Hindley [3, p. 431] and Manne [10, p. 113] regarded it as the ultimate external restraint protecting the interests of shareholders. There is a substantial body of theories regarding the motivations and logic behind the buying and selling of corporate control.[1] There has also appeared a number of studies examining the efficiency of the market for corporate control (Kuehn, [7]; Hindley, [4]; Singh, [14]; Kuehn, [8]). A relatively recent US study (Holl [6]) was aimed at identifying which large management controlled firms had evaded market discipline, and comparing the profitability performance of these firms with that of a matched sample of all owner controlled firms.

However, very little effort has been directed at the question of how the character of control affects the working of this market mechanism. Investigations in the area can yield insights into the way that the capitalist system operates, and help to predict the effects that current trends—the spread of multinational corporations, increasing inter-corporate shareholdings, the rise of financial institutions and a decline in private ownership control—will have on the mechanics and efficiency of the resource allocation process. Policy prescriptions could eventually be expected in the areas of anti-trust, securities regulation, and regulation of foreign investment.

In this paper, section I derives a number of hypotheses relating to the effectiveness of the market for corporate control. In section II some tests of these hypotheses are performed using a model based on Holl's [6] earlier analysis of U.S. corporations, but employing a sample of listed Australian corporations. Since this approach is found to be defective, section III proposes an alternative test which obtains results not inconsistent with our hypotheses. The final section summarises the results and outlines the implications for future research.

I

If there existed a frictionless and perfect market in corporate control, resources would be allocated in an optimal manner as far as stockholders and

* This paper is based on portions of the author's doctoral dissertation, "Managers and Markets" [9]. He would like to thank David Round, Ian McLean and John Hatch for their comments, while retaining responsibility for any errors.

[1] See Hindley [5] for a review of the literature in this area.

the capital market are concerned. That is, internally inefficient managers would be displaced through takeovers. But this requires, *inter alia*, that the market be able to determine whether the observed performance of a firm is indeed due to sub-optimal performance by management, which in turn requires intimate knowledge of internal operations in a target company. In fact, experience suggests that many company stocks may be persistently over- or under-valued by the stock market (see Nerlove, [12]). Information costs, transactions costs and the rationalization costs will be non-negligible. Considering these costs Williamson [18, p. 317] concluded that "the market for corporate control would appear to be imperfect".

Ceteris paribus, the ease with which a successful takeover bid can be mounted will be a function of the size of the target corporation. A large firm has more complex organizational structure, which raises the capital and information costs facing a bidder. The bidder will normally need to be larger than the target, which for large firms reduces the number of potential market raiders. Finally, larger firms will have greater resources with which to organise a defence.

Holding other things (including firm size) constant, the ease of takeover will also be a function of the distribution of share ownership, that is, of the character of control. This factor is often mentioned by researchers (for example, see Hannah, [2]; Kuehn, [8]), but is seldom expanded upon.[2] In unlisted private ownership companies takeovers often arise out of changes in family circumstances. By selling control owners can capitalize their future earnings stream as capital gains rather than as dividends, which are taxed at a higher rate. Family circumstances may also have some bearing on closely held listed companies—especially those in which first generation owners are still active in management—although a takeover bid would be conditional upon family acceptances. Hence, the attitude of the board would be crucial, and, if it were known in advance to be hostile, a bid may not be considered.

Reporting the results of a major study of UK takeovers Kuehn [8, p. 40] found that over 90 per cent of offers were successful. There is no doubt that bidders were being careful to approach only those firms where they felt that their chances were best. However, it is interesting that three-quarters of the 44 unsuccessful offers were for firms with net assets of less than £5m. The reason was that in these firms voting control was firmly in the hands of the directors. Hence, in private ownership companies vulnerability to an uninvited market raid will depend more on the structure of shareholdings than on firm size. However, given the level of shareholdings controlled by incumbent directors, the ease of takeover would still diminish with size.

In a dispersed ownership (or management controlled) company top man-

[2] For example, consider the following statement of an experienced practitioner at a recent seminar on takeovers: ". . . it is essential to closely analyse the register of shareholders grouping large related holdings together, . . . The holding of institutions is also vital and broad links between the directors and the institutions should be studied.". (Marks, [11, p. 6]).

agement will be composed either of true professionals with a relatively small ownership stake, or of former owner-controllers who may have retained a substantial but proportionately small equity interest. Furthermore, the wealth of this latter group is likely to be much more highly diversified than that of owner-controllers. Since financial institutions often make up the bulk of holdings in such companies, and may be willing to sell their holdings if an attractive offer were made, these firms will be more vulnerable to a takeover bid. Small firms are most vulnerable because the dispersion of shareholdings is lower than in the case of large firms. Generally speaking, protection is afforded only by size, and this realization must place a good deal of pressure to perform on those managements of smaller companies which value their independence.

In the company controlled sector the *market* mechanism, of itself, will be ineffective in disciplining management through the threat of takeover bid. In analyzing the performance of one company controlled firm in our sample, Associated Pulp and Paper Mills Ltd., *Finance Week* (1972, March 17, p. 33) put it this way,

> ". . . some bad miscalculations have been made in the expansion programme and second rank management appears to have something to answer for . . . although asset backing is above the price of the shares, a takeover bid is highly unlikely because Wiggins Teape of Britain (part of the British American Tobacco group) now holds 24 per cent of APPM and two Collins miners, North Broken Hill and Broken Hill South own another 25 per cent".

Here the corrective discipline must come from *within*, either at the initiative of the board or the dominant stockholder company.[3] Once it has a dominant shareholding the parent company has considerable discretion over the firm's future. If difficulties are encountered it can institute reforms in management, increase its control by buying out minority shareholdings, or divest itself of the subsidiary's assets. In these circumstances the market may act as a barometer in notifying the parent that action is required. Also, since the parent already has effective control over the firm, size considerations will not play the same role that they do in, say, management controlled firms.

II

Holl [6] devised a test of the effectiveness of the corrective discipline of the market for corporate control in which it was argued that in the longer period a firm's management will take corrective action in order to avert takeover. Such

[3] As a postscript on future development in APPM it is interesting to note that in the second half of the 1978 interim profits reached record levels after growing for four years. In *The Age* (1979, February 15, p. 21) it was reported that ". . . directors said the most important elements in the profit improvement were the increased benefits from a management and structural reorganization started four years ago, from cost control and rationalization moves . . .".

action will eventually translate into a rising valuation ratio, so that if the market operates efficiently it will ensure that a firm "pursue policies which result in its valuation ratio moving towards the long run industry average". Hence, the basic relationship proposed by Holl was of the form,

$$\text{VAL}_{i,t} = \beta_0 + \beta_1 \text{VAL}_{i,t-1} + \varepsilon_{i,t} \qquad (1)$$

where

$\text{VAL}_{i,t}$	is the valuation ratio of the ith firm in time period t
$\text{VAL}_{i,t-1}$	is the valuation ratio of the ith firm in time period $t-1$
$\beta_0\ \beta_1$	are constants
ε	is the stochastic error term

A value of $0 > \beta_1 < 1$ would indicate that there is a movement towards the long run average for all firms over time periods $t-1$ and t. In other words, the corrective discipline of the market has succeeded *partially* in motivating policies designed to move firms' valuation ratios closer to the industry average. If $\beta_1 = 0$ the constraint is fully effective because firms with below average valuation ratios in period $t-1$ would have raised their valuation ratios to equal the industry average in period t. On the other hand, if $\beta_1 > 1$, the constraint is non-existent.

There are at least two problems with this formulation. The first is that the calculations were based on the movements of individual company valuation ratios relative to the average for the entire sample. In the UK Kuehn [8, p. 53] has argued that "since the vast majority of takeovers occur within the same or similar industries, it is the performance of the firm with respect to similar firms in the same industry which will single it out as takeover candidate". Therefore it may be irrelevant to ask how a firm is valued in relation to all firms in the quoted industrial population.[4] This observation may not be particularly valid in the case of the United States, where a large proportion of mergers have been of the conglomerate variety, but this is not the case in Australia (Stewart, [15]).

The second problem is that raw values of the valuation ratios in both periods were employed, and these will be sensitive to fluctuations in the stock market. Consider the case in which a representative company has a valuation ratio which is two-thirds of the industry (or population) average in period $t-1$. If the stockmarket is depressed in period t by a factor of 0.5 in relation to what it was in period $t-1$, but the representative company nevertheless maintains a valuation ratio in t which is two-thirds of the average valuation ratio in t, using raw values of VAL the slope coefficient would be 0.5 and indicate a functioning constraint when in effect the relativities of all companies have not changed. In these circumstances then, if the industry averages

[4] Inter-industry differences in valuation ratios in the United Kingdom are well documented in Singh and Whittington [13] and Singh [14].

in periods $t - 1$ and t were set to equal unity, and the positions of individual firms were calculated as proportions of these averages the resultant slope coefficient would also assume a value of unity, indicating that a corrective restraint was non-existent.

An alternative approach is to specify the relationship in the following manner,

$$\frac{VAL_{i,j,t}}{\overline{VAL}_{j,t}} = \beta_0 + \beta_1 \frac{VAL_{i,j,t-1}}{\overline{VAL}_{j,t-1}} + \varepsilon_{i,j} \quad (2)$$

where

$VAL_{i,j,t}$	is the valuation ratio of the *i*th firm in industry *j* in period *t*
$\overline{VAL}_{j,t}$	is the average valuation ratio for all firms in industry *j* in period *t*
$VAL_{i,j,t-1}$	is the valuation of the *i*th firm in industry *j* in period $t - 1$
$\overline{VAL}_{j,t-1}$	is the average valuation ratio for all firms in industry *j* in period $t - 1$
$\beta_0 \beta_1$	are constants
ε	is the stochastic error term
t	refers to the years 1972/73 to 1974/75
$t - 1$	refers to the years 1966/67 to 1968/69

This formulation allows us to take into account both the industry effects and general stock market effects which were not considered by Holl. To recapitulate, if we show that β_1 is not significantly different from unity, or that it is significantly greater than unity for a group of companies arranged by control-type, this is tantamount to showing that this control group was free to ignore the corrective discipline of the market for corporate control. Conversely, if we obtain an estimate of β_1 which is significantly less than unity we may conclude that the constraint is operating in some degree. However, to conclude that the constraint is *fully* effective we must be able to show that β_1 is significantly less than one *and* not significantly different from zero. Following Holl, our *a priori* hypothesis would be that the coefficient β_1 should increase with firm size. However, the results which are shown in Table I do not *appear* to support this hypothesis. Rather, in each size category the market was at least partially ineffective, and, contrary to expectations, the value of the β_1 coefficient *falls* marginally as we move from the small to the large firms category.

The analysis is repeated in Table II, where firms are grouped according to control-type. Here, Holl's hypothesis that the market is more effective in restraining owner controlled firms *appears* to be borne out. In owner controlled firms the β_1 coefficient of 0.131 is not significantly different from zero, and is

TABLE I

THE CORRECTIVE DISCIPLINE OF THE MARKET FOR CORPORATE CONTROL, BY FIRM SIZE

Equation Number	Size Category	n	$\overline{VAL}_{t-1}$	$\overline{VAL}_t$	β_0	β_1	t-ratio $Ho: \beta = 0$	t-ratio $Ho: \beta = 1$	r^2	$\bar{r}^2$	MCC
1.1	Small	63	1.034	1.114	0.704	0.397	(3.496)[a]	(5.322)[a]	0.167	0.153	?
1.2	Medium	81*	0.935	0.905	0.543	0.387	(3.104)[a]	(4.911)[a]	0.109	0.097	?
1.3	Large	49	1.065	0.980	0.614	0.344	(2.615)[b]	(4.991)[a]	0.127	0.108	?

Notes: *a* and *b* denote significance at the 0.01 and 0.05 levels respectively using a one-tail test.
? indicates that the market for corporate control (MCC) operated imperfectly.
* United Telecasters Ltd. was excluded from the sample since its adjusted valuation ratio had a value of 128.

almost four times smaller than the coefficient obtained in the management controlled sample. However, management controlled firms had valuation ratios which were on average between 6.2 and 9.6 points *above* their industry's average, while the valuation ratios of owner controlled firms were 10.4 and 6.2 points *below* average. The results for company controlled firms are similar to those for management control.

In Table III firms are grouped by size *and* control-type. The results reveal basic differences between owner controlled firms on the one hand, and management and company controlled firms on the other. In the first group the β_1 coefficient increases with size, and our statistical tests, applied literally, indicate that except in the case of large firms, the market applied a perfect restraint. However, in management and company controlled firms the opposite is found, since the β_1 coefficient decreases as firm size increases.

Our tests show that with the exception of large company controlled firms, the corrective restraint was an imperfect disciplinarian on non-owner controlled firms irrespective of firm size. Yet in the large firms group there is little separating the values of coefficients achieved in the three control-type subsamples. Also, with the exception of the large firms category, the average valuation ratios of owner controlled firms (in relation to their industry averages) were considerably lower than those of management controlled firms, and, to a lesser degree, lower than those of company controlled firms.

The results appear somewhat confusing. The major problem is that the test proposed by Holl is founded on logic which was employed by Stigler [16] and

TABLE II

THE CORRECTIVE DISCIPLINE OF THE MARKET FOR CORPORATE CONTROL, BY CONTROL-TYPE

Equation Number	Control Type	n	$\overline{VAL}_{t-1}$	$\overline{VAL}_t$	β_0	β_1	t-ratio $Ho: B = 0$	t-ratio $Ho: \beta = 1$	r^2	$\bar{r}^2$	MCC
2.1	OC	68	0.896	0.938	0.820	0.131	(1.068)	(7.059)[a]	0.017	0.002	+
2.2	MC	75	1.062	1.096	0.581	0.485	(4.455)[a]	(4.729)[a]	0.214	0.203	?
2.3	CC	50*	1.050	0.910	0.408	0.478	(3.525)[a]	(3.846)[a]	0.206	0.189	?

Notes: *a* denotes significance at the 0.01 level using a one-tail test.
\+ indicates that the market for corporate control (MCC) operated perfectly.
? indicates that the market for corporate control operated imperfectly.
* United Telecasters Ltd. was excluded from the sample since its adjusted valuation ratio had a value of 128.

TABLE III
THE CORRECTIVE DISCIPLINE OF THE MARKET FOR CORPORATE CONTROL, BY FIRM SIZE AND CONTROL TYPE

Equation Number	*Control-Type*	*n*	$\overline{VAL}_{t-1}$	$\overline{VAL}_t$	β_0	β_1	*t-ratio* $Ho: \beta = 0$	*t-ratio* $Ho: \beta = 1$	r^2	$\bar{r}^2$	*MCC*
	Small Firms:										
3.1	OC	31	0.882	1.001	1.025	−0.027	(0.158)	(5.957)[a]	0.001	<0	+
3.2	MC	18	1.226	1.360	0.759	0.492	(2.529)[b]	(2.611)[a]	0.286	0.241	?
3.3	CC	14	1.131	1.046	0.488	0.494	(1.657)[c]	(1.719)[c]	0.186	0.118	?
	Medium Sized Firms:										
3.4	OC	27	0.832	0.842	0.667	0.210	(0.838)	(3.156)[a]	0.027	<0	+
3.5	MC	28	0.960	1.028	0.542	0.507	(2.039)[b]	(1.984)[b]	0.138	0.105	?
3.6	CC	26*	1.015	0.837	0.369	0.461	(2.589)[b]	(3.027)[a]	0.218	0.186	?
	Large Firms:										
3.7	OC	10	1.112	1.001	0.640	0.324	(1.405)[c]	(2.930)[a]	0.198	0.098	?
3.8	MC	29	1.061	0.999	0.633	0.345	(1.872)[b]	(3.559)[a]	0.115	0.082	?
3.9	CC	10	1.026	0.907	0.565	0.333	(1.073)	(2.148)	0.126	0.017	+

Notes: *a*, *b* and *c* denote significance at the 0.01, 0.05 and 0.10 levels respectively using a one-tail test.
+ indicates that the market for corporate control (MCC) operated perfectly.
? indicates that the market for corporate control operated imperfectly.
* United Telecasters Ltd. was excluded from the sample since its adjusted valuation ratio had a value of 128.

Whittington [17], who were searching for evidence of persistent *profitability* performance. It was argued that the unimpeded operation of market forces should eliminate high profits in some uses, for example through new entry—and low profits in other uses, for example by the exit or takeover of unprofitable firms. Thus, with perfect factor mobility there should be a tendency for above or below average profitability of individual industries and firms to be eliminated over time. In the context of Holl's model it is crucial to recognize that the value of the β_1 depends not only upon how firms with below average valuation ratios are behaving, but also upon the behaviour of firms with above average valuation ratios.

It has been observed (for example by Singh, [14]) that a high valuation ratio does not necessarily provide protection from takeover. Also, Kuehn [8] has observed that for different firms there exists a unique valuation ratio at which the probability of takeover is unacceptably high. Our theoretical approach proposes that one factor which determines the value of this critical valuation ratio is the firm's character of control. With a given valuation ratio we expect a dispersed ownership company to be more vulnerable than an owner controlled company, and that this difference in relative vulnerability should decline as firm size increases. It is not surprising that in Table III we find the average valuation ratio of small management controlled firms to be almost 40 points higher than similar sized owner controlled firms, while in the medium size category the difference is only 16 points. Thus, in the small and medium sized firms categories management controlled firms had valuation ratios which were more highly persistent than in owner controlled firms, but they were also persistently higher. In our view this indicates that the market for corporate control was imposing greater discipline on management controlled firms—in order to survive they needed to achieve above average valuation ratios, and to maintain them at above average levels. By contrast, owner controlled firms which had above average valuation ratios in 1966–67 to 1968–69 did not appear to have the same pressure on them to maintain their above average valuation.

III

These propositions can be explored further by taking a different view of Holl's model, and examining the structure of actual takeover bids experienced in a subsequent period, 1975–76 to 1978–79. We can say with some assurance that firms which survive with below average valuation ratios over an extended period without raising their valuation ratio towards the industry average, and without experiencing a change in control must, in some way, have been able to avoid market discipline. These are firms which fall within the shaded area in Figure 1.

The *Australian Financial Review* was examined for reports of takeover bids for companies in the sample over the period from 1975/76 to 1978/79. A total of 55 bids representing 28.3 per cent of the continuing firms sample were identified. As in the United Kingdom a high success rate was evident, and most of the exceptions were bids for small and medium sized owner controlled firms. Table IV displays the prior performances (in terms of post-tax rate of return on equity assets averaged over the period 1966/67 to 1974/75) of firms which experienced bids, together with those of firms which we have defined as evading the market for corporate control (MCC). The main focus will be on

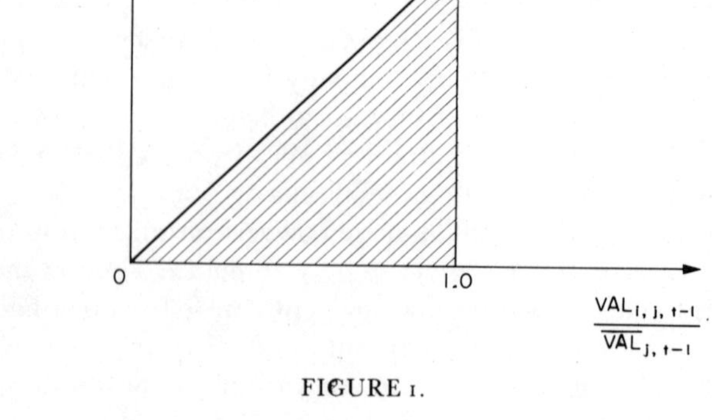

FIGURE 1.

comparing the effectiveness of market discipline on management, as opposed to owner controlled firms.

Our first hypothesis is that, given the size of the firm, the market's discipline will be more effective in restraining management controlled firms. Without reference to size we find that a higher proportion of owner controlled firms (38 per cent) than management controlled firms (28 per cent) could be said to have evaded the market's discipline. Yet the difference in proportions is particularly marked in the small firms category, is lower among medium sized firms, and is reversed in the large firms group.

The proportion of actual takeovers subsequent to 1974/75 is slightly higher among owner controlled firms (29.4 per cent as against 26.7 per cent). But we also find that the performance of companies experiencing a bid, relative to those which did not, differed on the basis of control-type. Owner-controlled firms which were subject to takeover earned higher profits than the average for all owner controlled firms in a given size category, while management controlled firms experiencing a bid generally had below average profitability. This can be explained by the fact that several of the owner controlled firms which were taken over did so as a result of "entrepreneurial" factors, while in management controlled firms a raider more often took control of a firm with lagging performance. Despite these entrepreneurial effects within owner controlled firms, the management controlled firms which were taken over had earned somewhat higher rates of return. Given that takeovers can occur for a variety of reasons, it is perhaps more relevant to consider the proportion of companies evading the market for corporate control which were able to survive without being contested. In each size category a higher proportion of owner controlled firms evading the market survived with control intact.

Our second hypothesis is that the effectiveness of the market restraint will diminish with size, but that this effect will be stronger in the case of management controlled firms. In Table IV we find that the proportion of management controlled firms able to evade the market increased with size, whereas in the owner controlled category the highest proportion was in medium sized firms. This pattern is replicated in the column showing firms which were subject to takeover. It is also of interest to note that only six of the 68 owner controlled firms had what could be considered a strong institutional component in their structure of shareholdings.[5] But five of these firms encountered a takeover offer, and only one (McEwens Ltd.) was able to survive with the original directors still in control.

Our hypothesis regarding company controlled firms is that the external market for corporate control and firm size will be less relevant. In Table IV it is apparent that the record for company control is unique in a number of respects. The proportion of firms which evaded market discipline was lowest

[5] A strong institutional shareholding was defined as one where institutional holdings among the largest 20 cohesive shareholder groups accounted for more than 50% of the groups' holdings, *and* the institutional holdings accounted for more than 15% of shares on issue.

TABLE IV

CORPORATE PERFORMANCE AND THE MARKET THE CORPORATE CONTROL, BY FIRM SIZE AND CONTROL-TYPE

Size Category	Control Type	n_1	Companies subject to a takeover bid n_2	$\frac{n_2}{n_1}$ %	REA	Companies not evading the MCC which were subject to a takeover bid n_3	$\frac{n_3}{n_1 - n_6}$ %	REA	Companies evading the MCC which were subject to a takeover bid n_4	$\frac{n_4}{n_6}$ %	REA	Companies evading the MCC which survived without a takeover bid n_5	$\frac{n_5}{n_6}$ %	REA	Companies evading the MCC n_6	$\frac{n_6}{n_1}$ %	REA	Average REA
Small	OC	31	9	29.0	11.7	6	30.0	13.9	3	27.3	7.4	8	72.7	7.7	11	35.5	7.6	10.4
Firms	MC	18	7	38.9	12.4	5	31.2	13.5	2	100.0	9.9	0	0.0	—	2	11.1	9.9	12.9
	CC	14	6	42.9	16.6	5	41.7	17.9	1	50.0	10.4	1	50.0	5.3	2	14.3	7.8	12.9
Sub-total		63	22	34.9	13.3	16	33.3	15.0	6	40.0	8.7	9	60.0	7.4	15	23.8	7.9	11.7
Medium	OC	27	10	37.0	7.9	5	35.7	8.0	5	38.5	7.7	8	61.5	6.	13	48.1	7.1	6.9
Sized	MC	28	8	28.6	8.3	4	21.1	9.0	4	44.4	7.5	5	55.6	8.4	9	32.1	8.0	9.5
Firms	CC	27	8	29.6	9.0	3	20.0	8.5	5	41.7	8.0	7	58.3	7.3	12	46.2	7.6	9.8
Sub-total		82	26	31.7	8.1	12	25.0	8.5	14	41.2	7.8	20	58.8	7.5	34	42.0	7.5	8.8
Large	OC	10	1	10.0	7.6	1	12.5	7.6	0	0.0	—	2	100.0	8.4	2	20.0	8.4	9.5
Firms	MC	29	5	17.2	8.5	3	15.8	9.9	2	20.0	6.3	8	80.0	7.9	10	38.5	7.6	8.6
	CC	10	1	10.0	14.3	0	0.0	—	1	33.3	14.3	2	66.7	8.2	3	30.0	10.2	8.9
Sub-total		49	7	14.3	9.2	4	11.8	9.3	3	20.0	9.0	12	80.0	8.0	15	32.6	8.2	8.8
All Companies		194	55	28.3	10.3	32	24.6	11.9	23	35.9	8.2	41	64.1	7.6	64	33.0	7.8	9.7

Note: the following identities hold; $n_3 + n_4 \equiv n_2$, $n_4 + n_5 \equiv n_6$.

in the small firms category. However, in relative terms, firms in this category experienced the greatest takeover activity. Another distinguishing feature is that in each size category the rate of return earned by those firms subject to takeover was higher than that of firms in other control-types which experienced bids.

Here changes in control must be viewed as investment decisions made by the controlling company. Of the fifteen firms which experienced a bid, in nine cases the controlling company was extending its shareholding, and in six of these control was already "strong" (i.e. more than 42 per cent of shares were held). In the six remaining instances the controlling firm was divesting itself of ownership in the company. In both the small and medium sized firms categories, firms in which the controlling company was expanding its ownership were on average at least 2.4 percentage points more profitable than those in which the takeover represented a divestiture. Thus, companies preferred to integrate reasonably profitable firms and discard the relatively unprofitable ones. The fact that absorptions and spin-offs of small firms are much easier to effect probably explains why they were involved in such a high proportion of takeovers. However, there remained several company controlled firms which had earned below average profits, and had evaded market discipline while not meeting with the same fate. Perhaps internal control measures were in the process of trying to improve performance, but since the period involved is quite long we cannot rule out the possibility that they were simply ineffective.

IV

Our results have suggested that the market for corporate control in Australia has been a somewhat imperfect disciplinarian. We have confirmed that in general the extent of ineffectiveness increases with firm size, however this relationship was most pronounced among management controlled firms. In owner controlled firms the incumbent ownership group could more often retain control despite prolonged periods of depressed earnings. Since this ability depended crucially on the composition of shareholdings it was more independent of firm size. In company controlled firms the external market for corporate control was of little consequence, except in so far as it provided a guide to decisions made by the parent concern. If subsidiaries were not performing up to the standards set for them they were disposed of in the market, while good performers were internalized.

The implications of our findings are as follows. First, future research on the effectiveness of the market for corporate control should incorporate a formal analysis of the influence that varying ownership structures can exert on its relationship with firm size and indicators of managerial performance. Second, the test proposed by Holl is not appropriate for this task. Third, differences in performance *between* control-types may arise from varying levels of external and internal restraints being imposed on management (given the managerial incentive structure), rather than from control-type *per se*. The market for corporate control is one such external restraint. Another is provided by the capital market's scrutiny of corporate borrowings and equity issues. Here also, recent Australian evidence (Lawriwsky, [9]) has indicated that the extent and effectiveness of the restraint is dependent on considerations of both firm size and control-type.

Michael L. Lawriwsky,
La Trobe University,
Department of Economics,
Bundoora,
Victoria,
Australia 3083

ACCEPTED DECEMBER 1982

DATA APPENDIX

A major source of data was the accounts of a sample of companies listed on the Sydney Stock Exchange over the period 1965/66 to 1974/75. The accounts had been arranged into a standardized format in *STATEX*, an investment service prepared and published by the Research and Statistics Department of the Sydney Stock Exchange. This data set relates to some 370 companies accounting for over 90 per cent of the capitalized value of all companies listed on that exchange. As a first measure, companies engaged in mining, finance, development and contracting, were eliminated. This left a sample of 317 companies. The most significant constraint on sample size was the need of detailed ownership and control data on individual companies, which had to be collected from primary sources. That is, it had to be gleaned from searches of share registers held throughout Australia. To minimize travelling expenses, 300 companies whose registers were kept in Sydney, Melbourne, Canberra or Adelaide were considered. A sample of 250 companies was drawn at random from this group, but was reduced by the omission of companies which had changed their accounting date or were not willing to cooperate. The final sample consisted of 226 companies which accounted for 49 per cent of the paid up capital of non-mining, non-finance, non-development and contracting companies listed on all Australian stock exchanges in 1975. Of these, 194 were listed continuously over the period. Companies were allocated to 2-digit ASIC industries utilizing several sources: the *Sydney Stock Exchange Investment Service Sheets*, *Jobson's Year Book*, and the *Journal of the Associated Stock Exchanges*.

Computation of financial variables followed closely the definitions employed by Singh and Whittington [13]:

Notation

m = last year of a period
p = first year of a period
o = year p *minus* one year
n = number of years in a period
$= m - o$

The values of m, p, o and n are:

"Whole period": $m = 9$, $p = 1$, $o = 0$, $n = 9$
"Sub-period 1": $m = 3$, $p = 1$, $o = 0$, $n = 3$
"Sub-period 2": $m = 6$, $p = 4$, $o = 3$, $n = 3$
"Sub-period 3": $m = 9$, $p = 7$, $o = 6$, $n = 3$

where "0" refers to 1965–66 and "9" to 1974–75.

The *valuation ratio* (VAL) was calculated as follows.

$$\frac{\sum_p^m(\text{shares on issue} \times \text{average post balance date price})}{\sum_p^m \text{ordinary equity}}$$

The *average post balance data price* is adjusted by *STATEX* for stock splits, bonus and cash issues, and is calculated by averaging the *average adjusted prices* over the three months following the balance sheet data. It is argued that the prices in this period will more accurately reflect the objective expectations of the market, since they will be based on current information released in the annual report. The average adjusted price for each month was calculated as follows.

$$\frac{\text{month end price} + \left(\dfrac{\text{month high} + \text{month low}}{2}\right)}{2}$$

The *post-tax rate of return on equity assets* (REA) was defined as:

$$\frac{\sum_p^m(\text{ordinary dividends} + \text{total retained})}{\text{aggregate equity assets}}$$

where *aggregate equity assets* was defined as:

$$\frac{(\text{equity assets})_m + (\text{equity assets})_o + \sum_p^m(\text{equity assets})}{2}$$

and *equity assets* was defined as:

$$\text{capital and reserves} - \text{minority interest} - \text{preferred capital}$$

Net assets was used as a measure of firm size. It was calculated as:

total assets – current liabilities – provisions

"Small" firms were defined as those with less than \$5m. in net assets in 1966, "Medium size" firms had net assets greater than \$5m. and less than \$20m., while "Large" firms had net assets of \$20m. or more. Admittedly, the terms "small", "medium" and "large" are somewhat arbitrary, and are always relative.

REFERENCES

[1] BERLE, A. A. and MEANS, G. C., *The Modern Corporation and Private Property*, (Macmillan Co., New York, 1932).

[2] HANNAH, L. "Takeover Bids in Britain Before 1950", *Business History*, 16 (January 1974), pp. 65–77.

[3] HINDLEY, B., "Capitalism and the Corporation", *Economica*, 36 (November, 1969), pp. 426–38.

[4] ——, "Separation of Ownership and Control in the Modern Corporation", *Journal of Law and Economics*, 13 (April, 1970), pp. 185 221.

[5] ——, "Recent Theory and Evidence on Corporate Merger", in Cowling, K. (ed.)., *Market Structure and Corporate Behaviour*, (Gray Mills, London, 1972), pp. 1–17.

[6] HOLL, P., "Control Type and the Market for Corporate Control in Large U.S. Corporations", *Journal of Industrial Economics*, 25 (June, 1977), pp. 259–73.

[7] KUEHN, D. A., "Stock Market Valuation and Acquisitions: An Empirical Test of One Component of Managerial Utility", *Journal of Industrial Economics*, 17 (April, 1969), pp. 132–44.

[8] ——, *Takeovers and the Theory of the Firm*, (Macmillan and Co., London, 1975).

[9] LAWRIWSKY, M. L., "Managers and Markets: Internal Organisation and External Market Restraints as Determinants of Australian Company Performance", unpublished Ph.D. Dissertation, University of Adelaide, 1980.

[10] MANNE, H. G., "Mergers and the Market for Corporate Control", *Journal of Political Economy*, 73 (April, 1965), pp. 110–20.

[11] MARKS, J. N., "Practical Implications of Takeovers", Paper presented at Seminar on Company Takeovers and Mergers held by The Securities Institute of Australia, Melbourne, November 1977.

[12] NERLOVE, M., "Factors Affecting Differences Among Rates of Return on Investments Individual Common Stocks", *Review of Economics and Statistics*, 50 (August, 1968), pp. 312–31.

[13] SINGH, A. and G. WHITTINGTON, *Growth, Profitability and Valuation*, (Cambridge University Press, Cambridge, 1968).

[14] SINGH, A. *Takeovers: Their Relevance to the Stockmarket and the Theory of the Firm*, (Cambridge University Press, London, 1971).

[15] STEWART, I. C., "Australian Company Mergers, 1960–1970", *Economic Record*, 53 (March, 1977), pp. 1–28.

[16] STIGLER, G. J., *Capital and Rates of Return in Manufacturing Industries*, (N.B.E.R., Princeton University Press, 1963).

[17] WHITTINGTON, G., *The Prediction of Profitability and Other Studies of Company Behaviour*, Cambridge University Press, Cambridge, 1971).

[18] WILLIAMSON, O. E., "Corporate Control and the Theory of the Firm", in H. G. Manne (ed.), *Economic Policy and the Regulation of Corporate Securities*, (American Enterprise Institute of Public Policy Research, Washington, 1969), pp. 281–336.

THE JOURNAL OF INDUSTRIAL ECONOMICS 0022-1821 $2.00
Volume XXXII March 1984 No. 3

THE ROLE OF MARKET STRUCTURE IN MERGER BEHAVIOR*

JOHN F. STEWART
ROBERT S. HARRIS
AND WILLARD T. CARLETON

I. INTRODUCTION

THE determinants of merger behavior have long been a topic of interest to academics and policy makers. The question is particularly relevant for policy because of the diversity of views concerning the ultimate impact of mergers on the economy. Mergers have been described by some as desirable transactions serving the purpose of efficiently reallocating productive, financial, and managerial resources within the economy. Alternatively, mergers have been attacked as undesirable transactions decreasing the competitive vigor of the economy and resulting in undesirable concentration of economic or political power. Mergers have also been described as "second best" transactions made by firms when natural or artificial market impediments (e.g., tax laws) prevent or discourage other types of transactions.[1] Each of these alternative views suggest entirely different, and potentially conflicting, roles for public policy toward mergers.

Public policy toward mergers has principally been concerned with issues relating to the potential anti-competitive impact of mergers. The acceptance of the hypothesis by regulatory agencies (and to a more limited extent by the courts) that the desire for market power motivates merger behavior, has resulted in restrictive public policy toward most horizontal and many vertical mergers. Conglomerate mergers, which have become the dominant type of merger as regulatory constraints tightened, are much harder to reconcile with either market power or efficiency theories of motivation.

Though there is not necessarily a direct link between merger motive and merger effect, an understanding of merger motives is important in shaping a reasonable public policy toward mergers. This task is complicated by the staggering variety of merger motives that have been proposed in the finance

* Partial funding for this research was provided by the Federal Trade Commission and Small Business Administration under FTC contract #L0636. The authors are grateful for this support. The opinions expressed are those of the authors and do not necessarily reflect the position of the FTC or SBA. The authors also wish to acknowledge the helpful comments of an anonymous referee.

[1] It has often been suggested that provisions in the tax law provide incentives for assets to be exchanged through merger rather than alternative types of transactions. A good summary can be found in Feld [3]. See also Bosland [1].

and industrial organization literatures. These hypothesized motives include mergers to readjust financial characteristics (e.g., liquidity, debt capacity), mergers for the purpose of diversification, mergers for scale economies, mergers for market power and other reasons too numerous to mention.[2] Unfortunately, empirical verification or rejection of hypothesized merger motivation has lagged substantially behind theorizing.

The majority of the empirical studies of merger behavior has followed one of two general strategies. A number of researchers have examined the differences between the pre-merger and post-merger performance of merged firms.[3] Other researchers have concentrated on identifying differences in the characteristics of firms involved in merger activity (typically acquired firms) and those not involved in merger activity.[4] Though both of these approaches have produced some valuable insights into merger behavior, each has its flaws.

When one firm absorbs another the identities of each become blurred in the data. This makes it very difficult to gain much of an insight into why the merger occurred by observing pre-merger and post-merger performance of the firms involved.[5] The principal problem for the second empirical strategy is that the existence of so many theoretically plausible, and often conflicting, merger motives makes the specification of empirical models of merger behavior extremely difficult. There are at least two dimensions of the specification problem. First, it is often very difficult to tie a particular measurable characteristic of a merger to a single theory of merger motivation.[6] What, for example, is the proper measure of market power that one should use to test the hypothesis that market power is a merger motive? In its general form, this problem is the Achilles heel of all empirical research; and we will not resolve it here. Second, it is possible that some factors may be important in some mergers and irrelevant in others, or have a positive effect on the likelihood of mergers in some circumstances and a negative impact in others. For example, some have suggested that firms with high price earnings ratios may be particularly desirable acquisition targets while others have suggested just the reverse. If both motivations in fact existed, it would be possible to find on average that there is no significant difference between the price earnings ratios of acquired and non-acquired firms. One might then infer incorrectly that neither explanation is important.

Though some studies have identified statistically significant differences in

[2] Rather than reproduce the entire laundry list of merger motives here, we direct the reader to the lists compiled by Scherer [12] and Steiner [15].

[3] See for example Hogarty [8], Gort and Hogarty [5], and Weston and Mansinghka [17].

[4] For a survey of the pre 1975 literature see Steiner [15]. Also see Stevens [16] and Carleton, Harris, and Stewart [2].

[5] Pre and post-merger comparisons can typically only be made using broad indicators of financial performance, which makes it difficult to determine the underlying motivation for the merger.

[6] For an excellent discussion of this issue see Steiner [15, Chapter 8].

the characteristics of acquired and non-acquired firms,[7] the empirical models have typically been weak in terms of explanatory power and the results must be interpreted with care. It should also be noted that these studies have typically ignored or failed to find any relationship between merger behavior and the market structure dimensions of merged firms, leaving us with little indication of the role of market structure related merger motives such as scale economies or market power.

In this paper we argue that empirical models typically used to explore merger behavior miss a crucial dimension of the problem by ignoring the pairings that occur in mergers. Though valuable insights can be gained from studying which firms are acquired and which are not, valuable information may be lost unless the matching of firms (who acquired whom) is also explored. The key conceptual points we wish to make in this paper are 1) that mergers may not be homogeneous phenomena, and, as a result, 2) valuable insights concerning merger motivation may be missed if all mergers are treated as being the same. Our goal is to explore the role that three elements of market structure (concentration, advertising intensity, and research and development intensity) play in merger behavior. Given the nature of our empirical method and of the data, we restrict our analysis to conglomerate mergers. Our reasons for this restriction are treated in more detail in Section III. For a sample of conglomerate mergers occurring between 1970 and 1977 our results show that there are relatively strong systematic relationships between certain dimensions of acquired and acquiring firms' market structures, even though previous studies have found no indication that market structure characteristics have any impact on the probability of a firm's acquisition.[8] These results suggest that the "real" dimensions of firm behavior (production, marketing, research and development strategy, etc.), as well as the financial dimensions of firm behavior, play a part in merger behavior. Specifically, we find a very strong positive relationship between the advertising intensity of the acquiring firm's industry and the advertising intensity of the acquired firm's industry. Building on this result, we find additional insights on the determinants of merger behavior can be gained by treating the acquisitions made by firms in advertising intensive industries as being qualitatively different from acquisitions made by firms in industries where advertising is a less important element of industry structure. These results are consistent with the hypothesis that some mergers may be at least partially

[7] Studies of mergers in the period between the mid 1950s and mid 1960s tended to find acquired firms to be relatively unprofitable and overly liquid. (See Hayes and Taussig [6], Singh [14] and Hindley [7]). These studies tend to support the "market for corporate control" hypothesis of Manne [9]. Studies of the late 1960s and early 1970s mergers tended to concentrate on the financial profiles of acquired firms: Monroe and Simkowitz [10] found that acquired firms (1968) were smaller, had lower price-earnings ratios, lower dividend payout and lower growth in equity. Carleton, Harris, and Stewart [2] found acquired firms (1974–77) were smaller and had lower price-earnings ratios but found the effect of liquidity and leverage to vary over time.

[8] See Carleton, Harris, and Stewart [2].

motivated by the desire to realize scale economies in advertising or that managements have very strong preferences to specialize in product market areas with similar marketing characteristics.

II. MARKET STRUCTURE AND MERGER PAIRINGS

The unifying element in most of the theories of merger motivation is the concept of value maximization.[9] When circumstances exist where the value of two firms when combined would exceed the sum of the values of the two firms operating independently, then a motive for merger is present. For some of the theories of merger motivation, the value maximization concept suggests firm characteristics that should be useful in dividing the universe of firms into two groups: those that are more likely to be acquired and those that are less likely to be acquired. Perhaps the best example of such a theory is the market for corporate control hypothesis.[10] If a firm is being inefficiently managed, the value of that firm can be increased by replacing the inefficient management with more efficient management. One way such a change can be effected is for an efficiently managed firm to acquire the inefficiently managed firm. Thus if one could construct a measure of management's efficiency, one could test the market for corporate control hypothesis by testing for a negative relationship between the efficiency measure and the probability of the firm's acquisition.

Under some other merger motivation theories, however, the characteristics of both the acquired and the acquiring firm will be important in determining whether or not a merger would augment the value of the firm. The matching phenomenon is likely to be of particular importance when one considers market power and scale economies as motives for merger. The remainder of this section will discuss the patterns of matching one might expect to observe in a world where market power and the realization of scale economies were among the possible motivations for merger.

Market Power

The desire to create market power or to exploit more fully existing market power is a very straightforward and historically significant motivation for merger. For horizontal mergers the reasoning is so well known that it need not be repeated here.

The theory of anticompetitive effects in non-horizontal combination is less direct and less developed than the theory of horizontal combinations.[11] A number of hypotheses have been forwarded. These include hypotheses that

[9] Not all theories of merger behavior rely on the value maximization concept. Nonprofit maximization behavioral motives such as a desire by management to "empire build" or grow for growth sake alone have been suggested.

[10] See Manne [9], Hindley [7] and Singh [14].

[11] See Scherer [12, Chapter 12].

conglomerate mergers may enhance the ability of firms to price discriminate[12] or to engage in "deep pocket" activities such as predation, and that conglomerate mergers may enhance the opportunities and rewards from mutual forbearance or reciprocity.

To the extent that there is a unifying element in the theories explaining mergers motivated by market power, it is market power itself. With the exception of horizontal mergers, where additional market power is created, the other mechanism presented in the literature might better be described as increasing the ability to exploit existing market power rather than as creating new market power. The ability to price discriminate, for example, has as a precondition some degree of market power. This line of reasoning suggests that some market power in the industries of the merging firms is necessary if the market power motivation for merger is to be plausible. In terms of degree of difficulty, it is hardest to find a plausible line of reasoning that would lead us to the conclusion that market power could be augmented by a non-horizontal combination of two firms in competitively structured industries; and easiest to find arguments that would lead us to the conclusion that market power could be augmented by a non-horizontal combination of two firms in oligopolistically structured markets. One reasonable proxy for existing market power is the concentration of a firm's industry. If market power were the dominant motive for merger, one would expect to find that most mergers were either horizontal or involved firms in concentrated industries. Neither appears to be the case.[13] If market power, however, is a partial explanation for merger behavior one might expect to find that firms in concentrated industries tend to pair with firms in concentrated industries (an indirect indication of market power motivation in these mergers) and that firms in unconcentrated industries tend to merge with firms in unconcentrated industries (an indication of motivations other than market power must be at work). The empirical manifestation of the above scenario would be some degree of correlation between acquired and acquiring firms' industry concentrations.

Scale Economies

Scale economies or other operating efficiencies of size or scope also provide a straightforward motivation for merger. If the total costs of doing business are less for the combined firm than for the independently operating firms, then an incentive for merger exists.

The industrial organization literature typically discusses scale economies in four different categories: 1) plant-specific scale economies; 2) product specific

[12] See Needham [11].

[13] Carleton, Harris, and Stewart [2] found no indication that firms in concentrated industries were more likely to be acquired than firms in unconcentrated industries for the 1974–77 period. Gort [4] found that merger rates in an earlier period (1951–59) tended to be higher in concentrated industries than unconcentrated industries but interpreted the results as indicating the likelihood of valuation discrepancies not as an indication of market power motivations. The current antitrust policy greatly limits the number of observed horizontal mergers.

scale economies; 3) vertical efficiencies; and 4) multiplant-scale economies. The first two of these have relatively little relevance to the present study since our method dictates the exclusion of horizontal mergers from the sample.[14] Furthermore, very few mergers have a direct effect of increasing plant size. The primary role for plant-specific economies through merger is for the combined firm to have the resources and the markets to build more efficient sized plants in the future. Note also that product-specific scale economies can only be realized in horizontal, or in market extension mergers. The technical efficiencies that can be realized through vertical integration (and thus vertical merger), though sometimes substantial, are not of great interest here because of the extremely small number of vertical mergers in the sample we will be using in the empirical work. This leaves multiplant scale economies to consider as a likely source of merger motivation in the mergers to be studied here.

When considering the combination of firms operating in different product markets, it is likely that cost saving would stem from efficiencies of size in activities ancillary to the production process.[15] These would include principally: marketing, research and development, finance, procurement, and the general management function. The two characteristics measured in this study are advertising intensity and research and development intensity. A general hypothesis might be that firms in which the ancillary activities described above represented a larger proportion of total cost would tend to be more prone to merger. The argument has two parts. First, if the potential for economies of size or scope in advertising and research and development exists, then the likely benefits from merger will be greatest for mergers between firms in industries where these activities represent a larger proportion of total cost. That is, a fifty percent reduction in per unit advertising cost for firms spending one percent of sales revenue on advertising has less of an impact on profits than a ten percent reduction in per unit advertising cost for firms spending ten percent of sales revenue on advertising, all else held equal. Second, the available evidence seems to suggest that the potential for realizing scale economies in advertising and R&D will be greatest in industries where advertising and R&D are an important part of conduct. Economies of size and scope in marketing and advertising are usually attributable to access by larger firms to media and rate structures not available to smaller firms, the ability of firms to transfer brand image and thus loyalty to a variety of products, and access to distribution channels unavailable to small firms. A similar case can be made for the proposition that the net benefits stemming from economies of size and scope in R&D are likely to be largest for a merger involving two firms in R&D intensive industries. It should be noted that our hypothesis is not that economies in advertising and R&D sufficient to motivate a merger can only occur between firms in advertising and R&D intensive industries; rather our hypothesis is that they are more likely in this case than in others.

[14] The success of antitrust authorities in successfully attacking horizontal and vertical combinations probably explains the relatively small numbers of such mergers in the sample.

[15] For a discussion of multiplant economies see Scherer, Beckenstein *et al* [13].

In earlier work, Carleton, Harris and Stewart [2] found no relationship between advertising intensity or research and development intensity and the likelihood that a firm would be acquired. However, a finding that, of those firms that did merge, firms in advertising intensive industries merged with firms also in advertising intensive industries and that firms in R&D intensive industries merged with firms also in R&D intensive industries would provide indirect support for the hypothesis that the realization of potential scale economies in advertising and/or research and development plays a role in merger behavior.

Management Specialization

One other point merits discussion. The net benefits of a merger will depend in part on the costs associated with absorbing the acquisition into the managerial organization of the firm. For example, the management of a firm operating in a market where product differentiation is not a part of industry conduct, may find it difficult, and thus costly, to operate a firm in a highly differentiated consumer market because management skills, experience, and organization are attuned to a different set of problems and environmental constraints. Each of the three market structure variables could be viewed as proxying for managerial environment, and the observed relationships between acquired and acquiring firm market structures could be indicative only of a preference of firms to merge with firms that are in some broad sense similar to themselves. We will not be able to eliminate entirely this alternative explanation of the patterns we find. We can only comment that diseconomies in certain forms of combination are only the opposite sides of economies in other forms of combinations.

III. MERGER PAIRINGS AND MARKET STRUCTURE

Model

To the extent that firms select merger partners based on a complementary matching of market structure characteristics, it should be possible empirically to "explain" a vector of observed acquired firm characteristics by the characteristics of the firms acquiring them. We model this matching with a system of linear regressions where, for each equation, the left hand side variable is a characteristic of the acquired firm and the right hand side variables are characteristics of the acquiring firm. The general form of the system can be written as:

$$Y_{1i} = a_1 + \beta_1 \bar{X}_{1i} + \varepsilon_{1i} \qquad i = 1, 2, \ldots, n$$

$$Y_{2i} = a_2 + \beta_2 \bar{X}_{2i} + \varepsilon_{2i}$$

$$\vdots$$

$$Y_{ji} = a_j + \beta_j \bar{X}_{ji} + \varepsilon_{ji}$$

where

Y_{ji} is the jth characteristic of the acquired firm in the ith merger,
$\bar{X}_{ji}$ is the vector of relevant characteristics of the acquiring firm in the ith merger,
ε_{ji} is the random error associated with the relationship between the jth acquired firm characteristic and acquiring firm characteristics in the ith merger, and
the a's and β's are the intercepts and vectors of slope coefficients in the relationships.

The interpretation of the model is that each characteristic of the acquired firm will be related to the characteristics of the firm that chose that firm as a merger partner. Given the expectation that there may be some correlation between the acquired firm's characteristics, the seemingly unrelated regression technique developed by Zellner [18] would be an appropriate estimation technique. In the current effort we are interested in the relationship between acquired and acquiring firm industry concentration, advertising intensity, and research and development intensity. We have no *a priori* reason to exclude any of the explanatory variables from any of the equations. In this case, where the vector of explanatory variable is identical for each equation, the Zellner technique and equation by equation ordinary least squares regression produce exactly the same results.

Data

The market structure data used in this study are industry measures of concentration, advertising intensity, and research and development intensity for 1) 83 firms acquired during 1970–77 and 2) the companies that acquired the 83 firms. Panel A of Table I lists variable names and definitions.

The data are part of a larger data set compiled by Carleton, Harris and Stewart [2]. Primary data sources are: (1) the COMPUSTAT Expanded Annual Industrial Tape (May 1979—Primary, Supplementary and Tertiary Files); (2) the COMPUSTAT Expanded Annual Industrial Research File (May 1979—Primary, Supplementary and Tertiary Files); (3) the Federal Trade Commission's Merger Series (Overall and Large); and (4) the 1972 Census of Manufacturers. The COMPUSTAT Industrial Research File covers firms that have been deleted from the COMPUSTAT Industrial File since 1970. It thus provides an excellent source of data for companies no longer in existence (e.g., as a result of merger or bankruptcy). The FTC merger series covers acquired firms classified in manufacturing and mining. The FTC definition of merger requires that (a) the acquisition must represent the purchase of 50.1 percent or more of the stock or assets of the company acquired and, (b) an independent company, subsidiary, or division of another company must be acquired.

TABLE I
VARIABLE DEFINITIONS

A. *Market Structure Variables*

CRAQG: 4 firm concentration ratio for acquiring firm's industry.
CRAQD: 4 firm concentration ratio for acquired firm's industry.
ADAQG: advertising intensity in acquiring firm's industry. (advertising expenditures as a percent of sales)
ADAQD: advertising intensity in acquired firm's industry. (advertising expenditure as a percent of sales)
RDAQG: research and development intensity in acquiring firm's industry. (R&D expenditures as a percent of sales)
RDAQD: research and development intensity in acquired firm's industry. (R&D expenditures as a percent of sales)

B. *Financial Variables**

CL1 = liquidity as measured by Net Working Capital ÷ Total Assets
NID2 = leverage as measured by Total Liabilities ÷ Total Assets (normalized)†
CPE1 = price earnings ratio
CA1 = activity as measured by sales divided by assets
CLG6 = size as measured by the log of assets.

* All financial variables are based on averages of 1972 73 data.

† To control for different industry leverage patterns the leverage variable NID2 is measured by dividing the firm's debt ratio by the average debt ratio for that firm's industry.

To be included in the study, the merger had to satisfy these general characteristics:

(1) COMPUSTAT information exists for the acquired firm and the acquiring firm,
(2) COMPUSTAT classifies the acquired and the acquiring firm as being in manufacturing (SIC 2000 to 3999), and
(3) the merger is recorded by the FTC (Overall and Large Merger Series).[16]

Industry concentration, advertising intensity and research and development intensity were constructed for each COMPUSTAT industry represented in the sample. COMPUSTAT industry definitions create something of a problem. COMPUSTAT uses a mixture of two, three and four digit SIC's. Thus some COMPUSTAT firms are assigned to very broadly defined industries and others to relatively narrowly defined industries. The 1972 Census of Manufacturing was used to construct four firm concentration ratios for each COMPUSTAT industry. Two and three digit sales weighted concen-

[16] Merger dates and the identity of the acquiring firm were also cross checked with data from Moody's Industrial Manuals. In a few cases, COMPUSTAT and the FTC gave different merger dates. Typically the dates were close (e.g. 1971 vs. 1970) and represent a different ruling on whether the merger was in late 1970 or early 1971. In these cases, the FTC date was used. In the one case where there was a large difference between FTC and COMPUSTAT dates and the merger would otherwise satisfy our screening rules the merger was eliminated from the sample.

tration ratios were constructed where appropriate.[17] Industry advertising and R&D intensities were constructed from COMPUSTAT data.[18]

For additional empirical work (reported later in the paper) another data set of 1279 manufacturing firms drawn from the same basic COMPUSTAT sources was used. This set included 1204 firms which were not acquired and 75 firms acquired during the period 1974–77. Using advertising intensity data, these acquired firms were further divided into two groups: 1) 59 firms which were acquired by firms in industries in which advertising expenditure was less than two percent of sales and 2) 16 firms which were acquired by firms in industries in which advertising expenditure was in excess of two percent of sales. In addition to market structure variables, certain financial variables for each company were calculated as is displayed in panel B of Table I.

Subsamples

The process described above produced complete data for 83 mergers that occurred between 1970 and 1977. The complete sample is denoted Sample 1 in the results section. The data present a significant problem in that there is a high potential for "spurious" correlations to appear. There are two reasons for this. First the complete sample contains a number of horizontal mergers. By definition these are mergers between firms in the same industry and thus the acquired and the acquiring firms have identical industry characteristics. This virtually guarantees that positive correlations between acquired and acquir-

[17] Some additional discussion of industry definition is required here. There is some method to the "madness" of the COMPUSTAT classification scheme. Typically, firms that produce a wide variety of products are assigned to two digit industries while firms producing more narrow product lines are assigned to three or four digit industries. Thus General Foods, which produces a wide variety of food products is assigned to COMPUSTAT industry 2000 (Packaged Foods), while Campbell Soup Co., which produces a less diverse line is assigned to 2030 (Canned Foods). With a few exceptions, the four digit industries used by COMPUSTAT tend to be relatively broad (e.g. 2844, cosmetics; 3221, containers—metal glass; 3428 hardware). In only a few cases is more than a single four digit industry listed by COMPUSTAT in the same three digit SIC, and in most of the cases there are substantial differences between the four digit products (e.g. 2082 Beverages—Brewers, 2085 Beverages—Distillers). Any construction of industry classifications will have the problem of over defining some industries and underdefining others. In constructing the data for this study an attempt was made to use roughly three digit SIC's. Some four digit industries were combined (e.g. cane and beet sugar refining are listed as separate COMPUSTAT industries) and some four digit industries were maintained (e.g. 3711, motor vehicles, and 3714, auto parts and accessories, were maintained as separate industries). In our judgment, the three and four digit industry classifications used in the study represent roughly similar degrees of market definition and the firms assigned to those industries have a major part of their business in the industry as defined. Firms assigned to two digit COMPUSTAT industries are generally operating in a number of different industries. Special note will be made of these cases in the later screening of the data. Sales weighted averages were used to aggregate the data where necessary.

[18] Industry advertising and R&D intensities were constructed using all firms covered by COMPUSTAT. Advertising and R&D intensities were also obtained from the Federal Trade Commission's Annual Line of Business Report but better coverage could be obtained from the COMPUSTAT data. Additionally, for those industries where data were available from both sources, a high degree of correlation was noted. (The correlation coefficient between COMPUSTAT and Line of Business Advertising intensity was .90. The correlation coefficient between COMPUSTAT and Line of Business R&D intensity was .82.)

ing firm characteristics would be found in a sample containing a substantial number of horizontal mergers. Second, while it may be true that an acquiring firm picks a firm as a desirable acquisition because it has a similar advertising intensity, it may also be true that firms pick acquisitions that are similar to themselves in a much broader sense. A firm in a closely related industry may be a more desirable acquisition, everything else held equal, because the acquiring firm's management has more information about production technologies, market conditions, distribution channels and so forth. Given that there is a tendency for such closely related industries to have similar market structures, a finding that elements of acquired and acquiring firm market structure are positively related may only be a result of these variables proxying for industry identification. An attempt to eliminate these problems was made by passing the data through a set of increasingly restrictive screens. In Sample 2 all mergers listed by the FTC as horizontal were omitted. It is also possible, however, that non-horizontal mergers can occur between two firms that would, in the COMPUSTAT data, be assigned to the same industry. Geographic market extension mergers and in some cases, where COMPUSTAT industries are broadly defined, product extension mergers could involve firms that were assigned identical market structure variables in the construction of the data. In Sample 3 all mergers where the COMPUSTAT SIC's for the acquired and acquiring firm are identical were eliminated. The use by COMPUSTAT of two, three, and four digit industries also creates a problem in the data in that a part of the data used to construct the market structure data for a firm in a two digit COMPUSTAT industry is also contained in the data for a firm in a three digit COMPUSTAT industry if the first two digits of the industry SIC's are the same. Sample 4 eliminated all such mergers. (e.g., A merger involving a firm in industry 3800 and a firm in industry 3890 would not be included in Sample 4.) The COMPUSTAT industry definition scheme requires the mixing of firms in broadly defined industries with firms in narrowly defined industries. In Sample 5 all mergers involving firms classified by COMPUSTAT into two digit industries were eliminated. The final sample thus contains relatively pure conglomerate mergers in the sense that it only included mergers between firms operating in different relatively well defined product markets. Though the results for all five samples are presented, the problem of spurious correlation is likely to be severe in samples 1, 2, and 3. Descriptive statistics for the five samples are displayed in Table II. It is interesting to note that there is little difference between the average market structure of acquired and acquiring firms in any of the samples.

Results

The results of the regression analysis for each of the five samples are reported in Table III. The reader is again cautioned to use care in interpreting the

TABLE II
DESCRIPTIVE STATISTICS ON THE MARKET STRUCTURE OF MERGING FIRMS

	Acquired Firms			*Acquiring Firms*		
	Concentration CRAQD	*Advertising Intensity ADAQD*	*R&D Intensity RDAQD*	*Concentration CRAQG*	*Advertising Intensity ADAQG*	*R&D Intensity RDAQG*
Sample 1 $n = 83$						
Mean	37	2.7	1.9	41	2.5	2.1
Std. Dev.	14	4.2	1.7	15	3.5	2.2
Sample 2 $n = 65$						
Mean	37	3.1	2.0	42	2.8	2.1
Std. Dev.	15	4.6	1.8	16	3.8	2.1
Sample 3 $n = 54$						
Mean	36	2.8	1.8	41	2.4	2.0
Std. Dev.	12	4.4	1.5	14	3.3	2.0
Sample 4 $n = 42$						
Mean	36	2.3	1.8	41	2.5	2.0
Std. Dev.	12	3.7	1.6	16	3.6	2.2
Sample 5 $n = 35$						
Mean	36	2.2	1.9	43	2.5	2.2
Std. Dev.	12	3.8	1.7	16	3.9	3.3

results of samples 1 and 2 and, to a lesser degree, the results in sample 3. In the unscreened samples there is a significant relationship between acquired and acquiring firm concentration ratios that disappears as the sample is screened to remove the "industry identification" effect. Though the data show that there is a tendency for firms in concentrated industries to merge with firms in concentrated industries, it is not possible to determine whether this tendency is completely spurious, represents a desire by firms to acquire firms in industries with concentration similar to their own or whether firms tend to acquire firms similar to themselves along broader dimensions. In the more stringently screened samples (3, 4 and 5), there is no significant relationship between the concentration of the acquired firm's industry and the concentration of the acquiring firm's industry. Thus for conglomerate mergers, there seems to be no indication that firms tend to pair in mergers based on market power considerations as measured by industry concentration.

The results for advertising intensity are much more consistent. In all of the samples a strong positive relation between acquired and acquiring firm advertising intensity appears, and none of the other variables in the model has a significant impact on acquired firm advertising intensity. This result holds

TABLE III

RESULTS OF REGRESSIONS RELATING CHARACTERISTICS OF ACQUIRED FIRMS TO CHARACTERISTICS OF ACQUIRING FIRMS, 1970–77 SAMPLE OF MERGERS

	Dependent Variables Acquired Firm					
Independent Variables Acquiring Firm	*Concentration CRAQD*		*Ad Intensity ADAQD*		*R&D Intensity RDAQD*	
Sample 1 $n = 83$ (all mergers)†						
constant	21.71	(4.53)*	0.70	(0.70)	0.12	(0.22)
Concentration CRAQG	0.34	(3.32)*	−0.01	(−0.46)	0.02	(1.90)*
Ad Intensity ADAQG	−0.23	(−0.49)	0.88	(9.02)*	0.10	(2.00)*
R&D Intensity RDAQG	0.90	(1.22)	0.82	(0.53)	0.32	(3.90)*
R^2, F		0.14, 4.5*		0.56, 33.7*		0.27, 10.0*
Sample 2 $n = 65$ (no horizontal mergers)†						
constant	23.72	(4.33)*	1.07	(0.86)	0.12	(0.22)
Concentration CRAQG	0.28	(2.54)*	−0.02	(−0.59)	0.03	(2.41)
Ad Intensity ADAQG	−0.37	(−0.73)	0.87	(7.51)*	0.11	(2.03)*
R&D Intensity RDAQG	1.35	(1.51)	0.12	(0.57)	0.35	(3.73)*
R^2, F		0.13, 3.2*		0.56, 25.9*		0.13, 3.2*
Sample 3 $n = 54$ (no mergers where SIC acquired equals SIC acquiring)†						
constant	36.58	(6.36)*	1.27	(0.78)	0.03	(0.05)
Concentration CRAQG	−0.05	(−0.42)	−0.02	(−0.48)	0.03	(2.09)*
Ad Intensity ADAQG	0.06	(0.12)	0.84	(5.53)*	0.02	(0.28)
R&D Intensity RDAQG	0.74	(0.86)	0.10	(0.42)	0.25	(2.44)*
R^2, F		0.02, 0.37		0.41, 11.7*		0.17, 3.3*
Sample 4, $n = 42$ (no mergers between firms in broadly and narrowly defined industries)†						
constant	35.97	(6.04)*	0.99	(0.91)	−0.15	(−0.19)
Concentration CRAQG	−0.03	(−0.26)	−0.02	(−0.89)	0.04	(2.19)*
Ad Intensity ADAQG	−0.03	(−0.06)	0.80	(7.96)*	0.04	(0.55)
R&D Intensity RDAQG	0.63	(0.70)	0.06	(0.35)	0.20	(1.74)*
R^2, F		0.02, 0.21		0.66, 24.6*		0.17, 2.6*
Sample 5 $n = 35$ (no mergers involving firms in broadly defined industries)†						
constant	39.55	(5.97)*	0.60	(0.54)	0.08	(0.08)
Concentration CRAQG	−0.08	(−0.62)	−0.01	(−0.68)	0.03	(1.74)*
Ad Intensity ADAQG	−0.15	(−0.25)	0.82	(8.88)*	0.01	(0.16)
R&D Intensity RDAQG	0.55	(0.56)	0.10	(0.64)	0.21	(1.65)*
R^2, F		0.03, 0.28		0.75, 31.4*		0.14, 1.7

Table entries: Regression coefficient (t ratio)

† See text.

* Significant at the 90% level.

even after all attempts to remove possible sources of spurious correlation have been made. It would appear that the degree to which an acquiring firm's industry is characterized by promotional expense and product differentiation (as proxied by advertising expenditure) has a significant effect on that firm's choice of merger partner (with respect to that acquired firm's characteristics in the same dimension of market structure). This result is consistent with the hypothesis that scale economies in advertising or specialization in management may, at least in part, provide motivation for merger.

Interesting results are also obtained in the research and development equation. Throughout all of the samples there is a positive significant relationship between the research and the development intensities of the acquired and the acquiring firms' industries. The more intensive the research and development effort is in the acquiring firm's industry, the higher the research and development intensity is likely to be in the acquired firm's industry. Again this finding would be consistent with scale economies or management/personnel specialization as an explanation of merger motivation. It is also interesting to note that there is a positive significant relationship between acquiring firm industry concentration and acquired firm research and development intensity, even in the highly screened samples. Firms in relatively concentrated industries are more likely to choose firms in research and development intensive industries than are firms in less concentrated industries. Several explanations of this result could be offered. Firms in concentrated industries may be seeking outlets for excess funds and choose technically advancing "growth" industries.[19] Firms in industries where market power is concentrated may be better able to exploit the advantages of technological progress.

It should be noted that, contrary to expectations, there is very little correlation between the market structure variables. Significant correlations between concentration and advertising intensity and between concentration and research and development intensity were not found in the sample. Some moderate correlation (coefficients on the order of .3) was found between advertising intensity and research and development intensity.

In summary, the following points should be noted. In our previous research (Carleton, Harris, and Stewart [2]) we found that there was no significant difference between the market structure characteristics of acquired and non-acquired firms and that, on average, the concentration, advertising intensity and research and development intensity of a firm's industry had no statistical effect on the likelihood that the firm would be acquired. By themselves these results would suggest that firms' market structures play no role in merger behavior. In this section we have found a strong pattern of relationships between the market structures of acquired and acquiring firms, even in samples where the acquired and acquiring firms are in different well-defined industries. These results strongly suggest that while market structure may have little effect on who gets acquired and who does not, market structure, and in particular advertising intensity, has a significant impact on the observed pairings that constitute mergers. Though we cannot, with certainty, state whether the observed pattern of acquired and acquiring firm advertising intensities is the result of a scale economies or management specialization motivation, we can conjecture that the strength of the relationship between acquired and acquiring firm advertising intensity suggests that, on average, a

[19] Unfortunately, the changing composition of the COMPUSTAT sample over time would not allow us to construct reliable measures of firm or industry growth rates to use in the analysis.

firm in an advertising intensive industry must either forego substantial benefits or incur substantial costs if it chooses to acquire a firm in an industry where advertising intensity is low.

IV. ADDITIONAL EVIDENCE ON ADVERTISING SCALE ECONOMIES AND MERGERS

In the previous section it was shown that there is a tendency for industry advertising intensity to have an effect on observed patterns of merger pairings. In this section we further investigate the effect of advertising on merger behavior by treating the acquisitions made by firms in industries with high advertising intensities as qualitatively different from acquisitions made by firms in industries characterized by low advertising intensities. This allows us to explore the possibility that a firm's characteristics may have different effects on the likelihood of its acquisition depending upon the type of acquiring firm. We can explore, for example, the possibility that while a firm's advertising-intensity may not be a good predictor of whether it will be acquired or remain single, it may yet be an excellent index of the probability that it will be acquired by an advertising-intensive firm.

We empirically model a world in which the characteristics of the individual firm results in one of three possible outcomes in a specified period of time:

(1) the firm is not acquired,
(2a) the firm is acquired by a firm in a low advertising intensity industry, or
(2b) the firm is acquired by a firm in a high advertising intensity industry.

An advertising intensity of two percent was used as the dividing line between high and low. Several critical comments should be made about our approach. First the outcomes 2a and 2b are not truly dichotomous and the dividing line is necessarily arbitrary.[20] Second, we are not explicitly analyzing firm by firm merger pairings, as was done in the previous section, but are looking at the observed merger patterns between the set of potential acquisitions and two qualitatively different *groups* of acquiring firms. Finally it should be noted that acquiring firms could have been divided into more than two groups if other characteristics of the acquiring firm were considered.[21]

[20] Though the correlation between the advertising intensities of the acquired and acquiring firms' industries for the entire sample is quite high ($P = 0.61$); when the two percent division point is used, the within group correlations drop substantially ($P = 0.19$ for the high advertising intensity group, $P = 0.26$ for the low advertising intensity group).

[21] It should be noted that acquiring firm industry advertising intensity is only weakly correlated with other characteristics of the acquiring firms. The highest correlation is with the price earnings ratio ($P = 0.26$). All other correlation coefficients are less than 0.2.

The Model

The conditional logit model considers the odds ratio for any bivariate choice:

$$\log \frac{P(2a)_t}{P(1)_t} = X_t B_2$$

$$\log \frac{P(2b)_t}{P(1)_t} = X_t B_3$$

$$\log \frac{P(2b)_t}{P(2a)_t} = X_t B_4 \qquad t = 1, 2, \ldots, T$$

where $P(i)_t$ is the probability of the ith outcome for firm t,
X_t is a $1 \times k$ vector of exogeneous variables for firm t,
and B_i $(i = 2, 3, 4)$ is a $k \times 1$ vector of unknown coefficients.

We can use the first equation as an example. The left hand side is simply the log of the ratio of two probabilities. The interpretation of a positive coefficient is that an increase in X_t causes state $2a$ (acquired by a firm in a low advertising intensity industry) to be more probable *relative* to state 1 (not acquired).

Estimation of this model can be accomplished by noting that $P(1)_t + P(2a)_t + P(2b)_t = 1$ for all t. Thus one of the above equations is redundant. If we solve the first two equations and the above identity for the probabilities we get:

$$P(1)_t = \frac{1}{c_t}$$

$$P(2a)_t = \frac{e^{X_t B_2}}{c_t}$$

$$P(2b)_t = \frac{e^{X_t B_3}}{c_t}$$

where

$$c_t = 1 + e^{X_t B_2 X_t B_3}.$$

The likelihood function for the observed random sample is:

$$L = \underset{\text{Outcome 1 observed}}{\Pi P(1)_t} \cdot \underset{\text{Outcome } 2a \text{ observed}}{\Pi P(2a)_t} \quad \underset{\text{Outcome } 2b \text{ observed}}{\Pi P(2b)_t}$$

The likelihood function can then be maximized with respect to B_2 and B_3. B_4 can then be calculated. An approximation to the asymptotic covariance matrix of the estimators can be obtained from the second derivatives of the likelihood function. This allows us to perform tests of hypotheses, using the normal distribution, that are asymptotically valid.

Data and Results

In previous work (Carleton, Harris, Stewart, [2]), the price earnings ratio, firm size, and less consistently liquidity, leverage and activity, were firm characteristics found to have an effect on the likelihood of acquisition. These variables are defined in Panel B of Table I and the sample is described in Section III. These variables and advertising intensity (advertising expenditure/sales) were used in the estimation of the logit model presented in Table IV. The last column of Table IV reports the coefficients of the model when only two outcomes are considered (1) not acquired, 2) acquired). Thus

TABLE IV
EFFECT OF CHARACTERISTICS OF ACQUIRED FIRMS ON PROBABILITY OF ACQUISITION BY FIRMS IN HIGH AND LOW ADVERTISING INDUSTRIES, 1974–77 SAMPLE OF MERGERS

	Log of Odds Ratios			
	Three Outcome Model			*Two Outcome Model Model*
Acquired Firm Characteristics	*Acquired by firm in low advertising industry vs. not acquired Log(P2a/P1)*	*Acquired by firm in high advertising industry vs. not acquired Log(P2b/P1)*	*Acquired by firm in high advertising industry vs. acquired by firm in low advertising industry Log(P2b/P2a*	*Acquired vs. not acquired Log(P2/P1)*
Constant	−2.753 (−3.025)*	−2.089 (−1.287)	0.664 (0.361)	−2.088 (−2.641)*
CL1 (liquidity)	2.810 (2.422)*	0.741 (0.354)	−2.069 (−0.876)	1.922 (1.915)*
NID2 (leverage)	−0.065 (−0.151)	0.515 (0.704)	0.581 (0.691)	−0.029 (−0.075)
CPE1 (price/earnings)	−0.035 (−1.798)*	−0.048 (−1.383)	−0.013 (−0.334)	−0.037 (−2.150)*
AD (ads/sales)	−0.503 (−2.650)*	0.219 (2.754)*	0.723 (3.515)*	−0.084 (−1.001)
CA1 (activity)	0.128 (0.977)	0.496 (2.937)*	0.368 (1.772)*	0.213 (1.987)*
CLG6 (log size)	−0.104 (−0.986)	−0.992 (−3.801)*	−0.888 (−3.181)*	−0.267 (−2.806)*

Events: 1 firm not acquired
2 firm acquired
2*a* firm acquired by firm in low advertising intensity industry
2*b* firm acquired by firm in high advertising intensity industry

* Significant at the 90% level.
t-ratios enclosed in parentheses.

on average, the probability of being acquired relative to the probability of not being acquired will increase as liquidity increases, as the price earnings ratio declines, as activity increases, and as firm size declines. These results provide an interesting contrast to the results in the first three columns which allow for differences in the advertising intensity of the acquiring firm's industry. For example, though advertising intensity has an insignificant effect on the probability of being acquired relative to the probability of not being acquired (column 4), increasing advertising intensity significantly increases the relative probability of being acquired by a firm in a high advertising intensity industry, and significantly decreases the relative probability of being acquired by a firm in a low advertising intensity industry (columns 1, 2, and 3). This corresponds directly to our findings in the previous section. Note also that while firm size has an overall negative impact on the probability of acquisition relative to nonacquisition, this effect is strongest when one considers the acquisitions made by firms in advertising intensive industries. In terms of probabilities, given our sample proportions, a naïve prediction would suggest that acquisition by a firm in a low advertising intensity industry (59 observations) is about 3.7 times more likely than acquisition by a firm in a high advertising intensity industry (16 observations). However, using our logit estimates, a hypothetical firm having the mean characteristics of the firms acquired by firms in high advertising intensity industries, is almost two times more likely to be acquired by a firm in a high advertising intensity industry than it is to be acquired by a firm in a low advertising industry.

The pattern that emerges is as follows: smaller firms in advertising-intensive industries and with higher sales to assets ratios are most likely to be acquired by firms that are also in advertising-intensive industries. The result that firms in high advertising intensity industries are more likely to be acquired by firms in high advertising intensity industries and firms in low advertising intensity industries are more likely to be acquired by firms in low advertising intensity industries is consistent with either a management specialization or scale economies hypothesis of motivation. The result that, everything else equal, a decrease in firm size has a larger and more significant positive effect on the probability that the firm will be acquired by an advertising intensive firm than it does on the probability that the firm will be acquired by a firm that is not in an advertising intensive industry is a finding more easily reconciled with a scale economy motivation than a management specialization motivation.

V. CONCLUSIONS

Our findings suggest that insight into the determinants of merger behavior can be gained by examining the relationships between the characteristics of acquiring firms and the characteristics of the firms they acquired. In particular, for a sample of mergers which took place between 1970 and 1977 there are significant positive correlations between the industry advertising intensity of acquired and acquiring firms, between the industry research and development intensities of acquired and acquiring firms, and between acquiring firm industry concentration and acquired firm industry research and development intensity. These results hold up even when attempts are made to screen the "industry identification" effect out of the data.

These results were used to divide all mergers into two groups that could have been made under different sets of motives. In particular, those acquisitions made by firms in industries characterized by high advertising intensity were assumed to be different from acquisitions made by firms in industries characterized by low advertising intensity. The conditional logit model showed that while "on average" advertising intensity had no significant effect on the probability of acquisition, when the advertising intensity of the acquiring firm's industry was qualitatively accounted for, industry advertising played a significant role in merger behavior. When this result is combined with findings that 1) firm size was strongly and negatively related to the probability of acquisition by a firm in an advertising-intensive industry and 2) the financial variables found to be important in "average" merger behavior play a less important role in mergers by firms in advertising-intensive industries, a strong circumstantial case appears for arguing that at least some mergers may be motivated by scale economies in advertising.

As we noted earlier, it is often very difficult to associate an observed empirical relationship between measurable variables with a single hypothesis of merger behavior. This is certainly true in the case of our results. Though it can be argued that our results are consistent with a hypothesis that mergers are to some extent motivated by scale economies in advertising, other explanations of the observed pattern of acquired and acquiring firms certainly exist. The finding of a consistent pattern of the acquired and acquiring firms' characteristics and of differences in the factors affecting the likelihood of acquisition when the sample is split by an acquiring firm characteristic strongly suggests a heretofore unexplored mechanism in the process by which merger partners are determined. In summary, our results support the general position that mergers are motivated by a complex combination of mechanisms rather than by a single mechanism.

John F. Stewart,
The University of North Carolina at Chapel Hill,
Department of Economics,
Gardner Hall 017 A,
Chapel Hill,
N.C. 27514,
U.S.A.

ACCEPTED JULY 1982

REFERENCES

[1] Bosland, C. C., "Has Estate Taxation Induced Recent Mergers?," *National Tax Journal* 16, 2 (June 1963), pp. 159–68.

[2] Carleton, W. T., R. S. Harris and J. F. Stewart, *An Empirical Study of Merger Motives.* (Federal Trade Commission and Small Business Administration, Washington, D.C., December 1980).

[3] Feld, A. L., "Tax Policy and Competition," (Federal Trade Commission, Washington, D.C., February 1979).

[4] Gort, M., "An Economic Disturbance Theory of Mergers," *Quarterly Journal of Economics* 83, 4 (November 1968), pp. 624–42.

[5] ——, and T. F. Hogarty, "New Evidence on Mergers," *Journal of Law and Economics* 13, 1 (April 1970), pp. 173–76.

[6] Hayes, S. L. and R. A. Taussig, "Tactics of Cash Takeover Bids", *Harvard Business Review* 45, 2 (March–April 1967), pp. 135–48.

[7] Hindley, B., "Separation of Ownership and Control in the Modern Corporation", *Journal of Law and Economics* 13, 1 (April 1970), pp. 185–221.

[8] Hogarty, T. F., "The Profitability of Corporate Mergers," *Journal of Business* 43, 3 (July 1970), pp. 317–27.

[9] Manne, H. G. "Mergers and the Market for Corporate Control", *Journal of Political Economy* 73, 2 (April 1965), pp. 110–20.

[10] Monroe, R. and M. Simkowitz, "A Discriminant Analysis Function for Conglomerate Targets," *Southern Journal of Business* 6, 4 (November 1971), pp. 1–16.

[11] Needham, D., *The Economics of Industrial Structure Conduct and Performance* (St. Martin's Press, New York, 1978).

[12] Scherer, F. M., *Industrial Market Structure and Economic Performance* (Rand McNally, Chicago, 1980).

[13] ——, A. Beckenstein, E. Kauter, and R. D. Murphy, *The Economics of Multiplant Operation: An International Comparisons Study* (Harvard University Press, Cambridge, 1975).

[14] Singh, A., *Takeovers: Their Relevance to the Stock Market and the Theory of the Firm* (Cambridge University Press, Cambridge, 1971).

[15] Steiner, P. O., *Mergers: Motives, Effects, Policies* (University of Michigan Press, Ann Arbor, 1975).

[16] Stevens, D. L., "Financial Characteristics of Merged Firms: A Multivariate Analysis", *Journal of Financial and Quantitative Analysis* 8, 2 (March 1973), pp. 149–58.

[17] Weston, J. F. and S. K. Mansinghka, "Tests of the Efficiency Performance of Conglomerate Firms," *Journal of Finance* 26, 4 (September 1971), pp. 929–36.

[18] Zellner, A., "An Efficient Method of Estimating Seemingly Unrelated Regressions and Tests for Aggregation Bias," *Journal of the American Statistical Association* 57, 298 (June 1962), pp. 348–68.

THE JOURNAL OF INDUSTRIAL ECONOMICS 0022-1821 $2.00
Volume XXXII March 1984 No. 3

SCALE ECONOMIES, IMPERFECT COMPETITION, AND PUBLIC POLICY

MARTIN K. PERRY*

ECONOMIES of scale give rise to a difficult tradeoff in evaluating the structure of an industry. Scale economies can be more fully exploited with fewer firms, but imperfect competition may emerge. On the other hand, scale economies are sacrificed when the number of firms is increased in order to foster competition. The free market outcome in such circumstances would typically involve a multi-firm industry with imperfectly competitive behavior as well as unexploited scale economies. If this market compromise is deemed unsatisfactory, regulation of a franchise monopolist might be considered. The argument for monopoly regulation is that any compromise between scale economies and imperfect competition can be avoided altogether by having a benevolent monopolist. However, in practice, regulation may be ineffective in restraining the monopolist's pricing or may introduce inefficiencies in production. Thus, there may well be cases for which neither the market outcome nor the regulated monopoly outcome are appealing.

This paper examines a second alternative for reducing the losses inherent in the market compromise between scale economies and imperfect competition. In so doing, it is useful to make the distinction between structural and behavioral policies toward an industry. A behavioral policy exercises direct control over the objective of the firms. Thus, monopoly regulation is a behavioral policy in that it attempts to suppress profit-maximization by the firm in order to achieve first-best marginal cost pricing or second-best average cost pricing. On the other hand, a structural policy exercises direct control over the structural environment of the firms. In the context of the oligopoly model used here, a structural policy would regulate the number of firms in the industry, but not their behavior.

What then would be the optimal structural policy relative to the market equilibrium? The market equilibrium is obtained by first defining the equilibrium industry output for any given number of firms. The number of firms is then allowed to increase until the profits of each are just non-negative. With imperfectly competitive behavior, this free entry market equilibrium will result in unexploited scale economies. The structural optimum can then be defined as the number of firms which maximizes consumer plus producer surplus *subject to the industry output equilibrium for any given number of firms.*

* I wish to thank Elizabeth E. Bailey, Robert D. Willig and John C. Panzar for helpful comments. This paper represents my own views and assumptions and not necessarily those of the Bell System.

The number of firms in the structural optimum may be greater than or less than the number which would arise in a free entry market equilibrium. Thus, the implementation of an optimal structural policy would differ correspondingly. If the number of firms in the structural optimum exceeds the free entry number, then large firms would need to be split into smaller firms, mergers prohibited, and subsidies designed to prevent exit by existing firms and to encourage new entry. On the other hand, if the number of firms in the structural optimum is less than the free entry number, mergers would need to be encouraged and entry prevented. Although both cases can arise in general, the analysis shows that an optimal structural policy "normally" requires entry restrictions. We derive a sufficient condition on the inverse demand function which guarantees that entry restrictions are optimal. This condition is satisfied for inverse demand functions which are linear or decline at an increasing rate. Since the constant elasticity inverse demand function violates the sufficiency condition, we consider this demand in conjunction with an exponential cost function. In this example, entry restrictions are more commonly optimal over the range of reasonable parameter values for the elasticity of demand and the degree of scale economies.

This analysis formalizes the policy tradeoffs discussed by Williamson [13] in his classic paper "*Economies as an Antitrust Defense: The Welfare Tradeoffs*". Furthermore, within the context of this model, we can actually conclude which of the two forces—scale economies or imperfect competition—predominates for given demand and cost conditions. The optimal structural policy typically requires entry restrictions because the efficiency gains from having each of the fewer firms more fully exploit the scale economies offset the dead-weight losses in consumer surplus from reduced competition and higher prices. In other words, we shall discover that the reduction in industry output from having fewer firms is minor relative to the increase in output per firm. However, since entry restrictions are generally viewed with disfavor, we shall closely examine both the distribution and magnitude of the welfare gains from an optimal structural policy in the context of the example.

I. THE MODEL

Let $P(X)$ be the inverse demand function for the industry's product X, where $P'(X) < 0$ of course. In addition, let $C(X_i)$ be the cost function of each firm, where $C'(X_i) > 0$. Economies of scale may be specified by assuming either that $C''(X_i) < 0$ or that there is a fixed cost F if $C''(X_i) = 0$. All firms and potential entrants are assumed to have the same cost function so that the number of firms is an unambiguous measure of industry structure. The profits of the ith firm can now be defined as a function of the firm's output X_i and the combined output X_0 of the other firms:

$$(1) \qquad \Pi(X_i; X_0) \equiv P(X_i + X_0) \cdot X_i - C(X_i).$$

It assumed that each firm chooses its output level in an attempt to maximize its profits. However, since its profits depend upon the output of the rest of the industry, the choice of X_i will depend upon the firm's perception about the response of X_0 to changes in its choice of X_i. In order to capture such behavioral perceptions, we assume that each firm has a simple conjectural variation on X_0:

$$\frac{dX_0}{dX_i} = \delta \qquad \text{where } -1 \leq \delta \leq (m-1) \tag{2}$$

If $\delta = 0$, each firm will attempt to maximize profits under the belief that the output of the rest of the industry will remain unchanged. This is the behavioral assumption introduced by Cournot [4]. The nonzero conjecture was introduced by Bowley [2] and recently discussed by Seade [9]. If $\delta > 0$, each firm expects the rest of the industry to expand in response to an increase in its output. If $\delta = (m-1)$, the industry behaves collusively maximizing joint profits given the number of firms. If $\delta < 0$, each firm expects the rest of the industry to contract. And if $\delta = -1$ each firm behaves competitively, expecting industry output $X_i + X_0$ and thus price $P(X_i + X_0)$ to remain unchanged. A conjectural variation is a convenient and useful method of capturing imperfectly competitive behavior in an oligopoly model. However, there remains the interesting problem of whether the conjectural variation should be endogenous. This issue is discussed in the concluding section.

Each firm's perceived rate of change of profits with respect to its output level can now be expressed as

$$\Pi'(X_i; X_0) = P(X_i + X_0) + (1+\delta) \cdot X_i \cdot P'(X_i + X_0) - C'(X_i). \tag{3}$$

In order for the firm to be in equilibrium, it must perceive no incentive to change its level of output, given the combined output of the other firms. Now suppose there are m firms.[1] In order for the industry to be in equilibrium, all firms must simultaneously perceive no incentive to change their output levels. Since all firms have the same cost function and conjectural variation, it is natural to restrict our attention to symmetric equilibria. Thus, in a symmetric equilibrium the industry output X is such that each firm perceives no incentive to change output when it chooses $X_i = X/m$ while the other firms are choosing the same, i.e., $X_0 = (m-1) \cdot (X/m)$. Using (3), a symmetric equilibrium must satisfy the following first order condition:

$$\Pi'\left(\frac{X}{m}; (m-1) \cdot \frac{X}{m}\right) = P(X) + (1+\delta) \cdot (X/m) \cdot P'(X) - C'(X/m) = 0 \tag{4}$$

[1] In the general analysis of this section, m will be treated as a real number to simplify the policy comparisons. However, in the example of section II, we explicitly deal with the minor problems of insuring that the number of firms is an integer.

Assuming the second order conditions are satisfied, the equilibrium condition (4) implicitly defines the equilibrium industry output $X(m; \delta)$ as a function of the number of firms m and the conjectural variation δ.

The second order condition on each firm requires that (X/m) is the output which indeed maximizes perceived profit function when $X_0 = (m-1) \cdot (X/m)$. Furthermore, we also impose the following stability condition:

$$\text{(5a)} \qquad \Pi'(X/m;\ (m-1) \cdot (X/m)) \gtrless 0 \qquad \text{as} \qquad X \lessgtr X(m; \delta)$$

Condition (5a) guarantees that the symmetric industry equilibrium is unique and stable. Uniqueness insures the functional relationship of $X(m; \delta)$, whereas stability implies that if all firms were at a symmetric output level X/m less than (greater than) the equilibrium level $X(m; \delta)/m$, then each would perceive an incentive to expand (contract) toward the equilibrium. A sufficient condition for (5a) to be satisfied is

$$\text{(5b)} \qquad \frac{d\Pi'}{dX} = D = [m + 1 + \delta] \cdot P'(X) + (1 + \delta) \cdot X \cdot P''(X) - C''(X/m) < 0 \quad \forall X.$$

Both of these firm and industry equilibrium conditions must be checked in particular examples.

Having characterized the industry equilibrium for m firms, we can now define the number of firms which would arise under free entry as well as the number of firms in the structural optimum. The profit of each firm as a function of the number of firms in the industry can be expressed as

$$\text{(6)} \qquad \Pi(m; \delta) \equiv P(X) \cdot [X/m] - C(X/m).$$

With free entry, the number of firms will increase until each is just earning nonnegative profits. Thus, the free entry number of firms is defined as

$$\text{(7)} \qquad \bar{m} \equiv \max\,\{m \colon \Pi(m; \delta) \geq 0\},$$

where $\Pi(m; \delta) > 0$ for $m < \bar{m}$ and $\Pi(m; \delta) < 0$ for $m > \bar{m}$. If there were no fixed cost and a constant marginal cost, $\bar{m}$ would be infinite. Thus, the specified scale economies enable $\bar{m}$ to be well-defined.

The number of firms in the structural optimum is obtained by maximizing consumer plus producer surplus along the equilibrium constraint $X(m; \delta)$. Assuming no income effects, the integral of inverse demand up to industry output is the total benefit or willingness to pay of consumers for this level of output. The surplus is the difference between these benefits and the industry costs:

$$\text{(8)} \qquad S(m; \delta) \equiv \int_0^{X(m;\, \delta)} P(v) \cdot dv - m \cdot C(X(m; \delta)/m).$$

The rate of change of surplus with respect to m is:

$$(9)\qquad S'(m;\delta) = [P(X) - C'(X/m)]\cdot\frac{dX}{dm} - \left(\frac{C(X/m)}{(X/m)} - C'(X/m)\right)\cdot\frac{X}{m}$$

where $X = X(m;\delta)$.

If a new firm is added to the industry, the first term is the increment in surplus from the competitive increase in output (assuming $(1+\delta)\cdot P' - C'' < 0$ so that $dX(m;\delta)/dm > 0$ as shown in Appendix 1). Working in the opposite direction, the second term is the increment in industry costs induced by the new firm (average costs exceed marginal costs since $C'' < 0$ or $F > 0$ when $C'' = 0$).

Assuming that $S(m;\delta)$ has a unique interior maximum on the number of firms m, the maximand $\hat{m}$ is the structural optimum and can be implicitly defined by

$$(10)\qquad S'(\hat{m};\delta) = 0.$$

The second order condition requires that surplus be increasing on $m < \hat{m}$ and decreasing on $m > \hat{m}$:

$$(11)\qquad S'(m;\delta) \gtreqless 0 \quad \text{as} \quad m \lesseqgtr \hat{m}.$$

Clearly $S''(m;\delta) < 0$ would be sufficient for (10), but there are no obvious and natural conditions which would insure such *a priori*. Thus, condition (10) is maintained as an assumption for the general analysis but should be verified for any example. However, we should suspect that $S'' < 0$ because with more firms the competitive impact of an additional firm on industry output should diminish while the new firm brings to the industry the same fixed costs as the previous firms.

Does the structural optimum call for more or fewer firms than the free entry equilibrium? Consider the rate of change of surplus evaluated at the free entry number of firms. This is obtained by substituting price for average cost in the second term of (9):

$$(12)\qquad S'(\bar{m};\delta) = [P - C']\cdot\left(\frac{dX(\bar{m};\delta)}{dm} - \frac{X(\bar{m};\delta)}{m}\right).$$

By condition (11), if $S'(\bar{m};\delta) > 0$, then $\hat{m} > \bar{m}$, but if $S'(\bar{m};\delta) < 0$, then $\hat{m} < \bar{m}$. Price must exceed marginal cost to satisfy the equilibrium condition (4) for $\delta \neq -1$ and to insure nonnegative profits. Thus, the first term of (12) is strictly positive. The sign of $S'(\bar{m};\delta)$ must then be the same as the sign of the second term of (12). Using (4) to define $dX(m;\delta)/dm$, we show in Appendix 1 that

$$(13)\qquad \left(\frac{dX}{dm} - \frac{X}{m}\right) \gtreqless 0 \quad \text{as} \quad P'(X) + (1+\delta)\cdot\frac{X}{m}\cdot P''(X) \gtreqless 0$$

where $X = X(m;\delta)$.

Since $\delta \leq (m-1)$, $P(X)$ such that $P' + X \cdot P'' < 0$ insures that both conditions in (13) are negative and thus $\hat{m} < \bar{m}$. When the latter condition is negative, exogenous increases in the output of the rest of the industry shift each firm's marginal revenue function downward in the neighborhood of the equilibrium. But more generally, with conditions (11) and (12), we see that $\hat{m} < \bar{m}$ as long as the second condition in (13) is negative when evaluated at $\bar{m}$, $P'(X(\bar{m}; \delta)) + (1+\delta) \cdot [X(\bar{m}; \delta)/\bar{m}] \cdot P''(X(\bar{m}; \delta)) < 0$.

Thus, we summarize with the following proposition:

Proposition: From the free entry equilibrium, an optimal structural policy would increase or decrease the number of firms in whichever direction increased output per firm and thus lowered the average cost of production:

$$\hat{m} \gtreqless \bar{m} \quad \text{as} \quad \frac{d[X(m; \delta)/m](\bar{m})}{dm} \gtreqless 0.$$

This result is obtained quickly by rearranging the second term of (12). But it provides a clear interpretation of the relationship between the structural optimum and the free entry equilibrium. An optimal structural policy moves the industry in the direction of lower average costs. In the case of entry restrictions this does not mean that the structural optimum maximizes output per firm because there is always the counterbalancing force of reduced competition. But if the output per firm at the free entry equilibrium can be increased some by *decreasing* the number of firms, then the structural optimum calls for *fewer* firms than the market. This would seem to be the normal case since it occurs for all $P(X)$ such that $P'' < 0$ or for which $-(P'/X) > P'' > 0$. When the inverse demand function is outside this class, we might find that output per firm can be increased by *increasing* the number of firms so that the structural optimum would call for *more* firms than the market. How likely is this case? In an attempt to answer this question, we consider the familiar constant elasticity inverse demand function which lies outside the above class. This example also enables a close examination of the welfare implications of an optimal structural policy.

II. AN EXAMPLE

Let the inverse demand function be

(14) $$P(X) = a \cdot X^{-1/\eta},$$

where $\eta > 0$ is the elasticity of demand. Note that $P' + X \cdot P'' = (a/\eta^2) \cdot X^{-1-1/\eta} > 0$ so that the sufficient condition for $\hat{m} < \bar{m}$ is not satisfied. The optimal structural policy will now depend upon the interaction of demand and cost. Let the cost function for each firm be

(15) $$C(X_i) = c \cdot X_i^e, \quad \text{where} \quad 0 < e < 1.$$

Both average and marginal costs decline with output, and the degree of scale economies increases as e declines. Although these specifications on demand and cost are restrictive, the rewards are substantial. The free entry equilibrium and the structural optimum can be characterized solely in terms of the meaningful parameters δ, η, and e. Over reasonable ranges of these parameters, we can then compare the industry output and surplus achieved under an optimal structural policy with that achieved under a policy of monopoly regulation.

With (14) and (15), we can now solve condition (4) for the equilibrium industry output function:

$$(16) \qquad X(m;\delta) = \left(\frac{a}{c \cdot e}\right)^{\eta/[1-\eta(1-e)]} \cdot \left(\frac{m\eta - (1+\delta)}{\eta \cdot m^{2-e}}\right)^{\eta/[1-\eta(1-e)]},$$

defined for $m > (1+\delta)/\eta$. In Appendix 2, we demonstrate that the second order conditions are satisfied. First, we require that $1 - \eta \cdot (1-e) > 0$ in order to satisfy condition (5a) for uniqueness and stability. Furthermore, we also insure that each *firm* is in equilibrium at a symmetric industry equilibrium yielding nonnegative profits. Thus, when the other firms are producing $(m-1) \cdot [X(m;\delta)/m]$, $X_i = X(m;\delta)/m$ is the only output level for which the remaining firm earns nonnegative profits and perceives no incentive to either expand or contract.

The number of firms in the free entry equilibrium and the structural optimum can now be calculated. Upon substituting (14), (15), and (16) into the profit function (6) and simplifying, we find that

$$(17) \qquad \Pi(m;\delta) \gtreqless 0 \quad \text{as} \quad m \lesseqgtr \bar{\mu}(\delta) \equiv \frac{1+\delta}{\eta \cdot (1-e)}.$$

The free entry number of firms is the largest integer less than $\bar{\mu}$:

$$(18) \qquad \bar{m} = \lfloor \bar{\mu}(\delta) \rfloor .$$

Clearly, $(1+\delta) > \eta \cdot (1-e)$ is necessary for a nontrivial free entry equilibrium. Now, in solving for the number of firms in the structural optimum, we first calculate the real number $\hat{\mu}(\delta)$ which is the solution to condition (10) for the specifications (14), (15), and (16). As shown in Appendix 3, $\hat{\mu}(\delta)$ is the positive root of a quadratic equation. The appropriate integral number of firms could be either the next smaller integer $\lfloor \hat{\mu}(\delta) \rfloor$ or the next larger integer $\lceil \hat{\mu}(\delta) \rceil$. Thus, the number of firms in the structural optimum is:

$$(19) \qquad \hat{m} = \text{argmax}\,\{S(\lfloor \hat{\mu}(\delta) \rfloor), S(\lceil \hat{\mu}(\delta) \rceil)\}.$$

Even in this simple example, $\hat{m}$ is neither always less than nor always greater than $\bar{m}$ for permitted values of the parameters. Thus, we directly compare $\hat{m}$ and $\bar{m}$ on a grid of plausible values for η, e, and δ. For the

TABLE I
THE NUMBER OF FIRMS IN THE STRUCTURAL OPTIMUM VERSUS THE NUMBER OF FIRMS IN THE FREE ENTRY EQUILIBRIUM ($\hat{m}/\bar{m}$)

η \ e	0.5	0.6	0.7	0.8	0.85	0.9	0.95
0.25	6/8	6/10	7/13	8/20	8/26	10/40	12/80
0.5	3/4	4/5	4/6	5/10	5/13	6/20	8/40
0.75	(3/2)	3/3	3/4	3/6	4/8	5/13	6/26
1.0	2/2	2/2	2/3	3/5	3/6	4/10	5/20
1.5	(2/1)	(2/1)	2/2	2/3	3/4	3/6	4/13
2.0	×	(2/1)	(2/1)	2/2	2/3	2/5	3/10
3.0	×	×	1/1	(2/1)	2/2	2/3	3/6

Cournot conjectural variation $\delta = 0$, Table I presents $\hat{m}$ and $\bar{m}$ for $\eta = 0.25 - 3.0$ and $e = 0.5 - 0.95$. The first entry of each cell is $\hat{m}$ and the second entry is $\bar{m}$, with the two separated by a slash. When demand is relatively elastic and scale economies are very pronounced, the stability condition $1 - \eta \cdot (1 - e) > 0$ is violated. These cells are crossed out in the lower left-hand corner of Table I. Now, if demand is somewhat less elastic or scale economies are somewhat less pronounced, $\hat{m}$ can be greater than or equal to $\bar{m}$. The cells for which the structural optimum would call for subsidizing new entry are circled in Table I.[2] Despite the existence of these cases, it is much more common in Table I for the structural optimum to call for entry restrictions.

This conclusion is not altered for conjectural variations other than $\delta = 0$. By examining $\bar{\mu}(\delta)$ from (17) and $\hat{\mu}(\delta)$ from Appendix 3, we see that:

$$\bar{\mu}(\delta) = (1 + \delta) \cdot \bar{\mu}(0), \quad \text{and} \quad \hat{\mu}(\delta) = (1 + \delta) \cdot \hat{\mu}(0). \tag{20}$$

When $\delta < 0$, firms are behaving more "competitively" and choosing larger output levels. Thus, the number of firms that can profitably exist in a free entry equilibrium is reduced. When $\delta > 0$, firms are behaving more "collusively" and the free entry number of firms is increased. Furthermore,

[2] Using the expression for $\bar{\mu}(\delta)$ from (17) and $\hat{\mu}(\delta)$ from Appendix 3, we find that before integer conversion, the structural optimum calls for more firms, $\hat{\mu}(\delta) > \bar{\mu}(\delta)$, whenever $\eta > e/(1 - e)$. The cell in Table 1 for $\eta = 0.75$ and $e = 0.5$ which seems to violate this condition is a case in which $2 < \hat{\mu} < \bar{\mu} < 3$ as argued but $\hat{m} = 3 > 2 = \bar{m}$ because the structural optimum maximizes surplus by rounding the number of firms upward.

the number of firms in the structural optimum responds in the same direction and in the same manner. Thus, except for the possibility of minor reversals due to the different ways in which $\bar{\mu}$ and $\hat{\mu}$ are converted into the integers $\bar{m}$ and $\hat{m}$, the comparisons in Table I would remain unchanged as the conjectural variation is altered.

Thus, the optimal structural policy may typically involve entry restrictions even when the inverse demand function violates the sufficient condition $P' + X \cdot P'' < 0$. And this conclusion is not altered over the reasonable range of conjectural variations. In reexamining Table I, note that when scale economies are minor and demand is inelastic, an optimal structural policy calls for a substantial reduction in the number of firms in the industry. This seeming anomaly raises questions concerning the source and magnitude of the welfare gains from an optimal structural policy. And this example provides a convenient format for addressing such questions. In considering whether optimal entry restrictions are a reasonable industrial policy, we ask (1) what happens to industry price and (2) how much of the potential gains from market intervention can be obtained by a structural policy.

Since there are scale economies, the first-best optimum would require marginal cost pricing by a monopolist. Thus, the surplus gain from having a benevolent monopolist is the maximum potential gain over the free entry industry structure. This is not to say that benevolent monopoly is feasible, but rather that it provides a meaningful and convenient reference point. With marginal cost pricing, the output of a monopolist is

$$(21) \qquad X_{mc} \equiv \left(\frac{a}{c \cdot e}\right)^{\eta/[1-\eta(1-e)]}$$

Since there are scale economies, marginal cost pricing results in negative profits for the monopolist. Thus, even though surplus is lower, it may be interesting to also consider second-best average cost pricing by the monopolist. For this case, output is

$$(22) \qquad X_{ac} \equiv \left(\frac{a}{c \cdot e}\right)^{\eta/[1-\eta(1-e)]} \cdot e^{\eta/[1-\eta(1-e)]}.$$

Both X_{mc} and X_{ac} are independent of δ because they are the product of behavioral policies which suppress the conjectural variation.

We can now compare industry output in the structural optimum and the free entry equilibrium with the output levels attained under average and marginal cost pricing by a monopolist. Upon examining (16), (21), and (22), we see that $X(m; \delta)$ and X_{ac} can be expressed as percentages of X_{mc} independent of the scale parameters a and c. Thus, for given δ, $100 \cdot X(\hat{m}; \delta)/X_{mc}$, $100 \cdot X(\bar{m}; \delta)/X_{mc}$, and $100 \cdot X_{ac}/X_{mc}$ (where $X_{mc} = 100$) are defined solely in terms of the elasticity of demand η and the degree of scale economies e. Table II(a) presents some comparisons of these percentages for $\delta = 0$. For example, when $\eta = 0.5$ and $e = 0.9$, industry output in

TABLE II(a)
INDUSTRY OUTPUT AS A PERCENTAGE OF $X_{mc} \equiv 100$

$$\left(\frac{X(\hat{m}; 0)}{X(\bar{m}; 0)} \; X_{ac} \right)$$

η \ e	0.5	0.7	0.8	0.9	0.95
0.5	$\frac{33}{40}$ 63	$\frac{52}{57}$ 81	$\frac{63}{68}$ 88	$\frac{74}{81}$ 95	$\frac{82}{89}$ 97
1.0	$\frac{13}{13}$ 25	$\frac{28}{35}$ 60	$\frac{46}{51}$ 76	$\frac{62}{69}$ 89	$\frac{73}{81}$ 95
2.0	×	$\frac{8}{3}$ 17	$\frac{24}{24}$ 48	$\frac{41}{51}$ 77	$\frac{59}{69}$ 89

TABLE II(b)
$X(\hat{m}; 2)/X(\bar{m}; 2)$

η \ e	0.5	0.7	0.8	0.9	0.95
0.5	23/28	43/48	55/61	69/76	79/86
1.0	4/4	20/22	33/38	54/61	69/76
2.0	×	2/2	10/12	34/39	54/61

TABLE II(c)
$X(\hat{m}; -1/2)/X(\bar{m}; -1/2)$

η \ e	0.5	0.7	0.8	0.9	0.95
0.5	50/50	59/65	63/74	76/84	83/90
1.0	25/25	37/37	59/59	67/74	78/84
2.0	×	×	38/38	49/60	69/75

the structural optimum, $\hat{m} = 6$, is 74% of the benevolent monopoly output; whereas, in the free entry equilibrium, $\bar{m} = 20$, industry output increases to 81% of this standard. Finally, the monopoly output with average cost pricing is 95% of that with marginal cost pricing. As in this case, we see from Table II(a) that an optimal structural policy which requires entry restrictions results in a lower industry output and a higher price. However, the decline in industry output is small relative to the reduction in the number of firms so that output per firm has increased as we expected from the proposition in Section I. The losses in consumer surplus are more than offset by increases in producer surplus which derive from the reduction in industry average costs.

The qualitative conclusions of Table II(a) concerning the structural optimum remain unchanged for conjectural variations other than $\delta = 0$. Differentiating $X(m; \delta)$ from (16) with respect to m, we find that

$$(23) \qquad \frac{dX(m;\delta)}{dm} > 0 \qquad \text{for } m < (2 - e) \cdot \bar{\mu}(\delta).^{3}$$

Since $e < 1$, $\bar{m} \leq \bar{\mu}(\delta) < (2 - e) \cdot \bar{\mu}(\delta)$, so that for any δ such that $\hat{m} < \bar{m}$, we see that $X(\hat{m}; \delta) < X(\bar{m}; \delta)$. Thus, nonzero conjectural variations do not alter the finding that an optimal structural policy involving entry restrictions would result in a lower industry output and a higher price than the free entry equilibrium. However, the conjectural variation does matter if one wishes to evaluate the industry output of either the free entry equilibrium or the structural optimum *relative* to the benevolent monopoly standards. Substituting $\mu(\delta)$ from (20) into (16) yields:

$$(24) \qquad X(\mu(\delta); \delta) = (1 + \delta)^{[-\eta(1-e)]/[1-\eta(1-e)]} \cdot X(\mu(0); 0).$$

The $(1 + \delta)$ term of (24) is the approximate fraction by which the industry output levels $X(\hat{m}; 0)$ and $X(\bar{m}; 0)$ from Table II(a) must be adjusted to get the output levels $X(\hat{m}; \delta)$ and $X(\bar{m}; \delta)$. For more "collusive" conjectural variations $\delta > 0$, both $X(\hat{m}; \delta)$ and $X(\bar{m}; \delta)$ are smaller and farther from X_{ac} and X_{mc}. Table II(b) calculates $X(\hat{m}; \delta = 2)$ and $X(\bar{m}; \delta = 2)$. On the other hand, for more "competitive" conjectural variations $\delta < 0$, $X(\hat{m}; \delta)$ and $X(\bar{m}; \delta)$ are larger and closer to X_{ac} and X_{mc}. Table II(c) calculates $X(\hat{m}; \delta = -1/2)$ and $X(\bar{m}; \delta = -1/2)$. However, even when $\delta = -1/2$, the industry output in the structural optimum or the free entry equilibrium is nontrivially less than that produced by a monopolist using either average or marginal cost pricing. Moreover, the percentage difference increases as scale economies become more pronounced, as demand becomes more elastic, and as the conjectural variation becomes less "competitive".

As we suspected, optimal entry restrictions do indeed reduce industry output and raise price. Thus, gains in producer surplus from more fully exploiting the scale economies must more than offset these losses in consumer surplus. As a result, we examine whether the gains from an optimal structural policy are at all significant relative to the potential gains from monopoly regulation which both reduces price and fully exploits scale economies.

In order to examine whether the gains in surplus from an optimal structural policy are significant, we shall again use the outcome of benevolent monopoly as a point of reference. We first calculate the surplus gains in

[3] The integer above or below $(2 - e) \cdot \bar{\mu}(\delta)$ is the number of firms which would maximize industry output, minimize industry price, and thus maximize *consumer* surplus.

moving from the free entry equilibrium to the structural optimum. We then calculate the surplus gains in moving from the free entry equilibrium to average cost pricing by a monopolist. Finally, we calculate the surplus gains in moving from the free entry equilibrium to marginal cost pricing by a monopolist. The latter is the largest possible surplus gain to be had. By measuring these welfare gains relative to the *revenues* obtained by a benevolent monopolist from marginal cost pricing, the effectiveness of an optimal structural policy can be examined solely in terms of the elasticity of demand η and the degree of scale economies e.[4]

An outline of the calculations is presented in Appendix 4, and the results for the conjectural variation $\delta = 0$ are summarized in Table III(a). For example, when $\eta = 1.0$ and $e = 0.9$, the surplus gain from an optimal structural policy is 5.9% of the revenues of a benevolent monopolist, the surplus gain from average cost pricing by a monopolist is 23.0% of the revenues of a benevolent monopolist, and the maximum surplus gain from having a benevolent monopolist itself is 23.6% of the resulting revenues. Because the units of measurement differ, the magnitudes in Table III(a) are not directly comparable across cells. However, we can examine the ratio of the gains from an optimal structural policy relative to the gains from marginal cost pricing by a monopolist. For differing values of η and e, this ratio measures the percentage of the potential gains that an optimal structural policy can capture. The percentage effectiveness of an optimal structural policy is also shown for each cell of Table III(a), e.g. 25% for $\eta = 1.0$ and $e = 0.9$.

We see from Table III(a) that the effectiveness of optimal entry restrictions declines as the scale economies become more pronounced and the demand becomes more elastic. What is the reason for this? When demand is inelastic and scale economies are minor, the free entry equilibrium can support a large number of firms. But moreover, we also find that the number of firms can be substantially reduced while causing only a minor reduction in the industry output. Thus, even though the scale economies are minor, the increase in output per firm causes substantial reductions in industry costs which more than offset the small losses in consumer surplus. This accounts for the anomaly that a structural policy designed to enable firms to more fully exploit scale economies is most effective when scale economies are minor.

On the other hand, when demand is more elastic or when scale economies are more pronounced, the free entry equilibrium supports fewer firms. The incentive for firms to contract output so as to accommodate entrants is dulled because the marginal and average costs rise more rapidly with

[4] This measurement also allows us to avoid dealing with the fact that consumer surplus is infinite for $\eta < 1$. Since consumer surplus is infinite no matter how little is consumed, this is simply a problem in the tail of the inverse demand function. Thus, we implicitly assume that there is some high price at which the quantity demanded falls to zero, making surplus finite. Furthermore, we assume that this price is so high as to be irrelevant to the industry policies being considered.

TABLE III(a)
RELATIVE SURPLUS GAINS FOR $\delta = 0$ FROM (1) OPTIMAL STRUCTURAL POLICY, (2) AVERAGE COST PRICING BY A MONOPOLIST, AND (3) MARGINAL COST PRICING BY A MONOPOLIST; AND THE PERCENTAGE EFFECTIVENESS OF (1) RELATIVE TO (3)

η \ e	0.5	0.7	0.8	0.9	0.95
0.5	$\frac{4.0}{186.5} = 2\%$ 204.0	$\frac{10.8}{93.3} = 11\%$ 97.1	$\frac{14.5}{66.0} = 22\%$ 67.4	$\frac{10.7}{36.1} = 29\%$ 36.4	$\frac{6.9}{20.4} = 34\%$ 20.4+
1.0	$\frac{0}{34.7} = 0\%$ 54.0	$\frac{0.1}{34.5} = 0\%$ 40.2	$\frac{5.3}{32.2} = 15\%$ 34.5	$\frac{5.9}{23.0} = 25\%$ 23.6	$\frac{4.8}{15.0} = 32\%$ 15.1
2.0	×	$\frac{4.1}{18.3} = 12\%$ 34.4	$\frac{0}{16.7} = 0\%$ 22.8	$\frac{3.0}{16.0} = 17\%$ 17.2	$\frac{3.2}{11.3} = 28\%$ 11.6

TABLE III(b)
THE EFFECTIVENESS OF AN OPTIMAL STRUCTURAL POLICY FOR $\delta = 2$

η \ e	0.5	0.7	0.8	0.9	0.95
0.5	1%	11%	16%	22%	27%
1.0	0%	4%	10%	17%	23%
2.0	×	0%	2%	11%	18%

TABLE III(c)
THE EFFECTIVENESS OF AN OPTIMAL STRUCTURAL POLICY FOR $\delta = -1/2$

η \ e	0.5	0.7	0.8	0.9	0.95
0.5	0%	17%	28%	38%	48%
1.0	0%	0%	0%	36%	39%
2.0	×	×	0%	18%	37%

stronger scale economies while the price rises less rapidly with a more elastic demand. Thus, the equilibrium is less conducive to new firms, and the output of existing firms does not decline as rapidly with new entry. Entry drives profits to zero more rapidly and the free entry equilibrium has fewer firms. As a result, the optimal structural policy nets fewer gains. Reducing the number of firms quickly reduces industry output in that the remaining firms do not increase their output to compensate for the reduction in output of the firms which exited. And since there are only a few firms anyway, their ranks cannot be reduced enough to generate much more than just offsetting cost savings from higher output per firm, even when scale economies are pronounced.

How then is the effectiveness of an optimal structural policy altered for other conjectural variations? For $\delta > 0$ firms are behaving more "collusively" with the consequent proliferation of firms in the free entry equilibrium as well as reduced industry output. This results in a larger distortion from the first-best optimum. Thus, since a structural policy is similarly confined by this behavior on the part of firms, the welfare gains from an optimal structural policy will be a smaller percentage of the larger potential gains. Table III(b) illustrates this for $\delta = 2$. On the other hand, when $\delta < 0$, firms are behaving more "competitively". The free entry equilibrium results in fewer firms, a larger industry output, and a reduced distortion from the first-best optimum. Since a structural policy also benefits from the more "competitive" behavior, optimal entry restrictions can capture a larger percentage of the smaller potential gains. Table III(c) illustrates this for $\delta = -1/2$. Entry restrictions are less worrisome when firms behave more "competitively".

Tables III(a)–(c) have shown that an optimal structural policy can result in nontrivial and even significant welfare gains. However, these gains are not overwhelming. In fact, for those parameter values of Table III(a) for which an optimal structural policy is most effective, average cost pricing by a monopolist can capture over 90% of the potential gains. Thus, in the concluding section which follows we briefly contrast the optimal structural policy with the behavioral policy of monopoly regulation.

III. CONCLUSIONS AND IMPLICATIONS

As we have seen, regulation of a monopolist with average cost pricing dominates the optimal structural policy. But monopoly regulation has disadvantages which were not explicitly considered in section II. Regulated monopoly requires behavioral as well as structural modifications to the industry, and this can prevent the welfare gains of average cost pricing from being fully realized. First, it is unclear how effective regulation can be in altering the unfettered monopoly outcome in the direction of average cost pricing, especially since the cost information would be held by the monopolist. Second, a regulatory process intended to achieve average cost pricing may instead induce productive inefficiencies such as the one discussed by Averch and Johnson [1].[5] And third, the administrative costs of regulation

[5] Callen, Mathewson, and Mohring [3] evaluate the efficacy of rate-of-return regulation on a monopolist for a comparable example. Their results indicate that the Averch-Johnson inefficiency can be significant and that the welfare gains from *optimal* rate-of-return regulation are substantially less than the potential gains from either average or marginal cost pricing by a monopolist. For $\eta = 2$ and $e = 0.8$, the gains relative to marginal cost pricing were only 40% when the capital share was 1/3 and 66% when capital share was 2/3.

may be substantial, primarily in an attempt to reduce the losses from each of the former. Thus, the calculations in Tables III(a)–(c) of the welfare gains from average cost pricing by a monopolist should be considered an overestimate.

An optimal structural policy of entry restrictions avoids the distortions of incentives inherent in the behavioral regulation of monopoly. The profits of firms remain positive so that neither subsidies nor output controls are required to implement this structural policy. Furthermore, the administrative difficulties of a structural policy would not seem to be as severe as those for monopoly regulation. First, a regulatory authority would have to solve for the optimal number of firms. In the context of this example, the optimal number of firms is simpler to calculate and requires less adjustment to exogenous changes than the regulated outputs for a monopolist. From Appendix 3, we found that $\hat{m}$ depended on the elasticities η and e but was independent of the scale parameters a and c. On the other hand, X_{mc} and X_{ac} from (21) and (22) crucially depend on a and c.

Second, the regulatory authority would have to prevent undesired entry. Licenses could be issued or auctioned. If auctioned, the price of a license would presumably be bid to the point where firms would earn zero profits net of the license fee. Alternatively, the regulatory authority could set an entry fee equal to the firm profits at the structural optimum and allow free entry to arrive at the optimal number of firms. Theoretically, an entry fee would be preferable to licenses in that it insures that only the most efficient firms enter and maintains the threat of entry to prevent subsequent collusion. But, with either auctioned licenses or an entry fee, the producer profits from restricted entry are recovered for the potential benefit of consumers.[6]

A structural policy can obviate some of the unexploited scale economies which result from imperfect competition and free entry. This theoretical finding takes on particular interest in light of the empirical results reported by Weiss [11] that suboptimal capacity is substantial in many industries.[7] However, with the myriad of practical considerations necessary in formulating an industrial policy, this analysis can only provide insights into the nature of an optimal structural policy and the rough welfare comparisons between it and regulated monopoly or the market equilibrium. Furthermore, the choice of policy would depend upon empirical findings concerning the applicability of this model to any particular industry under consideration. This invites a brief concluding discussion of three theoretical considerations not embodied in this model.

[6] If licenses are merely issued, the corporate income tax would result in a partial redistribution to taxpayers of the profits from a structural policy.

[7] Weiss [11] found that the majority of plants in the industries studied were suboptimal, that the percentage of shipments from such plants was often more than 30% of industry shipments, and that the average of such shipments over all the industries studied was around 50%.

Both the general discussion and the example explicitly assumed scale economies were pervasive over all ranges of output. However, even if scale economies could be exhausted, an optimal structural policy would still typically involve entry restrictions because an imperfectly competitive equilibrium would generate firm output levels below this minimum efficient scale. This fact has been illustrated by von Weizsäcker [12] in an example using linear demand and quadratic costs so that average costs are U-shaped. Of course, if competitive behavior arose in this case, no structural or behavioral policy could improve on the market outcome.

A second restriction on the analysis is that the conjectural variation was specified exogenously. We considered the impact of different conjectures, but we did not allow the conjectural variation to be endogenously determined along with industry output and the number of firms. This could be an important limitation in light of the traditional criticism of the conjectural variation equilibrium. As Friedman [5, chapter 4] points out, the actual behavior of the other firms around the equilibrium would generally not conform to the behavior conjectured by each firm. In the Cournot case of $\delta = 0$, the other firms would not hold their output fixed if one firm increased his output. However, this problem has been recently solved by imposing an addition condition, known as "consistency", on the equilibrium so that conjectured behavior is required to conform to some notion of how the other firms would react. When marginal costs are rising, Perry [7, proposition 2(b)] has shown that a consistent conjectural variation would be negative between competitive and Cournot, $-1 < \delta < 0$.[8] Furthermore, Perry [8, section II] also showed that with quadratic costs ($C''' > 0$) and quadratic demand (with $P' + X \cdot P'' < 0$) the consistent conjectural variation becomes less competitive and approaches Cournot behavior when the number of firms is reduced. This would suggest that an optimal structural policy of entry restrictions would be less desirable. However, Perry [8, section III] also found that entry restrictions did indeed remain optimal under the sufficiency condition $P' + X \cdot P'' < 0$ discovered in section I of this paper. The additional loss in consumer surplus from the yet higher prices caused by less competitive behavior is of a lesser order of magnitude than the gains from more fully exploiting the scale economics.

When marginal costs are declining as assumed in both the general treatment and the example, Perry [7, proposition 2(c)] has shown that any consistent conjectural variation must be positive. However, there are indications that a consistent conjecture may not even exist, and even if one did exist, computing it would be very difficult even in a simple example. Thus, it seems that this analysis would be intractable if the conjectural variation were made endogenous in a correct fashion.

[8] As discussed here, consistency is defined as if the number of firms is fixed. If consistency is redefined to take into account entry and exit, called "full" consistency, Perry [7, section III] has shown that only competitive behavior would arise. Thus, as mentioned the policy problem would disappear with U-shaped average costs.

Finally, this analysis has only considered the case of homogeneous products. Product differentiation generates an additional factor which would seem to undercut any finding of optimal entry restrictions. Reducing the number of firms narrows product diversity as well as reducing competition. In the spatial models of Willig [14], the structural optimal typically requires entry restrictions as we found for the homogeneous case. However, in the monopolistic competition model of Spence [10], the structural optimal calls for more firms than the free entry equilibrium, even when the products are nearly perfect substitutes. This seeming discrepancy was resolved by Koenker and Perry [6]. Spence's results were obtained under the implicit assumption of competitive behavior. Koenker and Perry showed that when non-competitive conjectural variations were specified, the structural optimum would involve entry restrictions when the products were close substitutes or when scale economies were substantial. This confirms the findings here for the homogeneous case.

Martin K. Perry,
Research Economist,
Bell Laboratories,
Murray Hill,
New Jersey

ACCEPTED JUNE 1982

APPENDIX 1

By totally differentiating (4) with respect to X and m, we find that

$$\frac{dX(m;\delta)}{dm} = \frac{X(m;\delta)}{m} \cdot \left(\frac{(1+\delta)\cdot P'(X) - C''(X/m)}{D}\right)$$

where $X(m;\delta)$ is abbreviated by X for the term in brackets. The denominator of this term is negative by the second order condition (5). Now, we see that

$$\frac{dX(m;\delta)}{dm} - \frac{X(m;\delta)}{m} = -X(m;\delta)\cdot\left(\frac{P'(X) + (1+\delta)\cdot(X/m)\cdot P''(X)}{D}\right)$$

The observation (13) follows immediately.

APPENDIX 2

We show that $\Pi'(X_i; (m-1)\cdot[X(m;\delta)/m]) \gtreqless 0$ as $X_i \lesseqgtr X(m;\delta)/m$ for X_i such that $\Pi(X_i; (m-1)\cdot[X(m;\delta)/m]) \geq 0$. Using (14) and (15), the firm's perceived rate of change in profits (3) becomes

$$\text{(A2-1)}\quad \Pi'(X_i; X_0) = (a/\eta)\cdot[X_i + X_0]^{-1/\eta} \cdot\left(\eta - \frac{(1+\delta)\cdot X_i}{X_i + X_0} - \frac{\eta\cdot e\cdot c\cdot[X_i+X_0]^{1/\eta}}{a\cdot X_i^{1-e}}\right).$$

Thus, $\Pi'(X_i; X_0)$ has the same sign as the term in brackets, define it as $B(X_i; X_0)$. At a symmetric position,

(A2-2) $B(X/m; (m-1)\cdot(X/m))$

$$= \eta - \frac{(1+\delta)}{m} - \left(\frac{\eta \cdot e \cdot c \cdot m^{1-e}}{a}\right) \cdot X^{[1-\eta\cdot(1-e)]/\eta}.$$

If $m \leq (1+\delta)/\eta$, $\Pi'(X/m; (m-1)\cdot(X/m)) < 0$ for all X and no symmetric equilibrium exists. Firms always perceive an incentive to contract just as a monopolist does when facing an inelastic demand. In addition, the exponent on X in (A2-2) reveals why $1-\eta\cdot(1-e) > 0$ is necessary for the stability condition (5). Thus, for $m > (1+\delta)/\eta$ and $1-\eta\cdot(1-e) > 0$, the equilibrium $X(m; \delta)$ in (16) is obtained by solving $B(X(m;\delta)/m; (m-1)\cdot[X(m;\delta)/m]) = 0$.

Now, consider X_i for which firm profits are nonnegative:

(A2-3) $\Pi(X_i; X_0) \geq 0$ for X_i such that $\dfrac{c\cdot[X_i + X_0]^{1/\eta}}{a\cdot X_i^{1-e}} \leq 1.$

Using (A2-3), we see that min $B(X_i; X_0) = \eta\cdot(1-e) - (1+\delta)$, and thus $\Pi'(X_i; X_0) > 0$ for all such X_i and X_0 when $(1+\delta) - \eta\cdot(1-e) < 0$. Firms always perceive an incentive to expand just as a competitive firm does under pervasive scale economies. For this reason, we require $(1+\delta) - \eta\cdot(1-e) > 0$. Since $\Pi(m;\delta) \gtreqless 0$ as $m \lesseqgtr (1+\delta)/[\eta\cdot(1-e)]$, this is equivalent to requiring that at least one firm be profitable in equilibrium. Also note that if $m > (1+\delta)/[\eta\cdot(1-e)]$, firms would shut down without subsidies designed to maintain their profitability in equilibrium. Thus, we are really confining our attention to the second order conditions on the firm for $1 \leq m \leq (1+\delta)/[\eta\cdot(1-e)]$.

With these restrictions, we can now examine the sign of $B(X_i; (m-1)\cdot[X(m;\delta)/m])$ for $X_i \neq X(m;\delta)/m$ such that $\Pi(X_i; (m-1)\cdot[X(m;\delta)/m]) \geq 0$. Note that (A2-3) implies that

(A2-4) $B(X_i; (m-1)\cdot[X(m;\delta)/m])$

$$\geq \eta - \frac{(1+\delta)\cdot X_i}{X_i + (m-1)\cdot[X(m;\delta)/m]} - \eta\cdot e.$$

$$> 0 \text{ for } X_i < \frac{\eta\cdot(1-e)\cdot(m-1)}{(1+\delta) - \eta\cdot(1-e)} \cdot \frac{X(m;\delta)}{m},$$

where $[\eta\cdot(1-e)\cdot(m-1)]/[(1+\delta)-\eta\cdot(1-e)] < 1$ from the restriction that $m < (1+\delta)/[\eta\cdot(1-e)]$. Now, upon differentiating $B(X_i; (m-1)\cdot[X(m;\delta)/m])$ with respect to X_i, we find it clearly declining for $X_i \geq [\eta\cdot(1-e)\cdot(m-1)]/[1-\eta\cdot(1-e)]\cdot[X(m;\delta)]/m$. If $\delta > 0$, we need to also consider what happens to $B(X_i; (m-1)\cdot[X(m;\delta)/m])$ for

$$\frac{\eta \cdot (1-e) \cdot (m-1)}{(1+\delta) - \eta \cdot (1-e)} \cdot \frac{X(m;\delta)}{m} \leq X_i < \frac{\eta \cdot (1-e) \cdot (m-1)}{1 - \eta \cdot (1-e)} \cdot \frac{X(m;\delta)}{m}.$$

For such X_i, the profit constraint of (A2-3) implies that

$$\text{(A2-5)} \quad \frac{dB(X_i, X_0)}{dX_i} < \frac{1}{X_i \cdot (X_i + X_0)^2} \cdot \left(-e \cdot [1 - \eta \cdot (1-e)] \cdot X_i^2 - \{[(1+\delta) - e \cdot \eta \cdot (1-e)] + e \cdot [1 - \eta \cdot (1-e)]\} \cdot X_0 \cdot X_i + e \cdot \eta \cdot (1-e) \cdot X_0^2\right).$$

The quadratic in (A2-5) is a declining function of X_i for all $X_i \geq 0$. When evaluated $X_0 = (m-1) \cdot [X(m;\delta)/m]$ and lower bound of X_i, the quadratic has the same sign as the terms $\{-[1 - \eta \cdot (1-e)] - \delta \cdot (1-e)\} \equiv \{-[(1+\delta) - \eta \cdot (1-e)] + \delta \cdot e\}$, the first negative for $\delta \geq 0$ and the second negative for $-1 \leq \delta \leq 0$. Thus,

$$\text{(A2-6)} \quad \frac{dB(X_i; (m-1) \cdot [X(m;\delta)/m])}{dX_i} < 0 \quad \text{for all } X_i \geq \frac{\eta \cdot (1-e) \cdot (m-1)}{(1+\delta) - \eta \cdot (1-e)} \cdot \frac{X(m;\delta)}{m}.$$

Expressions (A2-4) and (A2-6) imply that $B(X_i; (m-1) \cdot [X(m;\delta)/m]) \gtreqless 0$ as $X_i \lesseqgtr X(m;\delta)/m$ for X_i such that $\Pi(X_i; (m-1) \cdot [X(m;\delta)/m]) \geq 0$. By referring back to (A2-1), the argument is completed.

APPENDIX 3

Using the restrictions that $m > (1+\delta)/\eta$ and $1 - \eta \cdot (1-e) > 0$, we show that $\hat{\mu}(\delta)$ maximizes surplus

$$S(m;\delta) = \int_0^{X(m;\ \delta)} a \cdot v^{-1/\eta} \cdot dv - m \cdot c \cdot [X(m;\delta)/m]^e.$$

The fact that consumer surplus is infinite for $\eta < 1$ is of no consequence since the marginal conditions still indicate whether surplus has increased or decreased by altering the number of firms. The rate of change of surplus with respect to the number of firms m has the same sign as the following quadratic expression:

$$\operatorname{sgn} \frac{dS(m;\delta)}{dm} = \operatorname{sgn}\{-\eta^2 \cdot (1-e) \cdot [1-\eta \cdot (1-e)] \cdot m^2$$

$$+ (1+\delta) \cdot \eta \cdot (1-e) \cdot [2-\eta \cdot (2-e)] \cdot m$$

$$- (1+\delta)^2 \cdot (1-\eta-e)\}.$$

We can ignore the smaller root of the corresponding quadratic equation because it is less than $(1+\delta)/\eta$. So consider the larger root

$$\hat{\mu}(\delta) = (1+\delta) \cdot \frac{(1-e) \cdot [2-\eta \cdot (2-e)] + \{\eta \cdot e \cdot (1-e) \cdot [4-\eta \cdot (1-e) \cdot (4-e)]\}^{1/2}}{2 \cdot \eta \cdot (1-e) \cdot [1-\eta \cdot (1-e)]}.$$

When $1-\eta \cdot (1-e) > 0$, $\hat{\mu}(\delta)$ is a real number exceeding $(1+\delta)/\eta$. Now, when evaluated at $m = (1+\delta)/\eta$, the quadratic is positive. Moreover, the derivative of the quadratic with respect to m is negative at $m = (1+\delta)/\eta$, and becomes more negative for larger m. Thus, the quadratic is positive (and declining) for $(1+\delta)/\eta < m < \hat{\mu}(\delta)$ and negative (and declining) for $m > \hat{\mu}(\delta)$. Since the rate of change of surplus behaves similarly, $\hat{\mu}(\delta)$ does indeed maximize surplus.

APPENDIX 4

Let $\bar{x} = [\bar{m} \cdot \eta - (1+\delta)]/[\eta \cdot \bar{m}^{2-e}]$, $\hat{x} = [\hat{m} \cdot \eta - (1+\delta)]/[\eta \cdot \hat{m}^{2-e}]$, $x_{ac} = e$, and $x_{mc} = 1$. These terms are obtained from $X(\bar{m};\delta)$, $X(\hat{m};\delta)$, X_{ac}, and X_{mc} by raising each to the $[1-\eta \cdot (1-e)]/\eta$ power and then multiplying by $c \cdot e/a$. By so doing, the surplus gain (ΔS) in moving from the free entry equilibrium $(\bar{x}, \bar{m})$ to any of the other three optima (x, m) can be expressed as:

$$\Delta S(\eta \neq 1) = a^{\eta e/[1-\eta \cdot (1-e)]} \cdot (c \cdot e)^{(1-\eta)/[1-\eta \cdot (1-e)]}$$

$$\cdot \left\{ \left(\frac{\eta}{\eta-1}\right) \cdot [x^{(\eta-1)/[1-\eta \cdot (1-e)]} - \bar{x}^{(\eta-1)/[1-\eta \cdot (1-e)]}] \right.$$

$$\left. - (1/e) \cdot [m^{1-e} \cdot x^{(\eta \cdot e)/[1-\eta \cdot (1-e)]} - \bar{m}^{1-e} \cdot \bar{x}^{(\eta \cdot e)/[1-\eta \cdot (1-e)]}] \right\},$$

$$\Delta S(\eta = 1) = a \cdot \{(1/e) \cdot [\ln x - \ln \bar{x}]$$

$$- (1/e) \cdot [m^{1-e} \cdot x - \bar{m}^{1-e} \cdot \bar{x}]\}.$$

Both of these expressions contain at least one of the scale parameters a and c. However, note that a monopolist's revenues from marginal cost pricing are equal to the terms outside the braces in the above expressions. By then measuring the surplus gains relative to these revenues, we can avoid the scale parameters. Thus, Table III(a) reports the terms in braces for the structural optimum ($x = \hat{x}$, $m = \hat{m}$), the behavioral optimum ($x = x_{ac}$, $m = 1$), and the first-best optimum ($x = x_{mc}$, $m = 1$).

REFERENCES

[1] AVERCH, HARVEY and JOHNSON, LELAND L., "Behavior of the Firm under Regulation", *American Economic Review*, 52 (Dec. 1962), pp. 1053–69.

[2] BOWLEY, ARTHUR L., *The Mathematical Groundwork of Economics* (Oxford University Press, Oxford, 1924).

[3] CALLEN, JEFFREY, MATHEWSON, G. FRANK, and MOHRING, HERBERT, "The Benefits and Costs of Rate of Return Regulation", *American Economic Review*, 66 (June 1976), pp. 290–7.

[4] COURNOT, AUGUSTIN, *Researches into the Mathematical Principles of the Theory of Wealth*, English edition of Cournot (1838), translated by Nathaniel T. Bacon (Kelley, New York, 1960).

[5] FRIEDMAN, JAMES W., *Oligopoly and the Theory of Games* (North-Holland, Amsterdam, 1977).

[6] KOENKER, ROGER W. and PERRY, MARTIN, K., "Product Differentiation, Monopolistic Competition, and Public Policy", *Bell Journal of Economics*, 12 (Spring 1981), pp. 217–31.

[7] PERRY, MARTIN K., "Oligopoly and Consistent Conjectural Variations", *Bell Journal of Economics*, 13 (Spring 1982), pp. 147–205.

[8] PERRY, MARTIN K., "The Effect of Entry on a Consistent Oligopoly Equilibrium", Economic Discussion Paper #204, Bell Laboratories (September 1981).

[9] SEADE, JESUS, "On the Effects of Entry", *Econometrica*, 48 (March 1980), pp. 479–89.

[10] SPENCE, MICHAEL, "Product Selection, Fixed Costs, and Monopolistic Competition", *Review of Economic Studies*, 43 (June 1976), pp. 217–36.

[11] WEISS, LEONARD W., "Optimal Plant Size and the Extent of Suboptimal Capacity", in *Essays on Industrial Organization in Honor of Joe S. Bain*, edited by Robert T. Masson and P. David Qualls (Ballinger, Cambridge, Mass., 1976).

[12] VON WEIZSÄCKER, C. C., "A Welfare Analysis of Barriers to Entry", *Bell Journal of Economics*, 11 (Autumn 1980), pp. 399–420.

[13] WILLIAMSON, OLIVER E., "Economies as an Antitrust Defense: Welfare Tradeoffs", *American Economic Review*, 58 (March 1968), pp. 18–36.

[14] WILLIG, ROBERT D., "Welfare Analysis of Policies Affecting Prices and Products", Memorandum No. 153, Center for Research in Economic Growth, Stanford University, Sept. 1973.

THE JOURNAL OF INDUSTRIAL ECONOMICS 0022-1821 $2.00
Volume XXXII March 1984 No. 3

MARKET POWER AND REGULATION: A SIMULTANEOUS APPROACH*

ELI NOAM

AMONG THE reasons for limiting conglomerate mergers, none carries more political weight than the fear of the social and political influence which large firms may wield. The underlying assumption for this apprehension—that firms' size generates political power—has led to public policy proposals such as Sen. Kennedy's bill to restrict mergers.

Yet to economists and political scientists, the relation of economic size and political influence has never been unambiguously clear (Bartlett [1], Kaysen [12]) once they abandoned the broad sweep of general discussions (Lindblom [14]; Galbraith [11]). After all, some politically very powerful industries consist of small firms (e.g., the funeral business) while the giant firms of the automobile industry have experienced a long string of legislative defeats on matters of pollution, safety, and energy conservation.

Despite the importance of the question of economic size and political power, it has seen surprisingly little research. A review of the literature (Epstein [7]) states that

> since rigorous analytical research regarding the political and social activities of American Business has long been a backwater of intellectual effort among political scientists and other scholars, there is no tradition of scientific research which has generated a coherent body of theoretical and methodological writing in this area. . . . Similarly, most of the published research has not examined possible relationship between firm size, structure, and market position and business political influence. So there is much to learn. . . .

It is an important question which of the characteristics of market structure exerts an impact on regulatory policy. Firms size *per se*, as a measure of economic power, is often considered to provide the ability to influence public decision making, since large firms have a particularly large economic stake and the means for political action (Blake [3]). On the other hand, large and visible firms may arouse more opposition and legal restrictions to their activities. Similar arguments can be made for the size of the entire industry.

Market concentration is the other major measure that may facilitate political effectiveness. For one, possible monopoly rents may be available to influ-

* The author wishes to thank G. Tullock, J. Quigley, R. Ventre, and an anonymous referee for their help, and the Columbia University Center for Law and Economic Studies for its support.

ence the political process. More importantly, concentrated industries are easier to organize, with less of a free-ride problem.

Several empirical-statistical analyses have related market structure with political power. These include studies of lobbying (Mann and McCormick [16]), tariffs (McPherson [18]; Pincus [22]; Caves [4]; Saunders [27]), tax rates (Marx [17]; Salamon and Siegfried [26]; Coolidge and Tullock [5]), and political contributions (Pittman [23]; Mann and McCormick [16]). The ability of different occupations to secure licenses is also investigated by Stigler [32] within a broader discussion of the nature of regulation. The present note is distinct in several respects. First, it abandons the one-way approach to causality in which economic power, assumed as given, is taken to affect public policies unidirectionally. Instead, it is based on the notion that industry structure itself is in turn affected by political and regulatory decisions. This simultaneity has not been investigated before in an empirical setting, though its existence has been noted as a potential source of statistical problems in the interpretation of the previous non-simultaneous studies (Siegfried [31]).

Furthermore, no linearity in the effects of economic power over public policy is assumed. As was pointed out by Coolidge and Tullock [5], the "production" of political influence may exhibit efficiencies of scale over some range and inefficiencics of scale in others. One often assumes diminishing returns for most production activities, and there is no reason why this could not be true for political influence, too.

Thirdly, this note investigates the explanatory strength of *alternative* measures on industry structure, since it is not clear which measure is most effective on regulatory behavior: absolute or relative size of industry, industry concentration, number and size of firms, etc.[1]

The regulatory policy that is investigated is the codification of local building standards. Their setting is detailed in the following.

Building codes are the local standards for the quality, construction techniques, and materials in the buildings of residential and commercial structures. They are of great importance to the construction industry since they are normally required for an approval of labor saving techniques and of new types of building materials (House Subcommittee [34]; Nutt-Powell [19]). Because of the potential reduction in demand for the services of skilled craftsmen that comes with many of these techniques, construction unions have traditionally favored restrictive codes.

> "The provision in some building codes, for example, allowing 2″ × 4″ studs to be placed on 24 inch centers rather than 16 inch centers in nonload bearing walls reduces the amount of labor required for these

[1] The study also looks at local regulation and one industry, rather than at national policies and many industries, as Caves does for the Canadian tariff, Pincus for the 1924 United States Tariff Act, Rose for federal regulation of the banking industry, and Salamon and Siegfried for corporate tax avoidance. (The latter, however, also look in part of their study into state gasoline excise tax rates, and deal there with non-federal policies.)

> partitions significantly. A carpenter's union would benefit from opposing such a code provision and other similar labor saving code changes." (Keating [13])

Builders, on the other hand, usually benefit from liberal codes since they reduce the cost of construction and the reliance on unionized labor. In contrast to the intense concerns of builders and unions, the interest of the general public in building codes is limited, perhaps due to their low visibility and high technicality (President's Commission on Housing [25]).

Building codes are almost always subject to local regulation and are typically administered by building departments. Political pressures are pervasive in the process. "Code design and code enforcement do not take place within a political vacuum. Building codes have important economic meaning to those favored or not favored by the specific standard." (Field and Ventre [9]).

As these authors observe in their wide-ranging study of building departments, concerning the political nature of regulatory decision making

> Most local building officials . . . are very sensitive to political pressure. . . . Thus it is that building departments, by and large, have acquired reputations . . . for being responsive to the needs of their clients, the members of the local building community. Despite the tenuous hold that building officials have on their positions, their official actions have powerful economic consequences for a sizable portion of the local economy . . . builders are widely known for their aggressiveness and political sophistication. . . . One can readily visualize (the) pressures that converge on the local building officials in these circumstances. [9, p. 139]

Unions are similarly forceful: "When Kansas City changed . . . the building code to allow for the use of plastic and copper materials, the A.F.L.-C.I.O. cancelled a scheduled convention in the city and the local plumbers' union collected signatures to force a referendum on the issues." (Fortune, 1968). Similarly, the classic study of New York governance (Sayre and Kaufman [28]) finds that

> Without . . . allies of weight and influence, without opportunities to form a broadly supporting public opinion, each Commissioner of Buildings is brought back, whatever his initial aspirations, to the necessity of a settlement with the groups whose activities he regulates. It is with them that he must make his peace [28, p. 272].

Building codes are thus a good example of regulation in an environment affected by interest group politics. They also provide, by their local nature and wide variability (Seidel [29]), an excellent case for an empirical investigation. An unusually good data set is available, collected in a 1970 survey of building codes by the International City Managers Association (ICMA) for over 1100 American cities and towns, and described by Field and Rivkin [8] and Oster and Quigley [21];[2] the latter study investigates the diffusion of four innovations in construction and their regulatory constraint.

To test the hypothesis that industry structure and regulatory policy affect each other, let regulation R be given by

$$(1) \qquad R = b_0 + b_{1j}F_j + b_{2j}F_j^2 + b_3U + b_4U^2 + \sum b_i X_i$$

where

R = regulatory restrictiveness
F_j = measure j for the industry structure of construction firms
U = strength of construction unions
X_i = other factors that influence regulatory restrictiveness.

F_j is a vector of alternative industry structure variables. U is a variable describing the strength of the countervailing interest group, construction unions, without which the effect of F_j may well be incorrectly assessed. Because the effects of industry structure may diminish with size, a quadratic specification is used which allows to observe a non-linearity.

At the same time, it is possible and plausible that regulatory policy itself has an impact on industry structure and firm size. For example, if code regulations are very strict, they may reduce economies of scale, leading to a greater number of smaller firms. The relation of regulation to structure can be expressed by equations of the form

$$(2) \qquad F_j = c_0 + c_1R + c_2U + \sum c_m Y_m$$

where measures of industry structure F_j are explained by regulatory strictness R, union strength U, and other factors Y_m.

Equations (1) and (2) create a system of simultaneous equations that will be estimated, after a description of the variables.

The alternative variables for industry structure that are used are (a) the volume, in dollars, of annual construction activity by the local building industry; (b) the number of construction firms; (c) the number of large firms, defined as having more than 100 employees; (d) the industry market concentration, defined as the share of the large firms in total local construction industry employment; and (e) the average size of the firms.[3] These variables are expressed both in absolute terms and relative to the population figures, where appropriate.

The strength of the countervailing pressure group (construction unions) is defined as the percentage of unionized construction workers among regional construction workers.[4]

[2] Data made available by R. Ventre, National Bureau of Standards, and J. Quigley, both of whose help is gratefully acknowledged.

[3] Data from U.S. Dept. of Commerce, *City and County Data Book*, 1970.

[4] From Bureau of Labor Statistics, *Industry Wage Survey*, 1972, and U.S. Dept. of Commerce, 1974. Made available by J. Quigley.

The restrictiveness R of regulation is defined by the number of prohibitions among the major restrictive provisions listed by a Presidential Commission (the Douglas Commission on Urban Problems [6])[5] and their cost to builders.[6]

Several control variables X_i take account of factors that may also have a bearing on a locality's regulatory restrictiveness.[7] First, the extent to which local governments are susceptible to pressure may be related to their governmental system of governance, and a city manager form of government may be less affected by interest group strength than that of an elected mayor with executive powers. Second, the regulatory agency itself may be less insulated from politics when the agency head is a political appointee subject to continuous recall, rather than officiating with a secure term of office.

Third, the personal characteristics of the building official himself may have an effect on the regulatory policy adopted. This pertains, in particular, to his professional competence, expressed here by years of education (President's Commission on Housing [25]), and by a professional affiliation—and hence possible identification—with either of the two interest groups prior to his becoming a building official.

Furthermore, regulations may also be affected by the economic conditions in the housing market. Where housing is in short supply (as measured by the rate of vacancies), building codes may be less restrictive in order to encourage construction. Similarly, the density of population may be a factor in the setting of the code, since it may call for different types of construction.

Finally, the political attitudes of the locality and the regulatory standards that prevail in the surrounding area may influence regulatory strictness. Where the electorate is politically conservative,[8] an anti-regulatory attitude may exist that affects building codes. At the least, this is a testable subsidiary hypothesis. Similarly, if a locality is in a region in which the strictness of regulation is high, its own regulation may be affected by it, both because it may be a reflection of regional circumstances such as climate, and because there are efficiencies to builders in having local regulations that are similar to those of the adjoining localities (weighted average SMSA strictness was used).

In the second equation, market structure is explained by regulatory strictness, among other factors. The market structure variables F_j, such as size, concentration etc., and the regulatory strictness R are defined as before, as is

[5] These code provisions are: Nonmetallic sheathed electrical cable; prefabricated metal chimneys; preassembled electrical wiring; wood roof trusses placed 24″ apart; plastic pipe in plumbing systems; bathrooms or toilet continuous air space; single plates in non-load-bearing interior partitions; 2″ × 3″ studs in non-load-bearing interior partitions; 2″ × 4″ of 1″ in lieu of corner bracing; wood frame exterior walls in multi-family structures.

[6] Let regulatory strictness R_i be defined by an index $R_i = \sum_j C_j$ where C_j is the cost of the restriction to construction firms. Cost figures are from Douglas Commission [6, p. 271 ff]. Where no specific cost was given in that source, it was approximated by extrapolation of the ranking of seriousness surveyed from home manufacturers (Field and Rivkin [8, p. 82]), for the restrictions, with the Douglas figures of cost, where available, as the calibration.

[7] Data, unless noted otherwise, are from survey, note 2.

[8] Defined as percentage of vote in the 1964 presidential election for Barry Goldwater.

the countervailing union strength U. Market structure is also likely to be affected by the extent of the underlying business activity. Hence, several market variables are introduced. First, the size of the market may affect structure. Where it is small and/or stagnant, one is likely to encounter smaller and fewer firms. For the estimation, two variables are used to allow for market size: present size, as expressed by present construction volume; and the first derivative of size, i.e., the rate of increase of local population. Second, the location of the market may also play a role, since urban markets are likely to include the high-volume and specialized office and commercial construction that may result in a high concentration ratio. Accordingly, a dummy variable is used to allow for the effect of urban, and rural location. Thirdly, the labor market situation may affect market structure. If construction wages are high, labor will be substituted by capital. This will affect measures of size that are based on the number of employees, and may also lead to a higher concentration ratio if capital equipment is utilized more efficiently at a larger scale of operation. Consequently, a variable for SMSA-wide wage levels is introduced into equation (2).[9]

Finally, if the industry structure is shaped by regulation at all, such effect will require an extended period. A long-held code, one would assume, has affected the industry over a longer period than a recently enacted one. Its longevity may also reflect an equilibrium of satisfaction with its provisions. To allow for this element, a time variable is introduced, expressing the length which the present code has been in effect.

The results of the two-stage least square estimations for the 1073 observations are given in Tables I and II.

For the primary question of this paper, concerning the association of different measures of market structure with public policy in building regulation, the main findings are given in the top two rows of Table I. As can be seen, the linear associations of the different measures are usually negative and are mostly significant, meaning that greater industry concentration, as well as absolute firm and industry size are associated with liberalized regulation, i.e., with a more favorable policy to the industry. The most significant of the measures is the one for concentration. Similarly, the coefficients for size (in terms of employees, average business volume of firms, and total industry volume) are also statistically significant and have the predicted sign. The total number of firms and the number of large firms, on the other hand, are not significant for regulatory strictness.

As has been seen, the results are different for the different measures of industry structure. The strong association of industry concentration, relative to those of the other measures, is interesting, and it means that low industry

[9] Index of "Maintenance men", including building trades, reported by US Department of Commerce, Bureau of Labor Statistics, 1975, and regional measures. Data provided by J. Quigley and updated.

concentration is associated with a reduced effectiveness in achieving industry goals. The costs of organizing for political action, the difficulty of achieving agreement, the lack of a history of oligopolistic cooperation, the ease of free-ridership (Olson [20]), the potential presence of monopoly rents, and the greater incentive for dominant firms to take a leadership role (Siegfried [31]), all combine to give unconcentrated local industry problems in achieving its objectives. These effects apparently more than offset the potential advantages of unconcentrated industries to exert pressure at more numerous points (Caves [4]). The findings of greater political effectiveness of concentration parallel those of Mann and McCormick [16] who observe increasing lobbying expenditures on lobbying with greater concentration.

Similarly, the size of the industry and of firms is associated with more favorable regulation. This is not surprising, given the greater resources available for the production of influence. The coefficients of size relative to population, unlike those of absolute size, are not significant. Because there are scale economies and fixed costs in the generation of influence, advantages accrue to those with a high absolute size of resources, rather than relative to population. To give an illustration: a legal brief or an expert opinion are not appreciably cheaper to produce for a medium sized city than they are for a large metropolis.[10]

A second question is whether economic size exhibits diminishing returns in its effect on regulation. The results do not support such a hypothesis, at least for building code regulation. To be unrejected, the square of the term for economic power would have to be positive, good-sized, and significant. However, the coefficients for F^2 fulfil none of these conditions.[11]

If the results show that measures of economic size and power explain regulatory outcomes, so does the power of the *opposing* influence group. Construction unions prefer a strict building code, and the stronger they are, the stricter the code is found to be.

Most of the remaining control variables are not observed to contribute much to the explanation of regulatory strictness. A city manager form of government and a secure term appointment for the agency head are not

[10] Furthermore, the correlation of per capita size of industry and firms with concentration is uncertain. Average firm size per capita is a ratio of industry size and of the product of the number of firms with population. All of these parameters are positively correlated, i.e., denominator and nominator move in the same direction. The average firms size per capita grows only with industry size if the number of firms increases at a slower rate, holding population constant. A larger *per capita* industry may hence be less concentrated, at least often enough to result in an uncertain statistical association with policy outcomes. It may also be the case that there is a need, in the case of highly technical issues such as building code provisions, to persuade public decision makers rather than the public at large but both the ratios of decision makers to population and that of per capita industry decreases with city size. Hence, the two trends cancel each other out, causing an uncertain and weak statistical association of size per capita of population with regulatory strictness.

[11] The square terms can therefore be left out. When this is done, the remaining results are similar. Without the square terms, logarithmic equations can be estimated for the elasticities of regulation w.r.t. firm size, etc. These elasticities are, for concentration: -0.5179; for average firm size: -0.0519; and for industry volume: -0.3241.

TABLE I

STRICTNESS OF BUILDING CODES AND ALTERNATIVE MEASURES OF ECONOMIC SIZE AND MARKET STRUCTURE
DEPENDENT VARIABLE: STRICTNESS OF REGULATION R

Alternative Measures of Market Structure	*Total Business Volume of Industry (in mill $)*	*Number of Large Firms*	*Total Number of Firms*	*Concentration (Ratio of Large Firms)*	*Employees per Firm*
Measure of Market Structure (F)	−0.0061	−0.0029	−0.0042	−0.1368	−0.0722
	(2.0742)	(2.2607)	(0.4966)	(2.0943)	(1.8526)
F^2	−0.0000	0.0002	0.0000	2.2437	0.0064
	(0.4926)	(0.1615)	(1.2413)	(0.4162)	(1.2617)
Construction Union Strength (U)	0.0259	0.0248	0.0612	0.0433	−0.0265
	(1.3282)	(1.8260)	(1.8497)	(1.3106)	(1.3827)
U^2	−0.0003	−0.0008	−0.0005	−0.0005	−0.0002
	(0.7316)	(0.8272)	(0.1492)	(0.8248)	(0.0241)
City Manager Form of Government	0.0562	0.0244	−0.0124	−0.0076	−0.0142
	(0.2846)	(1.2433)	(1.4907)	(0.0416)	(1.0220)
Agency Chief Appointed to Fixed Term	−0.1243	−0.1421	−0.1627	−0.0582	−0.1992
	(0.5481)	(−0.8274)	(1.2419)	(0.4954)	(0.9460)
Agency Chief—Years of Education	−0.0009	−0.0027	−0.0012	−0.0047	−0.0041
	(1.9175)	(2.0759)	(1.8264)	(1.7902)	(2.1654)
Agency Chief—Prior Union Association	0.0002	0.0000	0.0009	0.0006	0.0010
	(0.2758)	(0.1541)	(0.2039)	(0.2611)	(0.5011)
Vacancy Rate	−0.3701	0.0491	−0.3062	0.8174	−0.5266
	(0.2041)	(0.1707)	(0.3611)	(0.4187)	(0.2344)
Political Conservativism	−0.0009	−0.0122	−0.0074	−0.0132	−0.0027
	(0.7256)	(0.4428)	(0.3461)	(0.4069)	(0.4220)
Regional Strictness	0.6029	0.8241	0.6043	0.8120	0.7734
	(4.1294)	(4.1648)	(4.2719)	(4.4297)	(4.8606)
R^2	0.3128	0.3892	0.3729	0.3572	0.3527

Alternative Measures of Economic Power	*Business Volume per Firm*	*Business Volume/ Capita Population*	*Employees per Firm/Capita Population*	*Large Firms/ Capita Population*
Measure of Economic	−0.1941	0.2147	0.5407	0.1927
Power (F)	(1.8727)	(0.1471)	(0.8743)	(0.2411)
F^2	−0.0004	−0.0000	−1.1603	−0.0278
	(1.2602)	(0.2092)	(0.3855)	(0.4112)
Construction Union	0.0032	0.0109	0.0272	0.0394
Strength (U)	(1.8964)	(1.6494)	(1.7254)	(1.6474
U^2	−0.0004	−0.0003	−0.0004	−0.0007
	(0.7282)	(0.4922)	(0.5671)	(0.3191)
City Manager Form	−0.0247	0.0182	−0.0127	−0.0942
of Government	(0.1751)	(1.2502)	(0.2523)	(1.2004)
Agency Chief—Appointment	−0.2719	−0.2729	−0.4177	−0.3511
to Fixed Term	(0.5922)	(1.2656)	(0.6741)	(0.5977)
Agency Chief—Years of	−0.0012	−0.0000	−0.0162	−0.0261
Education	(1.7426)	(1.6295)	(2.1346)	(1.8263)
Agency Chief—Prior Union	0.0271	0.0009	0.0001	0.0000
Association	(0.3677)	(0.2591)	(0.4267)	(0.2908)
Vacancy Rate	−0.4660	0.7212	−0.4739	−0.5192
	(0.5102)	(0.4100)	(0.3501)	(0.3966)
Political Conservativism	−0.0049	−0.0029	−0.0022	−0.0054
	(0.4697)	(0.5644)	(0.1260)	(0.2947)
Regional Strictness	0.6220	0.4166	0.7094	0.6624
	(4.0562)	(4.1593)	(4.3027)	(4.0277)
R^2	0.3722	0.3598	0.3619	0.3522

(t-statistics in parentheses).

TABLE II
STRICTNESS OF REGULATION AND FIRM SIZE AND MARKET STRUCTURE

Dependent Variable	Total Volume of Indust. (in thous.)	Number of Large Firms	Total Number of Firms	Concentration Ratio (Share of Large Firms)	Employees per Firm
Strictness of Code	−20958.4	−0.9258	10.3496	−0.0234	−1.0795
	(2.8243)	(2.1046)	(1.1462)	(2.2944)	(1.8618)
Construction Union	−40.379	−0.0109	1.1244	−0.0017	−0.2792
Strength	(1.7847)	(0.0944)	(2.0746)	(1.6592)	(2.6419)
Construction Volume		0.0251	0.4329	0.0006	0.0062
		(2.1095)	(1.3922)	(1.8599)	(2.0058)
Population Increase	92.11	0.0741	4.1864	0.0003	0.0037
	(1.3294)	(0.7519)	(1.5968)	(0.2172)	(1.4127)
Construction Wage	0.9162	−0.0026	−0.0041	−0.0013	−0.0015
Level	(2.3454)	(1.4275)	(1.4275)	(1.7983)	(1.6297)
Urban	14955.2	−6.1223	−472.78	0.0492	−0.6720
	(3.0074)	(2.2197)	(5.7194)	(1.4266)	(1.0940)
Age of Code	−131.79	0.7827	0.9224	0.0027	0.0472
	(1.2977)	(1.0462)	(0.2047)	(1.2884)	(1.8579)
R^2	0.6114	0.2034	0.4178	0.3051	0.3419

Dependent Variable	Business Volume per Firm (in thous.)	Business Volume/ Capita Population	Employees per Firm/Capita Population	Large Firms/ Capita Population
Strictness of Code	−19.0651	−0.0682	−0.0359	0.0296
	(1.7032)	(0.2473)	(0.7216)	(0.5293)
Construction Union	−2.4937	0.0022	−0.0041	−0.0071
Strength	(2.8740)	(0.3192)	(0.2743)	(0.8542)
Construction Volume	1.7598	−0.0007	−0.0001	0.0001
	(5.2627)	(0.3490)	(0.5031)	(2.7491)
Population Increase	−0.1827	0.0072	0.0019	0.0004
	(0.1653)	(1.7649)	(0.8266)	(0.3751)
Construction Wage	0.0247	0.0003	−0.0001	−0.0097
Level	(1.8271)	(1.2245)	(0.5982)	(0.2176)
Urban	147.4392	−0.2419	−0.2757	−0.0482
	(7.2419)	(2.2471)	(5.2644)	(0.7916)
Age of Code	−0.1298	0.0032	−0.0001	−0.0006
	(1.2041)	(0.9272)	(0.2841)	(0.4972)
R^2	0.5491	0.3274	0.3924	0.1970

clearly associated with changes in regulations, even though they may make an agency less susceptible to political pressures. Both the vacancy rate in the housing market, as a measure of the need for housing construction, and the political conservatism are weak explanations of regulatory strictness. There are, however, strong associations between the locally and the regionally prevailing strictness of regulation, and small, but notably significant coefficients for the educational level of the chief building official. His prior job associations, on the other hand, do not appear to have any effect.[12]

This brings us to the other side of the simultaneous equations, namely the

[12] The estimation uses a dichotomous variable for prior union affiliation of the official. An identical estimation used prior construction firm affiliations, with similarly insignificant results.

relation of public policy to the industry. It has been argued in this paper that regulation itself shapes market structures. Hence, these effects should be observable from the data. The results, given in Table II, do not reject this hypothesis. The first line of the table shows the coefficients of market structure with respect to regulatory strictness. There is a strong association of strictness with the concentration ratio. The coefficient is negative, meaning that with stricter regulation the share of large firms is smaller. This can be explained in that building code regulation may reduce the efficiencies of scale, e.g., by preventing large-volume preassembly (President's Commission on Housing 1982 [25], Keating [13]) thus helping small and middle sized firms to hold their own against large competitors. Similar results can be observed for the other industry measures. Strict building code regulation is associated with smaller sized firms, a smaller number of firms, and a smaller total volume of industry activity. Building codes therefore seem to act in part as barriers to entry, and a constraint on business activities. Again, the size measures per capita of population are statistically insignificant. Expressed as elasticities, the association of regulation is, on concentration: -0.7092; on average firm size: -0.0341; on industry volume: -0.4122.

It is interesting to observe, in the second line of Table II, the coefficients of construction unions on the market structure of firms. It is negative on firm size, concentration ratio and number of large firms. It is positive in its association with the total number of firms. This result is at odds with the Galbraithian theory of "countervailing power," according to which the strength of one interest group induces the development of the strength of the opposing group. Instead, we find that unionization is associated with smaller firms, at least in the building industry. A small and related effect can be observed for the SMSA-wide wage level for construction workers, which is associated, at moderate levels of significance, with a smaller number of firms, and a more concentrated industry.

Of the other variables, the size of the market has a positive and significant association with market strictness variables. Neither the growth of the market, nor the age of the code has such an effect.

SUMMARY

Findings for the building codes of more than 1100 American cities and towns show how different measures of construction industry structure explain the strictness of local building regulation. It is observed that most of these structural measures are in fact associated with the strictness of regulatory policy, and that several measures—industry concentration, total industry size, and average firm size—have a particularly significant statistical association. These effects appear to be linear, and diminishing returns for the effects of firm size are not observed.

What these results show about the effects of market structure on this particular form of regulation—Building codes—may not be necessarily unexpected. Nevertheless, the findings provide a rare opportunity for a statistical investigation of such effects on regulatory policy, and the possibility to examine the reverse effect of regulation on market structure.

Eli Noam,
Columbia University,
726 Uris Hall,
New York,
N.Y. 10027,
U.S.A.

ACCEPTED JULY 1982

REFERENCES

[1] BARTLETT, RANDALL, *Economic Foundations of Political Power* (Free Press, New York, 1973).

[2] BAUER, RAYMOND A., ITHIELD DE SOLA POOL and LOUIS A. DEXTER, *American Business and Public Policy: The Politics of Foreign Trade* (Atherton Press, New York, 1963).

[3] BLAKE, HARLAN, "Conglomerate Mergers and the Antitrust Laws," *Columbia Law Review*, 73 (March 1973), pp. 591–92.

[4] CAVES, RICHARD E., "Economic Models of Political Choice: Canada's Tariff Structure," *Canadian Journal of Economics*, 9:2 (May 1976), p. 278.

[5] COOLIDGE, CATHLEEN, and GORDON TULLOCK, "Firm Size and Political Power," in Siegfried [30].

[6] DOUGLAS COMMISSION (Report of the National Commission on Urban Problems), *Building the American City* (Government Printing Office, Washington, D.C., 1968).

[7] EPSTEIN, EDWIN M., "Firm Size and Structure, Market Power and Business Political Influence: A Review of the Literature," in Siegfried [30].

[8] FIELD, CHARLES G. and STEVEN R. RIVKIN, *The Building Code Burden* (D. C. Heath, Lexington, 1975).

[9] FIELD, CHARLES G. and FRANCIS T. VENTRE, "Local Regulation of Building: Agencies, Codes and Politics," in International City Management Association, *The Municipal Year Book 1971* (Washington, D.C., 1971), pp. 139–65.

[10] FREY, BRUNO, "Eine Theorie Demokratischer Wirtschaftspolitik," *Kyklos*, 31:2 (1978), pp. 208–34.

[11] GALBRAITH, JOHN KENNETH, *The New Industrial State* (New American Library, New York, 1967).

[12] KAYSEN, CARL, "The Corporation: How Much Power? What Scope?" in E. S. Mason, ed., *The Corporation in Modern Society* (Harvard University Press, Cambridge, 1959), p. 99.

[13] KEATING, BARRY P., "Standards: Implicit, Explicit and Mandatory," *Economic Inquiry*, XIX, 3 (July 1981), pp. 440–58.

[14] LINDBLOM, *Politics and Markets: The World's Political-Economic Systems* (Basic Books, New York, 1977).

[15] LOWI, THEODORE J., "American Business, Public Policy, Case Studies and Political Theory," *World Politics*, Vol. 16, XVI:4 (July 1964), p. 677.

[16] MANN, H. M., and K. MCCORMICK, "Firm Attributes and the Propensity to Influence the Political System," in Siegfried [30].

[17] MARX, T. G., "Political Consequences of Conglomerate Mergers," *Atlantic Economic Journal*, 8:1 (March 1980), p. 62.

[18] MCPHERSON, C. P., "Tariff Structure and Political Exchange," Ph.D. dissertation, University of Chicago (1972).

[19] NUTT-POWELL, THOMAS E., *Manufactured Homes* (Auburn House Publishing Company, Boston, 1982), p. 76.

[20] OLSON, MANCUR, *The Logic of Collective Action: Public Goods and the Theory of Groups* (Harvard University Press, Cambridge, 1965).

[21] OSTER, SHARON and JOHN QUIGLEY, "Regulatory Barriers of the Diffusion of Innovation: Some Evidence from Building Codes," *Bell Journal of Economics*, 8:2 (Autumn 1977), p. 361.

[22] PINCUS, J. J., "Pressure Groups and Patterns of Tariffs," *Journal of Political Economy*, 83:4 (August 1975), p. 757.

[23] PITTMAN, R., "The Effects of Industry Concentration and Regulation on Contribution in Three 1977 U.S. Senate Campaigns," *Public Choice*, 27 (Fall 1976), p. 71.

[24] PITTMAN, R., "Market Structure and Campaign Contributions," *Public Choice*, 31 (Fall 1977), p. 37.

[25] PRESIDENT'S COMMISSION ON HOUSING, *Final Report*, Washington, D.C., 1982.

[26] SALAMON, LESTER M., and JOHN T. SIEGFRIED, "Economic Power and Political Influence: The Impact of Industry Structure on Public Policy," *American Political Science Review*, 71:3 (September 1977), p. 340.

[27] SAUNDERS, RONALD S., "The Political Economy of Effective Tariff Protection in Canada's Manufacturing Sector," *Canadian Journal of Economics*, 13:2 (May 1980), p. 340.

[28] SAYRE, WALLACE S., and HERBERT KAUFMAN, *Governing New York City: Politics in the Metropolis* (Russell Sage Foundation, New York, 1960).

[29] SEIDEL, STEPHEN R., *Housing Costs and Government Regulation* (Center for Urban Policy Research, New Brunswick, 1978), p. 85.

[30] SIEGFRIED, JOHN J., ed., *The Economics of Firm Size, Market Structure, and Social Performance*, Bureau of Economics, Federal Trade Commission (Superintendent of Documents) Washington, D.C. (1980).

[31] SIEGFRIED, JOHN J., "The Effects of Conglomerate Mergers on Political Democracy: A Survey," in Roger D. Blair and Robert F. Lanzillotti (eds.), *The Conglomerate Corporation* (OGH, Cambridge, 1981).

[32] STIGLER, GEORGE J., "The Theory of Economic Regulation," *Bell Journal of Economics and Management Science*, 2:1 (Spring 1971), p. 3.

[33] TUFTE, EDWARD R., *Political Control of the Economy* (Princeton University Press, Princeton, 1978).

[34] U.S. CONGRESS, House of Representatives, House Subcommittee on Housing and Community Development, *Hearings: National Manufactured Home Construction and Safety Standards*, Parts 1 and 2 (U.S. Government Printing Office, Washington, D.C., September 1981).

[35] U.S. DEPARTMENT OF COMMERCE, Bureau of the Census, *U.S. Census of Population and Housing* (U.S. Government Printing Office, Washington, D.C., 1960, 1970).

[36] U.S. DEPARTMENT OF COMMERCE, *City and County Data Book* (U.S. Government Printing Office, Washington, D.C., 1972).

[37] U.S. DEPARTMENT OF LABOR, Bureau of Labor Statistics, *Industry Wage Survey:* Contract Construction, Bulletin 1853 (September 1972).

[38] U.S. DEPARTMENT OF LABOR, Bureau of Labor Statistics, *Handbook of Labor Statistics of 1975*, Reference Edition. Bulletin 1985, 1975.

[39] U.S. DEPARTMENT OF LABOR, *Employment and Earnings* (Government Printing Office, Washington, D.C., October 1977).

THE JOURNAL OF INDUSTRIAL ECONOMICS 0022-1821 $2.00
Volume XXXII March 1984 No. 3

REGULATION AND RISK PREFERENCES*

SHERRILL SHAFFER

I. INTRODUCTION

A NUMBER of economists in recent years have suggested that government regulation may have the effect of reducing the level of risk to the producing firms, their consumers, or some combination thereof. Peltzman [7] appears to be the first to have derived this implication in the context of a general theoretical model of regulation, with Owen and Braeutigam [5] concurring shortly thereafter. Empirical support for the hypothesis has been adduced by Hogan *et al.* [2].

It is generally agreed that any such reduction of risk constitutes an added, perhaps hitherto unacknowledged, benefit of regulation. For instance, Owen and Braeutigam [2, p. 25] note that "if the effect of regulation is to reduce the risks faced by individuals . . . then it is easily demonstrated that voters in a society of risk averse individuals will prefer a regulated economy to a free market economy, even if it costs something. . . ."

This result, derived for reductions in the riskiness of consumption quantities or of profit streams, is known to fail in some instances of price risk. That individuals who are risk averse in quantities may tend to prefer risky prices has been established by Waugh [12], Pazner and Razin [6], Flemming *et al.* [1], and Turnovsky *et al.* [11]. Oi [3] demonstrates conditions under which a firm's expected profits increase with the riskiness of its output price, and Rosse [9] has established properties of production technology which may be applied in a straightforward fashion to show that riskier input prices yield higher expected profits.

Thus it is incorrect to suppose that all economic agents will benefit from a reduction in the risk of any parameter. Risk preferences must be examined separately for each case. The purpose of this paper is to extend the investigation of quantity risk aversion to the cases of (a) consumers who have exogenous, differential information and (b) firms which maximize expected profits and are in that sense risk neutral.

II. CONSUMERS WITH DIFFERENTIAL INFORMATION

This section employs mean-variance analysis to characterize the effect of risk-reducing regulation on an agent's expected consumption, conditional on his

* This paper is adapted from a section of the author's Ph.D. dissertation. The author gratefully acknowledges helpful comments from Therese Flaherty, Sanford Grossman, David Kreps, Hajime Miyazaki, Bruce Owen, James Rosse, and two anonymous referees. This paper embodies the views of the author and does not represent the official views or policy of the Federal Reserve System or the Federal Reserve Bank of New York.

information. In this manner we also derive the effect of differential information on consumer preferences for regulation, and describe the information required for a regulator to decide whether to regulate.

Suppose that each consumer observes an exogenous signal in the current period which gives him further information about the vector that he will consume in the coming period. For example, future price levels are significant determinants of the individual's future consumption, and these price levels can often be predicted with some accuracy in the short run. Factors (signals) affecting next period's prices may include some combination of current prices and information about shifts in supply or demand. A drought over Kansas this year may signal slightly higher wheat prices worldwide next year, with each individual then reducing his consumption of wheat accordingly. Likewise, an individual's future income will affect his future consumption, while being itself affected by current variables, including some that are exogenous. An auto worker will revise downward his expected consumption in the coming year upon learning that his plant has just shut down; in this case, a relevant signal is the state of operation of his plant.

We can model this process in simplified form by specifying y_i to be a random, scalar variable having a joint distribution with the individual's (vector) consumption x_i. For purposes of this discussion we shall deal with the joint normal distribution. Regulation as a means of reducing quantity risk can then be represented in a straightforward way: using a standardized signal and omitting the consumer subscript, we have

$$\begin{bmatrix} \tilde{x}^r \\ \tilde{y} \end{bmatrix} \sim \mathcal{N}\left(\begin{bmatrix} \bar{x} \\ 0 \end{bmatrix}, \Sigma^r\right) \qquad \begin{bmatrix} \tilde{x} \\ \tilde{y} \end{bmatrix} \sim \mathcal{N}\left(\begin{bmatrix} \bar{x} \\ 0 \end{bmatrix}, \Sigma\right)$$

where

$$\Sigma^r = \begin{pmatrix} \sigma_1^2 & \rho_{12}\sigma_1\sigma_2 & \cdots & & \rho_1\sigma_1 \\ \rho_{12}\sigma_1\sigma_2 & \sigma_2^2 & \cdots & & \rho_2\sigma_2 \\ \vdots & & \ddots & & \vdots \\ & & & \sigma_G^2 & \rho_G\sigma_G \\ \rho_1\sigma_1 & \rho_2\sigma_2 & \cdots & \rho_G\sigma_G & 1 \end{pmatrix},$$

the regulated variance-covariance matrix; and

$$\Sigma = \begin{pmatrix} \sigma_1^2 + s_1^2 & \cdots & \cdots & \cdots & \rho_1\sqrt{\sigma_1^2 + s_1^2} \\ \vdots & \sigma_2^2 + s_2^2 & \cdots & \cdots & \rho_2\sqrt{\sigma_2^2 + s_2^2} \\ \vdots & \vdots & \vdots & \ddots & \\ \vdots & \vdots & & \sigma_G^2 + s_G^2 & \rho_G\sqrt{\sigma_G^2 + s_G^2} \\ \rho_1\sqrt{\sigma_1^2 + s_1^2} & \rho_2\sqrt{\sigma_2^2 + s_2^2} & \cdots & \rho_G\sqrt{\sigma_G^2 + s_G^2} & 1 \end{pmatrix},$$

the unregulated variance-covariance matrix. Then, for the jth good, we have the result

Proposition 1:

$$|E\tilde{x}_j^r|y - \bar{x}_j| \leq |E\tilde{x}_j|y - \bar{x}_j|.$$

That is, for each good, regulation weakly reduces the magnitude of deviation of the expected endowment conditional on the signal from the unconditional expected endowment. Thus, if the individual's signal indicates that he is likely to consume less of some commodity than he would have expected in the absence of a signal, the amount of that shortfall will be less (or, equivalently, the expected consumption of that commodity conditional on the signal will be greater) under risk-reducing regulation than without such regulation. Conversely, if a favorable signal is encountered, causing the individual to revise upward his expected consumption of a particular commodity over his pre-signal expectation, the amount by which he will revise his estimate upward will be less (as will the final expected consumption of the commodity conditional on the signal) under risk-reducing regulation than without such regulation.

Proof:

$$E\tilde{x}_j|y = \bar{x}_j + \rho_j y\sqrt{\sigma_j^2 + s_j^2}$$

$$E\tilde{x}_j^r|y = \bar{x}_j + \rho_j y\sigma_j$$

Let

$$A = E\tilde{x}_j^r|y - \bar{x}_j = \rho_j\sigma_j y,$$

$$B = E\tilde{x}_j|y - \bar{x}_j = \rho_j y\sqrt{\sigma_j^2 + s_j^2}$$

Now $\sqrt{\sigma_j^2 + s_j^2} \geq \sigma_j$ so that four cases arise:

(i) $\rho_j > 0, y > 0 \Rightarrow A \leq B,\ A > 0,\ B > 0 \Rightarrow |A| \leq |B|$

(ii) $\rho_j < 0, y > 0 \Rightarrow A \geq B,\ A < 0,\ B < 0 \Rightarrow |A| \leq |B|$

(iii) $\rho_j > 0, y < 0 \Rightarrow A \geq B,\ A < 0,\ B < 0 \Rightarrow |A| \leq |B|$

(iv) $\rho_j < 0, y < 0 \Rightarrow A \leq B,\ A > 0,\ B > 0 \Rightarrow |A| \leq |B|$

Q.E.D.

Proposition 2:

Where each good can be regulated separately to achieve $s_j = 0$ for an arbitrary good j, each consumer i will (strongly) prefer regulation of good j for all j such that $E\tilde{x}_j|y < \bar{x}_j$ (i.e., whenever his signal indicates a worse outcome than his pre-signal expectation). This result holds for risk neutral as well as risk averse individuals.

Proof:

Utility maximizers always prefer the larger of $E\tilde{x}_j^r | y$ and $E\tilde{x}_j | y$, and thus prefer regulation iff $Ex_j^r | y > E\tilde{x}_j | y$, assuming no risk-seeking behavior. Thus regulation is preferred iff $A > B$ (as defined in the proof of Proposition 1). This inequality holds, by Proposition 1, iff A and B are both negative; i.e., when $E\tilde{x}_j | y < \bar{x}_j$ (and $E\tilde{x}_j^r | y < \bar{x}_j$).

Q.E.D.

If each good cannot be independently regulated, then the decision rule given by Proposition 2 is inadequate and the consumer must compare his expected utility with and without regulation. A central planner is even worse off. The community decision to regulate is presumably based on some aggregation of individual preferences. If each good can be independently regulated, a central planner needs to know only the sign of the signal and of each ρ_j for consumer i in order to know whether i favors regulation of good j. Otherwise, he must know the magnitudes of these quantities, $\bar{x}_i$, and i's utility function as well. Thus it is in the interest of a central planner in this model to be able to regulate good by good, unless each individual can communicate his stand on regulation directly to the planner. (Then, of course, the planner no longer must infer i's stand, and becomes indifferent between blanket regulation and piecewise regulation as far as informational requirements go. It remains true that good-by-good regulation offers greater flexibility in maximizing social welfare here.)

A special case arises if the community goal is to maximize the expected social endowment (a rational goal if, for instance, distributional issues are settled independently). Define the community parameters

$$\tilde{X} = \sum_i \tilde{x}_i, \quad \tilde{Y} = \sum_i \tilde{y}_i, \quad S = \sum_i \Sigma_i.$$

Then by Corollary 2.2 of Raiffa and Schlaifer [8, p. 254],

$$\begin{bmatrix} \tilde{X} \\ \tilde{Y} \end{bmatrix} \sim N\left(\begin{bmatrix} \sum_i \bar{x}_i \\ 0 \end{bmatrix}, S \right)$$

A knowledge of $\bar{x}_i$ and Σ_i enables the planner simply to sum the individual signals and form a community conditional consumption expectation. The decision rule appropriate to the stated goal (as we may see immediately by applying Proposition 2 to the above distribution of $\tilde{X}$ and $\tilde{Y}$) is to regulate good j if and only if $E\tilde{X}_j | Y < \sum_i \bar{x}_{ij}$.[1] Note that for such a goal the analysis remains valid if we replace consumption vectors by endowment vectors, since trades sum to zero identically in a closed economy (abstracting from intertemporal trade or savings). That is, if regulation affects endowments rather

[1] Similarly, any risk-neutral social welfare function strictly increasing in x_{ij}, say $\sum_j \sum_i \alpha_{ij} x_{ij}$, yields the decision if and only if $E\tilde{x}_j | Y < \sum_i \alpha_{ij} x_{ij}$.

than consumption, then the social division rule for regulation still depends only on the sums of individual means, covariances, and signals. Note further that a voting rule, by aggregating only the signs of $E\tilde{x}_j|y_i - \bar{x}_j$, can never be sufficient to maximize a social utility function which is linear in the x_i's; information about the magnitudes is needed as well.

The question remains as to how $\bar{x}$ is determined. The naive assumption that $\bar{x}$ equals the status quo has several advantages over alternative assumptions. It is simple and not unreasonable. It allows our planner of the previous paragraph to replace $\sum_i \bar{x}_j$ by total current consumption or endowment (which may be proxied by GNP or some such regularly observed quantity). Proposition I becomes the condition that "regulation reduces movement away from the status quo," the view empirically supported in Owen and Braeutigam [5]. Economic interpretations of y are not difficult to find; people regularly alter their income expectations according to the state of the stock market, their health, and last month's tenure decisions. A scalar signal may be less realistic than a vector, but the model can easily accommodate the latter.

III. RISK NEUTRAL PRODUCERS

Moving from consumers to producers, we shall see in this section that expected profits rise as output quantity risk is reduced, *ceteris paribus*. This result is achieved when a firm faces random demand quantities at fixed prices, and rising per-unit costs for production unequal to demand. It implies that even a risk neutral firm may benefit from regulation that reduces quantity risk.

Consider a firm which must plan production at the beginning of a period, before it knows the exact quantity which will be demanded in that period. If it decides to produce too much, it will incur storage costs for the excess, and may have to reduce the price in order to sell the excess at all. A lower per-unit profit results either way. Alternatively, or in addition, there may be costs of rapid quantity adjustment if production is reduced as demand becomes known. Contracts may require that the firm continue its original rate of input consumption, for instance, at least in the short run. It is reasonable to expect that such costs, on a per unit basis over all units produced, would rise with the amount by which production exceeds demand.

Likewise, if demand exceeds production then the firm may incur higher costs if, for example, it has a common carrier obligation. In that case the regulatory agency could be expected to enforce the common carrier obligation through a system of rewards and penalties. The firm then faces the choice of a rapid adjustment of output to meet the higher demand, with attendant increases in average cost, or a direct penalty resulting from a failure to meet its obligations. It is not necessary for our result that the firm suffer such a direct cost of failing to meet demand, but we include the condition in our model here for the sake of realism.

For simplicity we assume constant marginal cost, and no fixed cost. Thus average cost equals marginal cost. The result to be shown will still hold under more general assumptions, as discussed later; for now it will suffice to point out that the result would be strengthened if the marginal cost increases with quantity produced.

The following notation applies to each firm individually; firm subscripts have been omitted for clarity.

$x =$ production quantity: a bounded, real, scalar variable

$\tilde{q} =$ demand quantity faced by the firm at the given, fixed prices: a bounded, continuous, real, random, scalar variable

$q =$ a realization of $\tilde{q}$

$a =$ profit per unit: the bounded, real scalar equal to price minus average cost for each good produced

$w = q - x =$ the difference between demand and production

$f(w) =$ the penalty function: real, continuous, strictly concave, with $f(0) = 0 = f'(0)$. Thus $f(w)$ is negative for nonzero w (i.e., demand unequal to production) and $f''(w)$ is also negative as shown in Figure 1.

$\pi =$ profit $= a \cdot x + f(w)$

Then the firm will maximize expected profit, which is equal to the certain value, production times per-unit profit; plus the expected value of the random penalty. That is,

$$E\pi = E(a \cdot x + f(w))$$
$$= a \cdot x + E(f(w)).$$

Now suppose that regulation induces a mean preserving shrink on the demand quantity faced by the firm. We can think of entry and competing technology, for instance, as being regulated to reduce the possibility of random changes in a firm's market share, thereby removing a noise component from the firm's random demand. The transatlantic cable and satellite communications industry provides a good example of this behavior; (see Owen and Braeutigam [5, Chapter 2]. Formally, this gives $q = q^r + z$ where z is a real continuous, bounded, scalar, random variable. If we now assume that $E(z \mid q^r) = 0$ then we can prove

Proposition 3:

$$E(\pi^r) \geq E(\pi).$$

That is, a risk neutral firm benefits from risk-reducing regulation.

Proof:

$$w = q - x = q^r + z - x = w^r + z$$
$$E(z \mid w^r) = E(z \mid (q^r, x)) = E(z \mid q^r) = 0$$
$$E(w \mid x) = E(w^r \mid x) + E(z \mid x) = E(w^r \mid x)$$

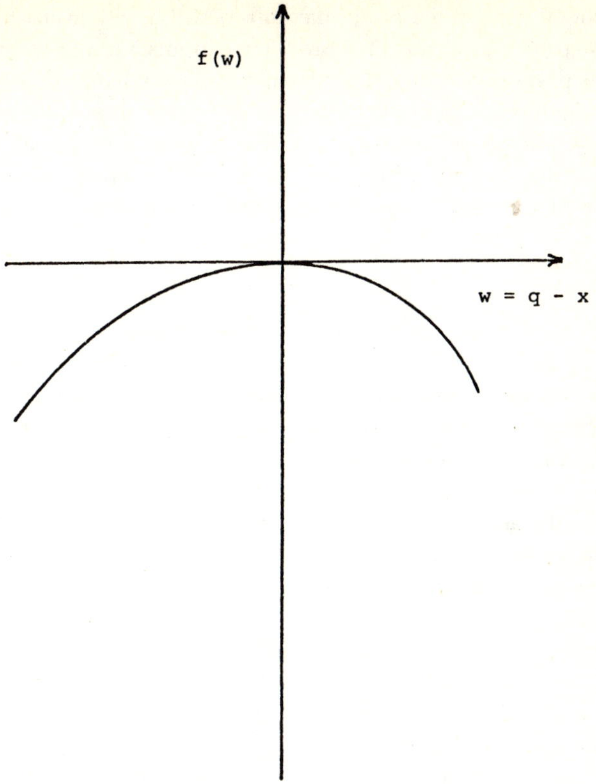

FIGURE I
Per-unit profit penalty function

so, by Rothschild and Stiglitz [10], $E(f(w^r)) \geq E(f(w))$ and

$$E(\pi^r) = a \cdot x + E(f(w^r)) \geq a \cdot x + E(f(w)) = E(\pi).$$

Q.E.D.

Here we have used assumptions on q and q^r to generate the properties of w and w^r needed to apply the Rothschild-Stiglitz theorem; this yields the result that the expected penalty is lower under regulation, giving a higher expected profit for the firm.

Note that this proof takes x as unaltered by regulation. In general, a firm's optimal production may vary with the riskiness of demand. Our result shows that even without an output change regulation increases the firm's expected profits. Thus regulation would be preferred even if it forces the firm to set its output levels as though it were not regulated. If autonomous output changes are allowed, such changes would only further increase expected profits, else no change would occur.

More generally, expected profit maximizers will be risk averse with respect to output quantities if (a) the set of productive inputs is a convex and compact subset of the positive orthant of Euclidean m-space for m inputs and (b) the set of feasible input–output combinations is a closed, nonempty, convex subset of Euclidean $(m + n)$-space for n outputs. These two conditions yield a minimum cost function that is convex in output quantities, as shown by Rosse [9], so that the profit function is concave in output quantities and therefore risk averse.

IV. SUMMARY AND CONCLUSIONS

Focusing on changes in risk apart from changes in the mean outcome, we have seen that a pure reduction in risk can be either beneficial or detrimental but rarely irrelevant to the welfare of the parties involved. We have applied the various cases of risk reduction to draw several tentative conclusions for public policy under the assumption, defended elsewhere by Owen and Braeutigam [5] and Peltzman [7], that government regulation of industry tends to reduce the riskiness of a number of economic parameters within the regulated industry.

The usefulness of the policy recommendations lies first in the *ex ante* fabrication of regulatory programs, in the event that risk reduction is a conscious and controlled objective of the regulation. If, as Peltzman hypothesizes, the reduction in risk is a byproduct of regulation rather than one of its central aims, then the conclusions set forth here are nevertheless useful in an *ex post* evaluation of ongoing regulatory programs.

The specific conclusions are as follows:

(1) The reduction of quantity risk is beneficial to consumers and producers alike, all else remaining equal.

(2) However, agent-specific information regarding the expected future outcome may create vested interests that oppose any reduction of quantity risk such as regulation might achieve.

(3) Such information may nevertheless be utilized in a decision rule to achieve such ends as the maximization of the overall community endowment through selective regulatory risk reduction, although a majority-rule voting mechanism fails to aggregate this information properly.

Sherrill Shaffer,
Banking Studies Department,
Federal Reserve Bank of New York,
33 Liberty Street,
New York, N.Y., 10045,
U.S.A.

ACCEPTED AUGUST 1982

REFERENCES

[1] FLEMMING, J. S., TURNOVSKY, S. J., and KEMP, M. C., "On the Choice of Numeraire and Certainty Price in General Equilibrium Models of Price Uncertainty," *Review of Economic Studies*, 44 (October 1977), pp. 573–83.

[2] HOGAN, W. P., SHARPE, I. G., and VOLKER, P. A., "Risk and Regulation: An Empirical Test of the Relationship," *Economics Letters*, 6 (1980), pp. 373–79.

[3] OI, W., "The Desirability of Price Stability Under Perfect Competition," *Econometrica*, 29 (January 1961), pp. 58–64.

[4] OI, W., "Rejoinder," *Econometrica*, 31 (January–April 1963), p. 248.

[5] OWEN, B. M., and BRAEUTIGAM, R., *The Regulation Game: Strategic Use of the Administrative Process* (Ballinger Publishing Company, Cambridge, 1978).

[6] PAZNER, E. A., and RAZIN, A., "Welfare Aspects of Exchange Rate Uncertainty," *Economica*, 41 (August 1974), pp. 256–68.

[7] PELTZMAN, S., "Toward a More General Theory of Regulation," *Journal of Law and Economics*, 19 (August 1976), pp. 211–40.

[8] RAIFFA, R., and SCHLAIFER, R., *Applied Statistical Decision Theory* (Division of Research, Graduate School of Business Administration, Harvard University, Boston, 1961).

[9] ROSSE, J. N., "Equivalent Structures of Production, Cost, and Input Demand with Multiple Inputs and Outputs," *Studies in Industry Economics*, No. 13 (June 1970), Department of Economics, Stanford University.

[10] ROTHSCHILD, M., and STIGLITZ, J. E., "Increasing Risk: I. A Definition," *Journal of Economic Theory*, 2 (September 1970), pp. 225–43.

[11] TURNOVSKY, S. J., SHALIT, H., and SCHMITZ, A., "Consumer's Surplus, Price Instability, and Consumer Welfare," *Econometrica*, 48 (January 1980), pp. 135–52.

[12] WAUGH, F. V., "Does the Consumer Benefit from Price Instability?" *Quarterly Journal of Economics*, 58 (August 1944), pp. 602–14.

THE JOURNAL OF INDUSTRIAL ECONOMICS 0022-1821 $2.00
Volume XXXII March 1984 No. 3

"POLLUTERS' PROFITS": AN EMPIRICAL NOTE

BRUCE YANDLE*

I. INTRODUCTION

IN AN insightful theoretical treatment of environmental regulation, Buchanan and Tullock (B-T) [1] described the possible conditions for profit enhancement caused when environmental regulations are imposed on a given industry. Their analysis focused on source standards where pollution was a joint product with a representative firm's output. Restrictions on pollution led to reductions in output, and the environmental authorities acted as cartel managers to make certain cheating did not occur.

The results of the B-T model were higher industry price, lower output, and, due to the lack of competitive entry, inefficient production. Polluter profits were enhanced in a regulation-induced equilibrium. There was no internal incentive for changing the regulatory institution to a system of charges, marketable permits or emission taxes.

The B-T analysis was later modified by Mumy [3] and used to develop an alternative regulatory strategy which might be palatable to polluters. Mumy effectively capitalized the polluter profits in his model, but introduced an incentive for the original polluters to exchange pollution rights with other firms which might place a higher value on them.

Koch and Leone [2] have used implicitly a version of the B-T analysis for a study of the tissue paper industry and the effects of water pollution control requirements on that industry's profits. Their case study supported the notion that profits can be enhanced by strict pollution control standards, especially when the standards are designed not to capsize the weaker firms in an industry.

As yet, however, no general test of the B-T theory has been reported. And that is the purpose of this note. The next section discusses the institutions which have been developed and applied to the pollution problem and relates those institutions to the theory. From the discussion, a testable model is developed. That and the results of a three-part search for B-T effects are reported in the section which follows.

* The opinions expressed here are those of the author and do not represent those of the Commissioners, Commission, or any of its staff. He expresses appreciation for comments from Robert E. McCormick and from an anonymous referee of this journal.

II. THE INSTITUTIONS

Since the legislative mandates of the 1970s, industries in the U.S. have been the direct objects of the environmental regulations.[1] That is, while individual firms and plants are considered in the developmental stages, effluent guidelines for water pollution control and emission standards for air pollution control are prepared and issued by the U.S. Environmental Protection Agency for industry and sub-industry categories. For example, there are guidelines for the iron and steel industry as well as for specialty steel manufacturers.

Generally speaking, EPA regulations call for point source controls. In other words, while a precise technology is not stated, levels of control are, and these are based on identified technologies which can be shown to achieve the level of control required at an identifiable cost. In addition to this general characteristic, EPA regulations require stricter control of new sources of pollution. The resulting bias in favor of old sources becomes an output restricting device for the affected industry.

At the firm level, economic gains can result from these institutions in several ways, neglecting the discovery of a net beneficial pollution control by-product. First, as suggested by the B-T analysis, cartel effects can cause the increased product price which accompanies output restrictions to exceed the increase in average costs associated with pollution control, especially when there is a bias against new entrants. In addition, some firms can gain economies of scale in pollution control leaving higher cost, marginal firms to determine industry price. Finally, firms adversely affected can choose to write off plant and equipment and thereby register a financial impact. In any case, intramarginal firms may gain economic rents, or polluters' profits.[2]

The B-T analysis gave no explicit treatment to regulatory-induced capital investments. Their point was carried by the assumption that output restrictions alone would meet the requirements for pollution reductions. In this sense, their analysis fails to meet the letter of the law that describes U.S. pollution control institutions. But, as is often the case, that lack of realism does not affect the predictive power of the B-T model.

The assumptions of the B-T model require that pollution be related to output. In a strict sense, environmental quality is achieved by having each firm in an industry reduce its output and thereby its effluent. Entry is controlled in order to maintain some targeted level of total pollution.

In actual practice, firms facing EPA regulations may reduce output to

[1] The relevant legislation is the Clean Air Amendments of 1970 and the amendments to the Federal Water Pollution Control Act, 1972. The air legislation, which established the requirements for point-source controls, was signed into law on December 30, 1970. Activities with respect to industry regulation began in 1971. The water legislation was signed in October 1972. In the analysis to follow, the period 1972–80 will be used as the time when regulation was effective. The selection of years is obviously imperfect.

[2] A successful cartel could also gain profits by specifying politically the kind of controls required, even to the point of reducing control expenditures below a level chosen in the absence of cartelizing regulation.

reduce pollution, but most often install capital equipment to control their environmental discharge. The installation of capital that contributes little to output raises the average cost of firms in the industry. That reduces the quantity demanded. In a growth economy, increases in demand pressing against industry supply will generate higher profits which would normally signal the entry of new firms or plants. However, if pollution standards are higher for new sources than for old, entry will be forestalled until the expected profit for the new entrant is high enough to cover all costs. A kind of blocked entry pricing results during the transition period, even if cartel control is not exerted. The result would be higher observable profits, lower investment in productive capital and equipment.

III. THE EMPIRICAL SEARCH

The empirical search for these predicted B-T effects involved a three-step procedure. First, a naive cross-sectional regression model of industry investment was posited which states that annual investment in nonpollution related capital by industry can be explained on the basis of industry profits lagged one year and investments in pollution control equipment in the same year. This prediction is based on both expansions of existing plants in an industry and on the entry of new firms.

Investments in pollution control equipment can be a substitute for other capital, if regulations are effective and if profits are so constrained that firms cannot afford both new plant capacity and pollution control. However, once expected rates of return are high enough, given sufficient demand and previously constrained investment, entry with pollution control will be positively related to other capital investments.

If the B-T effect is present, entry will be impeded and there will be significantly less investment in particular industries than predicted by the profit coefficient alone. That is, adjusting for profits and then examining a multi-industry estimate, for a given year, the unexplained residual for a given industry's investment in capital will be negative. Again, with profits held constant, further examination of residuals for a series of years would reveal runs of negative residuals for the constrained industry. In the absence of B-T effects, one would expect a random run of negative and positive residuals.

This first procedure identifies candidate industries for further analysis, with the important statistical finding turning on observed relative underinvestment in given industries. A second and related step in the search will involve a time series analysis of investment for each industry, and after adjusting for other specified variables requires that candidate industries have significantly negative association between investment and a dummy variable for the years when emission and effluent standards are in effect (1972–80).[3]

[3] See footnote 1.

The third and final step in the search for B-T effects is a stringent test that requires that each industry have positive profits whose rates of growth across the period of analysis exceed the average of the industries analyzed. If a particular industry survives all three tests that industry is declared a B-T industry. One that survives either step one or step two and has higher profit growth is termed a possible B-T industry.[4]

IV. THE THREE TESTS

The regression model used to identify industries which meet the first condition states:

$$\text{INV} = f(\text{PROFIT, AIR, WATER}),$$

where the dependent variable is nonpollution related capital investment, PROFIT is total after tax profits in the previous year, AIR is investment in air pollution control equipment, and WATER is investment in water pollution control equipment.

Data for 11 two-digit SIC code industries reported by the Department of Commerce were assembled for each year, 1973–80, and ordinary least squares regressions were run for each of the years.[5] The residuals were then examined and industries identified which had investment expenditures in a given year at least one standard deviation below the mean, and which had a dominant run of negative residuals. This procedure identified the first B-T candidates.

The regression results are shown in Table I, where the estimated par-

TABLE I
REGRESSION RESULTS

	1 *1974*	*2* *1975*	*3* *1976*	*4* *1977*	*5* *1978*	*6* *1979*	*7* *1980*
Intercept	0.776	1.736	1.161	0.4662	0.691	0.856	1.777
	(1.494)	(3.245)*	(1.771)	(1.505)	(0.709)	(0.690)	(0.878)
AIR	−1.443	−4.800	−0.333	1.583	4.801	−0.917	7.216
	(−0.589)	(−1.870)*	(−0.090)	(0.731)	(0.585)	(−0.110)	(0.556)
WATER	−0.667	4.533	1.334	1.359	−3.844	3.556	−1.452
	(−0.160)	(1.162)	(0.342)	(0.663)	(−0.402)	(0.266)	(−0.689)
PROFIT	0.0009	0.0005	0.0008	0.0007	0.0004	0.0010	0.0010
	(6.126)*	(3.420)*	(4.336)*	(12.06)*	(5.016)*	(4.452)*	(2.785)*
R^2	0.91	0.85	0.85	0.97	0.88	0.86	0.74
F	24.55	13.39	14.15	105.64	18.71	14.74	6.94

T statistics in parentheses. Asterisk indicates significant at 10 percent level.

[4] To satisfy the B-T hypothesis, it is not necessary that an industry earn positive profits. Indeed, an industry with negative profits could minimize its losses by means of a pollution control cartel.

[5] The analysis is limited by scant data on pollution control expenditures. These have been reported since 1973 at the 2-digit SIC code level. Some 2-digit industries were deleted because of inability to obtain compatible data on profits.

TABLE II
RESIDUALS OF ESTIMATED INVESTMENT

Industry	*1974*	*1975*	*1976*	*1977*	*1978*	*1979*	*1980*
Iron and Steel	−0.373	−0.183	−0.596	−0.516	−0.343	−0.849	−1.592
Nonferrous Metal	0.123	0.436	−0.114	−0.118	−0.283	−0.160	−1.976
Electrical Machinery	−0.537	−0.212	0.308	0.824	−0.150	−0.531	0.254
Machinery	−0.151	0.012	−0.831	−0.235	−2.281	−1.664	−1.946
Transportation	1.353	2.332	2.774	−0.368	3.229	4.839	8.136
Stone, Clay, Glass	−0.238	−0.187	−0.219	0.270	0.059	0.505	−1.781
Food	−0.249	−0.896	−0.895	−0.455	−0.222	−1.384	−0.335
Textile	−0.468	−1.265	−0.516	0.057	−0.147	−0.661	−1.706
Paper	0.837	−0.180	−0.322	0.377	0.702	1.149	1.888
Chemical	0.396	0.451	−0.007	−0.392	−0.586	−0.801	0.883
Petroleum	−0.691	−0.306	0.420	0.557	0.023	−0.442	−1.823
Standard Deviation	0.753	1.100	1.210	0.540	1.547	2.137	3.592

ameters of the model are reported. The sign and significance of the coefficient on AIR (1975) suggests a deterrent effect on investment in the earlier years, whereas the post-1976 period appears to be an entry period.[6]

The residuals of the estimate of new investment are reported in Table II, where Textiles (1975) and non-electrical machinery (1978) have residuals more than one standard deviation below the mean. An examination of the signs for the residuals across the tests shows dominant negative runs for iron and steel, non-ferrous metal, non-electrical machinery, food and textiles. When significant under-investment for a given year is considered with a series of negative runs, textiles and non-electrical machinery survive the first tests.

The next test was based on a time series analysis for the same 11 industries over the period 1967–80. Since data on investment in pollution control equipment were not maintained for the earlier years of the test, the basis regression model for each industry states:

$$INV = f(PROFIT, TREND, LAW),$$

where INV is total investment in new plant and equipment (including pollution control), PROFIT is net after tax profits lagged one year, TREND is an index variable to adjust for inflation and other unspecified trend effects, and LAW is a zero-one dummy variable denoting the years when pollution regulations were in effect for air and water; 1972–80 equals one.

Data for each industry were analyzed, and the results are reported in Table III. As shown by the F and Durbin-Watson statistics, each equation has a significant linear fit, and there are no strong indications of first order autocorrelation. An examination of the coefficients on LAW shows three cases where there is significantly negative association with the dependent variable, after

[6] The general lack of significance for AIR and WATER suggests that investment in non-pollution capital was not generally deterred by pollution control equipment, and that those expenditures were anticipated for planned alterations and expansions.

TABLE III
REGRESSION RESULTS, TIME SERIES 1967–80

Industry	*Intercept*	*Profit*	*Trend*	*Law*	R^2	*F*	*D.W.*
Iron and Steel	0.732	0.0006	0.140	−0.805	0.81	13.01	1.26
	(2.661)*	(3.732)*	(2.939)*	(−2.176)*			
Nonferrous Metal	0.113	0.0004	0.118	0.253	0.96	90.50	2.87
	(1.041)	(5.392)*	(5.550)*	(5.390)*			
Electrical Machinery	−1.369	0.0009	0.237	−0.177	0.96	95.38	1.87
	(−4.428)*	(5.331)*	(2.141)*	(−0.313)			
Machinery	0.612	0.0011	−0.242	0.399	0.95	69.15	1.118
	(1.411)	(4.486)*	(−0.994)	(0.536)			
Transportation	−4.435	0.0010	1.014	−2.031	0.93	43.82	1.118
	(−3.985)*	(2.885)*	(3.645)*	(−1.225)			
Stone, Clay, Glass	−0.3919	0.0013	0.1048	−2.311	0.97	118.36	2.408
	(−2.933)*	(5.621)*	(2.268)*	(−1.080)			
Food	0.2623	−0.0001	0.6239	−0.8931	0.97	142.10	2.392
	(1.071)	(−0.550)	(4.740)*	(−2.413)*			
Textiles	0.2395	0.0005	0.0486	0.0174	0.88	22.48	1.962
	(2.187)*	(2.400)*	(2.230)*	(0.127)			
Chemical	−0.609	0.0009	0.1227	0.5696	0.96	89.09	2.508
	(−1.193)	(3.130)*	(0.510)	(0.758)			
Paper	−0.0432	0.0012	0.1676	−0.4627	0.92	39.76	1.591
	(0.122)	(2.823)*	(1.156)	(−0.735)			
Petroleum	−1.917	0.0035	1.501	−6.353	0.96	81.31	1.226
	(−2.385)*	(2.567)*	(5.969)*	(−4.773)*			

T statistics in parentheses. Asterisk indicates significant at 10 percent level.

adjusting for profits and trend. The industries so identified are: iron and steel, food, and petroleum, with the latter industry having been subject to a number of shocks not controlled for in the model. The two industries which survived both parts of the first test are not included. However, iron and steel, and food had dominant negative residuals in the first test.

TABLE IV
INDUSTRY PROFITS, PERCENT CHANGE[a]
1973–80

Industry	*Percent Change*
Iron and Steel	39
Nonferrous Metal	105
Electrical Machinery	87
Nonelectrical Machinery	130
Transportation	−109
Stone, Clay, Glass	43
Food	117
Textiles	19
Paper	113
Chemicals	97
Petroleum	229
Mean	79.0

[a] Nominal dollars. Source: *Survey of Current Business*.

TABLE V
TEST RESULTS

Industry	Test One Part I	Test One Part II	Test Two	Test Three
Iron and Steel	N	Y	Y	N
Nonferrous	N	Y	N	Y
Electrical Machinery	N	N	N	Y
Non-electrical Machinery	Y	Y	N	Y
Transportation	N	N	N	N
Stone, Clay, Glass	N	N	N	N
Food	N	Y	Y	Y
Textiles	Y	Y	N	N
Paper	N	N	N	Y
Chemicals	N	N	N	Y
Petroleum	N	N	Y	Y

N: Did not pass the test.
Y: Passed the test.

The third and final hurdle to be jumped in the search for B-T effects requires that industry profits be expanding relative to the mean of the eleven industries analyzed. This would indicate an association between relative under-investment in plant and equipment, as shown by the first two tests, and higher growth in profits. The percentage change in nominal profits for each industry across 1973–80 is reported in Table IV. Of the industries analyzed and mentioned as candidates, non-electrical machinery, food, and petroleum have above average growth in profits. The caveat for petroleum is relevant here also.

TABLE VI
CAPITAL INVESTMENT BY MANUFACTURING SECTORS 1973–80
(BILLIONS)[a]

Industry	Total Non-Pollution Capital	Total Pollution Capital	Pollution's Share
Primary Metal	$37.7	6.9	18.4%
Fabricated Metal	18.6	0.7	3.7
Electrical Machinery	40.4	0.9	2.2
Non-Electrical Machinery	54.6	0.9	1.6
Auto	28.7	1.6	5.5
Aircraft	22.8	0.4	1.9
Stone, Clay, Glass	18.0	1.8	10.2
Food	39.7	1.9	4.8
Textiles	8.0	0.4	4.8
Pulp and Paper	27.7	3.1	11.4
Chemical	60.6	5.8	9.5
Petroleum	86.7	9.9	10.6
Rubber	12.8	0.4	3.0
Mining	63.4	2.3	3.6
Public Utilities	132.2	16.3	12.3

Source: Rutledge and O'Connor [4].
[a] Nominal dollars.

Based on the series of tests, no single industry survived each element. There are no clear-cut B-T industries. However, as shown in Table V, the food industries survived one part of the first test, negative runs, and two remaining tests. It is the closest candidate for nomination as a B-T industry. Nonelectrical machinery survived both parts of the first test and the third test. Petroleum survived tests two and three. They are termed possible B-T industries. The three candidates identified by these tests are listed along with 11 others in Table VI, which shows the proportion of total capital expenditures accounted for by pollution control investment during 1973–80. As indicated there, only the petroleum industry had relatively high pollution control capital expenditures. It should be noted, however, that large relative expenditures on pollution control equipment do not by themselves identify B-T industries. Capital expenditures can be the result of large scale entry. It can be argued that B-T industries could exist while spending very little on pollution control. Indeed, that is the essence of the argument put forward by Buchanan and Tullock.

V. SUMMARY

The first test described here related relative capital investment, a proxy for entry, for 11 industries to profits and pollution control expenditures. The second test examined each industry relative to its own time path, and sought to answer how that industry's expansion responded to a period environmental regulation. The two tests, when coupled with an examination of relative growth in profits, required a heavy burden of proof before accepting the B-T hypothesis. One industry "almost" survived the tests. Two industries ran very close in the search for "polluters profits."

Bruce Yandle,
Federal Trade Commission,
Washington, D.C., 20580,
U.S.A.

ACCEPTED SEPTEMBER 1982

REFERENCES

[1] Buchanan, J. M. and Tullock, Gordon, "Polluters' Profit and Political Response: Direct Controls versus Taxes," *American Economic Review*, Vol. 65, (March 1975), pp. 139–47.

[2] Koch, C. J. and Leone, Robert A., "The Clean Water Act: Unexpected Impacts on Industries," *Harvard Environmental Law Review*, Vol. 3, (1979), pp. 84–111.

[3] Mumy, G. E., "Long Run Efficiency and Property Rights Sharing for Pollution Control," *Public Choice*, Vol. 35, (1980), pp. 59–74.

[4] Rutledge, Gary L. and O'Connor, Betsy D., "Plant and Equipment Expenditures by Business for Pollution Abatement, 1973–80, and Planned 1981," *Survey of Current Business*, (June 1981), pp. 19–31.

THE JOURNAL OF INDUSTRIAL ECONOMICS 0022-1821 $2.00
Volume XXXII March 1984 No. 3

A NOTE ON THE USE OF INCORPORATION AS AN ESCAPE FROM USURY CEILINGS

W. J. Boyes and Dale Beck Furnish

I. INTRODUCTION

The structure of usury statutes varies from state to state. In particular some states have a limit on loan transactions involving unincorporated businesses while having no limit on transactions involving corporations. The purpose/policy behind this dichotomy stems from the industrial organization argument about relative bargaining strengths in a market. The unincorporated business is purported to involve people unsophisticated in financial transactions who, therefore, need protection. On the other hand, the corporation is large and sophisticated in financial matters and can fend for itself. The historical precedent for this distinction is the 1850 case of *New York Dry Dock Bank v. American Life Insurance & Trust Co.*[1] In the *Dry Dock Bank* Case a commercial borrower was able totally to evade repayment on a loan, both principal and interest being excused, because the court found that a 2000 pound discount on a 50,000 pound loan at 6 percent carried its charges past permissible interest rates of 7 per cent. The outcry was so great that the New York legislature created the corporate exemption to its usury statute so that no other commercially sophisticated lender like the Dry Dock Bank might hide behind the usury law to discharge its debts.[2]

The purpose of this brief paper is to suggest that the effects of the dichotomy may be slightly different from the salutary objectives of the critics of the *Dry Dock* decision or of the legislators of the corporate exemption. In particular, we present some evidence which suggests that the corporate exemption induced unincorporated firms to incorporate simply to avoid usury limits.

II. INCORPORATIONS AND USURY

The history of usury has been one of continual conflict between economic forces and the law.[3] At first, debate focused on whether any interest charges were proper for loans. Over time, interest became a commonplace element of exchange, whose propriety was above question, while debate shifted to the proper level for interest rates. A unitary level was initially sought, but broke

[1] See Boyes and Furnish [2, p. 88].
[2] See Boyes and Furnish [2, pp. 35–60, 125–56].
[3] For a very detailed historical review of the history of usury laws, see Boyes and Furnish [2, pp. 85–109].

down as credit usage extended to a broad variety of borrowers. Special categories were created and lawmakers accepted the necessity of distinct interest ceilings for different types of loans. Beginning with adoption of a small-loan act drafted by the Russell Sage Foundation early in this century, state legislatures created a series of special rates for particular loans. These categories include small consumer loans, larger personal loans, revolving credit loans, mortgage loans, unincorporated business loans, and corporation loans. Moreover, within each class of loans there are often sub-classifications, each having a different interest rate.[4]

These classifications are the legal response to economic forces, but they also create relative cost differentials which are bound to re-allocate resources, at least during time periods when one or more usury ceilings become binding. For example, the rapid inflationary period of the late 1970s drove market interest rates up against the usury limits in state after state, forcing lending institutions to ration credit by means other than interest rates. As several studies have pointed out,[5] the usury limit on individual loans forced consumer finance companies to refuse to loan to the higher risk individuals—those with insecure jobs or low incomes. The limit on single-family home mortgages was, whenever possible, avoided by requiring higher points, more initial costs, and higher down payments. Institutions altered their portfolios, refusing to loan for mobile homes, condominiums, and other categories of riskier loans. The unincorporated business was often crowded out of the market. Yet, as mentioned previously, many states had dichotomized the usury statutes between incorporated and unincorporated businesses. Hence, there was a path open to the unincorporated business which would enable it to obtain access to the credit markets. The question was whether the costs of following this path were less than the benefits.

In most states incorporation is a relatively easy and inexpensive process. State incorporation codes and case law set minimum standards for corporate charters by requiring that stockholders be granted certain rights. Once incorporated in a particular state, a corporation may do business in any other state, and generally, continue to be governed by the corporate code of the state of incorporation. According to the critics, the history of state corporation law is a "race to the bottom."[6] In fact, the history is largely one of the reduction of legal restrictions on management. Restrictions on the longevity of the corporation, the businesses in which it can engage, the authorization of stock, the classes of stock issued, dividend policy, discretion as to the holding of shareholder's meetings, the means of electing directors, the sales of assets, and the indemnification of officers are among the restrictions that have been eliminated or diminished by amendments to state corporation codes as states competed for the chartering business. As corporations have sought charters in

[4] See American Bankers Association [1].
[5] See Boyes and Furnish [2, pp. 61–85] for a review of the literature.
[6] See Cary [3] and Hazen [5].

states with less restrictive codes, other states have adopted similar codes in response. The similarity of incorporation statutes across states implies that firms need not move to Delaware or New Jersey, the earliest competitors for charters, to operate under the relaxed corporation codes.[7]

The relative cost of incorporating should have dropped significantly during the period of the late 1970s. The cost of incorporating had been reduced through state competition and the cost of not incorporating had risen because usury limits restricted an unincorporated business's access to the credit market. If this is the case we should find the rate at which firms incorporate to be substantially higher in states in which the usury statute is dichotomized between unincorporated and incorporated businesses than in states which treat these two classes uniformly.

We separated states into two samples, one consisting of those states whose usury statutes permitted higher interest rate charges on loans to incorporated than to unincorporated firms, and another made up of those states whose statutes created no dichotomy. We then calculated the mean rate of growth of new incorporations in each of the two groups over two significant time periods. The first period examined was 1978–79, when market rates bounced up against or exceeded the usury ceilings in virtually every state. The second period we selected was 1974–77, when market rates on loans remained substantially below almost all usury ceilings (and a period during which the usury statutes were not altered).[8] We expected that in the 1978–79 period there would have been substantial demand pressure by private businesses to maintain their access to loan funds by incorporating,[9] while in the other period no benefit would have accrued to business borrowers based on the corporate status of their enterprise.

During the 1978–79 period the rate of new incorporations in the states with a dichotomy in usury limits between incorporated and unincorporated businesses grew 56 percent while in the other states the rate of growth was only 23 percent. We used a test of means to examine the hypothesis of no difference between the two groups of states. Under the assumption that the two groups are random samples from normal distributions having the same variance, the null hypothesis of identical means can be tested with a t-test where the t distribution has $n + m - 2$ degrees of freedom and where $n + m$ is the size of the combined samples.[10] The difference was significant at any reasonable level

[7] See Nader *et al.* [7].

[8] Data on incorporations are from Dun and Bradstreet, Inc. and data on usury limits are from American Bankers Association [1]. While a few states have "floating ceilings" where the general usury statute ties the ceiling rate to a market rate, most have a general usury limit that is changed only very seldom. Most states altered their statutes in 1973–early 1974 and in 1979–80 but only after credit virtually dried up as market rates escalated past the ceilings. For further discussion see Boyes and Furnish [2, particularly pp. 35–64].

[9] Indeed, we talked to officers of financial institutions who indicated to us that they sometimes suggested to rejected private applicants for business loans that if they would incorporate, then loans would be available at higher interest rates.

[10] See Hogg and Allen [6, pp. 301–303].

for the 1978–79 period. However, during the 1974–77 period the differences were not significant. The growth rate for states without a dichotomy was 22 percent while it was 20 percent for the states whose usury statutes differentiated firms by corporate status.

III. CONCLUSIONS

Perhaps one could rationalize the dichotomy of the usury treatment between unincorporated and incorporated business by noting that it works like a form of price discrimination. The unincorporated firm must make the decision to enter the world of corporations and give up the usury statutes applicable to the unincorporated business. In the sense of the law, the firm has moved from unsophisticated to sophisticated market agent.[11]

In addition, perhaps one might defend a dichotomy based on corporate status on the grounds that the liability of a corporation is limited to its business assets, so that a lender decides to loan to a corporation based on carefully defined collateral, aware that it cannot reach personal resources of the principals. There may be a higher risk to the lender, justifying higher interest rates on such loans. On the other hand, owners of unincorporated businesses hazard not only the assets of the specific business for which they borrow money, but *all* of their other personal assets save those few items exempted by law from execution. Since such borrowers may lose virtually all of their estate, and guarantee their business loans with their personal assets, perhaps they represent less of a credit risk for lenders and deserve a lower interest rate than the corporate debtor. In both cases, however, a free market would properly evaluate these risks and price accordingly. There would be no need for the law to specify a price differential faced by incorporated and unincorporated firms. However, a market effect which pushes a prospective debtor to incorporate may have the salutary effect of protecting the debtor from excessively encumbering personal assets for the high-risk purpose of a business loan[12] and in this sense reduce social costs.

In any event, it is highly unlikely that legislators intended the usury statutes to work as an incentive for incorporating. In fact, in recent years there was a great deal of concern over the ease with which a firm could be incorporated. Much of the legal literature decried the move toward less restrictive incorporation codes. Competition among states for corporate charters has been criticized in the legal literature where it was viewed as "unhealthy" because it

[11] For a review of these arguments, see Cary [3], Dodd and Leftwich [4], and Nader *et al.* [7].

[12] It is possible, of course, for an individual owner to sign personal guarantees for loans made to his incorporated business, thus giving away the benefits of limited liability. A lender thus might use the personal guaranty of its debtor to charge the corporation-loan interest rate on credit secured by all debtor's personal assets.

supposedly results in a trend toward pro-management statutes.[13] It is alleged that in their quest to make statutes more appealing to corporate management, some states provide management with so much freedom from stockholder control that shareholders receive inadequate protection. Thus, to the extent that usury restrictions have acted as an incentive for less sophisticated borrowers to incorporate, they have run counter to a growing concern to impose more restrictions on the act of incorporating.

It is likely that the incorporation loophole for evading usury limits was created inadvertently by legislators who did not realize that it would bring about the reallocation of resources during periods of binding usury constraints. The legislative purpose for the dichotomy was to hold a sophisticated class of debtors to interest rates for which they had bargained. The incorporation loophole temporarily disappeared in 1980 as most states and then the Federal Government, by the Monetary Control Act of 1980, removed virtually all usury ceilings. However, the federal legislation, and that of most states, carried a sunset provision which will force reconsideration of the usury question by 1984. The outcome of the reconsideration will depend on how the legislatures weigh the political benefits and costs. We would expect that as legislatures confront the issue of usury laws afresh, if the fact of unsophisticated parties' incorporation to evade usury ceilings comes to their attention, some may find added reason to increase controls on the process of incorporation or to support federal incorporation statutes. Others may do away with the dichotomy while still others may accept the effect which has evolved through the loophole, and leave it as a salutary control.

W. J. Boyes and Dale Beck Furnish,
Arizona State University,
Tempe,
A.Z., 85287,
U.S.A.

ACCEPTED SEPTEMBER 1982

REFERENCES

[1] AMERICAN BANKERS ASSOCIATION, *Analysis of State Usury Statutes*, May 1979.

[2] BOYES, W. J. and DALE BECK FURNISH (eds.), "Usury and the Monetary Control Act of 1980," Special Project, *Arizona State Law Journal*, Vol. 1981, No. 1, pp. 32–292.

[3] CARY, W. L., "Federalism and the Corporate Law: Reflections Upon Delaware," *Yale Law Journal* 83, No. 4 (1974), pp. 663–707.

[4] DODD, P. and R. LEFTWICH, "The Market for Corporate Charters: Unhealthy Competition versus Federal Regulation," *Journal of Business*, Vol. 53, No. 3 (July 1980), pp. 259–84.

[13] That this change in status is left to the discretion of the individuals involved is consistent with other areas of the law. See, e.g., Uniform Commercial Code §2-104(1), which defines "merchant" as "a person . . . who *holds himself out* as having knowledge or skill peculiar to the practices or goods involved in the transaction." (Emphasis added).

[5] HAZEN, THOMAS L., "Corporate Charting and the Securities Markets: Shareholder Suffrage, Corporate Responsibility and Managerial Accountability," *Wisconsin Law Review* (1978), pp. 389–439.

[6] HOGG, ROBERT V. and ALLEN T. CRAIG, *Introduction to Mathematical Statistics* (The Macmillan Co., New York, 1970).

[7] NADER, RALPH M., MARK GREEN and J. SELIGMAN, *Taming the Giant Corporation*, (Norton, New York, 1976).

THE JOURNAL OF INDUSTRIAL ECONOMICS 022–1821 $2.00
Volume XXXII March 1984 No. 3

SUB-CONTRACTING BETWEEN SMALL-SCALE ENTERPRISES IN DEVELOPING COUNTRIES: A NOTE

JAN J. P. VAN HEEMST*

THE development of sub-contracting practices is often referred to as one of the ways to stimulate the growth of small-scale enterprises and the creation of employment opportunities. However, in most of the writings proposing such sub-contracting practices, the kind of sub-contracting patterns aimed at relate in most cases implicitly or explicitly to situations in which the sub-contracting firm (i.e. the principal or parent firm) is of a relatively larger size than the sub-contractor, i.e. the small-scale firm. Indeed, in many cases, the parent firm is supposed to be situated in the modern sector, operating on a larger scale and sometimes being of foreign origin and ownership. But it can be argued that the potential of sub-contracting relationship between firms of a small size should in this respect not be overlooked, and deserves to be given more attention.

In the literature dealing with sub-contracting, various categories of reasons are presented for which a parent firm may involve a sub-contractor in its productive activities. The three major categories[1] to be found in this respect may be summarised as:

(1) cost considerations;
(2) scarcity or absence of necessary inputs;
(3) shorter-term capacity considerations.

In our opinion all three categories apply to a large extent—at least in principle—also to situations in which both parent firm and sub-contractor are small in size, as will be argued below.

Beginning with cost considerations, this reason for sub-contracting relates to cases in which the sub-contracting firm is in a position to carry out a certain task in a less costly manner because it can make use of certain factors of production more efficiently, or because it pays lower prices for its factor inputs, e.g. it pays a lower wage rate. A more efficient use of factors of production may occur, for example, when the sub-contracting firm is in a position to employ—on a more permanent, longer term basis—a piece of equipment or machinery at a higher utilisation rate, or when the services of staff employed can be more fully utilised.

* The author would like to thank his colleagues Prof. C. Cooper, Prof. S. Sideri and Mr. B. Helmsing for their encouraging comments on a previous version.

[1] See for a more detailed discussion in this connection for example Watanabe [9, pp. 56–58]; or UNIDO [8, pp. 24–32].

Within the context of two small-scale firms this reasoning may apply to situations in which one small-scale firm wishes to sub-contract a certain stage of its production process to another small-scale firm which specialises in carrying out that stage, because it is for the former firm, given its normal level of production, uneconomical to purchase the equipment needed for carrying out that stage in its own factory. Whenever it is possible from an organisational or technical point of view to break down the production process into a number of discrete stages, sub-contracting may in this case lead to a reduction in production costs of the small-scale enterprise responsible for the final product. Especially in developing countries, where small-scale firms often face high cost of capital, the savings obtained in this context through sub-contracting may be substantial.

Re scarcity or absence of certain vital inputs, one should in the first place think here of those cases in which the contractor lacks specific technical know-how or skills. But also the cases in which the contractor does not possess certain machinery or equipment that is needed in the production process, and thus has to rely on the services of a sub-contractor, fall under this heading.

Small-scale firms, particularly in developing countries, frequently suffer from lack of financial resources, for which reason it may not be possible to purchase all the equipment needed for carrying out the various stages of the production process. In such circumstances the producer has to look for certain alternatives, one of which may be the sub-contracting of the stage for which the equipment needed cannot be secured.[2] The firm to which that—normally somewhat capital intensive—stage is sub-contracted may also be a small-scale one, which specialises in carrying out that particular stage for those firms which are not able (or willing) to do it by themselves. It should be said, however, that the circumstances leading to this kind of sub-contracting relationship, i.e. lack of financial resources of the parent firm, may at the same time form a risk for the sub-contractor. This, because a weak financial position of the parent firm may negatively affect its ability to meet its financial obligations in time, thus affecting the financial and economic position of the sub-contractor.

In general, shorter-term capacity considerations play a role when the parent firm is confronted with levels of demand, for example during peak seasons, which can in the short term not be met by its existing production capacity; it may then fall back on the services of a sub-contractor for producing a part of the output. It is clear that also in this case the parent firm may be a small one, sub-contracting a part of the productive activities to be carried out to another small firm. However, since sub-contracting which takes place for capacity reasons normally is on a short-term basis, it seems less

[2] The forming of a producers' cooperative, which may be another alternative in these circumstances seems in a number of cases an unattractive one. Referring to the informal sector, Sethuraman [7] argues that informal sector entrepreneurs (in Africa) are generally reluctant to form cooperatives. Another source from which it becomes clear that certain types of co-operatives are often no success, at least in Africa, is Gosselin [3].

suitable for the development of a more permanent, continuous economic relationship between the contractor and the sub-contractor.

The little empirical evidence available[3] suggests that some sub-contracting practices among small-scale entrepreneurs can be found in Africa, Asia and Latin America. As far as Africa is concerned, one example which can be given relates to practices of small-scale, informal sector undertakings active in the field of wood working in Lomé, Togo, which make use of the services of other small entrepreneurs, owning a combine, for carrying out certain operations.[4] In Ghana similar practices can also be found on a fairly wide scale in the branches of automobile repair, metal work and shoe manufacture.[5] Re footwear production, especially sandal making, it may be mentioned that a large number of small-scale, informal sector producers in Ghana sub-contract several stages (notably sewing, pressing and finishing) to other small-scale enterprises.[6] Consequently, several small-scale firms are involved in producing a pair of sandals, with each firm needing only a small amount of fixed capital. One advantage of these practices is the relatively low cost of production for the contractor, as has been demonstrated elsewhere.[7] Another aspect of it is the reduction in quality differences between large-scale firm products and small-scale firm products. This is because the sub-contracting practices of the small-scale firms have made it possible for them to manufacture a product through a number of mechanised operations that make the product as such more comparable to those produced by larger-scale firms.[8]

Other evidence, related to other continents, cites Singapore as an example of an Asian country where sub-contracting practices between small-scale enterprises can be found,[9] while as far as Latin America is concerned we would mention here the evidence existing on Peru. With regard to the latter country it may be said that sub-contracting between small-scale firms in Lima cannot only be found in the production of footwear and clothing, but also in relation to the manufacture of stationery products, transport vehicles, etc.[10] In addition, it may be said that small-scale firm sub-contracting relationships to be found in Lima in fact form part of a larger chain of relationships involving firms of various size, at least as far as certain types of products are concerned.

A final point worth mentioning in connection with the empirical evidence

[3] A rather extensive survey by us of empirical literature dealing with small-scale industry and with the informal sector, rendered only very little relevant evidence, most of which is referred to below.

[4] See Nihan, Demol and Jondoh [6, p. 644].

[5] See Sethuraman [7, p. 347].

[6] See Aryee [1, p. 16 and p. 47]. These sub-contracting practices between small-scale footwear producers in Ghana has also been dealt with in our own work. See van Heemst [4].

[7] See van Heemst [4].

[8] *Cf.* Aryee [1, p. 47].

[9] See Fong [2, p. 21].

[10] See MacEwan Scott [5, pp. 114–15].

is the observation that the development of sub-contracting relationships between informal sector enterprises results in a clustering together of these enterprises.[11] In this regard it may be argued that in order to have a proper functioning sub-contracting relationship maintained between small-scale enterprises of a durable nature, the parties involved should certainly be located in the same town, and preferably even in the same area (e.g. a market area or an industrial estate). In policy terms this would imply that any measures that facilitate a close location to each other of the firms concerned should be considered as favourable for the maintenance and development of sub-contracting practices.

From what has been said above it may be deduced that various situations can be hypothesized in which sub-contracting relationships between small-scale enterprises would develop which are of a more than incidental nature, while moreover such relationships may be beneficial, at least in principle, to both the contractor and the sub-contractor, and in addition may have certain positive aspects from a socio-economic point of view. More empirical research in this field seems desirable in order to obtain more conclusive evidence.

Jan J. P. van Heemst,
Institute of Social Studies,
P.O. Box 90733,
2509 LS The Hague,
Holland.

ACCEPTED JULY 1982

REFERENCES

[1] ARYEE, G. A., *Income Redistribution, Technology and Employment in the Footwear Industry*, working paper World Employment Programme Reseach, ILO, Geneva, 1981.

[2] FONG, H. D., *Small Industry in Singapore*, Institute of Business Studies, Nanyang University Singapore, 1971.

[3] GOSSELIN, G., *Developpement et Tradition dans les Societés Rurales Africaines,* ILO, Geneva, 1970.

[4] VAN HEEMST, J., *Scale, Organisation and Efficiency in Footwear Production: An Analysis of Some Ghanaian Data*, Occasional paper no. 95, Institute of Social Studies, The Hague, 1982.

[5] MACEWAN SCOTT, A., 'Who are the Self-employed?' in Bromley, R., and Gerry C. (eds), *Casual Work and Poverty in Third World Cities*, pp. 105–29 (John Wiley & Sons New York, 1979).

[6] NIHAN, G., DEMOL, E. and JONDOH, C., 'The Modern Informal Sector in Lomé', *International Labour Review*, 118, 5, (September–October 1979) pp. 631–44.

[7] SETHURAMAN, S. V., 'The Urban Informal Sector in Africa', *International Labour Review*, 116, 3, (November–December 1977), pp. 343–52.

[8] UNIDO, *Sub-contracting for Modernizing Economies,* Vienna, 1974, ID/129.

[9] WATANABE, S., 'Sub-contracting, Industrialisation and Employment Creation'. *International Labour Review*, 104, 1 (July–Aug. 1971), pp. 51–76.

[11] *Cf.* Sethuraman [7, p. 347].

THE JOURNAL OF INDUSTRIAL ECONOMICS 0022–1821 $2.00
Volume XXXII March 1984 No. 3

TESTING STIGLER'S INTERPRETATION OF "THE DIVISION OF LABOR IS LIMITED BY THE EXTENT OF THE MARKET"*

DAVID LEVY

GEORGE Stigler [21] has written one of the few papers on the topic of vertical integration which provides empirical implications and evidence.[1] The implications follow from his interpretation of Adam Smith's theorem, "The division of labor is limited by the extent of the market". In support of the implications, Stigler presents evidence of changes in the level of vertical integration in the textile industry and in the U.S. manufacturing sector as a whole.

In a recent article in this journal, Tucker and Wilder [23] present empirical results which they claim are consistent with Stigler's hypothesis. They conduct an interindustry study using firm level and industry level data. Their industry level study uses data collected by the Census of Manufacturers at the plant level. Tucker and Wilder provide no justification for using plant level data and, as Eckard [7] points out in a recent note, vertical integration within a plant need not be related to vertical integration of the firm.

Another and possibly more serious shortcoming of Tucker and Wilder's paper is the lack of a clear statement of the relationship between their empirical tests and Stigler's hypothesis. Early in the article, they state Stigler's hypothesis as "vertical integration should be the typical development in growing industries, with vertical disintegration more prominent in declining industries" [23, p. 82]. However, in their regression equations they include firm size and firm growth rate variables claiming that these variables are "more representative of Stigler's maturity concept" [23, p. 85] than industry size and growth rate. They do not explain why this is true. They go on to claim that both of these variables are expected to have negative signs according to Stigler's hypothesis, again without explanation. They also include concentration ratios in their estimated equations without any justification.

In this paper, Stigler's hypothesis is reexamined in an attempt to provide a clearer link between the theory and the empirical tests. The first section summarizes Stigler's analysis and argues that his stated assumptions are not sufficient to justify his conclusions. In Section II, Stigler's analysis is

* Special thanks go to the Research Program in Competition and Business policy, UCLA, directed by J. Fred Weston for the use of their data. I would also like to thank Benjamin Klein, Harold Demsetz, Kwang Chung, Hugh Rockoff, Irvin Tucker, Ronald Wilder and an anonymous referee for comments on earlier drafts of this paper.

[1] A recent review of the theoretical literature on vertical integration can be found in Kaserman [10] but there is no discussion of empirical evidence for the different rationales.

reformulated to provide specific implications. An empirical test of the implications is contained in Section III. The tests are conducted using industry level data collected at the corporate level. Separate equations are estimated to explain the level of vertical integration in different industries and changes in the level of integration over time. Section IV summarizes the empirical results and compares them with the results obtained by Tucker and Wilder and others. The results are consistent with the implications from our reformulation of Stigler's analysis.

I. STIGLER'S INTERPRETATION OF ADAM SMITH'S THEOREM

Stigler interprets Smith's theorem in terms of the relationship between vertical integration and the "extent of the market". Production of a final good is viewed as "a series of distinct operations" or "functions".[2] Vertical integration is then defined as the production of different functions in the same firm and specialization is the production of different functions in separate firms.[3] Stigler's use of the term, extent of the market, is less clear. He generally seems to be referring to industry demand for the final product and, except where otherwise indicated, this meaning is presumed in our discussion.

Stigler analyzes the effect of changes in the extent of the market on the vertical integration of functions subject to increasing and decreasing costs in the relevant range. According to his analysis, the firm starts out vertically integrated. As demand increases, firms vertically disintegrate. They spin off the decreasing cost functions and purchase from new firms entering to meet the demand for the increasing cost activities' products. The process reverses itself as demand declines. Stigler concludes, "Vertical disintegration is the typical development in growing industries, vertical integration in declining industries" [21, p. 135].

Stigler is not explicit about the conditions assumed in arriving at his conclusions. To justify initial integration of the decreasing cost acitivity, he states that "the scale of the product may be too small to support a specialized firm or firms" [21, p. 133; see also p. 136]. This statement might follow from a specific set of assumption about the setup costs of a new firm and demand conditions. However, Stigler does not explicitly state such assumptions. Therefore it is not clear why a specialized firm does not produce the decreasing cost function from the start to take advantage of scale economies.

[2] In his graphical analysis, Stigler explicitly assumes that a constant proportion is maintained between the rate of output of each function and that no complementarity exists between the costs of each function. He claims to make these assumptions for expository convenience, but it becomes clear in our discussion below that complementarities play an essential role in justifying his conclusions.

[3] Stigler's use of the term, specialization, is unusal. Clearly, Adam Smith's notion of the division of labor as described in the pin factory did not imply the production of distinct operations in separate firms. In fact, increased specialization may in general take place within a firm or in separate firms (see Levy [14] for further discussion). Nevertheless, Stigler's use of the term is accepted here to be consistent with his discussion.

Without further restrictions on the analysis, it could also be argued that the integrated firm would never spin off the decreasing cost function. While continuing to produce for itself the integrated firm could also sell to others (as demand increases) in order to take advantage of scale economies.[4] The same basic objections can be raised against Stigler's analysis of the increasing cost function. Without further specification, there is no basis for determining whether the increasing cost function will be performed in a specialized firm or in an integrated firm.

In order to derive more definite implications, the advantages of vertical integration and specialization must be clearly specified. In the next section, specific factors affecting the costs of vertical integration and specialization are examined.[5]

II. TESTABLE IMPLICATIONS SUGGESTED BY STIGLER'S ANALYSIS

Testable implications are suggested here by drawing upon and extending Stigler's analysis. The hypotheses relate the effects of three separate facets of the "extent of the market" to costs associated with specialization and integration. Two hypotheses are developed by modifying Stigler's analysis of the decreasing cost activity to allow for changes in the number of firms and to incoporate the effects of demand growth. Another hypothesis is based on Stigler's discussion of managerial anticomplementarities.

In his discussion of the decreasing cost activity, Stigler provides a basis for the assertion that firms start out vertically integrated. He argues:

> . . . Young industries are often strangers to the established economic system. They require new qualities of materials and hence make their own; they must overcome technical problems in the use of their products and cannot wait for potential users to overcome them; they must persuade customers to abandon other commodities and find no specialized merchants to undertake this task. These young industries must design their specialized equipment and often manufacture it, and they must undertake to recruit . . . skilled labor. [21, p. 136].

[4] Williamson [31, pp. 15–19] has criticized Stigler's analysis for similar reasons. He also argues that Stigler's analysis requires further specification of the costs associated with vertical integration and market alternatives.

[5] Coase [5] has stated that firms will continue to add activities to their production schedule until "the costs of organizing an extra transaction within the firm are equal to the costs involved in carrying out the transaction in the open market, or, to the costs of organizing by another entrepreneur" [5, p. 340]. The approach in the next section is closely patterned after this framework.

The importance of Coase's article has also been mentioned by Stigler who later (in his book of readings [21]) appends to his original article the statement, "Reference should have been, and now is, made to R. H. Coase" [21, p. 141].

The analysis in the next section makes explicit transactions cost considerations as discussed by Coase and later developed by Williamson [31], [32].

This statement implies that producers at different stages have asymmetric information about technology and market conditions and that vertical integration facilitates information transfer between stages. However, Stigler does not explain why this capability is present within the firm but not present between firms. Nor does he explicitly relate the argument to industry scale. He merely claims that effective information transfer is a problem in "young" industries.

In a discussion of Stigler's analysis, Adelman [1] has expanded upon the effect of industry age. Associating young industries with rapid growth and mature industries with slow growth, he argues:

> As the firms and their industry grow, they do so under the forced draft of demand chronically in excess of supply at prevailing prices . . . A sluggish response (by input suppliers) will often force the growing firm to provide its own supplies and/or marketing outlets. [1, p. 319].

According to this statement, supply reliability problems arise in young industries experiencing rapid growth. This might occur due to an inability to transfer information about quantity demanded (as suggested in this statement) or about product specification (as suggested by Stigler).[6] However, the argument again depends on the unstated assumption that information can be more efficiently transferred within the firm than between firms.[7] Given this assumption, we can accept Adelman's conclusion that the "expanding industry (is expected) to be more highly integrated than the relatively stable one" [1, p. 319]. Equivalently, vertical integration is expected to be positively related to industry demand growth.[8]

A rationale for vertical disintegration is suggested in Stigler's discussion of his complementary assumption. He states:

> Actually many processes will be rival . . . Sometimes the rivalry will be technological . . . but almost always it will be managerial; the wider the range of functions the firm undertakes, the greater the tasks of coordination.

[6] Investigation of the product life cycle (see e.g., Levitt [13] suggests that products tend to be less standardized in the earlier stages of the product life cycles (i.e., the introduction and growth stages). Lack of standardized technology and marketing practices would be expected to increase the requirements for efficient information transfer (as implied in Stigler's discussion).

[7] For justification of the view that vertical integration facilitates information transfer, see Williamson [31, esp. pp. 31–37] or Arrow [3]. Williamson argues that coding systems within the firm, internal auditing capabilities and contingent reward schemes facilitate information flows.

[8] Demand growth is a proxy here for stages in the industry life cycle. Another proxy might simply be the industry's age. However, Gold [8] found that industries have widely varying life cycle patterns over time. Evidence in the marketing literature (see e.g. Polli and Cook [19]) also suggests that age does not correspond very well with the product life cycle. In industries experiencing continual technological change, there may even be a series of life cycles. As an alternative for age, Polli and Cook use industry demand growth to classify stages in the life cycle (see also Simon [20] for a recent application).

Stigler [21] elaborates on the effect of managerial diseconomies in a later discussion: "When a firm supplies only a part of its needs for some process . . . the rising costs of internal coordination are in fact the basic explanation for partial recourse to purchase" [21, p. 171]. This latter statement would follow when internal costs increase with firm size and the costs of managing dissimilar activities increase more than the costs of managing a uniform activity.[9] Under these conditions, vertical integration will be inversely related to the scale of the maintained activities.

Another important (and measurable) aspect of the extent of the market that might be expected to affect vertical integration is the number of firms in an industry. For example, Williamson [31], [32] maintains that "small numbers bargaining problems" create incentives for vertical integration. Small numbers situations occur when economies of scale arising with experience, location or production of a specialized component confer cost advantages on a producing firm (see also Klein, Crawford and Alchian [11]). Because of the lack of alternative buyers and sellers, firms are able to take advantage of their bargaining position. To internalize the associated costs, firms vertically integrate. Williamson [32] states:

> As generic demand grows and the number of supply sources increases exchange that was once transaction-specific loses this characteristic and greater reliance on market-mediated governance is feasible [32, p. 260].

Hence, vertical integration will be positively related to the fewness of firms.

This relationship between vertical integration and the fewness of firms can also be justified by extending Stigler's discussion of the decreasing cost activity. As in Stigler's analysis, assume that the decreasing cost activity is vertically integrated initially and that the output of this activity is used only in the firm. These assumptions can be justified by informational considerations and small numbers bargaining problems of the type discussed above. Now it is also assumed that the scale at which the vertically integrated firm produces each maintained function is held constant so that the number of firms producing at each stage increases as industry demand increases. Under these conditions, the incentives for a firm to specialize in the decreasing cost activity increases as the relative advantages of scale economies increase.

The argument is illustrated using Figure 1 where Y_{VI} represents the average costs to an integrated firm engaging in the decreasing cost activity and Y_S represents the average costs of a specialist firm. Initially, the integrated firms produce the quantity Q_1 at an average cost of C_1 and the specialist firm would produce the same quantity Q_1 at a higher average cost

[9] Further discussion of managerial diseconomies associated with firm size can be found in Williamson [31, see esp. chapter 7]. The claim that the costs of managing dissimilar activities add disproportionately to internal costs has also been made by Coase [5, p. 343] and Alchian and Demsetz [2, p. 343, fn. 18].

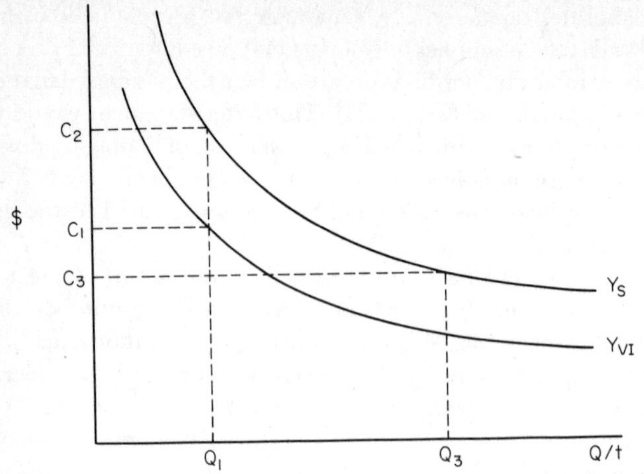

FIGURE 1
Production of the Decreasing Cost Activity.

of C_2 (due to small numbers bargaining problems and information costs). The specialist firm does not find it profitable to produce. As industry demand increases and new firms enter the downstream industry, the specialist firm can expand its production and move to a point such as Q_3 with costs of C_3. Meanwhile, the integrated firm continues to produce Q_1 since the amount produced of the maintained functions is held constant. Because the specialized firm can produce at lower costs than the integrated firm, the integrated firm spins off the decreasing cost activity and buys from the specialized firm at a price lower than its average costs.[10] Hence, vertical integration is again expected to be positively related to the fewness of firms producing at the different stages of production.[11]

III. EMPIRICAL RESULTS

In the preceding section, the "extent of the market" was decomposed into three distinct characteristics, each hypothesized to have a separate effect on vertical integration. The hypotheses have been tested using the following regression equation:

$$\mathrm{VI}_{it} = \beta_0 + \beta_1 \mathrm{AVGFS}_{it} + \beta_2 \mathrm{DG}_{it} + \beta_3 \mathrm{CONC}_{it}$$

[10] As pointed out by an anonymous referee, this argument does not require that economies of scale continue indefinitely for the decreasing cost activity. It is only necessary that there is some point at which average costs of the specialized firm are below C_1.
[11] Carlton [4] investigates economies associated with risk pooling. His analysis also suggests that the level of integration will be positively related to the fewness of firms.

where

VI_{it} = level of vertical integration in industry i at time t
$AVGFS_{it}$ = average firm size in industry i at time t
DG_{it} = demand growth in industry i at time t
$CONC_{it}$ = concentration (fewness of firms) in industry i at time t

β_1 is expected to be negative since average firm size creates a disincentive to integrate due to rising costs of internal control. Firms are expected to integrate vertically in the faster growing industries in order to reduce information costs, implying β_2 will be positive.[12] Since fewness of firms at each stage leads to an increased likelihood of small numbers bargaining problems among nonintegrated firms and less incentives for specialized firms to take advantage of scale economies, β_3 is expected to be positive.

The vertical integration, firm size and demand growth variables were created using data obtained from the Census-Link publications. The Link enterprise data relates establishment level data collected by the Census of Manufacturers to the financial statistics of the owning companies (as reported to the IRS), so that the data are at the corporate level. The data are then aggregated to about the three-digit industry level. To create the vertical integration variable, the ratio of value added to sales was calculated. This measure is subject to systematic biases, but special precautions described below were taken in our estimation procedures.[13] Firm size[14] was measured

[12] Demand growth is a proxy for life cycle effects. Along with demand growth, Tucker and Wilder [23] also included age variables in their equations to capture life cycle effects. Age variables were not included in this study because of the extremely tenuous relationship of age with industry life cycle effects (see footnote 8) and difficulties in accurately determining the age for industries. Furthermore, in an earlier study (Levy [14]) where firm level data were used, statistical tests indicated nonhomogeneous age effects across firms.

[13] The value added/sales ratio depends on the final stage of production of the firm and treats backward and forward integration asymmetrically. For further discussion of these problems, see Adelman [1] or Levy [14, Chapter 3].

Another problem, arising with the use of LINK data, is that value added does not include wholesale, retail and service industries. Although the sample here includes firms primarily engaged in manufacturing, this omission will bias the value added measure for firms integrated into those sectors. I would like to thank I. Tucker and R. Wilder for pointing out that measurement problem.

Recently, Maddigan [17] proposed an alternative measure that avoids the asymmetric treatment. However, the proposed measure does not account for partial integration within the industries as they are defined. This problem is likely to be especially severe in our study, since the data are collected at the three digit industry level and firms producing at different stages are often contained in the same industry.

[14] Industry sales is an imperfect measure of the scale of activities, since it is affected by the level of forward integration, i.e. forward integration would increase sales even if the scale of activities remained unchanged. However, this measurement error would tend to bias β_1 in a positive direction (since the error would induce a positive correlation between AVGFS and VI) and thus bias the results against the hypothesized effect.

The equations reported below were also estimated with value added per firm as an alternative measure of firm size. The results were substantively the same (e.g. the signs of the coefficients were in the same direction), but in some cases the coefficients became insignificant. The coefficient on the average firm size variable was negative but insignificant in the difference equation and negative but significant in the levels equation. These results are not reported here, because the value added measure of firm size is susceptible to bias from changes in both forward and backward integration.

as industry sales divided by the number of firms in the industry and deflated by the producer price index (from the 1978 *Statistical Abstract* p. 484). Demand growth was calculated as present deflated sales divided by preceding period deflated sales.[15]

Fewness of firms was measured by an industry concentration ratio. Four-firm concentration ratios of four-digit industries were available in the Census of Manufactures reports. To obtain industry concentration ratios corresponding to the IRS industries, four-digit concentration ratios were weighted by the number of employees in each of the constituent four-digit SIC industries of firms in the Link industries.[16]

The Census-Link and concentration data were available for the years 1963, 1967 and 1972. However, many industries were excluded from the original sample because data required to construct a particular variable were unavailable, industries became more aggregated[17] or because of dramatic changes in the classification of firms in a particular industry.[18] The final data set contained 38 industries for each of the three years. The final industries are listed in Table I and the means of the variables for particular years are listed in Table II. It is interesting to note that the mean level of vertical integration declined slightly from 1963 to 1972 for the industries in our sample.

Two sets of regressions were estimated to test the empirical implications. In the first set of equations, the variables were all estimated in levels form and the cross sectional data were pooled for the three years. The variables were differenced in the second set of equations, so that each variable was measured in terms of its percentage change over the period from 1963 to 1972.[19] Although estimation of the equations in difference form involves a loss of degrees of freedom, it acts as a check on the sensitivity of the results to omitted time-invariant cross sectional variables and cross sectional biases in the vertical integration measure.[20] The levels and difference equations were estimated in log and linear form. Only the equations in log form are reported here, but the choice of functional form did not substantially affect the results.

[15] The percentage change in sales is an appropriate measure of demand growth when the demand curve is unit elastic in the relevant ranges.

[16] The employee weights were originally obtained from the Census-Link publications. The number of employees was used as weights rather than sales since it is not sensitive to how close the stage production is to the final production stage.

[17] Originally there were 117 industries in 1963. Of these the classification of 45 became more aggregated over time. To make industries comparable, the data for earlier years were aggregated to the level of later years.

[18] The IRS classifies corporations into the industry accounting for the largest percentage of sales. However, these classifications often change over time (e.g., due to merger or changes in product composition). To correct for this problem, industries which tended to display extreme instability over time were excluded from the sample.

[19] The variables were differenced over the longer period 1963–72 rather than over the two shorter periods, 1963–67 and 1967–72, in order to better capture long run effects.

[20] See Maddala [16, p. 326] for further discussion and Cowling and Waterson [6] for an example of its use.

TABLE I
LINK ENTERPRISE INDUSTRIES COMPRISING THE FINAL DATASET

Link SIC	*Industry Name*	*Corresponding 2, 3, or 4 Digit Census SIC*
2020	Dairy Products	202
2040	Grain Mill Products	204
2050	Bakery Products	205
2082	Malt Liquors and Malt	2082, 2083
2086	Bottled Soft Drinks and Flavorings	2086, 2087
2100	Tobacco Manfacturers	21
2228	Weaving Mills & Textile Finishing	221, 222, 223, 226
2250	Knitting Mills	225
2310	Men's & Boys' Clothing	231, 232
2380	Miscellaneous Apparel & Accessories	237, 238
2430	Millwork, Plywood & Prefabricated Structural Products	243
2510	Household Furniture	251
2620	Pulp, Paper & Board	261, 262, 263, 266
2712	Periodicals	271
2715	Books, Greeting Cards & Miscellaneous Publishing	2731, 274
2830	Drugs	283
3098	Miscellaneous Plastic Products	307
3140	Footwear, except Rubber	314
3198	Leather & Leather Products Not Elsewhere Classified	311, 312, 313, 315, 316, 317, 319
3240	Cement, Hydraulic	324
3270	Concrete, Gypsum & Plaster Products	337
3298	Other Nonmetallic Mineral Products	325, 326, 328, 329
3310	Ferrous Metal Processing & Basic Products, & Primary Metal Products Not Elsewhere Classified	331, 332, 3391, 3399
3410	Metal Cans	341
3450	Screw Machine Products, Bolts, & Similar Products	345
3461	Metal Stampings	346
3530	Construction, Mining, & Materials Handling Machinery & Equipment	353
3550	Special Industry Machinery	355
3570	Office & Computing Machines	357
3580	Service Industry Machines	358
3598	Other Machinery, Except Electrical	351, 359
3698	Other Electrical Equipment & Supplies	361, 362, 364, 369
3730	Ship & Boatbuilding & Repairing	1929, 193, 194, 195, 196, 199, 373
3798	Transportation Equipment, Not Elsewhere Classified	374, 375, 379
3810	Scientific & Mechanical Measuring Instruments	381, 382
3830	Optical, Medical, & Opthalmic Equipment	383, 384, 385
3860	Photographic Equipment & Supplies	386
3980	Ordnance, Except Guided Missiles	191

For the equations measured in levels form, there were sufficient degrees of freedom to control for industry-specific and time-specific effects. One commonly used method to incorporate these effects is to include separate dummy variables for each cross sectional unit and each time period. Another increasingly popular method is the variance components model. This model

TABLE II
MEANS BY YEAR

Variable	*1963*	*1967*	*1972*
VI	0.426	0.411	0.409
AVGFS	97.2	118.2	122.3
CONC	31.9	32.5	34.0
DG	1.52	1.52	1.21

uses fewer degrees of freedom than the dummy variable model and is more appropriate if the results obtained with a randomly chosen sample are used to make inferences about a larger population (see Maddala [16] and Mundlak [18] for further discussion). For these reasons, the results from the error components model are reported instead of those from the dummy variables model.

Using the error components model, the results are:

$$\underset{}{VI_{it}} = \underset{(-4.34)}{-0.673} - \underset{(-7.23)}{0.151}\ AVGFS_{it} + \underset{(2.23)}{0.070}\ DG_{it} + \underset{(1.91)}{0.093}\ CONC_{it}$$

$$\text{Transformed M.S.E.} = 0.0044$$

$$\sigma_i^2 = 0.0035$$

$$\sigma_t^2 = 0.0001$$

$$\sigma_{it}^2 = 0.0044$$

The *t*-statistics are reported in parenthesis. The coefficient of AVGFS is negative and significantly different from zero at the 0.01 level. The effects of DG and CONC are both positive. Respectively, they are significantly different from zero at the 0.05 and the 0.10 level. Since the ratio of the variance components for the cross section (σ_i^2) to the variance component for the error (σ_{it}^2) is large and the ratio of the variance component for the time series (σ_t^2) to the variance component for the error (σ_{it}^2) is small, the results are close to those which would be obtained from estimating a model with industry-specific dummy variables but without time-specific dummy variables (see Madalla [16] for further discussion).

Estimation of the equation in differenced form yields the following results:

$$\Delta VI_i = \underset{(1.79)}{0.057} - \underset{(-3.94)}{0.217}\ \Delta AVGFS_i + \underset{(1.57)}{0.078}\ \Delta DG_i + \underset{(2.23)}{0.149}\ \Delta CONC_i$$

$$R^2 = 0.394$$

$$DF = 34$$

The effect of AVGFS on VI is again negative and significantly different from zero at the 0.01 level. The effects of DG and CONC are both positive, with the former significant at the 0.15 level and the latter at the 0.05 level.

IV. SUMMARY AND CONCLUSIONS

By expanding upon Stigler's analysis, specific testable implications were suggested. Equations were then estimated both in levels and difference form to check for sensitivity of the results to specification bias and measurement problems. In both equations, the empirical results were consistent with the hypotheses. The negative relationship between vertical integration and firm size was significant at the 0.01 level. A positive relationship was found between vertical integration and the variables, concentration and demand growth. With one slight exception, these effects were all significant at the 0.10 level.

Similar results were obtained in the study by Tucker and Wilder [23].[21] As pointed out above, they used a firm growth variable rather than industry growth and their industry level data were collected at the plant level. Nonetheless, they did find a positive and significant relationship between industry concentration and vertical integration in most of their equations. The firm size variable had a negative, though not always significant effect. The sign of the coefficient on firm growth varied.[22]

Others have also provided evidence pertaining to Stigler's implications. Adelman [1] reported an "apparent rough correlation" [1, p. 318] between vertical integration and firm size which he claims is contrary to Stigler's hypothesis. He did not provide statistical tests of this relationship. Furthermore, he did not control for other effects such as concentration and industry growth and, hence, his study may be susceptible to specification bias from omitted explanatory variables.

In his study, Stigler finds evidence that vertical integration has declined over time in the manufacturing sector. He claims this result is consistent with his hypothesis. Since his study, others have investigated broad trends in vertical integration with mixed results. Adelman [1] and Laffer [12] find no apparent trend over long periods of time. On the the other hand, Tucker and Wilder [23], Livesay and Porter [15] and Maddigan [17] conclude that vertical integration has shown a slight upward trend. This evidence is again subject to specification bias from omitted variables. It is also susceptible to

[21] Using the firm level data set, Tucker and Wilder adjusted the value added/sales measure of vertical integration by subtracting out net income and taxes from the numerator and denominator. They state, "(w)e believe that the adjusted index is a more conceptually sound method of measuring trends in vertical integration, since it removes the effects of trends in profitability and taxation" [23, p. 87]. While their adjusted index may remove economic profits, it also removes returns to inputs, such as part of the returns to capital (i.e. those which would accrue to stockholders) and monopoly rents to owners of the firm. Furthermore, their reported results indicate that, although the significance of coefficients is affected by the choice of vertical integration measure, the signs of the coefficients are unaffected.

[22] Tucker and Wilder included lagged vertical integration as an explanatory variable in most of their equations. Since the coefficient on this variable was generally close to one, their equations were structurally very close to equations where the dependent variable is differenced. Consequently, the negative sign on the firm growth variable may be due to a negative effect of firm size on integration. Note that when the lagged integration variable is omitted, the firm growth coefficient becomes positive while in those equations where lagged integration is included the firm growth coefficient is negative (see [23, p. 91]).

aggregation bias. While many industries in the economy have matured, it is also true that many new industries have emerged and others have declined. The net effect of changes in the scale or even the average age of markets is thus uncertain.

In conclusion, empirical implications which have roots in a theorem proposed by Adam Smith were tested here. The results of a cross-sectional and time series study of manufacturing industries support the implications and are consistent with those of an earlier study by Tucker and Wilder. However, the variance component for the cross-sections was large relative to that of the error in our estimated equation, indicating that there are substantial industry-specific effects yet to be explained. Further research incorporating other explanatory variables would seem warranted.

David Levy,
Department of Economics,
Rutgers University,
New Brunswick,
N.J. 08903.

ACCEPTED DECEMBER 1982

REFERENCES

[1] ADELMAN, MORRIS A., "Concept of Statistical Measurement of Vertical Integration", in Stigler, G. J. (ed.), *Business Concentration and Price Policy* (Princeton University Press, Princeton 1955).

[2] ALCHIAN, ARMEN A., and DEMSETZ, HAROLD, "Production, Information Costs and Economic Organization", *American Economic Review*, LXII, 5 (December 1972), pp. 777–95.

[3] ARROW, KENNETH J., "Vertical Integration and Communication", *Bell Journal of Economics*, VI, 1 (Spring 1975), pp. 173–83.

[4] CARLTON, DENNIS W., "Vertical Integration in Competitive Markets under Uncertainty", *Journal of Industrial Economics*, XXVII, 3 (March 1979), pp. 189–209.

[5] COASE, RONALD H., "The Nature of the Firm", reprinted in *Readings in Price Theory*, G. Stigler and K. Boulding (ed.), pp. 331–51 (R. Irwin, Homewood, Ill. 1952).

[6] COWLING, KEITH and WATERSON, M., "Price-Cost Margins and Market Structure", *Economica*, XLIII, 3 (August 1976), pp. 267–74.

[7] ECKARD, E. WOODROW JR., "A Note on the Empirical Measurement of Vertical Integration", *Journal of Industrial Economics*, XXVIII, 1 (September 1979), pp. 105–7.

[8] GOLD, BELA, "Industry Growth Patterns: Theory and Empirical Results", *Journal of Industrial Economics*, XIII, 2 (November 1964), pp. 53–73.

[9] GORT, MICHAEL, *Diversification and Integration in American Industry* (Princeton University Press, Princeton, 1962).

[10] KASERMAN, DAVID L., "Theories of Vertical Integration: Implications for Antitrust Policy", *Antitrust Bulletin*, XXIII, 3 (Fall 1978), pp. 483–510.

[11] KLEIN, BENJAMIN, CRAWFORD, ROBERT G. and ALCHIAN, ARMEN A., "Vertical Integration, Appropriable Rents, and the Competitive Contracting Process", *Journal of Law and Economics*, XXI, 2 (October 1978), pp. 297–326.

[12] Laffer, Arthur B., "Vertical Integration by Corporations, 1929–1965", *Review of Economics and Statistics*, LI, 1 (February 1969), pp. 91–93.

[13] Levitt, Theodore, "Exploit the Product Life Cycle", *Harvard Business Review*, XLIII, 6 (November-December 1965), pp. 81–94.

[14] Levy, David T., *The Transactions Cost Approach to Vertical Integration: An Empirical Examination*, Unpublished Ph.D. Dissertation, UCLA, 1981.

[15] Livesay, Harold C. and Porter, Patrick, "Vertical Integration in Manufacturing, 1899–1948", *Journal of Economic History*, XXIX, 3 (September 1969), pp. 494–500.

[16] Maddala, G. S., *Econometrics* (McGraw-Hill Book Company, New York, 1977).

[17] Maddigan, Ruth J., "The Measurement of Vertical Integration", *Review of Economics and Statistics*, LXIII 3 (Aug 1981), pp. 328–35.

[18] Mundlak, Yairi, "On the Pooling of Time Series and Cross Section Data", *Econometrica*, XLVI, 1 (January 1978), pp. 69–85.

[19] Polli, Rolanda and Victor Cook, "Validity of the Product Life Cycle", *Journal of Business*, XLII, 4 (October 1969), pp. 385–400.

[20] Simon, Hermann, "Dynamic of Price Elasticity and Brand Life Cycles: An Empirical Study", *Journal of Marketing Research*, XVI, 5 (November 1979), pp. 439–52.

[21] Stigler, George J., "The Division of Labor is Limited by the Extent of the Market", reprinted in Stigler, *The Organization of Industry* (Richard D. Irwin, Inc., Homewood: 1968).

[22] ———, *The Theory of Price* (Macmillan Company, New York, 1966).

[23] Tucker, Irvin B., and Wilder, Ronald P., "Trends in Vertical Integration in the U.S. Manufacturing Sector", *Journal of Industrial Economics*, XXVI, 1 (September 1977), pp. 81–94.

[24] U.S. Bureau of the Census, *Enterprise Statistics: 1963*, Pt. 3, *Link of Census Establishment and IRS Corporation Data* (U.S. Government Printing Office, Washington, D.C., 1976).

[25] ———, *Enterprise Statistics: 1967*, Pt. 3, *Link of Census Establishment and IRS Corporation Data* (U.S. Government Printing Office, Washington, D.C., 1973).

[26] ———, *Enterprise Statistics: 1972*, Pt. 3, *Link of Census Establishment and IRS Corporation Data* (U.S. Government Printing Office, Washington, D.C., 1976).

[27] U.S. Congress, Senate, *Concentration Ratios in Manufacturing Industry, 1963.* 89th Cong., 2nd Sess., Committee Print, *Report Prepared by the Bureau of the Census for the Subcommittee on Antitrust and Monopoly of the Committee on the Judiciary, Pt. I* (U.S. Government Printing Office, Washington, D.C., 1966).

[28] U.S. Bureau of the Census, *Census of Manufactures, 1967, Special Report Series: Concentration Ratios in Manufacturing* (U.S. Government Printing Office, Washington, D.C., 1970).

[29] ———, *Annual Survey of Manufacturers: 1970, Value of Shipment Concentration Ratios* (U.S. Government Printing Office, Washington, D.C. 1972).

[30] ———, *Statistical Abstract of the United States* (U.S. Government Printing Office, Washington, D.C. 1978).

[31] Williamson, Oliver E., *Markets and Hierachies: Analysis and Antitrust Implications* (Free Press, New York, 1975).

[32] ———, "Transaction-Cost Economics: The Governance of Contractual Relations", *Journal of Law and Economics*, XXII, 2 (October 1979), pp. 233–61.

THE JOURNAL OF INDUSTRIAL ECONOMICS 0022-1821 $2.00
Volume XXXII March 1984 No. 3

TRENDS IN VERTICAL INTEGRATION: REPLY

RONALD P. WILDER AND IRVIN B. TUCKER

DAVID Levy's article [1], in addition to reformulating George Stigler's work on vertical integration, also offers comments on our 1977 article. In this reply we would like to make a few remarks on conceptual and empirical issues.

The first issue is whether the firm or the industry is the more appropriate unit of observation. Stigler's 1951 article [2] is not definitive on this point, as the section on vertical integration begins with the passage, "Many economists believe that, with the growth of firms (and industries?), functions are usually taken over from previous independent industries". [2, p. 189] At the end of that section, Stigler concludes, "These remarks are not intended to constitute a theory of vertical integration. There is doubt, indeed, that we want a theory of vertical integration except as part of a theory of the functions of a firm" [2, p. 191]. Stigler's discussion thus appears to apply to firms as well as industries.

In our 1977 article, we argue that observing vertical integration trends at the firm level is less subject to measurement problems because one can adjust for trends in profitability and income taxes. Our analysis of firm-level data led to the conclusion that "individual firms show significant changes over time in vertical integration, and in both directions" [3, p. 92]. Aggregation tends to mask this diversity of trend found at the level of the individual firm.

An additional problem related to aggregation and the use of the enterprise data is the non-comparability of the value-added and sales measures in that data source. The value added measure is not available for wholesale, retail and service industries, while sales data are available for all sectors. As a result, Levy's observed declining trend in the mean value-added/sales ratio could be due entirely to the secular shift in the economy toward services and the growing diversification of firms over the study period. (Although Levy's sample consists entirely of manufacturing industries, it is likely that many companies included in those industries are diversified firms whose sales data include some sales by subsidiaries in trade or services lines of business).

A general problem with empirical studies of trends in vertical integration is that the observed trend in the value-added/sales ratio may reflect diversification as well as integration, especially with the increasing importance of conglomerate mergers in recent American economic history. Most large firms of today are multi-establishment, multi-industry firms, with a variety of life cycle effects at work within each firm. Although we would expect (with Stigler) that vertical disintegration would be the dominant trend for most firms and industries, this trend may be concealed by the effects of diversification on conventional measures of vertical integration.

ACCEPTED DECEMBER 1982

Ronald P. Wilder,
Department of Economics,
College of Business Administration,
University of South Carolina,
Columbia, S.C. 29208.

Irvin Tucker,
Department of Economics,
College of Business Administration,
University of North Carolina—Charlotte,
Charlotte, N.C. 29223.

REFERENCES

[1] LEVY, DAVID, "Testing Stigler's Interpretation of 'The Division of Labor is Limited by the Extent of the Market,'", *Journal of Industrial Economics*, XXXII, 3 (March 1984), pp. 377–89.

[2] STIGLER, GEORGE J., "The Division of Labor is Limited by the Extent of the Market", *Journal of Political Economy*, LIX, 3 (June 1951), pp. 185–93.

[3] TUCKER, IRVIN B. and WILDER, RONALD P., "Trends in Vertical Integration in the U.S. Manufacturing Sector", *Journal of Industrial Economics* XXVI, 1 (September 1977), pp. 81–94.

THE JOURNAL OF INDUSTRIAL ECONOMICS
Volume XXXII March 1984 No. 3

PUBLICATIONS RECEIVED

Agenda for Britain 1: Micro Policy for the 80's, edited by C. D. Cohen. Published by Philip Allan Publishers Ltd., 1982, £14.00 (hardback), £6.95 (paperback).

The Alcohol Economy (Fuel Ethanol and the Brazilian Experience), by Harry Rothman, Ron Greenshields, and Francisco Rosillo Calle. Published by Frances Pinter (Publishers), 1983.

The Analysis of Value and Volatility in Financial Futures, by Martin L. Leibowitz. Published by New York University, 1982.

Business and Academia (Partners in New England's Economic Renewal), by John C. Hoy, and Melvin H. Bernstein. Published by University Press of New England, 1982, £8.50.

Business Taxation, Finance and Firm Behaviour Proceedings of a Symposium at IUI, Stockholm, August 28–29, 1978, by Gunnar Eliasoon, and Ian Sodersten. Published by The Industrial Institute for Economic and Social Research, Stockholm, 1982, Skr 140:–.

Change and Choice in Indian Industry, edited by Amiya Kumar Bagchi, and Nirmala Banerjee. Published by K. P. Bagchi & Co., Calcutta, 1982, Rs. 85.00.

Conflicts of National Laws with International Business Activity: Issues of Extraterritoriality, by A. H. Hermann. Published by British-North American Research Committee, London, 1982, £3.00, $6.00.

Current Problems of Monetary Policy. Would the Gold Standard Help?, by Phillip Cagan. Published by American Enterprise Institute for Public Policy Research, 1983.

Do Stock Prices Reflect the Adjustment of Earnings for Inflation?, by Phillip Cagan. Published by Salomon Brothers Centre for the Study of Financial Institutions, 1982.

The Economics of Industrial Innovation, 2nd Edition, by Christopher Freeman. Published by Frances Pinter (Publishers) Ltd., 1982, £15.50.

Economic Regulation: Essays in Honour of James R. Nelson, edited by Kenneth D. Boyer and William G. Shepherd. Published by Michigan State University, 1982, $18.00.

The Emergence of Industrial America, by Peter George. Published by Savoy, 1982, $33.50 (Cloth), $10.95 (Paper).

Energy Strategies for the U.K., by S. C. Littlechild, and K. G. Vaidya. Published by George Allen and Unwin, 1982, £15.00.

Entrepreneurs in Red, by Kalman Rupp. Published by Suny (New York), 1982, $39.50 (Cloth), $14.95 (Paper).

Evaluating the Reliability of Macro Economic Models, edited by Gregory C. Chow, and Paolo Corsi. Published by John Wiley & Sons Ltd., 1982, £22.50.

French Planning in Theory and Practice, by Saul Estrin, and Peter Holmes. Published by George Allen and Unwin, 1983, £15.00.

The Gateway: U.S. Imigration Issues and Policies, edited by Barry R. Chiswick. Published by American Enterprise Institute for Public Policy Research, 1982, $22.95 (Cloth), $12.95 (Paper).

Industrial Policy and Shipbuilding—Changing Economic Structures in the Low Countries 1600–1980, by C. A. de Feyter. Published by HES Publishers B.V. (Netherlands), 1982, Hfl. 40,00.

The Liberation of Capital, by Folkert Wilken. Published by George Allen and Unwin, 1982, £12.00.

Longman Dictionary of Business English, by J. H. Adam. Published by Longman York Express, 1982, £5.95.

Low Pay, Occupational Mobility, and Minimum-Wage Policy in Britain, by David Metcalf. Published by American Enterprise Institute Studies in Economic Policy, 1981, $4.25.

Macroeconomics in Question, by Malcolm Sawyer. Published by Harvester Press Ltd., 1982, £18.95 (Cloth), £5.95 (Paper).

Management of Industrial Change in Germany, by Ernst-Jürgen Horn. Published by Sussex European Papers No. 13, (Sussex University), 1982, £5.00.

Managerial Economics, by Ken Randall. Published by Heinemann Educational Books, 1982, £4.95.

Market Mechanisms and Central Economic Planning, by Milton Friedman. Published by American Enterprise Institute for Public Policy Research, 1981.

Measuring the Importance of Small Business in the American Economy, by Lawrence J. White. Published by New York University, 1982.

Microelectronics and Women's Employment in Britain, edited by SPRU Women and Technology Studies. Published by Science Policy Research Unit, University of Sussex, 1982, £2.50.

Multinational Companies and Economic Concentration in Europe, by Frank Fishwick. Published by Gower, 1982, £12.50.

The Newly Industrializing Countries: Adjusting to Success, by Neil McMullen. Published by The British-North American Committee, 1983, £3.50.

Of Bread and Guns; the World Economy in Crisis, by Nigel Harris. Published by Pelican, 1983, £2.95.

On Britain, by Ralph Dahrendorf. Published by BBC Publications, 1982, £7.25 (Hardback), £2.95 (Paperback).

On the Complete Systems Approach to Demand Analysis, by N. Anders Klevmarken. Published by The Industrial Institute for Economic and Social Research, 1982, Skr 125:–.

Participatory and Self-Managed Firms, edited by Derek C. Jones and Jan Svejnar. Published by Lexington Books—Toronto, 1982, £27.50.

Patterns of Regional Economic Decline and Growth: The Past and What Has Been Happening Lately, by Mark Perlman. Published by American Enterprise Institute, 1982.

Perspectives on a Decade of Small Business Research Bolton Ten Years On, edited by John Stanworth, Ava Westrip, David Watkins, and John Lewis. Published by Gower, 1982, £16.50.

Perspectives on Political Economy, Alternatives to the Economics of Depression, edited by R. J. Barry Jones. Published by Frances Pinter (Publishers) Ltd., 1983.

The Political Economy of Austria, edited by Sven W. Arndt. Published by American Enterprise Institute for Public Policy Research, 1982.

Production, Purpose and Structure, by Jeremy Bray. Published by Frances Pinter (Publishers) Ltd., 1982, £8.95.

Public and Private Control in Mass Product Industry: The Cement Industry Cases, by P. Bianchi. Published by Martinus Nijhoff Publishers, 1982.

The Rational Expectations Revolution in Macro Economics Theories and Evidence, by David K. H. Begg. Published by Philip Allan Publishers Ltd., 1982, £16.00 (Hardback), £7.95 (Paperback).

Regional Dimensions of Industrial Policy, by Michael E. Bell and Paul S. Lande. Published by Lexington Books, 1982, £17.00.

Scale in Production Systems, edited by John A. Buzacott, Mark F. Cantley, Vladimir N. Glagolev, and Rolfe C. Tomlinson. Published by Pergamon IIASA Proceedings Series, 1982.

Schumacher on Energy, by Geoffrey Kirk. Published by Jonathan Cape, London, 1982, £7.95.

Stimulating Small Firms, edited by David Watkins, John Stanworth, and Ava Westrip. Published by Gower, 1982.

Studies in Labor Market Behaviour: Sweden and the United States, edited by Gunnar Eliasson, Bertil Holmlund, and Frank P. Stafford. Published by IUI, Stockholm, 1982, Skr 140.

Tax Policy and Corporate Concentration, by Alan L. Feld. Published by Lexington Books, 1982, £16.00.

Toward a Positive Theory of Insurance, by David Mayers and Clifford W. Smith Jr. Published by Salomon Brothers Centre for the Study of Financial Institutions—Graduate School of Business Administration, New York University, 1982.

Trade Issues in the mid 1980s, by Sidney Golt. Published by British-North American Research Association, London, 1982, £3.50, $7.00.

Under Japanese Management, by Michael White and Malcolm Trevor. Published by Heinemann Educational Books Ltd., 1983, £14.50 (Hardback), £6.50 (Paperback).

Unemployment Insurance Financing An Evaluation, by Joseph M. Becker. Published by American Enterprise Institute Studies in Economic Policy, 1981, $14.25 (Cloth), $6.25 (Paper).

Unemployment and Technical Innovation, by Christopher Freeman, John Clark and Luc Soete. Published by Frances Pinter (Publishers) Ltd., 1982, £15.00.

The Unequal Struggle? British Socialism and the Capitalist Enterprise, by Jim Tomlinson. Published by Methuen & Co. Ltd., 1982, £8.95 (Hardback), £3.95 (Paperback).

Work in Crisis—Dilemma of a Nation, by Roger Clarke. Published by Saint Andrew Press, Edinburgh, 1982, £4.75.

The World Zinc Industry, by Satyadeu Gupta. Published by Lexington Books, 1982, £18.50.

THE JOURNAL OF INDUSTRIAL ECONOMICS

Published first in October 1952, the Journal has a very wide international circulation, and has established itself as the leading journal in the field of industrial economics. It was founded to promote the analysis of modern industry, particularly the behaviour of firms, and the functioning of markets. More specifically it seeks to bring the tools of modern economic analysis to bear on the analysis of real problems of industrial economies.

Contributions are welcomed covering all the major areas of industrial economics. One such area is the relationship between market structure and market behaviour in the areas of pricing, product differentiation, advertising and the dissemination of information and R and D. Another area focuses more directly on the firm, its objectives, finance, investment and growth. A third area comprises the background environment within which industrial firms operate: the changing structure of industry, public policy on monopoly and restrictive trade practices, regulation, fiscal and monetary policy as they affect firms, and underlying changes in productivity and international competitiveness.

The Journal has a tradition of publishing a blend of theory and evidence. Theoretical discussion is welcomed provided that the more abstract theory includes sufficient introduction and other explanation to convey the significance of the material to the general reader who wants to decide whether to follow the analysis through. Empirical analysis, and especially econometric analysis, should include an explanation of the data sources used, of the methods applied and of the underlying theoretical basis of the study. The Journal has a particular tradition of case studies of firms and industries, which the Editors would wish to continue. However contributors of such studies are asked to remember that a study will be of interest to the international readership of the Journal only if it makes a particular contribution to the methodology of such studies, or if the empirical results are exceptionally interesting.

Alongside articles of more normal length, the Editors are ready to publish shorter notes, especially where these give interim results of important research studies, or where they report significant new empirical results. Books are not reviewed, although books received will be listed, sometimes with a short note: but substantial review articles will be considered.

Information for contributors

Typescripts from North America should be sent to Professor H. Michael Mann, Department of Economics, Boston College, Chestnut Hill, Massachusetts, 02167, U.S.A. Typescripts from *all* other countries should be sent to the General Editor, Journal of Industrial Economics, Institute of Economics and Statistics, The University of Oxford, St. Cross Building, Manor Road, Oxford, OX1 3UL, U.K. Detailed Information for Contributors is available from the General Editor. Contributors are asked to send an Abstract, not exceeding 100 words, with their article. No payment is made for articles accepted, but authors are provided with 25 free offprints.

Information for subscribers

The journal is published four times a year, in September, December, March and June, by Basil Blackwell Publisher Ltd., 108 Cowley Road, Oxford OX4 1JF, England. Prices are as follows:

	UK	Overseas	USA	Canada
Institutions	£24.00	£29.40	$59.50	$72.90
Individuals	£14.95	£18.30	$35.00	$43.25
Single issue prices for:				
Institutions	£6.50	£7.75	$16.00	$19.50
Individuals	£4.75	£5.75	$11.00	$13.50

CONTRIBUTORS TO THIS NUMBER

W. H. DAVIDSON: Associate Professor of Business Administration, The Colgate Darden Graduate School of Business Administration, University of Virginia.

DONALD G. McFETRIDGE: Professor of Economics, Carleton University, Ottawa, and Associate Editor of this Journal.

STEVEN SCHWARTZ: Assistant Professor of Economics, Miami University, Oxford, Ohio.

MICHAEL L. LAWRIWSKY: Lecturer in Economics, La Trobe University, Bundoora, Victoria, Australia.

JOHN F. STEWART: Associate Professor, Department of Economics, University of North Carolina—Chapel Hill.

ROBERT S. HARRIS: Associate Professor, School of Business Administration, University of North Carolina—Chapel Hill.

WILLARD T. CARLETON: Kenan Professor, School of Business Administration, University of North Carolina—Chapel Hill.

MARTIN K. PERRY: Research Economist, Bell Laboratories, Murray Hill, N.J.

ELI NOAM: Associate Professor, and Director of the Research Program in Telecommunications and Information Policy, Columbia University in the City of New York.

SHERRILL SHAFFER: Economist, Banking Studies Department, Federal Reserve Bank of New York.

BRUCE YANDLE: Executive Director of the Federal Trade Commission, Washington, D.C., on leave from Department of Economics, Clemson University.

W. J. BOYES: Professor of Economics, Arizona State University, Tempe.

DALE BECK FURNISH: Professor of Law, Arizona State University, Tempe.

JAN J. P. VAN HEEMST: Senior Lecturer in Economics, Institute of Social Studies, The Hague.

DAVID LEVY: Assistant Professor, Department of Economics, Rutgers University.

RONALD P. WILDER: Professor of Economics, University of South Carolina.

IRVIN B. TUCKER: Assistant Professor of Economics, University of North Carolina—Charlotte.

US Mailing: Second class postage paid at New York. Postmaster: Send address corrections to: Journal of Industrial Economics, c/o Expediters of the Printed Word Ltd., 527 Madison Avenue, Suite 1217, New York, NY 10022 (US Mailing Agent).

Set by Santype International Ltd., Salisbury, Wilts.
Printed and bound by Whitstable Litho Ltd., Whitstable, Kent

THE JOURNAL OF INDUSTRIAL ECONOMICS

Volume XXXII JUNE 1984 No. 4

JAMES L. BOTHWELL, THOMAS F. COOLEY and THOMAS E. HALL
A New View of the Market Structure–Performance Debate 397

MARIE-PAULE DONSIMONI, PAUL GEROSKI and ALEXIS JACQUEMIN
Concentration Indices and Market Power: Two Views 419

ROGER CLARKE, STEPHEN DAVIES and MICHAEL WATERSON
The Profitability–Concentration Relation: Market Power or Efficiency? 435

A. J. BUXTON, S. W. DAVIES and B. R. LYONS
Concentration and Advertising in Consumer and Producer Markets 451

STEPHEN C. FARBER
Cyclical Price Flexibility: A Test of Administered Pricing 465

LARRY L. DUETSCH
Entry and the Extent of Multiplant Operations 477

JAMES E. ANDERSON
Identification of Interactive Behavior in Air Service Markets: 1973–76 489

JOHN E. KWOKA, Jr.
Market Power and Market Change in the U.S. Automobile Industry 509

PETER SCHWARZ
The Estimated Effects on Industry of Time-of-Day Demand and Energy Electricity Prices 523

ISSN 0022-1821
BASIL BLACKWELL OXFORD ENGLAND

THE JOURNAL OF INDUSTRIAL ECONOMICS 0022–1821 $2.00
Volume XXXII June 1984 No. 4

A NEW VIEW OF THE MARKET STRUCTURE—PERFORMANCE DEBATE*

JAMES L. BOTHWELL, THOMAS F. COOLEY AND THOMAS E. HALL

I. INTRODUCTION

Because economics is a non-experimental science, the data that economists work with are generated by measurement of uncontrolled systems. In order to make use of such data it is necessary to have some basis for placing restrictions on the models which generate the observations. This is the role of deductive reasoning in economics. Theories about the behavior of individuals, markets, firms, and even sectors of the macroeconomy place restrictions on the data that are observed, and statistical methods are used in lieu of experimental controls in testing these restrictions. While there is often debate about the validity of the deductive foundations and the credibility of the implied restrictions (e.g., Sims [40]) such foundations provide at least a framework within which meaningful debate can take place. Occasionally, however, the foundations are virtually non-existent or at best very weak and yet statistical work proceeds, often on a very large scale, in the hope that statistical regularities will appear in the data that either confirm or refute informal conjectures. This paper is concerned with one area of economics in which this latter practice has been widespread, namely the debate about the relationship between market structure and performance.

While the relationship between competition and market performance on the one hand and pure monopoly and performance on the other have been well established in the literature since the 18th century, the vast middle ground has remained relatively unsusceptible to theoretical analysis. Nevertheless, there has developed over the past thirty years an area of research based initially on the following two conjectures. The first is that the more concentrated an industry is, that is the more it is dominated by a few firms, the easier it is for firms to coordinate their policies. Firms operating in more concentrated industries thus find it easier to collude either explicitly or implicitly than do firms operating in less concentrated industries, and successful collusion should lead to higher profits. The second conjecture is that measurable characteristics of market structure are exogenous with respect to measures of profitability. These two conjectures form the basis of the widely

* We are indebted to William Comanor, H. E. Frech III, Wesley Magat and James Vanderweide for helpful comments. James L. Bothwell would also like to acknowledge the support of the Center for the Study of Business Regulation, Fuqua School of Business, Duke University. The views expressed in this paper are strictly those of the authors and do not represent any official position of the U.S. General Accounting Office.

influential work of Bain [1], which searched for statistical regularities in the relationship between profitability and concentration over a cross section of U.S. manufacturing industries. Over time, Bain's original work inspired a vast proliferation of empirical studies of the relationship between various measures of market structure or firm characteristics and economic performance.

Obviously, the original Bain conjecture has great intuitive appeal. Successful collusion need not be overt since firms which deviate from the accepted market norms do so in the face of likely retaliation by other firms with at best uncertain consequences. At the same time, the prisoners' dilemma argument is equally compelling on *a priori* grounds because the gains from acting individually can be great and policing of the collusive arrangement may be difficult or costly (Stigler [41]). The variations on the static oligopoly model are numerous. The existence of asymmetric information, non-homogeneous products, non-contiguous markets and differences in technology all influence whether the equilibrium solution to the oligopoly problem in a given industry is more likely to be competitive, monopolistic or a Nash-Cournot equilibrium. The result is that there is no real consensus about what generalities are likely to emerge in the study of the relationship between market structure and performance.[1]

While there is no consensus about the foundations of the market structure—performance paradigm, there are clearly many who believe in the basic Bain conjectures. The many studies which have been conducted in the Bain tradition have mostly been attempts to unveil the particular generality conjectured by Bain—a positive correlation between measures of profitability and measures of concentration for a cross section of industries or firms. This search for empirical generalities marked a significant departure from the earlier tradition in industrial organization. This approach was originated by Mason [28], who argued that the relationship between industry characteristics and performance could best be understood by conducting detailed case studies of industries in the hope that useful generalizations would emerge. Thus, in the case study approach, the search for generalities is a secondary objective conditioned on the richly detailed information about the industry. In the Bain approach the conditioning information set is quite limited, although as the tradition evolved, new entrants have expanded the information set by examining the correlation between concentration and profits conditional on additional characteristics of firms that are measurable for cross sections of firms.

By now the Bain tradition is quite well developed. In a recent survey, Weiss [44] discusses some fifty-four empirical studies of the relationship between concentration and profits and there undoubtedly have been many more since.

[1] The fact that some industries are dominated by a few large firms can be quite consistent with competitive equilibrium in a world with adjustment costs, or a skewed distribution of managerial talent (Lucas [23], [24]).

There are three basic controversies that are involved in discussions of this research: (1) The exogeneity of measures of market structure or firm characteristics with respect to profitability; (2) The appropriate selection of data to test the Bain conjecture; (3) The role of specification uncertainty and prior beliefs in the interpretation of the results. This paper addresses only the last of these issues, not because we think the others are unimportant, but because we believe the latter problem has been the most neglected in the literature and is probably the most important source of scepticism about the results.[2]

Given the vast number of market structure—performance studies, it is unlikely that any new empirical results will alter significantly the beliefs of those who are interested in this line of research. All of the empirical evidence is based on projections of the data that are heavily conditioned by the prior beliefs of the researcher. If the results are not robust over alternative projections, then there is little reason to accept the evidence as reflecting the information content of the data rather than the prior beliefs of the researcher. In this paper we analyze the relationship between profitability and market structure using methods which make explicit the role of prior beliefs and specification uncertainty. This methodology is based on the work of Chamberlain and Leamer [8] and Leamer [20].

In the next section of the paper, we identify several prominent classes of alternative prior beliefs that have appeared in the literature. The third section presents a brief discussion of the methodology used in this paper. The following two sections discuss the data and the results. The major conclusion that emerges from our analysis is that specification uncertainty plays a critical role in market structure—performance studies. When this uncertainty is accounted for, the data appear to be largely uninformative about the relationship between concentration and profits. This is in contrast to the claim of Weiss [44, p. 363] that, ". . . the fairly simple econometric techniques applied in the field over the past 10 to 15 years have yielded a set of conclusions that, to my mind, surpass in concreteness and certainty those attained by the preceeding case studies." For some classes of prior belief, the data do appear to be informative. Thus, the positive correlations between market share and profitability and advertising and profitability do not appear terribly sensitive to specification uncertainty. However, it is by now well established that the causal direction of these correlations is at least questionable and that there is no obvious connection between these and the Bain hypothesis.

The results presented here suggest to us that, at the level of theoretical abstraction typically considered in market structure—performance studies, data on cross sections of firms or industries are unlikely to be sufficiently

[2] The question of data selection has been discussed fairly thoroughly by Weiss [44] and Demsetz [15] among others, although there appears to be little agreement on the direction of bias in the most commonly used samples. The question of exogeneity has been less thoroughly discussed, although in specific instances (e.g., Schmalensee [37], Martin [27]) it has been dealt with explicitly.

informative to make such empirical analysis useful. It may, therefore, be more productive to return to industry specific analysis. There will undoubtedly be some who are unconvinced by this argument and for them we offer the observation that further empirical studies based on weak deductive foundations are likely to be convincing only to the extent that they account explicitly for the role of prior beliefs and specification uncertainty.

II. DETERMINANTS OF PROFITABILITY

The conventional market structure—conduct—performance paradigm has guided vast amounts of empirical research in the field of industrial organization for the past three decades. Like empirical research in other areas of economics, the maintained hypotheses that are considered reflect to a large extent the prior beliefs of the researchers. The result is that there is always a suspicion that what is being engaged in is more advocacy than objective empirical analysis.

In the market structure—performance literature, the most important, alternative prior beliefs (maintained hypotheses) appear to fall into six categories which we characterize as follows:

1. Seller concentration explains profits. High rates of return are thought to be caused by monopoly power conferred by high degrees of seller concentration. This is the basic collusion specification of Bain [1].
2. Seller concentration and entry barriers explain profits. High rates of return are thought to reflect monopoly power resulting from both high seller concentration and high barriers to entry. This prior comes from the traditional market structure—performance paradigm of industrial organization and accounts for the peristence of collusive gains. It is prevalent in the work of Mann [26], Weiss [45, 46], Comanor and Wilson [11], Qualls [34], [35] and many other researchers.
3. Absolute or relative firm size explain profits. This prior reflects the Demsetz [14], [15] and Peltzman [33] notion that high rates of return result from superior firm efficiency or innovativeness, and not from oligopolistic collusion and joint profit maximization. This prior has also been adopted by others (e.g., Shepherd [39], Gale [17]) who assume that high market shares indicate high barriers to entry.
4. Risk differentials explain profitability differences. This reflects the notion that high rates of return reflect neither monopoly power nor superior efficiency, but the payment of positive risk premiums to risk averse investors. It underlies much of the work of Stigler [41], Fisher and Hall [16], Cootner and Holland [13], and many others. There are, however, considerable differences in beliefs about which measure of risk—variability of return over time, financial leverage, or nondiversifiable risk—is relevant.

5. Advertising intensity explains profits. This reflects the notion of Bloch [4] and others that differences in reported accounting profit rates result from differences in the amounts of omitted, intangible capital resulting from advertising expenditures. Because advertising is assumed by some to be a source of product differentiation, this prior also may reflect the belief that the extent of product differentiation is a major determinant of profitability (Comanor [10], Schmalensee [37]).
6. Growth explains profits. This reflects Brozen's [6], [7] disequilibrium hypothesis that profitability differences result not from monopoly power, but from adjustments in capacity lagging behind changes in demand.

Given a particular maintained hypothesis about the most important determinant of profitability, there remains uncertainty about the rest of the specification of the model. If the results are not robust with respect to uncertainty about the conditioning set of variables then it cannot be concluded that the data are very informative about the hypothesis in question. The next section discusses the methodology used to determine whether the results are robust to such specification uncertainty.

III. SPECIFICATION UNCERTAINTY

The hypotheses discussed in the previous section all specify the primary determinants of profitability. In each case, however, the investigator must have in mind a set of possible conditioning variables that may or may not belong in the regression. Although uncertainty about the inclusion or exclusion of such variables is not often explicitly acknowledged, it is an inevitable and important aspect of virtually all empirical investigations. The primary concern for the problem at hand is the extent to which this specification uncertainty leads to uncertainty in the estimated parameters of primary interest.

Consider the regression model

$$y_i = \beta x_i + \sum_{j=1}^{k} \gamma_j z_{ji} + u_i \tag{1}$$

where the maintained hypothesis is that y_i is related to x_i, the focus variable, and β is the parameter of primary interest. The z_i represent the uncertain conditioning set whose inclusion in the regression is regarded as doubtful. When there are k uncertain variables, there are 2^k possible regressions that are defined by the inclusion or exclusion of some or all of the variables that are uncertain. If k is at all large, only a subset of the possible regressions can be examined. What is finally reported is usually a still smaller subset, generally those that are confirmatory of the non-explicit prior beliefs of the researcher. If it were possible to specify doubts about the role of possible conditioning variables explicitly in terms of a well defined prior distribution, with the prior location and covariance matrix specified, then there would be no particular problem since integration of such a distribution with a sample likelihood function would lead to a well defined posterior distribution on the parameters of interest.[3] But, while what is usually meant by doubt about a variable's inclusion is a prior location of zero, it is generally difficult to specify the covariance matrix of the prior distribution. The approach adopted in this paper is based on results of Chamberlain and Leamer [8] and Leamer [20] which show that specification of the prior location and the sample covariance matrix is sufficient to constrain the posterior means to lie within a particular ellipsoid. Thus it is possible to consider how the parameters of interest vary over all possible prior covariance specifications.

To illustrate this, consider the special case of equation (1) in which there are two doubtful variables:

$$y_i = \beta x_i + \gamma_1 z_{1i} + \gamma_2 z_{2i} + u_i . \tag{2}$$

We can define a composite variable,

$$w_i(\theta) = z_{1i} + \theta z_{2i}, \tag{3}$$

and rewrite this equation as

$$y_i = \beta x_i + w_i(\theta)\Gamma + u_i . \tag{4}$$

where $\Gamma = \begin{pmatrix} \gamma_1 \\ \gamma_2 \end{pmatrix}$.

For suitably defined θ this regression will yield any of the four regressions defined by including both doubtful variables, deleting one or the other or both. These four points are noted in Figure 1.[4] There is no obvious reason to restrict our attention only to these four points, however, since they are only a subset of the regressions which incorporate general linear restrictions among the doubtful variables. Each value of θ in equation (4) will define a different regression and yield a different estimate of the parameter of interest $\hat{\beta}(\theta)$. Varying θ over the real line yields the ellipse of constrained estimates shown in Figure 1. This ellipse contains all possible posterior means that can result from integration of the prior distribution centered at the origin with the sample likelihood function.

One measure of the effect of specification uncertainty on the uncertainty about the parameter of interest is to simply consider the extreme values of $\hat{\beta}(\theta)$ over this ellipse. Alternatively, since extreme values of the ellipse of constrained estimates may occur at locations in the parameter space which are unlikely given the sample, it is possible to consider extreme values over this ellipse that are constrained to fall within any given likelihood ellipse. For

[3] A compendium of Bayesian terminology is in Appendix I.

[4] The four values of θ and their corresponding points are: $\theta = 0$, $(\hat{\gamma}_1, 0)$; $\theta = \infty$, $(0, \hat{\gamma}_2)$; $\theta = b_{yz_2 \cdot xz_1}/b_{yz_1 \cdot xz_2}$, $(\hat{\gamma}_1, \hat{\gamma}_2)$; and $\theta = -b_{z_1y \cdot x}/b_{z_2y \cdot x}$, $(0, 0)$ where $b_{cd,e}$ is the least squares estimated coefficient of d as an explanatory influence of c in a model that also has e.

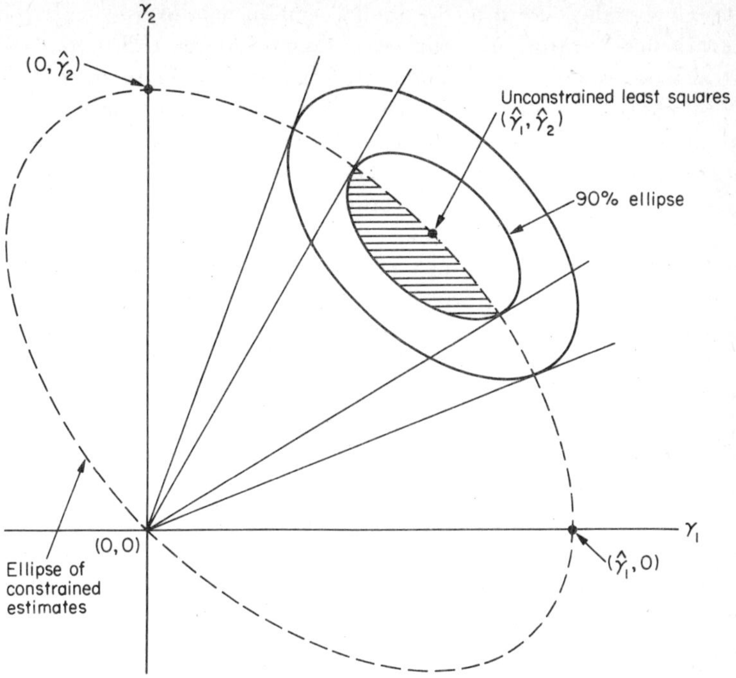

FIGURE 1
Ellipsoids of Constrained Estimates

example, these extreme values would be defined within the set indicated by the shaded region in Figure 1 for the 90 percent likelihood ellipse, which is generated in the usual way under the assumption that all doubtful variables enter the regression. By examining the extreme values of the parameter of interest over a sequence of likelihood ellipsoids (representing various values of the data confidence), we can examine how specification uncertainty varies for different possible relative weights on the sampling and prior distributions.

In Section V we present the upper and lower bounds on the parameter of interest for various values of the data confidence. In addition we perform this analysis for prior distributions which isolate different parameters as being of primary interest in accord with the scheme discussed at the end of the previous section. This analytical procedure has the advantage that consumers, even those with strong prior convictions, can judge how informative the data are about various hypotheses in the face of specification uncertainty.

IV. THE DATA SET

For the purpose of this analysis, it is important to have a data set roughly comparable to those used in previous empirical studies of the concentration—

profits relationship. Most of the studies contained in Weiss' [44] extensive review of this literature use cross section data on large U.S. manufacturing firms or industries over periods of several years during the 1950s or the 1960s. The estimation procedure almost always involves a single equation, ordinary least squares regression of some measure of profitability on a measure of seller concentration. Major differences among specifications result primarily from differences in the number and type or other explanatory variables included in the various models.

The present study uses a sample of 156 large U.S. manufacturing firms over the period 1960–67. These firms are a subset of the 231 firm sample used by Shepherd [39] and are taken primarily from the *Fortune Directory* of the 500 largest U.S. industrial corporations. In compiling his sample, Shepherd excluded firms which he considered were either experiencing a major disequilibrium or merger during the 1960s, operating subject to regulatory constraints, or highly diversified, and for which, in his opinion, adequate market structure data were not available. In order to capture the full variety of different specifications appearing in the literature, it was necessary to have data on measures of firm and industry attributes not considered by Shepherd. The additional data constraints we encountered account entirely for the reduced sample size. The resulting 156 firm subsample is approximately the same as the 158 subset of Shepherd's sample subsequently used by Bothwell and Keeler [5].

Profitability Measures

Prior studies have used several different measures of profitability. Most, based on the general economic principle that rates of return on investment will tend, in the long run, toward equality under competition, use either the rate of return on equity or the rate of return on total assets (for firms or industries) averaged over periods of several years. Some researchers (see Hall and Weiss [18]) have preferred the former measure on the basis that it corresponds to what entrepreneurs, or managers acting in the best interest of owners, should seek to maximize. Capital structure is viewed as an element of input mix, with the optimal amount of debt varying among firms or industries because of differences in such factors as stability and growth. As a result, they argue that although rates of return on equity will tend toward equality under competition, rates of return on assets will differ among firms or industries even in a perfectly competitive long run equilibrium.

Stigler [41], however, has argued that lenders also seek to maximize the present value of their future income streams and differ from entrepreneurs only in placing a higher value on security relative to earnings. To the extent that lenders are risk averse, he thought that the realized rate of return on assets should be expected to be larger the greater the proportion of debt in the capital structure, but with a partially offsetting reduction in the risk premium demanded by equity holders. Stigler, however, preferred to leave open all questions concerning the effect of interfirm or interindustry differences in capital structure on realized rates of return by considering total assets as the investment basis and the sum of interest payments, dividends and undistributed profits net of income taxes as the return on this capital.[5]

Regardless of which of these measures is used, both are subject to several well known problems stemming from the lack of correspondence between accounting and economic profits. First, depreciation practices vary considerably among firms and industries and do not adjust asset valuations for changes in price levels. Accounting rates of return are thus affected by interfirm and interindustry differences in accounting conventions and the age and durability of capital assets. Second, advertising and research and development expenditures are treated as current expenses rather than as investment in depreciable, intangible capital stocks. Third, executive salaries and emoluments may, to varying degrees, contain a portion of economic profits as well as a payment for labor services. Fourth, economic profit is net of all opportunity costs, including the opportunity cost of invested capital, while accounting profit is not.

Because of this continuing disagreement over what the appropriate rate of return to use is, and the fact that different measures of profitability have significantly affected the results of several prior empirical studies, we use both the after tax rate of return to stockholders' equity (RE) and the after tax rate of return to total assets (RA) as alternative dependent variables. Each of these is derived from individual firm, annual accounting data taken from the Compustat tape and averaged over the period 1960–67.

Explanatory Variables

The various specifications and priors discussed in Section II imply that profitability can be related to a large number of firm specific and industry specific attributes. Since it would be impractical to collect data on all of the diverse measures appearing in prior empirical studies, we focus on the principal ones. Specifically, the full set of explanatory variables considered in this study includes the following:[6]

Seller Concentration (SC)

By far the most frequently used measure is the ubiquitous four firm concentration ratio for three or four digit Standard Industrial Code (SIC) industries.

[5] If accounting rates of return are reflective of market rates, this approach is consistent with the capital structure irrelevance theorem of Modigliani-Miller which suggests that while the rate of return on equity is positively related to the ratio of debt to equity, the rate of return on assets will be unaffected by the degree of financial leverage.

[6] A data appendix listing the firms in the sample, their primary industry classification, and the basic market structure data are available on request, for a reasonable length of time, from the authors.

Since many of these industry definitions do not correspond closely with the product and geographical bounds of theoretically meaningful markets, many researchers adjust the raw concentration data supplied by the Census of Manufacturers for over- or under-inclusion. In addition, because of firm diversification, weighted average concentration ratios are often computed on an individual firm basis with the weights based on either product line sales data or plant employment statistics. Shepherd followed both of these procedures in calculating firm specific, weighted averages of four firm concentration ratios based on adjusted SIC concentration ratios. These estimates were available to us and are used here without alteration.

Advertising Intensity (ADVS)

The conventional measure used by Comanor and Wilson [11], Shepherd [39] and others is the ratio of advertising outlays to industry sales revenues. Data are from the 1965 *Internal Revenue Service Corporation Source Book of Statistics of Income* for IRS "minor industries", which are roughly comparable to 3-digit SIC industry groups. This measure, as well as all other measures of industry-specific attributes used except seller concentration, is determined for each firm on the basis of the most important industry in which that firm produced.[7]

Economies of Scale in Production (SCALE)

We use the same measure of economies of scale in production relative to market size as that first developed and used by Comanor and Wilson [11]. Following their procedure, it is calculated by dividing the average plant size among the largest establishments accounting for half of industry output by total output. Data on the size and output of establishments within four digit SIC industries are from the 1963 *Census of Manufacturers* and the 1963 *Census of Mineral Industries.*

Absolute Capital Requirements (LOGCAP)

The amount of capital necessary for a single efficient plant. This measure is also computed by following the procedure used by Comanor and Wilson [11] and multiplying the average output level of plants at estimated minimum efficient scale by the ratio of total assets to gross sales for the industry. The variable is expressed in logarithmic form. Data on industry assets and sales are from the 1963 *IRS Statistics of Income: Corporation Income Tax Returns*, which is also the source of correspondence between IRS and census defined industries.

[7] Firms were assigned to primary 3-digit industries according to the classification appearing in *Mergers and Super Concentration* [42].

Leverage (*AEIC*)

Leverage has been used as a measure of risk in several empirical studies, including Hall and Weiss [18], Gale [17], Baker [3] and Hurdle [19]. The usual supposition is that a leveraged firm with relatively more borrowed capital represents a greater financial risk to equity holders than a firm with relatively less debt. Gale, however, argues that firms have low debt because they operate in industries with high degrees of business risk and thus expects a negative leverage-return relationship if owners are risk averse. We use annual accounting data on each firm's financial structure taken from the Compustat tapes to measure leverage inversely as the ratio of common equity to total invested capital, averaged for the period 1960–67.

Profit Variability (*STD*)

Another frequently used measure of risk reflects the amount of variation in rates of return over time. Following Fisher and Hall [16] and Shepherd [39], we use the standard error of a trend line fitted to each firm's annual rate of return on equity for the period 1960–67. Annual accounting data are from the Compustat tapes.

Non-Diversifiable Risk (*BETA*)

Recently, a measure of risk based on the capital asset pricing model of Sharpe [38] and Lintner [21] has been incorporated into a market structure-profitability model by Bothwell and Keeler [5]. The basic supposition is that risk averse investors will seek to reduce risk by holding diversified portfolios. If so, the only measure of risk that should matter for any given investment is that which cannot be eliminated through diversification, and the cost of equity capital to a firm, i.e., the expected return required by investors in order for them to continue to hold that firm's stock in their portfolios, becomes a function of the degree of non-diversifiable systematic risk associated with the return on the firm's stock. This risk measure, the well known "beta coefficient", is estimated by regressing the actual monthly rate of return on the stock of each firm on the monthly return of an index representing a market portfolio for the period 1960–67. The necessary stock market data are from the data tapes supplied by the Center for Research in Security Prices of the University of Chicago School of Business. (For a more detailed discussion of the estimation procedure see Bothwell and Keeler [5, p. 76]).

Firm Growth (*GD*)

Measured as the percentage change in each firm's sales revenue over the period, 1960–67. Prior studies have used either this measure, or one based on the growth of physical output. (See, for example, Hall and Weiss [18], Shepherd [39]). Sales data are from the Compustat tapes.

Firm Size (CLOGA)

We use a common measure of firm size, the logarithm of total year end assets (in millions of dollars) averaged over the period of the analysis (e.g., Hall and Weiss [18], Shepherd [39]). The data are again taken from the Compustat tapes.

Market Share (MS)

Shepherd [39] calculated weighted average market shares in 1961 and 1968 for each of the 231 firms in his sample. We use the average of these estimates for our 156 firm subsample.

V. RESULTS OF THE ANALYSIS

Table I presents the results of the ordinary least squares estimates of the basic equations including all of the possible explanatory variables for both measures of profitability. The least squares estimates of most of the coefficients appear to be reasonable and the degree of explanatory power is acceptable for cross sectional data. The sample confidence intervals for some of the coefficients are quite wide and the effect of seller concentration (SC) is obviously poorly defined.

Our primary concern is to analyze the effect of specification uncertainty on these results for a variety of priors. Each of the priors defines a focus variable or variables whose coefficient(s) are of primary interest and assigns a prior distribution that is uninformative about those variables. The remaining vari-

TABLE I
ORDINARY LEAST SQUARES ESTIMATES
STANDARD ERRORS IN PARENTHESIS

(1)
$$\begin{aligned} RE = &-0.003597 + 0.01874\,SC + 0.5680\,ADVS + 0.00197\,LOGCAP \\ &\;(0.0337)\quad\;\;(0.0235)\qquad\;(0.119)\qquad\quad(0.00267) \\ &+ 0.01779\,SCALE + 0.07752\,AEIC + 0.1619\,STD - 0.01186\,BETA \\ &\;\;(0.106)\qquad\qquad(0.0264)\qquad\;(0.237)\qquad(0.0131) \\ &+ 0.01944\,GD + 0.1653\,MS - 0.00759\,CLOGA \\ &\;\;(0.00479)\quad\;(0.0306)\quad\;(0.00717) \\ &R^2 = 0.5656 \qquad SEE = 0.0370 \end{aligned}$$

(2)
$$\begin{aligned} RA = &-0.00609 + 0.02028\,SC + 0.2641\,ADVS + 0.00163\,LOGCAP \\ &\;(0.0213)\quad(0.0149)\qquad(0.0755)\qquad(0.00169) \\ &-0.07513\,SCALE + 0.0896\,AEIC + 0.003061\,STD - 0.0106\,BETA \\ &\;\;(0.0673)\qquad\quad(0.0167)\qquad(0.150)\qquad\quad(0.00830) \\ &+ 0.00866\,GD + 0.09871\,MS - 0.00862\,CLOGA \\ &\;\;(0.00303)\quad\;(0.0194)\quad\;(0.00454) \\ &R^2 = 0.5914 \qquad SEE = 0.0234 \end{aligned}$$

ables in each equation are treated as doubtful and the prior distribution assigns them a location of zero. The upper and lower extreme bounds (denoted U and L) on the coefficient(s) of primary interest are reported for various values of data confidence in Tables II and III for each of the measures of profitability.

The first prior considered is the basic collusion hypothesis of Bain. The focus variable is seller concentration (SC) and all other variables are regarded as doubtful. The extreme bounds are presented in the first row of Tables II and III. The extreme bounds over the entire ellipsoid of constrained estimates is extremely wide (0.237 to −0.026) when rate of return on equity is the dependent variable (Table II). While the upper bound of this coefficient is quite large at the prior, its lower bound is negative and remains negative for values of data confidence that give much more weight to the data. Since larger values of the data confidence mean less weight to the data, the uncertainty in this coefficient that is due to specification uncertainty is very large indeed and is everywhere larger than the sampling uncertainty in the coefficient. This result is obtained for both of the measures of profitability considered. Since the upper bounds of the interval are always positive, it is clear that there are some specifications which will yield a positive conditional correlation between concentration and profits. It is nevertheless clear that such a finding would be a property of the researcher's prior, not of the data.

The second prior considered treats both seller concentration and two common measures of barriers to entry, the extent of scale economies (SCALE) and capital requirements (LOGCAP), as focus variables. All other variables are regarded as doubtful. The second row of Tables II and III shows the extreme bounds on the coefficient of SC for this barriers to entry prior. The third row shows the extreme bounds on the sum of the coefficients of the barriers to entry measures for the same prior. The results in row 2 suggest that inclusion of some measure of barriers to entry as a focus variable is sufficient to bound the conditional correlation of concentration and the rate of return on equity or assets above zero. This may appear to lend support to the barriers to entry hypothesis, but it should be noted that the lower bound is still very close to zero and the uncertainty in the coefficient of SC due to specification uncertainty is quite large and is greater than the sampling uncertainty for all values of the data confidence. Moreover, the extreme bounds on the sum of the coefficients of the barriers to entry measures (SCALE and LOGCAP) are quite wide with a negative lower bound for most values of the data confidence. Thus, the data do not seem terribly informative about the conditional correlation of these two barriers to entry measures and profitability. On the whole, these results suggest to us that the support for the barriers to entry hypothesis is at best very weak.

The third prior considered treats only firm size (CLOGA) as a focus variable with all other variables treated as doubtful. This is a prior that seems implicit in much of the work of Demsetz. The results presented in row 4 of

TABLE II
EXTREME BOUNDS WHEN RETURN ON EQUITY (RE) IS THE DEPENDENT VARIABLE

	Prior Focus Variables	Bounds on Coeff. of	Bounds	Data confidence						
				0.0	0.250	0.500	0.750	0.900	0.990	1.00
1	SC	SC	U	0.0187	0.0823	0.0931	0.150	0.116	0.136	0.237
			L	0.0187	−0.0169	−0.0205	−0.0235	−0.0253	−0.026	−0.026
2	SC, SCALE,	SC	U	0.0187	0.0748	0.0844	0.0946	0.104	0.122	0.228
	LOGCAP		L	0.0187	0.00069	0.00011	0.00010	0.00010	0.00010	0.00010
3	SC, SCALE,	SCALE &	U	0.0198	0.114	0.129	0.146	0.162	0.191	0.564
	LOGCAP	LOGCAP	L	0.0198	−0.0438	−0.0539	−0.0641	−0.0732	−0.0884	−0.129
4	CLOGA	CLOGA	U	−0.00759	0.0132	0.0166	0.0202	0.0237	0.0300	0.0820
			L	−0.00759	−0.0225	−0.0249	−0.0274	−0.0296	−0.0332	−0.0420
5	MS	MS	U	0.165	0.238	0.252	0.266	0.280	0.305	0.527
			L	0.165	0.125	0.122	0.120	0.118	0.118	0.118
6	ADVS	ADVS	U	0.568	0.803	0.843	0.887	0.928	1.00	2.93
			L	0.568	0.482	0.471	0.461	0.453	0.441	0.432
7	GD	GD	U	0.0194	0.0303	0.0321	0.0341	0.0360	0.0395	0.109
			L	0.0194	0.0144	0.0137	0.0131	0.0126	0.0118	0.0108
8	AEIC	AEIC	U	0.0775	0.144	0.156	0.168	0.180	0.200	0.257
	BETA		L	0.0775	0.0194	0.0111	0.0029	−.0041	−0.0148	−0.0249
9	AEIC	BETA	U	−0.0118	0.0139	0.0182	0.0266	0.0266	0.0335	0.0489
	BETA		L	−0.0118	−0.0362	−0.0400	−0.0438	−0.0471	−0.0526	−0.0606
10	STD	STD	U	0.162	0.722	0.815	0.913	1.01	1.18	5.23
			L	0.162	−0.171	−0.226	−0.283	−0.334	−0.442	−0.788

TABLE III
EXTREME BOUNDS WHEN RETURN ON ASSETS (RA) IS THE DEPENDENT VARIABLE

Prior #	*focus Variables*	*Bounds on Coeff. of*	*Bounds*	*Data confidence* P.O	0.250	0.500	0.750	0.900	0.990	1.00
1	SC	SC	U	0.0203	0.0610	0.0678	0.0751	0.0821	0.0950	0.165
			L	0.0203	−0.0022	−0.0048	−0.0070	−0.0085	−0.0096	−0.0096
2	SC, SCALE, LOGCAP	SC	U	0.0203	0.0563	0.0623	0.0688	0.0749	0.0862	0.159
			L	0.0203	0.00814	0.00739	0.00714	0.00714	0.00714	0.00714
3	SC, SCALE, LOGCAP	SCALE & LOGCAP	U	−0.0735	−0.0127	−0.0029	0.00759	0.0176	0.0360	0.294
			L	−0.0735	−0.114	−0.121	−0.128	−0.134	−0.145	−0.183
4	CLOGA	CLOGA	U	−0.0086	0.00493	0.00706	0.00933	0.0115	0.0155	0.0550
			L	−0.0086	−0.0173	−0.0188	−0.0203	−0.0216	−0.0239	−0.0299
5	MS	MS	U	0.0987	0.143	0.151	0.160	0.169	0.185	0.362
			L	0.0987	0.0733	0.0714	0.0699	0.0691	0.0688	0.0688
6	ADVS	ADVS	U	0.264	0.413	0.438	0.465	0.491	0.539	1.98
			L	0.264	0.208	0.200	0.193	0.187	0.177	0.163
7	GD	GD	U	0.00866	0.0154	0.0166	0.0179	0.0191	0.0213	0.0748
			L	0.00866	0.00516	0.00467	0.00418	0.00375	0.00305	0.00153
8	AEIC BETA	AEIC	U	0.0896	0.132	0.139	0.146	0.153	0.164	0.184
			L	0.0896	0.0516	0.0462	0.0408	0.0363	0.0297	0.0249
9	AEIC BETA	BETA	U	−0.0106	0.0053	0.0078	0.0103	0.0126	0.0162	0.0207
			L	−0.0106	−0.0264	−0.0289	−0.0313	−0.0335	−0.0370	−0.0413
10	STD	STD	U	0.00306	0.372	0.430	0.492	0.551	0.660	3.61
			L	0.00306	−0.188	−0.222	−0.258	−0.291	−0.347	−0.619

Tables II and III lend little support to this hypothesis. The value of the coefficient at the data is negative for both of the profitability measures and the extreme bounds span zero for all values of the data confidence.

The next prior considered focuses on market share (MS) as the primary determinant of profitability; all other variables are regarded as doubtful. The results presented in row 5 of Tables II and III show that, although the specification uncertainty leads to substantial uncertainty in the coefficient, the existence of a strong positive correlation between market share and profitability is fairly robust to specification uncertainty. A similar result is obtained when the advertising-sales ratio (ADVS) is treated as the focus variable. Those results, presented in row 6, show strong positive correlation between advertising intensity and profitability. Thus, both of these hypotheses show some sensitivity (in terms of the magnitude of the effect) to uncertainty in the specification, but the direction of the effect is supported by the data. This does not, of course, imply anything about the causal direction of the relationship.

The notion that disequilibrium in an industry, as measured by the growth in demand (GD), is the primary factor affecting profitability is represented by a prior which focuses on GD as the primary variable of interest. These results are presented in row 7 of Tables II and III. Again, while there is substantial uncertainty in the coefficient due to the uncertain specification, the data seem to support a positive correlation between growth and profitability.

The final priors consider measures of risk as the primary determinant of profitability. The first regards both non-diversifiable risk (BETA) and leverage (AEIC) as focus variables. These results are presented in rows 8 and 9 of Tables II and III. The extreme bounds are presented for the coefficients of the two focus variables. The last prior considered focuses on business risk as measured by the variability of a firm's rate of return on equity over time (STD) as the primary determinant of profits. The results presented in row 10 of Tables II and III suggest that there is no support for this hypothesis in the data.

Theory would predict that the sign of the coefficient of BETA should be positive (assuming the measure of profitability is correct) while the coefficient of AEIC should be negative if it is a measure of financial risk and positive if it is a measure of business risk. There is, thus, little interpretation that can be placed on the results for AEIC except to note that the effect of specification uncertainty on the uncertainty in this coefficient is very large. When the effect of the specification uncertainty is accounted for, the data appear uninformative about the coefficient of BETA.

VIII. CONCLUDING REMARKS

The presence of specification uncertainty in studies of the relationship between market structure and performance must be acknowledged. That uncertainty can be accounted for in a way that makes explicit both the maintained hypothesis of the researcher and the incomplete specification of prior uncertainty about the set of conditioning variables. The results of the previous section suggest that when these factors are accounted for, the data examined in this paper do not support the basic collusion hypothesis of Bain. Neither do they lend any convincing support to the barriers to entry hypothesis (i.e., the extended Bain "monopoly power" hypothesis), the absolute firm size hypothesis, or the various "risk premium" hypotheses.

The data offer the strongest support for the hypotheses that advertising and profits are positively correlated and market share (relative firm size) and profits are positively correlated. There are some who would interpret the former finding as evidence in favor of the Bain hypothesis, because they interpret advertising intensity as indicating product differentiation barriers to entry. Alternative, quite different interpretations are offered by Nagle [32]. The robust positive correlation between market share and profits is also subject to two interpretations, one due to Demsetz and Peltzman that firm size is an indication of efficiencies, and the other that large firm size indicates a large capital requirements barrier to entry. The latter would seem to be suspect in this context where capital requirements are used as an additional variable, but the possibility of multiple interpretations itself suggests the limitations of the basic hypothesis considered at this level of abstraction.

There are some who believe that an inductive research program still holds promise (e.g., Scherer [36, p. 295]). Our own view is that stronger theoretical restrictions on the data than are typically offered in market structure—performance studies will make it easier to interpret the conditional correlations that emerge. Whatever course one pursues, it seems clear that the substantial role played by specification uncertainty at the very least counsels caution in the acceptance of empirical results from regressions such as those considered here, particularly if the results of such studies are used to support or advocate changes in public policy. Finally, however, it seems to us that the best way to lend credibility to studies of market structure and performance is to ground them more firmly in economic theory.

James L. Bothwell,
Office of the Chief Economist,
United States General Accounting Office
Washington, D.C., 20548

ACCEPTED APRIL 1983

APPENDIX I

Compendium of Bayesian Terminology

Doubtful variables: The explanatory variables that the researcher is uncertain whether to include or exclude from the regression.

Ellipse of constrained estimates: the set of all estimated values of the coefficients of the doubtful variables resulting from estimation of the regression under all possible linear constraints among the doubtful variables. Each point on this ellipse corresponds to a different estimate of the coefficient of the focus variable.

Likelihood ellipse: the ellipse summarizing the sample information, centered around the unconstrained least squares point (the values of all estimated coefficients when all of the doubtful variables are included in the regression). The ellipse traces out the set of all possible values for the estimated coefficients of the doubtful variables (which implies corresponding values of the coefficients of the focus variables) for a constant sum of squared residuals and a certain probability (data confidence). The larger the probability is, the larger the ellipse is. This corresponds to the classical F test.

Posterior distribution: the estimates resulting from the combination of the prior distribution with the sample likelihood function. These Bayesian posterior estimates will reflect the researcher's prior beliefs about the parameter's values. In pure classical statistics, estimates are formed solely from the sample information—prior information is not explicitly acknowledged.

Prior distribution: the prior location (mean) and prior covariance matrix which summarize the state of ignorance or knowledge about a parameter before the sample data are analyzed.

Prior location: the mean of the prior distribution. Since the researcher is uncertain about including the doubtful variable in the regression, this uncertainty is expressed by setting the prior location of the coefficient of the doubtful variable equal to zero. If the researcher strongly believes that a variable belongs in the regression, then the prior location is unspecified.

Specification uncertainty: the uncertainty of the researcher about what explanatory variables to include in a regression. The effects of specification uncertainty are that every time a regression is estimated with a different set of explanatory variables, the coefficient of the variable of interest (focus variable) will be different.

Upper (Lower) bound: the highest (lowest) value of the coefficient of a focus variable that corresponds to coefficients of the doubtful variables laying within both the ellipse of constrained estimates and a certain confidence ellipse. The data confidence corresponding to each set of extreme bounds indicates the relevant confidence ellipse. The specification uncertainty at each level of data confidence is measured by the distance between the corresponding upper and lower bounds.

APPENDIX II

Summary Characteristics of the Data

Variable	*Mean*	*Standard Deviation*	*Minimum Value*	*Maximum Value*
BETA	0.88837	0.27020	0.31184	1.65872
SC	0.64622	0.17144	0.25000	0.96000
RA	0.08805	0.03549	0.01680	0.22450
RE	0.12582	0.05432	0.02560	0.35740
ADVS	0.02236	0.02814	0.00100	0.11780
CLOGA	2.57779	0.53190	1.32250	4.09120
AEIC	0.81556	0.13395	0.36510	1.00000
GD	0.86853	0.66688	−0.26400	3.97700
MS	0.22551	0.12640	0.04000	0.75000
STD	0.01710	0.01462	0.00141	0.11384
SCALE	0.02444	0.02999	0.00020	0.15570
LOGCAP	3.49367	1.42383	−0.66165	5.92693

REFERENCES

[1] BAIN, JOE S., "Relation of Profit Rate to Industrial Concentration: American Manufacturing, 1936–1940", *Quarterly Journal of Economics*, **65** (August 1951), pp. 293–324.

[2] ——, *Barriers to New Competition* (Harvard University Press, Cambridge 1956).

[3] BAKER, SAMUEL H., "Risk, Leverage, and Profitability: An Industry Analysis", *Review of Economics and Statistics*, **55** (November 1973), pp. 503–507.

[4] BLOCH, HARRY, "Advertising and Profitability: A Reappraisal", *Journal of Political Economy*, **82** (March/April 1974), pp. 267–86.

[5] BOTHWELL, JAMES L. and KEELER, THEODORE E., "Profits, Market Structure, and Portfolio Risk", *Essays on Industrial Organization in Honor of Joe S. Bain*, R. Mason and P. Qualls (eds.) (Ballinger, Cambridge, 1976).

[6] BROZEN, YALE, "The Anti-Trust Task Force Deconcentration Recommendation", *Journal of Law and Economics*, **13** (October 1970), pp. 279–92.

[7] ——, "Bain's Concentration and Rates of Return Revisited", *Journal of Law and Economics*, 14 (October 1971), pp. 351–70.

[8] CHAMBERLAIN, G. and LEAMER, E., "Matrix Weighted Averages and Posterior Bounds", *Journal of the Royal Statistical Society, Series B*, **38** (1976), pp. 73–84.

[9] COMANOR, WILLIAM S., "Comment", *Frontiers of Quantitative Economics*, M. Intriligator (ed.) (North-Holland, Amsterdam, 1971).

[10] ——, *Advertising and Market Power*, (Harvard University Press, Cambridge, 1974).

[11] COMANOR, WILLIAM S. and WILSON, THOMAS A., "Advertising, Market Structure and Performance", *Review of Economics and Statistics*, **49** (November 1967), pp. 423–40.

[12] COOLEY, THOMAS F. and LEROY, S. F., "Identification and Estimation of Money Demand", *American Economic Review*, **72** (December 1981), pp. 825–44.

[13] COOTNER, PAUL and HOLLAND, D., "Rate of Return and Business Risk", *Bell Journal of Law and Economics and Management Science*, **1** (Fall 1970), pp. 211–26.

[14] DEMSETZ, HAROLD, "Industry Structure, Market Rivalry, and Public Policy", *The Journal of Law and Economics*, **16** (April 1973), pp. 1–10.

[15] ——, "Two Systems of Belief about Monopoly", *Industrial Concentration: The New Learning*, H. Goldschmid, H. Mann, and J. Weston (eds.) (Little Brown, Boston, 1974).

[16] FISHER, I. N. and HALL, G. R., "Risk and Corporate Rates of Return", *Quarterly Journal of Economics*, **83** (Februaty 1969), pp. 79–92.

[17] GALE, BRADLEY T., "Market Share and Rate of Return", *Review of Economics and Statistics*, **54** (November 1972), pp. 412–23.

[18] HALL, MARSHALL and WEISS, LEONARD W., "Firm Size and Profitability", *Review of Economics and Statistics*, **49** (August 1967), pp. 319–31.

[19] HURDLE, GLORIA J., "Leverage, Risk, Market Structure and Profitability", *Review of Economics and Statistics*, **56**, (November, 1974).

[20] LEAMER, EDWARD E., *Specification Searches: Ad Hoc Inference with Nonexperimental Data*, (John Wiley and Sons, New York, 1978).

[21] LINTNER, JOHN, "Security Prices, Risk, and Maximal Gains from Diversification", *Journal of Finance*, **20** (December 1965), pp. 587–616.

[22] LITZENBERGER, ROBERT and JOY, O., "Interindustry Profitability Under Uncertainty", *Western Economic Journal*, **25** (September 1973), pp. 338–49.

[23] LUCAS, ROBERT E., "Adjustment Costs and the Theory of Supply", *The Journal of Political Economy*, **75** (August 1967, part 1), pp. 321–34.

[24] ——, "On the Size Distribution of Business Firms", *The Bell Journal of Economics*, Vol. 9, No. 2 (Autumn 1978), pp. 508–23.

[25] MACAVOY, PAUL W., MCKIE, JAMES W. and PRESTON, LEE E., "High and Stable Concentration Levels, Profitability, and Public Policy: A Response", *Journal of Law and Economics*, **15** (October 1971), pp. 493–99.

[26] MANN, H. MICHAEL, "Seller Concentration, Barriers to Entry, and Rates of Return in Thirty Industries", *Review of Economics and Statistics*, **48** (August 1966), pp. 296–307.

[27] MARTIN, STEPHEN, "Advertising, Concentration, and Profitability: The Simultaneity Problem", *Bell Journal of Economics*, Vol. 10, No. 2 (Autumn 1979), pp. 639–47.

[28] MASON, EDWARD S., "Price and Production Policies of Large-Scale Enterprise", *American Economic Review*, Supplement 29 (March 1939), pp. 61–74.

[29] MCGEE, JOHN S., *In Defense of Industrial Concentration*, (Praeger, New York, 1971).

[30] MODIGLIANI, FRANCO, "New Developments on the Oligopoly Front", *Journal of Political Economy*, **66** (June 1958), pp. 215–32.

[31] ——, and MILLER, MERTON H., "The Cost of Capital, Corporation Finance, and the Theory of Investment", *American Economic Review*, **48** (June 1958), pp. 261–79.

[32] NAGLE, THOMAS, "Do Advertising-Profitability Studies Really Show That Advertising Creates a Barrier to Entry?" *Journal of Law and Economics*, Vol. XXIV, (October 1981), pp. 333–49.

[33] PELTZMAN, SAM, "The Gains and Losses from Industrial Concentration", *The Journal of Law and Economics*, XX, No. 2, (October 1977), pp. 229–53.

[34] QUALLS, DAVID, "Concentration, Barriers to Entry and Long Run Economic Profit Margins", *Journal of Industrial Economics*, **12** (April 1972), pp. 146–68.

[35] ——. "Stability and Persistence of Economic Profit Margins in Highly Concentrated Industries", *Southern Economic Journal*, **40** (April 1974), pp. 604–12.

[36] SCHERER, F. M., *Industrial Market Structure and Economic Performance* (2nd Ed.), (Rand, McNally, Chicago, 1980).

[37] SCHMALENSEE, RICHARD, *The Economics of Advertising*, (Amsterdam: North Holland, 1972).

[38] SHARPE, WILLIAM F., "Capital Asset Prices: A Theory of Market Equilibrium Under Conditions of Risk", *Journal of Finance*, **19** (September 1964), pp. 425–42.

[39] SHEPHERD, WILLIAM G., "The Elements of Market Structure", *Review of Economics and Statistics*, **54** (February 1972), pp. 25–38.
[40] SIMS, CHRISTOPHER A., "Macroeconomics and Reality", *Econometrica*, **48** (January 1980), pp. 1–48.
[41] STIGLER, GEORGE, J., *Capital and Rates of Return in Manufacturing Industries*, (Princeton University Press, Princeton, 1963).
[42] U.S. House of Representatives, Select Committee on Small Business, *Mergers and Super-Concentration*, (November 1962).
[43] VERNON, JOHN M., *Market Structure and Industrial Performance: A Review of Statistical Findings* (Allyn and Bacon, Boston, 1972).
[44] WEISS, LEONARD W., "The Concentration-Profits Relationship and Antitrust", *Industrial Concentration: The New Learning*, H. Goldschmid, H. M. Mann and J. F. Weston (eds.) (Little Brown, Boston, 1974).
[45] ——, "Quantitative Studies of Industrial Organization", *Frontiers of Quantitative Economics*, M. Intriligator (ed.) (North Holland, Amsterdam 1971).
[46] ——, "Advertising, Profits and Corporate Taxes", *Review of Economics and Statistics*, **51** (November 1969), pp. 421–36.

THE JOURNAL OF INDUSTRIAL ECONOMICS 0022–1821 $2.00
Volume XXXII June 1984 No. 4

CONCENTRATION INDICES AND MARKET POWER: TWO VIEWS*

MARIE-PAULE DONSIMONI, PAUL GEROSKI AND ALEXIS JACQUEMIN

INTRODUCTION

Many industrial economists believe that, despite being a little crude and frequently somewhat *ad hoc*, concentration indices can be useful in assessing the state of competitiveness in markets. We too believe this to be the case, but discern that there exist two rather different views on why this might be. Though these two views have been frequently discussed, usually it has been independently of each other and an attempt at synthesis seems necessary. Hence, the purpose of this paper is to compare them systematically in order to derive their respective implications for the measurement of concentration, for empirical work on market performance, and for antitrust policy.

THE STRUCTURALIST VIEW

Dating from the early work of Mason, a number of economists have advanced the proposition that the 'performance' of firms in any industry is largely determined by the 'structure' of the market they operate in. The definition of structure used in these arguments is somewhat loose, but there is widespread agreement that the various features of importance needed to account for variations in industry performance include: the number and size distribution of buyers and sellers, entry conditions, product characteristics, the nature of international competition, and so on (for seminal expositions of this position, see Bain [1951], [1956], [1959]). Since many of these structural features are interdependent (e.g., extensive scale economies give rise to high levels of concentration, highly concentrated markets frequently are highly differentiated, and so on), the structuralist hypothesis is fundamentally a *joint* hypothesis about the *combined* effects of a number of factors on industry performance: ". . . concentration is simply one determinant of industry structure and is not of itself a measure of monopoly or market power . . ." (Comanor and Wilson [1967; p. 423]). However, over time the notion that 'industry structure determines industry performance' has become increasingly identified with the *partial* hypothesis that more concentrated oligopolies enjoy significantly larger

* We wish to dedicate this paper to the memory of Elizabeth Brunner in recognition of her efforts on behalf of this journal and her contributions to Industrial Economics. Useful remarks from J. Cubbin and an anonymous referee are gratefully acknowledged.

rates of profit than less concentrated ones (this might be described as a triumph of t over F statistics!). The corollary of this somewhat restrictive version of the structuralist hypothesis is that: "... the purpose of a measure of concentration is to predict the extent of the departure of price ... from the competitive level" (Stigler [1968; p. 30]).[1]

To make even the restricted structuralist hypothesis operational requires an extensive measurement exercise, and this applies particularly to industry concentration (for a good discussion, see Curry and George [1983; pp. 204–15]). Bain used four firm Concentration Ratios in his original 1951 study, but the gradual easing of data constraints has led to the construction of alternate measures (such as Herfindahl or Entropy indices) which utilize information on the entire distribution of firm sizes. Since the structuralist hypothesis is founded on the causal argument that structure affects performance primarily by determining behavior or conduct, the choice amongst these various concentration indices should be made by modelling how structure affects conduct (for an effort along these lines, see Stigler [1964]), but this has proved too difficult. As a consequence, a large literature has devoted itself to examining the comparative statistical properties of different concentration indices conceived as summary statistics of the distribution of firm sizes in an industry (Hart [1975] and Davies [1979] are interesting examples of this type of work), and choice is usually made on such criteria.

However its components are measured, the structuralist hypothesis is potentially *falsifiable* since it posits a systematic association between performance and the combined effect of various exogenous structural features of an industry. This has naturally led to the estimation of equations involving performance being regressed on as many structural variables as possible, and to a lot of concern with 'overall explanation'. However, in the absence of theorizing to assist the construction of precise functional relationships, the structuralist hypothesis is actually rather weak since it is hardly conceivable that there would be no correlation between some element of structure and industry performance.[2] In fact, the existence of a statistical link between structure and performance does not fully address the crucial issue of the direction of causality between the two. Since the mechanism through which structure affects

[1] The "structure-performance" hypothesis has been further refined to account for intra-industry variations in performance (see, for example, Porter [1979], Oster [1982] and Donsimoni and Leoz-Arguelles [1982]), but this extension involves no revision of those characteristics of the structuralist hypothesis that we are concerned with here.

[2] Econometric implementation of the structuralist approach is discussed in Weiss [1974], Scherer [1980], Phillips [1976], Sawyer [1982], and Cowling [1976]. The multicollinearity endemic to these regressions provides good support for rejecting the restricted structuralist view focusing solely on concentration, since it clearly indicates the interdependence of all the elements of market structure. Measuring performance is another difficulty which must be faced (Scherer [1980] or Weiss [1974] are excellent discussions; Fisher and McGowan [1983] focus on a somewhat particular definition of performance). The well known Demsetz [1974] market power-efficiency ambiguity is basically concerned with the welfare implications of structure-performance (although his notion of 'efficiency' is disconcertingly broad), and the extreme version of Demsetz's counter-hypothesis seems inconsistent with the data; see Caves and Pugel [1980], for example.

performance is via the impact of structure on conduct, controlled experiments are probably the appropriate means to use to ascertain this causality (Plott [1982] provides a survey of these experimental approaches; Scherer [1980] discusses the extensive case study literature looking at the impact of structure on various forms of inter-firm co-operations).[3] The importance of this last point emerges when one considers the *two implications for antitrust* that emanate from the structuralist hypothesis, for neither has much appeal in the absence of strong causal links in the hypothesized direction.

Since variations in structure are thought to cause systematic variations in performance, the nature of this association can clearly be used to guide antitrust intervention. That is, if it is the case that the association between the two is monotonically increasing, then an obvious intervention rule is to attack those industries which have the highest levels of concentration, since these are the ones most likely to exhibit systematically high and persistent excess profitability.[4] However, the structuralist hypothesis implies considerably more than just an intervention rule, it also suggests the type of antitrust policy which is appropriate; viz., the manipulation of market structure. Since it is the latter which is seen as the ultimate determinant of how firms conduct their affairs and so of eventual market performance, then it is at this primal feature of the market that policy makers ought to direct their attention.[5]

To sum up, the structuralist hypothesis (at least in its more sensitive versions) is a joint hypothesis outlining the causal determination of performance through the collective interdependent effects of several facets of market structure on conduct. Concentration levels are one of a number of independent predictors of performance. In the absence of specific information on precisely how the different dimensions of the size distribution of firms affect conduct, the *appropriate concentration index is not well defined* and, in the absence of precise information on the inter-relationships between the various facets of structure, its total effect on performance cannot be assessed with any accu-

[3] Conventional thinking on this issue points towards the use of multiequation models, but this is not really a solution to the problem at all. Simultaneity bias is a concern with consistency in estimation; that is, with whether one needs supplementary equations in order to get unbiased estimates of the parameters of the profits equation (for multi-equation models, see Strickland and Weiss [1976], Geroski [1982b], and others). Exogeneity in a statistical sense is a somewhat stronger concept (e.g., Engle *et al.* [1983]), involving the notion of whether such additional equations would also increase the efficiency of estimating the parameters of the profits equation. Neither is the same as testing causal direction in a controlled experiment.

[4] It follows that empirically determining the appropriate functional form is an important issue, since it is that which embodies the intervention guidance rule (this point is made in Geroski [1982a]). The practical importance of the point can be found in the various non-linear profit-concentration empirical models which are beginning to abound in the literature, many of which suggest the considerably simplified policy rule of monitoring only those industries where concentration exceeds some 'critical' level.

[5] See, for example, Kaysen and Turner [1965]. While structuralist policies have, in the main, concentrated on anti-merger activity, the Neal Committee of 1968 and Senator Hart (with his Industrial Reorganization Acts of 1974 and 1976) have pushed much further towards actually breaking down intrenched monopoly positions; for some reactions, see Goldschmidt *et al.* [1974, pp. 340–426).

racy. Nevertheless, a correlation between profits and concentration forms the basis, in this view, of a rough and ready predictor of industry performance and of the likely benefits of structural antitrust intervention.

A NEW VIEW

1. *The Basic Paradigm*

What might be called the 'non-causal' alternative asserts that the level of industry concentration is not an exogenous determinant of conduct, but that it is useful for assessing industry performance despite its endogeneity (e.g., Saving [1970], Cowling and Waterson [1976], Encaoua and Jacquemin [1980], Geroski [1982a], Clarke and Davies [1982]).

The argument starts with a precise definition of performance. *At the level of a firm* it is natural to focus on the Lerner index of monopoly power, viz. the discrepancy between price and marginal cost. Defining performance *at the industry level* requires additional considerations. To see the problem, consider two duopolies which involve pairs of Lerner indices: (0.4, 0) and (0.2, 0.2), respectively. The first industry could be considered to show lower levels of performance because of the high level of power exercised by the first firm, the second industry could be considered worse because, while no one firm has 'excessive' power, all firms have substantial power, or both industries could be considered equally bad because 'on average' they involve equal elevations of price above marginal cost. Evidently, industry performance is a notion which depends not only on the average extent of power exercised by all firms, but on the distribution of power within the industry; it involves explicit normative judgments concerning how the performance of the individual industry members is to be 'added up' to an overall summary figure. To fix ideas, assume that there are N firms, indexed by subscript n, in a homogeneous goods industry. A fairly general overall index of industry performance, $P = P(l_1, \ldots, l_N)$, can be constructed from individual firm Lerner indices, l_n, using weights α_n:

$$P(l_1, \ldots, l_N) \equiv \sum_{n=1}^{N} \alpha_n l_n, \tag{1}$$

and this is what we shall work with hereafter.

Having defined industry performance, it is clear that direct observation of individual firm Lerner indices plus selection of the weights renders P observable. In such circumstances, there is clearly no need for concentration indices or, indeed, any structural measure whatsoever to predict performance. Hence, concentration indices will be useful only if performance cannot be directly observed. They can be used to proxy market performance under conditions of data paucity by using standard economic theory. Assume, for simplicity, that the N industry members maximize profits, that they know cost and demand conditions, and that they hold beliefs concerning their rivals' reactions. In the homogeneous-goods case,[6] the outputs selected by each firm determine the industry price, and the first-order conditions describing the determinants of these output levels can be rewritten as:

$$(2) \qquad l_n \equiv \frac{f(q) - c_n'(q_n)}{f(q)} = \frac{\beta_n s_n}{\eta}, \qquad n = 1, \ldots, N,$$

where $p = f(q)$ is the price prevailing in the industry, $q = \sum_{n=1}^{N} q_n$ is the output level of the industry, c_n' is firm n's marginal cost, s_n is its market share, β_n is unity plus the sum of its conjectural variations concerning the response of its $(N - 1)$ rivals to changes in its own output, and η is the absolute value of industry demand elasticity. Then, aggregating the right hand-side of (2) using the same weights that defined P, the *appropriate concentration* index which best reflects performance (with a factor of proportionality η) is, $S = S(l_1, \ldots, l_N)$:

$$(3) \qquad S(l_1, \ldots, l_N) \equiv \sum_{n=1}^{N} \alpha_n (s_n \beta_n).$$

Thus, having started from the definition (1) we have, using the theoretical model reflected in (2), deduced what is the appropriate concentration index to proxy unobserved performance.[7] As can be seen in (3), the concentration index so derived depends on market conduct and the normative judgments which are embodied in the definition of industry performance.

2. *Implementation Problems*

It is instructive to contrast this new approach with the structuralist one. When concentration is conceived as an exogenous determinant of performance, it can be used to *predict* it; when the two are considered to be jointly determined, then one can only be seen as a *proxy* for the other. In terms of correlations, the new approach is interested not so much in whether some particular concentration index is correlated to performance as with selecting that concentration index which maximizes the correlation. A second difference is that the appropriate concentration index defined in (3) is a *sufficient statistic.* That is, when concentration is viewed as endogenous, it includes, at equilibrium, *all* the

[6] For some explorations of concentration indices which may be useful to reflect the localized competition characteristic of markets with extensive product differentiation, see Schmalensee [1983]. Geroski [1983] produces an analogue to (3) below for differentiated goods. Obviously when products are differentiated, one is liable to wish to place far more stress on distributive evaluations of performance relative to the usual efficiency considerations, and so weight firms according to *what* as well as *how much* they produce.

[7] This contrasts with the axiomatic approach of Hannah and Kay [1977] or Encaoua and Jacquemin [1980] which involves making some relatively mild assumptions about what industry performance ought to be, and using this to rule out a number of measures which are inconsistent with even such weak restrictions. The correspondingly stronger assumptions made here about what performance consists of is what enables us to reduce the set of 'acceptable' measures of concentration to a single 'appropriate' measure.

various exogenous factors (scale economies, product differentiation advantages or absolute cost advantages) embodied in cost and demand conditions which together determine the performance of firms and so of the industry as a whole. Hence, it is *the only* piece of information needed to proxy performance. By contrast, in the structuralist view, concentration is *only one* of several structural features which determine performance and so it can hardly be relied upon to predict accurately alone.

In order to appreciate more fully the differences between the two approaches, it is necessary to spend some time considering the two elements involved in constructing appropriate concentration indices: the normative judgments which define the exercise from the outset (i.e., the α's) and the nature of the necessary empirical work involved in assessing conduct (i.e., the β's). We consider each in turn.

2.1 *Normative Judgments*

The natural theoretical approach to choosing the weights α_n to use in policy discussion is to carefully specify a social welfare function. This automatically determines the weights (e.g., Dansby and Willig [1979], Dixit and Stern [1982] and others), but frequently involves defining P in terms of α's which require a good deal of information not usually available. From the point of view of applied workers, one wishes to restrict attention to that class of industry performance measures which are defined by weighting systems whose components, the α's, are relatively simple to compute. The two important choices in this regard to be made are the *base* of the α's, and their *relative size.*

One obvious easily implementable base for the α's are market shares, involving a judgment: $\alpha_n = f(s_n)$ to discriminate between firms by their relative size. The usual course of affairs in applied work is to select weights: $\alpha_n = s_n$, so that industry performance is defined as the market share weighted average of the individual firm Lerner indices. When unit costs are constant, this becomes nothing more than the industry profit-sales ratio, and obviously is fairly easy to observe. Indeed, its easy observability seems to be its main attraction, and it is worth emphasizing that that also implies that there will be little need to develop appropriate concentration indices to proxy it.

From (1) and with additional information on η, one can also use l_n as a base, forming a judgment: $\alpha_n = g(l_n)$ which can be implemented with market share data. That there is a difference between using s_n and l_n follows from noting that: $l_i > l_j$, but $s_j > s_i$ if: $(s_i/s_j) > (\beta_j/\beta_i)$; the substantive basis of the difference between using weights based on l_n or on s_n is that the former penalizes firms on the basis of actual market power exercised regardless of size, while the latter penalizes size per se regardless of performance.[8] Normative

[8] Weights based upon l_n also have the advantage of being negative when l_n is, a desirable property since deviations above *and* below price equals marginal cost are inimical to welfare; see Cowling and Mueller [1978] in a related context.

concern solely with allocative efficiency dictates choices of weights based on l_n (as in Dansby and Willig [1979]), and so the use of *size based weights* involves *additional* normative judgments about the distribution of output across firms. For example, one may decide that having all output supplied by a monopolist is inferior to a situation where several firms supply the same market, even if in both situations the equilibrium price is equidistant from marginal cost.[9]

Having chosen a basis for the α's, the second question to be faced is their relative size. The most subtle aspect of this question is whether one can reasonably neglect small firms altogether, assigning them zero weight. This corresponds to a normative decision to ignore any welfare loss created by small firms elevating their prices, and is not an unreasonable course to follow (if only because such distortions are unlikely to affect many consumers). In a sense, it is the underlying justification for applying a "rule of reason" in antitrust policy. Such a normative decision makes reasonable the omission of perhaps even large parts of the distribution of firm sizes in constructing concentration indices because it defines industry performance in a way which steers attention away from *any* actions such firms may choose to take.[10] The remaining question concerned with relative size is whether to make the weights non-linear in their base. One obvious situation in which this would be desirable is when there is some concern over inequality of outcomes. For example, one might believe that relatively equal sized firms are conducive to increased research or to competition in some other non-price dimension and elect to use weights: $\alpha_n = (s_n - 1/N)^2$ which penalize unequal outcomes directly.[11]

2.2 *Measuring Market Conduct*

The first necessary step in computing appropriate concentration indices is setting the α's, and this reflects various normative choices. The α's are, in some sense, a given for the individual researcher and need only be made explicit. Defining the β's is, by contrast, *basically an empirically issue*. In practical terms,

[9] Such additional judgments are likely to arise because one believes that performance ought to be assessed on grounds wider than just price and its relation to marginal cost. Blackorby *et al.* [1982] advocate forming social value judgments directly on the distribution of industry output across firms, and we are willing to follow this as far as to suggest a presumption towards having a reasonably large number of firms even when circumstances can be contrived to make a monopolist produce a competitive output.

[10] Such a case is examined, for instance, by d'Aspremont and Jacquemin [1984] who use Shapley values to measure the power to monopolize. Firms with no ability to induce a shift from a competitive to a co-operative regime through coalitions are considered as "null-firms", in spite of their non-null market share.

[11] In this case,

$$S = \sum_{n=1}^{N} s_n^3 - \frac{2}{N} H + \frac{1}{N} \quad \text{if} \quad \beta_n = 1 \quad \text{for all } n$$

(i.e., all firms are Cournot), where $H \equiv \sum_{n=1}^{N} s_n^2$ is the Herfindahl index of concentration. Such welfare judgments present an interesting instance where a *single* concentration index (such as H or $1/N$) is *insufficiently* sensitive to reflect what is a fairly sophisticated notion of performance.

this involves assessing the extent to which each firm is willing to contribute to the output restriction necessary for all to jointly achieve monopoly profits; the lower bound (i.e., $\beta_n = 0$ for all n) corresponds to perfectly competitive behavior which involves no output restriction. Particular values of the β's correspond to different solution concepts and this implies that, for a given set of weights α's, different concentration indices correspond to different solution concepts. Thus, a Cournot industry generates a different appropriate concentration index from industry pricing which follows a Dominant Firm pattern (one may find that a Herfindahl index is appropriate in the first case, and a Concentration Ratio in the latter).

There are obviously a great many difficulties involved in assessing conduct, and a number of ways in which the exercise can be performed. The two most basic questions to be addressed are: (i) "do all firms contribute to output restriction?", and (ii) "do all those who do (i.e., who are characterized by strictly positive β's) do so to an equal extent (i.e., are characterized by the same value of β)?" Simple answers to these questions (based, perhaps, on a distinction between different groups of firms within an industry[12]) facilitate the rapid construction of rough indices of market structure, although more sophisticated techniques will obviously yield more precise information. What one wishes to do is to estimate particularly the distribution of the β's across industry members for some year t (which, with market shares for t, can be used to proxy unobserved performance in t). Obviously a times series of data on l_n and s_n for a number of years up to n for each firm i can be used with (2) to produce estimates of β_n which can be taken as an estimate of the true β_{in} in t.[13] One need not estimate constant values of β_n for the pre-test period of course, and it is easy to model and estimate simple yearly variations in β_n over time (firm or industry specific) to improve one's prediction of β_{nt}; it is also possible to use times series data involving aggregates (industry profits or the profits of the leading group taken together) to make rough and ready estimates of most of the β_n's (Geroski, [1983], considers this type of data constrained problem). If time variation is thought not to be important, cross section data for pre-t years can be used (although for a single year cross-section sample we cannot estimate very many different values for the β_n). Finally, case study work and qualitative studies are perfectly acceptable methodologies provided that attention is directed to at least ranking firms correctly by the extent of their contribution to output restriction and getting a rough feel for relative contributions. From the point of view of (3), any reasonable proxies $[\beta_1/\gamma, \ldots,$

[12] Suppose that one was able to separate the industry into three homogeneous groups (I_i, $i = 1, 2, 3$) such that $\beta_3 > \beta_2 > \beta_1 = 0$. Then, if one defines performance using $\alpha_i = s_i$, it follows that $S = \beta_2 \sum_{i \in I_2} s_i^2 + \beta_3 \sum_{i \in I_3} s_i^2$ (i.e. the appropriate concentration index is a weighted sum of two of the intra-group Herfindahl indices). This reduction of N unknown β's to two obviously considerably simplifies computation of S.

[13] One need not use profits data; indeed, it would be preferable to use data directly relating to prices and marginal cost to avoid the familiar monopoly power-efficiency problem. For references to empirical work along these lines, see Geroski, [1983].

β_N/γ] for the true vector of β_n's gives an index proportional to the appropriate one, and that is good enough for most purposes.

The contrast with the empirical work suggested by the structuralist approach can be usefully made explicit at this point. In that methodology, one seeks a correlation between concentration and profits to infer that, because of market structure, market power exists. When performance cannot be directly observed, one could use such a correlation (together with information on other structural factors) to predict it, but the exercise is evidently poorly defined from this point of view since it provides no assurance that the predictor so used is anything like the best possible. In the new approach, the focus of attention is turned completely away from the testing of causal propositions towards the construction of sufficient proxy variables. Given a definition of performance (including the normative judgments it involves), economic theory is used not so much to design experiments as to guide the construction of estimates of important unobservables. In the context of concentration indices, this involves assessing conduct which, though interesting in its own right, is purely instrumental. That is, choice of the optimal concentration index involves assessing conduct because this is exactly the information one needs in order to make the leap from relative firm size to firm performance, and it is performance which is the object of the exercise.

SOME IMPLICATIONS OF THE NEW VIEW

We have contrasted two views about the nature of the relationship between concentration and industry performance, showing differences in the way economic theory is used empirically and stressing that, as with any evaluator of economic performance, concentration indices are not value free. There seem to be three implications of this new view which are worth remarking upon.

The first implication is that the new approach places relatively more stress on *intra-industry* work than on *inter-industry* work. The reason is that conduct is likely to be industry specific to some degree, and thus that each industry is correspondingly liable to require its own concentration index. This, of course, does not rule out using a single concentration index to proxy performance in different industries; what is required is that explicit attention be paid to the *errors of measurement* which arise from incorrect assessment of industry conduct when the "wrong" concentration index is applied to a particular industry. From a practical point of view, such errors can be minimized when the same appropriate index is applied only to industries which are likely to behave in fairly similar ways. As with any errors in variables problem, what is of supreme importance is that steps are taken to insure that such errors are purely random and uncorrelated with variables of interest.

The second implication is that the use of any particular concentration index requires both normative and empirical justification. For example, what is one to make of a statement like: "the four-firm Concentration Ratio of industry *i* has risen in the past few years"? If one is concerned only with the leading firms in the industry from the point of view of welfare, or if one genuinely believes that they are the only firms which cause welfare loss, then one is implicitly using a set of α's and β's which are such as to make the too often criticized four-firm Concentration Ratio the appropriate proxy for performance, and one ought rightfully be concerned by such movements in it. However, if one believes: (i) that the market is "contestable" (i.e. $\beta_n = 0$ for all n; see Baumol *et al.* [1982]); (ii) that one ought to use performance based weights and that, for the industry in question, η is very large; or (iii) that asymmetry in market shares is undesirable per se, then movements in the four-firm Concentration Ratio can be viewed with some equanimity since, under these circumstances, it is unlikely to be highly related to the appropriate concentration index.

The problem can also be illustrated with a few simple exercises. Suppose first that the industry is Cournot (i.e., $\beta_n = 1$) for all n. Then from equation (3), if the weights are: $\{\alpha_n = 1, n = 1, \ldots, 4, \text{ and } \alpha_n = 0, n = 5, \ldots, N\}$, then the four-firm Concentration Ratio is appropriate; if the weights are $\{\alpha_n = s_n, n = 1, \ldots, N\}$, the Herfindahl index is appropriate; if the weights are $\{\alpha_n = l_n, n = 1, \ldots, N\}$, then the appropriate index is the Herfindahl divided by η; and if $\{\alpha_n = |\log s_n|\}$, then the Entropy index is appropriate. Suppose now, by contrast, that the four leading firms ($n = 1, \ldots, 4$) are Dominant and that the rest are competitive (i.e., $\beta_n = \beta > 0$, $n = 1, \ldots, 4$ and zero otherwise). Then, optimal indices corresponding to the four sets of normative judgments above are:

$$\beta \sum_{n=1}^{4} s_n,\ \beta \sum_{n=1}^{4} s_n^2,\ (\beta/\eta) \sum_{n=1}^{4} s_n^2, \text{ and } \beta \sum_{n=1}^{4} [\log s_n] s_n \text{ respectively}$$

(further computations are described in the Appendix). The general points that follow from these examples are: that the same index (e.g., the four-firm Concentration Ratio) is consistent with rather different sets of normative judgments and explicit beliefs about industry conduct; that performance based normative weights reintroduce the elasticity of demand as a crucial element in constructing the appropriate concentration index; and that, for a given set of normative judgments about performance (explicit beliefs about industry conduct), apparently minor changes in explicit beliefs about conduct (normative judgments about performance) can have a noticeable effect on the definition of the appropriate index. In short, there is no such thing as an "optimal" index of concentration, both because different industries behave differently as well as because no obvious widely accepted normative judgments exist to guarantee its optimality.

Finally, it is worth considering the antitrust implications of the new approach. As can be expected, they differ markedly from those of the structuralist approach. In the first place, it is clear that choice of the α's carries with it some implications of where, within an industry, attention ought to be centered. Inspection of equation (2) reveals that α_n is the marginal gain in overall industry performance P achieved by reducing l_n by one unit, and so the entire system of weights which define P also determine a presumption about the "ideal" distribution of power within the industry. Those firms which are assigned a higher weight are those calling for most attention should the industry be deemed to need antitrust intervention. There remain two further questions. First, in terms of *policy standards*, is it opportune for the antitrust authorities to use concentration indices to guide intervention? Second, in terms of *policy enforcement*, what role can structural remedies play? In answer to the first question, it is clear that appropriate concentration indices make sense as useful screening devices to aid the selection of cases where the probability of adverse welfare effects is high. As we have seen, such indices really require only very simple evaluations of conduct, and so represent the kind of inexpensive first step towards the full and very complex analysis of industry performance (which includes, *inter alia*, accurate measurement of performance itself) necessary for reasonable antitrust intervention. Rather than simply selecting some concentration index on the basis of habit or out of fondness for its statistical properties, it seems sensible for the authorities to construct approximate appropriate indices. The second question concerns the possible role of structural manipulations (such as dissolution and divestiture) in antitrust policy. Strictly speaking (and in contrast to structuralist antitrust policy), such concerns seem misplaced. *Conduct* is, in this new view, the basic exogenous variable giving rise to market power and excess profits, and it ought to be the *subject of direct policy attention* whenever intervention is thought necessary. This view, evident in the context of static oligopoly models, is even more compelling when one considers dynamic strategic competition in which firm's actions have, over time, an indirect effect by altering market structure in a way which constrains rivals subsequent actions (see Encaoua *et al.* [1982]). Of course, it is hard to imagine that current structure does not affect future conduct,[14] and so one may see in such dynamic links a role for structural manipulations; in practice, however, it is hard to imagine a blunt tool such as structural manipulation usefully effecting delicate alterations in business conduct.

CONCLUSION

We have contrasted two views concerning the usefulness of concentration indices and have traced the implications of each for empirical work and policy implication. It ought not be too big a surprise to discover that, in analysing

[14] That current structure affects future conduct is an eminently reasonable proposition which does not affect the view of conduct as exogenous in the slightest, for it is current period conduct (however determined) which jointly determines current structure and performance. If current structure affects future conduct, then (in the sense of a reduced form) it affects future performance and structure jointly, and such a relationship could be written as 'explaining' either structure or performance at any time t in terms of their own respective histories.

market performance, the assumption one makes about what is exogenous has an enormous impact on the goals and methods of empirical investigation and on the kinds of policy advice one may wish to give. The choice between the two schools of thought discussed here is really quite simple: either structure is to be taken as exogenous and as a determinant of conduct and thus performance; or, conduct is taken to be the important exogenous variable which jointly determines both structure and performance.

What can be said about the choice between these two views? Obviously traditional oligopoly theory lies in the second tradition. Like most of economic theory, it takes as given the tastes, beliefs and goals of agents, and traces the consequences of their choices in a parametrically given environment: ". . . since conduct involves setting quantities, it is hard to see how any theory of oligopoly could take concentration indices to be exogenous" (Dixit and Stern [1982, p. 123]). Of course, this association with orthodoxy need not compel one to reject the view that it is structure which is exogenous; indeed, there is no doubt that the structure of markets in some broad sense affects firms' behavior (the often discussed sleepiness of Dominant Firms is a familiar example of the type of phenomena under consideration). What it does do, it seems to us, is firmly to divorce the notion of market structure from concentration indices based on current or medium run flow variables. The research problem of the structuralist school has always been that of developing satisfactorily conceptualisations and measurements of "market structure" in order practically to operationalize the notion that human behavior can be determined by the circumstances surrounding choice. Leaping over this very considerable step to the rather more exciting task of "testing the theory" has led to the widespread use of concentration indices in conceptually inappropriate ways. The structuralist hypothesis seems to us to be valid and interesting and concentration indices seem to us to be useful for assessing market performance, but the two are very different animals.

M. P. Donsimoni, P. Geroski and
Alexis Jacquemin,
C.R.I.D.E.
3 Place Montesquieu,
Louvain la Neuve, 1348,
Belgium

ACCEPTED AUGUST 1983

APPENDIX

Thinking of appropriate concentration indices parametrized by the α's and β's suggests exploration of how the two trade-off in determining any one particular index. The purpose of this appendix is to provide two examples which are suggestive in this respect.

TABLE I

Types of Market Conduct	Types of Weights		
	I: Relative to all the firms		
	Mean $(1/N)$	*Value* (s_{nm})	*Log inverse* $\lvert \log s_{nm} \rvert$
$\beta_{nm} = \beta$	$\beta(1/N)$	βH	βE
$\beta_{nm} = \beta_m$	$\sum_{m=1}^{M} \beta_m s_m (1/N)$	$\sum_{m=1}^{M} \beta_m s_m^2 H_m$	$\sum_{m=1}^{M} \beta_m [s_m E_m - s_m \log(1/s_m)]$
	II: Relative to subgroups		
	Mean $(1/NM)$	*Value* (s_{nm}/s_m)	*Log inverse* $\lvert \log s_{nm}/s_m \rvert$
$\beta_{nm} = \beta$	$\beta \sum_{m=1}^{M} s_m^2 (1/NM)$	$\beta \sum_{m=1}^{M} s_m^2 H_m$	$\beta \sum_{m=1}^{M} s_m^2 E_m$
$\beta_{nm} = \beta_m$	$\sum_{m=1}^{M} \beta_m s_m^2 (1/NM)$	$\sum_{m=1}^{M} \beta_m s_m^2 H_m$	$\sum_{m=1}^{M} \beta_m s_m^2 E_m$

Note: E and H are the traditional Entropy and Herfindahl indices computed on the whole population, while E_m and H_m are respectively the same computed on the subpopulation.

To get a feel of how the appropriate index is affected by alternative normative judgments, or beliefs about conduct, assume that there are M groups of firms (indexed by subscript m) and that each group contains firms with the same β_m (this corresponds loosely to the notion of "strategic groups"). Let s_{nm} be the market share of firm n in group m, and s_m the market share of group m. Table I displays a number of simple appropriate concentration indices which emerge by varying β or α. In the first two rows, the weights are based on s_{nm}: the first column imputes mean values, the second market shares, and the third their logs. Symmetrically the last two rows correspond to the same type of weighting schemes multiplied by the group market share. In addition, rows 1 and 3, assume the β's to be the same over the whole population; while rows 2 and 4 assume the β's to be the same per group of firms. As can be seen, traditional measures of concentration like H and E emerge in very special cases, i.e., cases where all firms behave in a similar manner and normative judgments solely rely on market shares. In all other cases, it appears that *more* than one index of concentration is called for.

To illustrate further the implications of choice of the β's and the α's, it is worth considering the trade-offs between beliefs (the β's) and normative judgments (the α's) that different individuals can adopt which is consistent with their use of the *same particular concentration index*. This is difficult to do in general, but is revealing in the particular case where the empirical worker decides to take observed market shares as a guide to conduct variations within the industry and where we restrict attention to normative judgments based on size only. In particular, suppose that the range of beliefs and judgments considered reasonable for individuals to hold are given by:

$$(\text{A.1}) \qquad \alpha_n = a\, s_n^A, \qquad a > 0, \qquad A \in (-\infty, +\infty)$$

$$(\text{A.2}) \qquad \beta_n = b\, s_n^B, \qquad b > 0, \qquad B \in (-\infty, +\infty)$$

The second equation is a rearrangement of the first order conditions of (2): when goods are homogeneous and every firm has identical cost functions, differences in β are the only cause of differences in s, and (A.2) represents the inverse of this association. Clearly the restrictions: $A + B = 1$ produces the Herfindahl index as appropriate. Suppose some particular individual felt that welfare weights ought to rise at an increasing rate ($A > 1$); then, if that individual uses the Herfindahl, it follows that he/she believes that the β's fall with market share. ($B < 0$), i.e., believes that large firms behave more competitively. Alternatively, if one felt that conduct was more or less uniform across firms ($B = 0$), then to use the Herfindahl index is to imply that one believes that the weights one ought to attach to firm size must rise at a constant rate. Finally, if some individual felt both that larger firms ought to attract more weights and that smaller firms behavior is liable to be more competitive, then, for the Herfindahl to be appropriate, the elasticities of α and β must both be less than unity, i.e., that the two must both rise at decreasing rates. These conditions do not seem so obviously appealing as to justify the recent surge of interest in the Herfindahl index. Two final remarks about the above equations can be made. First, this system will never produce either a Concentration Ratio or an Entropy index as appropriate; however, the number of firms will suffice as an appropriate index if $A = -B$, i.e., when the fall in α 'due to' s is exactly offset by the proportional increase in l via β 'due to' s. Finally, the above specification implies that for a given set of beliefs (b and B) and judgments (a and A), only one concentration index will ever be necessary to reflect performance.

REFERENCES

BAIN, J. S., 1951, 'Relation of Profit Rate to Industry Concentration', *Quarterly Journal of Economics*, 65, **3** (August), pp. 293–324.

BAIN, J. S., 1956, *Barriers to Entry* (Harvard University Press, Cambridge Mass.).

BAIN, J. S., 1959, *Industrial Organisation* (Wiley, New York).

BAUMOL, W., J. PANZAR and R. WILLIG, 1982, *Contestable Markets and the Theory of Industry Structure* (Harcourt Brace Jovanich Inc., New York).

BLACKORBY, C., D. DONALDSON and J. WEYMARK, 1982, 'A Normative Approach to Industrial Performance Evaluation and Concentration Indices', *European Economic Review*, 19, **1**, (September), pp. 89–112.

CAVES, R. and T. PUGEL, 1980, Intraindustry Differences in Conduct and Performance: Viable Strategies in U.S. Manufacturing Industries. Monograph Series in Finance and Economics, New York University Graduate School of Business Administration.

Clarke, R. and S. Davies, 1982, 'Market Structure and Price-Cost Margins', *Economica*, 49, **3** (August), pp. 277–88.

Comanor, W. and T. Wilson, 1967, 'Advertising, Market Structure and Performance', *Review of Economics and Statistics*, 49, **4** (November), pp. 423–40.

Cowling, K., 1976, 'On the Theoretical Specification of Structure-Performance Relations, *European Economic Review*, 8, **1** (January), pp. 1–14.

Cowling, K. and M. Waterson, 1976, 'Price-cost Margins and Market Structure', *Economica*, 43, **3** (August), pp. 267–74.

Cowling, K. and D. Mueller, 1978, 'The Social Costs of Monopoly Power', *The Eonomic Journal*, 88, **4** (December), 727–48.

Curry, B. and K. George, 1983, 'Industrial Concentration: A Survey', *The Journal of Industrial Economics*, 31, **3** (March), 203–55.

d'Aspremont, C. and A. Jacquemin, 1984, Measuring the Power to Monopolize: A Simple Game-Theoretic Approach, forthcoming, European Economic Review.

Dansby, R. and R. Willig, 1979, 'Industry Performance Gradient Indexes', *American Economic Review*, 69, **3** (June), 186–93.

Davies, S., 1979, 'Choosing Between Concentration Indices: The Iso-concentration Curve', *Economica*, 46, **2** (May), 67–75.

Demsetz, H., 1974, 'Two Systems of Belief About Monopoly', In Goldschmid, H. *et al.* (eds), *Industrial Concentration: the New Learning*, (Little Brown, Boston).

Dixit, A. and N. Stern, 1982, 'Oligopoly and Welfare: A Unified Presentation With Applications to Trade and Development', *European Economic Review*, 19, **1** (September), 123–44.

Donsimoni, M-P. and V. Leoz-Arguelles, 1982, Strategic Groups: An Application to Foreign and Domestic Firms in Spain. In Geroski, P. and A. Jacquemin (eds), Symposium on Domestic Industrial Organization and International Competition. *Recherches Economiques de Louvain*, 47, **3–4** (December), 291–306.

Encaoua, D., P. Geroski and A. Jacquemin, 1982, 'Strategic Competition and the Persistence of Dominant Firms: A Survey', Forthcoming in Matthewson, F. and J. Stiglitz (eds.), *New Developments in the Analysis of Market Structure.* (MIT Press, Cambridge Mass.)

Engle, R., D. Hendry and J-F. Richard, 1983, 'Exogeneity', *Econometrica*, 51, **2** (March), 277–304.

Fisher, F. and J. McGowan, 1983, 'On the Misuse of Accounting Rates of Return to Infer Monopoly Profits', *American Economic Review*, 73, **1** (March), 82–97.

Geroski, P., 1982a, 'Interpreting a Correlation Between Profits and Concentration', *Journal of Industrial Economics*, 30, **3** (March), 305–318.

Geroski, P., 1982b, 'Simultaneous Equations Models of the Structure Performance Paradigm', *European Economic Review*, 19, **1** (September), 145–58.

Geroski, P., 1983, 'Some Reflections on the Theory and Application of Concentration Indices', *International Journal of Industrial Organization*, 1, **1** 79–84.

Goldschmid, H. M. Mann and J. F. Weston, (eds), 1974, *Industrial Concentration: the New Learning*, (Little Brown, Boston).

Hannah, L. and J. A. Kay, 1977, *Concentration in Modern Industry.* (McMillan, London).

Hart, P., 1975, 'Moment Distributions in Economics: An Exposition', *Journal of the Royal Statistical Society, Series A*, 134, Part 1, 423–34.

Kaysen, K. and D. Turner, 1965, *Antitrust Policy: an Economic and Legal Analysis.* (Harvard University Press, Cambridge Mass.)

Oster, S., 1982, 'Intra-Industry Structure and the Ease of Strategic Change', *Review of Economics and Statistics*, 64, **3** (August), 376–383.

Phillips, A., 1976, 'A Critique of Empirical Studies of Relations Between Market Structure and Profitability', *Journal of Industrial Economics*, 24, **2** (June), 241–249.

PLOTT, C., 1982, 'Industrial Organization Theory and Experimental Economics', *Journal of Economic Literature*, 29, **4** (December), 1485–1527.

PORTER, M., 1979, 'The Structure Within Industries and Companies Performance', *Review of Economics and Statistics*, 61, **2** (May), 214–227.

SAVING, T., 1970, 'Concentration Ratios and the Degree of Monopoly', *International Economic Review*, 11, **1** (February), 139–146.

SAWYER, M., 1982, 'On the Specification of Structure-Performance Relationships', *European Economic Review*, 17, **1** (March), 295–306.

SCHERER, F. M., 1980, *Industrial Market Structure and Economic Performance.* 2nd Edition. (Rand McNally, Chicago).

SCHMALENSEE, R., 1983, 'The New Industrial Organization and the Economic Analysis of Modern Markets, in W. Hildenbrand (ed), *Advances in Economic Theory*, (Cambridge University Press, Cambridge).

STIGLER, G., 1968, *The Organization of Industry.* (Irwin, Homewood Ill.).

STIGLER, G., 1964, 'A Theory of Oligopoly', *Journal of Political Economy*, 72, **1** (February), 44–61.

STRICKLAND, A. and L. WEISS, 1976, 'Advertising, Concentration, and Price-Cost Margins', *Journal of Political Economy*, 84, **5** (October), 1109–1121.

WEISS, L., 1974, 'The Concentration Profits Relationship and Antitrust'. In Goldschmid, H. *et al.* (eds), *Industrial Concentration: the New Learning.* (Little Brown, Boston).

THE JOURNAL OF INDUSTRIAL ECONOMICS 0022–1821 $2.00
Volume XXXII June 1984 No. 4

THE PROFITABILITY-CONCENTRATION RELATION: MARKET POWER OR EFFICIENCY?*

Roger Clarke, Stephen Davies and Michael Waterson

Industrial economists have been studying the relationship between profitability and concentration using cross-industry samples for many years now. However, as sometimes happens, once it appeared that some consensus had been achieved: "With few exceptions, market concentration and industry profitability are positively correlated" (Peltzman, [1977, p. 229]), people began to question the interpretation of those results. In particular, Demsetz (e.g. [1973], [1974]) and others suggested that, rather than concentration/market power leading to higher prices and profits, the causal direction in fact ran from greater efficiency to both higher profits and, incidentally, to higher concentration.

Our purpose here is to subject these conflicting hypotheses to cross-industry empirical test using U.K. data. In order to do this, we first develop a model which is sufficiently general to allow for both alternative explanations of a positive concentration-profitability correlation. In the light of this model we then examine the implications for the *within-industry* relation between market share and firm-level profitability. More specifically we explore Demsetz's claim that the empirical form of this relationship should signal which of the alternative hypotheses is consistent with the *between-industry* profitability concentration correlation.

Our model suggests that, in certain special circumstances, this claim is partly justified, in that it should be possible to assess the relative strengths of the market power and efficiency effects from the within industry relation. More generally, however, factors such as product differentiation and scale economies may seriously impair the information content of the relation, with at least a strong suspicion that the estimates will tend to exaggerate the evidence in favour of the efficiency hypothesis.

In the event, our results tend to confirm that, for most industries, the within-industry data offer little conclusive support for either hypothesis. But, for a not insignificant minority of industries, the evidence suggests some support for the view that both efficiency and market power are at work simultaneously.

Our model is detailed in section II and estimated on U.K. data in section III, after which we offer a few comments in section IV. First, however, we provide a backcloth to the later analysis.

* We should like to thank Paul Geroski and an anonymous referee for helpful comments.

I. A BRIEF OUTLINE OF THE DEBATE

For some commodities it is the case that prices can be observed and are comparable directly and there have been studies on such data.[1] In that situation, if price is found to be positively related to concentration, the most likely explanations come from a relatively restricted set of market power hypotheses suggested by oligopoly theory. Either firms find it easier to collude or to follow a dominant firm when they become small in number, *or*, for any given conjecture about rivals' reactions, the equilibrium outcome will involve a restriction of output proportional to the degree of "concentration", *or* some mixture of these explanations prevails.

Things become considerably more difficult if prices cannot be compared without reference to their margin above costs. Then a larger price-cost margin can logically come either from a higher price or a lower level of costs.[2] Any explanation which gives rise to one or both of these, together with an increase in concentration, will fit a set of observations for which the price cost margin and concentration are positively related.

One possible explanation has been covered, that coming from oligopoly theory. For example, horizontal merger will increase concentration and may allow the constituent firms more latitude in pricing. Alternatively, a largely chance mechanism (e.g. the Gibrat process) could give rise to a concentrated structure and thence to oligopolistic pricing behaviour. In some simple cases, all firms would have equal cost levels and prices, so one might observe all firms in concentrated industries having higher price-cost margins. The difficulty for those in the industry (and therefore for theory) is how other firms are kept out.

This problem was recognised in later studies of the concentration-profitability kind by incorporating variables designed to measure "barriers to entry". Published work for the U.K., for example, has normally included both concentration and barrier to entry variables, but with mixed results; for a review see for example Devine *et al.*, [1979]; Clarke, [1984]. Although there are some difficulties in disentangling the separate effects, the general *interpretation* seemed uncontroversial (though see Cooley, [1982], and subsequent discussion).

However, Demsetz has pointed to a completely different view of similar studies in the United States. In essence this supposes that some industries become concentrated because one or more firms have a strong *efficiency* advantage over their competitors (both actual and potential). It is this greater efficiency which leads to the concentration of a large part of the market within the hands of those leading firms and also to greater profitability. The public

[1] Scherer [1980, pp. 287–88] provides a short survey, and a recent example is Geithman, Marvel and Weiss [1981]. Others, such as Nickell and Metcalf [1978] have made less direct attempts to do this, though their success in capturing pure price effects is less easy to establish.

[2] An alternative comparison, often employed in the U.S., is that between profit and capital employed. The problems with using this type of measure are arguably more severe than with the price-cost margin, since the extent to which, say, monopoly profits have been capitalised is difficult to discover.

policy implications of this and the earlier market power hypotheses could hardly be more different; for example, a policy of "deconcentration" would benefit society in the form of lower prices according to the market power view, whereas it would punish efficiency if Demsetz is right.

Since neither hypothesis has been refuted on the basis of deductive logic, it is not surprising that much of the controversy has moved on to examine the empirical means by which we can deduce the superiority of one hypothesis over the other. On this, Demsetz argues as follows: "if efficiency is associated with concentration, there should be a positive association between concentration and the difference between the rate of return earned by large firms and that earned by small firms . . ." [1973, p. 5]. Thus, if the efficiency explanation is correct, we should expect to observe a within-industry positive relation betwen the profitability and market share of firms. On the other hand, if the exercise of market power hypothesis is correct, the higher prices should benefit all firms equally and, in the absence of efficiency differences, on the Demsetz hypothesis, there should exist little or no differences in the profitability of different sized firms within the industry. Empirical work by Demsetz himself (on profitability) and by Carter [1978] (on price-cost margins) has tended to support his predictions.

A number of commentators have expressed doubts concerning this methodology, suggesting that other mechanisms could generate the within-industry results which Demsetz offers as support for the efficiency hypothesis. For example, a simple explanation flowing via lower costs is provided by Scherer [1980, pp. 280–1]. If the firms in an industry operate according to a production function exhibiting economies of scale, there would be a natural tendency over time for the larger firms to be more successful and for the industry to become more concentrated. High industry profitability could arise solely from the lower cost position of the large firms. In that case, breaking up the large firms would still have deleterious consequences, though disallowing mergers need not if the economies can as easily be gained through internal growth. But moreover, how is one to distinguish those situations where scale economies only have efficiency effects, from those where the firms enjoying such economies realise entry into the industry is difficult (for whatever reason) and thus set high prices? In both cases industry profitability is higher in concentrated industries and, within these, is higher among the larger firms. Other possibilities which would fit these observations include the case of vertical integration which could benefit the integrator's position, increase concentration and also give rise to lower costs and prices, and the rather different case where the large firms produce no more cheaply but enjoy product differentiation advantages or first-mover advantages which allow them to charge higher prices (see Bond and Greenberg, [1976]). Recently also Porter [1979] has shown how the concept of "barriers to mobility" may provide the means by which to explain inter-industry variations in profitability.

Thus, Demsetz's test of comparing profitability amongst large and small firms and identifying high large firm profits with efficiency is defective, in that their efficiency would imply higher profits, but their higher profits do not necessarily imply their efficiency.[3] As he later admits (but is unwilling to accept), one could conceive of a more complex explanation arising from the same data: "Large firms in concentrated industries have lower cost because there are scale economies in these industries or because of some inherent superiority of the larger firms in these industries. Nonetheless they succeed in colluding so that *their* profit rates are relatively high. The prices they set in this collusion are not so high as to yield high profits for . . . smaller firms" (Demsetz, [1974, p. 178]).

An alternative general approach is to employ a tightly-specified theoretical model to produce a more sophisticated test. There are dangers in this, exemplified by Peltzman's [1977] work. He developed a very complex model of cost-reducing process innovation bringing about concentration and efficiency increases and estimated it satisfactorily. However, despite the detailed specification, the interpretation of the model is subject to several difficulties. The basic framework relating concentration (MS) to prices (p) and industry unit costs (c), namely:

$$(1) \qquad \frac{dp}{dMS} = \frac{\partial p(.)}{\partial MS} + \frac{\partial p(.)}{\partial c} \cdot \frac{dc}{dMS}$$

is somewhat at variance with the idea that cost changes initiate the causal chain. Also, the regression equations he derives to use in (1) are difficult to interpret since the effects of concentration are bound up in multiplicative terms in each of which industry growth also appears. Lustgarten [1979] suggested the model could be simplified without real loss and did this, while Scherer [1979] noted that most recent concentration increases in the U.S. had in fact come about through product innovations or successful advertising campaigns in conjunction with scale economies, rather than through process innovations.

The lesson we can draw is that whilst there may be gains from imposing more structure on the model than Demsetz was willing to, if the underlying purpose is to develop a cross-industry model, one must avoid being overly specific in detailing the mechanism involved within than structure. In fact the model we develop below has, as its basic framework, the eclectic view proposed by Demsetz [1974] in the quotation above, that is we take account of scale economies, efficiency, collusive behaviour, and also product differentiation (which he seemed unconcerned about). Some writers (e.g. Scherer, [1980, chapter 9]) have tended to blur the scale economies/efficiency distinc-

[3] To be sure, one could define "superior efficiency" widely enough to encompass all these cases to make Demsetz's test tautological, but this is unlikely to be very useful; one is essentially interested in real rather than pecuniary economies.

tion, but we feel that since the policy implications may differ, it is useful to be quite explicit on this point. In developing our model we concentrate upon the influence of structure rather than (as in Porter, [1979]) the means by which that structure may have been generated.

II. A THEORETICAL FRAMEWORK

Our starting point in this section is a model within the mainstream tradition of oligopoly theory, namely that developed by Clarke and Davies [1982] from Cowling and Waterson [1976].

Assuming an industry of N firms producing a homogeneous good, with the firms differing only in the height of their marginal cost curves, c_i, Clarke and Davies derive a relationship (their equation (9)) between price and marginal cost for firm i. This may be re-written in terms of the price cost margin as:

$$\frac{p - c_i}{p} = \frac{\alpha}{\eta} + \frac{(1 - \alpha)}{\eta} s_i \tag{2}$$

where η is the modulus of the price elasticity of demand, s_i is the share of firm i in industry output, and α is the degree of implicit collusion, being the proportionate extent to which each firm believes each other firm will react to its output changes.[4]

Then multiplying (2) throughout by s_i, making the assumption that marginal and average variable costs coincide, and summing across the industry yields (their equation (10)):

$$\frac{\Pi}{R} = \frac{\alpha}{\eta} + \frac{(1 - \alpha)}{\eta} H \tag{3}$$

where Π/R is the industry gross profit-revenue ratio (the numerator being total revenue minus total variable costs) and H is the Herfindahl index of concentration. Finally, Clarke and Davies show (in their equation (13)) that the Herfindahl exceeds the value $1/N$ to an extent directly proportional to the coefficient of variation in marginal costs.

This model is particularly convenient for present purposes since it allows us to formalize the alternative hypotheses discussed above in a very simple way.

Consider first industries free of collusive practices. This corresponds to $\alpha = 0$, and as is evident from (3), profitability at the industry level and concentration are positively related ($\Pi/R = H/\eta$). This is just as Demsetz predicts. In addition, within each industry, from (2) profitability is pro-

[4] Thus $dX_j/dX_i = \alpha(X_j/X_i)$ for $j = 1 \ldots \neq i \ldots N$, for all i. The α values could differ between firms, but this type of formulation is probably closest in spirit to Demsetz (see Hause, [1977]).

portionate to market share and, again as suggested by Demsetz, there are larger profit rates for the larger firms.[5]

Turning to the alternative view, namely that higher concentration leads to higher industry profits because it facilitates collusion, this can be represented in our model as the assumption that $0 < \alpha \leq 1$ and $\partial\alpha/\partial H > 0$. Since it is clear from (3) that, as α is raised, so is industry profitability, this too is consistent with a positive profitability-concentration correlation across industries.[6] Within collusive industries, as shown by (2), it is still the case that larger firms earn higher profits, but the relationship becomes flatter (i.e. less pronounced) as collusion increases.

To a large extent these results confirm what might be termed the Demsetz empirical methodology. There are two conflicting explanations of a positive correlation between industry profitability and concentration, in order to choose between the two we must examine the within industry relationship between market share and profitability. But his methodology can be extended in one important respect. While it is true that, if the collusion effect dominates, the within-industry relationship is less pronounced, in general it persists to some extent in all but the, presumably rare, cases of perfect collusion ($\alpha = 1$). This suggests to us an important refinement to the necessary empirical tests. Having established, within a given industry, that market share and profitability are related, we should move on to derive a measure of *how pronounced the relationship is*. In terms of equation (2) this might sensibly be the estimate of α which can be recovered from a linear regression of profitability against market shares. "Large" values of α would then confirm an important collusion (market power) dimension, while low values would not. As a further test of the collusion hypothesis, one could then test whether there is, indeed, a positive correlation across industries between α and concentration. This we do in the following section.

But, before doing this, it is necessary to consider the theoretical complications introduced by product differentiation and scale economies. In particular, our interest concerns the impact of these phenomena on the information value of the within industry profitability/market share relation.

We introduce *product differentiation* as simply as possible by now supposing that each of the N firms in the industry produces a different brand, selling at

[5] By way of an explanation of these two results, it is illustrative to contemplate an industry of initially equal cost, and thus equal sized, firms. If one of these firms discovers and applies a method of lowering costs, it is able to increase its market share and mark-up. The coefficient of variation in marginal costs will rise (from zero) and, with it, the Herfindahl concentration index. Since the innovating firm now forms a larger part of the industry, the aggregate price-cost margin also rises, and we therefore observe increased profitability and concentration without any collusion.

[6] In fact in addition to the positive relation between Π/R and α as shown in (3), it is also the case that, as α increases, so too does the equilibrium value of H (Clarke and Davies, [1982, p. 280]).

price p_i. The extent of differentiation is reflected in the magnitude of the k parameter in:

$$(4) \qquad \frac{\partial p_i}{\partial x_j} = k \frac{\partial p_i}{\partial x_i} \qquad 1 \geq k \geq 0$$

Since price may now vary across firms, we re-define firm size in value terms with market share,

$$s_i = p_i x_i \Big/ \sum^N p_i x_i$$

Correspondingly, the definition of our collusion parameter is now modified to read:

$$(5) \qquad \frac{dx_j}{dx_i} = \alpha \frac{s_j}{s_i} \qquad 1 \geq \alpha \geq 0$$

Firm i's gross profits and first order maximization condition are, respectively:

$$\Pi_i = p_i x_i - c_i x_i$$

and

$$(6) \qquad \frac{d\Pi_i}{dx_i} = p_i + x_i \left(\frac{\partial p_i}{\partial x_i} + \sum_{j \neq i} \frac{\partial p_i}{\partial x_j} \frac{dx_j}{dx_i} \right) - c_i = 0$$

Inserting (4) and (5) into (6), firm i's margin is:

$$(7) \qquad \frac{p_i - c_i}{p_i} = \frac{1}{s_i \eta_i} \{\alpha k + (1 - \alpha k) s_i\}$$

where η_i is the firm's own price elasticity of demand, written as a positive number. Aggregating (7) across firms, the industry profits-revenue ratio is:

$$(8) \qquad \frac{\Pi}{R} = \sum \frac{1}{\eta_i} \{\alpha k + (1 - \alpha k) s_i\}$$

Equation (7) bears a strong resemblance to (2). It shows that similarity of brands gives the same signal as collusion. This seems intuitively sensible since k represents the degree of closeness in the way consumers view the various brands on offer, while α represents the extent to which firms view their product decisions as moving together.

On the other hand, there is no certainty that the basic predictions of the previous homogeneous product model will carry over. By this we mean that (7) need not imply a monotonic relationship between profitability and market share and (8) need not imply a monotonic relationship between industry profitability and concentration. Without more specific information on the relation between s_i and η_i (i.e. the nature of the firm demand curve) therefore there is no certainty that the Demsetz methodology is appropriate.[7] Nevertheless, it is instructive to consider a special case where these predictions *do* carry over: this is where $s_i \eta_i$ is constant across firms. Retaining assumption (4), this implies:

$$x_i = A_i + B/p_i - k \sum_{i \neq j} x_j \tag{9}$$

where $s_i \eta_i = \sum p_i x_i / B = R/B$.

In this special case,

$$\frac{p_i - c_i}{p_i} = \frac{R}{B} \{\alpha k + (1 - \alpha k) s_i\} \tag{2a}$$

and

$$\frac{\Pi}{R} = \frac{R}{B} \{\alpha k + (1 - \alpha k) H\} \tag{3a}$$

Comparison with (2) and (3) confirms that the only substantive difference is the replacement of α by αk. What this means is that within industry variations in profitability still provide *qualitatively* the same evidence on the market power versus efficiency hypotheses, but *quantitatively* the relative importance of the market power effect will be understated where differentiation is pronounced (k low). This follows fairly obviously, of course, from our observation above about the similarity of signals from collusion and differentiation.

Turning finally to *scale economies*, there are two points of issue. *First*, one might argue, with Scherer [1980], that in industries with pronounced scale economies, large firms will be more profitable, and thus appear more efficient, merely because they are further along the same scale curve. This will tend to increase the chance of accepting a Demsetz view even although larger firms do not operate on a lower cost curve. We are not convinced by this argument: if all firms have access to the same scale curve, but some have chosen less sensible points on it, this is one manifestation of inefficiency, and can be represented by different levels of short-run costs as in our original model.

A *second*, essentially empirical, consideration requires some attention however. In common with most studies, we shall measure profitability using the price-average variable cost margin, while our model concerns the price-marginal cost margin. However, this creates a problem which we shall illustrate by positing the following total variable cost function which gives rise to "U"-shaped average variable costs:

$$TVC_i = c_0 x_i^3 + c_1 x_i^2 + c_{2i} x_i \qquad c_0 \geq 0,\ c_1 \leq 0,\ c_{2i} > 0 \tag{10}$$

[7] For example, if s_i and profitability are to be positively monotonically related, it is necessary (but not sufficient) that s_i be inversely related to η_i. There exists a wide range of possible demand curves for which this condition is not satisfied.

Here pure efficiency differences are represented by different c_{2i} values, while c_0 and c_1 reflect the degree of scale economies. While the use of such a cost curve in either of the above models does not affect the linear relation between market share and the price-marginal cost margin, it does mean that marginal cost $(3c_0x_i^2 + 2c_1x_i + c_{2i})$ and average variable cost $(c_0x_i^2 + c_1x_i + c_{2i})$ no longer coincide. Rather, since

$$\frac{p_i - AVC_i}{p_i} = \frac{p_i - MC_i}{p_i} + \frac{MC_i - AVC_i}{p_i}$$

$$= \frac{p_i - MC_i}{p_i} + \left(\frac{2c_0X^2}{p_i}\right)s_i^2 + \left(\frac{c_1X}{p_i}\right)s_i \quad (\text{where } X = \sum x_i),$$

the empirically testable relation to emerge in the homogeneous product case (for example) is:

$$(11) \qquad \left(\frac{p - AVC}{p}\right)_i = \frac{\alpha}{\eta} + \left\{\frac{(1-\alpha)}{\eta} + \frac{c_1X}{p}\right\}s_i + \left\{\frac{2c_0X^2}{p}\right\}s_{i2}$$

Thus an (upward sloping) quadratic relationship is now appropriate.[8] What this suggests, empirically, is that the large-small firm differences are likely to be accentuated. Fitting a straight line to data generated by such a process will result in an upward bias in the estimate of the coefficient on s_i. In our terms, this implies on overstatement of the efficiency component relative to the market power effect.

To extent that scale economies are important and a cost function like (10) captures their nature, this suggests that previous studies may have been biased towards the Demsetz hypothesis. In our own work we can avoid this problem by estimating a quadratic relation and this we do in the following section. But note that where a quadratic relation is observed we will be unable to assess the relative strengths of the efficiency and market power hypotheses since an estimate of α (or αk in the differentiation case) is not recoverable (i.e. identifiable) from the regression coefficients of the quadratic (because of the extra component on the term in s_i).

III. EMPIRICAL RESULTS: U.K. MANUFACTURING

As a preliminary to conducting the tests suggested by the previous section, we first follow the similar, if rather cruder, empirical methodology used by Demsetz himself and later Carter [1978]. This amounts to comparing average margins for small and large firms within "concentrated" industries and within "unconcentrated" industries (as in Table I).

[8] If the formulation for total variable cost did not include a cubic term, this would not be true, but that would lead to rather implausible shapes for the marginal and average variable cost curves.

TABLE I
ANALYSIS OF MARGINS AND CONCENTRATION, 1971 AND 1977

	Concentration Ratio		
	below average	*above average*	
1971			
PR top 5 firms	0.2194	0.2025	(−1.249)
PR rest	0.2095	0.2082	(−0.093)
	(1.858)*	(−0.333)	
PN top 5 firms	0.4603	0.5040	(1.983)**
PN rest	0.4707	0.5207	(2.607)**
	(−1.352)	(−1.114)	
1977			
PR top 5 firms	0.2282	0.2220	(−0.432)
PR rest	0.2373	0.2267	(−0.880)
	(−0.842)	(−0.435)	
PN top 5 firms	0.4594	0.5470	(1.886)*
PN rest	0.5215	0.5882	(2.647)**
	(−1.379)	(−1.865)*	

Source: Census of Production Summary Tables 1971 and 1977.
Significant at the 5%** and 10%* levels on a 2-tailed test.

More precisely, for two different years, 1971 and 1977, samples of 147 and 155 three digit manufacturing industries respectively have been classified into above and below average concentration, and average margins for large firms (the top 5 firms) and small firms (the rest) within those industries have been computed. Two alternative performance indicators have been used for the comparisons in table 1:

PR: the ratio of gross profits to sales

PN: the ratio of gross profits to net output.[9]

On the basis of these measures, standard t tests for differences between means have been employed, and appropriate t values are shown in brackets in the table.[10]

The Demsetz expectation (i.e. assuming that the efficiency hypothesis provides a complete explanation) is that the relatively small firms will tend to have similar profitability regardless of concentration, but differences between small and large firm profitability should be larger as concentration increases.

In fact, the data offer little support for this hypothesis, at least when analysed in this way. In the first place, evidence for similar margins for small firms in high or low concentration industries is mixed. Reading across the rows in Table I, it is true that the PR measure shows similar *small* firm

[9] This is a less usual measure than PR, though Hart and Morgan [1977] provide some arguments in favour of its use.

[10] Where calculations suggested that the assumption of equal variances was violated, appropriate corrections were applied (see Dixon and Massey, [1957, chapter 9]).

margins for the two concentration groups, but using the PN measure they are significantly higher in the high concentration group. This latter result supports a collusion effect. Secondly, and less equivocally, there is no evidence that differences between large and small firm margins are larger in more concentrated industries. Thus, reading down the columns in the table, in both concentration groups there is no significant evidence of a difference between small and large firm margins. Indeed, if anything, and contrary to both Demsetz's results and predictions, margins tend to be higher on average amongst smaller firms. These conclusions remain broadly true when the split between high and low concentration industries is made at a variety of concentration values other than the mean.

Given that these results constitute the first known attempt to test the Demsetz hypothesis using his methodology on U.K. data, and since the U.S. experience is not duplicated, they are of some interest. However, in the light of our models of the previous section, we do not find them either surprising or particularly illuminating. As argued earlier, the experience of different manufacturing industries is likely to be complex and general relationships between margins and concentration are unlikely to be exhibited in simple comparisons of averages for all industries.

Therefore we now turn to our empirical examinations based on the theory expounded in Section II. To this end, we estimated linear and quadratic relationships between average margins and market shares, taking margins as the left hand variable. In symbols, we estimated:[11]

$$\left(\frac{p - AVC}{p}\right) = a + bs_i + cs_i^2 + u_i \quad \text{with } c \neq 0 \text{ and } c = 0 \tag{12}$$

for each of 104 suitable MLH industries. The data employed were taken from census size class distributions for 1971–77 (excluding the smallest size class) and data on average margins and market shares for each year were pooled in an attempt to improve estimates obtained. As expected, a variety of cases were observed, with 29 instances of a significant positive linear relationship; 19 of a significant negative linear relationship; and 11 and 13 instances respectively of inverted U and U-shaped relationships (using a 10% two tailed test). The remaining cases exhibited no relationship.

Let us now attempt to interpret these results in terms of our models. *First*, the industries for which no significant relationship, or for which negative linear or inverted U shaped relationships were found, clearly offer no support for the Demsetz hypothesis. Equally however they are not easily explained in terms of our model. This may be either because our neo-classical equilibrium approach is inappropriate, or because product differentiation is an altogether more complex phenomenon than suggested by our special case analysis, or for other reasons. In any event, one might argue that any or all of these reasons

[11] Note that the theory suggests that this is an equilibrium relationship, so no direction of causation is to be implied here necessarily.

are sufficient to render any rigorous test of the Demsetz *hypothesis* impossible. (They certainly suggest that Demsetz's empirical *methodology* is a long way from being universally appropriate.) We therefore remove these industries from our sample. *Second*, the 11 industries for which we found a U shaped (i.e. rising) quadratic relationship are consistent with our scale economies modified model. Here, given sufficient information about the cost curve (i.e. the values of c_0 and c_1 in equation 10) we *would* be able to evaluate the relative strengths of the efficiency and market power effects. But in the absence of such information, no judgement is possible and these, too, are removed from our sample for further analysis.

Third, there remain the 29 cases for which a significant positive market share profitability relationship was observed. In terms of our model, this is the group of industries for which the efficiency and market power effects can be distinguished. In Table II, we report the estimates of a and b for each of these industries. According to our homogeneous product model (equation (2)), the ratio $\hat{a}/(\hat{a} + \hat{b})$ provides an estimate of α for each industry. (It is worth recal-

TABLE II
ANALYSIS OF MARGINS AND MARKET SHARES, 1971–77: POSITIVE LINEAR CASES

	MLH Industry	$\hat{a}$	$\hat{b}$	$\hat{\alpha}$
211	Grain Milling	0.156 (10.52)	0.73 (2.91)	0.178
214	Bacon Curing, etc.	0.149 (25.55)	0.93 (4.48)	0.138
218	Fruit and Vegetables	0.234 (30.75)	0.44 (2.08)	0.347
231	Brewing	0.221 (38.10)	0.46 (3.72)	0.324
271(1)	Inorganic Chemicals	0.257 (28.09)	0.93 (5.67)	0.216
272	Pharmaceuticals	0.438 (31.22)	0.95 (2.06)	0.316
276	Synthetic Resins	0.286 (29.61)	0.50 (1.71)	0.364
277	Dyestuffs	0.315 (36.74)	0.83 (7.80)	0.275
279(1)	Polishes	0.245 (10.25)	1.95 (6.88)	0.112
279(2)	Adhesives, etc.	0.273 (19.78)	0.92 (4.12)	0.229
279(5)	Printing Ink	0.379 (28.21)	0.33 (1.95)	0.535
338	Office Machinery	0.290 (9.31)	1.02 (1.72)	0.221
363	Telegraph and Telephones	0.324 (22.92)	0.28 (1.74)	0.536
364	Radio Components,	0.372 (42.81)	0.44 (1.83)	0.458
367	Radio, Radar, etc.	0.404 (38.36)	0.64 (2.77)	0.387
382	Motor Cycles	0.190 (6.76)	0.71 (2.38)	0.211
391	Hand Tools, etc.	0.308 (39.67)	1.06 (6.19)	0.225
392	Cutlery	0.343 (30.60)	1.67 (7.11)	0.170
412	Spinning and Doubling	0.178 (24.04)	0.57 (2.98)	0.238
419	Carpets	0.218 (26.47)	0.67 (2.99)	0.246
422(1)	Household Textiles	0.196 (11.98)	0.74 (1.82)	0.209
449(1)	Corsets and Misc.	0.272 (37.58)	1.45 (7.10)	0.158
449(2)	Gloves	0.227 (16.50)	0.69 (2.89)	0.248
450	Footwear	0.242 (40.22)	0.87 (3.09)	0.218
463	Glass	0.315 (40.60)	0.68 (3.81)	0.317
474	Shop and Office Fittings	0.246 (15.32)	6.02 (3.41)	0.039
483	Manufactured Stationery	0.292 (41.55)	1.71 (7.58)	0.146
492	Linoleum, etc.	0.210 (12.21)	1.32 (4.75)	0.137
493	Brushes and Brooms	0.265 (13.68)	1.27 (3.54)	0.173

Source: see text. *t* values in brackets.

ling, however, that where the differentiation model (equation (2a)) is appropriate, these are estimates of αk and will thus underestimate the extent of collusion.) In our terms, larger values of $\hat{\alpha}$ indicate industries in which the collusion or market power effect is more pronounced. More generally however it is clear that $\hat{a}/(\hat{a}+\hat{b})$ is a useful indicator of the similarity of margins between firms of different size. Thus, even without the rationale provided by our model, this statistic may provide a useful pointer to collusion within an industry.

As can be seen, there is considerable variation in the value of $\hat{\alpha}$, with apparently high levels of collusion observed in the printing ink, telegraph and telephone, and radio components industries, with, at the other extreme, almost Cournot-like competition in the shop and office fittings industry. These findings are not without intuitive appeal, and hence lend support to the method employed.

However, the key to the controversy lies in the existence, or otherwise, of a systematic general relationship between the $\hat{\alpha}$ estimates and concentration in the industries concerned. According to the market power hypothesis (as in Stigler [1964] for example), we should expect a positive relationship. According to Demsetz's efficiency hypothesis we should expect either a negative, or no, relationship. In fact, as in the earlier quotation [1973, p. 4], Demsetz himself implies a negative inter-industry relationship (since he expects more pronounced profitability-market share relationships, i.e. low $\hat{a}/(\hat{a}+\hat{b})$, in our terms $\hat{\alpha}$, values in more concentrated industries). According to our model, however, in the absence of any collusion, the slope of the profitability-market share relationship is determined only by η (see equation (2)) and need not be related in any simple way to the level of concentration. Therefore, we suggest that a non-positive relation between concentration and $\hat{\alpha}$ would favour the Demsetz view.

In the event, we find that the $\hat{\alpha}$ and concentration are *positively* related measuring the latter by either the Herfindahl index or the 5 firm concentration ratio (CR).

$$(13)\qquad \hat{\alpha}_j = 0.110 + \underset{(2.57)}{0.003}\, CR_j \qquad R^2 = 0.196$$

$$(14)\qquad \hat{\alpha}_j = 0.170 + \underset{(2.53)}{1.682}\, H_j \qquad R^2 = 0.191$$

where $j = 1 \ldots 29$,[12] using 1974 concentration data, (t values in parentheses).

[12] Since this sample of industries includes 8 (MLHs: 211, 276, 338, 367, 422(1), 450, 483, 493) for which a significant quadratic effect was also found, one might argue that they include the potentially distortionary effects of scale economies (thus leading to biased $\hat{\alpha}$). The results were substantively unchanged, however, when excluding these 8 industries from the sample:

$$\hat{\alpha}_j = 0.098 + \underset{(2.26)}{0.003}\, CR_j \qquad R^2 = 0.211$$

and

$$\hat{\alpha}_j = 0.163 + \underset{(2.29)}{1.788}\, H_j \qquad R^2 = 0.216$$

On the evidence of these results then, at least part of the reason why concentration and industry profitability are correlated is that more concentrated industries tend to be more collusive. Moreover, to the extent that concentrated industries tend to involve higher levels of product differentiation (lower values of k in our second model), these results may *underestimate* the strength of the collusive effect.

Taking these results at face value however and inserting (14) into (3) (or 3a if $\hat{\alpha}$ is taken as an estimate of αk), the relationship between industry profitability and concentration for this set of industries is found to be:

$$\left(\frac{\Pi}{R}\right)_j = \eta_j^{-1}\{0.170 + 2.512\ H_j - 1.682\ H_j^2\}$$

which implies a positive relation with a declining slope over the range of H_j values observed in the present sample.[13]

IV. CONCLUDING REMARKS

If anything, the evidence of the previous section is more sympathetic to the traditional market power explanation of profitability-concentration correlations at the industry level than to Demsetz. We find no evidence for the U.K. that differences between small and large firm profitability tend to be larger in high concentration industries. This is true, both when considering our entire sample of industry and for the sub-sample for which a discernible linear firm size-profitability effect exists. This is in contrast to some results found by Demsetz for the U.S. and is in conflict with his predictions were the efficiency explanation to be valid. On the contrary, we find significant evidence, for the sub-sample, that small firm-large firm differences are *less* pronounced in concentrated industries, as expected by the market power hypothesis.

On the other hand, our model does confirm that, without any collusion, a positive profitability concentration relationship might still be expected as Demsetz suggests, and while we have evidence of market power effects, these clearly vary between industries and in some cases are not pronounced. This suggests to us that, in general, both efficiency and market power effects are at work.

Finally, both on theoretical and empirical grounds, we suggest that the within-industry empirical methodology is of limited value. Not only is it the case that, for most industries, the data do not exhibit a pattern amenable to tests for choosing between the alternative hypotheses, but also our theory shows why this should be so. Once we relax the twin assumptions of product

[13] It is interesting to note that when Π/R was regressed linearly against H for this sample of industries, the latter attracted a positive coefficient which was not quite significant at the 10% level. This perhaps illustrates the problems involved in attempting to examine the profitability-structure relationship at the industry level when η is unknown and an arbitrary functional form is employed.

homogeneity and constant costs, there is no certainty that large firms will achieve higher profit rates in industries without collusion as suggested by Demsetz.

ACCEPTED MAY 1983

Roger Clarke,
Division of Economic Studies,
The University of Sheffield,
Crookesmoor Building, Conduit Street, Sheffield S10 1FL

S. W. Davies,
School of Economic and Social Studies,
University of East Anglia,
Norwich NR4 7TJ

Michael Waterson,
Department of Economics
University of Newcastle,
Newcastle upon Tyne NE1 7RU

REFERENCES

BOND, P. S. and GREENBERG, W., 1976, "Industry Structure, Market Rivalry and Public Policy: A Comment", *Journal of Law and Economics*, 19, **1**, (April), pp. 201–204.

CARTER, J. R., 1978, "Collusion, Efficiency and Antitrust", *Journal of Law and Economics*, 21, **2** (October), pp. 435–44.

CLARKE, R., 1984, "Profit Margins and Market Concentration in U.K. Manufacturing Industry: 1970–76", *Applied Economics*, 16, **1** (February), pp. 57–71.

CLARKE, R. and DAVIES, S. W., 1982, "Market Structure and Price Cost Margins", *Economica*, 49, **195** (August), pp. 277–87.

COOLEY, T. F., 1982, "Specification Analysis with Discriminating Priors: An Application to the Concentration Profits Debate", *Econometric Reviews*, **1**, No. 1, pp. 97–128.

COWLING, K. and WATERSON, M., 1976, "Price-Cost Margins and Market Structure", *Economica*, 43, **171** (August), pp. 267–74.

DEMSETZ, H., 1973, "Industry Structure, Market Rivalry and Public Policy", *Journal of Law and Economics*, 16, **1** (April), pp. 1–9.

DEMSETZ, H., 1974, "Two Systems of Belief About Monopoly" in H. S. Goldschmid, H. M. Mann and J. F. Weston (eds), *Industrial Concentration: the New Learning* (Boston, Little, Brown).

DEVINE, P. J., LEE, N., JONES, R. M. and TYSON, W. J., 1979, *An Introduction to Industrial Economics* (third edition), (London, Allen and Unwin).

DICKSON, V. A., 1982, "Collusion and Price-Cost Margins", *Economica*, 49, **193** (February), pp. 39–42.

DIXON, W. J. and MASSEY, F. J. JR., 1957, *Introduction to Statistical Analysis*, (second edition), (New York: Mc-Graw-Hill).

GEITHMAN, F. E., MARVEL, H. P. and WEISS, L. W., 1981, "Concentration, Price and Critical Concentration Ratios", *Review of Economics and Statistics*, 63, **3** (August), pp. 346–53.

Hall, M. and Weiss, L., 1967, "Firm Size and Profitability", *Review of Economics and Statistics*, 49, **3** (August), pp. 319–31.

Hart, P. E. and Morgan, E., 1977, "Market Structure and Economic Performance in the United Kingdom", *Journal of Industrial Economics*, 25, **3** (March), pp. 177–93.

Hause, J. C., 1977, "The Measurement of Concentrated Industrial Structure and the Size Distribution of Firms", *Annals of Economic and Social Measurement*, 6, **1**, pp. 73–107.

Lustgarten, S., 1979, "Gains and Losses from Concentration: A Comment", *Journal of Law and Economics*, 22, **1** (April), pp. 183–90.

Nickell, S. and Metcalf, D., 1978, "Monopolistic Industries and Monopoly Profits or, Are Kellogg's Cornflakes Overpriced?", *Economic Journal*, **88**, (June), pp. 254–68.

Peltzman, S. 1977, "The Gains and Losses from Industrial Concentration", *Journal of Law and Economics*, 20, **2** (October), pp. 229–63.

Porter, M. E., 1979, "The Structure Within Industries and Companies' Performance", *Review of Economics and Statistics*, 61, **2** (May), pp. 214–27.

Samuels, J. M. and Smyth, D. J., 1968, "Profits, Variability of Profits and Firm Size", *Economica*, 35, **2** (May), pp. 127–39.

Scherer, F. M., 1979, "The Causes and Consequences of Rising Industrial Concentration", *Journal of Law and Economics*, 22, **1** (April), pp. 191–208.

Scherer, F. M., 1980, *Industrial Market Structure and Economic Performance*, (second edition), (Chicago, Rand McNally).

Stigler, G. J., 1964, "A Theory of Oligopoly", *Journal of Political Economy*, 72, **1** (February), pp. 44–61.

THE JOURNAL OF INDUSTRIAL ECONOMICS 0022-1821 $2.00
Volume XXXII June 1984 No. 4

CONCENTRATION AND ADVERTISING IN CONSUMER AND PRODUCER MARKETS*

A. J. BUXTON, S. W. DAVIES AND B. R. LYONS

INTRODUCTION

THE effect of concentration on advertising has long been the subject of debate. On the theoretical side two approaches may be distinguished. Starting with Kaldor [1949–50], an analysis in which the assumed purpose of advertising is to make profits, but not necessarily maximum profits, has been developed by Sutton [1974]. Additionally, building on the original work of Dorfman and Steiner [1954] and others, Cable [1972] has provided a profit maximising model of the way in which concentration affects the optimal amount of advertising. Both approaches predict a systematic, non-linear, relationship between concentration and advertising. In Sutton's terms this is rationalised by pointing to the different opportunities and incentives for advertising under different market structures; Cable's analysis is based on various hypotheses concerning the magnitudes of the price and advertising demand elasticities and reactions under different market structures. Basically, they both argue that it is difficult to internalise the benefits of advertising in low concentration industries, and monopoly gives no incentive for competitive advertising. In between, oligopoly provides the structure most conducive to advertising.

As reviewed in a later section, however, the empirical evidence is somewhat conflicting. Some reject the hypothesis of a positive relationship, but other evidence has confirmed the existence of a linear or inverted U-shaped relation. Three main issues have been examined in these studies; the existence and shape of the underlying relationship between concentration and advertising; the influence of product and market characteristics; and more recently the direction of causality. The second though has probably been the source of most debate. The issue has been that differences in product and market characteristics will, *ceteris paribus*, affect the amount of advertising carried out. Samples are then chosen (and/or variables included) which attempt to account for these differences. In particular, researchers generally attempt to distinguish between consumer and non-consumer goods samples. It is argued in this paper that such apparently judicious selection of samples may be misguided and seriously affect the results. The main reason is that, even if it were possible to define a consumer good in principle, in general, firms as well

* This paper is part of an S.S.R.C. sponsored project. The authors are grateful to Dr. R. Clarke, Mr. A. J. McGuiness, Prof. M. K. Wickens and an anonymous referee for helpful comments.

as consumers buy such goods. Crucially, the proportion going to each varies among products, and firms, it is generally believed, are affected differently by advertising than are consumers. *Quite simply it is the belief that consumers are different from producers rather than that consumer goods are different from producer goods which is important as far as marketing is concerned.* Furthermore, the type of advertising expenditure will differ when selling to firms. For instance, the employment of sales representatives will be more appropriate when a given value of output is sold to a few purchasers, but general advertising will be more cost effective when purchasers are diffused as in consumer markets. This must be taken into account systematically in the empirical work.

The aim of this paper is therefore to look at the relationship between advertising and concentration, focusing mainly on this issue in an attempt to avoid the biases that afflict previous studies. Evidence for the U.K. is provided which shows that concentration affects advertising positively, but (i) only up to a maximum beyond which the relation is negative; and (ii) only in that part of each market which is concerned with sales to consumers.

CONSUMERS, PRODUCERS AND ADVERTISING

The basic hypothesis which has been examined in the industry advertising/concentration literature is that advertising intensity rises then falls as concentration increases. Such a relationship may be represented as quadratic in concentration. Thus:

$$\frac{A}{S} = \alpha_0 + \beta_0 C + \gamma_0 C^2 \tag{1}$$

where C is concentration, A is industry advertising, S is industry sales, and $\beta_0 > 0$ and $\gamma_0 < 0$.

However, this equation is not expected to apply to all markets. The most widely held general view appears to be that expressed by Mann: "whatever *a priori* theorising is brought to bear, the predicted relationship would be expected to be confined to consumer goods industries".[1] He argues that, whatever the informative aspects of advertising, consumer purchasers are more susceptible than producer purchasers to brand image effects. Furthermore, in frequently purchased goods, consumers, more so than producers, treat advertising as a substitute for experimentation where there is no obvious basis for choice between brands. Cable [1972] argues that search behaviour will be different for consumer and producer purchasers, and that quite simply the number of purchasers will generally be greater in consumer industries. From the supply side, Boyer [1974] suggests that the nature of the advertising may differ according to whom it is aimed.

[1] Mann [1974, p. 139].

The most common response to these market differences among goods has been to attempt to remove their effect by some form of sample restriction. Thus equation (1) is assumed to apply mainly to consumer markets and is therefore tested with samples designed to include only consumer goods. However, only if the sample were restricted to industries where *all* advertising and sales were to consumers, would straightforward estimation be possible. Unfortunately, examination of input-output tables (for the U.K. at least) reveals *no* such industries. Many apparently consumer goods are also sold to producers, certain foodstuffs, for instance, being sold to restaurants.

If overall advertising is the sum of the advertising directed at consumers and at producers, it may be possible to treat these as individual activities, the amount spent on each having a different relation to concentration. Thus:

$$\frac{A_c}{S_c} = \alpha_1 + \beta_1 C_c + \gamma_1 C_c^2 \qquad (2)$$

$$\frac{A_p}{S_p} = \alpha_2 + \beta_2 C_p + \gamma_2 C_p^2 \qquad (3)$$

where A_c, A_p, S_c and S_p are advertising and sales to consumers and producers, and C_c and C_p are concentration in the consumer and producer parts of the market respectively. It is expected that β_1 and γ_1 will be larger (in absolute terms) than are β_2 and γ_2.

This formulation requires two qualifications. Firstly, advertising is only one element of total promotional activity, and it is the latter to which the theory primarily relates.[2] Advertising should therefore be taken to include complementary non-media spending. Secondly, Porter [1976] has argued that consumer spending can be further sub-divided into "shopping" and "convenience" goods, depending on whether or not customers seek a retailer's advice before purchase. Although this distinction is not made explicit in either the theoretical or our empirical framework, this is not because it is believed to be potentially unimportant. Rather, we prefer to focus on the prior issue of bias in existing work, even within the conventional model of a relatively simple consumer/producer split.

EXISTING STUDIES

Equations (2) and (3) can now be used to re-interpret existing studies. First note that:

$$\frac{A}{S} \equiv \frac{S_c}{S}\frac{A_c}{S_c} + \frac{S_p}{S}\frac{A_p}{S_p} \qquad (4)$$

[2] Cable [1972, p. 118].

and substituting (2) and (3) into (4) gives:

$$(5)\qquad \frac{A}{S} = \alpha_1 \frac{S_c}{S} + \alpha_2 \frac{S_p}{S} + \beta_1 \frac{S_c}{S} C_c + \beta_2 \frac{S_p}{S} C_p + \gamma_1 \frac{S_c}{S} C_c^2 + \gamma_2 \frac{S_p}{S} C_p^2$$

Greer [1971] uses samples from three classes of consumer goods and therefore attempts three separate estimates of (2). His data though are for *all* industry sales and advertising, so that some of the advertising and sales of these "consumer goods" may actually go to producers. Greer classifies an industry as a consumer industry if the *majority* of its sales go to final consumers. This imples the inclusion of industries also selling to producers, and the effect can be seen by considering (5). If it is assumed that concentration is the same for both parts of each market, then $C_p = C_c = C$. This assumption may appear restrictive, but data limitations effectively prevent its relaxation in empirical work. Rearranging (5) gives

$$(6)\qquad \frac{A}{S} = \alpha_1 + \beta_1 C + \gamma_1 C^2 + (\alpha_2 - \alpha_1) \frac{S_p}{S} + (\beta_2 - \beta_1) \frac{S_p}{S} C + (\gamma_2 - \gamma_1) \frac{S_p}{S} C^2$$

Estimation of (6), in an attempt to estimate (2) (i.e. using only C and C^2 as explanatory variables) relegates the last three terms to the error. The resultant quasi-error term will be uncorrelated with the included variables *only if* either $S_p = 0$; or if each of the corresponding coefficients in (2) and (3) are equal. Greer's estimates will therefore be biased if one of these two conditions is not satisfied. The former is inconsistent with the sales pattern of most industries. The latter is clearly not expected given that the attempt to use samples of consumer goods is *precisely because* the relationships are expected to differ between consumers and producers.[3]

A similar conclusion applies to Sutton's estimates. He uses U.K. industries in which "consumer goods are believed to account for a significant proportion of total sales, although the latter may also include industrial sales".[4] An inspection of the input-output tables [C.S.O., 1972] shows that the sales of Sutton's industries do indeed include industrial sales, in fact his sample includes one industry, Man-made Fibres, in which *none* of the sales are to final consumers. Cable uses more narrowly-defined industries, designed to approximate true consumer markets, but he cannot claim that all sales are to consumers so the problem of bias may again be present. Reekie [1975] does use data for sales to consumers, but not for advertising to consumers, and so problems remain.

[3] Ornstein's [1976] reworking of Greer's data does not tackle this criticism.
[4] Sutton [1974, p. 67].

Finally, Strickland and Weiss [1976] include S_c/S as an explanatory variable in their regressions. Since $S_c = S_p = S$, (6) may be rearranged to give:

$$\text{(7)} \qquad \frac{A}{S} = \alpha_1 + \beta_1 C + \gamma_1 C^2 + (\alpha_1 - \alpha_2)\frac{S_c}{S} + (\beta_2 - \beta_1)\frac{S_p}{S}C + (\gamma_2 - \gamma_1)\frac{S_p}{S}C^2$$

The estimated coefficient on S_c/S is, given this interpretation, an estimate of $(\alpha_1 - \alpha_2)$, which they find to be positive and significant. This suggests that at least the constant terms in (2) and (3) are significantly different from each other. However, the last two terms in (7) are again included in the quasi-error term and will bias the estimated coefficients under the same conditions as those discussed above.

Given the data which are being employed, all the existing studies therefore suffer, to a greater or lesser extent, from incorrect specification. None has managed to take full account of the existence of sales (or advertising) to both producers and consumers. This makes interpretation of their results somewhat difficult, but, for comparative purposes, their findings are briefly summarised here.

First the ordinary least squares estimates. For each of three years Greer [1971], for the U.S. finds a significant quadratic for his first two classes of consumer goods and for the whole sample, but not for his third class. Mann *et al* [1973] subsequently argue that Greer's findings are highly sensitive to the inclusion of a single industry. When this industry is removed from the sample, the quadratic is reduced in significance in every case and becomes insignificant for two in three of the previously significant cases. A positive linear relation remains. Sutton [1974], finds a significant quadratic for the U.K. as does Cable [1972], although in the case of the latter, only the Herfindahl index of concentration was found to be significant. Strickland and Weiss [1976], for the U.S. find a significant quadratic for both the full sample and for a subsample of industries with sales of more than 50% to consumers. Entered as an additional explanatory variable, the share of sales going to consumers is also highly significant. Reekie [1975], however, finds no evidence of a quadratic or even any significant positive relation for the U.K.,[5] and neither does Ornstein [1976] for the U.S.

[5] It must be noted though that Reekie approximates concentration with recalled brand market density ratios, calculated by asking samples of consumers "Which brand do you use most often?". The percentage of consumers answering for a given brand gives that brand its market share. Since many consumers use two brands "most often", the resultant five brand market density ratios, the recalled brand share of the top five brands, are in most cases much greater than 100%. As Reekie says, "the figures are biased" (Reekie [1975, p. 16]) which must cast further doubt on his results.

AN ALTERNATIVE APPROACH

While there have been considerable differences in the theoretical and empirical approaches and findings of existing studies, the fundamental difficulty has been how to choose the sample and variables in order to test the basic relationship between advertising and concentration. The alternative which suggests itself is to estimate a general equation which permits a sample of industries which sell both to consumers and to producers. The basis for such an equation is clearly (5) which can provide estimates of *all* the coefficients in (2) and (3). If, as has been believed, the relation between concentration and advertising applies only to consumer sales, then this will show up in the estimated coefficients. The equation is flexible in that it *permits*, but does not *impose* that the relation (i) holds for the sales of a product going to consumers but (ii) does not hold for the sales of the same product going to producers or vice versa.

Estimation of (5) requires data on industry advertising, sales, concentration and the proportion of sales going to final consumers. The first three were obtained for 51 industries from the 1968 Census of Production, while the sales proportions were obtained from input-output tables in C.S.O. [1972].[6] Equation (5) contains no constant term, so for estimation and presentation purposes, it was rearranged. Setting $C_c = C_p = C$ (as discussed above) gives:

$$\frac{A}{S} = \alpha_2 + (\alpha_1 - \alpha_2)\frac{S_c}{S} + \beta_1\frac{S_c}{S}C + \beta_2\frac{S_p}{S}C + \gamma_1\frac{S_c}{S}C^2 + \gamma_2\frac{S_p}{S}C^2 \qquad (8)$$

Various estimates of (8) together with an estimate of the basic equation (1) are shown in Table I.

Regression 1 shows the complete absence of a quadratic relation for the raw data. The inclusion of the share of consumers' expenditure in regression (2) improves the fit: the coefficients on C and C^2 are significant on a 5% one-tail significance test, and the $\bar{R}^2$ is considerably improved. The equation is similar to that of Strickland and Weiss. It assumes that $\beta_1 = \beta_2$ and $\gamma_1 = \gamma_2$ and tests whether $\alpha_1 = \alpha_2$. The result suggests that $\alpha_1 > \alpha_2$: that consumer sectors of industries, for any concentration level, have greater advertising intensities than producer sectors. *However, this result does not hold when the full equation is estimated.* Regression (3) shows that while β_1 and γ_1 are significantly different from zero, β_2 and γ_2 are not. That is, no concentration effect exists in the producer sector. Furthermore, the hypothesis that $\hat{\alpha}_1 = \hat{\alpha}_2$ cannot be rejected, and, given the insignificant constant term, $\hat{\alpha}_1 = \hat{\alpha}_2 = 0$. These results are supported in the last two regressions in Table I. Regression (4) imposes that $\beta_2 = \gamma_2 = 0$ and finds, again, that $\hat{\alpha}_1 = \hat{\alpha}_2 = 0$ cannot be rejected. (5) includes both of these restrictions and provides strong evidence of a quadratic relation between concentration and advertising intensity for sales of a good to consumers. The negative part of this function, however, should be treated with

[6] The appendix contains a list of data sources and of industries in the sample.

TABLE I
DEPENDENT VARIABLE A/S. t VALUES IN PARENTHESES.

	Constant	C	C^2	S_c/S	$(S_c/S)C$	$(S_p/S)C$	$(S_c/S)C^2$	$(S_p/S)C^2$	$\bar{R}^2$
1.	0.1566 (0.1013)	0.0723 (1.0728)	−0.007 (−1.1229)						−0.020
2.	−1.6958 (−.0916)	0.1179 (1.8400)	−0.0011 (−1.8661)	3.7110 (3.0347)*					0.133
3.	1.2858 (0.5722)			−0.0402 (−0.8990)	0.3438 (2.4609)†	−0.0156 (−0.1599)	−0.0030 (−2.4113)†	0.0008 (0.0877)	0.164
4.	0.7916 (1.8367)			−0.0324 (−1.1400)	0.3341 (2.6428)*		−0.0030 (−2.6052)*		0.192
5.	0.6922 (1.6349)				0.2078 (3.4057)*		−0.0020 (−2.7219)*		0.193

* Indicates significance at the 1% level on a two-tailed test.
† Indicates significance at the 5% level on a two-tailed test.

great caution. Only Tobacco and Soaps and Detergents have both high concentration and substantial sales to consumers. The effect of excluding these two observations is discussed below. A discussion of quantitative effects is postponed until an extended model is developed (see Tables II and III below).

The explanatory power of the Table I regressions is not high, suggesting that other product and market characteristics may have an important part to play in the explanation of advertising intensities. Support for this view is given by a regression in which the "extreme" observations are removed from the sample.[7] The scatter of A/S and $(S_c/S)C$ shows four such industries.[8] The regression corresponding to (5) in Table I was therefore carried out for this sub-sample of 47 industries:

$$\frac{A}{S} = 0.4889 + 0.1279(S_c/S)C - 0.0013(S_c/S)C^2 \qquad \bar{R}^2 = 0.495$$

$$(3.7863) \quad {}^*(6.1185)^* \qquad (3.9649)^*$$

The result suggests that, far from reducing the evidence of a quadratic relation, *more* support is given. It also suggests positive advertising even in competitive industries ($C \to 0$) and in producer markets ($S_c \to 0$). The four "extreme" observations apparently lie some way from the average relation and reduce the explanatory power of the model when they are included in the sample. Explanation of these observations and of the unexplained variance of the full sample requires further consideration of product and market characteristics which may shift the quadratic relationship.

Until now, the remaining product and market characteristics have been subsumed into the error term. Yet clearly the omission of such variables may reintroduce the sort of bias which this approach is trying to eliminate.

Following previous work by Cable, Greer and Strickland and Weiss, four additional variables are introduced: a "personal goods" dummy variable (P), corresponding to Cable's "sensitive areas" variable; a durability dummy variable (D) to reflect repeat purchases; rate of growth of sales ($\dot{S}/S$), and rate of return on sales (π/S).[9] The question must be asked whether these variables affect advertising to consumers and producers in different ways. If they do, then they should be included separately in (2) and (3) and then combined to give an equation similar to (5) explaining total advertising. Furthermore, the growth of, and return on, sales may be different in the two sectors of any market. Obviously an equation that included all these permutations would

[7] As noted above, Mann *et al.* argue that Greer's quadratic result was largely due to extreme observations. Sutton also rejects three industries which he suggests are exceptional, but does not publish the results of regressions including these data.

[8] Tobacco, Soap, Pharmaceuticals, and Toilet Preparations. The last two have much higher advertising intensities than all the remaining industries.

[9] See the appendix for a description of these variables. A fuller justification for their inclusion is given in the studies cited.

soon become unmanageable in econometric terms. Fortunately, the problem is not as great as it first appears. The theory underlying the quadratic is based on the incentive and opportunity to advertise, both of which are highly sensitive to the nature of the buyer. The influence of profitability, however, whether as a measure of liquidity or of the demand elasticity, is not expected to be so sensitive. Similarly, the other variables may reasonably be introduced as follows:

$$\frac{A}{S} = \alpha_3 + \alpha_4 P + \alpha_5 D + \alpha_6 \frac{\dot{S}}{S} + \alpha_7 \frac{\pi}{S} + \beta_1 \frac{S_c}{S} C + \gamma_1 \frac{S_c}{S} C^2 \tag{9}$$

The results of various estimations of (9) are given in Table II.[10] Both P and π/S are highly significant in all cases and considerably improve the $\bar{R}^2$.[11] The quadratic relationship improves in significance in all the regressions,

TABLE II
DEPENDENT VARIABLE A/S. (t-VALUES IN PARENTHESES).

	Constant	P	D	$\dot{S}/S$	π/S	$(S_c/S)C$	$(S_c/S)C^2$	$\bar{R}^2$
1.	0.4201	9.8042				0.1679	−0.0015	0.703
	(1.6346)	(9.2214)*				(4.5332)*	(−3.3616)*	
2.	0.7825		−0.2868			0.2048	−0.0020	0.170
	(1.3935)		(−0.3938)			(3.3021)*	(−2.6985)*	
3.	0.1669			0.3684		0.2075	−0.0019	0.169
	(0.0967)			(0.3143)		(3.3683)*	(−2.6637)*	
4.	−4.6146				0.2650	0.2142	−0.0016	0.538
	(−5.0116)*				(6.1430)*	(4.6639)*	(−2.9896)*	
5.	−1.1539	7.4172	−0.4262	−0.5571	0.1350	0.1769	−0.0015	0.747
	(−1.0506)	(6.0465)*	(−1.0335)	(−0.8206)	(3.2683)	(5.1037)*	(−3.5748)*	
6.	−1.8975	7.6578			0.1187	0.1795	−0.0014	0.746
	(−2.3532)†	(6.3064)*			(3.0075)*	(5.2121)*	(−3.5334)*	

* Indicates significance at the 1% level on a two-tailed test.
† Indicates significance at the 5% level on a two-tailed test.

[10] Equation (9) and Table II include the restriction of a zero effect of concentration in producer markets as suggested by Table I. When product and market characteristics are added to (8) in which no restrictions are made on the coefficients the results are very similar to those of Table I, in the sense that $\beta_2 = \gamma_2 = 0$ and $\hat{\alpha}_1 = \hat{\alpha}_2$, and Table II in the significance of the coefficients. For instance the equivalent of equation (5), the full model, in Table II is:

$$\frac{A}{S} = \underset{(-0.4810)}{-0.9102} + \underset{(5.9152)^*}{7.6436P} - \underset{(-0.4676)}{0.2170D} - \underset{(-0.9733)}{0.7054\dot{S}/S} + \underset{(2.7700)^*}{0.1232\pi/S} - \underset{(-0.7617)}{0.0204S_c/S}$$

$$+ \underset{(3.0383)^*}{0.2620(S_c/S)C} - \underset{(-2.7451)^*}{0.0022(S_c/S)C^2} + \underset{(0.1227)}{0.0069(S_p/S)C} - \underset{(-0.1331)}{0.0000(S_p/S)C^2}$$

[11] The measurement of π/S may cause some concern since the numerator is gross profit including current advertising. In this respect we follow the existing literature. The reason, since we are dealing with industry figures, is that net profit would be very difficult to calculate because of the measurement of depreciation, and interpretation of a profit figure between gross and net which simply excludes advertising would seem a little difficult.

but D and $\dot{S}/S$ are never significant. These results are in general agreement with those of previous studies.[12]

Table III gives an idea of the order of magnitude of the concentration effect. The results are based on regression 6 of Table II for a non-personal goods industry with mean return on sales (19%).[13]

TABLE III
PREDICTED PERCENTAGE A/S RATIO FOR INDUSTRIES DIFFERING BY CONCENTRATION AND SHARE OF SALES TO CONSUMERS

4-Firm Concentration Ratio (%)	15	30	43	64	85
Share of Sales to Consumers (%)					
0	0.36	0.36	0.36	0.36	0.36
50	1.55	2.43	2.93	3.24	2.93
100	2.74	4.49	5.50	6.11	5.50

Three general points may be made. Firstly, above mean concentration (43%), there is no substantial rise in the advertising ratio. This is because the latter is at a maximum at $C = 64\%$, and the slope of the quadratic is shallow around this point. Secondly, below mean concentration, there is a substantial effect of market structure on the advertising intensity. As long as there are significant sales to consumers, the advertising ratio doubles between $C = 15\%$ and $C = 64\%$. Since 8 of the 51 industries have $C < 20\%$ and 33 have $C < 45\%$, this result is of some economic importance. In 1982 prices a one percentage rise in an average size industry's advertising intensity represents some £15 million. Thirdly, the share of sales going direct to consumers is critical. Without consumer sales, concentration has no effect on advertising.

Two further results, using the unweighted quadratic in concentration, are in order to make comparison with existing work. First the simple quadratic with the product and market characteristic variables gives:

$$\frac{A}{S} = \underset{(0.0503)}{0.0805} + \underset{(5.6003)^*}{8.9575\,P} - \underset{(-1.3338)}{0.7738\,D} - \underset{(-0.6069)}{0.5559\,\frac{\dot{S}}{S}} + \underset{(1.4061)}{0.0736\,\frac{\pi}{S}}$$

$$+ \underset{(0.9225)}{0.0431\,C} - \underset{(-0.8957)}{0.0004\,C^2} \qquad \bar{R}^2 = 0.557$$

[12] The "personal goods" variable can in no sense be interpreted as "explaining", in a causal sense, advertising intensity, and in this case therefore is rightly called a dummy. It does nothing other than permit the relationship between advertising and concentration to be shifted for these goods from that for the remainder, and hence "explains" in the statistical sense some of the variance of advertising intensity. The variable says nothing about why the relationship is different.

[13] The last column of the table should be taken as illustrative because the sample includes only one industry, tobacco, which has both significant sales to consumers and a concentration ratio substantially above 64%. The last row should be treated with similar caution since only 5 observations have consumer sales greater than 75%.

The relation between concentration and advertising is insignificant and this "standard" model is clearly inferior to the model advocated above. Second, the regression similar to that of Strickland and Weiss, including the proportion of sales going to consumers:

$$(10)\qquad \frac{A}{S} = -3.3783 + 3.8537\frac{S_c}{S} + 7.3365\,P - 0.4954\,D - 0.4982\frac{\dot{S}}{S}$$

$$(-2.3377) + (5.1053)^{*} \quad (5.5769)^{*}(-1.0625) \quad (-0.6813)$$

$$+ 0.1406\frac{\pi}{S} + 0.0927\,C - 0.0008\,C^2 \qquad \bar{R}^2 = 0.718$$

$$(3.2105)^{*} \quad (2.4034)^{\dagger}(-2.3027)^{\dagger}$$

The inclusion of S_c/S considerably improves the fit and the quadratic in concentration becomes significant. In terms of t values and $\bar{R}^2$, however, it remains inferior to regression (5), in Table II. Furthermore, given these results, the inference that it is the constant terms rather than the concentration effect that makes consumer and producer markets differ, is incorrect and misleading.

Finally, some comments can be made about the issue of simultaneity which may arise if advertising "causes" concentration, perhaps by creating an entry barrier. An examination of reverse causality between concentration and advertising ideally requires the formulation of a complete model of structure and performance, which is outside the scope of this paper. An alternative, which can be used to provide provisional results, is to employ an instrumental variable which is correlated with concentration but is independent of the error term in the advertising equation. In principle any series could be used which satisfies this criterion. However a more usual approach is to employ a variable which makes some theoretical sense. It may be argued that such a variable in this case is minimum efficient size. This will reflect exogenously—given cost conditions in different industries but may be expected to be a possible determinant of concentration (for instance Guth [1971]). Also minimum efficient scale is a likely exogenous contender in a simultaneous model of structure and performance, as for instance in Strickland and Weiss [1976]. The variable used here is therefore minimum efficient plant size as a proportion of industry size (taken from Lyons [1980]), in a first attempt to purge the estimate of possible bias. The estimation procedure is not straightforward,[14] but using this method, the results suggest that the instrumental variable estimates broadly

[14] An equation system which is non-linear in endogenous variables cannot be estimated directly by TSLS. The reduced form equation must be approximated by a polynomial function of the exogenous variables. This gives a set of instruments which will produce consistent estimates using two-stage-least-squares. Kelejian [1971], contains a formal proof. We follow Strickland and Weiss in using second-degree polynomial approximations. The estimation is slightly different though, because the variables in the advertising equation are $(S_c/S)\,C$ and $(S_c/S)C^2$. In this case, given the reduced form equations, each exogenous variable in the second-degree polynomial approximation to the reduced form, must be multiplied by S_c/S.

replicate the OLS results in terms of both statistical significance and the size of the coefficients. For instance, the preferred specification, and the straight quadratic (including S_c/S) give results as follows (asymptotic standard errors in parentheses):

$$\frac{A}{S} = -\underset{(0.8574)}{2.0683} + \underset{(1.2364)}{7.6900}\, P + \underset{(0.0414)}{0.1250}\, \frac{\pi}{S} + \underset{(0.0373)}{0.1983}\, \frac{S_c}{S}\, C - \underset{(0.0004)}{0.0017}\, \frac{S_c}{S}\, C^2$$

$$\frac{A}{S} = -\underset{(6.3993)}{15.1906} + \underset{(1.3993)}{6.0970}\, \frac{S_c}{S} + \underset{(1.4056)}{6.9794}\, P + \underset{(0.0426)}{0.1342}\, \frac{\pi}{S} + \underset{(0.0267)}{0.0545}\, C - \underset{(-0.0002)}{0.0005}\, C^2$$

The ratio of every coefficient to its asymptotic standard error is greater than two, suggesting that both equations are well determined. Once more, however, the concentration effect appears better specified in the first equation. This preliminary finding that simultaneity may be less important than is often feared, is supported by the work of Greer [1971] and Strickland and Weiss [1976].

CONCLUSIONS

This paper has examined the literature concerning the quadratic relationship between advertising intensity and concentration. It has pointed out some of the problems in existing work and has suggested an alternative method of accounting for possible differences between consumers and producers by arguing that the relevant difference should be between sales to consumers and sales to producers rather than between so-called consumer and producer goods. This alternative framework produces an alternative quadratic relationship between advertising and concentration which, when estimated for the U.K. for 1968, produces significant results compared to insignificant results using an ordinary quadratic. The reason is that concentration only affects advertising in respect of sales to consumers.[15] Extending this framework to account for other product and market characteristics, the results are found to be similar to those of other researchers; namely that "personal goods" and the return on sales have significant positive effects on advertising, but that durability and sales growth are insignificant. When the model is estimated by TSLS to allow for the possibility of a simultaneous relation between advertising and concentration, the results are found to be very similar to those obtained from the OLS estimation. Finally, the quantitatively important part

[15] It is interesting to speculate whether or not this quadratic might also apply to sales representatives, "free" meals, gifts and entertainments, and other forms of promotional activity in respect of sales to other producers; and even, perhaps, lobbying costs in respect of sales to government departments.

of the relationship is for industries of less than average concentration, where an increase in the concentration ratio leads to a substantial increase in the advertising intensity, the more so, the greater are sales to consumers.

ACCEPTED FEBRUARY 1983

A. J. Buxton,
Department of Economics,
University of Salford,
Salford, M5 4WT

S. W. Davies
Department of Economics
University of East Anglia
Norwich NR4

B. R. Lyons
St. John's College
Cambridge CB2 1TP

APPENDIX: DATA SOURCES

The data relate to 51 of the 144 MLH (3 digit) U.K. manufacturing industries in 1968. The 51 industries are the total number of MLH's for which data on advertising are available. All other MLH's are aggregated into product groups which are too broad for our purposes. As the following list suggests, this sample provides a substantial, and representative cross-section of the major sectors (Orders) of manufacturing. 1968 was chosen for the detailed Census of that year and for its stability relative to the 1970s.

Sample industries (with MLH number): 214 bacon curing, 216 sugar, 217 cocoa, chocolate and sugar confectionery, 218 fruit and vegetable products, 221 vegetable and animal oils, 231 brewing and malting, 239(1) spirit distilling, 240 tobacco, 272 pharmaceutical chemicals and preparations, 273 toilet preparations, 274 paints, 275 soap and detergents, 276 synthetic resins and plastics, 321 aluminium, 331 agricultural machinery, 332 machine tools, 333 pumps, valves and compressors, 334 industrial engines, 335 textile machinery, 336 construction equipment, 337 mechanical handling equipment, 338 office machinery, 341 industrial plant and steelwork, 354 scientific and industrial instruments and systems, 361 electrical machinery, 362 insulated wires and cables, 366 electronic computers, 368 electric appliances primarily for domestic use, 369 miscellaneous electrical goods, 370 shipbuilding and marine engineering, 382 motor cycles, tricycles and pedal cycles, 383 aerospace equipment manufacturing and repairing, 390 engineers' small tools and gauges, 395 cans and metal boxes, 411 man-made fibres, 412 spinning and doubling, 413 weaving, 414 woollen and worsted, 417 hosiery and other knitted goods, 419 carpets, 423 textile finishing 442 men's and boys' outerwear, 443 women's and girls' outerwear, 445 dresses, lingerie, infants' wear, etc., 450 footwear, 461 bricks, etc., 462 pottery, 463 glass, 464 cement, 481 paper and board, 491 rubber.

Advertising: Table 4 of B.S.O. [1974]; market research is included as a complementary expenditure.

Sales: B.S.O. [1974]

Concentration: 4-firm concentration ratio calculated from B.S.O. [1974] as by Sawyer [1971].

Consumer purchases: Table B of C.S.O. [1972]: input-output data are often more aggregated than the MLH level, in which case the same consumer sales ratio is assumed to apply to all constituent MLH's.

Profits: value added minus wages and salaries, B.S.O. [1974].

Durable goods: dummy variable = 1 if machinery, carpets or pottery (MLH 331–361, 336–390, 419, 462); = 0 otherwise.

Personal goods: dummy variable = 1 if MLH 272 or 273; = 0 otherwise.

REFERENCES

BOYER, K. D., 1974, "Informative and Goodwill Advertising", *Review of Economics and Statistics*, LVI2 (November), pp. 541–48.

B.S.O., 1974, *Report on the Census of Production, 1968* (HMSO, London).

CABLE, J., 1972, "Advertising Policy and Intermarket Differences in Advertising Intensity", in Cowling, K., ed., *Market Structure and Corporate Behaviour*, (Gray-Mills, London).

C.S.O., 1972, *Input-Output Tables for the United Kingdom, 1968.* Studies in Official Statistics No. 22 (HMSO, London).

DORFMAN, R. and STEINER, P. O., 1954, "Optimal Advertising and Optimal Quality", *American Economic Review*, **44** (December), pp. 826–36.

GREER, D., 1971, "Advertising and Market Concentration", *Southern Economic Journal*, **38** (July), pp. 19–32.

GUTH, L. A., 1971, "Advertising and Market Structure Revisited", *Journal of Industrial Economics*, **19** (April), pp. 186–94.

KALDOR, N., 1950, "The Economic Aspects of Advertising", *Review of Economic Studies*, **18**, No. 1, pp. 1–27.

KELEJIAN, H. H., 1971, "Two-Stage Least Squares and Econometric Systems Linear in Parameters but Non-linear in the Endogenous Variables", *Journal of the American Statistical Association*, **69** (June), pp. 373–74.

LYONS, B. R., 1980, "A New Measure of Minimum Efficient Plant Size in U.K. Manufacturing Industry", Economica, **47** (February), pp. 19–34.

MANN, H. M., 1974, "Advertising, Concentration, and Profitability", in Goldschmid, H. J. *et al.*, ed., *Industrial Concentration: The New Learning*, (Little, Brown, Boston).

MANN, M. HENNING, J. and MEEHAM, J., 1973, "Advertising and Market Concentration: Comment", *Southern Economic Journal*, XXXIX (January), pp. 448–51.

ORNSTEIN, S. I., 1976, "The Advertising-Concentration Controversy", *Southern Economic Journal*, **26** (December), pp. 151–60.

PORTER, M.E., 1976, *Interbrand Choice, Strategy and Bilateral Market Power*, (Harvard University Press, Cambridge, Mass.).

REEKIE, W. D., 1975, "Advertising and Market Structure: Another Approach", *Economic Journal*, **85** (March), pp. 156–76.

SAWYER, M. C., 1971, "Concentration in British Manufacturing Industry", *Oxford Economic Papers*, **23** (November), pp. 352–83.

STRICKLAND, A. D. and WEISS, L. W., 1976, "Advertising, Concentration and Price-Cost Margins", *Journal of Political Economy*, **84** (No. 5), pp. 1109–21.

SUTTON, C. J., 1974, "Advertising, Concentration and Competition", *Economic Journal*, **84** (March), pp. 56–59.

THE JOURNAL OF INDUSTRIAL ECONOMICS 0022–1821 $2.00
Volume XXXII June 1984 No. 4

CYCLICAL PRICE FLEXIBILITY: A TEST OF ADMINISTERED PRICING

STEPHEN C. FARBER*

I. INTRODUCTION

THE study of cyclical price behavior has been a debate over the extent to which prices behave in a classical manner: falling in recessions and rising in expansions. At one extreme in this debate, the proponents of administered prices state that "In recessions administered prices tend to fall less than market dominated prices; . . . similarly, since administered price does not fall as much in recession, it rises less in recovery" [8, p. 292]. Some proponents [4][1][7, p. 11] have suggested a response lag in administered price industries, resulting in countercyclical price behavior in these industries. At the other extreme in this debate, Stigler and Kindahl (S&K) [15] argue that industrial prices do behave in a classical manner. It will be shown below that there is a substantial justification for expecting the relation between concentration and price flexibility to be U-shaped in upswings and inverted U-shaped in downswings.

There has been little evidence in the literature of the proposed U-shape relation of concentration to cyclical price flexibility. In only one year during 1967–72 did Qualls [9] find a significant U-shape relation between concentration and the annual magnitude of wholesale price changes.

However, the data were list price BLS data, not actual transactions data; and annual data do not exactly test cyclical hypothesis. Rice [11] used three concentration intervals and found little relation to the standard deviation of the percentage change in average annual prices. He used both BLS list price data and NBER transactions price data. His test is also biased against any cyclical hypotheses since business cycles are not annual phenomena. If the relation between price changes and concentration is U-shaped the concentration intervals selected will be crucial to any U-shape test. Also, a Chi-square test of this sort is weaker than the parametric tests which could have been used on the same data.

Weiss investigated the relations between concentration, percentage price changes, and deviation from trend for the NBER transactions price series over different stages of the business cycle using three concentration groups. He found that in recessions prices in the least concentrated industries were more likely to fall both absolutely and relative to trend then other price series but there was no distinction between price behavior in the two most concentrated

* The author is grateful for the suggestions of Adrienne McElwain and an anonymous referee.

industries. He also concluded there was no distinction between the three categories for recoveries [18, p.617]. Again, the concentration intervals chosen are crucial to testing U-shape relations and the Chi-square test is weak. His parametric analysis of the correlation between concentration and price changes is even weaker since correlation analysis is only valid for monotonic relations.[1]

Lustgarten's [6] study of the magnitude of annual price changes is also marred by some measurement and specification errors. First, his price data are not transaction price data. Second, the does not include a quadratic term in concentration. Third, if the "lag and catch up" behavior of administered pricing firms is true, the independent regressions of annual price changes [6, p. 200] are not unrelated and the estimate of each annual equation will be inefficient, resulting in the possible rejection of a significant concentration effect. Finally, as in other studies, annual data do not test the cyclical character of administered pricing hypotheses.

The purpose of this study is to use the S&K NBER transactions price data to investigate determinants of the magnitude of price changes over the business cycle. The theoretical justification for a U-shaped relation between concentration and the magnitude of price changes will be proposed and tested across separate stages of the business cycle. Since NBER data are used, these hypotheses can be tested exactly for each stage of the business cycle. Section II of this paper presents the theoretical justification for an estimating model which considers the U-shaped concentration effect. Section III presents the empirical results using the S&K NBER transactions price data. Section IV is a summary of results.

II. THE MODEL

In the debate over cyclical price flexibility, three major models have been proposed to explain price changes: the classical independent profit maximizing model; the conjectural variation model of oligopolistic industries; and the administered price model. Each of these is discussed separately below.

As S&K have noted:

> Classical theory leads one to expect prices to fall in competitive industries during a business contraction, because both demand and marginal production costs fell, and that reverse movements will occur in expansions. This expectation was not subjected to elaborate analysis

[1] It is not clear from Weiss' explanation whether the measure of price changes was an average across industries of the percentage change in the NBER price index from the trough month to the peak month, or an average across industries of the average monthly change in price during the recovery. However, the magnitude of the numbers in his Table 5 and a comparison of these numbers with Stigler and Kindahl's Tables 6–8 [15, p. 82] support the former interpretation. This measure makes the price change sensitive to the beginning and end months, increasing the variance in the measure of price changes across industries and weakening any concentration-price change test.

> perhaps because a similar pattern was expected under monopoly. Here too, marginal cost would fall and there was no strong reason to expect marginal revenues to rise, although a price reduction was no longer a necessary result of a leftward shift in demand and cost functions. [15, pp. 60–61.]

It is well known that simple individual profit maximization under imperfect competition could result in any price change in response to changes in demand depending on elasticities [12, p. 351]. There is no net expectation that monopoly prices would behave differently from competitive prices.

Several extensions of the simple imperfect competition models have implications for the relative price flexibility of monopolistic and competitive industries. If imperfectly competitive firms engage in limit pricing to maximize the present value of the firm, cyclical price flexibility will depend on the relation between the short run profit maximizing price and the limit price. High barriers to entry increase the likelihood that the limit price exceeds the short run profit maximizing price, increasing the range of upward short run price variability. To the extent that industry structure is a result of barriers to entry, highly concentrated industries may have as much upward price flexibility as unconcentrated ones.

Barro [3, p. 20] has shown that the gain from price adjustment to changing demand will increase with the price elasticity of demand. For a perfectly monopolistic firm, demand elasticity is less than that for a competitive firm, implying less incentive to change price for the monopoly when there are costs of changing prices to their equilibrium short run profit maximizing levels. If oligopolists have at least as elastic demands as monopolists, they have at least as much to gain from price adjustment as monopolists when costs of adjustment are not considered. However, one adjustment cost is the oligopolistic rival response to price signals which result from price changes. This cost would be greater for oligopolists than monopolists, implying a possible non-monotonic relation between price flexibility and concentration.

Schramm and Sherman provide justification for a U-shaped effect of concentration on price flexibility. They show that a firm must trade off a capital profit risk premium for an employment instability wage premium. A firm may choose price stability in order to reduce profit risk at the expense of the wage premium. They prove that a lower average price in relation to the short run profit maximizing price increases incentives for price stabilization [13, p. 131]. An implication is that since competitive firms and monopolistic firms with high entry barriers can hold their average price at a short run profit maximizing level the incentive for price stabilization is weak. However, oligopolistic firms which may use limit pricing, will have average prices less than the short run profit maximizing price; therefore, satisfying the Schramm and Sherman condition for price stability.

Conjectural variation models of price behavior consider the interdependence of price decisions. In competitive industries this interdependence does not exist, and in very tighly knit oligopolies conjectural uncertainties can easily be resolved through collusion or flows of information. For intermediate market structures, interdependencies exist but are more costly to deal with. As Bain has noted, "Moderate concentration . . . should tend to give rise to imperfect collusion (and) kinked demand curve conformations . . . whereas high concentration should provide an environment conducive to effective collusion or its equivalent." [2, p. 43]. Qualls has suggested a loosely knit oligopoly environment creates "Uncertainties of conjectural variations and mutual mistrust of motives and actions (which) lead firms to adopt uniform pricing rules such as 'standard unit cost plus customary markup', (resulting in) prices (which) are held at this level in the face of random or cyclical fluctuations in demand" [10, p. 306.] For these reasons, Qualls suggests a relation between concentration and price flexibility which is U-shaped in expansions and inverted U-shape in contractions. There may not be inflexibility forever in loosely knit oligopolies. Since it may be costly for a single oligopolistic firm to undertake a price policy independently of others in the industry, oligopolistic firms may wait until it has become clear to all firms that market conditions have changed. The result may be a lagged response to any changes in market conditions.

The third model of price changes, the administered price thesis, was originally proposed as the result of observations that some industries had inflexible prices over the business cycle [8, p. 292]. As Scherer has noted, a major difficulty with this thesis is whether it has any testable implications [12, p. 355]. Simply observing inflexible prices and ascribing them to administered pricing is tautological. However, identifying cyclically inflexible prices by industry in one cycle and testing whether this inflexibility exists in all other cycles for these industries and not for others is a non-tautological test of the thesis.[2]

There is some justification for considering capital intensity as a determinant of price flexibility. Average costs are less variable with respect to variable input prices for more capital intensive industries; so one would expect less downward flexibility in downturns and less upward flexibility in upturns for more capital intensive industries. Schramm and Sherman suggest that capital intensive firms would be concerned with profit risk, and, according to their model, could tend to reduce price variability [13, p. 133]. If capital intensity is positively related to entry barriers, limit price models would suggest that capital intensive industries are likely to have short run profit maximizing

[2] A testable form of the thesis would be the inclusion of lagged price behavior in a model predicting current price behavior. The S&K test of the thesis is essentially of this type. Their sample consists only of those industries "in which the charge of inflexible prices has been heard most frequently: ferrous and nonferrous metals, chemicals, and drugs." [15, p. 23]. The 1957–66 price behavior of these historically define administered price industries is then analyzed over business cycles to determine whether there is classical price behavior within this entire set and across all business cycle stages.

prices which are below their limit prices; so they could have more flexible prices than less intensive industries.

The above capital intensity effects are symmetric over the cycle; i.e., either always more flexible or always less flexible. Barro has indirectly provided a justification for asymmetric capital intensity effects. Barro, in his adjustment cost model, has shown that the gain from price adjustment increases with the slope of marginal cost [3, p. 20]. Suppose that marginal costs are more steeply sloped above capacity and less steeply sloped below capacity for more capital intensive industries.[3] When firms are operating below capacity in the trough of a business cycle, capital intensive firms with flat marginal costs would have smaller gains from upward price adjustment than less capital intensive firms as demand expanded toward capacity levels. On the other hand, when industries are operating above capacity in the peak of a business cycle, the steep marginal cost of capital intensive firms would suggest greater gains from price reduction for the more capital intensive firms as demand falls toward capacity levels. If the above is true, one would expect more downward price flexibility in early stages of downturns for capital intensive industries, and less upward price flexibility in early stages of upturns for such industries. If information or decisions about demand changes lag actual demand changes, capital intensity may be observed to have these effects over the entire upswing or downswing.[4]

Although one may argue about the capital intensity–MC assumption above, the result of this argument corresponds with the intuitive notion that capital intensive firms would be anxious to use their capital to capacity and not wish to discourage demand increases during expansions by raising prices; and they would wish to encourage demand if it is falling during contractions in order to maintain capacity operations.

In summary, the Barro disequilibrium model, the Schramm and Sherman risk model, and the conjectural variation model provide a theoretical justification for an inverted U-shape relation between concentration and price changes in recessions. These models and the limit pricing model provide justification for a U-shape relation during upturns. The limit pricing model also suggests that capital intensive industries, having higher limit prices, would permit greater upward price flexibility during upturns. On the other hand, less sensitivity to variable input prices for capital intensive industries may result in less price variability at all stages of the cycle. If marginal costs

3 This is an admittedly arguable assumption. A justification is indirectly provided by Stigler [14]. An unadaptable plant is one which cannot easily vary the quantity of variable factors using the specific types of fixed factors; i.e., one with fixed coefficient production functions. One thinks of mechanized processes as consisting of very distinct machines, each with its own fixed input requirement; e.g., one man — one shovel. The machine can process material inputs at a constant cost up to the point where its engineering capacity causes increased costs. The assumption in the text implies that more capital intensive processes are less adaptable, therefore are more likely to have reverse L-shaped short run marginal costs.

4 This suggests that the long run trend of price increases would be inversely related to capital intensity. The regression shown in footnote 8 suggests this is true.

for more capital intensive industries are flatter below capacity and steeper above capacity, the Barro model suggests that capital intensity creates a smaller likelihood of price increases when demand rises from trough levels and more downward price flexibility when demand falls from peak levels. The Schramm and Sherman model suggests that more capital intensive industries will be more sensitive to profit risk, and therefore, would be more likely to stabilize prices.

III. DATA AND ESTIMATION

The theory presented above suggests the following system of equations:

$$
\begin{aligned}
&\dot{p}_{1i} = \alpha_{10} + \alpha_{11}CR_{1i} + \alpha_{12}CR_{1i}^2 + \alpha_{13}K/L_i + \varepsilon_{1i} \\
(1)\quad &\dot{p}_{2i} = \alpha_{20} + \alpha_{21}CR_{2i} + \alpha_{22}CR_{2i}^2 + \alpha_{23}K/L_i + \varepsilon_{2i} \\
&\vdots \\
&\dot{p}_{ni} = \alpha_{n0} + \alpha_{n1}CR_{ni} + \alpha_{n2}CR_{ni}^2 + \alpha_{n3}K/L_i + \varepsilon_{ni},\ i = 1, \ldots, N
\end{aligned}
$$

where $\dot{p}_{ni}$ is the price change for industry i in business cycle stage n, CR_{ni} is the concentration at time n, and K/L_i is capital intensity measured as an average intensity over several stages of the business cycle in order to avoid simultaneity problems due to the potential effect of $\dot{p}$ on output, variable inputs, and, therefore K/L. For downturns, theory suggests that $\alpha_{n0} < 0$, $\alpha_{n1} > 0$, $\alpha_{n2} < 0$; and in upturns we expect $\alpha_{n0} > 0$, $\alpha_{n1} < 0$, $\alpha_{n2} > 0$. Theory is inconsistent about the effects of capital intensity, so it is impossible to sign α_{n3} *a priori*.

Under some interpretations of administered pricing, the error terms, ε_{ni}, are related. For example, suppose industries which reduce prices in downturns by less than would be predicted by concentration and capital intensity alone also raise prices less than other similar industries in upturns. In this case, $E[\varepsilon_{ji}\varepsilon_{ki}] > 0$. Means original formulation of administered pricing was simply that some firms always changed prices less than others, and this was not simply related to market structure. Even though one could criticize these formulations of administered pricing for being atheoretical, if it is true empirically it means the equations in system (1) are not independent. In this case, estimating efficiency can be improved by using seemingly unrelated equation (SURE) estimating techniques [5].

Theoretically, it would be optimal to include variables representing cyclical demand and direct cost changes. However the price data used are the S&K five-digit product data and direct cost data are not available at this level of disaggregation. Unless some exogenous measure of demand change could have been found at the five-digit level the usual method of including output change would create simultaneity problems.[5] The exclusion of demand and

[5] Lustgarten [6] uses an index of demand based on input-output methods at the four-digit level. One could argue that his method does not remove all simultaneity bias if industry i's prices affect equilibrium output of its buyers.

direct cost variables may not be a severe problem in this study. First, it is not clear that cyclical demand changes would be systematically related to concentration. Second, the S&K sample includes only staple industrial materials. Demand and cost changes should vary less across these industries than across a more generally defined set of industries. Third, although cost changes may be related to concentration, including capital intensity may control somewhat for the effect of direct cost variability on price changes. Also, if we adjust price changes for trends in price we should control for cost related trend effects of concentration. Finally, if cyclical demand and cost changes consistently affect industry i, the exclusion of these variables will make $E[\varepsilon_{jk}\,\varepsilon_{ki}] \neq 0$ in system (1). A SURE method of estimation should control somewhat for these excluded variables.

Price changes in cycle stage n are measured by the average monthly percentage change in the NBER price index over stage n [15]. There is controversy over the definitions of the various business cycle stages. S&K [15] use a different definition for some stages than Means [8]. We will compare the results of estimating system (1) with both sets of definitions. Capital intensity is measured as the simple average of the 1957 and 1962 ratio, Gross Book Value ÷ Production Workers [15].[6]

Concentration was measured using the value of shipments ratios for 5-digit SIC product classes [17]. SIC industries were assigned to the NBER industries using the BLS-WPI link.[7] Concentration ratios for only 61 of S&K's 68 industries could be obtained for 1963 and 1958. Value of shipment weighted ratios were derived for multiple SIC products. The Appendix shows a comparison of the 1963 4-firm value of shipments concentration ratios in the S&K sample and a random sample of 94 five-digit industries. A Chi-square test showed that the S&K sample was significantly different from the random sample at the 0.01 level. The S&K sample overrepresents high concentration levels. This is expected since they selected industries that were prominent in discussions of administered price industries. Only in 53 cases could a capital intensity measure be derived, so the estimating sample consists of 53 products.

Table I shows single equation OLS estimates of system (1) for each cycle stage using unadjusted average monthly percent changes in price for that stage as the dependent variable. Equations (1)–(4) show estimates for each cycle stage using the S&K cycle definitions [15, p. 43]. For the first downturn, the 1958 4-firm concentration ratio yielded the higher R^2. In the first upturn and second downturn the 1963 8-firm ratio yielded the highest R^2, while the

[6] Other measures of capital intensity, such as Gross Book Value ÷ Value of Shipments or Horsepower per Production Worker generally resulted in poorer estimates.

[7] The relevant concentration ratio may change over time and the 4- or 8-firm ratios are equally preferable, *a priori*. Accordingly, we allow the relevant ratio to be changed over time and select the particular 4- or 8-firm ratio which maximizes the R^2 for each single equation estimate. Concentration is supposed to be generally reflective of the market structure in a particular cycle stage. In all instances, for later business cycles the best fitting concentration measures were also chronologically later.

TABLE I

SINGLE EQUATION, OLS ESTIMATES OF AVERAGE PERCENTAGE NBER PRICE CHANGES, UNADJUSTED FOR TREND, BY BUSINESS CYCLE STAGE ($N = 53$)*

Business Cycle Stage	*Intercept*	*CR*	CR_3^2 ($\times 10^3$)	K/L ($\times 10^8$)	R^2	F
S&K Downturns						
(1) 7/57 – 4/58	−0.0108	0.00038	−0.00313	−0.4991	0.06	0.94
	(−1.51)[c]	(1.57)[c]	(−1.57)[c]	(−0.65)		
(2) 5/60 – 2/61	−0.0073	0.00024	−0.00224	−1.4701	0.13	2.42
	(−0.82)	(0.90)	(−1.13)	(−2.48)[aa]		
S&K Upturns						
(3) 4/58 – 5/60	0.0102	−0.00034	0.00277	−0.9439	0.19	3.72
	(1.49)[c]	(−1.63)[c]	(1.81)[b]	(−2.06)[bb]		
(4) 1/61 – 12/66	0.0004	0.00005	−0.00419	−0.5457	0.06	0.82
	(0.12)	(0.32)	(−0.33)	(−1.56)[cc]		
Means Downturns						
(5) 7/57 – 4/58	−0.0108	0.00038	−0.00313	−0.4991	0.06	0.94
	(−1.51)	(1.57)[c]	(−1.57)[c]	(−0.65)		
(6) 1/60 – 1/61	−0.0101	0.00033	−0.00274	−1.1748	0.15	2.80
	(−1.44)[c]	(1.56)[c]	(−1.75)[b]	(−2.50)[aa]		
Means Upturns						
(7) 4/58 – 6/59	0.0164	−0.00053	−0.00418	−0.5822	0.12	2.29
	(−1.84)[b]	(−1.98)[b]	(2.10)[a]	(−0.98)		
(8) 1/61 – 3/62	0.0113	−0.00045	0.00339	−0.7916	0.15	2.16
	(1.41)[c]	(−1.81)[b]	(1.88)[b]	(−1.37)[cc]		

* *t*-values in parentheses.
[a] one-tail significance at 0.01; [b] one-tail at 0.05; [c] one-tail at 0.10.
[aa] two-tail at 0.01; [bb] two-tail at 0.05; [cc] two tail at 0.10.

1967 4-firm ratio fit best for the second upturn. Therefore, later ratios fit later cycle stages best, as expected. In equations (1)–(3) the signs for the constant and the concentration terms are as expected. In equations (2) and (4) these coefficients are not significant and in equation 4 the concentration coefficients have the wrong sign. Capital intensity appears to reduce upward price flexibility in upturns and increase downward price flexibility in downturns.

Equations (5)–(8) show the OLS estimates using Means' cycle definitions [8, p. 296]. Means' and S&K's definitions for the first downturn are the same. Comparing *t*-values, it is clear that Means' definitions result in more significant and correctly signed effects of concentration on price changes than S&K's definition. In the second downturn and upturn Means' definitions yield higher *R*'s over the 53 observations than S&K's definitions. Capital intensity has the same effects as in equations (1)–(4).

Average monthly price changes were adjusted for price trends by subtracting from average monthly changes the elasticity coefficient, b_i, estimated from the equation, $p_{ti} = ae^{b_i t}$, for each industry. The resulting OLS regressions using these trend-adjusted price changes are shown in Table II. Comparing Tables I and II we see that the expected quadratic effect of concentration

TABLE II
SINGLE EQUATION, OLS ESTIMATES OF AVERAGE PERCENTAGE NBER PRICE CHANGES, ADJUSTED FOR TREND, BY BUSINESS CYCLE STAGE ($N = 53$)*

Business Cycle Stage	*Intercept*	*CR*	CR^2 ($\times 10^3$)	K/L ($\times 10^8$)	R^2	*F*
S&K Downturns						
(1) 7/57 – 4/58	−0.0114	0.00040	−0.00296	0.5442	0.06	0.96
	(−1.49)[c]	(1.52)[c]	(−1.40)[c]	(0.66)		
(2) 5/60 – 2/61	−0.0088	0.00031	−0.00266	−0.5138	0.04	0.74
	(0.84)	(0.96)	(−1.13)	(−0.73)		
S&K Upturns						
(3) 4/58 – 5/60	0.0086	−0.00027	0.00235	0.0124	0.14	2.56
	(1.77)[b]	(−1.84)[b]	(2.14)[b]	(0.38)		
(4) 1/61 – 12/66	−0.0005	0.00011	−0.00087	0.4034	0.13	1.72
	(−0.12)	(0.73)	(−0.66)	(1.08)		
Means Downturns						
(5) 7/57 – 4/58	−0.0114	0.00040	−0.00296	0.5442	0.06	0.96
	(−1.49)[c]	(1.52)[c]	(−1.40)[c]	(0.66)		
(6) 1/60 – 1/61	−0.0113	0.00038	−0.00299	−0.2041	0.04	0.71
	(−1.20)	(1.32)[c]	(−1.41)[c]	(−0.32)		
Means Upturns						
(7) 4/58 – 6/59	0.0148	−0.00047	0.00376	0.3742	0.12	2.19
	(2.14)[b]	(−2.22)[b]	(2.40)[a]	(0.81)		
(8) 1/61 – 3/62	0.0081	−0.00033	0.00266	0.1696	0.09	1.21
	(1.38)[c]	(−1.81)[b]	(1.99[b])	(0.44)		

*See Table I for the key to symbols.

remains. In some cases the *t*-values rise and in some cases they fall, but none are reduced to below ten percent significance by this trend adjustment. Capital intensity becomes insignificant in Table II. This could have occurred if more capital intensive industries had lower trends in price increases, perhaps reflecting less sensitivity to rising wages over the period.[8] Lower price trends in capital intensive industries could also occur if these industries had smaller price increases in upturns and greater price decreases in downturns as the Barro adjustment model and *L*-shaped marginal costs would suggest.

Table III presents the SURE estimates of the unadjusted price change equations using the Means business cycle definitions. The SURE technique should yield more efficient estimates of the equations than single equation estimation. In each equation of Table III, *t*-values are higher for most coefficients than for corresponding equations in Table I.[9] Table IV shows the

[8] The OLS regression across the 53 sample industries of average capital intensity on trend values was:

$$\text{TREND} = \underset{(-2.10)}{-0.00079} - \underset{(-3.5)}{9.489 \times 10^{-9}}\, K/L,\ R^2 = 0.20.$$

[9] Although they are not shown, the SURE equations comparable to equation system (1)–(4) in Table I, the S&K cycle definition, raise the *t*-values for *CR* and CR^2 in equation (1) to 2.01 and −2.02, respectively. The other coefficients do not increase as dramatically.

TABLE III
SURE ESTIMATES OF AVERAGE PERCENTAGE NBER PRICE CHANGES, UNADJUSTED FOR TREND, BY BUSINESS CYCLE STAGE, USING MEANS' CYCLE DEFINITIONS ($N = 53$)*

Business Cycle Stage	*Intercept*	*CR*	CR^2 ($\times 10^3$)	K/L ($\times 10^8$)
Downturns				
(1) 7/57 – 4/58	−0.0117	0.00042	−0.00350	−0.5276
	(−1.67)[c]	(1.78)[b]	(−1.82)[b]	(−0.68)
(2) 1/60 – 1/61	−0.0111	0.00036	−0.00296	−1.1866
	(−1.61)[c]	(1.74)[b]	(−1.91)[b]	(−2.51)[bb]
Upturns				
(3) 4/58 – 6/59	0.0171	−0.00056	0.00436	−0.5721
	(1.92)[b]	(−2.06)[b]	(2.17)[b]	(−0.95)
(4) 1/61 – 3/62	0.0111	−0.00044	0.00343	−0.7440
	(1.39)[c]	(−1.81)[b]	(1.90)[b]	(−1.42)

*See Table I for the key to symbols.

SURE estimates using the trend adjusted price changes for Means cycle definitions. As expected, the SURE technique improves t-values for the equations in Table IV compared to the corresponding OLS estimates of Table II.[10]

IV. SUMMARY

It is difficult to deny that a quadratic effect of concentration on cyclical price changes exists. This study has used monthly average percentage transaction price changes over each business cycle to test the U-shape and inverted

TABLE IV
SURE ESTIMATES OF AVERAGE PERCENTAGE NBER PRICE CHANGES, ADJUSTED FOR TREND, BY BUSINESS CYCLE STAGE, USING MEANS' CYCLE DEFINITIONS ($N = 53$)*

Business Cycle Stage	*Intercept*	*CR*	CR^2 ($\times 10^3$)	K/L ($\times 10^8$)
Downturns				
(1) 7/57 – 4/58	−0.0124	0.00045	−0.00352	0.4896
	(−1.73)[b]	(1.85)[b]	(−1.79)[b]	(0.60)
(2) 1/60 – 1/61	−0.0129	0.00043	−0.00335	−0.2141
	(−1.46)[c]	(1.60)[c]	(−1.69)[b]	(−0.34)
Upturns				
(3) 4/58 – 6/59	0.0157	−0.00049	0.00393	0.3792
	(2.32)[b]	(−2.41)[a]	(2.59)[a]	(0.82)
(4) 1/61 – 3/62	0.00871	−0.00035	0.00279	0.1776
	(1.50)[c]	(−1.94)[b]	(2.12)[b]	(0.46)

* See Table 1 for the key to symbols.

[10] Comparable SURE estimates using the S&K definitions raised t-values dramatically above their levels in Table II. The CR and CR^2 t-values rose to 2.15 and −2.09, respectively, in equation (1); to −2.02 and 2.32 in equation (3); and to 1.30 and −1.45 in equation (2).

U-shape concentration effects consistently predicted by several oligopoly models. Using transaction prices and measuring price variability exactly during each cycle stage provides a more accurate test of these hypotheses than other studies which have used list prices or annual price changes. Even simple OLS estimates establish validation of the predicted quadratic concentration effects. Recognizing possible intercyclical dependencies of error terms, theoretically preferred SURE estimates of equation systems resulted in even stronger evidence for the expected quadratic effects than the OLS estimates. Table IV which is a SURE estimate of price changes adjusted for price trends, illustrates the strength of the quadratic relation. All second order terms for concentration are significant and of the correct sign at least at the five percent level. Inflection points, where $\partial p/\partial CR = 0$, occur at concentration levels between 62 and 64 for all equations in Table IV. Similar inflection points occur for all equations in the remaining tables. Although capital intensity appears to have a price stabilizing effect in upturns and a destabilizing effect in downturns for unadjusted price changes, when price trends are removed the capital intensity effect disappears, implying no purely cyclical effect of capital intensity.

Stephen C. Farber,
Department of Economics/2107 CEBA,
College of Business Administration,
Louisiana State University,
Baton Rouge, LA, 70803

ACCEPTED AUGUST 1982

APPENDIX

FREQUENCY DISTRIBUTION OF 1963 4-FIRM VALUE OF SHIPMENTS CONCENTRATION RATIOS IN THE S&K SAMPLE AND A RANDOM SAMPLE OF 5-DIGIT INDUSTRIES

Value of Shipments Concentration Ratio	*Frequency*	
	S&K Sample (*1*)	*Random Sample*[a] (*2*)
0–9	0	4
10–19	1	20
20–29	5	13
30–39	11	16
40–49	10	15
50–59	17	13
60–69	9	5
70–79	3	3
80–89	3	4
90–99	2	1
	61	94

[a] One 5-digit industry was selected at random from each page of the *1967 Census of Manufacturers, Concentration Ratios in Manufacturing*, Part 2.

REFERENCES

[1] Ackley, Garner, "Administered Prices and the Inflationary Process," *American Economic Review*, **49**, 2 (May 1959), pp. 419–61.

[2] Bain, J. S., "Workable Competition in Oligopoly", *American Economic Review*, **40**, 2 (May 1950), pp. 35–47.

[3] Barro, Robert, J., "A Theory of Monopolistic Price Adjustment", *Review of Economic Studies*, **39**, 1 (January 1972), pp. 17–26.

[4] Galbraith, John K., "Market Structure and Stabilization Policy", *Review of Economics and Statistics*, **39**, 2 (May 1957, pp. 124–33.

[5] Johnston, J., *Econometric Methods* (McGraw-Hill, New York, 1972).

[6] Lustgarten, Steven, "Administered Inflation: A Reappraisal", *Economic Inquiry*, **13**, 2 (June 1975), pp. 191–206.

[7] Means, Gardiner, C., *Administrative Inflation and Public Policy* (Anderson Kramer Associates, Washington, D.C., 1959).

[8] ——, "The Administered-Price Thesis Reconfirmed", *American Economic Review*, **62**, 3 (June 1972), pp. 292–306.

[9] Qualls, David, "Market Structure and Price Behavior in U.S. Manufacturing, 1967–72", *Quarterly Review of Economics and Business*, **18**, 4 (Winter 1978), pp. 35–37.

[10] ——, "Market Structure and the Cyclical Flexibility of Price-Cost Margins", *Journal of Business*, **52**, 2 (April 1979), pp. 305–25.

[11] Rice, Edward M., "Price Stability in Concentrated Industries: Comment", *Southern Economic Journal*, **45**, 3 (January 1979), pp. 190–94.

[12] Scherer, F. M., *Industrial Market Structure and Economic Performance* (Rand McNally, Chicago, 1980).

[13] Schramm, Richard and Sherman, Robert, "A Rationale for Administered Pricing", *Southern Economic Journal*, **44**, 1 (July 1977), pp. 125–35.

[14] Stigler, George J., "Production and Distribution in the Short Run", *Journal of Political Economy*, **47**, 3 (June 1939), pp. 305–27.

[15] ——, and Kindahl, James K., *The Behavior of Industrial Prices* (National Bureau of Economic Research, New York, 1970).

[16] U.S. Bureau of the Census, *Annual Survey of Manufacturers, 1964–65* (Washington, USGPO, 1969).

[17] ——, *Census of Manufacturers, 1972*, Volume I, (Washington, D.C., USGPO, 1976).

[18] Weiss, Leonard, W., "Stigler, Kindahl, and Means on Administered Prices", *American Economic Review*, **67**, 4 (September 1977), pp. 610–19.

THE JOURNAL OF INDUSTRIAL ECONOMICS 0022–1821 $2.00
Volume XXXII June 1984 No. 4

ENTRY AND THE EXTENT OF MULTIPLANT OPERATIONS

LARRY L. DUETSCH*

There have been many studies of the effects of entry conditions on industry profitability, but few studies of the direct effects of entry conditions on entry. The number of empirical studies of the determinants of entry has been small despite the importance of entry conditions in microeconomic theory. Orr's [7] study of the determinants of entry in Canadian manufacturing industries has been the most comprehensive work to date. This paper reports on a similar study of the determinants of entry in U.S. manufacturing industries between 1963 and 1972. Among the potential determinants of entry that are examined, one of the most significant appears to be the extent of multiplant operations among established firms. The effect that the extent of multiplant operations can be expected to have on the prospects of potential entrants is explained in the next section of the paper. In subsequent sections a model of entry is adopted, the variables used to estimate the model are specified, and the empirical results are assessed.

I. MULTIPLANT OPERATIONS AND THE PROSPECTS OF POTENTIAL ENTRANTS

Scherer *et al.* [8] have identified two types of industries in which it appears that multiplant firms are often able to achieve lower average costs than single-plant firms. The first type of industry is one that serves a large geographic area and produces a product with relatively high transportation costs. In such an industry real transportation economies are likely to result from a mode of operation in which each plant serves a single region or locality. In most of the industries studied by Scherer *et al.* there was evidence of a potential for additional cost reductions if a single firm operated plants in several regions or localities. These potential economies appeared to stem from real and/or pecuniary advantages of the multiplant firm over single-plant firms in spreading risks, raising capital, procuring materials, supporting research and development, and engaging in sales promotion activities. The actual savings realized from these advantages appeared to be slight in most industries.

The second type of industry in which multiplant firms are able to achieve lower average costs is one that is segmented along complex product lines. In such an industry, real economies often result from a mode of operation in

* I thank H. Michael Mann and an anonymous referee for their helpful comments on a previous draft of this paper.

which each plant is specialized in a particular product line. Again, the potential for cost reductions often appeared to be greater if several of these specialized plants were operated by a single firm. Scherer *et al.* found that the economies that are actually achieved by multiplant firms that operate several specialized plants were often due entirely to longer production runs and could also be achieved by specialized single-plant firms. The actual savings that could only be realized by firms that operate more than one of these specialized plants generally appeared to be slight.

Since these two types of industries are fairly common, it seems reasonable to expect that there is a potential for slight multiplant economies in many industries. When real, not merely pecuniary, economies result, multiplant operations appear to be a socially desirable consequence of basic market conditions. Unfortunately, the existence of multiplant firms may be an aspect of industry structure that subsequently deters the entry of new firms. Two possible effects on entry seem likely.

First, if multiplant firms do have a potential for achieving somewhat lower average costs than single-plant firms, new entrants could expect to suffer from a cost disadvantage if they serve only one region or produce only one product line. New entrants would generally face the prospect of much larger capital requirements if they wish to avoid such a cost disadvantage. Since a large capital requirement for a single plant of minimum efficient size appears to deter entry (Orr [7]), it is expected that a multiplant capital requirement would have an even greater deterrent effect on entry. Of course, if established multiplant firms do sometimes fail to realize their potential for lower costs, as Scherer *et al.* report, this multiplant capital requirement barrier to entry may be less effective in deterring entry.

Second, even if multiplant firms do not have a significant potential cost advantage over single-plant firms, segmentation of the industry along geographic lines because of high transportation costs or along complex product lines because of single-plant production economies is quite likely to lead to the formation of multiplant firms (Duetsch [5]).[1] Although potential entrants into one segment of such an industry would not suffer from a cost disadvantage, they would naturally fear that established multiplant firms would be willing to reduce their price-cost margin temporarily in that segment in order to prevent successful entry. Entry into a single industry segment in which multiplant firms are more common may be perceived as being more risky because of the greater likelihood that one of the multiplant producers will initiate price reductions, more intense promotional expenditures, or other measures intended to block entry now and forestall it in the future. If one

[1] Firms that seek an opportunity to grow are likely to perceive an attempt to enter an unrelated industry as being more risky than an attempt to enter another regional market or an attempt to produce and market a closely related product. In other words, risk aversion favors the formation of multiplant operations within an industry, since this would appear to involve less uncertainty than diversification.

established firm initiates such measures, others would be likely to follow and the attempt to enter would be more likely to fail. This perceived risk may be sufficient to deter many potential entrants.

In summary, then, less entry is expected in industries in which multiplant operations are more common, both because the extent of multiplant operations often reflects multiplant cost advantages which increase the capital requirement for successful entry and because multiplant firms are perceived as being more likely to take action to counter attempted entry in one segment of the industry. This study estimates the apparent overall effect of multiplant operations on entry and also the apparent effects of other plausible deterrents to entry.

II. A MODEL OF ENTRY

The general form of the model employed here to assess the relative importance of various determinants of entry into U.S. manufacturing industries has been borrowed, with certain modifications, from Orr [7]. Stated simply, the amount of entry that occurs is expected to be determined by the prospects of potential entrants. The number of new entrants (E) observed in an industry is expected to be positively correlated with the industry's profitability (P), the rate of growth of industry output (G), and the industry's size (S). In addition, E is expected to be negatively correlated with the capital requirement for a plant of minimum efficient size (K), advertising intensity in the industry (A), high industry concentration (C), the importance of scale economies in the industry (X), and the extent of multiplant operations (M). The general form of the model, with expected signs, is as follows:

$$E = f(\overset{+}{P}, \overset{+}{G}, \overset{+}{S}, \overset{-}{K}, \overset{-}{A}, \overset{-}{C}, \overset{-}{X}, \overset{-}{M}) \tag{1}$$

This specification of the model roughly follows Orr's formulation.[2]

Most of these variables have straightforward interpretations as determinants of the number of new entrants. Higher profitability for established firms can be expected to attract more potential entrants, but more actual entry can be expected in growing markets and/or large markets. On the other hand, high capital requirements can greatly reduce the number of potential and actual entrants. Intense ongoing advertising by established firms can also increase the difficulty of entry. Even though advertising is sometimes employed by newcomers as a means of entry, intense advertising is generally expected to discourage entry. Particularly high industry concentration is expected to discourage entry, since established firms in highly concentrated

[2] Orr did not include S in the general formulation of his model but did include S in his estimating equations. On the other hand, Orr included X in his general formulation but not in his estimating equations. Because of data limitations, two variables that Orr included are omitted here. They are the intensity of research and development activity and the degree of risk in the industry. In Orr's study they appeared to be weak barriers to entry. Of course, Orr omitted M.

industries are better able to signal a credible threat of retaliation against new entrants. Significant economies of scale, such that new entrants must either capture a substantial market share or suffer much higher costs at a suboptimal size, can also be expected to discourage entry. Finally, as discussed above, the prospects of potential entrants are likely to be diminished if it is common for established firms to have multiplant operations.

III. THE DATA AND THE SPECIFICATION OF THE VARIABLES

Equation (1) has been estimated for four-digit industry samples drawn from the *Census of Manufactures*.[3] Samples were obtained for each of three time periods: 1963–72, 1963–67, and 1967–72. The size of each sample was determined by the availability of the necessary data. Since the present model purports to explain entry, not exit, each sample includes only industries in which the number of firms increased during that time period. Many industries appear in all three samples but others appear in only one or two of the samples. All data were taken from the *Census* except as indicated below. Each of the specific measures used here to estimate equation (1) will be described in turn.

The number of new entrants, E, during each time period has been estimated by calculating the *net* increase in the number of firms classified in the industry. This estimate of E is subject to two measurement errors. First, changes in the primary product of plants could affect the number of plants (and firms) classified in any industry. If some firms have just one plant that produces the product and those plants also produce other products, even small changes in the product mix in those plants could cause them to be reclassified in other industries at certain times. The frequency with which such changes in classification occur is not known, but is probably small and may vary somewhat from one industry to another because of differences in plant specialization. Second, this net measure of E underestimates the actual amount of entry that has occurred. E may be considerably less than the gross number of new entrants if the number of firms that have exited the industry is large. Since the specific barriers and prospects that determine the number of entrances and exits in an industry can differ (Caves and Porter [3]), a gross measure of entry would have been preferable, but it is not possible to obtain a gross measure from *Census* data. Net entry data could easily conceal instances of entry that have a significant effect on competition. Even though meaningful entry and exit may occur when a substantial firm is taken over by an outsider, no net change in the number of firms appears in *Census* data. Or if a new firm enters at the same time that two established firms in the industry merge, again no net change in the number of firms appears in *Census* data. The extent to

[3] In order to avoid particularly unreliable or misleading observations, no industry was included if its title contained the phrase "not elsewhere classified" or if its definition had been irreconcilably changed during the time period.

which E underestimates the gross amount of entry varies from industry to industry, depending on the number of firms that have left the industry and the manner in which they left. Naturally, these measurement errors can be expected to reduce the explanatory power of the model employed here.

The profitability of each industry, P, has been estimated by adjusting the price-cost margin for the costs of capital and advertising at the beginning of the time period. An unusually high price-cost margin may not constitute an unusually attractive incentive for entry if the industry is capital-intensive and/or advertising-intensive. In order to obtain a measure of profitability that more accurately reflects the incentive for entry, the price-cost margin was regressed on the assets/shipments ratio and the advertising/sales ratio. Residuals from this regression have then been used as the measure of P. Since the samples for the three time periods consist of different industries, this procedure had to be repeated for each of the samples. The price-cost margins were calculated by subtracting payroll from value added and then dividing by industry shipments. Data on the current book value of assets were taken from the *Annual Survey of Manufactures* and the advertising/sales ratios were taken from Ornstein [6, pp. 77–85].

The growth rate of industry output, G, has been measured by calculating the percentage growth in value of shipments during the time period.

The size of the industry, S, has been measured by the value of shipment at the beginning of the time period.

The capital requirement for a plant of minimum efficient size, K, has been estimated in the initial year of each time period according to the method employed by Comanor and Wilson [4, p. 438]. The average shipments of the largest plants accounting for 50 percent of industry shipments was multiplied by the industry assets/shipments ratio to obtain K for each industry. Data on the current book value of assets were again taken from the *Annual Survey of Manufactures*.

The advertising intensity in each industry, A, at the beginning of the time period was again taken from Ornstein [6, pp. 77–85].

High industry concentration, C, has been measured by a dummy that indicates a sufficiently high degree of market power so that established firms may be expected to have formed a cooperative industry equilibrium that would be threatened by entry. Confronted by this, potential entrants should come to expect that established firms would retaliate if they were to attempt entry. This dummy was given a value of one if the four-firm concentration ratio was at least 0.60 and was given a value of zero otherwise.[4] The values of the dummy were based on 1966 concentration ratios that have been adjusted by Shepherd [9, pp. 263–67] for the importance of imports, industry defini-

[4] Bradburd and Over [1] recently presented evidence which indicates that a cooperative industry equilibrium is likely to be formed when the four-firm concentration ratio has risen to 0.68. Since they also report that others have estimated a somewhat lower critical concentration ratio, a critical value of 0.60 was chosen here.

tions that appeared to be too broad or too narrow, and the local or regional scope of markets.[5] These adjusted concentration ratios more accurately reflect the degree of market power in many industries.

Scale economies in the industry, X, are expected to constitute a significant barrier to entry only if the minimum efficient size of a plant is large relative to the size of the market *and* the cost disadvantage of suboptimal plants is substantial. Furthermore, as a practical matter, the minimum efficient plant size estimates that were used to calculate K cannot simply be divided by S to determine X for each industry without producing multicollinearity between S, K, and X. In view of these considerations, X has been measured using a method that should be sensitive to the dimensions of the scale economy barrier and yet minimize the potential for multicollinearity. Following the suggestion of Caves *et al.* [2, p. 137], X was given a value of zero unless the cost disadvantage of suboptimal plants appeared to be greater than 10 percent at the beginning of the time period.[6] If the cost disadvantage of suboptimal plants did appear to be greater than 10 percent, X was given the value of the minimum efficient plant size estimate divided by S, all in the initial year of the period. No attempt was made to further adjust these estimates of X for the existence or size of local or regional markets.

The extent of multiplant operations, M, should reflect the potential for multiplant economies in each industry. The multiplant economies that may deter entry have been found by Scherer *et al.* [8] to generally be more significant for firms that operate several plants *within* an industry, either plants located in geographically segmented markets or plants specialized in complex product lines. Therefore, M has been measured by estimating the proportion of the firms classified in an industry that conduct *intra*-industry multiplant operations. Unfortunately, the *Census* does not distinguish purely diversified multiplant firms from those that operate in segmented markets or produce complex product lines. Consequently, M was estimated at the beginning of the time period in two ways. First, the number of single-plant firms was simply subtracted from the total number of firms, and the result was expressed as a fraction of the total number of firms. This clearly provides an upper-bound estimate of M, since some firms may have operated only one plant within the industry. In fact, for most industries in the three samples, the difference between the total number of firms and the number of single-plant firms exceeded the difference between the total number of plants and the total

[5] These adjusted 1966 concentration ratios have been used to assign values to this dummy for each of the industry samples, even though 1963 and 1967 are the initial years of the time periods. This should not introduce a significant error, since industry concentration generally changes little during such short periods and this dummy is insensitive to nearly all small changes in concentration.

[6] Caves *et al.* [2] have suggested that the cost disadvantage of small, presumably suboptimal, plants can be estimated by comparing value added per worker in the largest plants accounting for about 50 percent of industry output to value added per worker in the remaining plants. In suggesting this approach, they very strongly emphasized the limited reliability of these estimates of the cost gradient.

number of firms. This apparently occurred whenever the number of purely diversified firms was large relative to the number of *intra*-industry multiplant firms. A second estimate of M was obtained by subtracting the total number of firms from the total number of plants and expressing the result as a fraction of the total number of firms. This also provides an upper-bound estimate of M, since some firms may have operated more than two plants. Nevertheless, for most industries this second estimate of M was smaller than the first estimate and therefore the second estimate was used.[7] In the remaining industries the first estimate was used.

IV. EMPIRICAL RESULTS

Equation (1) has been estimated in the same form as that employed by Orr [7, pp. 62–64].[8] Use of this functional form seems appropriate, since it specifies the relationships between entry and each of the independent variables in percentage terms, either by defining the variable in percentage terms or by using logarithmic values of the variable. In this cross-section of industries, *percentage* variations in any of the independent variables are expected to be linearly related to *percentage* variations in the number of entrants that appear. Ordinary least squares estimates of equation (1) for U.S. manufacturing industries are presented in Table I.

Sample 1 consists of 95 industries in which net entry was positive between 1963 and 1972. $\bar{R}^2$ is quite high for a cross-section study of this type. G, $\ln S$, and M are each highly significant determinants of $\ln E$. P and $\ln K$ are somewhat less significant determinants of $\ln E$ in sample 1. The sign of each of these five variables is consistent with prior expectations. The fact that C does not appear to deter entry in the U.S. is somewhat surprising since high concentration was found to strongly deter entry in Canadian industries. Neither A nor X appear to be determinants of $\ln E$, but since the role of advertising continues to be a subject of theoretical and empirical controversy, the insignificance of A is less surprising. Perhaps A has complex effects that depend on the nature of the market.[9]

It seems likely that the insignificance of X may be due to the limited reliability of the cost disadvantage measure that was used here to determine the value of X.[10] For this reason the importance of scale economies has also been measured without regard for the cost disadvantage of suboptimal plants.

[7] By using the second estimate, M was adjusted for the presence of purely diversified firms in 71 of the 95 industries in sample 1.

[8] Simultaneity should not pose a serious estimation problem. Entry may well influence subsequent profitability, concentration, and even advertising, but the model has been estimated with entry data for a period subsequent to the measurement of these independent variables.

[9] When equation (1) was estimated for the subsample of 77 producer goods industries in sample 1, the coefficient of A was positive and barely significant at the 10 percent level, suggesting that product promotion may be a means of entry rather than a barrier to entry.

[10] The significance of X was not enhanced if X was allowed to equal zero when the cost disadvantage of small plants appeared to be 20 percent or less.

TABLE I
REGRESSION EQUATIONS EXPLAINING ENTRY (natural log of E)

sample	constant	P	G	ln S	ln K	A	C	X	M	R^2	$\bar{R}^2$	n
1 1963–72	−0.61	0.27[b]	0.86[a]	0.63[a]	−0.28[b]	0.05	0.39	−1.58	−3.81[a]	0.55	0.51	95
	(0.77)	(2.40)	(5.93)	(4.73)	(2.40)	(0.66)	(1.44)	(0.47)	(4.41)			
2 1963–72	−0.31	0.26[b]	0.86[a]	0.58[a]	−0.24[c]	0.04	0.39	−2.19	−3.87[a]	0.55	0.51	95
	(0.29)	(2.35)	(6.01)	(3.47)	(1.66)	(0.57)	(1.46)	(0.56)	(4.38)			
3 1963–72	0.11	0.21[c]	0.88[a]	0.54[a]	−0.16	−0.00	0.23	1.18	−3.69[a]	0.54	0.50	95
	(0.13)	(1.85)	(6.01)	(3.94)	(1.25)	(0.01)	(0.86)	(0.35)	(4.11)			
4 1963–72	−1.12	0.31[a]	0.98[a]	0.63[a]	−0.37[a]	0.07	0.15			0.45	0.41	95
	(1.34)	(2.62)	(6.45)	(4.50)	(3.07)	(0.91)	(0.54)					
5 1963–67	−2.11[b]	0.17	0.62	0.85[a]	−0.59[a]	0.15	0.42	2.30	−1.79[c]	0.41	0.35	89
	(2.39)	(1.28)	(1.07)	(6.03)	(4.77)	(1.57)	(1.34)	(0.64)	(1.78)			
6 1967–72	0.39	0.35[b]	1.32[a]	0.41[a]	0.11	−0.01	−0.43	−6.48	−2.73[b]	0.37	0.31	96
	(0.43)	(2.09)	(3.99)	(2.75)	(0.75)	(0.23)	(1.28)	(1.35)	(2.41)			

Note: t statistics are shown in parentheses; a, b and c indicate significance at 1%, 5% and 10% levels.

To obtain this alternative measure for comparison, the minimum efficient plant size estimate that was used to calculate *K* has simply been divided by *S* to obtain *X* for each industry. This alternative produces somewhat greater multicollinearity between *S*, *K*, and *X* but has the advantage of being less complex. When this simpler *X* is used in sample 2, it performs no better than its more complex counterpart in sample 1 and it causes both ln *S* and ln *K* to be less significant determinants of ln *E*. These results seem to indicate that scale economies are not an important deterrent to entry in typically large U.S. industries, but this conclusion must be regarded as tentative since the importance of scale economies may not be well measured by either the complex or simple versions of *X*.

Although *M* is highly significant in sample 1, this result does not indicate whether extensive multiplant operations deter entry because of multiplant cost advantages or because multiplant firms are perceived as particularly threatening by potential entrants. If the primary deterrent to entry was simply the threat posed by the "deep pocket" of established firms, however, one would expect that the threat posed by the presence of purely diversified firms would deter entry as effectively as the presence of *intra*-industry multiplant firms. To examine this possibility further, in sample 3 *M* has been estimated by simply subtracting the number of single-plant firms from the total number of firms and expressing the result as a fraction of the total number of firms. Unlike *M* in sample 1, *M* in sample 3 has not been adjusted to try to exclude purely diversified firms with only one plant in any industry.[11] If entry is deterred primarily by the "deep pocket" threat of established firms, the unadjusted *M* in sample 3 could be expected to be more closely associated with ln *E* than the adjusted *M* in sample 1. The results are equivocal in that both versions of *M* are highly significant determinants of ln *E*, although *M* in sample 3 is somewhat less significant than *M* in sample 1. These results seem to be consistent with the further possibility that potential entrants are deterred *either* by cost advantages or the "deep pocket" of established firms that have multiplant operations. No conclusive interpretation of these results seems justified, however.

Sample 4 consists of the same industries as sample 1, but the two variables that were appended to Orr's model in this study have been deleted in order to facilitate comparisons. The results obtained for sample 4 differ somewhat from those obtained by Orr, who concluded that industry size, capital requirements, advertising intensity, and high concentration were most closely associated with entry in Canada. *P*, *G*, ln *S*, and ln *K* are most closely associated with ln *E* in sample 4. Comparing the results for samples 1 and 4, it is clear that the addition of *M* to the model greatly increases $\bar{R}^2$.

[11] This affects most observations of *M*. See footnote 7.

Sample 5 consists of 89 industries with positive net entry between 1963 and 1967 and sample 6 consists of 96 industries with positive net entry between 1967 and 1972. $\bar{R}^2$ is much lower for either of these short periods than it is for the longer period from 1963 to 1972. Ln S and M have customarily acceptable levels of significance in each of the short time periods, but M has a lower t statistic in either short period than it has in the longer period. P and G only appear to be significant determinants of ln E in the later period. The estimated coefficients for ln K, A, C, and X change sign from the earlier period to the later period, but among these only ln K is significant in either period. Clearly, the model performs best in accounting for entry between 1963 and 1972. Perhaps the market forces that determine entry operate more predictably during longer periods, or perhaps measurement errors are less serious during longer periods, especially errors in measuring entry.

V. CONCLUSIONS

The model employed here seems to perform well in accounting for the number of entrants into U.S. manufacturing industries between 1963 and 1972. The evidence indicates that more entry occurred in large, rapidly growing industries with relatively high price-cost margins, relatively low capital requirements, and limited multiplant operations. The model does not perform as well in accounting for entry between 1963 and 1967 or between 1967 and 1972, but even in these shorter periods more entry occurred if multiplant operations were less extensive.

Although the determinants of entry appear to differ somewhat in importance in the U.S. and Canada, the similarities between Orr's results and those presented here are striking. In both studies, profitability, industry growth, industry size, and capital requirements appear to have the effects on entry that one would expect. Differences between these two studies could easily be due to differences in the composition of the industry samples and/or differences in the specification of the variables.

Finally, the performance of this model of entry is improved considerably by controlling for the extent of multiplant operations found in industries. As expected, it appears that slight multiplant cost advantages and/or grave concerns about the reaction to entry deter many potential entrants when multiplant operations are extensive. In such industries the number of actual entrants is certainly smaller.

Larry L. Duetsch,
Division of Social Sciences,
University of Wisconsin—Parkside,
Post Office Box 2000,
Kenosha, WI 53141, USA.

ACCEPTED DECEMBER 1982

REFERENCES

[1] BRADBURD, R. M. and OVER, A. M. JR., "Organizational Costs, 'Sticky Equilibria', and Critical Levels of Concentration", *Review of Economics and Statistics*, LXIV, 1 (February 1982), pp. 50–58.

[2] CAVES, R. E., KHALILZADEH-SHIRAZI, J. and PORTER, M. E., "Scale Economies in Statistical Analyses of Market Power", *Review of Economics and Statistics*, LVII, 2 (May 1975), pp. 133–40.

[3] CAVES, R. E. and PORTER, M. E., "Barriers to Exit", R. T. Masson and P. D. Qualls, eds., *Essays on Industrial Organization in Honor of Joe S. Bain* (Ballinger, Cambridge, 1976).

[4] COMANOR, W. S. and WILSON, T. A., "Advertising, Market Structure and Performance", *Review of Economics and Statistics*, XXXXIX, 4 (November 1967), pp. 423–40.

[5] DUETSCH, L. L., "Geographic Market Size and the Extent of Multiplant Operations", *Review of Economics and Statistics*, LXIV, 1 (February 1982), pp. 165–67.

[6] ORNSTEIN, S. I., *Industrial Concentration and Advertising Intensity* (American Enterprise Institute for Public Policy Research, Washington, D.C., 1977).

[7] ORR, D., "The Determinants of Entry: A Study of the Canadian Manufacturing Industries", *Review of Economics and Statistics*, LVI, 1 (February 1974), pp. 58–66.

[8] SCHERER, F. M., BECKENSTEIN, A., KAUFER, E. and MURPHY, R. D., *The Economics of Multiplant Operation: An International Comparisons Study* (Harvard University Press, Cambridge, 1975).

[9] SHEPHERD, W. G., *Market Power & Economic Welfare: An Introduction* (Random House, New York, 1970).

THE JOURNAL OF INDUSTRIAL ECONOMICS 0022–1821 $2.00
Volume XXXII June 1984 No. 4

IDENTIFICATION OF INTERACTIVE BEHAVIOR IN AIR SERVICE MARKETS: 1973–76*

JAMES E. ANDERSON

I. INTRODUCTION

The industrial organization literature has a well-known story about determinants of oligopoly behavior. Consideration of the costs and benefits of coordination yields a list of factors contributing to the presence of tacit or explicit collusion (see Scherer, [6]). Empirical evidence on the relevance of the story is weak. Either adequate measures of collusion are missing (as in regressions of profits on four-firm concentration ratios) or incidents of explicit collusion are analyzed across markets so heterogeneous that the *ceteris paribus* assumption is hard to defend (see Hay and Kelley [4]).

Air service markets in the 1973–76 period are an ideal environment for the construction of a test. Anderson and Kraus [1] develop conjectural variation estimates for flight scheduling rivalry in 64 city-pair markets for 138 flight offers. Interactive behavior is defined as a conjecture that rivals' output (flight offers) will vary positively with one's own. It is not necessarily associated with tacit or explicit collusion, but it can be shown that equilibrium industry output will fall with a *ceteris paribus* rise in any conjectural variation (for example, from the Cournot level to an interactive level). Douglas and Miller [3] and Schmalensee [7] have theorized that Cournot behavior was the norm in air service markets in this period. Anderson and Kraus [1] reject Cournot behavior in favor of interactive behavior in about 15% of the cases. If the standard story is at all useful, it should be able to explain the division into two groups.

The present study relates the presence (or absence) of interactive behavior to measures of market environment drawn from the standard story. By using closely related markets in an entry-restricted era, the extraneous factors which plague studies like Hay and Kelley [4] can be eliminated, and the standard story convincingly tested. The results below give it strong confirmation. They also give indirect confirmation of the validity of the Anderson-Kraus [1] model of air service markets. Several critics have pointed out that the airline case for 1973–76 is so special that the test may be low powered—failure-to-reject the standard story based on airline data gives little assurance that

* The work supporting this paper was carried out with support from the CAB. It has benefitted from criticism given an earlier version in a seminar at the Board. John Ciccolo and Marvin Kraus have also made helpful comments. The author alone is responsible for errors. A version of it was presented to the Econometric Society, Denver, September 1980, where it received valuable comments from E. Patrick Marfisi.

failure-to-reject would occur if analogous work were done on other industries. Unknown, but probably low power of hypothesis tests is ubiquitous in econometric work. Different data sets or small specification changes frequently reverse the outcome of hypothesis tests. There is no reason to assume that the present test of the collusion factors story is more subject to this problem than other work. The low power problem, as usual, implies that future work should attempt to replicate results.

The conjectural variation approach to oligopoly behavior and the story tested here are remarkably simple-minded in light of the deep considerations of game theory. Their success in explaining behavior should help overcome pessimism about ever doing good empirical work on oligopoly behavior, at least in limited circumstances.

Part II briefly reviews the Anderson-Kraus [1] model. Part III sets out the factors hypothesized to influence ease of coordination in the literature. These prior beliefs are then compared to the results of the empirical work. Part IV presents the empirical results. Appendix A sets out the statistical model of this study.

II. THE ANDERSON-KRAUS MODEL

The major methodological innovation of Anderson-Kraus is an attempt to deal with oligopolistic behavior of carriers. Most traffic in 1973–76 was in markets served by two or three carriers, and little was served by more than 5 or 6. Neither joint monopoly nor Cournot nor purely competitive behavior can be safely assumed for explaining carrier decisions on flight offers. This section describes the method used to test for different types of oligopolistic behavior on the part of carriers. See Anderson and Kraus for further details.

The Anderson-Kraus model is an elaboration of the Douglas-Miller model of carrier behavior in the price-constrained period. It stresses sheduling rivalry, in which airlines are aware of the effects of their flight offers on market demand and (possibly) on their rivals' flight offers. Anderson and Kraus specialize it to markets defined by non-stop flights in directional city-pair markets. Other aspects of carrier decision-making are excluded from the study by assuming they enter separately. See Anderson and Kraus for a defense of the assumption.

The carrier's flight offer each month is assumed to be the one which maximizes short run profits. We make the following assumptions about how carriers perceive their marginal profits from flights: (1) the airlines have conjectures as to the effect of changes in their own flight offers on each rival's flight offer; (2) their conjectural variations are constant; (3) they have conjectures as to the effect on their market shares of changes in their own plus the induced change in their rivals' flight offers; (4) these conjectured share variations are constant; (5) they assume that CAB fares are independent of their flight offers. In addition, following Theodore Keeler's [5] evidence on airline cost functions, long run marginal cost of flights and of passengers served is constant.

The short run profit function is:

$$(1) \qquad \pi = PQ\theta - C(Q\theta, f) - \frac{1}{2}\frac{1}{e}(\hat{f} - f)^2.$$

P is the fare, Q is market demand, θ is market share, f is the flight offer, $C(\ )$ is the long run cost function, $\hat{f}$ is a forecast capacity variable upon which long run costs are based, e is a positive parameter, and $\frac{1}{2}(1/e)(\hat{f}-f)^2$ is a convex cost function which captures the added cost incurred by departing from planned capacity. The first order condition is:

$$(2) \qquad \frac{d\pi}{df} = (P - C_{Q\theta})Q\frac{d\theta}{df} + (P - C_{Q\theta})\theta\frac{dQ}{dF}\frac{dF}{df} - C_f + \frac{1}{e}(\hat{f} - f) = 0,$$

where F is the market aggregate number of flights, subscripts denote partial differentiation, $d\theta/df \equiv \delta$ is the constant conjectural share variation, $dF/df \equiv \gamma$ is the constant conjectural flight variation, and dQ/dF is the market demand derivative with respect to flights.

It is in principle possible to estimate dQ/dF and assume that carriers use this correct value. Since it is a complicated function the parameters of which can be estimated only by an elaborate procedure (see Anderson and Kraus [2]), we assume instead that carriers have a conjecture as to its value, Ψ. Solve (2) for f

$$(2') \qquad f = \hat{f} + (P - C_{Q\theta})Q[e\delta] + (P - C_{Q\theta})\theta[e\Psi\gamma] - C_f[e].$$

The right hand side of (2′) is essentially the equation estimated by Anderson and Kraus [1][1] over monthly data for 138 flight offers in 64 markets. e, $(e\delta)$, $(e\Psi\gamma)$ are the parameters of interest ($\hat{f}$ is a forecast function, the parameters of which are also estimated).

The Cournot behavioral assumption asserts that firms are aware of the demand constraint, but do not assume others will react to their service changes.[2] Cournot behavior implies $\gamma = 1$. γ is not identified (appearing only in the product $e\Psi\gamma$), but notice that any reasonable market state should have the perceived aggregate flight elasticity $[\Psi(F/Q)]$ for each carrier bounded between zero and one. Aircraft type is assumed exogenous in Anderson-Kraus. Thus, elasticity greater than one implies an increase in flights raises

[1] Anderson-Kraus is slightly more complicated since the focus is on seat offers rather than flight offers.

[2] Another case in the literature on airline behavior yields a restriction on (2′) which can be tested. De Vany's version of a competitive airline market asserts that $\partial Q\theta/\partial f = Q/F$, carriers assume that adding a flight will add traffic at the market load factor. In terms of (2′) this implies at each sample point t

$$\omega \equiv e - (e\delta)F_t - \theta_t(e\Psi\gamma)\frac{F_t}{Q_t} = 0.$$

Evaluating F, Q, and θ at the sample mean; and replacing e, $(e\delta)$, $(e\Psi\gamma)$ with their estimated values, we can form an asymptotic t-test statistic to see whether behavior differs significantly from the competitive model. For 75 out of 138 cases, competitive behavior could be rejected. Work along the lines explained below attempted to test for significant differences in the rejection and non-rejection groups. No success in explaining the division was achieved. Probably all markets are non-competitive, but random influences produce realizations of t such that competition cannot be rejected in a substantial number of cases.

load factors. Elasticity less than zero implies a decrease in flights raises traffic. A conservative test of interactive behavior vs. Cournot behavior can be created by taking the highest possible value of the perceived elasticity, unity, and rejecting Cournot behavior in favor of interactive behavior only if $\hat{\varepsilon} \equiv \hat{e} - (e\hat{\Psi}\gamma)(\bar{F}/\bar{Q}) < 0$ in a statistically significant sense, where ˆ denotes estimated value and ¯ denotes the sample mean. It can be shown that total flights (F) in a market in long run equilibrium fall monotonically as the magnitude of interactive behavior rises. While some interactive cases are not picked up by the test (since the perceived elasticity typically will lie well below unity), it does pick out the worst ones from a policy standpoint, *ceteris paribus*. Non-Cournot behavior in which conjectural variations are perversely interactive (carrier i assumes rivals will decrease flights in response to his increase in flights) results in long equilibrium between pure competition and Cournot, and is thus of limited policy interest. Therefore, the one-tailed test used picks out the most interesting cases.

The flight offer equations were estimated for 138 cases in 64 markets. Results for 36 equations in 16 markets are presented in Anderson and Kraus [1]. For the purposes of this paper 6 of the 138 cases were eliminated due to insignificant (usually negative) values of $\hat{e}$. Of the remaining 132, 55 had negative t-ratios for the reject-Cournot test ($\hat{\varepsilon} < 0$), with 20 t-ratios being less than minus 1.65 (0.05 probability). Under the null hypothesis, the t-ratios should be asymptotically normally distributed about zero. The relative frequency of negative 1.65 and under values is about 3 times what it should be under the null hypothesis. A crude but reasonable alternative hypothesis is that there are two sample universes, one centered on a negative value for interactive flight offers and the other centered on a non-negative value (perhaps zero but more likely positive in light of the construction of the test) for Cournot flight offers. Factors suggested by economic theory will be used in the remainder of this paper to explain the division of outcomes into 2 groups.

III. FACTORS ASSOCIATED WITH INTERACTIVE BEHAVIOR

This section will set out a list of factors affecting the likelihood of finding interactive behavior and comment on their fit with the results. In effect, it is discussing the right hand side of a regression equation. The left hand side, the dependent variable, measuring the likelihood of interactive behavior based on the Anderson-Kraus t-values, is discussed in Appendix A. With small distortion to intuitive understanding, the casual reader can skip Appendix A save for its last two paragraphs (which rule out joint determination of the factors and the interactive behavior in the cross-section). The discussion of this section should be read referring to the table in Part IV. A smaller (more negative) value of the dependent variable in the table means a greater likelihood of interactive behavior.

The industrial organization literature has a story about oligopoly behavior which yields a list of factors contributing to the presence of tacit or explicit cooperation.[3] Essentially they enumerate costs and benefits of coordination. While usually developed for the classic price-quantity dimensioned market, the insights easily carry over to the quantity-quality dimensioned market that characterized air service in the 1973-76 period.

First are a group of four *factors which facilitate cooperative behavior. Fewness of sellers* has always been granted great importance in aiding cooperation on theoretical grounds, and it appears to have some validity empirically. Fewness makes communication through parallel behavior easier and also makes cheating on tacit rules easier to detect. In the 1973–76 airline case, all markets are marked by fewness (the four firm concentration ratios are nearly all 100%). On prior grounds one might not expect to be able to discriminate between them on this basis. Results not shown in Part IV confirm this: number of sellers had no explanatory power.

A second facilitator of cooperation is *homogeneity*. By homogeneity is meant: (1) homogeneity of the product (and absence of close substitutes) in demand; (2) homogeneity of sellers' production functions; and (3) stability of market conditions over time.

For the air service case, product heterogeneity at a point in time exists mainly in the existence of two sorts of travellers: business and pleasure. Markets which are heavily one or the other might be expected to be easier to coordinate since demand should be easier to predict, and since all carriers might then carry a similar mix. The results of Part IV show that pleasure markets, *ceteris paribus*, are more likely to have interactive behavior. Results not shown reveal that heavily business and mixed markets, *ceteris paribus*, are no more likely to have interactive behavior than the average: these market characteristics have no explanatory power. The reason has to do with a separate characteristic of demand: elasticity. This is the third facilitator of cooperation in Scherer's taxonomy. *Ceteris paribus*, the lower the elasticity the greater the rewards to cooperation. The elasticity of total traffic with respect to total flights should be lowest in pleasure markets, where scheduling convenience matters least, and highest in business markets, where it matters most.[4] The two influences go in the same direction for pleasure markets, but in opposite directions for business markets.

[3] We follow here a development due to Scherer [6] and Hay and Kelly [4].

[4] It is helpful to analytically relate the flight elasticity to the value of time, the price elasticity, and the fare. Pleasure markets have low value of time and high price elasticity, which have opposite effects on flight elasticity. In the regulated period the fare was high enough so that pleasure markets had low price and flight elasticity on balance. With deregulation, pleasure markets experienced more price competition, hence lower fares, and this raised the flight elasticity, *ceteris paribus*. The likelihood of interactive behavior in tourist markets should now (post-1976) be lower. This discussion follows from an analytical decomposition of the aggregate flight elasticity.

Let demand be $Q = Q(P + Wt(Q, F))$ where $P + Wt$ is the full trip price, t is the travel-plus-delay time function, W is the value of time and P is the fare. The aggregate flight elasticity is:

$$\Psi \equiv \frac{dQ}{dF}\frac{F}{Q} = \frac{(\partial t/\partial F)F}{\dfrac{(P/W) + t}{\varepsilon} + \dfrac{\partial t}{\partial Q}Q}, \text{ where } \varepsilon \equiv -Q'\frac{P + Wt}{Q}, \text{ the price elasticity.}$$

We can see that *cetris paribus*, $\partial\Psi/\partial P < 0$, $\partial\Psi/\partial\varepsilon > 0$, $\partial\Psi/\partial W > 0$.

Returning to considerations of homogeneity, distance between city-pairs may signal a product heterogeneity related to network effects. With shorter distances, there may be more through traffic and there are likely to be more close substitutes via other routings for the chosen direct flight city-pair. This will make coordination more difficult, and will raise the flight elasticity of demand. Surface competition also raises the short-haul flight elasticity. The results of Part IV show that longer distance increases (but not significantly) the likelihood of finding interactive behavior, as this explanation indicates it should.

Instability of markets over time is very important in air service. Entry and permanent shifts in equipment type are not significant in our sample, though classically they should make coordination difficult. But large seasonal variations in demand cause related shifts in flight offers, in equipment type, and traffic related costs. *Ceteris paribus*, coordination should be easier the less the variation in demand. Increases in the coefficient of variation of market demand in Part V is found to reduce the likelihood of finding interactive behavior.

On the supply side, product heterogeneity occurs mainly due to differential network effects (flight costs in a given market do not vary with great significance). In Anderson-Kraus, we develop a model based on ignoring such effects. Nevertheless, the presence of large differences in the connectedness of different carriers' networks may complicate the task of coordination. In well connected sections of the country, all carriers are likely to be reasonably equal in their ability to service through traffic. In less well connected cities, important differences will emerge.[5] The results of Part IV show that interactive behavior is more likely to occur in well connected markets. Another aspect of differential network effects lies in the presence of regional carriers. For our data set, this is mainly Allegheny. *Ceteris paribus*, one anticipates that the presence of such carriers would make coordination more difficult. Instead, the results of Part V show that generally their presence contributes significantly to the occurrence of interactive behavior on the part of the major trunk carriers (no flight offer equations were estimated for regional carriers). Our tentative explanation is that regional carriers (or at least Allegheny) tend to be in a client relationship with the majors due to connections at the boundaries of their networks. This creates an environment conducive to leader-follower behavior (which is consistent with an interactive value for the conjectural variation of the leader).

[5] This argument abstracts from the complication that connectedness is carrier *and* market specific. For example, Delta and Eastern both hub at Atlanta and have an advantage relative to other carriers there. Moreover, both should respond differently to each other than to third parties. The practical reason for abstracting from detail of this sort is that dummy variables for carrier and market specific characteristics eat degrees of freedom at a great rate. Furthermore, while the Atlanta case is clearcut, other markets have less sharp differences, so that classification is highly subjective.

The consequence is that there may be some specification bias in the coefficient associated with this variable. There should be only weak relation between connectedness and the other independent variables, so bias should be limited to the connectedness coefficient.

The final facilitator of coordination is a *benign industry social structure.* The presence of a dominant firm and the absence of a maverick are the two factors usually mentioned. In the air service case, National was our candidate for maverick status. Neither variable affects the likelihood of finding interactive behavior. In Part V we present results using a number of variables related to market structure. The market shares of the largest, next largest, and third largest carriers are used as explanatory variables (with the fourth being the remainder). Concentration might plausibly contribute to a benign structure, *ceteris paribus.* All three shares are positively associated with the likelihood of finding interactive behavior. A complicating factor in the association of shares with finding interactive behavior emerges when the Anderson-Kraus flight offer equations are considered. Appendix B shows that reject-Cournot cases with low probability of the Type I error tend to be concentrated in low market share cases. The reason is that the variance of the regressors relative to the regress and is higher for low market share cases. *Ceteris paribus*, while the estimator is consistent, there is a better chance of discovering a significant negative value of the reject-Cournot statistic for low market shares. The text following Table B-II further develops this line of reasoning. The results of Part IV thus show that the likelihood of finding interactive behavior falls with one share, *ceteris paribus.*

The presence of various carriers might also contribute to the likelihood of finding interactive behavior. The use of a set of carrier presence dummies shows that all firm effects are very weak.

The other relevant factors in explaining coordination are a *group of three factors which increase the cost of non-cooperating*.

Two related factors are *lumpiness* and *infrequency* of sales, which are hardly problems in air service markets of reasonable size, the only ones studied here. Thin air service markets will face such problems. The final factor in the standard industrial organization story is *a high proportion of fixed costs.* The burden of excess capacity in periods of slack makes it costly not to cut back supply cooperatively. In air service markets there are no fixed costs allocable to markets outside of the very short run, but excess capacity (less than 100% load factor) is ubiquitous. The average cost of carrying a passenger is the marginal cost of his presence on the aircraft plus average per passenger flight cost $C_f(f/Q\theta)$. Carrier i's decision to cut back flights decreases average per passenger cost for carrier j by increasing j's load factor. Flight costs act like fixed costs in increasing the desirability of cooperation. The results of Part IV show that, *ceteris paribus*, the likelihood of finding interactive behavior increases with $C_f(f/Q\theta)$.

Finally, departing from the factors associated with costs or benefits of cooperation in the standard model, six added features of air service markets may be associated with the likelihood of interactive behavior. Absolute size may matter, with perhaps more careful attention paid to flight scheduling in bigger markets, thus enhancing the likelihood of interactive behavior. Average flights per month is seen in Part IV to have no relation to the likelihood of interactive behavior. Second, load factors have a close relation to profits and appear to be carefully watched. $C_f(f/Q\theta)$ is inversely related to load factors, and the likelihood of interactive behavior is positively associated with $C_f(f/Q\theta)$. On the other hand, high load factors may signal benign structural factors omitted in the preceding list. In Part IV, the likelihood of finding interactive behavior is positively associated with average load factor, *ceteris paribus* (which in this case means a change in C_f and $f/Q\theta$ so that $C_f(f/Q\theta)$ remains constant.)[6] The second moments of load factors may also be associated with the likelihood of finding interactive behavior. *Ceteris paribus*, we might expect it to be more difficult to figure out rivals' responses and coordinate behavior if load factors are highly variable. In Part IV, higher values for the coefficients of variation for own load factors and for market load factor are found to reduce the likelihood of finding interactive behavior. Fourth, it is interesting to see whether "profit margins" (calculated as average revenue per flight minus the average cost per flight over the average cost per flight) have any relation to the likelihood of finding interactive behavior. In Part IV, the likelihood decreases as the "profit margin" increases, *ceteris paribus*. One tentative explanation is that managers work harder (at figuring out rivals' behavior *inter alia*) in more threatening environments. This is consistent with other findings (see Scherer, [6, p. 176]). High profits may also proxy other variables unfavorable to interaction.

Finally, two institutional features of air service markets in the period 1973–76 might contribute to interactive behavior. For a few months at the beginning of the period, explicit collusion was approved by the CAB in a few markets (in order to reduce fuel consumption). There is no evidence based on our methods that this created interactive behavior—Anderson-Kraus cannot reject Cournot behavior for those cases. The second institutional feature is more significant. Peak load problems at Washington, Chicago, and New York have created an airport constraint on the total number of arrivals during some hours of the day. Carriers in effect own landing rights. This may lead to greater likelihood of co-ordination in markets with one of the 3 cities as a destination, since the constraint makes it easier to identify what rivals do in substituting along the constraint line. Also, the omission of the shadow price as an explanatory variable in the Anderson-Kraus regression equation creates bias tending to spuriously indicate interactive behavior. Anderson and Kraus argue this bias will be negligible. At any rate, results not shown in Part IV indicate that destination in Washington, Chicago, or New York has no explanatory power for the likelihood of finding interactive behavior.

[6] Another interpretation of the sign of this coefficient is through simultaneous determination of the conjectural variation estimate and the load factor. In principle, successful interaction increases load factors, *ceteris paribus*. In Appendix A, it is argued that load factors are predetermined with respect to measured conjectural variations, hence bias can be ruled out. Positive sign then results from omitted exogenous variables proxied by load factors.

IV. RESULTS

The dependent variable is LNODDS, the log of the odds of the Type I error associated in the standard normal distribution with the t-ratio $\hat{\varepsilon}/\hat{\sigma}_{\varepsilon}$. It is calculated for 132 flight offer equations estimated by Anderson-Kraus on monthly data for 1973–76. Appendix B lists the markets and carriers in Table B-I and the cases where negative estimates of $\hat{\varepsilon}$ were found in Table B-II. For values in the interactive range, the dependent variable is related to the independent variable by a linear regression. As explained in Appendix A, for values above the interactive range the true value of LNODDS, given the interactive sample universe, is unobservable. We select three limiting values above which LNODDS is unobserved corresponding to probabilities of the Type I error of 0.05, 0.10, and 0.50. For values above the limit, LNODDS is set at its limiting value. For these observations, the normal distribution is used to calculate the cumulative (from the right tail) probability associated with the linear regression disturbance for that observation. The maximum likelihood TOBIT estimator is then implemented.

The independent variables are the distance for the city-pair market (DIST) and either descriptive statistics for the monthly time series or dummy variables. The statistics are:

SHR, the average own traffic share;
SHRi, the average traffic share of the ith largest carrier in the market, $i = 1, 2, 3$; in logs
LDF, average own load factor (traffic carried/seats offered);
SF, average own flights offered;
CFVRBQ, the coefficient of variation of market traffic;
CFVRMKLDF, the coefficient of variation of market load factors;
CFVRLDF, the coefficient of variation of own load factors;
AVCST, the mean of monthly flight cost per passenger; in logs;
PIMGN, the average "profit" margin.

The dummy variables are:

OTHCR, equal 1 for a market in which a regional carrier has an important share, and 0 otherwise;
RTSTR, equal 2 for well-connected markets, 1 for moderately well-connected markets, and 0 for the least well-connected markets;
AMMK, equal 1 if American is in the market, and 0 otherwise;
EAMK, equal 1 if Eastern is in the market, and 0 otherwise;
UNMK, equal 1 if United is in the market, and 0 otherwise;
DEMK, equal 1 if Delta is in the market, and 0 otherwise;
PLSDUM, equal 1 if the market is pleasure dominated (more than 75%), and 0 otherwise;
MAJCR, equal 1 if the own carrier is one of American, Eastern, United, or Delta;
MINCR, equal 1 if the own carrier is one of TWA, Braniff, or Western.

TABLE I

Dependent Variable	*SHR*	*LDF*	*SF*	*DIST*	*OTHCR*	*RTSTR*	*SHR1*	*SHR2*
Limit = ln(0.05/0.95) = −2.94	2.22	−7.0165	0.4360	−1.022	−5.120	−3.988	−35.51	−5.170
	(0.670)	(2.88)	(0.617)	(1.260)	(2.04)	(1.57)	(14.9)	(7.01)
	2.707	−8.750	0.537	−2.648	−7.24	−5.19	−51.37	−5.83
	(0.7943)	(3.533)	(0.767)	(1.58)	(2.48)	(1.69)	(17.29)	(9.19)
Limit = ln(0.10/0.90) = −2.19	1.35	−2.15	0.229	−0.0396	−1.88	−2.04	−6.157	2.09
	(0.415)	(1.69)	(0.463)	(0.638)	(0.840)	(1.12)	(6.24)	(4.71)
	1.37	−1.50	0.363	−0.196	−1.97	−2.18	−8.93	−0.846
	(0.470)	(1.79)	(0.5206)	(0.673)	(0.853)	(1.19)	(6.92)	(6.33)
Limit = ln(0.50/0.50) = 0	1.017	0.673	0.563	0.1360	−0.731	−0.433	4.26	7.40
	(0.292)	(1.09)	(0.317)	(0.388)	(0.398)	(0.411)	(3.48)	(3.47)
	1.442	0.7050	0.421	0.285	−0.625	−0.249	1.476	6.36
	(0.344)	(1.16)	(0.330)	(0.400)	(0.407)	(0.426)	(3.68)	(3.76)
	SHR3	*AMMK*	*EAMK*	*UNMK*	*DEMK*	*CFVRBQ*	*CFVRMKLDF*	*CFVRLDF*
Limit = ln(0.05/0.95) = −2.94	−47.182					30.477	16.718	7.578
	(18.86)					(15.26)	(17.39)	(3.925)
	−60.46	−0.4354	0.708	0.6606	1.31	42.32	35.30	8.705
	(20.27)	(0.771)	(0.718)	(0.915)	(0.706)	(18.17)	(19.21)	(4.36)
Limit = ln(0.10/0.90) = −2.19	−8.66					6.29	3.39	7.30
	(7.38)					(7.93)	(13.25)	(3.61)
	−9.69	−0.555	0.399	−0.225	0.3911	7.53	8.36	7.76
	(7.95)	(0.578)	(0.507)	(0.560)	(0.447)	(8.01)	(13.6)	(3.7)
Limit = ln(0.50/0.50) = 0	3.08					9.98	−10.17	11.46
	(3.70)					(4.09)	(6.59)	(3.16)
	1.855	−0.278	0.819	0.215	0.766	9.39	−11.175	11.55
	(3.90)	(0.312)	(0.343)	(0.305)	(0.318)	(4.27)	(6.76)	(3.27)

	PLSDUM	*AVCST*	*MAJCAR*	*MINCAR*	*PIMGN*	R^2	*Prob* ($y <$ lim | *ave. x*)	*Observed Freq.* ($y < lim$)
Limit = ln(0.05/0.95) = −2.94	−3.430	−2.891	38.205	49.89	0.1904	0.8367	0.000	0.1515
	(1.688)	(1.183)	(18.14)	(34634)	(0.0321)			
	−5.99	−2.80	54.78	67.37	0.0041	0.8786	0.000	0.1515
	(2.12)	(1.29)	(21.54)	(30513)	(0.00136)			
Limit = ln(0.10/0.90) = −2.19	−1.29	−1.28	7.71	16.46	0.00240	0.7567	0.007	0.1970
	(1.11)	(0.829)	(6.97)	(43334)	(0.00105)			
	−2.26	−1.029	9.35	18.44	0.002714	0.8160	0.007	0.1970
	(1.29)	(0.829)	(7.43)	(41402)	(0.00112)			
Limit = ln(0.50/0.50) = 0	−0.654	−1.61	−2.96	−1.783	0.00063	0.6733	0.453	0.4167
	(0.419)	(0.544)	(3.94)	(3.96)	(0.00048)			
	−1.004	−1.516	−1.47	0.1961	0.000853	0.7417	0.457	0.4167
	(0.440)	(0.561)	(4.10)	(4.144)	(0.000504)			

Two equations for each limit on LNODDS are presented in the table, one with and one without the carrier presence dummies. The intercept is suppressed, since the unit vector equals MAJCR + MINCR. The terms in brackets under the coefficient estimates are standard errors. The coefficients are normalized (deflated by the estimated standard deviation of the disturbances). An R^2 between observed and predicted values is also presented. The last two columns give an alternative measure of explanatory power. The calculated probability of the dependent variable lying below the limit given average values for the independent variables is contrasted with the observed frequency. The gain in the first over the second measures the average gain over the pure ignorance alternative classification.

The results presented in the table give confirmation of the story told in Part III. For limits of ln (0.05/0.95) and ln (0.10/0.90), all point estimates have the right sign and generally are more than 2 standard errors from zero. Exceptions are the size variable SF, the distance variable DIST for ln (0.10/0.90), and the carrier presence dummies. Qualitatively these equations are very similar. In contrast, with limit = ln (0.50/0.50) = 0, the results are somewhat more muddled. Notably, the ranked market share variables change sign. Undoubtedly the below-limit group now includes a number of observations from the Cournot sample universe. In this light, the model is surprisingly robust as the limit is raised. The goodness-of-fit measures show that the equations are very successful in sorting out interactive and Cournot behavior.

James E. Anderson,
Boston College,
Chestnut Hill,
Massachusetts, 02167

ACCEPTED OCTOBER 1982

APPENDIX A. THE STATISTICAL MODEL

The task of this paper is to explain the incidence of interactive (reject Cournot) behavior in light of factors enumerated in the last section. This appendix considers the choice of a dependent variable which will imply a statistical model.

t-ratios $(\hat{\varepsilon}/\hat{\sigma}_{\varepsilon})$, are not a satisfactory measure of the likelihood of interactive behavior, since they assign as much importance to each increment of t from, say -1.5 to -2.5. An extreme remedy is to define a dummy dependent variable based on finding t-values above and below some critical value. This throws away information. A better measure is the probability of the Type I error associated with the t-ratio in the standard normal table. This probability will be roughly triangularly distributed under the null hypothesis, symmetrically about 0.50 in the interval (0, 1). Still nicer is the log of the odds of the Type I error. It will, under the null hypothesis, by symmetrically distributed about zero (from $+\infty$ to $-\infty$) and, while non-normal, will not deviate very much from the normal, based on calculations with representative variances. The log of the odds is used below as the dependent variable.

It has one major disadvantage. The dependent variable will be assumed to equal a mean explained by the characteristics vector plus a normal zero mean disturbance. The normal probability density function for the dependent variable is thus assumed to slide back and forth on the horizontal axis as the conditioning characteristics shift—the disturbance pdf is constant. The problem with this is that the true pdf for those observations which come from the interactive (reject-the-null-hypothesis) universe cannot be a simple horizontal translation of the null hypothesis pdf. The interactive sample universe(s) will not yield a symmetric distribution (nor will the Cournot unless it is in fact centered on $\varepsilon = 0$) for the dependent variable, the log of the odds of finding a t-ratio as small given the null hypothesis. The degree of asymmetry depends on the distance of the center of the alternative distribution(s) from zero. In what follows we nevertheless assume the disturbance term has zero mean and is normally distributed. This is based on rough calculations that indicate departure from symmetry and normality is mild even for fairly extreme cases.[7]

For values in the interactive range ($-\infty$ to Y_{LIM}, where Y_{LIM} is a critical value such as $\ln(0.05/0.95)$) we assume that Y_i, the observed log of the odds for observation i, is related to X_i, a vector of market characteristics by $Y_i = X_i\beta + U_i$, where β is a parameter vector and U_i is a realization of a zero mean normally distributed random variable. For values outside the interactive range (values greater than Y_{LIM}), the "true" value of Y, the log of the odds *given the interactive sample universe*, is unobserved. So we set Y at its limiting value. For observations j where Y is at its limit we can use the normal distribution for U to calculate the cumulative (from the right tail) probability associated with $Y_{\text{LIM}} - X_j\beta$. The maximum likelihood TOBIT estimator of β can then be implemented.

A possible weakness of this procedure is that it assumes the "true" value of Y is observed for $Y < Y_{\text{LIM}}$. The alternative is to assume no "true" Y's are observable and use a critical value of the log of the odds (hence a critical value

[7] For example, if the mean value of t in the interactive sample universe is -1.65, the true distribution of the log of the odds of the Type I error has its median at -2.94 ($\ln(0.05/95)$). Twothirds of its values lie between -4.595 ($\ln(0.01/0.99)$ and 0 ($\ln(0.5/0.5)$). 5% of its values should lie below -6.907 ($\ln(0.001/0.999)$), and 5% above 2.94 ($\ln((0.95/0.05)$). The mean is hard to calculate, but it is algebraically greater than the median, so that shifting the distribution up so that the new mean $= 0$ would leave the median on a negative value. If the distribution is for simplicity shifted to the right by 2.94 so that the median $= 0$, 5% of realizations will have values of 5.88 or more and 5% will have values of -3.97 or less. The normal approximation would assign 5% probability to the range outside the median value $\pm 1.65\sigma$; where σ is the standard deviation. Considering that the median shift will put the mean at a positive value and that σ, the standard deviation for the assumed shift by 2.94 will lie between 3.97/1.65 and 5.88/1.65, the probability assignment of the normal approximation does not grossly err in the tails. A further check in practice comes from examining the histograms of the residuals from the results in Part V. Without exception, they are symmetric and unimodal, and do not appear markedly non-normal. Normality cannot be rejected using the chi-square test.

of "t") to create a dummy dependent variable equal to 1 when $Y > Y_{\text{LIM}}$ and 0 when $Y \leq Y_{\text{LIM}}$. With $Y_i = X_i\beta + U_i$ as the underlying model, but Y_i unobserved, and U_i normally distributed; the maximum likelihood PROBIT estimator of β can be implemented. Results not reported below show that the PROBIT and TOBIT procedures are qualitatively identical—all coefficient signs are preserved and much of the significance of the equations. TOBIT makes more efficient use of information and thus naturally gives a somewhat better fit. The comparison with PROBIT indicates the conclusions are robust with respect to possible distortions created by the construction of the Y's.

A source of uncertainty in the procedures is the proper limit value to be selected. In principle this could also be estimated but how to do it is still an unsolved problem (raised in Tobin's original paper, [8]). In what follows, we present results for limits associated with probabilities of the Type I error of 0.05, 0.10, and 0.50. The histogram of the log of the odds in Table A-I illustrates the problem. It is likely that there are at least two sample universes, one centered in the significantly negative range and one or more centered in the higher (algebraically) range. With the minimum of two, the overlap of the tails of the two resulting distributions creates the middle accumulation of the histogram. The proper limit value is not obvious, but the results of Part V show that at least the move from a limit of -2.19 [ln(0.10/0.90)] to -2.945 [ln(0.05/0.95)] does not change the qualitative results.

In using the TOBIT estimator, the U's must be distributed independently of the X's. The X's are either market statistics such as means or variances across the time series of variables like market shares or carrier flight offers, or they are dummy variables. Y, the log of the odds, is constructed from t-statistics estimated from time series regressions. If the asymptotic unbiasedness assumption of estimation is met, there should be no systematic relation between the realization of t and the realizations of moments of market time series as we move across markets. Thus the independence of U and the X's is reasonable on this ground.

Another possible source of violation of independence and hence specification bias is more interesting. Why would not interactive behavior and variables like profits and load factors be jointly determined? More formally, the hypothesized relationship purports to explain the likelihood of interactive behavior by the characteristics of the environment. But suppose actors could select the environment on the basis of its characteristics. Then an initial configuration of long run market statistics could be shifted as carriers of differing behavior patterns entered and exited the market. Y and the X's would be jointly determined, and simultaneous equations bias would exist through correlation of the X's and U. It is significant to see that this possibility can be rejected. For air service in 1973–76, entry was strictly controlled. Exit was not controlled, but in our sample did not occur other than by carriers with trivial market share. Carriers may not choose markets, and single equation techniques are appropriate. This statement does not deny the implicit

TABLE AI

HISTOGRAM OF THE LOG OF THE ODDS

```
BCT.     N
0.129 17 I
0.129 17 I
0.121 16 I
0.121 16 I
0.121 16 I
0.114 15 I
0.114 15 I
0.114 15 I
0.106 14 I
0.106 14 I
0.106 14 I
0.099 13 I                                                      X
0.099 13 I                                                      X
0.099 13 I                                                      X
0.091 12 I                                 X                    X
0.091 12 I                                 X                    X
0.091 12 I                                 X                    X
0.083 11 I                                XX                    X
0.083 11 I                                XX                    X
0.083 11 I                                XX                    X
0.076 10 I                                XX                    X
0.076 10 I                                XX                    X
0.076 10 I                                XX                    X
0.068  9 I                                XX                    X
0.068  9 I                                XX                    X
0.068  9 I                                XX                    X
0.061  8 I                                XX   X                X
0.061  8 I                                XX   X                X
0.061  8 I                                XX   X                X
0.053  7 I                              X XXX  X                X
0.053  7 I                              X XXX  X                X
0.053  7 I                              X XXX  X                X
0.045  6 I                             XXXXXX  XX               X
0.045  6 I                             XXXXXX XX                X
0.045  6 I                             XXXXXX  XX               X
0.038  5 IX                            XXXXXXX XXX              X
0.038  5 IX                            XXXXXXX XXX              X
0.038  5 IX                            XXXXXXX XXX              X
0.030  4 IX                          X XXXXXXXXXXX X      X     X
0.030  4 IX                          X XXXXXXXXXXX X      X     X
0.030  4 IX                          X XXXXXXXXXXX X      X     X
0.023  3 IX                          X XXXXXXXXXXXXXX X   X     X
0.023  3 IX                          X XXXXXXXXXXXXXX X   X     X
0.023  3 IX                          X XXXXXXXXXXXXXX X   X     X
0.015  2 IX                    X XX  X XXXXXXXXXXXXXX X X X     X
0.015  2 IX                    X XX  X XXXXXXXXXXXXXX X X X     X
0.015  2 IX                    X XX  X XXXXXXXXXXXXXX X X X     X
0.008  1 IX                  XXXXXX XX XXXXXXXXXXXXXXXXXXXX     X    X
0.008  1 IX                  XXXXXX XX XXXXXXXXXXXXXXXXXXXX     X    X
0.008  1 IX                  XXXXXX XX XXXXXXXXXXXXXXXXXXXX     X    X
         I---------I---------I---------I---------I---------I---------I
-       23.0 -    16.1 -    9.21 -    2.30      4.61      11.5      18.4
```

theoretical dependence of, for example, the mean load factor in a single market on the true value of the conjectural variation parameters in that market. But since the latter *are* parameters, mean load factors across the cross-section are predetermined with respect to the measured conjectural variation and hence its transform, Υ.[8]

[8] Formally, we argue that the model implies $\Upsilon(\gamma) = X(\gamma^*, \theta)\beta + U$, where γ is the measured conjectural variation and γ^* is the true value.

APPENDIX B. MARKETS AND CARRIERS COVERED, AND CLASSIFICATION WITH MARKET SHARES

TABLE B-I: FLIGHT OFFER EQUATIONS USED

City-Pair	*Carriers*	*City-Pair*	*Carriers*
BOS-NY	AM, EA, DE	CHI-CLE	UN
NY-BOS	AM, EA, DE	CLE-CHI	UN
BAL-NY	AM, EA, DE	DAL-DEN	BR
NY-BAL	EA	DEN-DAL	BP
CHI-LV	TR, UN	CHI-PHNX	AM, TR
LV-CHI	TR, UN	PHNX-CHI	AM, TR
LA-NY	AM, TR, UN	CHI-DEN	TR, UN
NY-LA	AM, TR	DEN-CHI	TR, UN
ATL-BRM	EA, DE	ATL-CHI	EA, DE
BRM-ATL	EA, DE	CHI-ATL	EA, DE
CHI-INDY	AM, DE	NY-SFO	AM, TR, UN
INDY-CHI	AM, DE	SFO-NY	AM, TR, UN
MIA-NY	EA, DE	BOS-MIA	EA, DE
NY-MIA	EA, DE	MIA-BOS	EA, DE
NY-TMPA	EA, DE	CHI-TMPA	EA, DE
TMPA-NY	EA, DE	TMPA-CHI	EA
CHI-MIA	EA, DE	ATL-NY	EA, UN, DE
MIA-CHI	EA	NY-ATL	EA, UN, DE
CHI-SFO	AM, TR, UN	CHI-DET	AM, UN, DE
SFO-CHI	AM, TR, UN	DET-CHI	AM, UN, DE
ATL-WAS	EA, DE	ATL-TMPA	EA, UN, DE
WAS-ATL	EA, DE	TMPA-ATL	EA, UN, DE
CHI-WAS	AM, TR	CHI-PITTS	TR, UN
WAS-CHI	AM, TR, UN	PITTS-CHI	TR, UN
CHI-CNCY	AM, DE	LA-PHNX	TR, WE
CNCY-CHI	AM, DE	PHNX-LA	TR, WE
BOS-CHI	AM, TR, UN	NY-STL	AM, TR
CHI-BOS	AM, TR, UN	STL-NY	AM, TR
NY-PITTS	TR	BOS-PHIL	DE
PITTS-NY	TR	PHIL-BOS	DE
		CLE-NY	AM, TR, UN
		NY-CLE	AM, TR, UN

Table B-II has market shares (average for 73–6) for the cases shown in parentheses. Out of 26 cases with 5% or 10% confidence level, 10 have market shares less than or equal to 11%, with 5 in the 3% to 6% range. 13 cases have shares greater than or equal to 21%. The largest share for any case is 57%.

A troublesome question is whether we have a statistical artifact due to the large number of small share rejections (and complete absence of big share rejections). There are two separate answers to this.

The first is statistical and gives a reasonable statistical case for it being harder to determine non-Cournot behavior for larger carriers. *Ceteris paribus*, the bigger carriers in a market need proportionally bigger variances for the right-hand side variables to have an equal chance at a precise determination

TABLE B-II
CARRIERS REJECTING COURNOT BEHAVIOR AT VARIOUS CONFIDENCE LEVELS, BASED ON NORMAL DISTRIBUTION PROBABILITIES, WITH MARKET SHARES

Carrier/ Confidence Level	0–0.05	0.05–0.10	0.10–0.20	0.20–0.30	0.30–0.40	0.40–0.50
AM 24 offers estimated	BAL-NY(0.11) BOS-NY (0.21) CHI-SFO (0.33) CHI-CINCY (0.18)		NY-BOS (0.20) NY-LA (0.39)	NY-SFO (0.34) STL-NY(0.27)	SFO-CHI (0.35)	CINCY-CHI (0.23) CHI-WAS (0.38) SFO-NY (0.31)
EA 24 offers estimated	BAL-NY (0.11) NY-BAL (0.11) TMPA-CHI (0.16)	ATL-NY (0.39) −CHI-ATL (0.34)		ATL-CGI (0.35)	TMPA-ATL (0.32) ATL-TMPA (0.30)	BOS-MIA (0.35) NY-ATL (0.39)
UN 28 offers estimated	LA-NY (0.23) PITTS-CHI (0.35) NY-ATL (0.04) ATL-NY (0.03) SFO-NY (0.33) NY-SFO (0.32) WAS-CHI (0.40)	CHI-DET (0.25) DET-CHI (0.24)	CHI-PITTS (0.35)	BOS-CHI (0.36) SFO-CHI (0.41)	CHI-SFO (0.44) CHI-LV (0.56)	
DE 30 offers estimated	BOS-NY (0.09) NY-BOS (0.10) BAL-NY (0.05) CHI-MIA (0.45) DET-CHI (0.06) CHI-DET (0.05)	−BIRM-ATL (0.57) −MIA-NY (0.14)	NY-MIA (0.14)		NY-TMPA (0.29) CHI-TMPA (0.36)	
TR 28 offers estimated			CHI-LV (0.44) SFO-CHI (0.24) LA-PHNX (0.24)	LV-CHI (0.41)	CHI-SFO (0.24) CLE-NY (0.07)	CHI-DEN (0.21)

of the coefficients. To see this recall that in the simple OLS bi-variate case, the variance of the slope coefficient is $\sigma^2/\text{var}(x)$, where σ^2 is the variance of the disturbance and x is the right-hand side variable. With larger numbers for Y (the dependent variable) and x, variance increases. Suppose (plausibly) that the variance of flight or seat offers increases in proportion to the square of the mean of Y. Thus σ^2 rises in this proportion. To have an equal chance at determining the slope coefficient, the sample variance of x must also rise in proportion to the square of the mean. In the Anderson-Kraus flight offer regressions (neglecting for simplicity the contribution of 1/cap, where cap is the number of seats per aircraft) the variable associated with $(e\Psi\gamma)$ is θ, the market share. It turns out that the time series variance of market shares rises less than proportionally to the square of the mean market share when we look across our cross section. θ has a relatively small variance anyway, which causes trouble. The above reasoning indicates this problem will be worse for the bigger mean shares, *ceteris paribus*. Furthermore, aside from the lagged dependent variables, the other two right-hand size variables of interest are Q (market demand), associated with $e\delta$, and C_f (cost of flights), associated with e. Neither Q nor C_f will increase in variance for larger carriers in a market. Thus the entire triplet of variables associated with determining $d\pi/d$ (seats) will have proportionately less variance for larger carriers in a market. *Ceteris paribus*, e, $e\Psi\gamma$, and $e\delta$ will be harder to pin down. The precision of this reasoning is blurred when we take account of the influence of 1/cap, of the lagged dependent variables, of covariation among the regressors, and of the fact that instruments are used for f_{t-1}, Q, and θ via 2 stage least squares. Nevertheless, the insight from the simple case ought frequently to hold true. Thus there is a "good" (in the sense of not implying an inappropriate model) reason why $[\hat{e} - e\hat{\Psi}\gamma(F/Q)] < 0$ occurs disproportionately often for smaller carriers. The table shows that the 28 negative values with confidence levels 0.10–0.50 have 26 market shares greater than or equal to 0.20. This tends to verify the above reasoning.

The second reason lies more in the realm of economic storytelling. Larger carriers in a market may in fact often behave in Cournot fashion, reacting quickly to changes in small rivals' offers and assuming passivity on their part in return. This is because they aggressively protect market share, and assume that their power to punish transgression ensures passive behavior by their rivals. The small rival, on the other hand, is well aware of the aggresive nature of the big rival, and hence may have a value of $[\hat{e} - e\hat{\Psi}\gamma(F/Q)] < 0$. Is there any prior reason to rule out this type of story, or to make it less likely than the other pairing (small-Cournot, large-reject-Cournet)?

REFERENCES

[1] ANDERSON, J. E., and KRAUS, M., "An Econometric Model of Regulated Airline Flight Rivalry", *Research in the Economics of Transportation*, **2** (1984), forthcoming.

[2] ANDERSON, J. E., and KRAUS, M., "Quality of Service and the Demand for Air Travel", *Review of Economics and Statistics*, **63** (November 1981), pp. 533–40.

[3] DOUGLAS, GEORGE W., and MILLER, JAMES C., "Quality Competition, Industry Equilibrium, and Efficiency in the Price Constrained Airline Market", *American Economic Review*, **64** (September 1974), pp. 657–69.
[4] HAY, G. A., and KELLEY, D., "An Empirical Survey of Price Fixing Conspiracies", *Journal of Law and Economics*, **17** (April 1974, pp. 13–38.
[5] KEELER, T. E., "Airline Regulation and Market Performance", *Bell Journal of Economics and Management Science*, **3** (Autumn 1972), pp. 399–424.
[6] SCHERER, F. M., *Industrial Market Structure and Economic Performance*, 2nd edition, (Chicago: Rand-McNally, 1980), Chapters 6, 7.
[7] SCHMALENSEE, R. L., "Comparative Static Properties of Regulated Airline Oligopolies", *Bell Journal of Economics*, **8** (Autumn 1977), pp. 565–76.
[8] TOBIN, JAMES, "Estimation of Relationships for Limited Dependent Variables", *Econometrica*, **26** (January 1958), pp. 24–36.

THE JOURNAL OF INDUSTRIAL ECONOMICS 0022-1821 $2.00
Volume XXXII June 1984 No. 4

MARKET POWER AND MARKET CHANGE IN THE U.S. AUTOMOBILE INDUSTRY

JOHN E. KWOKA, JR.*

I. INTRODUCTION

SINCE 1970 there has been a virtual revolution in the United States automobile industry. The four American companies that began the decade have been confronted with huge fluctuations in the level and composition of demand, rising imports, unprecedented financial losses, and effective bankruptcy for two of their number. The companies' difficulties are generally attributed to oil price increases, economic recessions, increasing government regulation, and changing cost conditions relative to foreign producers. Less often recognized, however, is the crucial underlying role of monopoly power in the industry, and in particular the long-standing dominance of General Motors. The concentration of the automobile market, this paper will argue, has led to distortions of decision making, which rendered the companies vulnerable to outside forces and ultimately induced responses that proved damaging to the entire U.S. industry.

To establish the context for the argument, we begin with a brief overview of the economic characteristics of the U.S. automotive industry. Then an intensive examination of three major corporate decisions is undertaken to see how monopoly power adversely conditioned the outcomes. These decisions are: (1) the pricing response to imports in the late 1970s, (2) the product response to that and earlier import waves, and (3) the choice of product quality. The paper concludes with some observations concerning the present and future state of competition in the industry.

II. ECONOMIC BACKGROUND

The United States automotive industry is one of the most highly concentrated in the manufacturing sector. The two-firm concentration ratio has ranged from 60 percent to 80 percent for the entire postwar period, and indeed for the 1930s as well. General Motors itself has had at least 40 percent of domestic sales each year since 1948. The profitability record of the domestic manufacturers, and GM in particular, has been impressive. In the period 1946 through

* Gratitude is expressed to P. Jaynes, J. Langenfeld and F. M. Scherer for helpful comments. Special thanks is due to an anonymous reviewer for many constructive suggestions.

1973, GM's average rate of return on net worth was 19.7 percent, compared to an all-manufacturing average of 9.2 percent. Ford earned 12.3 percent and Chrysler 10.7 percent, while American Motors earned 7.3 percent. [25, p. 168]. The turbulent 1970s have seen sizeable swings in profitability, but as recently as 1978, GM earned $3.5 billion after taxes for a 20.0 percent return on stockholders equity. Ford earned $1.6 billion, a 16.4 percent return and 1.4 percentage points above the all manufacturing average [7], [11]. Even in 1979, those two firms earned a total of over $4 billion in profit, and GM in a single quarter amassed $1.2 billion.

Such statistics confirm the impression of both size and profitability of the domestic automobile industry. Unfortunately, they do not reveal much of what one needs to know in order to make an economic policy judgment concerning the industry. For diversified, multinational corporations like Ford or General Motors, aggregate profit figures do not necessarily reflect domestic automotive performance. Occasionally, the companies disclose the latter, but publicly available data generally do not permit subtracting out, e.g., GM's locomotives, Ford's overseas operations, Chrysler's military division (recently sold), or American Motors' Jeeps. Until this is done on a consistent and systematic basis, one is operating with imprecise measures of economic performance.[1]

If such disaggregation were possible, and supernormal profits for the industry, and in particular for its leaders, remained, the fundamental issue is joined: Does that profitability result from cost advantages of large size, or is it the result of the exercise of monopoly power so as to exclude or disadvantage smaller rivals? There is a wealth of alternative explanations in the literature. With respect to cost advantages, virtually every conceivable difference between General Motors and the other companies has been alleged to be important. Table I documents the basis for the following possible sources:

(1) Production scale economies, given the wide disparity in the companies' annual volume.
(2) Numbers of models, reducing risks of demand shifts or product failure.
(3) Numbers of dealers, providing superior market exposure; or larger sales per dealer, providing financially stronger and more exclusive dealers.
(4) Advertising economies, so that expenditures per unit are lower.
(5) Transportation cost advantages for more widely dispersed manufacturers.
(6) Cost savings from greater vertical integration, measured by the value-added-to-sales ratio.

[1] A consistent and systematic basis would also have to include corrections for differences between economic and accounting rates of return and for the "monopoly wage effect". See, respectively, Solomon [21] and Pugel [18].

TABLE I
CHARACTERISTICS OF FOUR LEADING U.S. AUTO COMPANIES (1980)

	GM	FORD	CHRYSLER	AMC
(1) Sales (000)[a]	4,066	1,446	625	151
(2) Number of Models[a]	124	59	42	22
(3 Dealers[a]	11,425	6,514	4,419	1,701
Sales/Dealer	356	222	146	89
(4) Advertising ($M)[b]	250	280	150	46
Advertising/Unit ($)	61	194	241	302
(5 No. Assembly Plants[a]	23	11	5	1
No. more than 500 mi. from Detroit	15	5	2	0
(6) Value added/sales[c]	0.406	0.379	0.192	0.328
(7) "Upsize" Market Sales (000)[a]	2,127	326	138	0
(8) Installation Rates (%)[a]				
Air conditioning	77	70	64	52
Automatic transmission	87	78	82	81

Sources: [a]*Automotive News Market Data Book Issue, 1981*, April 29, 1981.
[b]*Automotive News*, August 17, 1981.
[c]GM, Ford, Chrysler, AMC *1980 Annual Reports.*

Additional cost effects are sometimes said to arise as the result of superior product quality, product development, or management at GM. But other hypotheses center on that company's possible use of its market power:

(1 As the industry price leader, GM may succeed in setting a monopoly price, or, given differences between the firms, the price most advantageous to itself.
(2) GM is particularly dominant in the more profitable "upsize" (larger) car segments, as well as in options and aftermarket parts.[2] See lines (7) and (8) of Table I for evidence of this.
(3) The largely exclusive dealership system may constitute an impediment to the expansion of small firms and to the entry of new firms.
(4) Vertical integration into component production may reduce sources of supply to nonintegrated manufacturers, raising risks and/or capital costs.
(5) Rapid styling and model changes may impose excess costs on small producers, due to product development costs and incomplete usage of dies. (Menge, [17]).
(6) GM's large size may permit the exercise of monopsony power against its suppliers.

Clearly we do not lack hypotheses with regard to the auto industry. We lack facts—facts in the form of engineering studies of production scale economies, profits by model or carline, evidence of cost savings from integration, rationale

[2] Evidence of large car profitability is contained in DeLorean [6]; *Los Angeles Times*, "Chrysler Set to Produce Luxury Line" [15]; and Bresnahan [3]. Regarding aftermarket parts, see Crandall [5]. For somewhat dated evidence on parts and accessories, see FTC *Report on the Motor Vehicle Industry* [8].

for exclusive dealerships, motivation behind style and model changes, and so forth. Despite the extensive literature on the industry, most of these issues are imperfectly understood. What we seek to address in the remainder of this paper is how this market concentration and these profit differentials affected industry decision-making with regard to pricing and product issues during the last decade.

III. PRICING STRATEGIES

The concentrated U.S. auto industry has always been more interested in larger, more profitable vehicles than in small cars. Where the latter have been offered, it traditionally has been to facilitate large car sales. Smaller cars created customer loyalty so that when buyers "traded up", they would purchase the company's more profitable vehicles. Small cars also helped maintain the dealer body and built showroom traffic, all designed ultimately to sell larger cars. But these purposes were indeed secondary, and they have made the small car segment of the auto market more expendable to the U.S. companies. As we shall now see, the pricing decisions of those companies in 1977 and 1978 indeed did yield up that segment to imports.

During the 1970s, imported cars, especially from Japan, constituted a "competitive fringe" in the U.S. industry. Japanese imports rose from about 600,000 in 1972 to 1.9 million in 1980. All imports simultaneously doubled their market share from about 14 percent to 28 percent. Remarkably, this occurred during a time when the slow devaluation of the dollar relative to the yen should have made Japanese imports ever more expensive relative to their domestic counterparts.

This phenomenon of a growing fringe in the face of a potential cost advantage can be explained by two factors. The first is that part of the cost advantage apparently conferred by dollar devaluations was illusory. Japanese auto production technology was rapidly improving during this period, offsetting part of the nominal cost change. In addition, U.S. hourly compensation in the automotive industry increased substantially during the decade at a rate apparently not matched abroad. And as will be discussed later, the lower quality of domestic vehicles meant that costs per equivalent quality product would be greater than the incurred costs to U.S. producers. Together these factors imply that the U.S. probably never enjoyed more than a modest advantage at any time.[3]

The second explanation is that domestic producers were almost certainly following a strategy of dynamic limit pricing (Gaskins [12], [13]; Scherer [19, pp. 241–42]) versus foreign small car competition. This theory predicts that if a dominant firm—or cooperating core of firms—has little (or no) cost

[3] Divergent estimates of the magnitude of the current cost differential certify to the difficulty of the measurement issue. See, e.g., FTC [9], Abernathy *et al.* [1], and Gomez-Ibanez and Harrison [14].

advantage over a fringe, its long-run profit-maximizing strategy is to raise price and thereby permit growth of the fringe. Thus at least initial excess profit can be obtained, even if ultimately market share is less. By contrast, to deter entry and preserve initial share, price would have to be held so low (given the modest cost advantage) as to yield a lesser profit stream over time. If the U.S. auto companies were in such circumstances, they would be expected to raise their small car prices and thereby forego market share.

One recent episode confirms this in the most striking manner. In January 1977, the yen cost. 0.344¢ (approximately 290 ¥/$). By September of that year the dollar had lost 10 percent of its value, with the yen costing 0.375¢. Over the next thirteen months, the dollar sank to 0.545¢/¥, for a further decline of nearly one-third. The direct consequence of this was that Japanese goods imported into this country had their prices raised commensurately. Thus, a $3000 vehicle, whose landed price was approximately $2000, would be repriced to the range of $3500 to $3750.[4] This phenomenon conferred a swift and substantial incremental advantage to domestic producers. Their response choices are indicated by the theory of dynamic limit pricing. The evidence bears scrutiny.

We shall focus on large-selling small cars of the four leading producers—GM's Chevette, Ford's Pinto, Toyota's Corolla, and Datsun's B-210. In addition, we restrict our attention to the 1978 model year (approximately October 1977 to October 1978) to avoid complications associated with vehicle changes between model years. Fortunately, this coincides with the period of rapid dollar devaluation. At the beginning of the model year, the base prices of these vehicles stood as follows:[5]

Chevette	$3354
Pinto	3338
B-210	3146
Corolla	3048

During the next ten months, import prices were increased four times, resulting in a price of $3498 for the Corolla and $3485 for the B-210. General Motors and Ford had a choice of holding their prices and underselling the importers, or raising price for greater short-term profitability even at the expense of market share.

Both companies chose the latter strategy, that of the dominant firm or core.

[4] That is, the $2000 port-of-entry price, denominated in yen, would rise to $2600 if the dollar dropped 30 percent. The $1000 margin consisted of costs incurred in this country and should not be affected by currency fluctuations.

[5] Data are from the *Wall Street Journal* [23] and *Automotive News*, [2]. Prices are for regular two-door sedans of each vehicle, excluding the stripped, low-selling Chevette Scooter and Pinto Pony.

GM raised the price on the Chevette in nearly lockstep fashion with Toyota and Datsun, resulting in a price of $3734. Chevette began the model year two or three hundred dollars above the Japanese models; it concluded at $250 above both. True, Chevette sales strengthened early in the 1978 model year, due to shifting demand and some vehicle changes that had been made. Yet production exceeded sales for each month beginning with January 1978, and price continued to increase. Even clearer was Ford's strategy. Because of adverse publicity about gas tank fires, its Pinto sales were stagnating and inventories were burdensome. It nonetheless raised its prices a total of $300, foregoing only one of four price increases initiated by the Japanese.

The price rounds themselves are of interest because they demonstrate the deliberate nature of domestic producers' price responses. As shown in Table II, each round was led by Toyota, quickly matched by Datsun, and typically followed by General Motors within two to four weeks.[6] Ford delayed longest, and passed up the last price round altogether. The domestic producers were taking nearly every opportunity to raise price, even though the clear effect would be to concede market share to the Japanese.[7]

TABLE II
ROUNDS OF PRICE INCREASES ON 1978 MODEL YEAR SMALL CARS

Date	*Toyota Corolla*	*Datsun B-210*	*GM Chevette*	*Ford Pnto*
Initial Prices	$3048	$3148	$3354	$3338
12/05/77	3128			
12/12/77		3196		
1/02/78			3454	
1/11/78				3473
2/27/78	3188			
3/06/78		3258		
3/27/78			3549	
4/18/78				3536
4/24/78	3388			
4/24/78		3398		
6/05/78			3644	
6/05/78				3629
7/10/78	3498			
7/17/78		3485		
8/07/78			3734	

Source: Wall Street Journal [23] and *Automotive News* [2].

[6] Domestic firms were followers in this application of dynamic limit pricing, due to the fact that the triggering events were cost increases incurred by the fringe.

[7] The *Wall Street Journal* [23] reported:

> If prices of the competing domestic models were left unchanged, some of them would enjoy huge price advantages over some of the best-selling imports. But it has become clear in recent months that at least two companies—Ford and General Motors Corporation—are willing to sacrifice some of that advantage by raising prices and enlarging profits on their small car models.

"Ford Motor Co. Again Increases Small Car Prices", April 18, 1978, p. 3.

Corroboration of such behavior by the domestic industry can be found in their response to more recent price increases on Japanese compact pickup trucks. Price increases of $800 to $900 per unit resulted from an August 1980 Customs reclassification of imported pickups, sought by Ford and the UAW. Compared to year-earlier levels, in the final quarter of 1980, total Japanese pickup sales fell by 16 percent, and non-captive import sales declined nearly one-quarter.[8] Although the domestic companies at that time offered no directly comparable vehicles, they did raise prices on their smallest pickups. Indeed, they managed to more than fully offset their sudden price advantage: over the entire 1981 model year, the domestic share of imported plus domestic light-duty pickup sales actually *declined*.[9]

Contrary to their public pronouncements, these experiences suggest that the dominant domestic manufacturers of motor vehicles have essentially permitted the increase in imported cars and trucks. Faced with clear opportunities to increase or at least maintain share, their pricing strategy may have been profit-maximizing, but it inevitably led to increased imports. A more competitively structured U.S. industry would not have been able to raise prices under such circumstances, and would have ended up with ultimately larger domestic output and market share.

IV. PRODUCT STRATEGIES

Insights from the theory of dynamic limit pricing also aid understanding the domestic manufacturers' earlier responses to imports. In 1955, imports constituted less than 1 percent of domestic sales. They virtually doubled in each of the next four years, to a high of 10.2 percent—609,000 units—in 1959. This import wave resulted from the demise of a number of independent producers of small cars in this country in the early 1950s, plus the reluctance of GM, Ford, and Chrysler to enter the small car segment.[10] A similar scenario ensued during the 1960s. After being beaten back early that decade, imports grew steadily up to 1970. Both episodes resulted in the near simultaneous introduction of small cars by the U.S. manufacturers. Here we are concerned with the behavior of the companies after these introductions.

Again, we draw on the theory of dynamic limit pricing, but with two extensions. The first concerns the predictions of the theory when the dominant firm or core begins with a substantial cost advantage over a significant size fringe. Then the present value of profits are maximized when the firm first *increases* its dominance by lowering price so as to drive some of the fringe producers out. Subsequently, the firm proceeds to raise price and profitability,

[8] Data are from *Automotive News* [2]. "Captive" pickups are Japanese-made vehicles marketed through domestic dealer networks.

[9] Data from *Automotive News* [2] and from the Motor Vehicle Manufacturers Association supplied to author.

[10] For a detailed account of company behavior prior to new model introductions, see White [26].

letting entry occur in the usual fashion. (See Scherer [19]) Secondly, though the theory focuses on price, in principle the dominant firm's strategy need not be limited to that variable. Any attribute which is finely differentiable—like price, but also size, weight, etc., for cars—may be similarly employed. Indeed, if non-price attributes involve slower responses by the fringe, e.g., due to product development lags, the dominant firm is likely to prefer to manipulate these other characteristics in order to maximize profitability.

Joining these two extensions, we predict that when a dominant firm or core begins with a substantial advantage over the fringe, we would expect an initial effort to drive the fringe down in size through strategic product policy, followed by product alterations which increase profitability while permitting some entry. The facts associated with the import waves of 1960 and 1970 are remarkably consistent with this dynamic product strategy. The smallest sedan built by the Big Three U.S. automobile companies grew from 189 inches in overall length in 1953 to 208 inches in 1959.[11] This corresponded to the period of a twenty-fold increase in imports' market share. The new small cars introduced in 1960 by the major domestic companies are described in Table III. By cutting size, weight, and price, they caused imports' sales to decline by 18 percent in 1960, an additional 24 percent in 1961, and 10 percent more in 1962. The result was that the overall share of imports was cut in half, to 4.9 percent in 1962 [2].

TABLE III
GROWTH OF DOMESTIC SMALL CARS

A. 1960–69

	Corvair		*Falcon*		*Valiant*	
Model Year	*length (in)*	*weight (lb)*	*length (in)*	*weight (lb)*	*length (ib)*	*weight (lb)*
1960	180.0	2305	181.2	2288	183.7	2635
1963	180.0	2335	181.1	2345	186.2	2535
1966	183.8	2530	184.3	2677	188.3	2770
1969	183.2	2585	184.3	2865	188.4	2855

B. 1970–76

	Vega		*Pinto*		*Gremlin*	
Model Year	*length (in)*	*weight (lb)*	*length (in)*	*weight (lb)*	*length (in)*	*weight (lb)*
1970–71	169.7	2202	163.0	2030	161.2	2575
1973	172.2	2268	164.1	2216	165.5	2702
1976	175.4	2523	169.0	2625	169.4	2761

Source: Wards Automotive Yearbook, [24].

[11] *Ward's Automotive Yearbook* [24]. The Studebaker Lark at 175 inches was the smallest vehicle built by any domestic manufacturer.

Now with the leading firms' dominance enhanced, the domestic core was in a position to capitalize on its market power. Table III documents the growth in size and weight of the Big Three's smallest cars starting in 1963 and continuing throughout the decade. By 1966, the Corvair had grown by 3.8 inches, the Falcon, by 3.1 inches, and the Valiant by 4.6 inches. By the end of the 1960s, these vehicles would weigh from 250 to 600 pounds more than at introduction, and it was doubtful consumers perceived them as small cars any longer. Not surprisingly, while imports' share had stabilized in the five-to-six percent range up until 1965, their share rose to 7.3 percent in 1966, and rose again in each subsequent year to a new high of 15.1 percent in 1971. This coincided precisely with the period in which domestic small cars were being redesigned into larger vehicles. This strategy, therefore, could scarcely be justified as a response to consumer demand, but is readily understood as a dynamic product policy by the dominant domestic core.

Remarkably, the same phenomenon occurred with the new product introduction of model years 1970 and 1971. By the late 1960s, the major U.S. companies had partially withdrawn from the small car market. The Valiant, for example, was an imperceptible half inch shorter than the basic Plymouth of fifteen years earlier. A new attack was mounted on the import share by the domestic manufacturers, but again, only to secure a temporary advantage. As shown in Table III, GM's new Vega began at 167.4 inches but grew to 175.4 inches in four years. Ford's Pinto was enlarged by a full six inches in the same period of time. AMC's Gremlin, introduced at 161.2 inches, grew to 169.4 inches by 1976. Vehicle weights increased by from 180 to nearly 600 pounds and once again—after serving their immediate purpose—the domestic manufacturers were moving away from the production of these small cars.

The immediate results of this product strategy in the 1970s did differ, however, from the previous experience. Better dealer networks and name recognition for imports kept them from being beaten back. The domestic small cars did, however, manage to halt the growth of imports for about five years. Then the redesign of these cars, together with other important factors, caused import share again to grow substantially. In both of these episodes, then, dramatically smaller domestic cars were used essentially to attack the competitive fringe and thereby regain market dominance. There was no commitment to small car production and none to keeping the import fringe small. Rather, dominance was used to raise profitability while vehicle redesigns subsequently permitted imports to increase their share.

V. PRODUCT QUALITY

The dominant product issue in recent years has been vehicle quality. Traditionally, U.S. auto manufacturers have shunned technological improvements in favor of frequent and expensive cosmetic changes in the vehicle. This, they have claimed, was in response to consumer preferences. Yet when faced with new foreign alternatives, American consumers shifted massively away from poorer quality domestic vehicles. The roots of this quality problem, we shall see, lie in part in the nature of oligopoly rivalry in the traditional domestic automobile industry.

The quality gap between U.S. produced and foreign cars is beyond dispute. Evidence comes from all sides of the market.

(1) *Consumer Reports* [4] surveys owners' repair experience with approximately 160 models each year. Ratings for domestic and Japanese imported vehicles in two representative years are summarized in Table IV. The evidence could scarcely be more striking that Japanese cars achieve quality standards vastly different than those of GM, Ford, Chrysler, and AMC.

(2) A different perspective is offered by a trade publication's 1980 survey of several hundred automotive engineers in the U.S. companies. Almost half (47.4 percent) stated that the highest quality cars were produced in Japan. Only 27.4 percent thought the U.S. did so, while Germany was a close third at 23.0 percent [16].

(3) Perhaps a more objective measure of quality is manufacturers' warranty cost per vehicle. It is currently reported that domestic vehicles on average cost $175 under warranty, while similar Japanese vehicles average only $80 [1, p. 37].

TABLE IV
CONSUMER REPORTS REPAIR RATINGS FOR 1979 AND 1981 CARS
(Percent of Models in Each Rating Category)

	1979		*1981*	
	Domestic	*Japanese*	*Domestic*	*Japanese*
Much better than average	0%	94%	0%	96%
Better than average	15	6	5	4
Average	39	0	49	0
Worse than average	18	0	15	0
Much worse than average	28	0	31	0

Source: Computed from *Consumer Reports* [4], April 1980 and April 1982.

What is less apparent than the quality difference itself is why it should have arisen. This can be traced back to three interrelated factors. First, it is important to recognize that the United States auto market for much of the postwar period was not fundamentally different than decades earlier. The companies were the same, the products in many ways similar, and marketing strategies almost unchanged. When Alfred Sloan shaped General Motors in the 1920s, he operated on the belief that automobile customers wanted four things—"comfort, convenience, power, and style" [20, pp. 87–88]. GM launched annual style changes at that time, and as other firms sought to emulate its success, they too moved towards extensive style and model changes. In an oligopoly setting, style changes were a safer outlet for rivalrous instincts than engineering and technological advances (See White [25, ch. 12]).

Quality was nowhere on Sloan's list. Along with engineering and technological improvements, it was seen as too uncertain and too subtle to be an effective marketing device. This view was nearly unanimous among the few domestic producers, based on Sloan's teachings and reinforced by decades of experience emphasizing styling. The American consumer had few realistic alternatives for most of this time, given the extent of concentration in the U.S. industry.

As opposed to quality, styling dominated for a second reason. As the vehicle market came to be primarily replacement rather than sales to new customers, any technique that shortened the average period of ownership promised more sales. Styling was such a strategy. By persuading present owners that there were significant psychic benefits from ownership of a new model, they could be convinced to purchase another vehicle sooner than if they focused more on the old vehicle's transportation function. Replacement demand could thereby be enhanced. By releasing more vehicles to the used car market, this strategy lowered prices there and made such cars available to additional individuals. Hence the entire stock of outstanding vehicles was enlarged.

Quality clearly could not serve such a purpose. Far from stimulating replacement demand, it raised the risk of lengthening the average period of ownership, keeping used car prices up, and preventing the stock-increasing effect upon which the industry came to rely. Quality competition thus actually posed a threat to the demand-enhancing strategy of the industry.[12]

Third and finally, on the production side, there is evidence that quality and style change conflict with each other. The complexity associated with frequent model changes and model proliferation appears to undermine the quality achievable by standardization. Long model runs permit a variety of cumulative volume economies, whereas varying models raises costs of coordination, increases necessary inventories, and reduces the opportunity for substitution of capital for labor inputs.[13] Japanese automotive production processes, for example, attain high quality on exceedingly long model runs. Their products are not so much technologically superior, but their manufacturing processes are highly standardized.[14] By contrast, until very recently, U.S. manufac-

[12] White [25, ch. 12] and Scherer [19, ch. 14] detail the role of style change in a replacement demand market. In this context, Gerald Myers, while President of AMC, spoke out in favor of "planned obsolescence" through more rapid changes in vehicles. *Wall Street Journal* [23], "People Are Keeping Cars Longer as Costs Rise and Attitudes Change", January 7, 1982, p. 23.

[13] The effects of Toyota's "kanban" system of minimal inventories is detailed in Abernathy *et al.* [1, p. 34] and in *Wall Street Journal* [23], "Auto Makers Have Trouble With 'Kanban,'" April 7, 1982, p. 35.

[14] With the exception of work on the rotary engine by Toyo-Kogyo (Mazda) and perhaps the stratified charge by Honda—neither of them industry leaders in Japan—few important new product technologies can be traced to that country. The need for standardization is increased, if not dictated, by the long "pipeline" through which the product must pass before reaching the U.S. customer.

turers have changed entire models on a three-year cycle, with more minor alterations annually. They offer over 250 models in total, each with an overwhelming variety of engines, transmissions, colors, accessories, and options. This strategy requires substantial and frequent changes in capital equipment and labor set-up costs.

Further evidence of this phenomenon is provided by Volkswagen's experience in its new production facility in the United States. At the outset, VW produced only a single model here, and early reports on its quality were very favorable. A company official stated that the quality of U.S.-built vehicles was at least as high as those imported from Germany [22, p. 42]. But when the plant began producing different models with multiple options, quality immediately declined [10].

Thus it would appear that the inferior quality of U.S. produced vehicles has resulted in no small part from the oligopolists' preference for style competition over more fundamental improvements. Style change and model proliferation enhanced replacement demand, even as it reduced standardization and the achievement of scale economies. Producers in other countries adopted different strategies for two reasons: (1) Less of their home country demand was due to replacement, and (2) their home industries were less concentrated, with (e.g.) Japan having nine automobile companies. Thus both supply and demand factors led to different products being built abroad, products which had great customer appeal when the previously-insulated American market was opened up.

VI. CONCLUSIONS

This review has sought to demonstrate how the absence of competition in the U.S. automobile industry has affected decision-making and contributed to some of the industry's current problems. Crucial pricing and product decisions have followed from the concentrated nature of the industry, and in turn have led to the decline in U.S. production, the rise in imports, and the poor quality of domestically produced vehicles. This is not to say that other influences were not at work in these matters. But the role of monopoly power seems clear and too often overlooked.

The importance of recognizing the role of monopoly power stems not only from a desire better to understand the past. Competition problems are obscured but not necessarily eliminated by the industry's current financial difficulties. GM's market share, for example, has remained at its historic level of about 45 percent, while its nearest rivals have slipped much farther back. Ford's 1980 share of 16.5 percent was down six to eight percentage points in five years, and Chrysler's 7.1 percent share was barely half of its 1974 level. The vagaries of exchange rate fluctuations and of the political process have made imports a less-than-completely certain source of competition. There seems abundant reason for continuing concern over the long-run competitive properties of the U.S. auto industry.

John E. Kwoka, Jr.,
Department of Economics,
The George Washington University,
Washington, D.C. 20052.

ACCEPTED SEPTEMBER 1982.

REFERENCES

[1] Abernathy, William, Harbour, James, and Henn, Jay, "Productivity and Comparative Cost Advantages: Some Estimates for Major Automotive Producers", Report to the U.S. Department of Transportation, February 13, 1981.
[2] *Automotive News*, various issues.
[3] Bresnahan, Timothy, "Departures from Marginal Cost Pricing in the American Automobile Industry", *Journal of Econometrics*, **17** (2), (November 1981), pp. 201–27.
[4] *Consumer Reports*, Annual Auto Issue, various years.
[5] Crandall, Robert, "Vertical Integration and the Market for Repair Parts in the U.S. Automobile Industry", *Journal of Industrial Economics*, XVI (3), (July 1968), pp. 212–34.
[6] DeLorean, John M., Corp., "Automobile Marketing Strategies, Pricing, and Product Planning", Report to National Highway Traffic Safety Administration, (National Technical Information Service, Springfield, Virginia, April 1978).
[7] *Economic Report of the President* (USGPO, Washington, D.C., 1980).
[8] Federal Trade Commission, *Report on the Motor Vehicle Industry* (FTC, Washington, D.C., 1939).
[9] ——, "Comments of the Staff of the Federal Trade Commission Before the International Trade Commission", (FTC, Washington, D.C., October 6, 1980).
[10] *Fortune*, "Don't Blame That Lemon on the Workers", (June 16, 1980), p. 86.
[11] *Fortune Directory of the Largest Industrial Corporations*, various years.
[12] Gaskins, Darius W., Jr., "Optimal Pricing by Dominant Firms", unpublished Ph.D. dissertation, University of Michigan, 1970.
[13] ——, "Dynamic Limit Pricing: Optimal Pricing Under Threat of Entry", *Journal of Economic Theory*, **3** (3), (September 1971), pp. 306–22.
[14] Gomez-Ibanez, Jose, and Harrison, David, "Imports and the Future of the U.S. Automobile Industry", *American Economic Review*, **72** (2), (May 1982), pp. 319–23.
[15] *Los Angeles Times*, "Chrysler Set to Produce Luxury Line" (September 26, 1979), p. 13.
[16] Maus, Erwin, and Waddell, Richard, "U.S. Engineers Rank Imports Tops—In Quality, Not Technology", *Ward's Auto World* (April 1980), pp. 48–54.
[17] Menge, J. A. "Style Change as a Market Weapon", *Quarterly Journal of Economics*, LXXVI (4), (November 1962), pp. 632–47.
[18] Pugel, Thomas, "Profitability, Concentration, and the Interindustry Variation in Wages", *Review of Economics and Statistics*, LXII (2), (May 1980), pp. 248–53.
[19] Scherer, F. M., *Industrial Market Structure and Economic Performance* (Rand McNally, Chicago, 1980).
[20] Sloan, Alfred P., Jr., *My Years With General Motors* (Doubleday, New York, 1963).

[21] SOLOMON, EZRA, "Alternative Rates of Return Concepts and Their Implications for Utility Regulation", *Bell Journal of Economics and Management Science*, **1** (1), (Spring 1970), pp. 65–81.

[22] U.S. House of Representatives, *Auto Situation 1980* (Subcommittee on Trade of the Ways and Means Committee, Washington, D.C., June 6, 1980).

[23] *Wall Street Journal*, various issues.

[24] *Ward's Automotive Yearbook*, various issues.

[25] WHITE, LAWRENCE, J., *The Automobile Industry Since 1945* (Harvard University Press, Cambridge, 1971).

[26] ——, "The Automobile Industry", in Walter Adams, ed., *The Structure of American Industry*, (MacMillan, New York, 6th ed., 1982), pp. 136–90.

THE JOURNAL OF INDUSTRIAL ECONOMICS 0022-1821 $2.00
Volume XXXII June 1984 No. 4

THE ESTIMATED EFFECTS ON INDUSTRY OF TIME-OF-DAY DEMAND AND ENERGY ELECTRICITY PRICES*

PETER SCHWARZ

I. INTRODUCTION

INDUSTRIAL electricity tariffs usually contain two types of consumption-related charges—the energy charge, assessed on total kilowatthours, and the demand (or capacity) charge, assessed on maximum kilowatts. Both charges can be differentiated by time of day, applying a premium to kilowatts and kilowatt-hours consumed during specified peak hours. The costs of both these dimensions—energy and maximum demand—vary by time of day and by season. Plant capacity must be constructed to meet the maximum, or peak, demand. Also, capacity is comprised of plants of varying fuel efficiencies.[1]

Figure 1 depicts a typical firm's pattern of demand, or load curve, over 24 hours. Under traditional electricity prices, the firm pays, usually on a monthly basis, an energy price P for total energy ($\int_{t=0}^{1} E\,dt$) and demand price P^* for maximum demand (E^*). If these charges are used in a time-of-day tariff, they will be at a higher level during potential utility system peak hours. Defining the interval (t_0, t_1) as peak, intrapeak maximum demand equals E_p^* and peak energy use equals $\int_{t_0}^{t_1} E\,dt$. If both prices are differentiated by time-of-day, then $P_p > P_0$ and $P_p^* > P_0^*$, where the subscripts denote the peak and off-peak periods.[2]

Time-of-day demand and energy charges can have differing effects. The peak energy charge encourages, within the peak hours, a reduction in the area beneath the load curve, that is, a reduction in peak energy (kilowatthour) use. It does not explicitly encourage a rearrangement of the load pattern within this interval, and so may not reduce the maximum intrapeak demand. The peak demand charge encourages a reduction in the maximum demand; this can be accomplished directly by flattening peak period use, or less directly by reducing use at each instant within the peak. Hence, the peak demand charge has its primary effect on the pattern of use, while the energy charge primarily affects the level of use.

*This paper is an extension of my Ph.D. dissertation. I wish to acknowledge the members of my thesis committee: William Oakland, J. Stephen Henderson, and Richard Tybout. For helpful comments on this paper, I wish to thank Tom Taylor of the Duke Powei Company. While these individuals share in the contributions of this paper, any remaining errors are my responsibility.

[1] Wenders [16] explicitly describes the costs of base, intermediate, and peaker units.

[2] The utility may set the off-peak demand charge equal to zero since off-peak use of capacity requires no system expansion

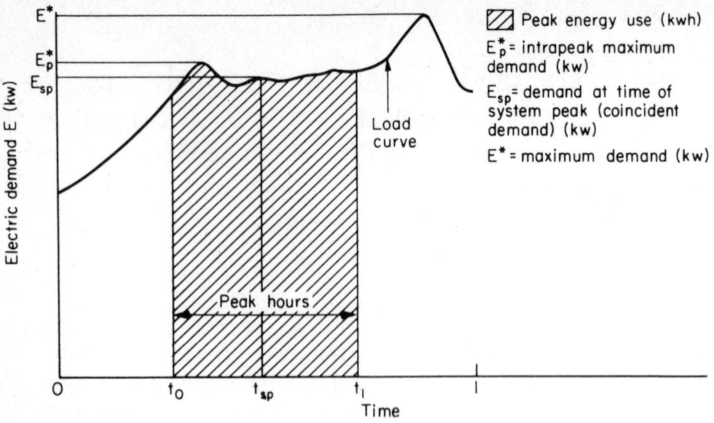

FIGURE 1
A Typical Firm's Load Curve.

These apparent differences in the effects of the two charges have received little attention in the peak load pricing or industrial electricity literature. Most existing studies make reference to peak load prices or an electricity price without differentiating the effects of demand and energy charges. Most estimates of traditional (non-time-of-day) industrial demand elasticities, such as Baxter and Rees [1], lump together the two charges. The few available estimates of time-of-day elasticities, including the initial estimates by Cargill and Meyer [2][3], as well as very recent time-of-day estimates for the industrial sector, by Mitchell, Manning and Acton [9] and Chung [3], use an average price, rather than separate inclusion of each price.

Some recent works have included separate demand and energy charges. Henderson [7] estimated the effects of traditional demand and energy charges. Spann and Beauvais [14] have developed a model which they believe gives guidance in estimating the effects of time-of-day demand and energy charges. In comments on that paper, Bridger Mitchell finds the model appropriate for non-time-of-day rates only, since Spann and Beauvais include only a traditional demand and energy price in their model; i.e. implicit in their model are the assumptions that peak and off-peak energy charges are equal, and peak and off-peak demand charges are equal. Mitchell closes his comments with ". . . there is so far no forecasting model that is able to analyze the effect of peak load rate structures that have time-differential charges for both energy (kwh) and power (kw). A pressing task for new research is to begin to fill this major gap."

[3] They use utility level load curves, and average prices based on residential, commercial, and industrial sectors.

The intent of this study is to contribute to this area. This study presents separate estimates of time-of-day demand and energy charges for a cross section of Michigan firms subject to mandatory time-of-day prices. In part II, the effects of the two charges on the firm's level and pattern of electric use are outlined, leading to hypotheses as to the expected effects of the two charges on industrial users. Part III presents the methodology, part IV describes the data. Part V reports the empirical estimates. Part VI contains the summary and conclusions.

II. THE EFFECTS OF TIME-OF-DAY DEMAND AND ENERGY CHARGES ON THE FIRM'S PATTERN OF ELECTRICITY USE

Following the terminology of Dansby [4], the effects of the charges are presented for two cases: flat demand, in which demand within the peak interval is constant, and fluctuating demand, in which intrapeak demand is not constant.

A. Flat Demand

Consider a firm with the load curve shown in Figure 2. Let this firm be subject to peak prices from time 0 to t_0, off-peak prices elsewhere. Then, within the peak period, the firm's demand is flat.

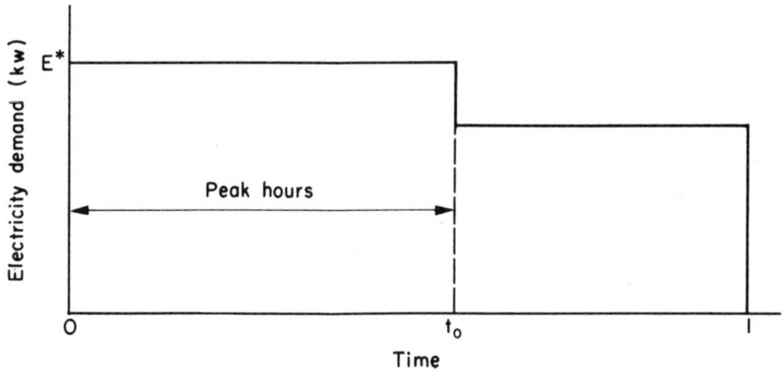

FIGURE 2
A Firm With Flat Intrapeak Demand

The peak energy charge is assessed on kilowatthours consumed within the tariff peak; this is measured by the area beneath the load curve over the interval 0 to t_0, i.e. $\int_{t=0}^{t_0} E\,dt$. Evaluation of the integral yields TE^*, where T is the number of hours in the peak interval. Thus, the effect of the peak energy charge is:

$$\frac{d\int_{t=0}^{t_0} E\,dt}{d\,P_p} = T\frac{dE^*}{dP_p}.$$

That is, the reduction in peak energy use due to the energy charge is equal to the reduction in maximum demand, E^*, times the number of peak hours.

The peak demand charge is assessed directly on maximum demand, E^*. Its effect is dE^*/dP_p^*. To reduce the demand component of the tariff, the firm must reduce demand at each instant within the peak. Hence a firm with flat intrapeak demand is indifferent between a demand charge P_p^* and an energy charge P_p, where $P_p = P_p^*/T$. If flat demand was optimal prior to the price increases, such a pattern will continue to be optimal when the rates are increased. The level of demand will decrease in response to either charge, but the pattern will remain flat. Therefore, when demand is flat, the two charges are essentially equivalent.

B. Fluctuating Demand

Suppose now that the peak period extends from t_1 to t_2, as shown in Figure 3. (The firm's load curve is the same as Figure 2.)

While the stylized load curve of Figure 3 is still very much simplified as compared to an actual load curve, it is sufficient for demonstrating fluctuating intrapeak demand. A possible scenario for this case is for the interval 0 to t_0 to represent the firm's day shift, while the utility system peak hours extend from the afternoon (t_1 to t_0) through the evening (t_0 to t_2). Another possibility is that the firm's electric use is at a higher level between 0 and t_0 due to hotter temperatures (and larger cooling requirements) than at other times.

It is important to note that the load pattern of industrial demand can differ from that of the utility, which contains the residential and commercial sectors in addition to the industrial sector.

To compare the effects of peak demand and energy charges on fluctuating demand the tariff peak period is split into two intervals of flat demand: t_1 to t_0, and t_0 to t_2. Within each of these intervals, the flat demand analysis can be applied.

Between t_1 and t_0, an energy charge P_p is essentially equivalent to a demand charge P_p^*, where $P_p = P_p^*/T$, and T is the number of hours in the interval t_1 to t_0.[4] Within the interval t_0 to t_2, the effect of the energy charge is again to

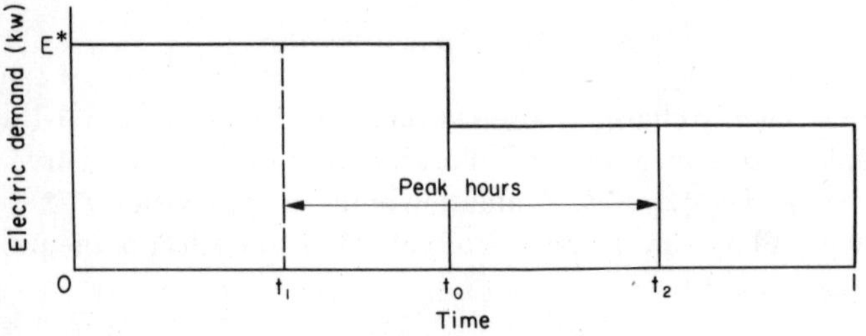

FIGURE 3
A Firm With Fluctuating Intrapeak Demand

reduce the area beneath the load curve. The demand charge does not have a uniform effect. The firm's intrapeak maximum demand occurs between t_1 and t_0, so the peak demand charge will reduce demand, and indirectly energy, within that interval. If E^* remains above demand from t_0 to t_2, then the demand charge is effectively zero from t_0 to t_2; i.e., it need have no effect on demand or energy from t_0 to t_2. If the peak demand charge is strong enough to reduce E^* below the level from t_0 to t_2, then the peak demand charge will be effective in the interval t_0 to t_2 as well, causing reductions in demand and energy.

Hence, when intrapeak demand fluctuates, the two charges have differing effects. Both charges reduce maximum demand and energy use in interval t_1, t_0, but only the energy charge is certain to reduce demand and energy from t_0 to t_2.

It should be noted that each of the charges has cross-interval effects as well as own-interval effects. The peak energy charge increases the cost of electricity throughout the tariff peak, encouraging off-peak use. The peak demand charge increases electricity cost over only part of the tariff peak, encouraging an increase in demand (and indirectly energy) elsewhere in the peak as well as in the off-peak.

Much of the peak load literature has ignored the issue of whether demand is flat or fluctuating. Steiner [15], Mohring [10], Panzar [11] and Wenders [16], use a single demand curve to relate peak demand to peak price. They do not specify whether this demand curve holds at each instant of the peak (equivalent to assuming flat demand) or whether it is an average of the demand curves at each instant. Each of these authors derives a single peak period price, but does not specify whether it is a demand or an energy charge. As has been demonstrated here, a single price is sufficient only under the assumption of flat demand, when either type of charge can be used.

There is no *a priori* reason to impose the assumption of flat demand; reference to industrial load curves contained in EPRI's "Modeling and Analysis of Electricity Demand by Time-of-Day"[5] show some industry loads exhibit substantial fluctuation. For such firms, the estimated effects of the two charges on the level and pattern of use are likely to differ.

The objectives of peak load pricing, as set out earlier, are to properly price energy and *system* capacity. The peak energy price, by reducing demand at each instant of the peak, should reduce the firm's peak energy use and its demand at the time of the system peak. The peak demand charge, which is effective at only some instants within the peak, may not reduce peak energy. In addition, it need not reduce the firm's demand at the time of system peak.

[4] Note that for a demand charge of given magnitude, its effect on E^* increases as the duration of E^* decreases. If the duration decreases to a single instant, the demand charge applies at that instant only.

[5] See EPRI [5], especially pages 13-18 through 13-24, 13-38 through 13-46, 13-59 through 13-61. Also, see Mitchell, Manning, and Acton [9].

It will do so if system peak falls within the interval t_1 to t_0, but can increase the customer's contribution if system peak falls inside the interval t_0 to t_2.

The effects of the two charges on three aspects of the firm's demand for electricity will be estimated. These three aspects are: peak period energy use, the firm's own intrapeak maximum demand, and the firm's demand at the time of the system peak, or coincident demand. The peak energy charge is expected to reduce each of these variables. The demand charge is expected to reduce the firm's own intrapeak demand, but its effect on peak energy use and coincident demand cannot be predicted *a priori*.

III. METHODOLOGY

The determinants of peak period energy use, intrapeak maximum demand, and coincident demand were estimated in separate equations. Each of the three aspects of peak use was regressed using two different functional forms; the first form employs the absolute level of electric use, while the second form uses a ratio of peak to total use. The six equations are:

$$(1)\qquad \text{KWHPK} = \alpha_0 Q^{\alpha 1} PE^{\alpha 2} PD^{\alpha 3} M^{\alpha 4} \varepsilon_1$$

$$(2)\qquad \text{KWMAX} = \beta_0 Q^{\beta 1} PE^{\beta 2} PD^{\beta 3} M^{\beta 4} \varepsilon_2$$

$$(3)\qquad \text{KWSP} = \gamma_0 Q^{\gamma 1} PE^{\gamma 2} PD^{\gamma 3} M^{\gamma 4} \varepsilon_3$$

$$(4)\qquad \text{LFPK} = \delta_0 EI^{\delta 1} PE^{\delta 2} PD^{\delta 3} M^{\delta 4} \varepsilon_4$$

$$(5)\qquad \text{LFMAX} = \zeta_0 EI^{\zeta 1} PE^{\zeta 2} PD^{\zeta 3} M^{\zeta 4} \varepsilon_5$$

$$(6)\qquad \text{LFSP} = \eta_0 EI^{\eta 1} PE^{\eta 2} PD^{\eta 3} M^{\eta 4} \varepsilon_6$$

where KWHPK is peak energy use (kwh),
KWMAX is intrapeak maximum demand (kw),
KWSP is coincident demand (kw),
LFPK is the ratio of average hourly energy use to peak hourly energy use,
LFMAX is the ratio of average hourly energy use to intrapeak maximum demand,
LFSP is the ratio of average hourly energy use to coincident demand.
Q is output ($),
PE is peak energy price (¢/kwh),
PD is peak demand price ($/kw),
M is manhours index,
EI is energy intensity (BTU/$),
ε is disturbance term.

Equations (1) through (3) relate, for each of 191 firms, the absolute level of an aspect of peak electric use to the firm's output level, the two peak prices, and a manhours index used as a proxy of the industry's economic well-being.

Equations (4) through (6) regress for each of 191 firms, a type of load factor on the two peak prices, the manhours index, and the industry's energy intensity. The log forms of equations (1) through (6) were used for estimation.

The log forms of equations (1) through (3) allow the resulting coefficients to be interpreted as elasticities. The quality of these estimates, however, is compromised by two problems. The main problem is with the way that the firm's output Q was estimated. Output was unavailable on an individual firm basis.[6]

As a proxy, output was calculated as:

$$(7) \qquad Q = \frac{\int_{t=0}^{1} E\, dt}{EI}$$

where $\int_{t=0}^{1} E\, dt$ is total energy use, and EI is electric intensity in firm i's industry.

Assuming a fixed-proportions production function, the ratio in equation (7) is a reasonable proxy for output. Energy intensity represents the total energy use per dollar of output, and is available for ninety sectors which approximate 2-digit SIC's.[7]

This proxy, however, is likely to be correlated with the error term and so will produce biased estimates, since:

$$(8) \qquad Q = \frac{\int_{t=0}^{1} E\, dt}{EI} = \int_{t=0}^{t1} E\, dt + \int_{t=t_1}^{1} E\, dt = \frac{\text{KWHPK} + \text{KWHOFF}}{EI}$$

where KWHOFF is the energy use during the off-peak period.

Also implicit in the use of this output measure is that total energy use is perfectly inelastic with respect to the peak charges; that is, the firm adjusts its time of use, but not its overall use, in response to the peak charges. This assumption is certainly questionable, both intuitively and from evidence on residential time-of-day experiments. One possible way to reduce peak use in response to peak rates is to reduce overall use.[8] With the available data, no better proxy could be found.

Equations (4) through (6) estimate the determinants of relative peak electric use. Since the dependent variable is a relative rather than absolute measure, output need not be included as an independent variable. That is, the absolute level is strongly related to output, whereas the load pattern need not be. Also, equations (4) to (6) avoid the assumption that total use is constant. The estimated coefficients indicate whether the peak prices have a stronger effect on peak use than on average use.

Energy intensity is included in equations (4) through (6). A firm with an energy-intensive production process has a higher percentage of its total costs accounted for by electricity costs. Such firms should have a larger incentive to smooth load since the cost savings are relatively high.

[6] Firms were identified only to three or four digit standard industrial classifications.
[7] See Penner, Herendeen, and Milke [12].
[8] This occurred in several residential peak load experiments, for example, Hausman, Kinnucan and McFadden [6].

The index of manhours was included in all six equations as a measure of the industry-specific excess capacity. The index is the ratio of man-hours hired in the firm's industry in a particular month to the manhours hired in an arbitrarily chosen base month. A high index value reflects full use of capacity.[9] If the firm is fully using its capacity, it will have a relatively flat load curve, so that for a given kilowatt demand level, the firm will consume a relatively large amount of energy. If there is excess capacity the firm will demand less energy per kilowatt. Hence, a firm's load factor is affected by the state of the economy for the firm as well as by the demand and energy prices.

Demand and energy prices are from the tariff schedules. Sample tariff schedules for each utility are contained in Table I. While the energy price is a flat rate charge, the demand price has a declining block structure. That is, an increase in intrapeak maximum demand leads to a decrease in the demand price. This interdependency between maximum demand and the demand price necessitates estimation of equations (2) and (5) by two-stage least squares (2SLS) along with a demand price equation.

TABLE I
SAMPLE TARIFF SCHEDULES

Consumer Power[a]
Monthly Rate:
Demand Charge:
\$6.65 per kw for the first 2,000 kw of billing demand
\$5.30 per kw for the next 18,000 kw of billing demand
\$4.70 per kw for all over 20,000 kw of billing demand
Energy Charge:
1.90¢ per kwh for all kwh consumed during the on-peak period
1.70¢ per kwh for all kwh consumed during the off-peak period
Detroit Edison[b]
Monthly Rate:
Service Charge:
\$160.00 per customer per month
Demand Charge:
\$6.00 per kilowatt for the first 1,000 kilowatts
\$5.90 per kilowatt for the next 9,000 kilowatts
\$5.70 per kilowatt for all over 10,000 kw.
Energy Charge:
1.5¢ per kwh for all kwh consumed during the on-peak period
1.3¢ per kwh for all kwh consumed during the off-peak period

[a] Effective May 21, 1976, Commercial and Industrial Primary Service.
[b] Effective March 31, 1976, Primary Supply Rate.

[9] The information was supplied by the Michigan Employment Security Commission for all manufacturing and some non-manufacturing SIC's. The variable has several advantages over value-added as proxy for the strength of the economy. It is available monthly by state, whereas value-added is available only quarterly and at the national level. I thank Syed Taqi for the data.

As set forth by Wilder and Willenborg [17];

> "The existence of decreasing block rates means that the average price paid . . . is negatively related to the quantity purchased. This relationship makes necessary the inclusion of a price equation in the model in order to insure identification of the demand relationship."

Because there were five different tariffs paid by different firms in the cross section, it was necessary to approximate the declining block structure, using dummy variables to represent the different tariffs. The exponential form (equation (9)) provides a good approximation of the declining block structure:

$$PD = \exp(\ln \alpha_0 - \alpha_1 \ln \text{KWMAX} + \alpha_2 D_1 + \cdots + \alpha_5 D_4 + \varepsilon), \tag{9}$$

where PD and KWMAX have been defined previously, and D_i is a shift parameter for tariff i, $i = 1, \ldots, 4$.

Figure 4 shows the relationship between the declining block structure and the negative exponential approximation.

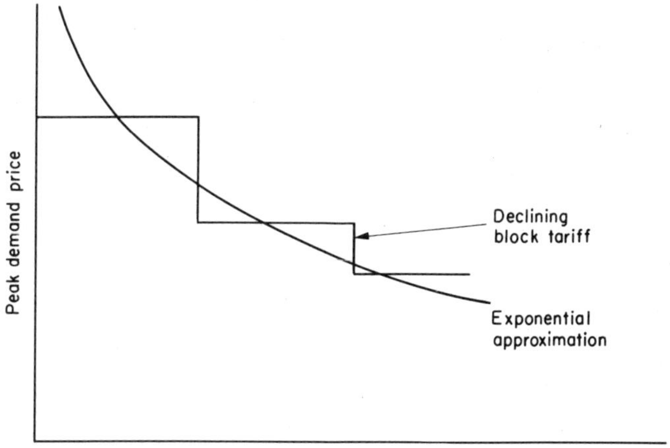

FIGURE 4
A Declining Block Tariff Structure.

Equations (1) and (3) were estimated using ordinary least squares, while equations (2) and (9), in which both KWMAX and PD appear, were estimated simultaneously using two-stage least squares. Similarly, equations (4) and (6) were estimated by OLS, while equations (5) and (9) were estimated simultaneously.[10]

[10] Other equations were also estimated with the demand price equation. Here, the two equations formed a recursive, rather than a simultaneous, system.

IV. THE ELECTRICITY DATA

The Consumers Power Company of Michigan and Detroit Edison supplied data on the three aspects of electricity use for each of 191 firms. Information on both sets of firms is available for eight months: August 1976 through March 1977. The two utilities also supplied tariff schedules, hour of monthly system peak, and a three- or four-digit SIC code for each firm. There are subtle differences in the data for each utility that require some discussion.

A. *Peak Energy Use*

Peak energy use is monthly energy use during the tariff peak hours, but the two utilities had different peak hours. In addition, Consumers Power used seasonal pricing, whereas Detroit Edison did not. In August 1976, September 1976 and March 1977, the Consumers Power tariff peak was 1000–1700 hours; in October 1976 through February 1977, it was 1700–2100 hours. The Detroit Edison peak was 0900–2100 hours in all eight months.

To get a comparable peak energy figure for customers of both utilities, it is necessary to aggregate months from each "season," i.e. August 1976 and October 1976. The sum of the peak energy use over the two months is then divided by the number of peak hours in the two months. For Consumers Power firms, the hourly average reflects the hours 1000–2100; for Detroit Edison firms, the average reflects the hours 0900–2100.[11]

As an example, consider two customers, one from each utility, shown in Table II.

TABLE II

	Consumer Power Customer Peak Energy Use	*Tariff Peak*	*Number of Peak Hours Per Month*	*Detroit Edison Customer Peak Energy Use*	*Tariff Peak*	*Number of Hours Per Month*
August 1976	24,506	1000–1700	154	28,439	0900–2100	264
September 1976	12,460	1000–1700	147	31,920	0900–2100	252
October 1976	6,501	1700–2100	76	26,289	0900–2100	252
January 1977	4,671	1700–2100	84	26,517	0900–2100	240
February 1977	4,254	1700–2100	76	28,293	0900–2100	240
March 1977	14,890	1000–1700	161	24,708	0900–2100	276
Hourly Average	96.4			109.0		

The hourly average peak energy use is 96.4 kwh for the Consumers Power firm, 109.0 kwh for the Detroit Edison firm. The calculation covers an equal number of months from each Consumers Power "season" so the resulting CP average is evenly weighted for the hours 1000–1700 and 1700–2100 hours.

[11] As indicated in footnote 4, the effect of the demand charge is not independent of the length of the tariff peak. Thus, part of the estimated effect of the peak demand charge may be due to the differing lengths of tariff peaks. This effect cannot be separated with the present data. To do so would require that all customers face the same peak hours.

This figure should be comparable to the Detroit Edison firm, which reflects 0900–2100 hours in all months.[12]

B. *Intrapeak Maximum Demand*

The Detroit Edison Company supplied, for each firm, both the maximum monthly demand and the intrapeak maximum demand. Consumers Power supplied the maximum monthly demand only, along with the date and hour of that demand. When the Consumers Power Tariff peak was 1000–1700 hours, most monthly maximum demands fell within the peak hours. When the tariff peak was 1700–2100 hours most maximum demands fell outside the peak. Hence, only the former set of months—August 1976, September 1976, and March 1977—contained usable information on the direct effect of the peak prices on intrapeak maximum demand. Intrapeak maximum demand was derived as an average of the three "summer" months.[13] Consumers Power firms with monthly maximum demand outside the tariff peak were deleted from the sample. The omitted firms are likely to have higher elasticities than firms in the sample, since they are apparently willing to operate at a high level off-peak. Thus, the remaining sample will yield a conservative estimate of the price elasticities.

C. *Coincident Demand*

Table III lists the time of system peak for the months August 1975 through November 1977.

TABLE III
TIME OF SYSTEM PEAK

Month/ Year	*Consumer Power*	*Detroit Edison*	*Month/ Year*	*Consumers Power*	*Detroit Edison*
3/76	2000	2000	1/77	1900	1900
4/76	N/A	1400	2/77	1000	1100
5/76	N/A	1400	3/77	2000	1100
6/76	N/A	1400	4/77	N/A	1100
7/76	N/A	1400[a]	5/77	N/A	1700
8/76	1400	1600	6/77	N/A	1600
9/76	1400	1700	7/77	N/A	1400
10/76	1700	1100	8/77	N/A	1700
11/76	1900	1900	9/77	N/A	1700
12/76	1900	1900	10/77	N/A	1900
			11/77	N/A	1800

Note: N/A = not available.
[a] Detroit Edison coincident demands were unavailable for this month.

[12] The estimates may be influenced by differing weather conditions in the two service areas. Location of the firms was unavailable, so a cross section weather variable could not be included.
[13] Again, the differing lengths of the tariff peaks may partially confound the price effects.

Of the eight months (August 1976 through March 1977) for which both utilities supplied data, system peak was at the same hour (1900 hours) in three months (November 1976, December 1976, and January 1977). In other months, the Detroit Edison and Consumers Power System peaks were at different hours; in these months, differences in the firm's contribution to system peak could be due to the different hour of measurement as well as price differences. In March 1977, for example, the Consumers Power system peak occurred at 2000 hours, while the Detroit Edison peak was at 1100 hours. Industrial customers typically have higher demands at 1100 hours than at 2000 hours. To obtain additional information on the effects of peak prices on coincident demand, June 1976 Detroit Edison observations were merged with August 1976 Consumers Power observations to form a complete sample.[14] This cross-section permits estimation of the effects of peak prices on an afternoon peak.

V. EMPIRICAL FINDINGS

Table IV contains the estimated elasticities of peak energy use (KWHPK), intrapeak maximum demand (KWMAX), and demand coincident with system peak (KWSP), with respect to the peak prices for energy and demand, the output proxy, and the manhours index.[15]

The price elasticities, and their levels of statistical significance, are presented separately in Table V.

The peak demand charge elasticity is negative and statistically significant in all three equations. The charge has a stronger effect on intrapeak maximum demand than on peak energy use, as was expected. The charge also reduces the firm's contribution to system peak, so that there are savings to the electric utility of capacity as well as fuel. The reduction in coincident demand is approximately two-thirds as much as the reduction in the customer's own intrapeak maximum demand.

The peak energy charge reduces coincident demand, but does not have a significant elasticity in the equations for peak energy use or intrapeak maximum demand. Reference to the sample tariffs in Table I suggests a possible explanation for the lack of significance of the coefficient. First, there is relatively little difference in the energy charges of the two utilities and the peak/off-peak differential is identical. Second, the price is a flat rate charge, so that all customers served by a particular tariff pay the same marginal rate. Thus, it is likely that the insignificance of the energy price elasticity is due to the limited cross-sectional variation.

[14] Of the months in which the two system peaks were at 1400 hours, only these two months had comparable temperatures. Differing temperatures can also affect electricity demand, so it is desirable to combine months with similar temperatures.

[15] The estimated coefficients when equations (1) and (3) were estimated as part of a recursive system were similar to the OLS estimates. Also, the OLS estimate of equation (2) was similar to the two-stage estimate.

TABLE IV

PEAK ENERGY USE (KWHPK), INTRAPEAK MAXIMUM DEMAND (KWMAX), AND COINCIDENT DEMAND (KWSP) ELASTICITIES

Dependent Variable	*Intercept*	*Q*	*PE*	*PD*	*M*	*Miscellaneous Statistics*
KWHPK[a]	2.06	0.93 (49.68)	0.13 (0.40)	−1.09 (−5.69)	0.30 (3.53)	OLS $R^2 = 0.95$ $F = 666$
KWMAX[b]	3.24	0.83 (35.10)	0.29 (0.04)	−2.13 (−7.35)	0.30 (2.84)	2SLS $R^2 = 0.92$ $F = 359$
KWSP: 1900 hours[c]	2.87	0.90 (30.76)	−1.44 (−2.52)	−1.51 (−5.52)	0.17 (0.79)	OLS $R^2 = 0.90$ $F = 275$
1400 hours[d]	2.93	0.85 (31.22)	−1.02 (−1.94)	−1.41 (5.91)	−2.43 (−3.99)	OLS $R^2 = 0.92$ $F = 345$

Note: *T*-statistics are in parentheses.

[a] Peak energy is an hourly average using August 1976, September 1976, October 1976, January 1977, and March 1977 data.

[b] Intrapeak maximum demand is an average of August 1976, September 1976, and March 1977 data.

[c] Coincident demand (1900 hours) is an average of November 1976, December 1976, and January 1977 data.

[d] Coincident demand (1400 hours) uses June 1976 (Detroit Edison) and August 1976 (Consumers Power) data.

Output has a positive effect on peak energy use, intrapeak maximum demand, and coincident demand. The size of the *T*-statistics supports the contention that *Q* is highly correlated with the dependent variable. As one would expect, the correlation is highest with KWHPK and lowest with KWSP.

An increase in the manhours index, used as a proxy for capacity use, leads to equal increases in peak energy use and intrapeak maximum demand. It also is associated with an increase in coincident demand at 1900 hours, although the coefficient is not significant.

TABLE V

SUMMARY OF DEMAND ELASTICITIES WITH RESPECT TO PEAK DEMAND AND ENERGY CHARGES

	Peak Energy Price	*Peak Demand Price*
Peak Energy Use	0.13	−1.09†
Intrapeak Maximum Demand	0.29	−2.13†
Coincident Demand (1900 hours)	−1.44*	−1.51†
Coincident Demand (1400 hours)	−1.02	−1.41†

Note: * = Significant at 95% level of confidence.
† = Significant at 98% level of confidence.

TABLE VI
PEAK PERIOD LOAD FACTOR ELASTICITIES WITH RESPECT TO ENERGY USE (LFPK), INTRAPEAK MAXIMUM DEMAND (LFMAX), AND COINCIDENT DEMAND (LFSP)

Dependent Variable	*Intercept*	*EI*	*PE*	*PD*	*M*	*Miscellaneous Statistics (OLS)*
LFPK[a]	7.08	0.09	−0.07	0.09	−0.01	$R^2 = .02$
		(1.64)	(−0.36)	(0.66)	(−0.23)	$F = 0.73$
LFMAX[b]	−1.80	−0.06	−0.52	1.11	0.22	$R^2 = .21$
		(−0.58)	(−1.41)	(4.35)	(1.60)	$F = 10.08$
LFSP	−2.43	0.10	0.59	0.53	0.20	$R^2 = .03$
(1900 hours)[c]		(0.90)	(1.44)	(1.81)	(0.27)	$F = 1.04$
LFSP	−2.07	0.08	0.07	0.42	1.69	$R^2 = .10$
(1400 hours)[d]		(0.94)	(0.22)	(1.77)	(3.39)	$F = 4.12$

Dependent Variable First Equation	*Intercept*	*EI*	*PE*	*PD*	*M*	*Miscellaneous Statistics (2SLS)*
LFPK[a]	5.61	0.14	0.05	0.36	−0.02	$R^2 = .05$
		(2.43)	(0.23)	(2.29)	(−0.41)	$F = 1.92$
LFMAX[b]	−3.91	0.05	−0.24	1.72	0.22	$R^2 = .25$
		(0.44)	(−0.62)	(5.57)	(1.64)	$F = 12.91$
LFSP	−3.96	0.18	0.79	0.96	0.35	$R^2 = .05$
(1900 hours)[c]		(1.50)	(1.86)	(2.77)	(0.47)	$F = 2.14$
LFSP	−3.63	0.16	0.28	0.87	1.58	$R^2 = .13$
(1400 hours)[d]		(1.68)	(0.80)	(3.04)	(3.13)	$F = 5.58$

Dependent Variable in Second Equation	*Intercept*	*KWMAX*	*D1*	*D2*	*D3*	*D4*	*Miscellaneous Statistics (2SLS)*
		−0.04	0.02	−0.42	0.16	0.05	$R^2 = .90$
PD	3.85	(−13.24)	(0.53)	(−9.11)	(3.01)	(1.17)	$F = 251$
		−0.04	−0.53	−0.48	0.10	−0.01	$R^2 = .87$
PD	2.09	(−11.36)	(−0.58)	(−9.28)	(1.79)	(−0.08)	$F = 207$
		−0.04	0.06	−0.38	0.20	0.09	$R^2 = .90$
PD	2.03	(−14.62)	(1.48)	(−8.66)	(4.00)	(2.02)	$F = 287$
		−0.04	0.07	−0.38	0.20	0.09	$R^2 = .90$
PD	2.01	(−14.05)	(1.59)	(−8.53)	(4.15)	(2.15)	$F = 283$

Note: *T*-statistics are in parentheses.

[a] Peak energy use load factor is an average using August 1976, September 1976, October 1976, January 1977, February 1977 and March 1977 data.

[b] Intrapeak maximum demand load factor is an average of August 1976, and March 1977 data.

[c] Coincident demand load factor (1900 hours) is an average of November 1976, December 1976, and January 1977 data.

[d] Coincident demand load factor (1400 hours) uses June 1976 (Detroit Edison) and August 1976 (Consumers Power) data.

The sign of the manhours coefficient in the equation for coincident demand at 1400 hours is unexpected. An increase in capacity usage was expected to lead to an increase in coincident demand. A possible explanation for the unexpected sign is that in order to meet high demand, the firm adds an evening shift which allows a reduction in the intensity of use of the day shift. As data on the use of manhours by shift were not available, this conjecture cannot be confirmed or denied.

As alluded to earlier, the coefficients in Tables IV and V are likely to be biased due to the output variable. Also, the results are based on the implicit assumption that total energy use is constant. Table VI contains the estimates of equations (4) through (6), concerning load factors. Table VII contains the price effects only.

As the magnitude of the demand price effect differed between the OLS and 2SLS estimates, both sets of coefficients are reported. The inclusion of the price equation results in a larger demand charge coefficient, at a higher level of statistical significance. The price effects are consistent with those in Table V. Both the OLS and 2SLS results show the demand charge to have the largest effect on intrapeak maximum demand relative to average demand, an intermediate effect on coincident demand, and a smaller effect on peak energy use. All the two-stage coefficients are statistically significant at 95% or higher.

The peak energy charge coefficient approaches significance only for the two-stage estimate of coincident demand (both 1900 and 1400 hours), showing a greater effect on coincident than on average demand. This is consistent with the earlier finding that the only significant effect of the peak energy price was a reduction in coincident demand.

Energy intensity is significant in only one equation, the two-stage estimate of peak energy use. It approaches significance in the OLS estimate of peak energy use, and the 2SLS estimates of coincident demand. The positive coefficient indicates that energy-intensive firms have higher load factors, indicating relatively smooth load profiles. This is consistent with the stated expectation

TABLE VII
SUMMARY OF PRICE ELASTICITIES

	PE	*PD*	
LFPK	−0.07	0.09	*OLS*
	0.05	0.36*	*2SLS*
LFMAX	−0.52	1.11†	*OLS*
	−0.24	1.72†	*2SLS*
LFSP	0.59	0.53	*OLS*
(1900 Hours)	0.79	0.96†	*2SLS*
LFSP	0.07	0.42	*OLS*
(1400 Hours)	0.28	0.87†	*2SLS*

Note: * = Significant at 95% level of confidence.

† = Significant at 98% level of confidence.

that energy-intensive firms have a greater incentive to modify their load profile by reducing peak energy and intrapeak demand relative to off-peak energy and demand.

Manhours is positive in all significant cases. High use of capacity leads to a high load factor. The effect is especially strong for coincident demand at 1400 hours. This supports the contention that when the firm operates at a high level, it adds an evening shift, resulting in coincident demand decreasing relative to off-peak demand.

VI. SUMMARY AND POLICY IMPLICATIONS

The effects on industrial customers of two types of peak load prices were presented. The peak energy charge was expected to reduce peak energy use, intrapeak maximum demand, and coincident demand. The peak demand charge was expected to reduce intrapeak maximum demand, but the effect of the price on peak energy use or coincident demand could not be determined *a priori*. The estimated effects of the charges showed the peak demand charge reduced peak energy use, intrapeak maximum demand, and coincident demand, while the peak energy charge caused a significant reduction in coincident demand only.

From a policy standpoint, the effects of the charges on the utility system are of primary importance. This would require information on residential and commercial customers in addition to industrial customers. The evidence presented here pertains to the industrial sector only. However, the effects presented for industrial users suggest that the two charges have differing effects, both theoretically and empirically. These differences are likely to exist for other types of customers as well.

If utility system demand were examined, the effect of a peak demand charge on demand at the time of system peak and on peak energy use could not be determined *a priori*, since its effect on a single sector cannot be determined *a priori*. Empirical evidence is required to find the effect of this charge on system capacity; for the industrial customers in the Michigan sample, the peak demand charge had the desired effects.

The peak energy charge is likely to reduce utility system coincident demand and peak energy use, since its effects on each sector should be the same as for the industrial sector. The empirical evidence for the Michigan sample found a reduction in coincident demand, but not peak energy use; this suggests caution in accepting the theoretical expectation. Perhaps the energy charge differential was too small to have an effect. It is clear that there is need for additional work to discern the effects of peak demand and energy charges on the utility system as well as separate customer classes.

Peter M. Schwarz,
The University of North Carolina at Charlotte,
Department of Economics,
UNCC Station,
Charlotte, N.C. 28223, U.S.A.

ACCEPTED JULY 1982

REFERENCES

[1] BAXTER, R. and REES, R., "Analysis of the Industrial Demand for Electricity," *Economic Journal*, 78, 310, (June 1968), pp. 277–98.

[2] CARGILL, T. and MEYER, R., "Estimating the Demand for Electricity by Time-of-Day, *Applied Economics*, 3, (September 1971), pp. 233–46.

[3] CHUNG, C., "Econometric Modeling of the Industrial Demand for Electricity of Time-of-Day; An Application to the California Cement Industry," in Modeling and Analysis of Electricity Demand by Time-of-day, Electric Power Research Institute, EA-1304, Research Project 1050, Workshop Proceedings, December (Palo Alto, California, 1979).

[4] DANSBY, R., "Welfare Optimal Peak Load Pricing and Capacity Decisions with Intraperiod Time Varying Demand," Bell Labs Economic Discussion Paper No. 39, (November, 1975).

[5] ELECTRIC POWER RESEARCH INSTITUTE, *Modeling and Analysis of Electricity Demand by Time-of-Day*, Electric Power Research Institute, EA-1304, Research Project 1050, Workshop Proceedings, December (Palo Alto, California, 1979).

[6] HAUSMAN, J., KINNUCAN, J. and McFADDEN, D., "A Two-Level Electricity Demand Model Evaluation of the Connecticut Time-of-Day Pricing Test," *Journal of Econometrics*, 10, 3, (August 1979) pp. 263–89.

[7] HENDERSON, J. S., "Electric System Load Patterns and Demand Charges," mimeo., (July 1978), The Ohio State University, Columbus.

[8] LAWRENCE, A. and AIGNER, O. (eds), "Modeling and Forecasting Time-of-Day and Seasonal Electric Demands," *Journal of Econometrics*, 9, 6, (January 1979), pp. 1–240.

[9] MITCHELL, B., MANNING, W. and ACTON, J., *Electricity Pricing and Load Management: Foreign Experience and California Opportunities*, Rand Corporation Report R-2106-CERCDC (Santa Monica, California, 1977).

[10] MOHRING, H., "The Peak Load Problem with Increasing Returns and Pricing Constraints," *American Economic Review*, 60, 4, (September 1970), pp. 693–705.

[11] PANZAR, J., "A Neoclassical Approach to Peak Load Pricing," *Bell Journal of Economics*, 7, 2, (Autumn 1976), pp. 521–30.

[12] PENNER, P. S., HERENDEEN, R. A. and MILKE, T. "New Hybrid 1971 Energy Intensities Available," *Energy*, 4, 3, (1979) pp. 469–73.

[13] SCHWARZ, P., "The Effects of Peak Load Demand and Energy Charges on the Industrial Use of Electricity," unpublished Ph.D. dissertation, The Ohio State University, 1980.

[14] SPANN, R. and BEAUVAIS, E., Forecasting and Modeling Time-of-Day and Seasonal Electricity Demands, Special Report EPRI EA-578-SR, December (Palo Alto, California, 1977).

[15] STEINER, P., "Peak Loads and Efficient Pricing," *Quarterly Journal of Economics*, 71, 4, (November 1957), pp. 585–610.

[16] WENDERS, J., "Peak Load Pricing in the Electric Utility Industry," *Bell Journal of Economics*, 7, 1, (Spring 1976), pp. 232–41.

[17] WILDER, R. and WILLENBORG, J., "Residential Demand for Electricity: A Consumer Panel Approach," *Southern Economic Journal*, 42, 2, (October 1975), pp. 212–17.

Journal of Business Finance & Accounting

Vol. 11 No. 2 **Contents** Summer 1984

On the Effects of Inflation in the Stock Market: Empirical Evidence with Finnish Data 1968–1981
by VESA KANNIAINEN and VESA KURIKKA

The Trend Toward Efficiency For Less Developed Stock Exchanges: Hong Kong
by STEVEN M. DAWSON

Corporate Accounting Data, Capital Market Information and Wage Increases of the Firm
by D.A. PEEL and P.F. POPE

The Information Content of Dividends: An Other Test
by ALLAN L. RIDING

The Competitiveness of Lease Markets: An Empirical Investigation of the UK Local Authority Lease Market
by COLIN M. YOUNG

The Validity of Conventional Valuation Models Under Multiperiod Uncertainty
by ØYVIND BØHREN

ARR vs. IRR: A Review and an Analysis
by PETER F. LUCKETT

Cost Variance Investigation in a Linear Programming Framework
by PETER CHENG, FREDRIC JACOBS and RONALD MARSHALL

Some Notes on the Cost of New Equity
by WILLIAM L. BEEDLES

A Further Note on Discounting Deferred Taxes
by HARRY I. WOLK, LYNN K. SAUBERT and FRANK M. TIERNAN

On the Negative Risk Premium For Risk Adjusted Discount Rates: A Further Comment
by JOHN R. GRINYER

On the Negative Risk Premium For Risk Adjusted Discount Rates: A Reply and Extension
by R.H. BERRY and R.G. DYSON

1984 subscription £31.50 in UK and £38.60 elsewhere (or US $77.50 or Can $95) to library and business subscribers, or £16.95 in UK and £20.75 elsewhere (or US $41.70 or Can $51) to individual teachers and students. Order from *Journals Dept., Basil Blackwell Publishers, 108 Cowley Road, Oxford, OX4 1JF, UK. Editorial communications to JBFA/CRIBA University of Warwick, Coventry CV4 7AL, UK.*

THE JOURNAL OF INDUSTRIAL ECONOMICS

Published first in October 1952, the Journal has a very wide international circulation, and has established itself as the leading journal in the field of industrial economics. It was founded to promote the analysis of modern industry, particularly the behaviour of firms, and the functioning of markets. More specifically it seeks to bring the tools of modern economic analysis to bear on the analysis of real problems of industrial economies.

Contributions are welcomed covering all the major areas of industrial economics. One such area is the relationship between market structure and market behaviour in the areas of pricing, product differentiation, advertising and the dissemination of information and R and D. Another area focuses more directly on the firm, its objectives, finance, investment and growth. A third area comprises the background environment within which industrial firms operate: the changing structure of industry, public policy on monopoly and restrictive trade practices, regulation, fiscal and monetary policy as they affect firms, and underlying changes in productivity and international competitiveness.

The Journal has a tradition of publishing a blend of theory and evidence. Theoretical discussion is welcomed provided that the more abstract theory includes sufficient introduction and other explanation to convey the significance of the material to the general reader who wants to decide whether to follow the analysis through. Empirical analysis, and especially econometric analysis, should include an explanation of the data sources used, of the methods applied and of the underlying theoretical basis of the study. The Journal has a particular tradition of case studies of firms and industries, which the Editors would wish to continue. However contributors of such studies are asked to remember that a study will be of interest to the international readership of the Journal only if it makes a particular contribution to the methodology of such studies, or if the empirical results are exceptionally interesting.

Alongside articles of more normal length, the Editors are ready to publish shorter notes, especially where these give interim results of important research studies, or where they report significant new empirical results. Books are not reviewed, although books received will be listed, sometimes with a short note: but substantial review articles will be considered.

Information for contributors

Typescripts from North America should be sent to Professor H. Michael Mann, Department of Economics, Boston College, Chestnut Hill, Massachusetts, 02167, U.S.A. Typescripts from *all* other countries should be sent to the General Editor, Journal of Industrial Economics, Institute of Economics and Statistics, The University of Oxford, St. Cross Building, Manor Road, Oxford, OX1 3UL, U.K. Detailed Information for Contributors is available from the General Editor. Contributors are asked to send an Abstract, not exceeding 100 words, with their article. No payment is made for articles accepted, but authors are provided with 25 free offprints.

Information for subscribers

The journal is published four times a year, in September, December, March and June, by Basil Blackwell Publisher Ltd., 108 Cowley Road, Oxford OX4 1JF, England. Prices are as follows:

	UK	Overseas	USA	Canada
Institutions	£24.00	£29.40	$59.50	$72.90
Individuals	£14.95	£18.30	$35.00	$43.25
Single issue prices for:				
Institutions	£6.50	£7.75	$16.00	$19.50
Individuals	£4.75	£5.75	$11.00	$13.50

CONTRIBUTORS TO THIS NUMBER

JAMES L. BOTHWELL: Economist, U.S. General Accounting Office, Washington, D.C.

THOMAS F. COOLEY: Professor of Economics, University of California, Santa Barbara.

THOMAS E. HALL: Assistant Professor of Economics, Miami University, Oxford, Ohio.

MARIE-PAULE DONSIMONI: Associate Professor of Economics, University of Louvain.

PAUL GEROSKI: Lecturer in Economics, University of Southampton, and Visiting Professor of Economics, University of Louvain.

ALEXIS JACQUEMIN: Professor of Economics, University of Louvain, and Associate Editor of this Journal.

ROGER CLARKE: Lecturer in Economics, University of Sheffield, and Associate Editor of this Journal.

STEPHEN DAVIES: Senior Lecturer in Economics, University of East Anglia, and Editor of this Journal.

MICHAEL WATERSON: Lecturer in Economics, University of Newcastle upon Tyne.

A. J. BUXTON: Lecturer in Economics, University of Salford.

B. R. LYONS: Fellow of St. John's College, Cambridge.

STEPHEN C. FARBER: Associate Professor, Louisiana State University, Baton Rouge.

LARRY L. DUETSCH: Associate Professor of Economics, University of Wisconsin—Parkside.

JAMES E. ANDERSON: Professor of Economics, Boston College, Chestnut Hill, MA.

JOHN E. KWOKA, Jr: Associate Professor of Economics, George Washington University, Washington, D.C.

PETER SCHWARZ: Associate Professor of Economics, University of North Carolina at Charlotte.

US Mailing: Second class postage paid at New York. Postmaster: Send address corrections to: Journal of Industrial Economics, c/o Expediters of the Printed Word Ltd., 527 Madison Avenue, Suite 1217, New York, NY 10022 (US Mailing Agent).

Set by Santype International Ltd., Salisbury, Wilts.
Printed and bound by Whitstable Litho Ltd., Whitstable, Kent

CONTENTS

VOLUME XXXII

Number 1, September 1983 PAGE

BO CARLSSON
Industrial Subsidies in Sweden: Macro-Economic Effects and an International Comparison 1

R. DIXON
Industry Structure and the Speed of Price Adjustment 25

RAPHAEL KAPLINSKY
Firm Size and Technical Change in a Dynamic Context 39

HIROYUKI ODAGIRI
R & D Expenditures, Royalty Payments, and Sales Growth in Japanese Manufacturing Corporations 61

NEIL DORWARD, MIKE POKORNY and RAY BAYLDON
The UK Truck Market: An Investigation into Truck Purchasing Behaviour and Changing Market Shares 73

MARCEL BOYER and MICHEL MOREAUX
Consistent Versus Non-Consistent Conjectures in Duopoly Theory: Some Examples 97

Number 2, December 1983

FRÉDÉRIC JENNY and ANDRÉ-PAUL WEBER
Aggregate Welfare Loss Due to Monopoly Power in the French Economy: Some Tentative Estimates 113

G. F. MATHEWSON
Information, Search and Price Variability of Individual Life Insurance Contracts 131

R. W. SHAW and S. A. SHAW
Excess Capacity and Rationalisation in the West European Synthetic Fibres Industry 149

R. K. TURNER and D. DEADMAN
The UK Wastepaper Industry and its Long Term Prospects 167

MANFRED NEUMANN, INGO BÖBEL and ALFRED HAID
Business Cycle and Industrial Market Power: An Empirical Investigation for West German Industries, 1965–77 187

C. W. L. HILL
Conglomerate Performance Over the Economic Cycle 197

MARC R. REINGANUM and JANET KIHOLM SMITH
Investor Preference for Large Firms: New Evidence on Economies of Size 213

JOHAN ARNDT and JULIAN L. SIMON
Advertising and Economies of Scale: Critical Comments on the Evidence 229

R. CLARKE and P. K. ELSE
Optimal Adjustments to Restrictions on Advertising: A Comment 243

MICHAEL R. BAYE
Optimal Adjustments to Restrictions on Advertising: Some Further Comments 249

Number 3, March 1984

W. H. DAVIDSON and DONALD G. McFETRIDGE
International Technology Transactions and the Theory of the Firm 253

STEVEN SCHWARTZ
An Empirical Test of a Managerial, Life-Cycle, and Cost of Capital Model of Merger Activity 265

MICHAEL L. LAWRIWSKY
Some Tests of the Influence of Control Type on the Market for Corporate Control in Australia 277

JOHN F. STEWART, ROBERT S. HARRIS and WILLARD T. CARLETON
The Role of Market Structure in Merger Behavior 293

MARTIN K. PERRY
Scale Economies, Imperfect Competition and Public Policy 313

ELI NOAM
Market Power and Regulation: A Simultaneous Approach 335

SHERRILL SHAFFER
Regulation and Risk Preference 349

BRUCE YANDLE
Polluters' Profits: An Empirical Note 359

W. J. BOYES and DALE BECK FURNISH
A Note on the Use of Incorporation as an Escape from Usury Ceilings 367

JAN J. P. VAN HEEMST
Subcontracting Between Small-Scale Enterprises in Developing Countries: A Note 373

DAVID LEVY
Testing Stigler's Interpretation of 'The Division of Labor is Limited by the Extent of the Market' 377
RONALD P. WILDER and IRVIN B. TUCKER
Trends in Vertical Integration: Reply 391

Number 4, June 1984

JAMES L. BOTHWELL, THOMAS F. COOLEY and THOMAS E. HALL
A New View of the Market Structure–Performance Debate 397
MARIE-PAULE DONSIMONI, PAUL GEROSKI and ALEXIS JACQUEMIN
Concentration Indices and Market Power: Two Views 419
ROGER CLARKE, STEPHEN DAVIES and MICHAEL WATERSON
The Profitability–Concentration Relation: Market Power or Efficiency? 435
A. J. BUXTON, S. W. DAVIES and B. R. LYONS
Concentration and Advertising in Consumer and Producer Markets 451
STEPHEN C. FARBER
Cyclical Price Flexibility: A Test of Administered Pricing 465
LARRY L. DUETSCH
Entry and the Extent of Multiplant Operations 477
JAMES E. ANDERSON
Identification of Interactive Behavior in Air Service Markets: 1973–76 489
JOHN E. KWOKA, Jr.
Market Power and Market Change in the U.S. Automobile Industry 509
PETER SCHWARZ
The Estimated Effects on Industry of Time-of-Day Demand and Energy Electricity Prices 523